*Major Problems in the
History of American Technology*

MAJOR PROBLEMS IN AMERICAN HISTORY SERIES

GENERAL EDITOR
THOMAS G. PATERSON

Major Problems in the History of American Technology

DOCUMENTS AND ESSAYS
EDITED BY

MERRITT ROE SMITH

MASSACHUSETTS INSTITUTE OF TECHNOLOGY

GREGORY CLANCEY

MASSACHUSETTS INSTITUTE OF TECHNOLOGY

HOUGHTON MIFFLIN COMPANY   BOSTON   NEW YORK

Editor-in-Chief: Jean L. Woy
Senior Associate Editor: Frances Gay
Associate Project Editor: Rebecca Bennett
Associate Production/Design Coordinator: Deborah Frydman
Marketing Manager: Sandra McGuire
Manufacturing Coordinator: Andrea Wagner

Cover Designer: Sarah Melhado
Cover Image: River Rouge Plant, 1932. © 1996 Whitney Museum of American Art, New York.

Text credits begin on page 521.

Printed in the U.S.A.

Library of Congress Catalog Number: 97-72550

ISBN: 0-669-35472-4

6789-FFG-09 08 07 06 05

To Chiyuki and Kenta

Contents

CHAPTER 3
Arts, Tools, and Identities in Agricultural Regimes, ca 1680–1850
Page 62

CHAPTER 4
The Debate over Manufactures in the Early Republic, 1785–1820
Page 103

CHAPTER 5
Inside Factory Systems, 1820–1885
Page 144

CHAPTER 6
"Second Nature": Steam, Space, and a
New World Order, 1840–1900
Page 191

CHAPTER 7
Telephony, 1872–1914
Page 233

CHAPTER 12

The Military-Industrial-University Complex, 1945–1990

Page 427

CHAPTER 13

Countdown to Cyberspace: 1974–1990

Page 471

Preface

America is frequently called a "technological society." That common refrain suggests that the United States is better known and respected throughout the world for its technological accomplishments than for its democratic institutions. This volume seeks to establish the centrality of technology to American life by making available documents and readings that can be used in conjunction with either general American history survey courses or more specialized subjects treating the history of technology and industrialization of America.

The history of technology is a relatively new field of inquiry within the larger discipline of history. While the discipline of the history of science traces its roots to the period of World War I, the history of technology is a child of the Cold War. Sustained professional interest and institutional support for the subject came only during the late 1950s and early 1960s, largely in response to the successful Soviet launching of *Sputnik* and the widely held belief that the United States had fallen behind the Soviet Union in space as well as in other critical areas of engineering and technological endeavor. The establishment of the Society for the History of Technology (SHOT) in 1958 and publication of its journal, *Technology and Culture*, in 1960 mark the beginning of the field in North America.

Historians of technology have long been interested in the sources of invention and innovation and the spread of new technologies from one region or country to another, as well as how culturally influenced processes of transfer and dissemination have, in turn, altered the technologies themselves. Some of the most distinguished work in the field since the 1960s focuses on the origins of mass production, the rise of modern management, and the emergence of large technological systems in manufacturing, power distribution, and transportation industries. While "big technologies" continue to receive considerable attention, in recent years some of the freshest work has focused on smaller-scale technologies—consumer products, domestic systems, niche-oriented factories, and technologies of the body. Engagement with gender, race, ethnicity, and other categories of identity are expanding the field in other directions. Regardless of theme or focus, invariably the best work in the history of technology seeks to situate objects or devices in a human context, or in an understanding of how object and context were coproduced.

Major Problems in the History of American Technology seeks to provide readers with a general introduction to the history of technology in the United States. In addition to treating well-known topics such as the factory system and mass production, the volume highlights such themes as colonization, Native American technology, slavery, gender, the role of the military in technological change, agriculture, toys and play, feminism, and environmentalism. The literature on racial and ethnic diversity as it relates to technology is just now developing. We have touched on this matter, but more thorough coverage will have to await another edition.

Like the other volumes in this series, this anthology approaches its subject through both primary sources and the interpretations of scholars. We invite readers to examine critical issues through diverse viewpoints and approaches. Each chapter begins with an introduction that identifies the problem or theme, places it in a larger context, and poses several questions to think about as one reads the documents and essays. The headnotes for the documents and essays convey the intensity of debate and also suggest key questions. The documents allow students to immerse themselves in the issues, develop their own perspectives, and evaluate the explanations of others. The essays reveal how scholars can read documents in multiple ways, choose to examine different aspects of the same problems, and come to different conclusions about what happened. Each chapter ends with a brief bibliography to guide further investigation. The format of the books in this series enables students to appreciate the complexity not only of history itself but the *writing* of history and to see that people who lived in the past and the issues they confronted may still be meaningful for today's students as they become scholars and citizens.

This book proceeds from the editors' conviction that history is an open-ended, interpretive discipline. By this we mean that every generation revises and rewrites its history books in light of its own particular needs, problems, political ideologies, and cultural influences. History, in this sense, is a moving target and no historical study can therefore be considered definitive for all time. What was applauded as the last word on a subject twenty years ago is more often than not thought of today as being dated as historians unearth new sources of information and devise more sophisticated and complete models of the past.

The following pages advance some explicit themes that summarize and expand upon the current state of scholarship in the history of technology.

First, we hold that technology is more than industrial production. Indeed, many important technologies have little to do with industry as traditionally conceived. Nor is technology just about engineers and formal engineering. We have purposely limited our discussion of the history of engineering because that story has been so well-told elsewhere.

Second, some technologies are more important than others, but the idea that there are "leading-edge" technologies that somehow define each period—such as steam, railroad, or computer ages—emanates from a flawed nineteenth-century model of linear progress. We have tried, as much as possible, to treat several different technologies in each chapter.

Third, technological change is rarely revolutionary. It is often slow and subtle rather than dramatic and obvious. Nor is it necessarily cumulative; it frequently involves forgetting as well as learning.

Fourth, technologies are deeply intertwined with societies and cultures. There are, at any given time, a stunning array of possible paths that technological innovation and development can take. No technology has an "internal logic" or an "economic logic" that fully explains why it ends up looking and behaving the way it does.

Fifth, the benefits derived from any technology are unevenly distributed—hence the need for always asking, Progress for whom? Progress for what? or Who and what are linked together by a given technology, and why?

Sixth, because technology is part of the web of human culture and because there is no clear boundary between technology on the one hand and culture, society, and politics on the other, we hold to an interactive model of history. Technology is one of many intersecting forces. To speak about "technology's impact" thus becomes highly problematic. Such explanations can easily become overly simplistic, linear, unidirectional models of history and can lead to an indefensible technological determinist position.

Finally, technologies invented in one place are not merely deployed to many others. The process of construction and/or reinvention often continues after technical objects leave laboratories or factories for other destinations. The ultimate fate of technologies is not determined by their inventors, but is in the hands of later users—hence our interest in the unintended consequences of technological change.

We have accumulated many debts in the course of preparing this text. We are grateful to the series editor, Professor Thomas G. Paterson of the University of Connecticut, for recognizing that the history of technology belongs in larger discussions of American history and for encouraging us at every turn. We are especially indebted to Yaakov Garb who provided us with most of the material in Chapter 11, and to Rebecca Herzig and Karin Ellison who commented on the early drafts of many chapters. Greg Galer and Russell Olwell were involved in the early planning of this book and pointed us toward a number of selections. We also wish to acknowledge all the helpful comments and suggestions that came from Lindy Biggs, Michael Fischer, Deborah Fitzgerald, Slava Gerovitch, Loren Graham, Hannah Landecker, Kenneth Keniston, Judith McGaw, Pauline Maier, Patrick Malone, Leo Marx, David Mindell, Brian O'Donnell, George O'Har, and John Staudenmaier. We are also grateful to the following reviewers who provided detailed and extremely helpful comments on the table of contents: Colleen A. Dunlavy, University of Wisconsin–Madison; John W. Lozier, Bethany College, Bethany, West Virginia; Howard P. Segal, University of Maine; and William F. Trimble, Auburn University. The project started out with James Miller and Patricia Wakeley of D. C. Heath and ended up with Jean Woy, Frances Gay, and Rebecca Bennett of Houghton Mifflin. To them we owe a debt of thanks for their fine editorial advice and overseeing the book's production.

M. R. S.
G. C.

Major Problems in the
History of American Technology

CHAPTER
1

What Is Technology?

✢

Technology *is no easier to define than* art, politics, religion, *or* society; *the question that forms the title of this chapter is not meant to be answered so much as grappled with as one reads through the book. As Leo Marx points out in the first essay, the word is comparatively new, and, at the turn of the twenty-first century, increasingly omnivorous. Cells and language now aspire toward technology; "-tech" and "techno-" cleave onto words that once meant their opposite (consider "techno-culture"). Although one can still read intellectual positions "against technology" at the close of the twentieth century, we are past being able to bracket it off from the rest of life simply by naming it. Technology, however it is defined, is not autonomous.*

Like the terms modern *and* modernism, technology *is simultaneously a historical project consciously pursued by people of a particular time and place, and an analytic category historians use to describe those very same people, and even their predecessors who never heard of "technology." The essayists in this book have different ideas about whether this is fine or very wrong, unavoidable or to be avoided. We have taken the most generous position, namely that technology is whatever and wherever our essayists say it is, and that they are even allowed to write about it—or something very close to "it"—without necessarily using the term. We hope that the question "what is technology?" will remain open through the end of the book, even as other interesting and important questions compete with it for primacy.*

✢ *E S S A Y S*

In the first essay, Leo Marx presents a brief history of the word *technology* and a few related terms. In the second selection, philosopher Langdon Winner considers the relation between technology (which he calls "artifacts") and politics. Sociologist Donald MacKenzie then takes up the problem of "technological determinism" and the relation of technology to society. In the fourth essay, historian Nina Lerman questions basic assumptions about what constitutes "technology," suggesting a change in vocabulary to accompany a change in vision. In the fifth essay, historian Carroll Pursell analyzes technology through gender—in this case, masculinity. Last, sociologist Bruno Latour questions the practice of isolating "technology"—or "society" or "nature"—as analytic categories.

The essayists consider technology from several disciplines and methodologies. Although they don't directly argue with one another, neither do they perfectly agree. Whom would you group with whom in terms of style or concern?

The Invention of "Technology"

LEO MARX

When the Enlightenment project was being formulated, after 1750, the idea of "technology" in today's broad sense of the word did not yet exist. For another century, more or less, the artifacts, the knowledge, and the practices later to be embraced by "technology" would continue to be thought of as belonging to a special branch of the arts variously known as the "mechanic" (or "practical," or "industrial," or "useful")—as distinct from the "fine" (or "high," or "creative," or "imaginative")—arts. Such terms, built with various adjectival modifiers of "art," then were the nearest available approximations of today's abstract noun "technology"; they referred to the knowledge and practice of the crafts. By comparison with "technology," "the practical arts" and its variants constituted a more limited and limiting, even diminishing, category. If only because it was explicitly designated as one of several subordinate parts of something else, such a specialized branch of art was, as compared with the tacit uniqueness and unity of "technology," inherently belittling. Ever since antiquity, moreover, the habit of separating the practical and the fine arts had served to ratify a set of overlapping and invidious distinctions: between things and ideas, the physical and the mental, the mundane and the ideal, female and male, making and thinking, the work of enslaved and of free men. This derogatory legacy was in some measure erased, or at least masked, by the more abstract, cerebral, neutral word "technology." The term "mechanic arts" calls to mind men with soiled hands tinkering with machines at workbenches, whereas "technology" conjures up images of clean, well-educated technicians gazing at dials, instrument panels, or computer monitors.

These changes in the representation of technical practices were made in response to a marked acceleration in the rate of initiating new mechanical or other devices and new ways of organizing work. During the early phase of industrialization (ca. 1780–1850 in England, ca. 1820–1890 in the United States), the manufacturing realm had been represented in popular discourse by images of the latest mechanical inventions: water mill, cotton gin, power loom, spinning jenney, steam engine, steamboat, locomotive, railroad "train of cars," telegraph, factory. The tangible, manifestly practical character of these artifacts matched the central role as chief agent of progress accorded to instrumental rationality and its equipment. Thus the locomotive (or "iron horse") often was invoked to symbolize the capacity of commonsensical, matter-of-fact, verifiable knowledge to harness the energies of nature. It was routinely depicted as a driving force of history. Or, put differently, these new artifacts represented the innovative means of arriving at a socially and politically defined goal. For ardent exponents of the rational Enlightenment, the chief goal was a more just, more peaceful, and less hierarchical republican society based on the consent of the governed.

As this industrial iconography suggests, the mechanic arts were widely viewed as a primary agent of social change. These icons often were invoked with metonymical import to represent an entire class of similar artifacts, such as mechanical inventions; or the replacement of wood by metal construction; or the displacement of human,

From Leo Marx, "The Idea of Technology and Postmodern Pessimism," in *Does Technology Drive History?* M. R. Smith and Leo Marx, eds. (Cambridge, MA: MIT Press, 1994), pp. 242–252.

animal, or other natural energy sources (water or wind) by engines run by mechanized motive power; or some specific, distinctive feature of the era ("the annihilation of space and time," "The Age of Steam"); or, most inclusive, that feature's general uniqueness (the "Industrial Revolution"). Thus, when Thomas Carlyle announced at the outset of his seminal 1829 essay "Signs of the Times" that, if asked to name the oncoming age, he would call it "The Age of Machinery," he was not merely referring to actual, physical machines, or even to the fact of their proliferation. He had in mind a radically new kind of ensemble typified by, but by no means restricted to, actual mechanical artifacts. "Machinery," as invoked by Carlyle (and soon after by many others), had both material and ideal (mental) referents; it simultaneously referred to (1) the "mechanical philosophy," an empirical mentality associated with Descartes and Locke and with the new science, notably Newtonian physics; (2) the new practical, or industrial, arts (especially those using mechanized motive power); (3) the systematic division of labor (the workers as cogs in the productive machinery); and (4) a new kind of impersonal, hierarchical, or bureaucratic organization, all of which could be said to exhibit the power of "mechanism." Carlyle's essay is an early, eloquent testimonial to the existence of a semantic void and to the desire to fill it with a more inclusive, scientistic, and distinctive conception of these new human powers than was signified by the most inclusive term then available, "the mechanic arts."

During the nineteenth century, discrete artifacts or machines were replaced, as typical embodiments of the new power, by what later would come to be called "technological systems." It is evident in retrospect that the steam-powered locomotive, probably the nineteenth century's leading image of progress, did not adequately represent the manifold character or the complexity of the mechanic art of transporting persons and goods by steam-powered engines moving wagons over a far-flung network of iron rails. To represent such complexity, that image of a locomotive was no more adequate than the term "mechanic art." As Alfred Chandler and others have argued, the railroad probably was the first of the large-scale, complex, full-fledged technological systems. In addition to the engines and other material equipment (rolling stock, stations, yards, signaling devices, fuel supplies, the network of tracks), a railroad comprised a corporate organization, a large capital investment, and a great many specially trained managers, engineers, telegraphers, conductors, and mechanics. Because a railroad operated over a large geographical area, 24 hours a day, every day of the year, in all kinds of weather, it became necessary to develop an impersonal, expert cohort of professional managers, and to replace the traditional organization of the family-owned and -operated firm with that of the large-scale, centralized, hierarchical, bureaucratic corporation.

Between 1870 and 1920 such large complex systems became a dominant element in the American economy. Although they resembled the railroad in scale, organization, and complexity, many relied on new nonmechanical forms of power. They included the telegraph and telephone network; the new chemical industry; electric light and power grids; and such linked mass-production-and-use systems as the automobile industry (sometimes called the "American" or "Fordist" system), which involved the ancillary production of rubber tires, steel, and glass and which was further linked with the petroleum, highway-construction, and trucking industries. In the era when electrical and chemical power were being introduced, and when these huge systems were replacing discrete artifacts, simple tools, or devices as the characteristic material form of the "mechanic arts," the latter term also was being replaced by a new conception: "technology."

The advent of this typically abstract modern concept coincided with the increasing control of the American economy by the great corporations. In Western capitalist societies, indeed, most technological systems (save for state-operated utility and military systems) were the legal property of—were organized as—independently owned corporations for operation within the rules, and for the purposes, of minority ownership. Thus, most of the new technological systems were operated with a view to maximizing economic growth as measured by corporate market share and profitability. At the same time, each corporation presumably was enhancing the nation's collective wealth and power. Alan Trachtenberg has aptly called this fusion of the nation's technological, economic, and political systems "the incorporation of America." By the late nineteenth century, Thorstein Veblen, an exponent of instrumental rationality, ruefully observed that under the regime of large-scale business enterprise the ostensible values of science-based technology (matter-of-fact rationality, efficiency, productivity, precision, conceptual parsimony) were being sacrificed to those of the minority owners: profitability, the display of conspicuous consumption, leisure-class status, and the building of private fortunes. But the abstract, sociologically and politically neutral (one might say neutered) word "technology," with its tacit claim to being a distinctive, independent mode of thought and practice like "science," is unmarked by a particular socio-economic regime.

Although the English word "technology" (derived from the Greek *teckhne,* "art" or "craft") had been available since the seventeenth century, during most of the next two centuries it had referred specifically and almost exclusively to technical discourses or treatises. In view of the way historians now routinely project the word back into the relatively remote past, it is surprising to discover how recently today's broad sense of "technology" achieved currency. It was seldom used before 1880. Indeed, the founding of the Massachusetts Institute of Technology in 1861 seems to have been a landmark, a halfway station, in its history; however, the *Oxford English Dictionary* cites R. F. Burton's use of "technology" in 1859 to refer to the "practical arts collectively" as the earliest English instance of the inclusive modern usage. (It is important to recognize the exact nature of this change: instead of being used to refer to a written work, such as a treatise, about the practical arts, "technology" now was used to refer directly to the arts—including the actual practice and practitioners—themselves.)

That this broader, modern sense of "technology" was just emerging at the middle of the nineteenth century is further indicated by the fact that Karl Marx and Arnold Toynbee, who were deeply concerned about the changes effected by the new machine power, did not use the word. At points in his influential lectures on the Industrial Revolution (composed in 1880–81) where "technology" would have been apposite, Toynbee, an economic historian, relied on other terms: "mechanical discoveries," "machinery," "mechanical improvements," "mechanical inventions," "factory system." Yet within 20 years Veblen would be suggesting that the "machine technology" was the distinguishing feature of modernity. My impression is, however, that "technology" in today's singular, inclusive sense did not gain truly wide currency until after World War I, and perhaps not until the Great Depression.

The advent of "technology" as the accepted name for the realm of the instrumental had many ramifications. Its relative abstractness, as compared with "the mechanic arts," had a kind of refining, idealizing, or purifying effect upon our increasingly elaborate contrivances for manipulating the object world, thereby protecting them from Western culture's ancient fear of contamination by physicality and work. An aura of impartial cerebration and rational detachment replaced the sensory associations that formerly had bound the mechanic arts to everyday life, artisanal skills, tools, work, and the egalitarian ethos of the early republic. In recognizing the mastery of various technologies as a legitimate pursuit of higher learning, the universities ratified that shift from the craft ethos to the mechanic arts to the meritocratic aspirations of the engineering and management professions. The lack of sensuous specificity attached to the noun "technology," its bloodless generality, and its common use in the more generalized singular form make the word conducive to a range of reference far beyond that available to the humdrum particularities of "the mechanic arts" or "the industrial arts." Those concrete categories could not simultaneously represent (as either "technology" or, say, "computer technology" can and does) a particular kind of device, a specialized form of theoretical knowledge or expertise, a distinctive mental style, and a unique set of skills and practices.

Perhaps the crucial difference is that the concept of "technology," with its wider scope of reference, is less closely identified with—or defined by—its material or artifactual aspect than was "the mechanic arts." This fact comports with the material reality of the large and complex new technological systems, in which the boundary between the intricately interlinked artifactual and other components—conceptual, institutional, human—is blurred and often invisible. When we refer to such systems, as compared with, say, carpentry, pottery, glass-making, or machine-tool operating, the artifactual aspect is a relatively small part of what comes before the mind. By virtue of its abstractness and inclusiveness, and its capacity to evoke the inextricable interpenetration of (for example) the powers of the computer with the bureaucratic practices of large modern institutions, "technology" (with no specifying adjective) invites endless reification. The concept refers to no specifiable institution, nor does it evoke any distinct associations of place or of persons belonging to any particular nation, ethnic group, race, class, or gender. A common tendency of contemporary discourse, accordingly, is to invest "technology" with a host of metaphysical properties and potencies, thereby making it seem to be a determinate entity, a disembodied autonomous casual agent of social change—of history. Hence the illusion that technology drives history. Of all its attributes, this hospitality to mystification—to technological determinism—may well be the one that has contributed most to postmodern pessimism.

. . . As the first complex technological systems were being assembled, and as the new concept of technology was being constructed, a related change was occurring within the ideology of progress. It entailed a subtle redescription of the historical role of the practical arts. Originally, as conceived by such exponents of the radical Enlightenment as Turgot, Condorcet, Paine, Priestley, Franklin, and Jefferson, innovations in science and in the mechanic arts were regarded as necessary yet necessarily insufficient means of achieving general progress. To the republican revolutionaries of the Enlightenment (especially the radical *philosophes*), science and the practical arts were instruments of political liberation—tools for arriving at the ideal goal of progress: a more just, more peaceful, and less hierarchical republican society based on the consent of the governed.

The idea of history as a record of progress driven by the application of science-based knowledge was not simply another idea among many. Rather it was a figurative concept lodged at the center of what became, sometime after 1750, the dominant secular world-picture of Western culture. That it was no mere rationale for domination by a privileged bourgeoisie is suggested by the fact that it was as fondly embraced by the hostile critics as by the ardent exponents of industrial capitalism. Marx and Engels, who developed the most systematic, influential, politically sophisticated critique of that regime, were deeply committed to the idea that history is a record of cumulative progress. In their view, the critical factor in human development—the counterpart in human history of Darwinian natural selection in natural history—is the more or less continuous growth of humanity's productive capacity. But of course they added a political stipulation, namely that the proletariat would have to seize state power by revolution if humanity was to realize the universal promise inherent in its growing power over nature. To later followers of Marx and Engels, the most apt name of that power leading to communism, the political goal of progress—of history—is "technology."

But the advent of the concept of technology, and of the organization of complex technological systems, coincided with, and no doubt contributed to, a subtle revision of the ideology of progress. Technology now took on a much grander role in the larger historical scheme—grander, that is, than the role that originally had been assigned to the practical arts. To leaders of the radical Enlightenment like Jefferson and Franklin, the chief value of those arts was in providing the material means of accomplishing what really mattered: the building of a just, republican society. After the successful bourgeois revolutions, however, many citizens, especially the merchants, industrialists, and other relatively privileged people (predominantly white and male, of course), took the new society's ability to reach that political goal for granted. They assumed, not implausibly from their vantages, that the goal already was within relatively easy reach. What now was important, especially from an entrepreneurial viewpoint, was perfecting the means. But the growing scope and integration of the new systems made it increasingly difficult to distinguish between the material (artifactual or technical) and the other organizational (managerial or financial) components of "technology." At this time, accordingly, the simple republican formula for generating progress by directing improved technical means to societal ends was imperceptibly transformed into a quite different technocratic commitment to improving "technology" as the basis and the measure of—as all but constituting—the progress of society. This technocratic idea may be seen as an ultimate, culminating expression of the optimistic, universalist aspirations of Enlightenment rationalism. But it tacitly replaced political aspirations with technical innovation as a primary agent of change, thereby preparing the way for an increasingly pessimistic sense of the technological determination of history.

The cultural modernism of the West in the early twentieth century was permeated by this technocratic spirit. (A distinctive feature of the technocratic mentality is its seemingly boundless, unrestricted, expansive scope—its tendency to break through the presumed boundaries of the instrumental and to dominate any kind of practice.) The technocratic spirit was made manifest in the application of the principles of instrumental rationality, efficiency, order, and control to the behavior of industrial workers. As set forth in the early-twentieth-century theories of Taylorism and Fordism, the standards of efficiency devised for the functioning of parts within machines were applied to the movements of workers in the new large-scale factory system. The technocratic spirit also was carried into the "fine" arts by avant-grade practitioners of various radically innovative styles associated with early modernism. The credo of the Italian Futurists; the vogue of geometric abstractionism exemplified by the work of Mondrian and the exponents of "Machine Art"; the doctrines of the Precisionists and the Constructivists; the celebration of technological functionalism in architecture by Le Corbusier, Mies Van der Rohe, and other exponents of the international style—all these tendencies exemplified the permeation of the culture of modernity by a kind of technocratic utopianism.

Architecture, with its distinctive merging of the aesthetic and the practical, provides a particularly compelling insight into the modern marriage of culture and technology. The International Style featured the use, as building materials, of such unique products of advanced technologies as steel, glass, and reinforced concrete; new technologies also made it possible to construct stripped-down, spare buildings whose functioning depended on still other innovative devices (the elevator, the subway system, air conditioning). This minimalist, functional style of architecture anticipated many features of what probably is the quintessential fantasy of a technocratic paradise: the popular science-fiction vision of life in a spaceship far from Earth, where recycling eliminates all dependence on organic processes and where the self-contained environment is completely under human control.

Do Artifacts Have Politics?

LANGDON WINNER

In controversies about technology and society, there is no idea more provocative than the notion that technical things have political qualities. At issue is the claim that the machines, structures, and systems of modern material culture can be accurately judged not only for their contributions of efficiency and productivity, not merely for their positive and negative environmental side effects, but also for the ways in which they can embody specific forms of power and authority. Since ideas of this kind have a persistent and troubling presence in discussions about the meaning of technology, they deserve explicit attention.

Writing in *Technology and Culture* almost two decades ago, Lewis Mumford gave classic statement to one version of the theme, arguing that "from late neolithic times in the Near East, right down to our own day, two technologies have recurrently existed side by side: one authoritarian, the other democratic, the first system-centered, immensely powerful, but inherently unstable, the other man-centered, relatively weak, but resourceful and durable." This thesis stands at the heart of Mumford's studies of the city, architecture, and the history of technics, and mirrors concerns voiced earlier in the works of Peter Kropotkin, William Morris, and other nineteenth century critics of industrialism. More recently, antinuclear and prosolar energy movements in Europe and America have adopted a similar notion as a centerpiece in their arguments. Thus environmentalist Denis Hayes concludes, "The increased deployment of nuclear power facilities must lead society toward authoritarianism. Indeed, safe reliance upon

From Langdon Winner, "Do Artifacts Have Politics?" *Daedalus* 109 (1980): 121–128.

nuclear power as the principal source of energy may be possible only in a totalitarian state." Echoing the views of many proponents of appropriate technology and the soft energy path, Hayes contends that "dispersed solar sources are more compatible than centralized technologies with social equity, freedom and cultural pluralism.

An eagerness to interpret technical artifacts in political language is by no means the exclusive property of critics of large-scale high-technology systems. A long lineage of boosters have insisted that the "biggest and best" that science and industry made available were the best guarantees of democracy, freedom, and social justice. The factory system, automobile, telephone, radio, television, the space program, and of course nuclear power itself have all at one time or another been described as democratizing, liberating forces. David Lilienthal, in *T.V.A.: Democracy on the March,* for example, found this promise in the phosphate fertilizers and electricity that technical progress was bringing to rural Americans during the 1940s. In a recent essay, *The Republic of Technology,* Daniel Boorstin extolled television for "its power to disband armies, to cashier presidents, to create a whole new democratic world—democratic in ways never before imagined, even in America." Scarcely a new invention comes along that someone does not proclaim it the salvation of a free society.

It is no surprise to learn that technical systems of various kinds are deeply interwoven in the conditions of modern politics. The physical arrangements of industrial production, warfare, communications, and the like have fundamentally changed the exercise of power and the experience of citizenship. But to go beyond this obvious fact and to argue that certain technologies *in themselves* have political properties seems, at first glance, completely mistaken. We all know that people have politics, not things. To discover either virtues or evils in aggregates of steel, plastic, transistors, integrated circuits, and chemicals seems just plain wrong, a way of mystifying human artifice and of avoiding the true sources, the human sources of freedom and oppression, justice and injustice. Blaming the hardware appears even more foolish than blaming the victims when it comes to judging conditions of public life.

Hence, the stern advice commonly given those who flirt with the notion that technical artifacts have political qualities: What matters is not technology itself, but the social or economic system in which it is embedded. This maxim, which in a number of variations is the central premise of a theory that can be called the social determination of technology, has an obvious wisdom. It serves as a needed corrective to those who focus uncritically on such things as "the computer and its social impacts" but who fail to look behind technical things to notice the social circumstances of their development, deployment, and use. This view provides an antidote to naive technological determinism—the idea that technology develops as the sole result of an internal dynamic, and then, unmediated by any other influence, molds society to fit its patterns. Those who have not recognized the ways in which technologies are shaped by social and economic forces have not gotten very far.

But the corrective has its own shortcomings; taken literally, it suggests that technical *things* do not matter at all. Once one has done the detective work necessary to reveal the social origins—power holders behind a particular instance of technological change—one will have explained everything of importance. This conclusion offers comfort to social scientists: it validates what they had always suspected, namely, that there is nothing distinctive about the study of technology in the first place. Hence, they can return to their standard models of social power—those of interest group politics, bureaucratic politics, Marxist models of class struggle, and the like—and have everything they need. The social determination of technology is, in this view, essentially no different from the social determination of, say, welfare policy or taxation.

There are, however, good reasons technology has of late taken on a special fascination in its own right for historians, philosophers, and political scientists; good reasons the standard models of social science only go so far in accounting for what is most interesting and troublesome about the subject. In another place I have tried to show why so much of modern social and political thought contains recurring statements of what can be called a theory of technological politics, an odd mongrel of notions often crossbred with orthodox liberal, conservative, and socialist philosophies. The theory of technological politics draws attention to the momentum of large-scale sociotechnical systems, to the response of modern societies to certain technological imperatives, and to the all too common signs of the adaptation of human ends to technical means. In so doing it offers a novel framework of interpretation and explanation for some of the more puzzling patterns that have taken shape in and around the growth of modern material culture. One strength of this point of view is that it takes technical artifacts seriously. Rather than insist that we immediately reduce everything to the interplay of social forces, it suggests that we pay attention to the characteristics of technical objects and the meaning of those characteristics. A necessary complement to, rather than a replacement for, theories of the social determination of technology, this perspective identifies certain technologies as political phenomena in their own right. It points us back, to borrow Edmund Husserl's philosophical injunction, *to the things themselves.* . . .

. . . Anyone who has traveled the highways of America and has become used to the normal height of overpasses may well find something a little odd about some of the bridges over the parkways on Long Island, New York. Many of the overpasses are extraordinarily low, having as little as nine feet of clearance at the curb. Even those who happened to notice this structural peculiarity would not be inclined to attach any special meaning to it. In our accustomed way of looking at things like roads and bridges we see the details of form as innocuous, and seldom give them a second thought.

It turns out, however, that the two hundred or so low-hanging overpasses on Long Island were deliberately designed to achieve a particular social effect. Robert Moses, the master builder of roads, parks, bridges, and other public works from the 1920s to the 1970s in New York, had these overpasses built to specifications that would discourage the presence of buses on his parkways. According to evidence provided by Robert A. Caro in his biography of Moses, the reasons reflect Moses's social-class bias and racial prejudice. Automobile-owning whites of "upper" and "comfortable middle" classes, as he called them, would be free to use the parkways for recreation and commuting. Poor people and blacks, who normally used public transit, were kept off the roads because the twelve-foot tall buses could not get through the overpasses. One consequence was to limit access of racial minorities and low-income groups to Jones Beach, Moses's widely acclaimed public park. Moses made doubly sure of this result by vetoing a proposed extension of the Long Island Railroad to Jones Beach.

As a story in recent American political history, Robert Moses's life is fascinating. His dealings with mayors, governors, and presidents, and his careful manipulation of legislatures, banks, labor unions, the press, and public opinion are all matters that political scientists could study for years. But the most important and enduring results of his work are his technologies, the vast engineering projects that give New York much of its present form. For generations after Moses has gone and the alliances he forged have fallen apart, his public works, especially the highways and bridges he built to favor the use of the automobile over the development of mass transit, will continue to shape that city. Many of his monumental structures of concrete and steel embody a systematic social inequality, a way of engineering relationships among people that, after a time, becomes just another part of the landscape. As planner Lee Koppleman told Caro about the low bridges on Wantagh Parkway, "The old son-of-a-gun had made sure that buses would *never* be able to use his goddamned parkways."

Histories of architecture, city planning, and public works contain many examples of physical arrangements that contain explicit or implicit political purposes. One can point to Baron Haussmann's broad Parisian thoroughfares, engineered at Louis Napoleon's direction to prevent any recurrence of street fighting of the kind that took place during the revolution of 1848. Or one can visit any number of grotesque concrete buildings and huge plazas constructed on American university campuses during the late 1960s and early 1970s to defuse student demonstrations. Studies of industrial machines and instruments also turn up interesting political stories, including some that violate our normal expectations about why technological innovations are made in the first place. If we suppose that new technologies are introduced to achieve increased efficiency, the history of technology shows that we will sometimes be disappointed. Technological change expresses a panoply of human motives, not the least of which is the desire of some to have dominion over others, even though it may require an occasional sacrifice of cost-cutting and some violence to the norm of getting more from less. . . .

In cases like those of Moses's low bridges . . . one sees the importance of technical arrangements that precede the *use* of the things in question. It is obvious that technologies can be used in ways that enhance the power, authority, and privilege of some over others, for example, the use of television to sell a candidate. To our accustomed way of thinking, technologies are seen as neutral tools that can be used well or poorly, for good, evil, or something in between. But we usually do not stop to inquire whether a given device might have been designed and built in such a way that it produces a set of consequences logically and temporally *prior* to any of its professed uses. Robert Moses's bridges, after all, were used to carry automobiles from one point to another. . . . If our moral and political language for evaluating technology includes only categories having to do with tools and uses, if it does not include attention to the meaning of the designs and arrangements of our artifacts, then we will be blinded to much that is intellectually and practically crucial.

Because the point is most easily understood in the light of particular intentions embodied in physical form, I have so far offered [an] illustration that seems almost conspiratorial. But to recognize the political dimensions in the shapes of technology does not require that we look for conscious conspiracies or malicious intentions. The organized movement of handicapped people in the United States during the 1970s pointed out the countless ways in which machines, instruments, and structures of common use—buses, buildings, sidewalks, plumbing fixtures, and so forth—made it impossible for many handicapped persons to move about freely, a condition that systematically excluded them from public life. It is safe to say that designs unsuited for the handicapped arose more from long-standing neglect than from anyone's active intention. But now that the issue has been raised for public attention, it is evident that justice requires a remedy. A whole range of artifacts are now being redesigned and rebuilt to accommodate this minority.

Indeed, many of the most important examples of technologies that have political consequences are those that transcend the simple categories of "intended" and "unintended" altogether. These are instances in which the very process of technical development is so thoroughly biased in a particular direction that it regularly produces results counted as wonderful breakthroughs by some social interests and crushing setbacks by others. In such cases it is neither correct nor insightful to say, "Someone intended to do somebody else harm." Rather, one must say that the technological deck has been stacked long in advance to favor certain social interests, and that some people were bound to receive a better hand than others.

The mechanical tomato harvester, a remarkable device perfected by researchers at the University of California from the late 1940s to the present, offers an illustrative tale. The machine is able to harvest tomatoes in a single pass through a row, cutting the plants from the ground, shaking the fruit loose, and in the newest models sorting the tomatoes electronically into large plastic gondolas that hold up to twenty-five tons of produce headed for canning. To accommodate the rough motion of these "factories in the field," agricultural researchers have bred new varieties of tomatoes that are hardier, sturdier, and less tasty. The harvesters replace the system of handpicking, in which crews of farmworkers would pass through the fields three or four times putting ripe tomatoes in lug boxes and saving immature fruit for later harvest. Studies in California indicate that the machine reduces costs by approximately five to seven dollars per ton as compared to hand-harvesting. But the benefits are by no means equally divided in the agricultural economy. In fact, the machine in the garden has in this instance been the occasion for a thorough reshaping of social relationships of tomato production in rural California.

By their very size and cost, more than $50,000 each to purchase, the machines are compatible only with a highly concentrated form of tomato growing. With the introduction of this new method of harvesting, the number of tomato growers declined from approximately four thousand in the early 1960s to about six hundred in 1973, yet with a substantial increase in tons of tomatoes produced. By the late 1970s an estimated thirty-two thousand jobs in the tomato industry had been eliminated as a direct consequence of mechanization. Thus, a jump in productivity to the benefit of very large growers has occurred at a sacrifice to other rural agricultural communities.

The University of California's research and development on agricultural machines like the tomato harvester is at this time the subject of a law suit filed by attorneys for California Rural Legal Assistance, an organization representing a group of farmworkers and other interested parties. The suit charges that University officials are spending tax monies on projects that benefit a handful of private interests to the detriment of farmworkers, small farmers, consumers, and rural California generally, and asks for a court injunction to stop the practice. The University has denied these charges, arguing that to accept them "would require elimination of all research with any potential practical application."

As far as I know, no one has argued that the development of the tomato harvester was the result of a plot. Two students of the controversy, William Friedland and Amy Barton, specifically exonerate both the original developers of the machine and the hard tomato from any desire to facilitate economic concentration in that industry. What we see here instead is an ongoing social process in which scientific knowledge, technological invention, and corporate profit reinforce each other in deeply entrenched patterns that bear the unmistakable stamp of political and economic power. Over many decades agricultural research and development in American land-grant colleges and universities has tended to favor the interests of large agribusiness concerns. It is in the face of such subtly ingrained patterns that opponents of innovations like the tomato harvester are made to seem "antitechnology" or "antiprogress." For the harvester is not merely the symbol of a social order that rewards some while punishing others; it is in a true sense an embodiment of that order.

Within a given category of technological change there are, roughly speaking, two kinds of choices that can affect the relative distribution of power, authority, and privilege in a community. Often the crucial decision is a simple "yes or no" choice—are we going to develop and adopt the thing or not? In recent years many local, national, and international disputes about technology have centered on "yes or no" judgments about such things as food additives, pesticides, the building of highways, nuclear reactors, and dam projects. The fundamental choice about an ABM or an SST is whether or not the thing is going to join society as a piece of its operating equipment. Reasons for and against are frequently as important as those concerning the adoption of an important new law.

A second range of choices, equally critical in many instances, has to do with specific features in the design or arrangement of a technical system after the decision to go ahead with it has already been made. Even after a utility company wins permission to build a large electric power line, important controversies can remain with respect to the placement of its route and the design of its towers; even after an organization has decided to institute a system of computers, controversies can still arise with regard to the kinds of components, programs, modes of access, and other specific features the system will include. Once the mechanical tomato harvester had been developed in its basic form, design alteration of critical social significance—the addition of electronic sorters, for example—changed the character of the machine's effects on the balance of wealth and power in California agriculture. Some of the most interesting research on technology and politics at present focuses on the attempt to demonstrate in a detailed, concrete fashion how seemingly innocuous design features in mass transit systems, water projects, industrial machinery, and other technologies actually mask social choices of profound significance. . . .

From such examples I would offer the following general conclusions. The things we call "technologies" are ways of building order in our world. Many technical devices and systems important in everyday life contain possibilities for many different ways of ordering human activity. Consciously or not, deliberately or inadvertently, societies choose structures for technologies that influence how people are going to work, communicate, travel, consume, and so forth over a very long time. In the processes by which structuring decisions are made, different people are differently situated and possess unequal degrees of power as well as unequal levels of awareness. By far the greatest latitude of choice exists the very first time a particular instrument, system, or technique is introduced. Because choices tend to become strongly fixed in material equipment, economic investment, and social habit, the original flexibility vanishes for all practical purposes once the initial commitments are made. In that sense technological innovations are similar to legislative acts or political foundings that establish a framework for public order that will endure over many generations. For that reason, the same careful attention one would give to the rules, roles, and relationships of politics must also be given to such things as the building of highways, the creation of television networks, and the tailoring of seemingly insignificant features on new machines. The issues that divide or unite people in society are settled not only in the institutions and practices of politics proper, but also, and less obviously, in tangible arrangements of steel and concrete, wires and transistors, nuts and bolts.

The Social Shaping of Technology

DONALD MACKENZIE

. . . The idea that technological change is just "progress," and that certain technologies triumph simply because they are the best or the most efficient, is still widespread. A weaker but more sophisticated version of technological determinism—the idea that there are "natural trajectories" of technological change—remains popular among economists who study technology.

In my experience, the idea of unilinear progress does not survive serious engagement with the detail of the history of technology. For what is perhaps most striking about that history is its wealth, complexity, and variety. Instead of one predetermined path of advance, there is typically a constant turmoil of concepts, plans, and projects. From that turmoil, order (sometimes) emerges, and its emergence is of course what lends credibility to notions of "progress" or "natural trajectory." With hindsight, the technology that succeeds usually does look like the best or the most natural next step.

However . . . we must always ask "Best for whom?" Different people may see a technology in different ways, attach different meanings to it, want different things from it, assess it differently. Women and men, for example, may view the same artifact quite differently. Workers and their employers may not agree on the desirable features of a production technology.

Such discrepant meanings and interests are often at the heart of what is too readily dismissed as irrational resistance to technological change, such as that of the much-disparaged Luddite machine breakers. We must also ask "Best for whom?" even when we are discussing such apparently "technical" decisions as the best way to automate machine tools or typesetting. These two technologies were the subjects of now-classic studies of Cynthia Cockburn (who focused on the shaping of technology by gender relations) and David Noble (who focused on its shaping of relations of social class). . . .

From Donald MacKenzie, "The Social Shaping of Technology" originally appeared as "Underpinnings" in *Knowing Machines: Essays on Technical Change* (Cambridge, MA: MIT Press, 1996), pp. 5–8.

Nor is this issue—the different meanings of a technology for different "relevant social groups," and the consequently different criteria of what it means for one technology to be better than another—restricted to situations of class conflict or other overt social division. The customers for . . . supercomputers . . . for example, were all members of what one might loosely think of as the "establishment": nuclear weapons laboratories, the code breakers of the National Security Agency, large corporations, elite universities, and weather bureaus. Responding to their needs, but far from subservient, were the developers of supercomputers, most famously Seymour Cray. All were agreed that a supercomputer should be fast, but there were subtle differences among them as to what "fast" meant. As a consequence, the technical history of supercomputing can be seen, in one light, as a negotiation—which is still continuing—of the meaning of speed.

We also need to delve deeper even where there is agreement as to what characteristics make a technology the best. . . . Technologies, as Brian Arthur and Paul David point out, typically manifest increasing returns to adoption. The more they are adopted, the more experience is gained in their use, the more research and development effort is devoted to them, and the better they become. This effect is particularly dramatic in the case of "network" technologies such as telephones or the worldwide computer network called the Internet, where the utility of the technology to one user depends strongly on how many other users there are. But the effect can be also be found in "stand-alone" technologies. . . .

This means that early adoptions—achieved for whatever reasons—may give a particular technology an overwhelming lead over actual or potential rivals, as that technology enjoys a virtuous circle in which adoptions lead to improvements, which then spawn more adoptions and further improvements, while its rivals stagnate. Technologies, in other words, may be best because they have triumphed, rather than triumphing because they are best.

Hindsight often makes it appear that the successful technology is simply intrinsically superior, but hindsight—here and elsewhere—can be a misleading form of vision. Historians and sociologists of technology would do well to avoid explaining the success of a technology by its assumed intrinsic technical superiority to its rivals. Instead, they should seek, even-handedly, to understand how its actual superiority came into being, while suspending judgment as to whether it is intrinsic. . . .

. . . [E]xpectations about the future are often integral to technological success or failure. Most obviously, a belief in the future success of a technology can be a vital component of that success, because it encourages inventors to focus their efforts on the technology, investors to invest in it, and users to adopt it. These outcomes, if they then bear fruit, can reinforce the original belief by providing evidence for its correctness.

Self-validating belief—"self-fulfilling prophecy"—has sometimes been regarded by social scientists as pathological, as permitting false beliefs to become true. The classic example is the way an initially arbitrary belief in the unsoundness of a particular bank can produce a run on that bank and thus cause it to fail. Nevertheless, self-referential, self-reinforcing belief is pervasive in social life, as Barry Barnes has argued eloquently. The most obvious case is money, which can function as a medium of exchange only when enough people believe it will continue to do so; but all social institutions arguably have something of the character of the self-fulfilling prophecy. Some of the most striking phenomena of technological change are of this kind. One example . . . is "Moore's Law": the annual doubling of the number of components on state-of-the-art microchips. Moore's Law is not merely an after-the-fact empirical description of processes of change in microelectronics; it is a belief that has become self-fulfilling by guiding the technological and investment decisions of those involved.

Of course, I would not suggest that self-reinforcing belief is all there is to phenomena such as Moore's Law. Expectations, however widespread, can be dashed as technologies encounter the obduracy of both the physical and the social world. As a result, many technological prophecies fail to be self-validating—for example, the prophecy, widespread in the 1960s, that the speed of airliners would continue to increase, as it had in previous decades. In recent years even Moore's Law seems to have lost some of its apparently inexorable certainty, although belief in it is still a factor in the justification of the enormous capital expenditures (of the order of $1 billion for each of the world's twenty state-of-the-art chip fabrication facilities) needed to keep component density growing. . . .

Problems with "Skill"

NINA LERMAN

Machines and tools have been described, discussed, and classified, and the processes of their invention and manufacture carefully examined. By contrast, the words for the human side of technological activity—skill, know-how, technical knowledge, technological knowledge—evoke a range of associations, but offer little of the precision and subtlety applied to investigations of hardware. The term "skill," a favorite of labor historians and historians of technology alike, implies a coarse skilled/unskilled dichotomy, which is occasionally expanded, but hardly refined, by the problematic term "semi-skilled." Using these terms is comparable to describing "sophisticated" as opposed to "unsophisticated" or "semi-sophisticated" hardware. In addition to the coarseness of the classification, "unskilled" often connotes low "intelligence," ambition, or social status, which silently superimposes other hierarchies, clouding the issues at hand. "Know-how" is useful for its simplicity, but its ingenious mechanical connotations make it an unlikely description of either knitting or nuclear engineering.

Using the term "knowledge," on the other hand, elevates all interactions with hardware, from churning butter to building locomotives, into the realm of other cognitive activities. The choice of adjective, at this stage, seems largely arbitrary, but recent authors have used "technical" to apply to the more elite or "cutting edge" domains of science, medicine, and new technologies. In general, "technological knowledge," when broadly defined parallel to current usage of "technology," is—at least connotationally—more inclusive. Such a term also provides an effective means of shedding old assumptions; for example, labor historians have not written about the unionization of

From Nina Lerman, "The Problem with 'Skill,'" in "From 'Useful Knowledge' to 'Habits of Industry': Gender, Race, and Class in Nineteenth-Century Technical Education" (unpublished Ph.D. dissertation, University of Pennsylvania, 1993), pp. 3–7.

"technologically knowledgeable" workers or the "technological de-knowledging" of the labor market.

Most studies of the subject thus far have begun with the assumption that studying "skill" should be done by looking at people labeled "skilled." But that label has had enough rhetorical weight that its use refers implicitly to characteristics other than technological knowledge. Scholars' examples are frequently drawn from metal-working, machining, and large-scale heavy industry—domains which are relatively privileged, and predominantly or exclusively male. Like the search for a lost key under a streetlamp because the light is better there, this focus excludes much of the territory in which the objects of the study might be found. For a definition of "technology" to make sense it must include all possible tools and techniques, despite connotations of complexity or sophistication. "Technological knowledge" applies to tasks such as haying or sewing as aptly as to operating heavy machinery, or programming a computer.

The conscious inclusion of such activities as, for example, the building of haystacks, sheds new light on some definitions of "skill." Sociologists of work have suggested measuring training time as a quantitative measure of skill. But how does one define training time? For example, as soon as he was old enough, a boy growing up on a nineteenth century farm tagged along with his father and helped out in small ways where he could. All the while he was absorbing the ways of a working farm. Suppose he began going out with his father when he was 4, and by 14 he could build his own haystack. Should we therefore consider comparisons with 10-year industrial apprenticeships? Or say that haystack-building required no training because a 14 year old could do it? The definition of "training" itself becomes problematic.

Women's tasks such as needlework are also instructive. Discussions of technological knowledge often differentiate between "knowledge" and "workmanship," or articulated and "tacit" knowledge. For example, Steve Shapin has written that "skill is knowledge without a voice." "Voice," in this definition, is closely linked to verbalization. A small girl in early nineteenth-century Philadelphia might have been given scraps of fabric, a needle, and thread. With practice, she learned to sew. Such scraps are unlikely to survive, or to be written about. But suppose that when she was, perhaps, eight years old, she embroidered a sampler under the guidance of her mother or her teacher at school. Her mother saved this sampler, and it was passed down from generation to generation. The child who embroidered it was soon helping her mother with the mending—but we have no record of her increasing mastery. Do the words on the sampler, in the form of a brief verse and the child's name, count as a "voice"? Does the sampler reflect "knowledge" while the mending the girl did at 12 is "skill"?

Exploring the realm beyond the streetlamp raises fundamental questions. . . . What kinds of choices are made by whom in the acquisition and development of technological knowledge? Who learns how to do what, who is allowed to learn how to do what, what things can one readily learn how to do? What knowledge is commonplace, and what is unusual? What does it mean, in a particular context, to say that a particular person possesses a particular skill? As Steven Lubar has pointed out, technological knowledge can only be studied in its representations: in artifacts, actions, pictures, and words. But in other realms historians have developed a critical repertory of questions about how the nature of the source biases its presentation of information, and also how our own assumptions and expectations bias our reading of the source. Such questions have only recently been applied to technological knowledge, and not yet systematically.

Masculinity and Technology

CARROLL PURSELL

Masculinity, that is, what makes a male manly, is something that we can all recognize despite the fact that we might disagree widely on what precisely that something is. It has been suggested that in most, if indeed not all, societies, the mere facts of anatomy are not sufficient to make a man feel, or to get a community to agree, on that person's masculinity. Being a "real man" is always something earned or acquired, something that is socially defined and individually displayed. As a category of gender, masculinity always implies an Other, in some cases the category Woman, in others, Boy.

Masculinity is both socially constructed and historically contingent, and therefore there can be no such thing as a male essence. It is not necessary, or even possible, to explain at once the presence and import of masculinity in all phases of the history of technology in all places and times, for it has meaning only in specific historical contexts. In fact, gender itself is a flexible and changing construct, ideas of masculinity are constantly being negotiated and none, at any one time, is perfectly hegemonic. David Leverenz, for example, has argued that "three basic masculine ideals were available in the mid-nineteenth century. The genteel patrician was the cultured gentleman of the old school. The artisan valued personal independence and pride in work. The aggressive self-made man was at the center of the new business culture. He was preoccupied with power and force, imposing his will upon the world out of fear of being crushed by it." Alongside these three there were undoubtedly others, and many of them overlapped to some degree. . . .

The way in which styles of masculinity relate to styles of technology is also not straightforward. The roles of patrician, artisan, and entrepreneur, to take these categories, each immediately suggest appropriate and widely divergent technologies. . . .

I have been set on this quest for masculinity by Judith McGaw, who has recently insisted that "we can make a start toward serious gender studies by consistently recognizing and acknowledging that the male actors who predominated historically in American engineering, business, and manufacturing were men and not merely people. In other words, we can no longer afford to write the history of technology as though it were normal to be male and aberrant to be female." In taking up that challenge, I feel particularly the weight of Evelyn Fox Keller's observation that "the association of masculinity with scientific thought has the status of a myth which either cannot or should not be examined seriously. It has simultaneously the air of being 'self-evident' and 'nonsensical'—the former by virtue of existing in the realm of common knowledge (that is, everybody knows it), and the latter by virtue of lying outside the realm of formal knowledge, indeed conflicting with our image of science as emotionally and sexually neutral."

From Carroll Pursell, "The Construction of Masculinity and Technology," *Polhem* 11 (1993). pp. 206–217.

The same is certainly true of technology as well. On the one hand, technology is so obviously masculine that it hardly seems worth making the point. On the other, even though an increasing number of scholars are choosing to identify with the notion that technology is socially constructed, masculinity, which is itself socially constructed, has hardly found a place as one of the forces to be studied as a part of this process. It has not gone unnoticed that like those other powerful social categories class and race, gender has not been much used as an analytical tool to help us understand technology. When gender has been raised as an issue, it is women, not men, who have been studied.

As we study the role of masculinity in the history of technology, it is important to remember that gender is a matter of boundaries, and boundaries always have two sides. From the perspective of masculinity, women (and sometimes boys also) are the Other (so is Nature), at the same time attractive and threatening. One way to control women (and to emphasize their otherness) is to technologize them, that is, to see them as less than human (and specifically, as machines). . . .

The role of gender in the history of technology has probably been studied most intensively in the area of work. Perhaps because the sexual division of labor is older even than that discovered by Adam Smith, the interplay between changing technologies and seemingly eternal patriarchy is an obvious subject for study. Maxine Berg has shown that even before the Industrial Revolution, the adoption of new machines was gendered in often complex ways even if the design of the machine was not. Cynthia Cockburn has noted that while independence was seen to flow from a skilled trade and was linked to manhood, it "was a negative quality in women, threatening economic competition and sexual emergence." Employers played upon this fear, seeking to replace independence among male workers with the feminine attribute of docility through such techniques as lightening the physical burden of labor and by then threatening to replace the men with either women or boys.

The psycho-sexual roots of masculinized technology are powerful and not to be ignored, but we should also keep in mind Mort Sahl's surprise when told that Edsels did not sell because their front ends suggested the female vulva rather than the male penis. He had always assumed, he said, that it was because the Edsel cost more than a Pontiac and wasn't as good a car. American historians are familiar with the way in which race has been used to mask class interest in our society, and no doubt gender has been used in the same way. Losing one's job to a woman may be emasculating, but it is also impoverishing. Yet one is struck by the many times in which male workers appear to sacrifice class power to patriarchal advantage, giving every indication that the latter is more important to them than the former. And to complete the circle, there is no reason to believe that the employer who, for example, uses patriarchy to separate (for his own interests) the male workers from the female, himself believes any less in the importance of patriarchy for all his cynicism. As Cockburn insists, the two hierarchies of class and gender "are clearly Interactive."

The case of Frederick Douglass suggests that even when a man was not an independent producer, the possession of a craft skill provided a sense of manhood. Douglass, while still a slave, had been taught [to] caulk boats and for a while, worked side by side with white craftsmen. When he gained his freedom and went North, he noted that in the shipyards of New Bedford "every man appeared to understand his work, and went at it with a sober, yet cheerful earnestness, which betokened the deep interest which he felt in what he was doing, as well as a sense of his own dignity as a man." Though he often felt the deep wound of racism from these same men, Douglass clearly counted a craft skill as an indispensable ingredient of his own escape from slavery. With a technological skill, he was not only his own man, he was a Man.

"Strive on—The control of nature is won, not given," reads the motto above the door of the engineering building at the University of Wyoming. Control is the most important word in engineering: self-control, control of others, control of nature. Technology gives us control, but it also takes (self) control. Women especially need controlling, but so does Nature which is seen as female. Self-control is to resist the feminine (natural) in ourselves, and is something women are thought not to have much of. It is, of course, no surprise that engineering is the most male-dominated of all professions, and that even in our own time, women have found it extremely difficult, for both institutional and cultural reasons, to break into the field.

In America the golden age of the engineer as a cultural type was from the mid-19th to the mid-20th century. Partaking at once of the patrician, the artisan and the entrepreneur, increasingly collegiately educated but seen to be in his natural element on the Frontier, the engineer was a manly ideal. . . .

. . . Annette Kolodny has alerted us to the fact that the western mind feminized those places and peoples over which it gained intellectual and emotional control. In the 1960s the Atomic Energy Commission was able to make a film entitled "No Greater Challenge" designed to promote the use of nuclear powered desalting plants to irrigate the arid coastal lands of the world. In this award-winning film, the desert lands are described as fertile, but barren, awaiting and perhaps even desiring to be made fruitful by the engineering application of tools and irrigation waters. Women appear only as white American consumers, women of color with large families or Hispanic fruit-packing workers. The white (with one exception) male engineers design and impose what the film calls an "agro-industrial complex" on a feminized nature, making her productive at last, bristling no longer with cactii and scorpions, but now with nuclear power plants, aluminum sheet rolling mills, harvesting machinery and port facilities. This is the great challenge facing man today, we are told, and the overcoming of challenges is the very stuff of man's history.

The glorification of the engineer has permeated American cultural forms in the 20th century. Camel cigarettes and Velvet pipe tobacco both ran full pages magazine ads in the 1920s showing engineers at work, smoking their product, very much like the Marlboro Man of a later generation. In the opening chapter of H. Irving Hancock's book for boys, *The Young Engineers in Nevada* (1913), one happily entitled "Alf and His 'Makings of Manhood,'" the description of Tom Reade's physique borders on the homoerotic. As the engineer sucked in his stomach and expanded his chest, "Alf watched. For that matter he seemed unable to remove his gaze from the splendid chest development that young Reade displayed so easily." He looked, we are told, "a good deal more like some Greek god of old than a twentieth century civil engineer." In the 1958 juvenile book *Civil Engineering Is Fun,* we are introduced to "lean, clear-eyed engineers whose very calm confidence suggests high adventure in exciting places." They are responsible for "huge bridges being flung across mighty chasms, and mighty mountains blasted and gouged until they yield a place for man to move with machines." The adventure comes "to engineers who fight the wilderness, the desert, the unrelenting reluctance of an ancient, undisturbed nature to give way to man." Since masculinity is socially constructed rather than innate, it has to be constantly reproduced. The engineering ideal, held up to boys in countless volumes of juvenalia, was an important part of that reproduction. The evolution since the 1950s away from a view of idealized engineering masculinity is itself a significant cultural shift. . . .

. . . Masculinity is not merely another aspect of technology to be studied, it has the potential of changing the way we look at the entire field. I suspect that masculine attitudes and assumptions underlie much of the way we define our field and the way in which we formulate and choose topics. The History of Technology, as an academic field, represents our "formal knowledge" of technology, but there is also an informal knowledge—that knowledge which arises not from scholarly work but from our common cultural attitudes. Indeed, I wonder if this in itself is not gendered: that is, that men have been attracted to and have dominated the field because of the perceived masculinity of the subject (technology), and that in turn we have shaped it in masculine ways. What would we find if we took our informal knowledge seriously and studied those popular insights? In a society where rape is being talked about more openly, and seen more commonly as an expression of power and control and a crime of violence rather than sex, can we continue to ignore the obvious and universally acknowledged rape metaphor in much of the rhetoric of technology? And would it not be potentially important if we took seriously S. I. Hayakawa's crack in the 1950s that any car with a horsepower larger than that of the contemporary MG was used merely to suppress male fears of impotence? Surely charges, largely justified, that such connections are crudely made and lack theoretical rigor is no reason for not *subjecting* them to critical rigor.

. . . Why do we define production exclusively in terms of what men do, and at the same time ignore consumption, which we associate with women? Why do we shy away from all but the invention and design of machines and tools? If we ignore gender, we assume that technologies are designed to accomplish ungendered "human" ends, since purpose is always necessary. If we take account of gender, it suggests that much of our technology is designed not only by but for men. Can we find examples of this?

The history of technology, as a field, has always been interested in the artisan and master craftsman, working independently with his own tools and operating as an independent producer. Yet when that artisan, at some point in the industrializing process, became proletarianized, he became also labor history and of only marginal interest to historians of technology. I would suggest that we are accepting a masculine notion that the loss of skill and independence, and presumably of agency, is a feminizing process, and the now "womanly" worker is not as worthy of study as the inventor, engineer, entrepreneur or even manager. These are the actors, the feminized workers are merely acted upon. Because we deny agency to women, we do so also to workers, thus missing the many ways in which they might help shape the technologies presented to them. Ruth Schwartz Cowan has described a similar, female, agency among housewives. If one can think of technological systems (or cultures) as hegemonic, one can also expect to find counter-cultures, especially perhaps in liminal situations. Technological change always involves liminality and we are perhaps too Whiggish in ignoring the complexity of that process. Paul Forman has recently taken historians of science to task for trying to be "transcendent" rather than "independent"—for accepting the definition of their subject matter from scientists rather than creating it for themselves. It may be that in ways we have not yet realized, historians of technology do the same.

. . . The evidence is clear, I believe, that historians of technology would do well to add gender to the several analytical categories with which they now attempt to understand their subject. The feminist analysis of our field, as in the larger historical discourse, has added a rich, subtle and powerful set of meanings to our work. In a survey of historical writings on sex done over twenty years ago, John C. Burnham dryly noted that "it is a comment on male chauvinism in the profession that most of this work on sex . . . centers upon the history of women and women's status in America. It is neither fair nor accurate to continue to imply that like sex, gender is something that only women experience. Through time gender roles, for both men and women, have been as varied and numerous as technologies, and the way in which these two powerful forces have interacted is surely worthy of our attention.

The history of technology will be bountifully enriched by a willingness to admit that men sometimes act in their own self-interest as men, and that this often involves the creation, definition, and use of technology. Nor is the importance merely academic. Judy Wajcman, in her recent book *Feminism Confronts Technology,* has written that "gender is not just about difference but about power; this technical expertise is a source of men's actual or potential power over women. It is also an important part of women's experience of being less than, and dependent on, men." Both scholarship and justice, I think, will be served by a closer attention to the role played through time by the shifting and sometimes contradictory, but always significant, social constructions of masculinity.

The Proliferation of Hybrids

BRUNO LATOUR

On page four of my daily newspaper, I learn that the measurements taken above the Antarctic are not good this year: the hole in the ozone layer is growing ominously larger. Reading on, I turn from upper-atmosphere chemists to Chief Executive Officers of Atochem and Monsanto, companies that are modifying their assembly lines in order to replace the innocent chlorofluorocarbons, accused of crimes against the ecosphere. A few paragraphs later, I come across heads of state of major industrialized countries who are getting involved with chemistry, refrigerators, aerosols and inert gases. But at the end of the article, I discover that the meteorologists don't agree with the chemists; they're talking about cyclical fluctuations unrelated to human activity. So now the industrialists don't know what to do. The heads of state are also holding back. Should we wait? Is it already too late? Toward the bottom of the page, Third World countries and ecologists add their grain of salt and talk about international treaties, moratoriums, the rights of future generations, and the right to development.

The same article mixes together chemical reactions and political reactions. A single thread links the most esoteric sciences and the most sordid politics, the most distant sky and some factory in the Lyon suburbs, dangers on a global scale and the

From Bruno Latour, *We Have Never Been Modern* (Cambridge, MA: Harvard University Press, 1993), pp. 1–7.

impending local elections or the next board meeting. The horizons, the stakes, the time frames, the actors—none of these is commensurable, yet there they are, caught up in the same story.

On page six, I learn that the Paris AIDS virus contaminated the culture medium in Professor Gallo's laboratory; that Mr. Chirac and Mr. Reagan had, however, solemnly sworn not to go back over the history of that discovery; that the chemical industry is not moving fast enough to market medications which militant patient organizations are vocally demanding; that the epidemic is spreading in sub-Saharan Africa. Once again, heads of state, chemists, biologists, desperate patients and industrialists find themselves caught up in a single uncertain story mixing biology and society.

On page eight, there is a story about computers and chips controlled by the Japanese; on page nine, about the right to keep frozen embryos; on page ten, about a forest burning, its columns of smoke carrying off rare species that some naturalists would like to protect; on page eleven, there are whales wearing collars fitted with radio tracking devices; also on page eleven, there is a slag heap in northern France, a symbol of the exploitation of workers, that has just been classified as an ecological preserve because of the rare flora it has been fostering! On page twelve, the Pope, French bishops, Monsanto, the Fallopian tubes, and Texas fundamentalists gather in a strange cohort around a single contraceptive. On page fourteen, the number of lines on high-definition television bring together Mr. Delors, Thomson, the EEC, commissions on standardization, the Japanese again, and television film producers. Change the screen standard by a few lines, and billions of francs, millions of television sets, thousands of hours of film, hundreds of engineers and dozens of CEOs go down the drain.

Fortunately, the paper includes a few restful pages that deal purely with politics (a meeting of the Radical Party), and there is also the literary supplement in which novelists delight in the adventures of a few narcissistic egos ("I love you . . . you don't"). We would be dizzy without these soothing features. For the others are multiplying, those hybrid articles that sketch out imbroglios of science, politics, economy, laws, religion, technology, fiction. If reading the daily paper is modern man's form of prayer, then it is a very strange man indeed who is doing the praying today while reading about these mixed-up affairs. All of culture and all of nature get churned up again every day.

Yet no one seems to find this troubling. Headings like Economy, Politics, Science, Books, Culture, Religion and Local Events remain in place as if there were nothing odd going on. The smallest AIDS virus takes you from sex to the unconscious, then to Africa, tissue cultures, DNA and San Francisco, but the analysts, thinkers, journalists and decision-makers will slice the delicate network traced by the virus for you into tidy compartments where you will find only science, only economy, only social phenomena, only local news, only sentiment, only sex. Press the most innocent aerosol button and you'll be heading for the Antarctic, and from there to the University of California at Irvine, the mountain ranges of Lyon, the chemistry of inert gases, and then maybe to the United Nations, but this fragile thread will be broken into as many segments as there are pure disciplines. By all means, they seem to say, let us not mix up knowledge, interest, justice and power. Let us not mix up heaven and earth, the global stage and the local scene, the human and the nonhuman. "But these imbroglios do the mixing," you'll say, "they weave our world together!" "Act as if they didn't exist," the analysts reply. They have cut the Gordian knot with a well-honed sword. The shaft is broken: on the left, they have put knowledge of things; on the right, power and human politics.

. . . For twenty years or so, my friends and I have been studying these strange situations that the intellectual culture in which we live does not know how to categorize. For lack of better terms, we call ourselves sociologists, historians, economists, political scientists, philosophers or anthropologists. But to these venerable disciplinary labels we always add a qualifier: "of science and technology." "Science studies," as Anglo-Americans call it, or "science, technology and society." Whatever label we use, we are always attempting to retie the Gordian knot by crisscrossing, as often as we have to, the divide that separates exact knowledge and the exercise of power—let us say nature and culture. Hybrids ourselves, installed lopsidedly within scientific institutions, half engineers and half philosophers, *"tiers instruits"* . . . without having sought the role, we have chosen to follow the imbroglios wherever they take us. To shuttle back and forth, we rely on the notion of translation, or network. More supple than the notion of system, more historical than the notion of structure, more empirical than the notion of complexity, the idea of network is the Ariadne's thread of these interwoven stories.

Yet our work remains incomprehensible, because it is segmented into three components corresponding to our critics' habitual categories. They turn it into nature, politics or discourse.

When Donald MacKenzie describes the inertial guidance system of intercontinental missiles . . . ; when Michel Callon describes fuel cell electrodes . . . ; when Thomas Hughes describes the filament of Edison's incandescent lamp . . . ; when I describe the anthrax bacterium modified by Louis Pasteur or Roger Guillemin's brain peptides . . . , the critics imagine that we are talking about science and technology. Since these are marginal topics, or at best manifestations of pure instrumental and calculating thought, people who are interested in politics or in souls feel justified in paying no attention. Yet this research does not deal with nature or knowledge, with things-in-themselves, but with the way all these things are tied to our collectives and to subjects. We are talking not about instrumental thought but about the very substance of our societies. MacKenzie mobilizes the entire American Navy, and even Congress, to talk about his inertial guidance system; Callon mobilizes the French electric utility (EDF) and Renault as well as great chunks of French energy policy to grapple with changes in ions at the tip of an electrode in the depth of a laboratory; Hughes reconstructs all America around the incandescent filament of Edison's lamp; the whole of French society comes into view if one tugs on Pasteur's bacteria; and it becomes impossible to understand brain peptides without hooking them up with a scientific community, instruments, practices—all impedimenta that bear very little resemblance to rules of method, theories and neurons.

"But then surely you're talking about politics? You're simply reducing scientific truth to mere political interests, and technical efficiency to mere strategical manoeuvres?" Here is the second misunderstanding. If the facts do not occupy the simultaneously marginal and sacred place our worship has reserved for them, then it seems that they are immediately reduced to pure local contingency and sterile machinations. Yet science studies are talking not about the social contexts and the interests of power, but about their involvement with collectives and objects. The Navy's organization is profoundly modified by the way its offices are allied with its bombs; EDF and Renault take on a completely different look depending on whether they invest in fuel cells or the internal combustion engine; America before electricity and America after are two different places; the social context of the nineteenth century is altered according to whether it is made up of wretched souls or poor people infected by microbes; as for the unconscious subjects stretched out on the analyst's couch, we picture them differently depending on whether their dry brain is discharging neuro-transmitters or their moist brain is secreting hormones. None of our studies can re-utilize what the sociologists, the psychologists or the economists tell us about the social context or about the subject in order to apply them to the hard sciences—and this is why I will use the word "collective" to describe the association of humans and nonhumans and "society" to designate one part only of our collectives, the divide invented by the social sciences. The context and the technical content turn out to be redefined every time. Just as epistemologists no longer recognize in the collectivized things we offer them the ideas, concepts or theories of their childhood, so the human sciences cannot be expected to recognize the power games of their militant adoles-cence in these collectives full of things we are lining up. The delicate networks traced by Ariadne's little hand remain more invisible than spiderwebs.

"But if you are not talking about things-in-themselves or about humans-among-themselves, then you must be talking just about discourse, representation, language, texts, rhetorics." This is the third misunderstanding. It is true that those who bracket off the external referent—the nature of things—and the speaker—the pragmatic or social context—can talk only about meaning effects and language games. Yet when MacKenzie examines the evolution of inertial guidance systems, he is talking about arrangements that can kill us all; when Callon follows a trail set forth in scientific arti-cles, he is talking about industrial strategy as well as rhetoric . . . ; when Hughes ana-lyzes Edison's notebooks, the internal world of Menlo Park is about to become the external world of all America . . . . When I describe Pasteur's domestication of mi-crobes, I am mobilizing nineteenth-century society, not just the semiotics of a great man's texts; when I describe the invention-discovery of brain peptides, I am really talk-ing about the peptides themselves, not simply their representation in Professor Guillemin's laboratory. Yet rhetoric, textual strategies, writings, staging, semiotics—all these are really at stake, but in a new form that has a simultaneous impact on the na-ture of things and on the social context, while it is not reducible to the one or the other.

Our intellectual life is out of kilter. Epistemology, the social sciences, the sci-ences of texts—all have their privileged vantage point, provided that they remain separate. If the creatures we are pursuing cross all three spaces, we are no longer understood. Offer the established disciplines some fine sociotechnological network, some lovely translations, and the first group will extract our concepts and pull out all the roots that might connect them to society or to rhetoric; the second group will erase the social and political dimensions, and purify our network of any object; the third group, finally, will retain our discourse and rhetoric but purge our work of any undue adherence to reality—*horresco referens*—or to power plays. In the eyes of our critics the ozone hole above our heads, the moral law in our hearts, the autonomous text, may each be of interest, but only separately. That a delicate shuttle should have woven together the heavens, industry, texts, souls and moral law—this remains un-canny, unthinkable, unseemly. . . .

. . . The ozone hole is too social and too narrated to be truly natural; the strategy of industrial firms and heads of state is too full of chemical reactions to be reduced to power and interest; the discourse of the ecosphere is too real and too social to boil down to meaning effects. Is it our fault if the networks are *simultaneously real, like nature, narrated, like discourse, and collective, like society*? . . .

This would be a hopeless dilemma had anthropology not accustomed us to dealing calmly and straightforwardly with the seamless fabric of what I shall call "nature-culture," since it is a bit more and a bit less than a culture. . . . Once she has been sent into the field, even the most rationalist ethnographer is perfectly capable of bringing together in a single monograph the myths, ethnosciences, genealogies, political forms, techniques, religions, epics and rites of the people she is studying. Send her off to study the Arapesh or the Achuar, the Koreans or the Chinese, and you will get a single narrative that weaves together the way people regard the heavens and their ancestors, the way they build houses and the way they grow yams or manioc or rice, the way they construct their government and their cosmology. In works produced by anthropologists abroad, you will not find a single trait that is not simultaneously real, social and narrated.

If the analyst is subtle, she will retrace networks that look exactly like the socio-technical imbroglios that we outline when we pursue microbes, missiles or fuel cells in our own Western societies. We too are afraid that the sky is falling. We too associate the tiny gesture of releasing an aerosol spray with taboos pertaining to the heavens. We too have to take laws, power and morality into account in order to understand what our sciences are telling us about the chemistry of the upper atmosphere.

⋔ F U R T H E R   R E A D I N G

Bijker, Wiebe E., Thomas P. Hughes, and Trevor Pinch, eds. *The Social Construction of Technological Systems: New Directions in the Sociology and History of Technology* (Cambridge, MA: MIT Press, 1990).

Cockburn, Cynthia. *Machinery of Dominance: Women, Men, and Technical Know-How* (London: Pluto, 1985).

Cutcliffe, Stephen, and Robert Post, eds. *In Context: History and the History of Technology: Essays in Honor of Melvin Kranzberg* (Bethlehem: Lehigh University Press, 1988).

Foucault, Michel. *The Birth of the Clinic* (New York: Pantheon Books, 1973).

Kranzberg, Melvin. "The Newest History: Science and Technology," *Science* 136 (May 11, 1962): 463–468.

Latour, Bruno, *Science in Action: How to Follow Scientists and Engineers Through Society* (Cambridge, MA: Harvard University Press, 1987).

Law, John. *A Sociology of Monsters: Essays on Power, Technology, and Domination* (London: Routledge, 1991).

MacKenzie, Donald, and Judy Wacjman, eds. *The Social Shaping of Technology* (Milton Keynes, England: Open University Press, 1985).

Mumford, Lewis. *Technics and Civilization* (New York: Harcourt, Brace Co., 1934).

Noble, David. *Progress Without People: In Defence of Luddism* (Chicago: Charles H. Kerr Publishing Co., 1993).

Pacey, Arnold. *The Culture of Technology* (Cambridge, MA: MIT Press, 1983).

Smith, Merritt Roe, and Leo Marx. *Does Technology Drive History?: The Dilemma of Technological Determinism* (Cambridge, MA: MIT Press, 1994).

Staudenmaier, John M. *Technology's Storytellers* (Cambridge, MA: The MIT Press, 1985).

Wacjman, Judy. *Feminism Confronts Technology* (University Park, PA: Pennsylvania State University Press, 1991).

Winner, Langdon. *The Whale and the Reactor: A Search for Limits in an Age of High Technology* (Chicago: University of Chicago Press, 1988).

CHAPTER 2

New Worlds of Technique: Native Americans and Europeans, ca 1600–1770

╬

During the European conquest and colonization of the Americas, artifacts like horses, books, and guns did not always function as they did in Europe. In Cortes's campaign against the Aztecs, his horses "worked" much like the legendary Trojan horse, helping to foster enough wonder and confusion for a small group of Spaniards to penetrate and wreck havoc in the Aztec inner circle. In New France, the unfamiliarity of paper and print helped "convert" Algonquins to belief in French religion. English matchlock guns that worked perfectly well against massed European armies were unless against Native American warriors using the forest as a shield. European skills and objects sometimes accumulated new powers in the New World and were other times struck impotent.

Cultural perceptions often mediated how artifacts were received and used. Europeans admired Native American ways of making and doing things, even as they cultivated feelings of superiority through observation and description. Yet countless Europeans perished in the New World because their skills and tools no longer worked here. The survivability of the colonists increased as they adopted or confiscated Native American skills and local knowledge, much as they did land and natural resources. Native Americans also observed and adopted European tools, sometimes using them in new ways, sometimes turning them against their would-be conquerors. Numerous translations were possible, many of them perverse, many of them lost to us because of failures of communication and description.

The European conquest of the Americas was not a unified project or process; different European and Native American peoples faced each other in diverse places over a very long time. The bulk of the essays and documents in this chapter describe encounters, in the seventeenth century, of various Algonquin peoples with the colonists of New England and New France. Even this "early" contact has a complex prehistory. Some peoples, such as the Massachuset, had been decimated by European diseases (passed to them by more easterly tribes) even before Europeans actually arrived in human form. The surviving Massachuset were prominent recruits in John Eliot's "praying towns." Not only European diseases, but European trade goods—often bartered far into the interior—may have triggered political upheaval even before colonization began. European tools were never applied deftly and unproblematically, to a "virgin wilderness."

Economists write of technology "transfer" or "exchange" across boundaries, while some sociologists and anthropologists discuss the "translation" of technologies, and, still others, the creation of a "technological creole" (a third language) at boundaries themselves. What are the implications of each of these metaphors, and which, if any, best fits what occurred in the Eastern Woodlands?

𝔸 D O C U M E N T S

The first selection, by William Bradford, governor and first historian of Plymouth, describes how the colonists encountered Squanto, "a special instrument sent of God." Second is a description of Micmac culture by Nicolas Denys, governor of what is now Nova Scotia, published in Paris in 1672. Third are selections from various works by John Eliot, a Puritan missionary who resettled Indian converts ("praying Indians") in fourteen English-style villages ("praying towns") around the periphery of the Massachusetts Bay colony in the mid-seventeenth century. Although Indian conversion was a stated goal of the Puritan "errand into the wilderness," the praying towns were brutally dispersed during King Philip's War 1675–1676. The fourth selection is from William Wood's *New England's Prospect* (1634). What cultural and political assumptions lie behind Wood's account? What are its ironies? The final selections come from Peter Kalm's *Travels in North America* (1770), which describe journeys he made through the mid-Atlantic colonies in the 1750s, more than a century after initial settlement. Kalm, a Swede, traveled along a colonial seaboard bereft not only of Native Americans but of important strands of memory.

William Bradford on Squanto, 1620–1621

. . . [ye] Indians came skulking about them [the colonists], and would sometimes show them selves aloofe of, but when any approached near them, they would rune away. And once they stoale away their tools wher they had been at worke, & were gone to diner. But about ye 16. *of March* a certaine Indian came bouldly amongst them, and spoke to them in broken English, which they could well understand, but marvelled at it. At length they understood by discourse with him, that he was not of these parts, but belonged to ye eastrene parts, wher some English-ships came to fhish, with whom he was aquainted, & could name sundrie of them by their names, amongst whom he had gott his language. He became proftable to them in aquainting them with many things concerning ye state of ye cuntry in ye east-parts wher he lived, which was afterwards profitable unto them; as also of ye people hear, of their names, number, & strength; of their situation & distance from this place, and who was cheefe amongst them. His name was *Samaset;* he tould them also of another Indian whos name was *Squanto,* a native of this place, who had been in England & could

From William Bradford, *Bradford's History "Of Plimoth Plantation"* (Boston: Wright & Potter, 1898), pp. 114–116, 121.

speake better English then him selfe Being, after some time of entertainmente & gifts, dis mist, a while after he came againe, & 5. more with him, & they brought againe all ye tooles that were stolen away before, and made way for ye coming of their great Sachem, called *Massasoyt;* who, about 4. or 5. *days after,* came with the cheefe of his friends & other attendance, with the aforesaid *Squanto.* With whom, after frendly entertainment, & some gifts given him, they made a peace with him (which hath now continued this 24. years) . . .

After these things he returned to his place caled *Sowams,* some 40. mile from this place, but *Squanto* contiued with them, and was their interpreter, and was a spetiall instrument sent of God for their good beyond their expectation. He directed them how to set their corne, wher to take fist, and to procure other comodities, and was also their pilott to bring them to unknowne places for their profitt, and never left them till he dyed. He was a *native of this place,* & scarce any left alive besides him selfe. He was caried away with diveree others by one *Hunt,* a mr. of a ship, who thought to sell them for slaves in Spaine; but he got away for England, and was entertained by a marchante in London, & imployed to New-found-land & other parts, & lastly brought hither into these parts by one Mr. *Dermer,* a gentle-man imployed by Sr. Ferdinando Gorges & others, for discovery, & other designes in these parts. . . .

[After the bad weather and illness of early spring 1621] they (as many as were able) began to plant ther corne, in which servise Squanto stood them in great stead, showing them both ye maner how to set it, and after how to dress & tend it. Also he tould them excepte they gott fish & set with it (in these old grounds) it would come to nothing, and he showed them yt in ye midle of Aprill they should have store enough come up ye brooke, by which they begane to build, and taught them how to take it, and wher to get other provissions necessary for them; all which they found true by triall & experience. Some English seed they sew, as wheat & pease, but it came not to good, eather by ye badnes of ye seed, or lateness of ye season, or both, or some other defeete.

Governor Nicolas Denys on the Micmac, 1672

All that I have said so far about the customs of the Indians, and of their diverse ways of doing things, ought to be understood only as the way in which they did them in old times. To this I shall add their burials, and the ancient ceremonies of their funerals. When some one of them died, there was great weeping in his wigwam. . . .

After this it was necessary to make great tabagie, that is to say festival, and to rejoice in the great gratification the deceased will have in going to see all his ancestors, his relatives and good friends, and in the joy that each of them will have in seeing him, and the great feasts they will make for him. They believed that, being dead, they went into another land where everything abounded plentifully, and where they never had to work. The festival of joy being finished it was necessary to do some work for the dead.

The women went to fetch fine pieces of bark from which they made a kind of bier on which they placed him well enwrapped. Then he was carried to a place where they had a staging built on purpose, and elevated eight or ten feet. On this they

From Nicolas Denys, *The Description and Natural History of the Coasts of North America* (Toronto: The Champlain Society, 1908), pp. 437–444.

placed the bier, and there they left it about a year, until the time when the sun had entirely dried the body. . . .

The end of the year having passed, and the body [being] dry, it was taken thence and carried to a new place, which is their cemetery. There it was placed in a new coffin or bier, also of Birch bark, and immediately after in a deep grave which they had made in the ground. Into this all his relatives and friends threw bows, arrows, snow-shoes, spears, robes of Moose, Otter, and Beaver, stockings, moccasins, and everything that was needful for him in hunting and in clothing himself. All the friends of the deceased made him each his present, of the finest and best that they had. They competed as to who would make the most beautiful gift. At a time when they were not yet disabused of their errors, I have seen them give to the dead man, guns, axes, iron arrowheads, and kettles, for they held all these to be much more convenient for their use than would have been their kettles of wood, their axes of stone, and their knives of bone, for their use in the other world.

There have been dead men in my time who have taken away more than two thousand pounds of peltries. This aroused pity in the French, and perhaps envy with it; but nevertheless one did not dare to go take the things, for this would have caused hatred and everlasting war, which it was not prudent to risk since it would have ruined entirely the trade we had with them. All the burials of the women, boys, girls, and children were made in the same fashion, but the weeping did not last so long. They never omitted to place with each one that which was fitting for his use, nor to bury it with him.

It has been troublesome to disabuse them of that practice, although they have been told that all these things perished in the earth, and that if they would look there they would see that nothing had gone with the dead man. That was emphasised so much that finally they consented to open a grave, in which they were made to see that all was decayed. There was there among other things a kettle, all perforated with verdigris. An Indian having struck against it and found that it no longer sounded, began to make a great cry, and said that some one wished to deceive them. "We see indeed," said he, "the robes and all the rest, and if they are still there it is a sign that the dead man has not had need of them in the other world, where they have enough of them because of the length of time that they have been furnished them."

"But with respect to the kettle," said he, "they have need of it, since it is among us a utensil of new introduction, and with which the other world cannot [yet] be furnished. Do you not indeed see," said he, rapping again upon the kettle, "that it has no longer any sound, and that it no longer says a word, because its spirit has abandoned it to go to be of use in the other world to the dead man to whom we have given it?"

It was indeed difficult to keep from laughing, but much more difficult to disabuse him. For being shown another which was worn out from use, and being made to hear that it spoke no word more than the other,—"ha," said he, "that is because it is dead, and its soul has gone to the land where the souls of kettles are accustomed to go." And no other reason could be given at that time. Nevertheless, they have been disabused of that in the end, though with much difficulty, some by religion, [some by] the example of our own customs, and nearly all by the need for the things which come from us, the use of which has become to them an indispensable necessity. They have abandoned all their own utensils, whether because of the trouble they had as well to make as to use them, or because of the facility of obtaining from us, in exchange for skins which cost them almost nothing, the things which seemed to them invaluable, not so much for their novelty as for the convenience they derived therefrom. Above everything the kettle has always seemed to them, and seems still, the most valuable article they can obtain from us. This was rather pleasingly exemplified by an Indian whom the late Monsieur de Razilly sent from Acadia to Paris; for, passing by the Rue Aubry-bouché, where there were then many coppersmiths, he asked of his interpreter if they were not relatives of the King, and if this was not the trade of the grandest Seigniors of the Kingdom. This little digression must not make me forget to say here, before finishing this chapter on funerals, that to express a thing such as it is when it can be no longer of use, they say that it is dead. For example, when their canoe is broken, they say that it is dead, and thus with all other things out of service.

. . . The Indians to-day practise still their ancient form of burial in every respect, except that they no longer place anything in their graves, for of this they are entirely disabused. They have abandoned also those offerings, so frequent and usual, which they made as homage to their *manitou* in passing by places in which there was some risk to be taken, or where indeed there had happened some misfortune [or other]. . . . They are also cured of other little superstitions which they had, such as giving the bones to the Dogs, roasting Eels, and many others of that sort which are entirely abolished. [This is] as much through a spirit of self-interest as through any other reason; for they gave there often the most beautiful and rarest objects they had. But since they cannot now obtain the things which come from us with such ease as they had in obtaining robes of Marten, of Otter, or of Beaver, [or] bows and arrows, and since they have realised that guns and other things were not found in their woods or in their rivers, they have become less devout. Or, it would be better to say, [they have become] less superstitious since the time when their offerings have cost them so much. But they practise still all the same methods of hunting, with this difference, however, that in place of arming their arrows and spears with the bones of animals, pointed and sharpened, they arm them to-day with iron, which is made expressly for sale to them. Their spears now are made of a sword fixed at the end of a shaft of seven to eight feet in length. These they use in winter, when there is snow, to spear the Moose, or for fishing Salmon, Trout, and Beaver. They are also furnished with iron harpoons, of the use of which we have spoken before.

. . . The axes, the kettles, the knives, and everything that is supplied them, is much more convenient and portable than those which they had in former times, when they were obliged to go to camp near their grotesque kettles, in place of which to-day they are free to go camp where they wish. One can say that in those times the immovable kettles were the chief regulators of their lives, since they were able to live only in places where these were. . . .

As for their festivals, they make these as they did formerly. The women do not take part in them; and those who have their monthlies are always separate. They always make speeches there, and dances; but the outcome is not the same. Since they have taken to drinking wine and brandy they are subject to fighting. Their quarrelling comes ordinarily from their condition; for, being drunk, they say they are all great chiefs, which engenders quarrels between them. At first it needed little wine or brandy to make them drunk.

But at present, and since they have frequented the fishing vessels, they drink in quite another fashion. They no longer have any regard for wine, and wish nothing but brandy. They do not call it drinking unless they become drunk, and do not think they have been drinking unless they fight and are hurt. However when they set about drinking, their wives remove from their wigwams the guns, axes, the mounted swords [spears], the bows, the arrows, and [every weapon] even their knives, which the Indians carry hung from the neck. They leave nothing with which they can kill one another. They permit that without saying a word, if it is before they commence to drink: otherwise the women do not dare enter the wigwams. Immediately after taking everything with which they can injure themselves, the women carry it into the woods, afar off, where they go to hide with all their children. After that they have a fine time, beating injuring, and killing one another. Their wives do not return until the next day, when they are sober. At that time the fighting can be done only with the poles of their wigwams, which they pull to pieces to allow this use. Afterwards their poor wives must go fetch other poles, and other pieces of bark to repair their lodging. And they must not grumble, otherwise they would be beaten.

The Reverend John Eliot on the "Praying Indians," 1647–1677

. . . God stirred up in some of them a desire to come into the *English* fashions, and live after their manner, but knew not how to attain unto it, yea despaired that ever it should come to passe in their dayes, but thought that in 40. yeers more, some *Indians* would be all one *English,* and in an hundred yeers, all *Indians* here about, would so bee: which when I heard, (for some of them told me they thought so, and that some wise *Indians* said so) my heart moved within mee, abhorring that wee should sit still and let that work alone, and hoping that this motion in them was of the Lord, and that this mind in them was a preparative to imbrace the Law and Word of God; and therefore I told them that they and wee were already all one save in two things, which make the only difference betwixt them and us: First, we know, serve, and pray unto God, and they doe not: Secondly, we labour and work in building, planting, clothing our selves, &c. and they doe not: and would they but doe as wee doe in these things, they would be all one with *English* men: they said they did not know God, and therefore could not tell how to pray to him, nor serve him. I told them if they would learn to know God, I would teach them. . . .

You know likewise that wee exhorted them to fence their ground with ditches, stone walls, upon the banks, and promised to helpe them with Shovels, Mattocks, Crows of Iron; and they are very desirous to follow that counsell, and call upon me to help them with tooles faster then I can get them, though I have now bought pretty store, and they (I hope) are at work. The women are desirous to learn to spin, and I have procured Wheels for sundry of them, and they can spin pretty well. They begin to grow industrious, and find something to sell at Market all the yeer long: all winter they sell Brooms, Staves, Elepots, Baskets, Turkies. In the Spring, Craneberies, Fish, Stawberies; in the Summer Hurtleberries, Grapes, Fish: in the Autumn they sell Craneberries, Fish, Venison, &c. and they find a good benefit by the Market, and grow more and more to make use thereof; besides sundry of them work with the

From *Collections of the Massachusetts Historical Society,* Vol. III of the Third Series (Cambridge, MA: E. W. Metcalf, 1833), pp. 50, 59, 138, 178–179.

English in Hay time, and Harvest, but yet it's not comparable to what they might do, if they were industrious, and old boughs must be bent a little at once; if we can set the young twiggs in a better bent, it will bee Gods mercy. . . .

. . . We must also of necessity have a house to lodge in, meet in, and lay up our provisions and clothes, which cannot be in *Wigwams*. I set them therefore to fell and square timber for an house, and when it was ready, I went, and many of them with me, and on their shoulders carried all the timber together, &c. These things they chearfully do; but this also I do, I pay them wages carefully for all such works I set them about, which is a good encouragement to labour. . . . There is a great river which divideth between their planting grounds and dwelling place, through which, though they easily wade in Summer, yet in the Spring its deep, and unfit for daily passing over, especially of women and children; therefore I thought it necessary, that this Autumne we should make a foot Bridge over, against such time in the Spring as they shall have daily use of it; I told them my purpose and reason of it, wished them to go with me to do that work, which they chearfully did, and their own hands did build a Bridge eighty foot long, and nine foot high in the midst, that it might stand above the floods; when we had done, I cald them together, prayed, and gave thanks to God, and taught them out of a portion of Scripture, and at parting I told them, I was glad of their readiness to labour, when I advised them thereunto; and in as much as it hath been hard and tedious labour in the wafer, if any of them desired wages for their work, I would give it them; yet being it is for their owne use, if they should do all this labour in love, I should take it well, and as I may have occasion, remember it. . . .

. . . [T]he *Sachems* of the Country are generally set against us, and counter-work the Lord by keeping off their men from praying to God as much as they can; And the reason of it is this, They plainly see that Religion will make a great change among them, and cut them off from their former tyranny. . . .

. . . In our first war with the Indians, God pleased to shew us the vanity of our military skill, in managing our arms, after the European mode. Now we are glad to learn the skulking way of war. And what God's end is, in teaching us such a way of discipline, I know not. By our late eastern war it hath pleased God to shew us our weakness by sea, as formerly by land. The Indians took many of our fishing vessels and the men that belonged to them, and forced them to sail whither they desired; many of the men delivered themselves and their vessels; many Indians were slain, some English.

William Wood, " . . . much good might they receive from the English," 1634

These Indians being strangers to arts and sciences, and being unacquainted with the interventions that are common to a civilized people, are ravished with admiration at the first view of any such sight. They took the first ship they saw for a walking island, the mast to be a tree, the sail white clouds, and the discharging of ordinance for lightning and thunder. . . .

From William Wood, *New England's Prospect* (Amherst, MA: University of Massachusetts Press, 1977), pp. 96, 108–109.

They do much extol and wonder at the English for their strange inventions, especially for a windmill which in their esteem was little less than the world's wonder, for the strangeness of his whisking motion and the sharp teeth biting the corn (as they term it) into such small pieces, they were loath at the first to come near to his long arms, or to abide in so tottering a tabernacle, though now they dare go anywhere so far as they have an English guide. The first plowman was counted little better than a juggler: the Indians, seeing the plow tear up more ground in a day than their clamshells could scrape up in a month, desired to see the workmanship of it, and viewing well the coulter and share, perceiving it to be iron, told the plowman he was almost Abamacho, almost as cunning as the Devil. But the fresh supplies of new and strange objects hath lessened their admiration and quickened their inventions and desire of practising such things as they see, wherein they express no small ingenuity and dexterity of wit, being neither furthered by art [n]or long experience.

It is thought they would soon learn any mechanical trades, having quick wits, understanding apprehensions, strong memories, with nimble inventions, and a quick hand in using of the ax or hatchet or such like tools. Much good might they receive from the English, and much might they benefit themselves, if they were not strong fettered in the chains of idleness; so as that they had rather starve than work, following no employments saving such as are sweetened with more pleasures and profit than pains or care, and this is indeed one of the greatest accusations that can be laid against them which lies but upon the men (the women being very industrious). But it may be hoped that good example and good instructions may bring them to a more industrious and provident course of life, for already, as they have learned much subtlety and cunning by bargaining with the English, so have they a little degenerated from some of their lazy customs and show themselves more industrious. . . .

. . . Their canoes be made either of pine trees, which before they were acquainted with English tools they burned hollow, scraping them smooth with clam shells and oyster shells, cutting their outside with stone hatchets. These boats be not above a foot and a half or two feet wide and twenty foot long. Their other canoes be made of thin birch rinds, close ribbed on the inside with broad, thin hoops like the hoops of a tub. These are made very light. A man may carry one of them a mile, being made purposely to carry from river to river and bay to bay, to shorten land passages. In these cockling fly-boats, wherein an Englishman can scarce sit without a fearful tottering, they will venture to sea when an English shallop dare not bear a knot of sail, scudding over the overgrown waves as fast as a wind-driven ship, being driven by their paddles, being much like battledores. If a cross wave (as is seldom) turn her keel upside down, they by swimming free her and scramble into her again.

Peter Kalm, " . . . contempt of useful arts," 1750

North America abounds in iron mines, and the Indians lived all about the country before the arrival of the Europeans, so that several places can be shown in this country where at present there are iron mines, and where, not a hundred years ago, stood great towns or villages of the Indians. It is therefore very remarkable that the Indians did

From Peter Kalm, *Travels in North America* (New York: Dover, 1966), pp. 232–233, 363.

not know how to make use of a metal or ore which was always under their eyes, and on which they could not avoid treading every day. They even lived upon the very spots where iron ores were afterwards found, and yet they often went many miles in order to get a wretched hatchet, knife, or the like, as above described. They were forced to employ several days in order to sharpen their tools, by rubbing them against a rock, or other stones, though the advantage was far from being equal to the labor. They could never cut down a thick tree with their hatchets, and only with difficulty could they fell a small one. They could not hollow out a tree with their hatchets, or do a hundredth part of the work which we can perform with ease by the help of our iron tools. Thus we see how disadvantageous the ignorance and inconsiderate contempt of useful arts is. Happy is the country which knows their full value! . . .

Canoes are boats made of one piece of wood and are much in use among the farmers and other people upon the Delaware and some little rivers. For that purpose a very thick trunk of a tree is hollowed out; the red juniper or cedar (*Juniperus Virginiana*), the white cedar, the chestnut, the white oak and the tulip tree are commonly used. . . . The size of the canoes varies with the purposes for which they are destined. They can carry six persons, who, however must in no way be unruly, but sit at the bottom of the canoe in the quietest manner possible, lest the boat capsize. The Swedes in Pennsylvania and New Jersey, near the rivers, seldom have any other boats in which to go to Philadelphia, which they commonly do twice a week on market days, though they be several miles distant from the town, and meet sometimes with severe storms. Yet misfortunes from the overturning etc. of these canoes are seldom heard of, though they might well be expected on account of the small size of the boats. . . .

. . . The making of the boat took up half our time yesterday and all to-day. To make such a boat they pick out a thick tall elm, with a smooth bark, and with as few branches as possible. This tree is cut down, and great care is taken to prevent the bark from being hurt by falling against other trees or against the ground. With this view some people do not fell the trees, but climb to the top of them, split the bark and strip it off, which was the method our carpenter took. The bark is split on one side, in a straight line along the tree, as long as the boat it intends to be. At the same time the bark is carefully cut from the trunk a little way on both sides of the slit, that it may more easily separate. It is then peeled off very carefully, and particular care is taken not to make any holes in it. This is easy when the sap is in the trees, and at other seasons they are heated by fire for that purposes. The bark thus stripped off is spread on the ground in a level place, [with the smooth side down, later] turning the inside upwards. To stretch better, some logs of wood or stones are carefully put on it, which press it down. Then the sides of the bark are gently bent upwards in order to form the sides of the boat. Some sticks are then fixed into the ground, at the distance of three or four feet from each other, in a curved line, which the sides of the boat are intended to follow, supporting the bark intended for them. The sides are then bent in the form which the boat is to have, and according to that the sticks are either put nearer or further off. The ribs of the boat are made of thick branches of hickory, these being tough and pliable. . . .

𝓐 *E S S A Y S*

The first selection, from Karen Kupperman's *Settling with the Indians,* discusses the often detailed observations European travelers made of Native American technologies. Although American artifacts and methods were openly admired and their advantages recognized, the same authors often insisted on the overall superiority of European arts. How were both positions sustained?

In the second essay, from *The Skulking Way of War,* Patrick Malone illustrates how Englishmen and Native Americans borrowed and sometimes transformed each other's tools and skills as they struggled for position in seventeenth-century New England. Drawing on both contemporary writing and recent archaeological evidence, Malone challenges assumptions about the "European" and "Native American" essence of specific technologies.

The third selection, from Richard White's *The Middle Ground,* considers the French and Native American fur trade, long framed as the classic case of Native American integration with—and ultimate dependence on—a European economy. He argues that the Algonquins had a different conception of the fur trade than the French and did not trade away their own technologies for a dependence on French goods.

Do Kupperman, Malone, and White reach the same conclusions about the character of technological exchange across cultural lines? To what extent are they addressing different historical problems, different regions and peoples, and using different types of evidence? Do the appended historical documents support the arguments of the essayists or suggest further problems?

Native American Technology

KAREN KUPPERMAN

John Smith was stung by the "worlds blind ignorant censure" which fell on the heads of the Jamestown colonists because they had not sent back rich commodities. Because their colonies on the coast of North America lay in the same latitudes as southern Europe, early English writers believed that all the minerals and crops found in those latitudes in other parts of the world would also be found in their America. Gold and silver, wines, oils, silk, and pearls were some of the commodities originally expected. When the expected wealth did not materialize, it was the Indians, not the faulty geographical lore of the English, who were blamed. Smith explained that the Spanish conquerors of Latin America had happened, through no virtue of their own, on a land in which the natives were numerous and technologically advanced, both in agriculture and in precious metal processing. All the Spanish had to do was to pick up what they wanted.

> But had those fruitful Countries, beene as Salvage as barbarous, as ill peopled, as little planted, laboured and manured as Virgina, their proper labours (it is likely) would have produced as small profit as ours.

What Smith is saying is that the technological level of the inhabitants is more important than any other factor in determining what a country will produce. North America

---

From Karen Kupperman, "Indian Technology," in *Settling with the Indians* (Totowa, NJ: Rowman and Littlefield, 1980), pp. 80–91, 102–103.

had little to offer, not because the potential or the ores were not there, but because the people had not developed that potential. James Rosier said the same thing writing of New England. He calls the Indians a "purblind generation, whose understanding it hath pleased God so to darken, as they can neither discerne, use, or rightly esteeme the unvaluable riches in middest whereof they live sensually content with the barke and outward rinde . . ." It quickly became a commonplace that the land needed nothing but "industrious men" and "engins" to make it among the most fruitful in the world.

There are two issues here which are of interest to us. One is the assumption which was universal among Englishmen that their technology was obviously superior to that of the Indians, a judgement continued by many historians. Every writer had schemes for developing the rich resources which he thought must be hidden in America. Even though their geographical knowledge slowly became more realistic as they realized that latitude was not the sole determinant of climate, they continued to believe that superior European technology would develop America in a way which the Indians never could.

What did English colonists say about the actual technological level of the Indians among whom they lived? This is the other issue which is raised by statements like those of Smith and Rosier. When this question is asked we again see the contrast between the rhetorical flourishes which occur in general statements and the reporting of detailed observations. Smith is a particularly outstanding example of this because, despite the denunciation just seen, he not only refers again and again to Indian agriculture, but he also makes no secret of the fact that he and all of the Jamestown colonists lived almost entirely on corn which they got from the Indians during the time he was in Virginia.

Agriculture was not just one form of technology among many. It was of prime importance, because it makes settled life possible. Just as the shepherd is superior to the hunter, so town life supported by agriculture is the highest form of human life for these writers. Mankind is meant to live gathered together in towns. . . . Eyewitness evidence from America clearly placed the Indians on the side of civil humanity as town dwellers, not nomads ranging over the land hunting and gathering for their subsistence. . . .

Alongside the towns in the typical picture of Indian life transmitted by eyewitness writers were the cornfields and gardens in which they grew their basic food of corn, pease, and pulses. DeBry's engraving of the town of Secota from John White's drawing shows fields of corn in three stages of growth, patches of tobacco, a group of sunflowers, a pumpkin patch, and a garden with unidentifiable vegetables. Hunting was supplementary to the Indian basic diet of maize and beans. Neither of these two vegetables is a complete protein when eaten alone. That is, neither contains all of the eight amino acids which the human body cannot manufacture for itself. However, when eaten together, they do form superior complete proteins, increasing the protein content of the ingredients by fifty percent. Further, growing beans and corn together as the Indians did increases yield, because the beans, as legumes, fix nitrogen in the soil. Eyewitness reports from America refute the contention that the "colonials liked to regard the Indians as members of a nomadic hunting race with no fixed habitation, roaming over thousand of acres of virgin wilderness." Again and again writers from Virginia and New England refer to Indian corn and its cultivation. Several of the earliest writers actually presented several-page descriptions of methods of preparing the soil, cultivation, and storage and use of crops. Many writers make it clear that they have seen cornfields and gardens which extended to several hundred acres. The Indians are clearly people who are recognizable as fellow agriculturalist with the English.

When the Indians set out to clear a field, they did not cut down the trees and pull our their roots as the English did in order to plow in straight lines. The Indians killed the trees by girdling them or burning the roots, and then planted their crops in hills around and between the dead tree trunks. Both men and women worked on clearing new ground, but the tending of the crops was done by the women and children. Their method of clearing fields involved less work than the English method, but several writers remarked on the assiduousness with which the Indian women kept their fields free of weeds. William Wood said the fields looked more like gardens, the women "not suffering a choaking weede to advance his audacious head above their infant corne, or an undermining worme to spoile his spurnes."

Indian cultivation methods were portrayed as primitive, but English writers were extravagant in praise of the product, particularly the Indian corn, variously called maize or Turkey or Guinie wheat. It was commonly said to be superior to any European grain, mostly because of its larger yield and its greater variety of uses. For Hariot, its superiority came from the fact that the Indians had two harvests each year. He and the Plymouth colonists also remark on the beauty of its red, blue, yellow, and white kernels, "a very goodly sight." Several of the writers simply affirm that it is "good meat" and can be used in a variety of ways. One use for which some of the writers had great hopes was as a source of that precious commodity, sugar. The stalk was said to yield juice so sweet that Sir Thomas Gates says the colonists make a cordial of it.

The most important attribute of maize was its great yield. English writers try various formulas to convey the fact that one grain of maize will produce a very large stalk which will have several large ears on it. Several writers simply affirmed that Indian corn is the best grain in the world. Some specifically say it is better than any English grain. Others try to give figures, such as Gabriel Archer, who says each grain of corn produces a large stalk with 2 or 3 stems each having an ear "above a spann longe, besett with cornes at the least 300 upon an eare for the most part 5, 6, & 700." The marginal note beside this statement puts is more simply: "infinit increase."

Not only was their grain superior, but some of the writers indicated that Indian cultivation methods were also superior. George Percy told of being conducted by Indians through "the goodliest Corne fieldes that ever was seene in any Countrey." Writers from all areas tell of the Indians instructing them in the planting and tending of Indian corn, but the Plymouth colonists complained that they still had smaller harvests than the Indians did. One reason for the poor yields in Plymouth colony was apparently their unwillingness to do the arduous work that the Indian women did in their fields. Lynn Ceci argues, though, that the most famous instance of instruction, that in which Squanto taught the Pilgrims to plant corn with fish, was not a transmission of an Indian trait. He had learned this technique, Ceci believes, from other Europeans with whom he had lived. William Wood gave a vivid picture of all that was involved in Indian agriculture when he told of the instruction the colonists received:

> Many wayes hath their advice and endeavour beene advantagious unto us; they being our first instructers for the planning of their Indian Corne, by teaching us to cull out the finest seede, to observe the fittest season, to keepe distance for holes, and fit measure for hills, to worme it, and weede it; to prune it, and dresse it as occasion shall require.

Care for the morrow was a principle attribute which distinguished civilized man from the brutes. Such providence was implicit in reports of Indian agriculture. Several of the writers carried the point further and wrote of the techniques by which the Indians stored their harvest for the winter. In fact most of the food grown was stored for winter use. . . .

. . . Reports of Indian agriculture were . . . important because they indicated that the country was fruitful and would be good for Englishmen who went there to live. Beyond this, many eyewitnesses assumed the role of ethnographers and endeavored to give a detailed picture of Indian life. The wealth of information was designed to enable the reader to picture the Indians and the environment they created. It was the details of daily life, the Indians in their houses, at meals, and at their occupations, which constituted a good ethnographic record for these writers and their audience. They generally attempted to give their readers a mental picture by comparing American things or practices to familiar ones, to bring them home. These descriptions were not characterized by disgust or scorn as many historians allege. The immense detail and the analytical tool of comparison of Indian practices to European ones both testify to the interest of the eyewitnesses in the Indians as human beings, not to an attitude of contemptuous dismissal.

Though all the writers clearly assumed that European technology was superior to Indian, they took great pains to affirm that the Indians were extraordinarily competent in their own relationship to their environment. Thomas Hariot, in the earliest eyewitness description of North American Indians, stressed their ingenuity and "excellencie of wit." Affirmations of the Indians' skill and intelligence come from all areas and throughout the period. Frequently writers say they are trying to overcome the opinion in England that the Indians are, as Morton says, "dull, or slender witted people." Hariot's praise of their ingenuity is frequently echoed. The other qualities most often praised are their ability to learn quickly and their dexterity. Alexander Whitaker of Jamestown offered, in refutation of the opinion that the Indians are "simple," this description:

> they are a very understanding generation, quicke of apprehension, suddaine in their dispatches, subtile in their dealings, exquisite in their inventions, and industrious in their labour.

"Subtile," was not always a praise word in this period. It can mean crafty, and smacks of sharp practice. Still, the picture communicated here is of intelligent and competent people. Their very subtlety means that the English will have to be careful in dealing with them. Colonists back up this picture of intelligent and skilful Indians with detailed pictures of the Indians in their daily lives, working, hunting, cooking, and playing, and this included a description of the environment they created for themselves. . . .

As modern concern for the interaction between man and the environment grows, some writers have asserted that the first in a long chain of ecological disasters occurred with the entrance of Europeans into America. . . .

It is undeniable that English writers of this period thought of the natural world as given to man by God for man's use. Not to develop nature's resources was seen by them as sinful. Nature, to 17th century Englishmen, represented potential. That is, all nature is the raw material from which man can make products necessary and useful for life. For this reason, the products of man and nature in combination were considered superior to nature alone. . . . Artificial was a word of high praise, while natural meant simple, or simple-minded. . . .

Seventeenth century writers, then, celebrated man's exploitation of nature. They did not see man as taking from nature and spoiling it in the process. Rather, they saw man as part of nature, as having a crucial and God-designed role in the development of nature's potential. . . .

The English did not think of exploitation of nature in terms of ruthless depletion of resources. English writers exhibited real concern for the development and conservation of resources. Furthermore, they were sometimes critical of observed Indian practices as wasteful. One such practice was the annual or semi-annual burning of the woods. Many of the early writers remark on the open parklike quality of American woods, and the great open areas. They say that thick underbrush is seen only in swampy areas. Reports from Virginia and New England claim that a man can ride a horse at a gallop through the woods. In fact, it seems likely that, because pre-contact Indians burned the woods every year, wooded areas in present day eastern North America are thicker and more tangled with underbrush, more like people's idea of the forest primeval, than those seen by the early colonists. Burning was a beneficial practice. Not only did it facilitate movement and hunting, but it also made possible the growth of a great variety of food-producing plants—fruits, berries, and nuts—and attracted animals, such as deer, elk, and buffalo, which would not live in a dense forest. Finally, the burning also drove away some unwelcome animals, such as reptiles. . . .

More of a problem is Indian treatment of animals. Did the Indian as the "first ecologist" carefully harvest the deer according to his need alone? Several of the early English writers were concerned about this issue. Thomas Hariot was concerned over the impact of English desire for deer skins on the deer population. He reassures his readers that they can trade for thousands of skins yearly and cause no more to be killed than is done already. . . . [Ralph] Hamor was shocked by Indian hunting practices, as he said they kill deer "all the yeer long, neither sparing yong nor olde, no not the Does readie to fawne, not the yong fawnes, if but two daies ould." New Englanders reported finding carcasses of deer which had had only the horns taken off. So many deer are killed at hunting time, according to Thomas Morton, that the Indians "have bestowed six or seaven at a time, upon one English man whome they have borne affection to."

The evidence demonstrates that the Indians were not averse to making massive changes in the natural world, as in their burning, when they felt the result would favor their livelihood. It does not prove that the English were superior in their ecological concerns. What the evidence does demonstrate is that neither side has a unique grasp of natural environment. At least some 16th and early 17th century Englishmen were very concerned about establishing a responsible relationship to this environment. . . .

The single most popular product of Indian technology was the canoe. Many writers described the wonderful boats, and frequently they gave long descriptions of their manufacture as well. The canoes were of two types. The earliest descriptions, those from Virginia territory, were of dugout canoes. John White painted a picture of one of these being made. Hariot began his note to this picture: "The manner of makinge their boates in Virginia, is verye wonderfull." He was concerned to demonstrate that it is possible to make such a canoe without iron tools. The method he described, that of alternately burning out the center and scraping it with sea shells,

proved to his satisfaction that "god indueth thise savage people with sufficient reason to make thinges necessarie to serve their turnes." Hariot and Barlowe say these
canoes can carry up to 20 men, but John Smith says some of them have a capacity
of 40 though he admits the smaller ones are more common. Only William Wood of
New England mentioned dugouts.

It was the birchbark canoes which were seen as most marvelous. Martin Pringe
offered the first and one of the best descriptions of their manufacture. The canoes he
saw, one of which was brought back to Bristol, were 17 feet long and 4 feet wide:

> made of the Barke of a Birch-tree, farre exceeding in bignesse those of England: it was
> sowed together with strong and tough Oziers or twigs, and the seames covered over the
> Rozen or Turpentine little inferiour in sweetnesses to Frankincense, as we made triall by
> burning a little thereof on the coales at sundry times after our comming home: it was also
> open like a Wherrie, and sharpe at both ends, saving that the beake was a little bending
> roundly upward. And though it carried nine men standing upright, yet it weighed not at
> the most above sixtie pounds in weight, a thing almost incredible in regard of the large-
> nesse and capacitie thereof.

John Winthrop said the canoes of the Long Island Indians could hold 80 men.

The most startling characteristic of the canoe was its lightness for its size and capacity. Thomas Morton says that two men can carry a canoe that will hold ten to
twelve men. William Wood says one man can carry a canoe a mile, and he points out
that this is what makes canoes well-suited to the environment, that they can be carried overland from stream to stream. As John Guy says, ". . . every place is to them a
harborough; where they can goe ashoare themselves, they take aland with them their
Canoa." Allied with this lightness was the marvelous swiftness of the canoe. James
Rosier recounted an incident in which "they in their Canoa with three oares, would at
their will go ahead of us and about us, when we rowed with eight oares strong; such
was their swiftnesse, by reason of the lightenesse and artificiall composition of their
Canoa and oares."

There is a theme running through all English discussions of Indian technology
which emerges most clearly in descriptions of the canoe. This is the belief that the Indians were better adapted to life in America than the English were. Though the writers
believed in the general superiority of English technology, they were clearly aware of
the fact that they would have to learn from the Indian in order to survive. Not only did
they realize this, they made no attempt to disguise it from their English audience.
Concerning the canoe, they not only demonstrated that it was a faster craft than their
small boats, but they also showed that it was more useful in America, because it could
go where their small boats could not go, and was more flexible to use. William Wood
gives a vivid picture of the relative clumsiness of the Englishman and his boat:

> In these cockling fly-boates, wherein an English man can scarce sit without a fearefull
> tottering, they will venture to Sea, when an English Shallope dare not beare a knot of
> sayle; scudding over the overgrowne waves as fast as a winde-driven Ship, being driven
> by their padles; being much like battle doores; if a crosse wave (as is seldome) turn her
> keele up-side downe, they by swimming free her, and scramble into her againe.

Indian canoes easily navigated the rocky and swift-moving rivers for which English
boats were useless and they could easily be carried around obstacles. John Smith was
scornful of the equipment sent to Jamestown by the Virginia Company. He wrote them

specifically about a boat in four pieces which they sent to be carried in pieces above the fall line and then assembled and used for exploring the river. Smith explained the difficulty: "If he had burnt her to ashes, one might have carried her in a bag; but as she is, five hundred cannot, to a navigable place above the Falles." American conditions were going to require adaptation.

The Skulking Way of War

PATRICK MALONE

Although Indians welcomed many of the articles offered as gifts or as trade items, they were selective in their adoption of foreign products. Favored goods usually satisfied functional or symbolic needs already existing in the aboriginal culture. A particular object might be more durable, efficient, or attractive than an Indian artifact serving a similar purpose. The function and meaning of an artifact could, however, change dramatically as it passed from one culture to another. Indians flatly rejected a number of European items, made physical modifications to others before adopting them, and acquired some simply to make use of the raw material contained in them. Native American craftsmen acknowledged the value of imported metals but retained their respect for traditional forms and ornamentation when they cut up brass or iron goods to create products that were distinctly Indian in appearance. . . .

No European artifact adopted by the Indians had a more dramatic effect on their military system than did the firearm. . . .

. . . Yet, even in their rush to acquire the white man's guns, Indians showed excellent judgment in assessing the relative values of the several types of firearms which Europeans used in America.

The vast majority of firearms carried by early explorers and by the Pilgrims, who came to New England in 1620, were muskets called "matchlocks" after their firing mechanism. . . . During the first half of the century, colonists relied heavily on matchlocks for their military defense.

Matchlock muskets, standard equipment in European armies, were relatively inexpensive for prospective colonists. Simple in operation the lock lowered a lighted match, held in a device called a serpentine, into an open pan of priming powder. By pulling a trigger on some weapons or depressing a lever on others, the musketeer forced the serpentine to rotate against a restraining spring, thus bringing the match into contact with the priming powder and setting off an explosive train leading from the pan through a touch hole to the propellant charge in the barrel. The projectile, usually a large lead ball weighing a twelfth of a pound, was sent on its way with great force.

European armies found the matchlock musket an effective arm for massed formations. Although it weighed up to twenty pounds, was inaccurate beyond fifty yards, and had to be fired using a forked rest, it performed well during European infantry actions in which ranks of musketeers fired concentrated volleys at close

From Patrick Malone, *The Skulking Way of War: Technology and Tactics Among the New England Indians* (Baltimore: Johns Hopkins University Press, 1993) pp. 37–42, 44–46, 67–68, 73, 77–89, 95–106, 114–125.

range. However, a weapon suitable for the battlefields of Europe was not necessarily adequate for warfare in the forests of New England.

In Europe, soldiers fought opponents who were willing to accept battle under mutually advantageous situations and to forego actions in bad weather, darkness, or forested terrain. The militiamen of New England in the seventeenth century faced Indian warriors with a long tradition of success through stealth and surprise. Indians used the forest as an ally against their enemies. They attacked when and where they chose, striking when least expected and taking advantage of every weakness an enemy revealed.

Many characteristics of the matchlock proved to be liabilities in the New World. A musketeer had to light his match, a cord treated with saltpeter or gunpowder, in advance of any action. Failure to have a ready match could prove fatal, because attackers were not likely to give their enemies a chance to start a fire. A musketeer in a combat situation was expected to keep both ends of his match lighted, to adjust it frequently as it burned down, and to blow the ashes off the smoldering tip which was clamped in the serpentine of his musket. Since a match burned at a rate of up to nine inches an hour, considerable quantities of the special cord had to be carried into the field and kept in good condition.

In rainy weather a musketeer tried to keep his match dry in his hat or under cover in some other way. The effort was troublesome and the results often futile. . . .

As early as 1607, Indians recognized weaknesses in the ignition system of the matchlock musket. William Strachey, in his narrative of the voyage of Gilbert and Popham to Sagadahoc, explained that a group of Indians "subtilely devised how they might put out the fire in the shallop [boat], by which means they saw they should be free from the danger of our men's pieces, and to perform the same, one of the savages came into the shallop and taking the fire brand, which one of our company held in his hand there to light the matches, as if he would light a pipe of tobacco, as soon as he [the Indian] had gotten it into his hand he presently threw it into the water and leapt out of the shallop." Although these Indians had discovered the Achilles' heel of the matchlock, they were unwilling to bet their lives on their solution. When Gilbert ordered his men "to present their pieces" in a desperate bluff, the shaken warriors decided not to risk the possibility that the muskets could still fire without lighted matches. They took their bows and fled into the forest.

The flaws in the matchlock became more obvious to Indians as they tested weapons acquired in trade and as they witnessed the problems experienced by musketeers in some of the early skirmishes between white men and Indians. A warrior who suddenly darted from the brush was no easy target for a European whose weapon required a separate rest to support it in firing. Even worse, the musketeer might be surprised when he was unable to fire his matchlock at all because of an extinguished match or wet priming powder. His chances of ambushing the Indians in their own forests were minimal with a lighted match that not only glowed in shadows or darkness, but also gave off a recognizable odor. Even if he managed to fire his weapon, the process of reloading it was slow, complicated (over forty separate motions were prescribed in most military manuals), and dangerous.

Captain Myles Standish, an experienced professional soldier and an influential military leader in Plymouth Colony, preferred a type of firearm more advanced than the matchlock. He brought with him to New England a "snaphaunce," [flintlock] which was self-igniting and required no rest to steady it while firing. One advantage of this weapon was shown during an attack by Indians on Cape Cod in 1620; Standish was able to fire while some of his men were calling "for a firebrand to light their matches."

. . . The flintlock was a much better weapon for forest warfare than the matchlock, but the Indian was quicker to realize this than the average colonist.

Despite increasing evidence that the matchlock was unsuited for forest warfare, colonial governments were slow in requiring militamen to equip themselves with expensive flintlocks. The fact that European armies still fought with matchlocks had a powerful influence. The best musketeer of the day fired volleys on command, with little regard for aiming and with justified confidence in the capability of a lighted match to ignite dry powder. Formal battles in nice weather on open fields made the cumbersome matchlock appear effective; military commanders in England did not worry about ambushes, night attacks, or enemies who took cover behind trees. . . .

In sharp contrast to the majority of English colonists, New England Indians chose flintlocks over matchlocks almost immediately. They knew how to hunt and fight in the forested terrain of the eastern woodlands, and they knew at once that a weapon dependent on a lighted match did not compare with a self-igniting flintlock. The practices of trained European armies meant nothing to them; Indians simply chose the weapon best suited for their hunting and their military tactics. . . .

A man and his firearm form a weapons system in which the skill of the man is at least as important as the inherent accuracy of his weapon. Although the English colonists brought firearms with them to New England, very few of the men could shoot well. The average colonist had little or no familiarity with guns when he arrived and was slow to develop any proficiency as a marksman in the New World. Hunting practices and militia training on both sides of the Atlantic did not prepare colonists to shoot accurately and quickly at evasive targets. Indians, on the other hand, were trained from childhood in hunting and military skills that were readily adaptable to the use of firearms. The warriors of the forest quickly demonstrated superior abilities with the projectile weapons of the Europeans.

. . . The residual effects of [the colonists'] English cultural heritage, reinforced by constant communication and continuing immigration, remained strong in succeeding generations. The colonists' proficiency with guns in the seventeenth century is, therefore, best examined with a transatlantic perspective.

In sixteenth- and seventeenth-century England, men rarely acquired ability with firearms through hunting experiences. Hunting was the sport of the upper classes and was forbidden to most of the common people. There were numerous restrictions on who could hunt and on what methods could be used; hunting laws were usually designed to preserve game for the privileged few. The most socially respectable forms of the sport were riding behind a pack of hounds, coursing with swift greyhounds, and hawking. In these activities, the hunter was relying on animals to kill other animals and was not testing his marksmanship. . . .

From the late sixteenth to the mid-seventeenth century the important of musketry increased tremendously in European warfare, while the need for skilled marksmaship actually declined. The military requirements of the period called for musketeers to load and handle their matchlock weapons with precise movements, to level them in the direction of an enemy formation, and to fire on command in a volley. The critical element in this massing of firepower was the simultaneous discharge of all the muskets in one or more ranks.

. . . This type of massed firepower made a high degree of individual accuracy less important than rapidity in firing and reloading the musket. . . .

Although numerous incidents in warfare against New England Indians demonstrated the value of aiming one's musket at a single enemy, most colonial officers and musketeers did not recognize the critical importance of individual marksmanship until the last stages of King Philip's War. The Pilgrims' first skirmish with hostile Indians in 1620 should have convinced those early colonists of the need for improved accuracy. William Bradford told how an Indian shooting arrows from beside a tree "stood three shots of a musket, until one taking full aim at him . . . made the splinters of the tree fly about his ears, after which he gave an extraordinary shriek and away they went." Fifty-seven years after this occurrence, and after the horrors of King Philip's War, the authorities of Plymouth Colony finally instructed militia officers to "not only train their soldiers in their postures and motions but also at shooting at marks." . . .

One might assume that colonists living in or near a "wilderness" would become good marksmen because of experience in hunting, whether or not they received military training in shooting at targets. Unfortunately, our popular image of sharpshooting frontiersmen is questionable even for the early nineteenth-century settlers of Kentucky and is far removed from the reality of the seventeenth-century colonists in New England. The latter as we have seen, had little, if any, hunting experience when they arrived, and they were soon so busy creating villages and towns that they had few opportunities to hunt. Most became hard-working agriculturists or craftsmen, more concerned with homes, shops, and cultivated lands than with the pursuit of wild animals. . . .

William Wood admitted reluctantly that "every one's employment [did] not permit him to fowl." Recognizing the incompetence of some would-be fowlers, he wrote: "many go blurting away their powder and shot, that have no more skill to kill, or win a goose, than many in England that have rusty muskets in their houses knows what belongs to a soldier. . . ." Also, beavers and otters were "too cunning for the English" but not for the Indians, "those skillful hunters whose time [was] not so precious, whose experience-bought skill [had] made them practical and useful in that particular." Roger Williams said that Indians armed with guns killed an "abundance of fowl," because they were "naturally excellent marksmen; and also more hardened to endure the weather, and wading, lying, and creeping on the ground, etc." . . .

Because the Indians had superior talents as hunters, the colonists let them supply much of the wild game that was eaten in the settlements. Wildfowl and deer were prized as food by both the Indians and the English. John Josselyn said that although the deer were "innumerable," there were "but few slain by the English." William Wood believed that it upset the Indians more "to see an Englishman take one deer, than a thousand acres of land." Some Indians were, however, willing to put their deer-hunting abilities to use for the English and to supply venison for a price. In a poem on New England, William Bradford wrote: "For us to seek for deer it doth not boot, / Since now with guns themselves [Indians] can shoot." . . .

Wolves and deer were wary animals which clearly presented too great a challenge for average colonists. Some men did try their luck at fowl-shooting, a type of hunting that required no real accuracy in this period of New England history. A few shot large numbers of the waterfowl that frequented the New England coast from the fall to the early spring, but this activity took more time than most men were willing to spend away from their daily masks. Isaack de Rasieres said that the geese at Plymouth in 1627 were "easy to shoot, inasmuch as they congregate together in such large flocks." Wood claimed that some men had killed "50 ducks at a shot, 40 teals at another." His figures may have been inflated, but they show that men shot at entire flocks and not at individuals birds. Thomas Morton provided further evidence of this fact when he wrote: "I have had often 1000 [geese] before the mouth of my gun." . . .

. . . For more sport a colonist could shoot flying pigeons in flocks of "millions and millions." The vast flights seemed to have "neither beginning nor ending," and "the shouting of people, the rattling of guns, and pelting of small shot could not drive them out of their course." Actually men found it more effective to take these birds with nets as they roosted than to shoot into their crowded flights. By the 1670s, John Josselyn thought the number of pigeons was "much diminished," because of "the English taking them with nets." . . .

Archaeological excavations at the sites of eight seventeenth-century homesteads in Plymouth Colony have yielded valuable clues about the diets and hunting practices of the colonists. Few wild animal bones were found among a total of approximately ten thousand bone fragments from the sites; well over ninety percent of the fragments were from domestic animals slaughtered for food. Bones from wild ducks appeared fairly often, but excavators found none from turkeys and only a very few from wild mammals. Although none of the sites dates from the first thirty years of the colony's existence, the preliminary results of this faunal analysis lend support to the theory that hunting in New England was an infrequent practice usually limited to the relatively easy shooting of wildfowl. . . .

The Indians' choice of firearms and ammunition had a significant effect on their ability to hit what they were aiming at, particularly if their target was as elusive as a deer or an alert warrior from another tribe. In trade they demanded flintlocks, which allowed them to "snap shoot" at a moving target. They came to prefer firearms with relatively short barrels, weapons which a man could point rapidly and which were easy to use in thick vegetation. . . .

By . . . 1675 . . . , the New England colonists had made numerous adaptations in their militia system, but they were still restricted by allegiance to cultural traditions and to standard military practices of their age. They did not acknowledge the obvious advantage of multiple shot over full-size musket balls in the close-range encounters of forest warfare. They had finally given up the matchlocks still in use on European battlefields and had armed themselves with the flintlocks that Indians had preferred for half a century. Yet they still did not realize the crucial significance of their flintlock musket's potential for accurate fire at either stationary or moving opponents. Neither their militia drills nor their minimal hunting experience gave them any real training in marksmanship. It would take months of military defeat before the colonists would admit that the Indians' way of employing muskets in warfare was clearly better than their own.

An Indian in combat chose an opponent, aimed specifically at that individual, and used acquired abilities in marksmanship to kill or wound him. He often chose small balls for his flintlock and was, for that reason alone, more likely to score a hit than any musketeer firing only the standard single ball. An Indian was also more likely to be well-practiced in the aimed firing of his weapon than an English colonist. He had probably spent years snap-shooting at moving animals, testing the rapid igni- tion system of his flintlock and learning how to lead a moving target. He could fire his weapon from many different positions; he could even shoot with it steadied against a tree or rock that shielded most of his body from enemy bullets. He under- stood that he was both the potential target and the skilled operator of a deadly ma- chine. The colonist had brought the firearm to the New World; in King Philip's War, the Indian would demonstrate how to use this machine. . . .

The Indian military system in southern New England underwent dramatic changes during the seventeenth century as Europeans introduced Indians to new weapons, tools, technological skills, and military philosophies. Indians selectively adopted artifacts, crafts practices, and ideas to fit the perceived needs of a culture threatened by both colonial expansion and tribal rivalries. They gained confidence from their increasing understanding of European technology and lost whatever awe they may have initially felt at the sight of such European products as firearms and axes. Even in the early 1630s, William Wood of Massachusetts Bay notices that "fresh supplies of new and strange products hath lessn'd their admiration, and quickened their invention, and desire of producing such things as they see, wherein they express no small ingenuity, and dexterity of wit. . . ."

The prospect of Indians extensively adopting English material culture and prac- ticing English crafts aroused mixed feelings among the Puritans. . . . Colonial au- thorities allowed craftsmen to instruct trusted Indians in useful trades, but a royal proclamation in 1630 forbade anyone to teach an Indian "to make or amend" firearms "or anything belonging to them."

Southern New England Indians had many opportunities to learn English craft techniques. The language barrier, which frustrated the first efforts to convert the In- dians, had little effect on the transfer of technology between cultures. Craft tech- niques can spread easily across cultural boundaries without verbal communication. Indians already versed in traditional methods of manufacturing aboriginal artifacts could learn a great deal just by observing English products and experimenting with tools and materials acquired in trade. Since they moved freely through colonial set- tlements, Indians could also observe English craftsmen at work and perhaps receive some instruction. Thomas Shepard said that the Indians at Nonantum in 1647 were "very dextrous at any thing they see done once." In the previous decade, Wood had noted that Indians could "soon learn any mechanical trades, having quick wits, un- derstanding apprehensions, strong memories, with nimble inventions, and a quick hand in using of the axe or hatchet." . . .

Puritan missionaries, believing that a Christian should lead a useful and indus- trious life, made technological training an important part of the process of "civiliz- ing" their Indian converts. They provided both instruction and tools for Christian Indians and strongly encouraged them to learn a trade. For some Indians the promise of such an introduction to English technology many have been as great as incentive for conversion as any attractions of the English faith. . . .

Serious disputes with Plymouth Colony in 1671 caused the Wampanoags to pre- pare for possible military action. Hugh Cole visited the tribal headquarters at Mount Hope in that year and noted the presence of Narragansett craftsmen who were repairing the Wampanoags' firearms. These artisans were apparently experienced in working with muskets and other metal weapons. In their Rhode Island home, the Narragansetts had their own forge, and at least one member of the tribe was a skilled blacksmith.

Recent excavations at a seventeenth-century Narragansett cemetery in Rhode Island have revealed an Indian blacksmith kit. This set of tools, including a hammer and some chisel-like wedges, was apparently buried with a man who had skill in its use. Narragansetts believed that souls in their afterlife would have need for many of the same artifacts they possessed when alive. Iroquois (Seneca) sites in New York from the same general period have also yielded tools for working on firearms. In addition to normal blacksmithing tools and a great many flintlock parts, Iroquois graves contained a hand vise (probably for holding sears and tumblers in filing operations), a three-cornered file, and a whetstone. One mass of 426 flintlock parts found in a single Iroquois grave must have belonged to a very capable and busy repairman. . . .

Only a part of Indian military technology was devoted to weaponry; Indians also continued the aboriginal practice of building forts. The basic design and construction of most Indian fortifications remained unchanged after the arrival of the English, but Indians could build log palisades better and faster with European tools. In some cases colonists assisted Indian allies in the construction of their forts. The English may even have suggested minor modifications in this defensive technology. . . .

The Narragansetts build the largest and most impressive Indian fort in New England. Supportive of the Wampanoags from the early phases of King Philip's War, this tribe began the construction of its huge fort in the Great Swamp of Rhode Island in 1675. The design included certain features which strongly suggest the influence of European engineering practices. William Hubbard mentioned "a kind of block house" at one corner of the wooden stockade and a "flanker" at another point. The palisade of the fort was still incomplete when a force of one thousand colonists attacked on the night of December 19, 1675, but these formidable defenses caused the English to suffer heavy casualties in the assault. At least seventy colonial soldiers were mortally wounded while taking and burning the fort. Fire, as in the 1637 destruction of a Pequot fort, made the Narragansetts' losses much higher.

The tribe had successfully hidden their forge from the English until "The Great Swamp Fight." Nathaniel Saltonstall reported that the attacking soldiers killed "an Indian black-smith" who repaired Narragansett firearms. They also "demolished his forge, and carried away his tools." . . .

One band of Narragansetts did not flee the Rhode Island area but instead went into hiding in a stone fort west of the present town of Wickford. The Indians had constructed a secret refuge by using the natural boulders of a hilltop as part of their defenses and by adding connecting walls of carefully laid stone to complete the fortification. The impressive position is still easily recognizable. It is known as "the Queen's Fort," because Queen Quaiapen's Narragansett band probably built and occupied it.

The Indian most qualified to build a fort of stone for the Narragansetts had shown his talent with masonry in English settlements before the war. Saltonstall wrote that he was "famously known by the name of Stonewall, or Stone-layer John; for that being an active ingenious fellow he had learned the mason's trade, and was of great use to the Indians in building their forts, etc." His engineering skill probably accounts for the sophisticated plans of both the wooden fort in the Great Swamp and the queen's stone fort. The layout of the latter structure includes a semicircular bastion and a sharp flanker, features which conform to seventeenth-century principles of European military engineering.

English forces did not discover the Narragansetts' stone fort during the war, but they did surprise the female sachem and her followers at a temporary campsite in June 1676. Major Talcott's company from Connecticut killed most of the Indians, including Queen Quaiapen and Stonewall John. The Indian craftsman has been the subject of considerable folklore since his death.

According to one Rhode Island legend which insults the New England Indians, Stonewall John was a renegade military engineer from England. Some people, unaware of the level of technology among the southern New England Indians in the seventeenth century, have found it difficult to believe that he was really an Indian. His reputation has overshadowed the achievements of other Indian craftsmen with widely varying degrees of skill who performed essential services for their tribes. Stonewall John was no doubt an exceptional dry mason and architect of fortifications, but he was only one individual within an entire system of technological support. Narragansett fortifications, although impressive examples of military engineering, were in fact the Indians' least effective application of technology to warfare. Only the Narragansetts tried to defend a large fort against the English in King Philip's War; the result was the catastrophe of the Great Swamp.

. . . The violence inflicted on Indians was, in fact, even more terrible and less restrained than the horrors of the Thirty Year War, where Christians fought other Christians. To many of the English who went to war against New England Indians, their opponents were more like wolves than men. The attitudes of both officers and common soldiers were strongly affected by the moral dangers of combat against foes who seemed to possess some strange form of animal cunning, who treated prisoners cruelly, and who would not fight in expected ways. The escalation of the war against the Pequots in 1637 was accompanied by English accusations that the Indians were less than fully human. Some colonists actually suggested that the Pequots were agents of the devil.

The burning of the Pequot fort may have been the first example of total warfare in New England. After a series of accusations and violent incidents and one unsuccessful punitive expedition, troops from both Connecticut and Massachusetts Bay invaded the territory of the Pequots. The militiamen landed in Rhode Island and marched overland to the Mystic River in Connecticut where the Pequots had one of their fortified villages. The total force contained about ninety colonists, sixty Mohegans, and a number of Narragansetts who had been recruited to both guide and fight. The presence of Indian allies worried some of the English participants, but the Mohegans had already proven their willingness to kill Pequots in a previous action.

On May 26, 1637, the English and their Indian allies achieved a complete surprise with a dawn attack on the palisaded fortifications. The Pequots, who probably felt safe in their fort, awoke to the sound of a volley of musketry against the log walls. Immediately after opening fire, the English charged through the entrance of the fort and into the streets of the village. The colonial commander, Captain John Mason from Connecticut, led his men in setting fire to the highly flammable Pequot dwellings. Within seconds the entire village was ablaze. The English withdrew to form a ring around the doomed fort as the fire became an inferno. Mohegans and Narragansetts waited in a large circle beyond the soldiers.

These Indian allies were shocked by the horrible scene as hundreds of men, women, and children perished in the blaze or were cut down as they tried to escape. In the frenzied action, the English even mistakenly wounded some of their Indian supporters. An Indian with Captain John Underhill objected strenuously to this strange and terrible form of warfare, he "cried mach it, mach it; that is, it is naught, it is naught, because it is too furious, and slays too many men." A week before this massacre, Roger Williams had sent a note to the Puritan leaders in the Bay Colony explaining the Narragansetts' request "that women and children be spared."

Underhill, who commanded the small body of Massachusetts men with Mason, answered critics by insisting that the mass slaughter of both warriors and noncombatants was justified by biblical precedent:

It may be demanded, why should you be so furious? (as some have said). Should not Christians have more mercy and compassion? But I would refer you to David's War. When a people is grown to such a height of blood, and sin against God and man, and all confederates in the action, there He hath no respect to persons, but harrows them, and saws them, and puts them to the sword, and the most terriblest death that may be. Sometimes the scripture declareth women and children must perish with their parents. . . . We had sufficient light from the word of God for our proceedings.

The Narragansetts and Mohegans had no experience with this type of war. They must have been amazed and horrified by the idea of destroying an entire village. The death, in one place, of perhaps four hundred or more Pequots created a scene of incredible carnage. Underhill admitted that "great and doleful was the bloody site to the view of young soldiers that had never been in war, to see so many souls lie gasping on the ground, so thick in some places, that you could hardly pass along."

Word of the merciless actions of the English militiamen in the Pequot War spread rapidly among the native population. Conservative Puritan Philip Vincent published an account of the war in London in which he claimed that the New England colonists were "assured of their peace, by killing the barbarians." He thought the war would have a positive effect as a deterrent: "For having once terrified them, by severe execution of just revenge, they shall never hear of more harm from them, except perhaps the killing of a man or two at his work. . . . Nay they shall have those brutes their servants, their slaves, either willingly or of necessity and docile enough if not obsequious."

By the beginning of King Philip's War, many of the Indians in southern New England had indeed learned a lesson from the earlier demonstration of total warfare against the Pequots, but it was not the lesson that Vincent envisioned. Indians had learned that the traditional restraints which had limited deaths in aboriginal warfare were nothing more than liabilities in any serious conflict with the English colonists. Wars between Indians had become bloodier as the weapons and attitudes of the Europeans influenced the native culture. Now a great confrontation was starting, and the Indians who challenged the authority of the New England colonies were ready to fight in a new way.

The Wampanoags, Narragansetts, Nipmucs, and Pocumtucks who either joined or were swept into the war with the English and their Indian allies in 1675 followed the precedent set in the Pequot war. They waged war on all colonists, not just combatants, and they used every means at their disposal to defeat their enemies. The total warfare which the English had introduced to New England became a nightmare for frontier towns and militia bands. Although nothing that the Indians did ever approached the horror of the Pequot fort, King Philip's War showed the English how well and how fiercely Native Americans could fight.

The widespread use of fire arrows and torches against English houses was one demonstration of the Indians' new willingness to practice total warfare. Captain Thomas Wheeler, who lived through a Nipmuc attack on Brookfield, Massachusetts, in August 1675, told how the Indians wrapped special arrows with rags containing brimstone and "wild fire." Frustrated by the stubborn defense of the town's garrison house, the Nipmucs built two siege devices mounted on wheels and loaded with inflammable materials. To the relief of the trapped colonists, a rainstorm prevented the testing of this innovative equipment. Before the Indians left, however, they managed to burn every house except the defended one and one under construction. . . .

Until the English made good use of their Indian allies and began to adopt some Indian tactics, the warriors who opposed them were far superior in forest combat. Gookin said that the colonial soldiers were unprepared for fighting in which they "could see no enemy to shoot at, but yet felt their bullets out of the thick bushes where they lay in ambushment." The warriors sometimes camouflaged "themselves from the waist upwards with green boughs" so that "Englishmen could not readily discern them or distinguish them from the natural bushes." Colonists "had little experience" with such warfare, "and hence were under great disadvantages." Benjamin Thompson complained in a poem that "every stump shot like a musketeer."

Most disturbing to the colonists was the deadly effectiveness of Indian musketry, a result of careful aiming at individual opponents. The marksmanship and pragmatic military practices of the Indians put the leaders of militia bands in particularly perilous positions. Because in European combat the enemy usually made no effort to aim at anyone, and officer was as safe in a prominent position as were any of his soldiers in formation. The Narragansetts, who did not consider it unsportsmanlike to try to kill the leaders of their opponents, shot Captain Davenport three times during the "Great Swamp Fight."

. . . Six other captains were killed or died of wounds received in that action. . . .

The Indian mode of warfare, actually a blend of aboriginal and European elements, proved so successful in numerous engagements that perceptive officers and government officials began to urge changes in colonial military doctrine. There was, however, considerable resistance to suggestions of adopting the Indian tactics which seemed to work so well in the forests. William Hubbard after blaming the "Bloody Brook massacre" on the soldiers' failure to fight in a body, as expected of European musketeers, went on to criticize any imitation of the Indians' method of "skulking behind trees and taking their aim at single persons."

Field commanders noted the obvious fact that their Indian opponents would not conform to European concepts of battlefield conduct. It was futile to send out a general from the Bay Colony with specific orders to stop the enemy's "skulkings whereby he picks off the English." To defeat the warring tribes, the English would have to use tactics which they had long regarded with contempt and indignation. Although the process of borrowing methods from Indians was difficult for most officers and common soldiers, a few enterprising men began to depart from accepted European practices as soon as they faced well-armed and forest-wise opponents who knew the value of scouting, surprise, cover, concealment, mobility, and marksmanship. Soon a tactical and technological revolution was underway, and a new doctrine of forest warfare was evolving.

When "multitudes of Indians who possessed themselves of every rock, stump, tree or fence that was in sight" ambushed Captain Church and a party of Plymouth colonists on July 9, 1675, the Englishmen dove for any cover they could find in the barren spot where they were temporarily trapped. . . .

Governor Leverett of Massachusetts Bay correctly appraised the military situation as early as September 24, 1675, when he commented that many men were "lost by not taking heed to the ambushments of the enemy nor observing their methods." He ordered the companies of the Bay Colony "to attend the enemies' method, which though it may seem a rout to ours is the best way of fighting the enemy in this bushy wilderness." His order did not cause any immediate changes, particularly because Indian scouts had been recently removed from most of the colony's military units. However, by the end of the following summer, soldiers from all of the New England colonies were shooting at individuals, using cover when fired upon, and moving through the woods quietly and carefully. Their ability to find and attack the enemy had greatly improved as they gained experience in the forest and listened to the advice of Indian allies. Connecticut units had learned much from their Mohegan and Pequot comrades-in-arms, and Captain Church had finally gotten the mixed company of Indians and Plymouth colonists which he had wanted.

Church probably did the most to popularize the adoption of unconventional tactics by English forces. On July 24, 1676, Governor Winslow commissioned him to "raise a Company of Volunteers of about 200 men, English and Indians; the English not exceeding the number of 60." . . .

This unusual Plymouth company killed or captured hundreds of Indians by fighting in the Indian manner. Church carefully studied the methods of his opponents and interrogated prisoners to gather information on enemy locations and tactics. By acting on the advice of both friendly and hostile Indians, he created a combined force which could defeat the enemy on its own ground. His captives offered one suggestion which improved the movement of troops through the forest and reduced casualties in combat; they told him that "the Indians always took care in their manner and fights not to come too thick together. But the English always kept in a heap together, that it was as easy to hit them as to hit a house." . . .

The killing of Metacomet, or King Philip, on August 12, 1676, was a widely-publicized feat which demonstrated the value of Captain Church's Indian-like tactics. Church had learned from an informer that Metacomet was in a swamp below Mount Hope, where the war had begun. Rushing to the area with a small force, Church split his unit into a raiding party to drive the Wampanoag sachem and his few remaining followers from their camp and a blocking force to wait in ambush for any fleeing Indians. Church personally stationed his blocking force in the wooded wetlands near the Indian camp. In the semi-darkness before dawn, he placed pairs of one Indian and one Englishman behind trees at spots which seemed to almost insure interception. When the raiders fired into and then rushed the camp, the elusive sachem escaped into the swamp only to run toward a pair of waiting men. It was an Indian who shot Metacomet after his English partner's musket had misfired.

The ultimate defeat of the hostile tribes was inevitable long before the death of the man whom the English called King Philip. The Indians' tactical successes and their skillful use of European military technology were not enough to win a war against the far more numerous colonists, whose Indian allies, fortified garrison houses, and almost unlimited logistical support tipped the scales heavily.

By the fall of 1676, disease, starvation, lack of ammunition, and relentless pursuit had brought disaster to the scattered Indians survivors. The hostility of the Mohawks toward the insurgent tribes had been a boon for the colonial forces and an important factor in the English military success. There was little hope of escape to the west, where the Mohawks were waiting, and few places where the remnants of proud bands could hide in New England. Colonists had burned corn fields, destroyed food caches, and kept their enemies from traditional fishing spots. When starvation forced Indians to leave hiding places in search of food, they frequently fell prey to grim soldiers who were no longer bewildered in the forest. The English units, guided by Indian scouts, had begun to use the same ambush and raid techniques with which their opponents had terrified most of New England in the previous year.

The English had also borrowed from the military material of the Indians during King Philip's War. Colonists learned to paddle birchbark canoes and to travel with snowshoes and moccasins in the deep snows of the New England winters. Hatchets, or tomahawks, designed for the Indian trade became standard sidearms in some units, replacing the traditional swords. Even English food proved less suitable for forest warfare than standard Indian rations. Bitter experiences with moldy bread and heavy supplies on long expeditions prompted a militia committee in Massachusetts Bay to add the following item to a list of military provisions: "fifty bushels of Indian corn, parched and beaten to nocake." Each of these hundred soldiers was to carry his supply of this nourishing and durable meal in a small bag, as was the Indian practice.

Not every colonist was pleased that Indian allies and borrowed military practices had contributed so much to the success of the English forces, but almost everyone agreed by 1677 that warfare in the New England forests required departures from conventional European methods. John Eliot recognized the military changes which had occurred since the Pequot War:

> In our first war with the Indians, God pleased to show us the vanity of our military skill, in managing our arms, after the European mode. Now we are glad to learn the skulking way of war.

The Middle Ground

RICHARD WHITE

Trade goods served both symbolic and utilitarian purposes. The same kettle that served to cement an alliance also cooked venison. . . . Turning to trade goods as items of everyday use draws attention to another facet of exchange: the possibility of dependency. The question of dependency—the possibility that without European goods and the fur trade the Algonquians would no longer be able to feed, clothe, or house themselves—looms over recent studies of the trade. To determine if this possibility became fact during the French fur trade, it is necessary to assess the place and prevalence of trade goods in everyday material life and the dependence of Algonquians upon them.

From Richard White, *The Middle Ground* (Cambridge, England: Cambridge University Press, 1991), pp. 128–141.

Superficially, Algonquian statements and actions regarding these matters seem to mimic the terms of the marketplace and indicate a material dependence on the French. On closer examination, however, their views and actions make sense only in the context of the particular social relationships that the goods themselves helped to establish. In referring to exchange, Algonquians spoke in terms of their *besoins*— their needs or necessities—and they visualized exchange as a way of satisfying these needs. *Besoin,* as used by the Algonquians, was not simply a statement of desire; the term had a particular resonance in their society because, once an appropriate social relationship had been established, an assertion of need for something could become a special claim on the thing needed. To be needy is to excite pity and thus to deserve aid. Just as in addressing manitous Algonquians sought to portray themselves as weak and miserable, so in addressing Onontio, Jesuits, or traders, they usually stressed their own misery and need. The Algonquians' emphasis on exchange as a way of satisfying their *besoins,* therefore, had a meaning quite different from that expressed in the French view of commerce as a way of filling needs.

In stressing their *besoins,* the Algonquians were actually making a claim on the French. Because they needed goods and were friends and allies of the French, they deserved to have those goods that the French possessed but did not themselves immediately require. Indians, like the Fox at their first contact, thought that "whatever their visitors possessed ought to be given to them gratis; everything aroused their desires, and yet they had few beavers to sell." Among the Potawatomis at initial contact, the French demand for payments for goods that Indians received led to violence. According to Algonquian cultural logic, the French, as allies, should act as if they were kinspeople of the Algonquians. Each side would supply the other's needs. Each side would graciously bestow what the other lacked.

Such a conception of exchange makes it clearer why middleman status was a matter of relative indifference to the Algonquians. If the French chose to bring them goods at their villages, this was to be praised not opposed. These western Algonquians conceived of traders as men who came to supply their *besoins,* and they welcomed them for their presence which promised to enhance the prestige, wealth, and strength of their villages. What infuriated them was not the loss of the opportunity to make the long and arduous journeys to Montreal to obtain their *besoins,* but the French announcement in the late 1690s that they were withdrawing their traders from the *pays d'en haut* and that they expected the Algonquians to resume their trade journeys. Onanghisse, the Potawatomi leader whose people the French presumed to be potential middlemen, was outraged:

> Father! Since we want powder, iron, and every other necessary which you were formerly in the habit of sending us, what do you expect us to do? Are the majority of our women who have but one or two beavers to send to Montreal to procure their little supplies, are they to intrust them to drunken fellows who will drink them and bring nothing back? Thus, having in our country none of the articles we require and which you, last year, promised we should be furnished with, and not want; and perceiving only this—that nothing whatsoever is yet brought to us, and that the French come to visit us no more— you shall never see us again, I promise you, if the French quit us; this Father, is the last time we shall come to talk with you.

Significantly, Onanghisse said nothing about lower prices or potential profits; he spoke for the women, who, by implication, were a major force in exchange in the villages. They and the other Potawatomis relied on the French for their *besoins,* their "little supplies." Exchange in Montreal was the domain not of calculating middle-men out for profit but of "drunken fellows" who drank up their beaver and failed to bring home the *besoins* they had been sent to fetch. Although these *besoins* were highly valued goods, they were not yet essential to Potawatomi survival. For if they were, how could Onanghisse have spoken of never seeing the French again and thus, presumably, doing without them?

This orientation toward *besoins* rather than profits appears also in the reaction of the Ottawas and Huron-Petuns of Michilimackinac to the French domination of their old carrying trade to the western tribes. The Ottawas, Huron-Petuns, and vari-ous western Chippewa bands continued, as they had for years, to gather furs on the lakes, but they now operated on the margins rather than at the center of exchange. The Ottawas lost their old lucrative trade with the Crees, who had begun trading at Hud-son's Bay. Only the Saulteurs, who as allies of the Sioux carried French goods to that people, continued to tap a major source of prime beaver. To obtain their *besoins,* the Huron-Petuns and Ottawas of Michilimackinac, as well as the Potawatomis of Green Bay, became provisioners of the trade. They sold corn and fish to the French who, according to Cadillac, reequipped themselves once on the outward journey from Montreal and again on their return. They compensated for the huge charges the French made for their goods by setting prices on their own commodities that made the French howl in protest. As La Potherie recognized, they now

> [do] not need to go hunting in order to obtain all the comforts of life. When they choose to work, they make canoes of birch-bark, which they sell two at three hundred livres each. They get a shirt for two sheets of bark for cabins. The sale of their French straw-berries and other fruits produce means for producing their ornaments, which consist of vermillion and glass and porcelain beads. They make a profit on everything.

What La Potherie called their profit, however, was probably not understood by the Indians in these terms, for, as La Potherie also notes, all except the Huron-Petuns saved nothing and realized no lasting gain from such exchanges. "They would be ex-ceedingly well-to-do if they were economical," but the social and cultural demands of their own society prevented such accumulation. They gave away their last food to a visiting stranger and then did not hesitate to beg for food from the French who came among them. The underlying logic of such exchange patterns was that *besoins* took precedence over profits. They had an obligation to visitors, and the French had an obligation to them.

The actual demand for the goods that the Algonquians identified as their *besoins* was surprisingly limited during the century of the French fur trade that ended in 1760. Father Charlevoix observed in the 1720s that Indian wants were, by European standards, meager. When he asserted that the Indians were "true philosophers and the sight of all our conveniences, riches, and magnificence affects them so little that they have found out the art of easily dispensing with them," he was not simply in-dulging in the myth of the noble savage. Indian wants do appear to have remained limited even at the height of the trade and Indian demand remained relatively in-elastic. Unless presented with brandy, Algonquians traded largely to clothe and orna-ment themselves, buy some metals tools, and acquire enough gunpowder for the next hunt. An analysis of French account books for Michilimackinac, Ouiatenon, Detroit, and Green Bay between 1715 and 1750 reveals that cloth, blankets, gunpowder, and shirts were the dominant trade goods at all the posts. These, along with capotes and, at Detroit, brandy, accounted for between 60 and 75 percent of the trade. The Indians did not trade for the guns they used in the hunt, for such guns rarely appear on the trade manifests. Guns seem to have come largely as presents from the Crown. The increase in the scale of trade apparent after 1720 resulted largely from the wide-spread adoption of woolens and other cloth to replace fur robes and leather garments.

In local economics where trade goods satisfied limited *besoins,* the fur trade in-volved relatively little disruption of native subsistence systems. Production for the fur trade came from a hunt not yet separated from the larger subsistence cycle. Success in the hunt remained a function of the hunters' relations with the manitous who con-trolled the game. And a successful hunt yielded goods whose distribution proceeded according to the demands of the manitous and the *besoins* of kinspeople. This was not an economy in which the production or distribution of goods formed a separate sphere of practical activity. Nor was it an economy that had yet, in any meaningful sense, rendered the Algonquians politically dependent on the Europeans. All of these points obviously demand substantiation.

Taken as a whole, the material day-to-day existence of Indian people showed remarkable continuity during the seventeenth and early eighteenth centuries. The fur trade barely altered Algonquian housing, transportation, and diet. The fur trade did initially put a greater emphasis on beaver hunting. And certain groups such as the Ottawas and Huron-Petuns increased the scale of their hunt. But for most groups, the fur trade did not immediately or drastically alter hunting or subsistence patterns. Furs were the products of hunts in which men, women and children departed together and in which household units consumed the meat while processing and reserving the furs for market. The trade certainly increased the amount of labor women had to devote to preparing furs for exchange, but, on the other hand, the purchase of cloth and ready-made clothing lessened the labor involved in producing finished garments. How this balances out in the end is impossible to determine from the existing evidence.

Even when beaver failed and Indians turned to other game, the immediate con-sequences were not severe. Deer and bear, the staples of the fur trade of the Ohio Valley and lower Great Lakes, also yielded meat. Subsistence and the hunt for furs remained as closely linked as ever. When the distance of beaver from the villages and the scarcity of other game in the region did create a conflict, the demands of subsis-tence took priority. Even around Green Bay into the mid 1740s, Indians long in-volved in the trade still had to be actively recruited to hunt beaver in the Sioux borderlands instead of remaining nearer their villages to hunt deer and bear. The ties to the trade of tribes such as the Sioux, whose involvement in the trade was much more recent, were even weaker. The French feared that increases in prices for trade goods would cause the Sioux to "lose their ardor for coming to find the merchandise whose use they have known only for a little while." Only later in the eighteenth and nineteenth centuries, and even then only among some tribes, did production for mar-ket become a separate sphere in which men, leaving their families behind, departed on long hunts whose sole goal was the accumulation of furs for market.

If production did not demand immediate alterations in the society, neither did the European goods that entered the society transform it. Indians acquired trade goods at a surprisingly gradual rate. A preexisting native technology survived for a remarkably long time alongside the new technology. Kettles boiled water, knives cut meat, and guns killed game, but they did not chain their users inevitably, inexorably, and immediately to the will of the suppliers. A far less efficient, but still serviceable, native technology remained available if trade goods were lacking.

Given existing interpretations of the scale and importance of the fur trade, the assertion that European goods remained relatively scarce in the *pays d'en haut* for generations and that a native technology remained available is bound to be controversial. Basically, there are three major problems with assuming that European goods rapidly and nearly completely replaced native manufacturers in the *pays d'en haut.* First, according to the archaeological record, native technology persisted for a considerable time. Second, given the carrying capacity of French canoes and the limited number that departed annually for the West, there was simply no way to transport all the goods that would have been necessary to supply the native population. Third, when read carefully, contemporary accounts make it clear that European goods remained relatively scarce over much of the *pays d'en haut* well into the eighteenth century.

It is necessary here to cite only a few examples of this evidence. Stone tools persisted alongside metal tools in the Ojibwa sites on the north shores of Lake Huron and Lake Superior that were occupied during the late seventeenth and early eighteenth centuries. Sites in the Michilimackinac region, the nexus of the trade, show the same pattern. At the Lasanen site, probably an Ottawa and Huron-Petun burial site used primarily between 1690 and 1700, "projectile points, scrapers and stone knives imply the maintenance of the prehistoric technological and economic patterns." Similarly, at the late seventeenth-century Summer Island site in Green Bay, stone tools persisted alongside European metal tools. Farther south, the Zimmerman site that the Kaskaskias occupied between 1683 and 1691 shows the same pattern of stone technology lingering alongside metals tools. Even at the eighteenth-century Guebert site occupied by the Kaskaskias after 1719, there are vestiges of stone technology. The Jesuits could collect stone daggers in everyday use as late as 1687, and, according to Father Sebastian Rale, arrows tipped with stone remained the principal weapon into the 1690s. Native pottery persisted even longer; it is readily available at all late seventeenth- and early eighteenth-century sites.

Other goods penetrated the region even more slowly. By 1679 the Fox Indians, a tribe described only five years later as a major supplier of furs, had acquired firearms, but a 120-man war party encountered by the French that year possessed only eight muskets. Cloths remained so rare that when the Fox captured a coat from the French, they ripped off the buttons and cut up the material in order to divide the coat into the maximum number of pieces. If the Wisconsin Fox ever acquired large amounts of cloth, such supplies vanished after their estrangement from the French. In 1718 the men still wore "scarcely any garments made of cloth." Similarly, in the 1680s, members of the La Salle expedition reported that the Illinois, the best armed tribe south of Lake Michigan, had virtually no guns and that the peoples around them lacked metal knives and hatchets. In 1706, nearly half a century after the first guns appeared among them, the Peorias, one of the tribes of the Illinois confederation, attacked a Jesuit priest, Father Gravier. Not only did they shoot him with arrows, but the arrows were tipped with flint. It is equally notable that the French response was to cut off powder for such guns as the Illinois possessed. The incident is a clear example of the persistence of old technology alongside the new. When, toward the end of the French and Indian War, supplies of powder failed at Detroit, the Ottawas, Huron-Petuns, Potawatomis and Chippewas there resumed hunting with bows and arrows. They did it without enthusiasm, but they did it. When French traders during the same period failed to supply cloth to the Illinois, those Indians clothed themselves in skins.

This failure of European goods rapidly to displace native manufactures is more understandable when we examine estimates of available cargo space during the late seventeenth and early eighteenth centuries. The French could not transport the amount of goods necessary to provide Algonquians with the tools and clothes they would need to abandon native manufactures. The intendant Jean Bochart de Champigny estimated that about seventy canoe loads of goods reached the West in the late 1680s (see Table 1), with this number increasing dramatically in the early 1690s, when Governor de Frontenac, on the pretext of supplying Michilimackinac and other posts, allowed large amounts of additional trade goods, including brandy, to be shipped west.

When these cargoes are places next to estimates of the population they were meant to supply, the reasons for the persistence of native technology become apparent. Until some time after 1700, this was a population in decline from disease, displacement, and war, but it was still sizable. Considering only the major population clusters, there were 15,000–20,000 persons in the towns around Green Bay in the 1670s, nearly 20,000 in the Illinois, Miami, and Shawnee villages around Starved Rock during the 1680s, 3,200 in Chequamegon at its height in the mid 1660s, and an estimated 6,000–7,000 in Michilimackinac in 1695. Such estimates ignore the Sioux, Crees, Nippisings, Mississaugas, and other Ojibwa groups, except the Saulteurs, all of whom were served at least partially by the French fur trade. Knives and, perhaps, hatchets had probably begun to meet the demand by the end of the century, but other goods, even by the highest estimates, could not have replaced native manufactures.

Conditions did change after 1720 when English and French competition for the fur trade increased the number of goods moving west. By the 1720s the *canots de maître* had replaced the much smaller eighteenth-century canoes, and considering the

Table 1   Estimates of annual canoe loads and goods reaching the West

	1670s		1690	1680s–1690s		
	Low	High	*Congés*	Low	High	Extreme
Canoes (number)	40	55	70	85	100	130
Guns (number)	320	440	560	680	800	1,040
Blankets (number)	60	825	1,050	1,275	1,500	1,950
Tobacco (livres)	2560	3,520	4,480	5,440	6,400	8,320
Cloth (ells)	3,160	4,345	5,530	6,715	7,900	10,270
Hatchets (number)	1,440	1,980	2,520	3,060	3,600	4,680
Knives (number)	16,320	22,240	28,560	34,680	40,800	53,040

Note: The canoe numbers above come from the following estimates: *40:* the minimal trade for the early 1670s; *55:* the capacity based on the high range of fur receipts for the 1670s; *70:* Champigny's 1690 figure, which, since it is close to the estimated figure for combined fur receipts and furs smuggled to the English, is the best official estimate; *85:* the high figure based on fur receipts for the 1680s and 1690s; *100:* Hennepin's estimate for 1679 and probably the high figure for the 1690s; *130:* the extreme 1684 estimate.

number of *congés* for western posts, it appears that in a year such as 1739, the fifty-six canoes allowed under the *congés* could contain cargos of approximately 336,000 livres of goods by weight (56 @ 6,000 = 336,000) as against 175,000 transported west in the late 1690s (100 canoes @ 1,750 = 175,000). Since these cargo figures do not include that portion of the trade of the Illinois country that went down the Mississippi to New Orleans, the portion of trade at Forts Niagara and Frontenac that came from the West, the illegal trade of coureurs de bois operating without *congés,* or the trade at Oswego, even this substantial increase still obviously underestimates the total. A rough estimate would be that Niagara-Oswego-Frontenac normally supplied an additional ten canoe loads of goods to the *pays d'en haut* during the 1730s and 1740s.

This rise in the scale of trade seems to have been largely a function of an increase in Indian consumption of cloth and woolen goods. Cloth had been a significant trade item since the late seventeenth century, but during the early eighteenth century European cloth had yet to replace native clothing. In 1718 the Indians around Detroit, and presumably the peoples who bordered them, wore a mixture of European clothing and native garments. The Potawatomi men, for example, wore "red or blue cloth" in the summer, but their winter clothing was buffalo robes. Farther west, the men of the Illinois, the Fox, and presumably the other peoples of the region mostly continued to wear clothing fashioned from animal skins.

By the 1720s and 1730s, cloth clearly dominated the trade. (See Table 2.) Whether smuggled English cloth or imported French cloth, it was cloth and clothing that filled the canoes going west. An examination of four surviving lists of cargoes shipped to Detroit and Green Bay between 1732 and 1747 reveals that cloth and clothing dominated every cargo except the one shipped to Detroit in 1732, when ammunition was being sent west in preparation for war against the Fox.

Yet even with the increase in cargo capacity and the rapid spread of European clothing, Indian consumption of trade goods remained relatively low. When the cargoes shipped to Green Bay during the 1740s are analyzed in the context of total population served by the traders, it becomes clear that the fur trade at Green Bay would not suffice to supply every Indian in the Green Bay trade area with a blanket. The trade would, however, certainly supply them all with knives, a cloth garment—a

---

Table 2   Relative percentages of cargoes by category (in livres/value)

	TEXTILES AND CLOTHING	ARMS AND AMMUNITION	METAL IMPLEMENTS	ALCOHOL
Detroit 1732	358/25%	509/36%	200/14%	178/13%
Detroit 1736	504/57%	68/8%	20/2%	167/19%
Green Bay 1740	4,545/53%	2,549/30%	541/6%	421/5%
Green Bay 1747	14,938/73%	3,049/15%	1,133/5%	628/4%

Source: Dean L. Anderson, "Merchandise for the Pays d'en Haut: Eighteenth Century Trade Goods and Indian Peoples of the Upper Great Lakes," paper presented at the Canadian Archaeological Association Annual Meeting, April 24–27, 1986, Toronto, Ontario.

blanket, shirt, or capote—and powder. Farther east, where the abundance of imports was greater and sources of supply more varied, the trade probably did serve to clothe the Indians and to provide basic metal technology. It did so, however, only in the peak years; in other years, Indians had to be prepared to supply their own clothing and to rely on old knives, hatchets, and so forth, repaired by French blacksmiths. Excavations at Fort Michilimackinac indicate that even as the number of trade goods increased after 1725, reflecting the growth of trade at the site, native technology persisted. Pottery and work in bone, antlers, and even stone hung on after imports had become part of everyday life.

James Fitting has attempted to determine whether "the introduction of European trade goods, particularly axes, kettles, knives and guns, altered the subsistence patterns of the area to the point that social and ideological orientations changed as well." To do so, he compared the artifact connections from the two villages: the Juntunen site, a typical late prehistoric settlement on the straits of Mackinac, and Lasanen, an Ottawa and Huron-Petun burial and village site seven miles from Juntunen which was occupied approximately from 1671 to 1701. He concluded: "If the introduction of European trade goods had any effect at all on the subsistence base, it was to amplify the trends already present. . . . We must reject the hypothesis that European trade goods drastically altered the subsistence base of the peoples of the Straits of Mackinac."

Apparently, this was true not only at Mackinac but also at the Bell site, a Fox village occupied well into the eighteenth century. Here, too, "contact with the Whites had not yet drastically altered their mode of life," and Fitting, in evaluating the same site, sees the way of life as "similar to that of peoples of the Late Woodland period." Father north, at Lake Nipigon, K. C. A. Dawson concludes, with the introduction of European goods "no major discontinuity appears evident." And David Brose, while hypothesizing that the Summer Island site (1650–1700) in Green Bay was occupied as a direct result of the fur trade, also says that native manufactures remained more significant than European and that the native tools most closely associated with subsistence were the slowest to change.

There is no denying that European goods had become an integral part of Algonquian life, but by the end of the French period there was not, as yet, material dependence. In an emergency Algonquians remained able to feed, clothe, and shelter themselves without European assistance, and more significantly they had more than one source for the manufactures they wanted. Politically powerful Algonquian groups could not only obtain such goods, they could have them bestowed as gifts. An understanding of regional relationships and of the emerging links between French and Indians during the French period cannot, therefore, be based on a simple model of early and decisive material dependence of Indians upon the French. Instead it is the relationships—political and social—through which goods moved and which, in part, gave the goods their meaning and influence that must be kept in mind.

How intricate this network of exchange had become and how thoroughly it was integrated into the political and social relationships of the French and Algonquians is apparent in the journal of Joseph de la Malgue Marin for 1753–54. Marin was the commander at Green Bay and a member of the company that leased the post there. He thus acted both as an agent of the kind and as a trader, and he had virtually no dealings with the Indians in which goods did not change hands. On his arrival, meeting the inhabitants of the first small Menominee village on his route, he gave them "the gifts for their village." He repeatedly made such gifts, "commensurate with their number," to the inhabitants of each village of Fox, Sauks, Menominees, Winnebagos, and Sioux he visited. When such villages had suffered the loss of prominent inhabitants, he frequently made additional gifts to cover the graves of the dead.

Such gifts were the expected courtesies of allies, but Marin also had to disburse goods to achieve specific ends. He worked simultaneously, for example, to prevent wars between the Green Bay peoples and the Illinois, who had attacked a Sauk village in Illinois and killed a Frenchmen, and to keep the peace between the Sioux and Menominees and the western Chippewas. All these negotiations involved covering the dead, consoling the mourners with gifts of brandy, and rewarding Indian emissaries active in the negotiations. He also gave presents to turn back war parties and to reward those who had refused to organize war parties. Ultimately, to guarantee negotiations, he agreed to give the Sauks and Fox a large present to give to the Illinois so that they would consent to peace. When the peace was concluded, he clothed and provisioned the Illinois delegation and then made additional gifts to the Sauks and Fox. Marin estimated his cost in preventing the Illinois war alone at 10,000 livres.

While all this was going on, other goods changed hands through trade. French traders granted goods to the Indians on credit with payment to come in the spring after the hunt. Other French traders departed with the Indians to their hunting camps. Despite all Marin's efforts, the returns of this trade were problematic. That winter the Lake Sioux, fearful of Chippewa attacks, did not hunt, thus depriving the French of a major source of furs.

For both the Indians and the French all of these exchanges were of a piece; they bound the French and the Algonquians together. Conceptually trade and gift exchanges were different, but in actual social practice they could no longer be disentangled without the collapse of the entire exchange network. And when the network worked properly, the Algonquians could continue to conceive of it as a system designed to satisfy their *besoins* (just as the French traders thought of it as a source of profit). As a Sauk speaker, Weasel, told both the Sauks and the Fox, they must be obliged to the French

> for all they were doing to help them. They came from a long way off and endured many difficulties and much misery to bring them the things they needed. Not only that but they were good enough to take an interest in reconciling them with the people they warred against. And but for that their villages would soon be reduced to nothing. And if they would think about all that, they would be at a loss to how to show their gratitude to the French for all the trouble they take for them. They would all indeed be ungrateful if they didn't do as I wished, especially as I [i.e., Marin] only spoke for their own good.

In the exchange network, commerce was obviously a part but hardly the whole of a larger structure. And to understand Algonquian actions within this structure, sentiments such as those of Weasel must be taken seriously for they represent not the illusions of duped primitives but a powerful formulation of a reality Algonquians and French had called into being. Without the middle ground, Weasel was a fool; with it, he was a wise and perceptive man.

⨝ *FURTHER READING*

Axtell, James. *After Columbus: Essays in the Ethnohistory of Colonial North America* (New York: Oxford University Press, 1988).

———. *The European and the Indian: Essays in the Ethnohistory of Colonial North America* (New York: Oxford University Press, 1981).

Clifford, James. *The Predicament of Culture* (Cambridge, MA: Harvard University Press, 1988).

Cronon, William. *Changes in the Land: Indians, Colonists, and the Ecology of New England* (New York: Mill and Wang, 1983).

Crosby, Alfred. *The Columbian Exchange: Biological and Cultural Consequences of 1492* (Westport, CT: Greenwood Publishing Co., 1972).

Gutierrez, Ramon A. *When Jesus Came the Corn Mothers Went Away: Marriage, Sexuality, and Power in New Mexico, 1500–1846* (Stanford, CA: Stanford University Press, 1991).

Perrin, Noel. *Gving Up the Gun: Japan's Reversion to the Sword, 1543–1879* (Boston: D. R. Godine, 1979).

Trigger, Bruce G. *The Children of Aataentsic: A History of the Huron People to 1660* (Montreal: McGill-Queens University Press, 1976).

Viola, Herman, and Carolyn Margolis, eds. *Seeds of Change* (Washington, DC: Smithsonian Institution Press, 1991).

Wachtel, Nathan. *The Vision of the Vanquished: The Spanish Conquest of Peru Through Indian Eyes* (New York: Barnes & Noble, 1977).

Arts, Tools, and Identities
in Agricultural Regimes,
ca 1680–1850

✦

*In the seventeenth and eighteenth centuries, Americans commonly described
agriculture, medicine, and mechanical pursuits as "arts." But these "arts" were
never arranged in the form of a democracy. They were always unevenly distributed
and differently embodied. This chapter looks at a variety of arts (and tools) as they
were practiced, wielded, and discussed in rural America over two centuries of
expansive settlement.*

*Throughout this period most Americans lived on farms or plantations, or in
villages not far removed from cultivation. Despite the presence of water-powered saw-
and gristmills (at least in the northern colonies/states), rural work in America was
overwhelmingly dependent on some combination of people, tools, and often animals.
But these "agricultural regimes" varied over space and time. We saw in the last
chapter that European colonization involved technical relearning and adaptation. By
the late seventeenth century, there were agricultural regimes in America very
different from those of Europe—most strikingly the slave societies of the southern
colonies. They differed from one another as well. Interacting with distinctions based
on wealth, race, and gender, the distribution of tools and talents in the various
colonies helped to structure power and social cohesion at its most rudimentary level.*

Terms like labor, work, *and* farming, *which have long peppered discussions
of "preindustrial" landscapes, inadequately describe diversity in skill and tool use.
The following documents and essays describe explicitly what various people knew,
what they did, and what tools they used. What does Judith McGaw mean by "so
much depends upon a red wheelbarrow"?*

✦ D O C U M E N T S

In the first three documents, previously published in *American Negro Slavery* (Michael
Mullin, ed.), eighteenth-century Virginians describe their plantations. William Byrd
uses a mechanical analogy, George Mason lists all of the specialized slave artisans on

whom Gunston Hall depends, and a plantation account organizes slaves, animals, and tools in the form of a list. The fourth selection was published in 1822 in the *American Farmer,* a gentleman's journal. "Mr. Garnett," addressing a public meeting on the topic of agricultural reform, criticizes the common tools of American farmers. What is his purpose? The fifth passage is from *Peck's Guide for Emigrants,* which told potential western settlers what they were likely to encounter. (The "West" in Peck's book is Illinois and Michigan.) The guide describes each county in Illinois and its infrastructure in 1830. Morgan County was "agricultural," yet note the diversity of activities. The sixth selection is from *Farm Drainage* by Henry F. French, published in 1859. French prepared this textbook, he wrote, because ditching and draining land were not skills held by many American farmers. Irish immigrants, he claimed, knew much more about draining and its proper tools. French's focus is on farming, but many Irishmen (who began to immigrate in large numbers in the 1840s) were at that time digging canals and constructing railroad embankments all over the North.

William Byrd II, ". . . to set all the springs in motion," 1726

Besides the advantage of a pure air, we abound in all kinds of provisions without expence (I mean we who have plantations). I have a large family of my own, and my doors are open to every body, yet I have no bills to pay, and half-a-Crown will rest undisturbed in my pocket for many moons together. Like one of the patriarchs, I have my flocks and my herds, my bond-men and bond-women, and every soart of trade amongst my own servants, so that I live in a kind of independence on every one but Providence. However this soart of life is without expence, yet is attended with a great deal of trouble. I must take care to keep all my people to their duty, to set all the springs in motion and to make every one draw his equal share to carry the machine forward. But then 'tis an amusement in this silent country and a continual exercise of our patience and economy.

A Virginian Describes His Self-Sufficient Plantation

EDMUND S. MORGAN

. . . My father had among his slaves carpenters, coopers, sawyers, blacksmiths, tanners, curriers, shoemakers, spinners, weavers and knitters, and even a distiller. His woods furnished timber and plank for the carpenters and coopers, and charcoal for the blacksmith; his cattle killed for his own consumption and for sale supplied skins for the tanners, curriers, and shoemakers, and his sheep gave wool and his fields produced cotton and flax for the weavers and spinners, and his orchards fruit for the distiller. His carpenters and sawyers built and kept in repair all the dwelling-houses, barns, stables, ploughs, barrows, gates &c., on the plantations and the out-houses at the home house. His coopers made the hogsheads the tobacco was prized in and the tight casks to hold the cider and other liquors. The tanners and curriers with the proper vats &c., tanned and dressed the skins as well for upper as for lower leather to the full amount

From *Virginia Magazine of History and Biography* 32 (December 1924), pp. 26–28.

From Edmund S. Morgan, *Virginians at Home: Family Life in the Eighteenth Century* (Charlottesville, VA: University of Virginia Press, 1952), pp. 53–54.

of the consumption of the estate, and the shoemakers made them into shoes for the negroes. . . . The blacksmiths did all the iron work required by the establishment, as making and repairing ploughs, harrow, teeth chains, bolts &c., &c. The spinners, weavers and knitters made all the coarse cloths and stockings used by the negroes, and some of finer texture worn by the white family, nearly all worn by the children of it. The distiller made every fall a good deal of apple, peach and persimmon brandy. . . . All these operations were carried on at the home house, and their results distributed as occasion required to the different plantations. Moreover all the beeves and hogs for consumption or sale were driven up and slaughtered there at the proper seasons, and whatever was to be preserved was salted and packed away for after distribution.

A Plantation Accounting, 1784

PLANTATION ACCTS. WITH CH[ARLES] PAYNE, OVERSEER AT EFF[INGHAM] FORREST.

Taken March 18th 1784

Negroes	*stock*
old Charles	Horses 10 (mostly mares)
Betty	Black Cattle (including)
Greenwich	"1 Red butt with a white face," and
Peter	1 Pided Cow 8 yrs. old.
Frank	
Anthony	total: 33 No Cattle
Timmy a boy	Hogs: 34
Sam a boy	Sheep: 78
Cardis	
Milly	
Black Hannah	
Candis Child	

No. 12

Acct. of Plantation Tools: 4 old Dutch Plows, 4 pr. Iron Traces, 1 pr. Iron Wedges, 4 Narrow Axes—two barrs Iron, 1 Broad Axx, 4 hilling hoes, 3 old Do. for Weading, 4 old hoes M. Muse put here, 5 Mattocks of M. Muse 1 Grubing hoe, 2 Drawing Knives, 2 Chissels, 1 hand Saw 2 Augers, 1 adds, 1 froe, 1 Scthe, 3 Murren hides, Two of which are Calves Skins, 2 Spinning Wheels

Fowls in the Care of old Betty
10 guse, 7 Fatning for Mrs. Nortons Use
5 Turkies for breading
3 fatning for Mrs. Norton
5 Dungle hens
8 Ducks

From Michael Mullin, ed., *American Negro Slavery* (Columbia, SC: University of South Carolina Press, 1926), p. 68.

A Gentleman Farmer on
Common Farmer's Tools, 1822

Whilst we are on the subject of economizing, I will take this occasion to suggest, that a very general saving might be made in selecting the best implements of every kind—for the best are always the cheapest in the end; instead of the scandalous, make-shift tools, which are found on far too many of our farms; some of them, indeed, so little resembling the things for which they are intended, that a stranger, accustomed to good agricultural implements, would be puzzled to guess what they were. There cannot be a greater mistake in economy than this make-shift plan, which is as irrational, as it is common. For even admitting that a half-tool will do half-work, there is an irretrievable loss of time. But the fact is, that it is a physical impossibility, for even half-work to be executed in the same time, if at all, with an implement half worn out, or so illy made, as scarcely to answer half the purpose of a good one. Yet there are thousands, into whose heads you can never beat it, that economy means any thing but the immediate, direct saving of money. To tell them that the best mode often of economizing, is *to lay-out money,* provided it be done judiciously, would be to subject yourself with them, to a strong suspicion of lunacy. Such men never can be made to believe that they get their "money's worth" in any thing that they purchase; and if they can only contrive, no matter at what expense of time and labour, to cobble up ("within themselves," as they call it) some awkward imitation of what they want, they chuckle and exult in their own fancied ingenuity and thrift, and conceit themselves in the high road to agricultural wealth and distinction. Not that I would by any means check the wish to make what we want, instead of purchasing, if the saving is *real,* not *merely apparent.* But whenever this self-supplying fancy seizes us, we should take care never to forget, that the cost of the self-instructing scheme, in regard to the making of agricultural implements, is precisely the difference between the work of cobblers, and that of master-work-men—added to the time lost both in making and using tools of inferior quality. It would be well also to remember, that unless we buy of others such articles as *they make,* and *we want, they* cannot purchase of us such things as *we make,* and *they want.* "To live and let live," is a maxim of universal application; and if properly introduced into practice, forms one of the surest and strongest ligaments of society. Without this, indeed, the division of labor, which is one of the greatest advantages of the social state, would prove a curse instead of a blessing. This maxim in fact, contains within itself the essence of universal justice. Once establish it, as the rule of conduct for nations, as well as individuals, and not only would contention, slander, cheating, extortion, and theft, cease in private life, but war itself, that dreadful scourge, and greatest disgrace of human nature, would forever disappear from the fair face of creation.

I will conclude these observations, relative to the saving of time and expense, in the foregoing particulars, with a few remarks on economizing in the operations of fencing and ditching. In all open, level land, the latter process should be executed principally with the plough; the throwing out the dirt, and trimming the sides, being the only operations which require other tools.—These last should be spades and

---

ditching shovels, instead of hand hoes, which are most commonly used, and frequently so worn out, as not to hold more than a handful of dirt each.

Morgan County, Illinois
(A Guide for Emigrants), 1831

Morgan County is destined to become one of the richest agricultural counties in the
State, lying north of Greene, with the Illinois river on the left. In 1821, the tract of country embraced within the limits of this county, contained only twenty families. Its population in 1830 was 13,281. It is well proportioned into timber and prairie, tolerably
well watered, and contains the finest tract of farming land around Jacksonville, I have
ever seen. In this county are about thirty mills for sawing and grinding, carried by
animal power, water and steam. There are two large steam grist and saw mills, one at
Naples, and the other at Beardstown. In this county are forty-six schools, twenty-six
stores, of which eleven are in Jacksonville, eighteen physicians, six attorneys, six coal
banks opened, thirty-five blacksmiths, two coppersmiths, one tinner, thirty-one carpenters, fifteen cabinet makers, five waggon makers, one carriage maker, fifteen coopers,
ten millwrights, ten tanneries, six saddlers, twenty shoe makers, twelve tailors, one
cloth dresser, twenty brickmakers, twenty-nine bricklayers, six hatters, and one college.

Jacksonville, the seat of justice, is conveniently located in the centre of the county,
in a beautiful prairie, and contains a population of about 750, and rapidly increasing.
This will doubtless become one of the largest inland towns in the State. Here is a factory for making cotton yarn, which runs one hundred and twenty-six spindles.

Irishmen and Spades, 1859

HENRY F. FRENCH

What can an Irishman do with a chopping ax, and what cannot a Yankee do with it?
Who ever saw a Scotchman or an Irishman who could not cut a straight ditch with a
spade, and who ever saw a Yankee who could or would cut a ditch straight with any
tool? One man works best with a long-handled spade, another prefers a short handle;
one drives it into the earth with his right foot, another with his left. A laboring man,
in general, works most easily with such tools as he is accustomed to handle; while
theorizing implement-makers, working out their pattern by the light of reason, may
produce such a tool as a man *ought* to work with, without adapting it at all to the
capacity or taste of the laborer. A man should be measured for his tools, as much as
for his garment, and not be expected to fit himself to another's notions more than to
another's coat. . . .

Of all the tools that we have ever seen in the hands of an Irishman, in ditching,
nothing approximates to the true Irish spade. It is a very clumsy, ungainly-looking implement used in the old country both for ditching, and for ridging for potatoes, being
varied somewhat in width, according to the intended use. For stony soil, it is made

From J. M. Peck, *Guide for Emigrants, Containing Sketches of Illinois, Missouri, and the Adjacent Parts*
(Boston: Lincoln and Edmunds, 1831), pp. 300–301.

From Henry F. French, *Farm Drainage* (New York: A. O. Moore, 1859), pp. 227–228, 237–239.

narrower and stronger, while for the bog it is broader and lighter. The Irish blacksmiths in this country usually know how to make them, and we have got up a pattern of them, which are manufactured by Laighton and Lufkin, edge-tool makers, of Auburn, N.H., which have been tested, and found to suit the ideas of the Irish workmen.

This is a correct portrait of an Irish spade of our own pattern, which has done more in opening two miles of drains on our own farm, than any other implement.

The spade of the Laighton and Lufkin pattern weighs 5 lbs., without the handle, and is eighteen inches long. It is of iron, except about eight inches of the blade, which is of cast steel, tempered and polished like a chopping axe. It is considerably curved, and the workmen suit their own taste as to the degree of curvature, by putting the tool under a log or rock, and bending it to suit themselves. It is a powerful, strong implement, and will cut off a root of an inch or two diameter as readily as an axe. The handle is of tough ash, and held in place by a wedge driven at the side of it, and can be knocked out readily when the spade needs new steel, or any repair. The length of the handle is three feet eight inches, and the diameter about one and one-fourth inches. The wedge projects, and forms a "treader," broad and firm, on which the foot comes down, to drive the spade into the ground.

We have endeavored to have the market supplied with the Irish spades, because, in the hands of such Irishmen as have used them, "at home," we find them a most effective tool. We are met with all sorts of reasonable theoretical objections on the part of implement sellers, and of farmers, who never saw an Irish spade in use. "Would not the tool be better if it were wider and lighter," asks one. "I think it would be better if the spur, or "treader," were movable and of iron, so as to be put on the other side or in front," suggests another. "It seems as if it would work better, if it were straight," adds a third. "Would it not hold the dirt better if it were a little hollowing on the front," queries a fourth. "No doubt," we reply, "there might be a very good implement made, wider and lighter, without a wooden treader, and turned up at the sides, to hold the earth better, but it would not be an Irish spade when finished. Your theories may be all correct and demonstrable by the purest mathematics, but the question is, with what tool will Patrick do the most work? If he recognizes the Irish spade as an institution of his country, as a part of 'home,' you might as well attempt to reason him out of his faith in the Pope, as convince him that his spade is not perfect." Our man, James, believes in the infallibility of both. There is no digging on the farm that his spade is not adapted to. . . . And it is pleasant to hear James express his satisfaction with his national implement. "And, sure, we could do nothing at this job, sir, without the Irish spade! " "And, sure, I should like to see a man that will spade this hard clay with anything else, sir!" On the whole, though the Irish spade does wonders on our farm, we recommend it only for Irishmen, who know how to handle it. In our own hands, it is as awkward a thing as we ever took hold of, and we never saw any man but an Irishman, who could use it gracefully and effectively.

☩☩ *E S S A Y S*

These essays discuss skills and tools in three different American places between the late seventeenth and the mid-nineteenth centuries. In late seventeenth-century South Carolina, as described in the selection from Peter Wood's *Black Majority*, "agriculture" and "commerce" were firmly tied together by a powerful planter class, which raised rice for European markets. But both the skills and labor that made this economy possible were embodied in recently arrived African slaves, who, until the middle of the eighteenth century, constituted the majority of the colony's population.

The next selection, from Laurel Thatcher Ulrich's *A Midwife's Tale,* describes the midwifery practice of Martha Ballard of late eighteenth-century Hallowell, Maine, based on her remarkable diary. Ballard's skills, like most of the people in her community, had English roots; how does Ulrich's discussion of skill compare with Wood's account?

Last, Judith McGaw's essay from her book *Early American Technology* traces tool ownership in rural New Jersey and Pennsylvania from the early eighteenth to the mid-nineteenth centuries, using household inventories as primary evidence. Her findings complicate modern assumptions about the even texture of early American rural life.

In these cultures with few machines, what was the relationship between skill and identity? Is everybody in these accounts skilled? Were their skills and tools similar; were they equally valued? Did the ability to make or do something guarantee independence or status? Were these rural worlds less complicated than our own?

Slavery and Arts in South Carolina

PETER H. WOOD

No development had greater impact upon the course of South Carolina history than the successful introduction of rice. The plant itself, shallow-rooted and delicate, is now rare on the landscape it once dominated, but its historical place in the expansion of the colony and state is deep-seated and secure, hedged round by a tangle of tradition and lore almost as impenetrable as the wilderness swamps near which it was first grown for profit. Despite its eventual prominence, the mastery of this grain took more than a generation, for rice was a crop about which Englishmen, even those who had lived in the Caribbean, knew nothing at all. White immigrants from elsewhere in northern Europe were equally ignorant at first, and local Indians, who gathered small quantities of wild rice, had little to teach them. But gradually, after discouraging initial efforts, rice emerged as the mainstay of the lowland economy during the first fifty years of settlement, and the cultivation of this grain for export came to dominate Carolina life during the major part of the eighteenth century. . . .

Throughout the eighteenth century white Carolinians marveled at their own industry and good fortune in having conjured this impressive trade from a single bushel of rice, and they debated which Englishman should wear the laurels for introducing the first successful bag of seed. . . .

Since rice cultivation had a halting beginning which stretched over several decades, numerous bags of imported seed could have contributed to its growth. Documentary evidence is scanty, and it therefore seems likely that minor issues of individual precedence may never be fully resolved. One fact which can be clearly documented, however, and which may have considerably greater significance, is that

From Peter H. Wood, *Black Majority: Negroes in Colonial South Carolina from 1670 through the Stono Rebellion* (New York: Knopf, 1974), pp. 35–37, 56–62, 103–105, 116–124, 196–210, 228–229, 289–291, 324–325.

during precisely those two decades after 1695 when rice production took permanent hold in South Carolina, the African portion of the population drew equal to, and then surpassed, the European portion. Black inhabitants probably did not actually outnumber whites until roughly 1708. But whatever the exact year in which a black majority was established, the development was unprecedented within England's North American colonies and was fully acknowledged long before the English crown took control of the proprietary settlement in 1720.

The fact that the mastery of rice paralleled closely in time the emergence of a black majority in the colony's population has not been lost upon scholars of the early South. But while few have failed to note it, none can be said to have explained it adequately. What could either be a mere coincidence on the one hand, or a crucial interrelation on the other, has been bypassed with short passages carefully phrased. One author observed that in 1700 "The transition from mixed farming and cattle raising to rice culture was just beginning, and with it the development of negro slavery." Another stated that "South Carolina's especially heavy commitment to the use of Negro labor coincided closely with the development of rice as a new and profitable staple." Similarly, a third scholar concluded that despite an earlier preference for Negro labor, white "South Carolinians did not import Negroes in large numbers until after the introduction of rice in the 1690's." In short, there appears to be an ongoing consensus among the leading southernists that somehow "rice culture turned planters increasingly to slave labor," but the casual relationships suggested, or perhaps skirted, by such observations have received little analysis.

Were Negro slaves simply the cheapest and most numerous individuals available to a young colony in need of labor? Or were there other variables involved in determining the composition of the Carolina work force? . . .

. . . Scholars have traditionally implied that African laborers were generally "unskilled" and that this characteristic was particularly appropriate to the tedious work of rice cultivation. It may well be that something closer to the reverse was true early in South Carolina's development. Needless to say, most of the work for all colonists was what one Scotsman characterized as simple "labor and toyl of the body," but if highly specialized workers were not required, at the same time there was hardly a premium on being unskilled. It seems safe to venture that if Africans had shown much less competence in, or aptitude for, such basic frontier skills as managing boats, clearing land, herding cattle, working wood, and cultivating fields, their importation would not have continued to grow. Competence in such areas will be considered elsewhere, but it is worthwhile to suggest here that with respect to rice cultivation, particular know-how, rather than lack of it, was one factor which made black labor attractive to the English colonists.

Though England consumed comparatively little rice before the eighteenth century, the cheap white grain had become a dietary staple in parts of southern Europe by 1670, and Carolina's Proprietors were anticipating a profit from this crop even before the settlement began. . . . [A] single bushel or barrel of rice was shipped by the Proprietors along with other supplies aboard the *William & Ralph* early in 1672. This quantity may have been planted rather than eaten, for one of several servants who defected to St. Augustine two years later told the Spanish governor that the new colony produced "some rice" along with barrel staves and tobacco. But by 1677 the colonists still had little to show for their experimental efforts. . . .

During the 1680s, perhaps after the arrival of a better strain of rice seed from Madagascar, the colonists renewed their rice-growing efforts. The mysteries of cultivation were not unraveled quickly, however, as is shown by several letters from John Stewart in 1690. Stewart had been managing Gov. James Colleton's "Wadboo Barony" and was taking an active part in rice experimentation. He claimed to have cultivated the crop in twenty-two different places in one season to ascertain the best location and spacing of the plant. Stewart boasted, perhaps truthfully, that already "Our Ryce is esteem'd of in Jamaica," but even this arch promoter did not yet speak of the grain as a logical export staple. Instead he proposed that rice could be used for the distilling of beer and ale ("from what I observ'd in Russia"), and he went on to suggest that planters "throw by Indian corne to feed slaves with rice as cheaper.

The processing as well as the planting of rice involved obstacles for the Europeans, which may explain why they had discarded the crop initially. "The people being unacquainted with the manner of cultivating rice," recalled an Englishman during the eighteenth century, "many difficulties attended the first planting and preparing it, as a vendable commodity, so that little progress was made for the first nine or ten years, when the quantity produced was not sufficient for home consumption. Similarly, Gov. Glen would later claim that even after experimenters had begun to achieve plausible yields from their renewed efforts around 1690, they still remained "ignorant for some Years how to clean it." . . .

In contrast to Europeans, Negroes from the West Coast of Africa were widely familiar with rice planting. Ancient speakers of a proto-Bantu language in the sub-Sahara region are known to have cultivated the crop. An indigenous variety (*Oryza glaberrima*) was a staple in the western rain-forest regions long before Portuguese and French navigators introduced Asian and American varieties of *O. sativa* in the 1500s. By the seventeenth and eighteenth centuries, West Africans were selling rice to slave traders to provision their ships. The northernmost English factory on the coast, James Fort in the Gambia River, was in a region where rice was grown in paddies along the riverbanks. In the Congo-Angola region, which was the southernmost area of call for English slavers, a white explorer once noted rice to be so plentiful that it brought almost no price.

The most significant rice region, however, was the "Windward Coast," the area upwind or westward from the major Gold Coast trading station of Elmina in present-day Ghana. Through most of the slaving era a central part of this broad stretch was designated as the Grain Coast, and a portion of this in turn was sometimes labeled more explicitly as the Rice Coast. An Englishman who spent time on the Windward Coast (Sierra Leone) at the end of the eighteenth century claimed that rice "forms the chief part of the African's sustenance." He went on to observe, "The rice-fields or *lugars* are prepared during the dry season, and the seed sown in the tornado season, requiring about four or five months growth to bring it to perfection." Throughout the era of slave importation into South Carolina references can be found concerning African familiarity with rice. Ads in the local papers occasionally made note of slaves from rice-growing areas, and a notice from the *Evening Gazette,* July 11, 1785, announced the arrival aboard a Danish ship of "a choice cargo of windward and gold coast negroes, who have accustomed to the planting of rice."

Needless to say, by no means every slave entering South Carolina had been drawn from an African rice field, and many, perhaps even a great majority, had never seen a rice plant. But it is important to consider the fact that literally hundreds of black immigrants were more familiar with the planting, hoeing, processing, and cooking of rice than were the European settlers who purchased them. Those slaves who were accustomed to growing rice on one side of the Atlantic, and who eventually found themselves raising the same crop on the other side, did not markedly alter their annual routine. When New World slaves planted rice in the spring by pressing a hole with the heel and covering the seeds with the foot, the motion used was demonstrably similar to that employed in West Africa. In summer, when Carolina blacks moved through the rice fields in a row, hoeing in unison to work songs, the pattern of cultivation was not one imposed by European owners but rather one retained from West African forebears. And in October when the threshed grain was "fanned" in the wind, the wide, flat winnowing baskets were made by black hands after an African design.

Those familiar with growing and harvesting rice must also have known how to process it, so it is interesting to speculate about the origins of the mortar-and-pestle technique which became the accepted method for removing rice grains from their husks. Efforts by Europeans to develop alternative "engines" proved of no avail, and this process remained the most efficient way to "clean" the rice crop throughout the colonial period. Since some form of the mortar and pestle is familiar to agricultural peoples throughout the world, a variety of possible (and impossible) sources has been suggested for this device. But the most logical origin for this technique is the coast of Africa, for there was a strikingly close resemblance between the traditional West African means of pounding rice and the process used by slaves in South Carolina. . . .

In the establishment of rice cultivation, as in numerous other areas, historians have ignored the possibility that Afro-Americans could have contributed anything more than menial labor to South Carolina's early development. Yet Negro slaves, faced with limited food supplies before 1700 and encouraged to raise their own subsistence, could readily have succeeded in nurturing rice where their masters had failed. It would not have taken many such incidents to demonstrate to the anxious English that rice was a potential staple and that Africans were its most logical cultivators and processors. Some such chain of events appears entirely possible. If so, it could well have provided the background for Edward Randolph's comment of 1700, in his report to the Lords of Trade, that Englishmen in Carolina had "now found out the true way of raising and husking Rice." . . .

Within the slave population itself, it was not always easy to distinguish separate categories as yet. Charlestown was still too small and the majority of lowland estates were still too modest to generate those clear distinctions in Negro life-styles between city and country which became familiar in the nineteenth century. By that later era a whole class of blacks had been mired in the work of the rice fields for generations, isolated from a smaller and largely hereditary grouping of tradesmen and house slaves. But in the first half of the eighteenth century Negroes in South Carolina were more unified by the common ground of Old World ancestry and recent migration than they were set apart by contrasting routines. On the one hand, a great many plantation slaves had spent time in Charlestown, at least when they arrived from overseas; on the other hand, few urban slaves were totally exempt from some measure of agricultural routine, if only at planting and harvest time.

Advertisements for slaves in the *South Carolina Gazette,* which began publication in the 1730s, make it apparent that even then no sharp line yet separated those in livery from those in work clothes, and the number of persons with diverse talents

reflects the fact that jacks-of-all-trades were still at a premium in the widening settlement. Hercules, the slave of a Goose Creek lawyer-planter, "used to wait on his Master
in Charlestown, & is now by trade a Cooper"; Peter, auctioned by John Simmons in
1733, was experienced as "a Bricklayer, Plaisterer and White-washer." Subsequent
notices included such descriptions as: "has serv'd his time to a Barber, and is a good
Cool," "used to a Boat, and something experienced in the Butcher's Trade," "his chief
Time has been spent in the Kitchen, Stable, Garden and playing for the Dancing-
School," "can work at the Shoemaker and Carpenter's Trades." In 1739 a Charlestown
master put up for sale "a Negro Man who is a very good Cook, makes Soap and
Candles very well, has had the Small Pox, is healthy and strong, speaks good English,
and is fit for a Boat." Few were more versatile than Tartar, a slave auctioned the fol-
lowing year and acknowledged to be "a good Groom, waiting Man, Cook, Drummer,
Coachman, and hacks Deer Skins very well."

The demand for diverse kinds of labor continued to be obvious to European
arrivals. "Artificers are so scarce at present," reported the founder of Purrysburg in
1731, "that all sorts of Work is very dear." Not simply in the expanding rice fields,
but in numerous other places as well, white employers showed a widespread preference for Negro slaves in filling their labor needs. Brickell noted that numerous slaves
were active in trades "and prove good Artists in many of them." He added; "Others
are bred to no Trades, but are very industrious and laborious in improving their Plantations, planting abundance of Corn, Rice, and Tobacco, and making vast Quantities
of Turpentine, Tar and Pitch, being better able to undergo fatigues in the extremity
of the hot Weather than any Europeans." . . .

Basic considerations of health and cost were supplemented in certain ways by
the existence of appropriate skills among the Africans, and it is only from the more
closed society of later times, which placed a high premium upon fostering ignorance
and dependence within the servile labor force, that white Americans have derived
the false notion that black slaves were initially accepted, and even sought, as being
totally "unskilled." The actual conditions of the colonial frontier meant that workers
who were merely obedient and submissive would have been a useless luxury. The
white slaveholders, whose descendants could impose a pattern of mannered outward
docility upon their Negroes, were themselves dependent upon a pioneer pattern of
versatility and competence among their workers during these early years. . . .

It is worth observing that Negroes and Indians, despite natural differences and
white efforts to generate further antagonisms, had in common comparable personal
and ancestral experiences in the subtropical coastlands of the southern Atlantic.
Their ability to cope with this particular natural world was demonstrated, and reinforced, by the reliance Europeans put upon them to fend for themselves and others.
Early forms of Indian assistance and black self-sufficiency made a lasting impression upon less well-acclimated whites, and as late as 1775 we find an influential
English text repeating the doctrine that in Carolina "The common idea . . . is, that
one Indian, or dextrous negroe, will, with his gun and netts, get as much game and
fish as five families can eat; and the slaves support themselves in provisions, besides
raising . . . staples."

Moreover, not only were West Africans and Indians more accustomed to the flora
and fauna of a subtropical climate generally, but both possessed an orientation toward
the kinds of "extreme familiarity with their biological environment, the passionate

attention . . . to it and . . . precise knowledge of it" which Europeans in Africa and America have in turn admired, belittled, and ignored. Lawson expressed the thought that if white Carolinians "would be so curious as to make nice Observations of the Soil, and other remarkable Accidents, they would soon be acquainted with the Nature of the Earth and Climate, and be better qualified to manage their Agriculture to more Certainty." But he went on to confess, as would Jefferson and others after him, that Europeans seemed to become less careful and observant rather than more so in the unfamiliar verdancy of the American South.

Both their background and their subservient status put foreign slaves in a better position to profit from contact with Indians than their equally foreign masters. As the number of Indians declined and their once-formidable know-how dissipated, it was the Negroes who assimilated the largest share of their lore and who increasingly took over their responsibilities as "pathfinders" in the southern wilderness. Slaves were, of course, responsible for transporting goods to market by land and water. But an even more striking index of white reliance upon black knowledge is the fact that the primary means of direct communication between masters was through letters carried by slaves. . . .

Obliged to transport passengers, messages, and goods, slaves naturally became guides as well as carriers. . . .

In coping with their new environment, it is clear that Negroes not only drew upon their associations with Indians but also brought to bear numerous aspects of their varied African experience. The term "carryover" (which anthropologists have applied to objects as tangible as the banjo and to beliefs as vague as spiritualism) fits a range of techniques and insights which were probably retained in the eighteenth century and which will only be fully explored as we learn more about the parent cultures from which these slaves were taken. Unlike the local Indians, for example, numerous Negroes possessed a familiarity, as already noted, with the herding of stock and the cultivation of rice. Nor would indigo and cotton be strange plants to many Africans in later years, as they were to most European and American workers. . . .

The West African and Carolinian climates were similar enough so that even where flora and fauna were not literally transplanted, a great deal of knowledge proved transferable. African cultures placed a high priority on their extensive pharmacopoeia, and since details were known through oral tradition, they were readily transported to the New World. This applied not merely to such specific arts as abortion and poisoning, but also to more general familiarity with the uses of wild plants. Negroes regularly gathered berries and wild herbs for their own use and for sale. John Brickell noted of slaves in North Carolina, for example, that "on Sundays, they gather Snake-Root, otherwise it would be excessive dear if the Christians were to gather it." The economic benefits to be derived from workers with such horticultural skills were not lost upon speculative Europeans. In 1726 Richard Ludlam urged the collection and cultivation of cochineal plants, specific plants upon which the cochineal beetle (an insect used to produce red dye) might feed and grow. According to Ludlam:

> Two or Three Slaves will gather as many Spontaneous Plants in one day, as will in an-
> other Day regularly Plant Ten Acres, by the Same hands and for the Quantity of Plants
> Growing here on the Banks of Rivers & in the multitudes of Islands on the Sea Coasts,
> I can Safely Assure you . . . Thousands of Acres might, at a Little Charge, be Stockd
> with them.

A variety of plants and processes were known to both West African and south-eastern American cultures, and such knowledge must have been shared and reinforced upon contact. Gourds, for example, served as milk pails along the Gambia River in much the same way calabashes had long provided water buckets beside the Ashley. It is impossible to say whether it was Africans or Indians who showed white planters, around 1700, how to put a gourd on a pole as a birdhouse for martins (that would in turn drive crows from the crops) or who fashioned the first drinking gourd which would become the standard dipper on plantations. The weaving of elaborate baskets, boxes, and mats from various reeds and grasses was familiar to both black and red. "The Mats the Indian Women make," wrote Lawson, "are of Rushes, and about five Foot high, and two Fathom long, and sew'd double, that is, two together." He reported these items to be "very commodious to lay under our Beds, or to sleep on in the Summer Season in the Day-time, and for our Slaves in the Night."

The palmetto, symbol of the novel landscape for arriving Europeans, was well known to Africans and Indians for its useful leaf. They made fans and brooms from these leaves and may well have entered into competition with Bermudians who were already exporting baskets and boxes made of woven palmetto. South Carolina's strong basket-weaving tradition, still plainly visible along the roadsides near the coast, undoubtedly represents an early fusion of Negro and Indian skills. The "Palmetto chairs" and "Palmetto-bottom chairs" which appear frequently in early inventories may at first have been a particular product of black hands, as suggested by one surviving mortgage. In 1729 Thomas Holton, a South Carolina chair- and couch-maker, listed as collateral three of his Negro slaves: "by name Sesar, Will, and Jack by trade Chairmakers." . . .

Fish and fishing . . . represent a separate area of expertise. While some Africans had scarcely seen deep water before their forced passage to America, many others had grown up along rivers or beside the ocean and were far more at home in this element than most Europeans, for whom a simple bath was still exceptional. Lawson, describing the awesome shark, related how "some Negro's, and others, that can swim and dive well, go naked into the Water, with a Knife in their Hand, and fight the Shark, and very commonly kill him." Similarly, the alligator, a freshwater reptile which horrified Europeans (since it was unfamiliar and could not be killed with a gun), was readily handled by Negroes used to protecting their stock from African crocodiles. These same slaves were inevitably knowledgeable about the kind of marsh and cypress swamp which their masters found so mysterious. From the start they tended, along with local Indians, to dominate the fishing of the region, for Englishmen, while capable of hauling nets at sea from an ocean-going vessel, were not at home in a dugout canoe.

These slender boats, however, were the central means of transportation in South Carolina for two generations while roads and bridges were still too poor and infrequent for easy land travel. . . .

As the colony grew, the demand for experienced craftsmen of all sorts was intense enough so that such questions as whether workers were free, indentured, or slave, or whether they were red, white, or black, often mattered less than their availability and aptitude. Specific skills which a worker did not already possess could be developed under service to a master. In 1727 a Charlestown clockmaker owed £20 to "an Indjon for Cutting Clock Wheels." An ad in the *Gazette* somewhat later read: "Any white Man or Negro having a mind to learn the Coopers Trade, to correct spoiled Wine and to distill, may apply to PETER BIROT, who will teach them under reasonable conditions." After mid-century the *Gazette's* owner, Peter Timothy, having just fired a "villainous Apprentice," wrote to his fellow printer Benjamin Franklin, "I am, (and have been these 4 Months) the sole Inhabitant of my Printing office, (excepting a Negro boy, whom I'm teaching to serve me at the Press)."

Under such conditions, signs of useful initiative on the part of black slaves did not go totally ignored. Two Negro men from a group sold at public auction in 1743 were advertised as follows: "one understands the Dairy, and the other has an extraordinary Inclination to learn the Carpenter's Trade." Several years later Robert Pringle felt enough confidence in a slave girl named Peggy to pay £20 to board her for a year with a woman who would teach her sewing. The slave Equiano relates that the following conversation occurred after he was purchased in Montserrat by a Quaker merchant named Robert King, and similar discussions between slave and master must occasionally have taken place in colonial Charlestown:

> Mr. King soon asked me what I could do; and at the same time said he did not mean to treat me as a common slave, I told him I knew something of seamanship, and could shave and dress hair pretty well; and I could refine wines, which I had learned on shipboard, where I had often done it; and that I could write, and understand arithmetic tolerably well, as far as the Rule of Three. He then asked me if I knew anything of gauging; and on my answering that I did not, he said one of his clerks should teach me to gauge.

More often than not, slaves belonging to white artisans worked at the trade of their own master. . . .

Often slaves mastered their trade so thoroughly that their owners sold them, along with their tools, as accomplished artisans. . . . Over the ensuing years it became a common practice for urban tradesmen to train up slave apprentices with specific skills who could then be sold to planters for a high price. This pattern of exporting black artisans to the country helped further the self-sufficiency of plantations to such a degree that by the time of the Revolution it posed a real dilemma to the white artisans themselves, who had inadvertently undercut their long-term profits by the short-term maneuver of selling talented slaves. . . .

In Charlestown, an entire class of "fishing Negroes" had emerged early in the eighteenth century, replacing local Indians as masters of the plentiful waters. . . .

Many Negro fishermen also made use of a variety of nets, and the art of net casting, which became an established tradition in the tidal shallows of Carolina, may have derived directly from West Africa. The surgeon visiting the Gold Coast at mid-century recorded in his journal: "It is impossible to imagine how very dextrous the negroes are in catching fish with a net." The know-how of Afro-Americans skilled in fishing provided steady profits for colonial slaveowners. A Carolina planter from Wando Neck, deprived of these profits when one of the Negroes disappeared in 1737, offered a reward for the runaway named Moses: "he is well known in Charlestown, having been a Fisherman there for some time, & hath been often employed in knitting of Nets." Not surprisingly, even now, generations after the end of slavery, professional Negro fishermen continue to be prevalent along the southeastern coast. . . .

All these varied activities of the Negro majority, whether based on skills transmitted from Africa or acquired in Carolina, were controlled to serve the white economy. Slaves were obliged by law to submit to the fact that their labor could be directed arbitrarily to suit the designs of their owners or the needs of the white colony at large. Often, therefore, masters hired out their slaves to provide themselves with an additional source of revenue. At mid-century Gov. Glen went so far as to propose a tax of six pence per pound "upon the Gettings of Negroes who are good Tradesmen, and bring considerable Gains to their Masters." . . .

Most hiring . . . remained in the private sector, where white owners moved slaves about profitably in response to continuing demands for labor. Even hands to do regular household chores were often in short supply, and it was not strange for a Charlestown home-owner to seek notice of "Any Person that wants to let out by the Year, or dispose of, a Negro Wench that can wash and smooth Linnen." An ad in the *Gazette* early in 1743 offered an accomplished mustee house boy "to be hired by the Year," and another six months later mentioned "Two very good House Wenches to be hired out by the Month." Negro sawyers were generally owned and rented in pairs; a Charlestown hatter claimed to have four men who could "whet, set and lay Timbers." Patrick Brown, a storekeeper, must have planned to hire out the three skilled slaves which he bought in 1744 for more than £280 each: "Two Angola's and [one] Iboe known by the names of Carolina, Anthony and Prince one of the three being a Cooper and the other two Sawyers." Numerous Negro bricklayers were also in demand, and on at least one occasion the labor of several was actually bequeathed. It was the last wish of Mary Mullins that future proceeds from the work of her "two Negroe Bricklayers . . . employed about the Rebuilding of the Presbiterian Meeting House" be divided between the minister and the church. And yet not all the proceeds from such exertions entered the pockets of free whites, for South Carolina slaves showed remarkable enterprise in their efforts to salvage for themselves some small individual profit in a system designed to preclude it. Indeed, the two bricklayers (Tony and Primus by name) who appear in the will of Mary Mullins provide a case in point. Not long after they were assigned to the Presbyterian Church, it was discovered that both craftsmen were selling their services secretly for their own profit. . . .

When a black artisan's skill was uncommon his reputation could be widespread: Sampson, a West Indian-born slave who was finally executed for his repeated efforts to escape, was "well known in Town & Country for his painting and glazing." . . .

Frequently, slaves with marketable talents took occasional jobs, and wages, without their owner's required approval, as numerous newspaper notices illustrate. Jack, "by Trade a Ship-Carpenter," pretended to be free and received wages for work done aboard vessels in Charlestown Harbor after the death of his master in 1737. Several years later, Limas, a Negro carpenter who was sold after his owner died, slipped away from his new master and "for some Time wrought clandestinely about Town, and thereby defrauded his Master of several Sums of Money." . . .

. . . [D]iligence in earning and diligence in saving were two very separate matters, and social forces were organized even more strongly against the latter than the former. Though a small quantity of cash could be obtained through extra exertion, there was every chance it would be snatched away arbitrarily and almost no prospect of conserving or investing it profitably. Pressures were all toward spending such money quickly or else running the risk of never spending it at all. Thus slaves who were hired out by the week to accumulate a fixed amount for their masters and who succeeded in earning an additional margin of cash through their personal initiative or ingenuity were still likely to part with this pocket money immediately in what can only be considered a sound principle of investment under the circumstances.

Yet even in spite of the thoroughly negative incentives for thrift among black workers, whites were chagrined to find that some Negroes were cleverly working their meager earnings into investments which could yield an interest. There is clear evidence of slaves entering upon organized efforts to slice out a small wedge of profit from their masters' economic pie. By 1720 goods as well as services were being sold regularly to willing European colonists through a network of informal contacts. . . .

Such industriousness had unsettling effects upon the white minority. Labor rates appeared unstable and food prices seemed high. The concern of Europeans over the growing preponderance of blacks and their continuingly diverse activities was re-flected in the changing statutes of the colony. Examined together, the successive slave laws of the South Carolina colony reveal a gradual movement toward forced depen-dence, with slaves being allowed to manage fewer things for their own use or profit and masters being required to provide more. Rations of clothing material and food were to be made available by the owner as a means of curtailing black initiative, and time itself was a commodity of which the slaves were allowed only a limited amount for themselves. . . .

Tension between black and white workers, a recurrent theme in America's later history, increased with the number of whites, and the hard-earned predominance of the Negro majority in parts of the colony's varied labor force was called into ques-tion. When debate began on a new Negro bill in 1737 it was proposed that no Charlestown slaves "be permitted to buy or sell or to be employed for Hire as Porters, Carters or Fishermen." This was amended to allow that "the Negroes be at Liberty to fish and ply as Porters and Carters under Lycense from the Commissioners of the Work House." The owners of slaves sent out as carters and porters paid a weekly sum for the privilege, and every Negro fisherman was charged £5 per annum for a license. Each received a numbered badge for identification, and the fees were used in support of the town watch.

At the same time pressure mounted against the participation of slaves in a variety of skilled crafts. The Negro Act of 1735 imposed a fine of £50 upon any master who allowed slaves to maintain any "houses of entertainment or trade," whether in their own names or under his protection, and two years later a protest was issued against the "too common Practice" of barbers, many of whom were Negroes, shaving cus-tomers on Sundays. During the reappraisals which followed in the wake of the Stono Uprising, a "Committee appointed to consider the most effectual Measures to bring into this Province white Persons to increase our Strength and Security" reported to the Assembly "that a great Number of Negroes are brought up to and daily employed in mechanic Trades both in Town and Country." The committee recommended a statute "prohibiting the bringing up [of] Negroes and other Slaves to mechanic Trades in which white Persons usually are employed," but a formal prohibition was not enacted until 1755 and appears never to have been totally enforced. . . .

One specific result of these economic pressures is worth noting separately. Where blacks and whites had previously shared most activities, distinguished only by the fact that the latter gave the commands and took the proceeds, workers were now occasionally set apart by race. At the same time that Negroes were being forced away from certain skilled trades, they were receiving more exclusive custody of the society's most menial tasks. Jobs which were in various ways taxing or offensive became, as Byrd had feared, "unfit" for white labor. As slaves assumed the entirety of the onerous business of rice production, they were also made to take on other oppressive chores as well. . . .

African awareness of plants and their powers has already been mentioned, and it was plain to white colonists from an early date that certain blacks were particularly knowledgeable in this regard. In 1733 the *Gazette* published the details of a medicine for yaws, dropsy, and other distempers "for the Discovery whereof, a Negroe Man in Virginia was freed by the Government, and had a Pension of Thirty Pounds Sterling settled on him during his Life." Some of the Negroes listed by the name "Doctor" in colonial inventories had no doubt earned their titles. One South Carolina slave received his freedom and £100 per year for life from the Assembly for revealing his antidote to poison; "Caesar's Cure" was printed in the *Gazette* and appeared occasionally in local almanacs for more than thirty years.

In West Africa, the obeah-men and others with the herbal knowledge to combat poisoning could inflict poison as well, and use for this negative capability was not diminished by enslavement. In Jamaica, poisoning was a commonplace means of black resistance in the eighteenth century, and incidents were familiar on the mainland as well. At least twenty slaves were executed for poisoning in Virginia between 1772 and 1810. In South Carolina, the Rev. Richard Ludlam mentioned "secret poisonings" as early as the 1720s. The administering of poison by a slave was made a felony (alongside arson) in the colony's sweeping Negro Act of 1740. No doubt in times of general unrest many poisoning incidents involved only exaggerated fear and paranoia on the part of whites, but what made the circle so vicious was the fact that the art of poisoning was undeniably used by certain Africans as one of the most logical and lethal methods of resistance. . . .

Three additional clauses in the measure of 1751 [mandating death for any Negroes convicted of poisoning] suggest the seriousness with which white legislators viewed the poisoning threat. They attempted belatedly to root out longstanding Negro knowledge about, access to, and administration of medicinal drugs. It was enacted "That in case any slave shall teach or instruct another slave in the knowledge of any poisonous root, plant, herb, or other poison whatever, he or she, so offending, shall, upon conviction thereof, suffer death as a felon." The student was to receive a lesser punishment. "And to prevent, as much as may be, all slaves from attaining the knowledge of any mineral or vegetable poison," the act went on, "it shall not be lawful for any physician, apothecary or druggist, at any time hereafter, to employ any slave or slaves in the shops or places where they keep their medicines or drugs." Finally, the act provided that "no negroes or other slaves (commonly called doctors,) shall hereafter be suffered or permitted to administer any medicine, or pretended medicine, to any other slave; but at the instance or by the direction of some white person," and any Negro disobeying this clause was subject to "corporal punishment, not exceeding fifty stripes." No other law in the settlement's history imposed such a severe whipping upon a Negro.

A letter written five years later by Alexander Garden, the famous Charlestown physician, sheds further light on the subject of poisonings. The outspoken Garden was forthright in criticizing his own profession, observing to his former teacher in Edinburgh that among South Carolina's whites, "some have been actually poisoned by their slaves and hundreds [have] died by the unskilfulness of the practitioners in mismanaging acute disorders." He claimed that when local doctors confronted cases

> proving both too obstinate and complicated for them, they immediately call them poison-
> ous cases and so they screen their own ignorance, for the Friends never blame the doc-
> tors neglect or ignorance when they think that the case is poison, as they readily think
> that lies out of the powers of medicine. And thus the word *Poison* . . . has been as good
> a screen to ignorance here as ever that of *Malignancy* was in Britain.

Nevertheless, actual instances of poisoning intrigued Garden, and he put forward a scheme "To examine the nature of vegetable poisons in general." He took the association with Africa most seriously and requested from his colleague "assistance in giving me what information you could about the African Poisons, as I greatly and do still suspect that the Negroes bring their knowledge of the poisonous plants, which they use here, with them from their own country." Perhaps most conclusive of all is the fact that Garden listed explicitly as part of his plan "To investigate the nature of particular poisons (chiefly those indigenous in this province and Africa)."

But apparently neither strict legislation nor scientific observation could be effective in suppressing such resistance, for in 1761 the *Gazette* reported that "The negroes have again begun the hellish practice of poisoning." Eight years later several more instances were detected, and although the apparent "instigator of these horrid crimes," a mulatto former slave named Dick, made good his escape, two other Negroes were publicly burned at the stake. According to the account in a special issue of the *Gazette,* Dolly, belonging to Mr. James Sands, and a slave man named Liverpool were both burned alive on the workhouse green, "the former for poisoning an infant of Mr. Sands's, which died some time since, and attempting to put her master out of the world the same way; and the latter (a Negro Doctor) for furnishing the means." . . .

. . . [A] comprehensive Negro Act, which had been in the works for several years but about which white legislators had been unable to agree in less threatening times, was passed into law [in 1740] and stringently enforced. This elaborate statute, which would serve as the core of South Carolina's slave code for more than a century to come, rested firmly upon prior enactments. At the same time, however, it did more than any other single piece of legislation in the colony's history to curtail *de facto* personal liberties, which slaves had been able to cling to against formidable odds during the first three generations of settlement. Freedom of movement and freedom of assembly, freedom to raise food, to earn money, to learn to read English—none of these rights had ever been assured to Negroes and most had already been legislated against, but always the open conditions of life in a young and struggling colony had kept vestiges of these meager liberties alive. Now the noose was being tightened: there would be heavier surveillance of Negro activity and stiffer fines for masters who failed to keep their slaves in line. Even more than before, slaves were rewarded for informing against each other in ways which were considered "loyal" by the white minority (and "disloyal" by many blacks). The ultimate reward of manumission was now taken out of the hands of individual planters and turned over to the legislature, and further steps were taken to discourage the presence of free Negroes.

Finally, and most significantly, authorities took concrete steps to alter the uneven ratio between blacks and whites which was seen to underlie the colony's problems as well as its prosperity. Since the economy by now was highly dependent upon rice exports, and since the Europeans in South Carolina were dependent upon African labor at every stage of rice production, there was talk of developing labor-saving machinery and of importing white hands to take on some of the jobs which could not be mechanized. A law was passed reiterating the requirement for at least one white man to be present for every ten blacks on any plantation, and the fines collected from violators were to be used to strengthen the patrols. The most dramatic move was the imposition of a prohibitive duty upon new slaves arriving from Africa and the West Indies. . . .

Among all these simultaneous efforts by whites to reassert their hold over black Carolinians, no single tactic was entirely successful. There is little to suggest that treatment became notably less brutal among masters or that doctrines of submissive Christianity were accepted rapidly among slaves. Despite the Negro Act of 1740, slaves continued to exercise clandestinely and at great cost the freedoms which the white minority sought to suppress. Those who wished to travel or to congregate, those who wished to grow food, hunt game, practice a trade, or study a newspaper learned increasingly to do these things secretly, and since informants were well rewarded, it was necessary to be as covert among other blacks as among whites. The result was not stricter obedience but deeper mistrust; a shroud of secrecy was being drawn over an increasing portion of Negro life.

Nor could white dependency on Negro workers be effectively reduced. The technique of periodically flooding the rice fields to remove weeds without the use of slave labor (which came into practice sometime around mid-century) may have originated in part to serve this end. But machines which could supplant the slaves who pounded rice every autumn made little headway until after the Revolution.

A Midwife's Tale

LAUREL THATCHER ULRICH

Martha Ballard was a midwife—and more. Between August 3 and 24, 1787, she performed four deliveries, answered one obstetrical false alarm, made sixteen medical calls, prepared three bodies for burial, dispensed pills to one neighbor, harvested and prepared herbs for another, and doctored her own husband's sore throat. In twentieth-century terms, she was simultaneously a midwife, nurse, physician, mortician, pharmacist, and attentive wife. Furthermore, in the very act of recording her work, she became a keeper of vital records, a chronicler of the medical history of her town.

"Doctor Coney here. Took acount of Births & Deaths the year past from my minnits," Martha wrote on January 4, 1791. Surprisingly, it is her minutes, not his data, that have survived. The account she kept differs markedly from other eighteenth-century medical records. The most obvious difference, of course, is that it is a woman's record. Equally important is the way it connects birth and death with ordinary life. Few medical histories, even today, do that. . . .

In western tradition, midwives have inspired fear, reverence, amusement, and disdain. They have been condemned for witchcraft, eulogized for Christian benevolence,

From Laurel Thatcher Ulrich, *A Midwife's Tale: The Life of Martha Ballard, Based on Her Diary, 1785–1812* (New York: Knopf, 1990), pp. 40, 46–49, 52–66.

and caricatured for bawdy humor and old wives' tales. The famous seventeenth-century English physician William Harvey dismissed the loquacious ignorance of midwives, "especially the younger and more meddlesome ones, who make a marvellous pother when they hear the woman cry out with her pains and implore assistance." Yet a popular obstetrical manual published in the same century dignified their work by arguing that Socrates's mother was a midwife and that "the Judges of old time did appoint a stipend for those women that did practice Physick well."

In the early years of settlement, some American colonies did in fact provide free land, if not stipends, for midwives. Yet the most famous midwife in early America is remembered for religious martyrdom rather than obstetrics. Boston ministers commended Anne Hutchinson for the "good discourse" she offered women in their "Childbirth-Travells," but when her teachings threatened to disrupt their authority, they condemned and banished her. The Puritans took their contradictions directly from the Bible. The Book of Exodus celebrates the courage of the Hebrew midwives who when told to destroy the male children of Israel "feared God, and did not as the king of Egypt commanded them." But the Apostle Paul, while acknowledging the good works of women who "relieved the afflicted," condemned those who wandered about from house to house, "speaking things which they ought not." . . .

Samuel Richardson drew upon midwifery lore in creating the character of Mrs. Jewkes, the terrifying woman who holds the innocent Pamela captive in the novel that gave Martha Ballard's niece her name. Charles Dickens exploited the same body of myth to different effect in his comic portrait of Sairey Gamp in *Martin Chuzzlewit:*

> She was a fat old woman, this Mrs. Gamp, with a husky voice and a moist eye. . . . She wore a very rusty black gown, rather the worse for snuff, and a shawl and bonnet to correspond. . . . Like most persons who have attained to great eminence in their profession, she took to hers very kindly; insomuch, that setting aside her natural predilections as a woman, she went to a lying-in or a laying-out with equal zest and relish.

Martha Ballard had at least one thing in common with Sairey Gamp—she was very fond of snuff. Yet in eighteenth-century Maine, it was not necessary to set aside one's "predilections as a woman" in order to perform what Martha once called "the last ofice of friendship." Her diary tames the stereotypes and at the same time helps us to imagine the realities on which they were based. Midwives and nurses mediated the mysteries of birth, procreation, illness, and death. They touched the untouchable, handled excrement and vomit as well as milk, swaddled the dead as well as the new-born. They brewed medicines from plants and roots, and presided over neighborhood gatherings of women. . . .

. . . Hallowell had several male physicians. . . .

Martha was respectful, even deferential, toward the [male physicians'] work, but the world she described was sustained by women—Mrs. Woodward, Mrs. Savage, Mrs. Vose, Old Mrs. Ingraham, Sally Fletcher, Lady Cox, Hannah Cool, Merriam Pollard, and dozens of others, the midwives, nurses, afternurses, servants, watchers, housewives, sisters, and mothers of Hallowell. The diary even mentions an itinerant "Negro woman doctor," who briefly appeared in the town in 1793. Female practitioners specialized in obstetrics but also in the general care of women and children, in the treatment of minor illnesses, skin rashes, and burns, and in nursing. Since more than two-thirds of the population of Hallowell was either female or under the age of ten, since most illnesses were "minor," at least at their onset, and since nurses were required even when doctors were consulted, Martha and her peers were in constant motion.

When Martha went to the field to dig cold water root on August 7, 1787, she was acting out the primary ritual of her practice, the gathering of remedies from the earth. Although she purchased imported laxatives and a few rare ingredients (myrrh, "dragon's blood," galbanum, spermaceta, and camphor) from Dr. Colman, she was fundamentally an herbalist. "Harvested saffron," "Cut the sage," "Gatherd seeds & Cammomile mint & hysop": such entries scattered throughout the diary tie her practice to English botanic medicine. Three-quarters of the herbs in the diary appear in Nicholas Culpeper's *The Complete Herbal,* published in London in 1649 (and reprinted many times in America). Almost all can be found in E. Smith, *The Complete Housewife: OR, Accomplish'd Gentlewoman's Companion,* an early eighteenth-century English compendium. Martha administered herbs internally as teas, decoctions, syrups, pills, clisters, vapors, and smoke and externally in poultices, plasters, blisters, cataplasms, baths, ointments, and salves. "Find Dolly lame. Poultist her foot with sorril roasted," she wrote on October 11, 1787, and when Theophilus Hamlin came to the house feeling ill, she "made a bed by the fire & gave him some catnip tea." Presumably the warm drink and the fire would cure his cold by contraries. Sympathetic medicine also worked. When Martha used saffron to treat jaundice in newborn children, she was following the ancient doctrine of "signatures," the yellow plant being the obvious cure for yellow skin.

There is no evidence in the diary of direct borrowing—she never mentions reading a medical book—yet Martha's remedies obviously rested on a long accumulation of English experience. When she used dock root to treat "the itch" or applied burdock leaves to an aching shoulder, she was following Culpeper's practice whether she knew it or not. More difficult to determine is her attitude toward the astrological concepts that informed his herbal. She may not have been aware, when she gave a newly delivered woman feverfew tea, that "Venus had commended this herb to succour her sisters." But her quiet statement on July 26, 1788, "Dog Days begin this day," associates her with such ancient traditions. Since antiquity, the period in late summer when the Dog Star became visible in the heavens had been linked with illness. The almanacs, which had determined the very form of her diary, perpetuated such beliefs. In fact she had good reason for believing that dog days brought illness, for she consistently made more medical calls in late summer than at any other time of the year. Whether her neighbors were actually more sickly during August and September or simply more disposed to ask for help, we do not know.

Her remedies are even closer to those in Smith's book. Like the English woman, she accepted the medicinal as well as the culinary virtues of common garden plants like green beans, onions, and currants and of household staples like vinegar, soap, and flour. On October 14, 1790, for example, she was "Calld in great hast to see Mrs Hamlin who was in a fitt. I walkt there, applyd Vinagar to her Lips, temples, & hands & onions to her-feet & shee revivd." And on another day, "Mr Ballard is unwell. Has taken some soap pills." There is hardly an ingredient in Martha's diary that does not appear in Smith's compendium. Both women routinely used camomile, sage, and tansy. Both employed cantharides and Elixir Proprietas. Both concocted that most famous of all cures—chicken soup. Yet compared to Smith's receipts, Martha's medicines *are* "simples." The most elaborate remedies described in her diary employ at most three or four plants. In contrast, Smith's recipe for "Lady Hewet's water" contains seventy-five separate plants, seeds, roots, and powders. Nor is there any hint in Martha's diary of the zoological inventiveness that led Smith to recommend setting a bottle of newly made cordial "into a hill of ants for amonth," to combine goose dung, ground snails, and earthworms with saffron, or to wet bandages in the spawn of frogs. . . .

The eclecticism of English medicine encouraged the incorporation of Indian or African cures. An aura of mystery, if not magic, attached to persons who were otherwise stigmatized in colonial society. Smith's recipe book included "The Negro Ceasars Cure for Poison" reprinted from *The Carolina Gazette,* and Hallowell patients sought out the "Negro doctoress" during her brief sojourn in the town. (Mrs. Parker even borrowed Martha's horse "to go and see the negro woman doctor.") There is no evidence that Martha was curious about Indian or Afro-American medicine, however. She noted the presence of the black healer but did not bother to record—or perhaps even to learn—her name. Such attitudes help to explain why her remedies are closer to Culpeper's seventeenth-century herbal than to James Thacher's *The American New Dispensatory,* an early-nineteenth-century pharmacopoeia that attempted to evaluate and incorporate Indian physic.

In eighteenth-century terms, Martha was an "empiric," a person unconcerned with theory. Her own descriptions demonstrate that her most immediate concern was to make her patients feel better. . . .

It would be a mistake, however, to describe her as a fringe practitioner preserving ancient English remedies lost to professional medicine. Most of the therapies we now associate with "folk" medicine were still a part of academic practice in her time. One of the Kennebec's best-educated physicians, Dr. Moses Appleton of Waterville, Maine, left a manuscript collection of recipes that included, in addition to erudite Latin formulas, a cure for dropsy compounded of parsley roots, horseradish, and mustard seed and a treatment for "the malignant sore throat" that called for applying carded black wool wet with vinegar and salt, ear to ear. The most explicit reference to astrological (or, more precisely, lunar concepts) in Hallowell comes from Daniel Cony's family record. One Cony child, the doctor reported, was born on "the first day of the week, the first hour of the day and the first day of the moon," another on "the 5th day of the week, and the eleventh day of the moon."

The technological simplicity of early medicine meant that male doctors offered little that wasn't also available to female practitioners. The stethoscope had not yet been invented. Watches with second hands were so rare that no one as yet counted the pulse (though in a general way most practitioners observed it). Nor did the clinical thermometer exist. Even the simple technique of percussion (tapping the chest and abdomen to discover fluid or masses) was yet to come. A probate inventory taken after the death of Dr. Obadiah Williams included "A Quantity of Medicine & Bottles together with the Amputating Instruments." That brief sentence pretty well describes the medical arsenal available to an eighteenth-century physician—drugs and a few rudimentary surgical instruments. Williams *did* use his instruments. On March 5, 1789, Martha wrote, "There was a young man had his Legg Cutt off at Stirling by Doctor Williams. He brot it to Doctor Coneys & disected it." Martha didn't observe this dissection, but she did attend four autopsies in the course of her career, carefully recording the results in her diary. That fact alone suggests that Hallowell's physicians considered midwives part of the broader medical community, a subordinate part no doubt (doctors dissected; midwives observed), but a part nonetheless.

Midwives and doctors shared a common commitment to what Martha would have called "pukes" and "purges." Early medicine merged the two meanings of *physic* as "knowledge of the human body" and as "a cathartic or purge." Because all parts of the body were related, laxatives treated the entire organism, not simply the gastrointestinal system. "I was calld to see Lidia White who has had fitts this day, but had left her before I arivd. Shee complained of an opresion at her stomach and pain in her head, I left her a portion of senna and manna." Senna and manna were mild cathartics. When her daughter Dolly was ill, Martha noted that a combination of "Senna & manna with annis seed and Rhubarb . . . opperated kindly." She even used manna with infants.

The emphasis on expulsion derived from the ancient theory of humors, the notion that health was achieved by a proper balance of the four bodily fluids—blood, phlegm, choler (or yellow bile), and melancholy (or black bile). When Martha wrote that Lidia Bisbe was "sick of a bilious disorder" or that Mr. Savage's daughter "puked up a considerable quantity of phlegm," she was expressing that world view, as was Moses Appleton when he recommended black wool "to keep back the humors." . . .

The most dramatic of the humoral therapies was bloodletting, a remedy Martha seldom mentioned and never employed. Along the Kennebec, the lancet was clearly a male implement. "Mr Stodard seemed to have more feavour," Martha wrote on February 16, 1795. "Doctor Page Bled him in the feet this morning. He has been bled, phisicked and Blistered before in his sickness." She noted that Dr. Colman bled one of her patients in the late stages of pregnancy, though it seems not to have been at her request. One home medical guide recommended bleeding "for pregnant women about the sixth, seventh or eighth month, who are plethoric and full of blood," but added that "children bear purging better than bleeding." Martha seems to have preferred purging for both groups. One of the few descriptions of bleeding in the diary involved a horse. "Mr Ballard went to Mr Browns for his mare," Martha wrote. "Had her Bled in the mouth. She bled all the way home & Continued to bleed an hour or two after coming home. We at length filled the incision with fur & it Ceast."

That male physicians leaned toward dramatic therapies was only to be expected. Their status—and fees—required as much. Dr. Cony used rhubarb and senna, as Martha did, but he also prescribed calomel, the mercurial compound Benjamin Rush called the "Samson of medicine." One historian concludes that in large doses calomel "did indeed slay great numbers of Philistines." The impressive salivation that followed its violent purging was in fact one of the symptoms of mercury poisoning. Hallowell's physicians also used laudanum (a liquid opiate), purple foxglove (digitalis), and the bark (quinine), therapies associated with a newer "solidistic" overlay on humoral therapy. . . .

In twentieth-century terms, the ability to prescribe and dispense medicine made Martha a physician, while practical knowledge of gargles, bandages, poultices, and clisters, as well as a willingness to give extended care, defined her as a nurse. In her world, such distinctions made little sense. She sometimes acted under the direction of a doctor. More frequently she acted alone, or with the assistance of other women. . . . When scarlet fever broke out in Hallowell in June, [Daniel Cony] was in Boston attending the General Court. He was back on July 19 to deliver his sister, Susanna

Church, of a son, but was soon off to the interior settlements on business. On July 26 Martha was summoned to *his* house to treat a servant, Peggy Cool, who was suffering from the rash.

Ironically, when the doctor did show up in the diary it was in the context of delivery. Martha's quiet entry for August 22, 1787—"Mrs Shaw has Doctor Coney with her"—suggests more than a casual interest in the doctor's whereabouts. Mrs. Shaw was then nine months pregnant, and perhaps in labor, or at least experiencing some of the signs of imminent delivery, when the doctor was called. Why she called him we do not know. Perhaps she was worried about possible complications, perhaps frightened by the recent death of Susanna Clayton. As it turned out, Martha delivered the baby. "Put [Mrs. Shaw] safe to Bed with a daughter at 10 O Clok this Evinng," she wrote on August 23, and on the next day added drily, "Doctor Coneys wife delivrd of a dafter Last Evng at 10 O Clok"—that is, at exactly the same time as Mrs. Shaw. It would seem, then, that if his own child hadn't intervened, Cony might have delivered the Shaw baby. Still, whatever her original intent, Mrs. Shaw was apparently satisfied with her midwife: two years and one month later, she summoned Martha again.

Daniel Cony's presence at the bedside of Mrs. Shaw suggests that reverberations of the new scientific obstetrics had reached the Kennebec. Unlike the surgeons of an earlier era, who were called only in dire emergencies, usually to dismember and extract an irretrievably lost fetus, late-eighteenth-century physicians considered it appropriate to officiate at an ordinary delivery. Yet most of them limited their obstetrical practice to eight or ten cases a year, whatever they could conveniently fit into their practice. Significantly, Martha performed at least one delivery for Cony's sister Susanna Church and another for his sister-in-law Susanna Brooks.

Kennebec doctors were not only part-time midwives, they were part-time physicians. Daniel Cony was a land proprietor and politician as well as a physician— perhaps a politician most of all. A Portland associate complained after a visit, "He had not been in the house half an hour before my head turned round like a top with politics. I would not live in the same house with . . . Daniel Coney for ten thousand pounds per annum." Yet Cony knew how to use one specialty to reinforce another. In a letter to a Massachusetts congressman, he neatly dismissed his political opponents by offering a "chemical" analysis of their behavior. Such men, he wrote, "abound with 'vitriolic acid' with a certain proportion of 'aqua regia.'" He became a fellow of the Massachusetts Medical Society not so much because of his medical skills, which by the standards of his own time were ordinary, but because his election to the legislature put him in frequent contact with the gentlemen who ran such associations. He was also a justice of the peace, as were fellow doctors Moses Appleton of Waterville and Obadiah Williams of Vassalboro. . . .

The most successful Kennebec physicians were Federalist gentlemen, organizers of agricultural societies, builders of bridges, incorporators of banks. Their involvement in medical organizations was part of this general commitment to voluntarism and civic betterment. . . . They were successful practitioners not only because of their acknowledged status as learned gentlemen but because the town's other healers chose to defer to them in hard cases. There were no laws to prevent Martha or her neighbors from administering calomel or drawing blood, yet they did not do so. By custom and training, bonesetting, tooth-pulling, bloodletting, and the administration of strong drugs were reserved for self-identified male doctors. When Martha "misplaced a

Bone in the Great toe of my right foot," she was grateful for the help of Dr. Page, but most of the time she and her family got along quite well without him. It was no doubt part of the men's strength that they supported neighborhood practitioners, offering chemical compounds and venesection only when tansy failed. Even their inaccessibility was an advantage, a sign of their importance in the larger world.

Male physicians are easily identified in town records and, even in Martha's diary, by the title "Doctor." No local woman can be discovered in that way. Hallowell's female healers move in and out of sickrooms unannounced, as though their presence there were the most ordinary thing in the world—as it was. Historians have been dimly aware of this broad-based work, yet they have had difficulty defining it. Physicians who joined medical societies and adopted an occupational title can be recognized as professionals. But what shall we call the women? Persons who perambulated their neighborhoods hardly practiced *domestic medicine,* nor does *folk medicine* accurately describe the differences between them and male professionals. . . .

Professionals sought to be distinguished from the community they served (hence the need for the title "Doctor"). Social healers, on the other hand, were so closely identified with their public we can hardly find them. Professionals cultivated regional or cosmopolitan networks, joining occupational associations. Social healers developed personal affiliations and built local reputations. Professional training, even if only in the form of apprenticeship, was institutional, fixed in place and time. Social learning was incremental, a slow build-up of seemingly casual experience.

Florence Nightingale's famous statement that "every woman is a nurse" captures one element of social practice—its grounding in common duties—but it fails to convey the specialization that occurred even among female healers. Caring for the sick was a universal female role, yet several women in every community stood out from the others for the breadth and depth of their commitment. They went farther, stayed longer, and did more than their neighbors. It would be a serious mistake to see Martha Ballard as a singular character, an unusual woman who somehow transcended the domestic sphere to become an acknowledged specialist among her neighbors. She *was* an important healer, and without question the busiest midwife in Hallowell during the most active years of her practice, but she was one among many women with acknowledged medical skills. Furthermore, her strengths were sustained by a much larger group of casual helpers. . . .

. . . Martha Ballard probably started out . . . doing nursing as well as housework for her relatives or neighbors. Once married, she would have had less freedom for general nursing but more scope for perfecting the gardening and cookery that were so closely associated with herbal medicine. As a young matron she no doubt watched with sick neighbors and assisted at births, until in midlife, with her own child-rearing responsibilities diminished, she became a more frequent helper and eventually a healer and midwife. Midwives were the best paid of all the female healers, not only because they officiated at births, but because they encompassed more skills, broader experience, longer memory. "Mrs Patin with me." The social base of female medicine is apparent in the very casualness of the entry. A midwife was the most visible and experienced person in a community of healers who shared her perspective, her obligations, her training, and her labor.

There is no need to sentimentalize this "female world of love and ritual," to use Carroll Smith-Rosenberg's now famous phrase, to understand that birth, illness, and death wove Hallowell's female community together. Consider two bland sentences from the entry for August 14, the day of William McMaster's funeral: "Mrs Patten here," and then later, "I drank Tea at Mr Pollards." Both visits—Sally Patten to Martha Ballard and Martha Ballard to Merriam Pollard—were continuations of meetings at the bedsides of gravely ill children. . . . Merriam Pollard had "sett up" with Martha at the Howards' two days earlier, and . . . Sally Patten, who had come to the McMasters' to watch with Billy, had helped Martha prepare his body for burial. Since Merriam and Martha were old friends, their tea party is easily explained, but what of Sally Patten's visit to Martha? What led her up the path toward the mills? Presumably she had crossed the river to attend Billy McMaster's funeral, but Martha's house was three-quarters of a mile beyond the meeting house. Her visit cannot have been a casual one. Was it a practical errand that brought her there, or a deeper need to consolidate the experience she had shared a few hours before? Even for Martha, the nightwatch had been profoundly disturbing. What must it have meant for a young mother still new to the circle of matrons?

Eighteenth-century physicians, like twentieth-century historians, had difficulty distinguishing one social healer from another, yet they understood the power of their presence. William Smellie, who wrote an important English obstetrical treatise, displayed an acute consciousness of the female audience for any medical intervention. Cautioning young physicians not to do anything to make "the gossips uneasy," he explained the importance of reassuring both the patient and her "friends." The word "friends" appears repeatedly in doctors' writings from the mid-eighteenth to the mid-nineteenth century. The label is a telling one: female healers identified with the patients they served in ways that male physicians could not.

Little wonder that some physicians actively resented their presence. William Buchan, author of the immensely popular *Domestic Medicine,* published in London in 1769 and reprinted at least fifteen times in America, deplored the social dimensions of traditional childbirth:

> We cannot help taking notice of that ridiculous custom which still prevails in some parts of the country, of collecting a number of women together on such occasions. These, instead of being useful serve only to crowd the house, and obstruct the necessary attendants. Besides they hurt the patient with their noise: and often, by their untimely and impertinent advice, do much mischief.

Here, as elsewhere, Buchan distinguished between what was "necessary" and what was merely customary. Like other eighteenth-century reformers, he wanted to simplify as well as improve contemporary practice. Groups of women cluttered a room with their ideas as well as their bodies.

In rural America, however, Buchan's ideas were just another strand in the dominant eclecticism. Doctors might mistrust the ubiquitous friends, but they could not easily do without them. Female healers performed the messy, time-consuming tasks of healing and at the same time validated male practice. As long as both sets of practitioners shared the same basic assumptions, and as long as physicians were content with the income available from part-time practice, there could be little competition between them.

"So Much Depends upon a Red Wheelbarrow": Agricultural Tool Ownership in the Eighteenth-Century Mid-Atlantic

JUDITH A. MCGAW

My title derives from one of the best-known Imagist poems, by William Carlos Williams. The poem goes:

> so much depends
> upon
>
> a red wheel
> barrow
>
> glazed with rain
> water
>
> beside the white
> chickens.*

   I begin by invoking the Imagist spirit because their mission—replacing the generalizations and abstractions of Victorian poetry with what they called "direct treatment of the 'thing'"—is an approach historians studying early American agricultural technology might profitably emulate. Unfortunately, a salient characteristic of scholarship treating early American farming is nicely captured by a *Peanuts* cartoon a graduate student gave me some years ago. The strip features Sally standing in front of her class and holding a piece of paper. "This is my report on Mr. John Deere," she says. "In 1837, Mr. Deere invented the self-polishing steel plow which was a great help to farmers . . ." In the next panel she has been interrupted and replies: "Plow? No, Ma'am I've never seen a plow . . ." After a pause she adds, "I've never even seen a farmer!" Paraphrasing Williams, this essay argues that, for understanding technological change in America, much depends upon our seeing farmers and plows, red wheelbarrows and white chickens.

   The Imagists also set a standard worth emulating by insisting that writers "use the language of common speech, but . . . employ always the *exact* word, not the nearly-exact, nor the merely decorative word," to quote Ezra Pound. Alas, when we read the history of technology, we hear few echoes of common speech literally or metaphorically speaking. We have mostly studied technology as an expression of leaders—inventors, experimenters, large corporations, or governments; we have mostly ignored common people's technological expression—what tools they chose to own or generally employed, for example.

   Nowhere is our ignorance of the mundane more evident than in scholarship on early American agricultural technology. With a few noteworthy exceptions, secondary

From Judith A. McGaw, *Early American Technology* (Chapel Hill, NC: University of North Carolina Press, 1994), pp. 328–357.

literature tells us little about which tools, practices, and knowledge early farmers and farm wives customarily employed. Instead, the scholarship features famous firsts—inventors' contrivances and agricultural reformers' proposals, with little sense of how these tools and ideas fared after their debut. We have more often looked at the machine on the drawing board than at the wheelbarrow in the garden.

Despite our inattention to common practice, historians have not been reluctant to characterize early American tool ownership, albeit in highly generalized terms. Indeed, one noteworthy feature of our literature is the virtual absence of clear and specific images of preindustrial technology. Rather than deriving from records that feature farmers, farm wives, and their tools, most scholarship rests on several sorts of unsubstantiated generalizations. One approach has relied heavily on what agricultural reformers and European travelers wrote. It reiterates their claims that common farmers resisted innovation and their assessments of early farm technology as hopelessly primitive, especially on the frontier.

By contrast, the other principal approach portrays the early yeoman as a technological virtuoso. It assumes, albeit implicitly, that tool ownership and tool-wielding skill were common in the preindustrial era. That assumption underlies, for example, the Marxist contention that industrialization degraded work when it shifted tool ownership from tool users to the employers of tool users. It also undergirds revisionist scholarship that depicts industrialization as the demise of an earlier, subsistent, communitarian economy in favor of an increasingly impersonal market-oriented one. Likewise, accounts of women and industrialization contrast restrictive nineteenth-century mill or domestic work with a colonial role presumed to entail an enormous array of agricultural processing tasks, such as spinning, weaving, candlemaking, churning, cheese production, and pickling.

Scholars who assess industrialization more favorably also assume widespread preindustrial tool ownership. For example, one explanation of America's relatively swift industrialization has been that frontier living nurtured technological creativity. Frontiersmen, it argues, had to be jacks-of-all-trades—to know how to use all of the tools that specialists wielded in more settled communities. The unspoken corollary is, of course, that frontiersmen owned all those tools. Nor is this mythic jack-of-all-trades confined to scholarly claims about the frontier. Often, eighteenth- and nineteenth-century northern rural communities are presumed to have nurtured a youthful variant of the type—the Yankee whittling boy. This handy youth figures prominently in the literature celebrating inventors, much of it popular, but some of it scholarly.

My data on tool ownership in the eighteenth-century mid-Atlantic paint a very different picture. I find, for example, that only a little more than half of farmers or yeomen probably owned plows and that, among farm women, about 20 percent made do without either a pot or a kettle, those huge iron or brass caldrons that colonial restorations invariably hang over the fire. The artifact we most often envision in early American hands—the gun—actually existed in only about half of households. And frontiersmen were only slightly more likely to own firearms: about 60 percent versus about 50 percent for inhabitants of longer-settled regions. Nevertheless, early Americans were far more likely to own guns than to possess that other icon of early American life—the Bible—although, surprisingly, frontier households came closest to owning Bibles as often as guns.

These data are arresting. If many, even most, colonial Americans lacked items we have believed common, even essential, our image of America's traditional technology must be quite distorted: a composite of colonial revival stereotypes and an uncritical acceptance of surviving artifacts as representative. We must do better if we would understand what technological experiences and fingertip knowledge the offspring of American farmers brought to the early factories or assess how the shift to industrial production altered people's relationships to their tools.

This essay offers one strategy for doing better. It begins by enunciating why American historians and historians of technology need real knowledge of how early Americans farmed. After articulating the large questions that motivated my data collection and shaped my data selection and analysis, I outline a feasible and promising alternative to the uncritical, anecdotal approach that has predominated in the field. By summarizing my research strategy—describing the sources I exploit and the methods I employ—I hope to evoke emulation: to persuade additional scholars to cultivate the abundant household-level evidence that awaits those willing to venture into new terrain and to challenge yet more colleagues to seek out other promising scholarly resources. The methodological discussion also provides a context for assessing and appreciating the preliminary report of findings on colonial tool ownership to which the essay turns next. As a first step away from the unsubstantiated generalizations to which we have grown accustomed, I present concrete evidence drawn from my research in progress and propose some large conclusions that may be drawn from the presence or absence of winnowing fans, dung hoes, candle molds, and dough troughs in eighteenth-century households. Finally, I conclude with a few brief observations provoked by this look at small things—"red wheel barrows" and "white chickens"; I invite my various colleagues to question our accustomed academic approach to early American technology.

My study of early American agricultural tool ownership derives ultimately from one big question: What accounts for America's sudden, rapid, and comparatively successful early nineteenth-century industrialization? It has seemed to me that most accounts of the American Industrial Revolution, because they begin in 1790, miss a good part of the answer to that question. Likewise, by focusing on manufacturers and treating agriculture merely as a belated beneficiary or victim of industry's mechanical creativity, scholarship on technological change in the American Industrial Revolution has begged some critical questions, such as: How did a declining proportion of farm households become able to feed a growing nonfarm population, supply a burgeoning international market, and provide the raw materials most early industry processed? or, What sorts of technical expertise did the sons and daughters of farmers bring to industrial work? or, How did changes in the goods farm households purchased help to create a market for early industrial commodities? or, What toolmaking skills had become common before industrialization?

In contrast to the narrow focus and abbreviated chronology of American scholarship, studies of British industrialization have historically paid at least some attention to prior and simultaneous agricultural innovation. More recently, a number of scholars have given husbandmen a leading role in the British Industrial Revolution. They have shown that most agricultural innovation, both technical and organizational, occurred in the seventeenth and early eighteenth centuries, much earlier than previously believed. Although historians of industry have simultaneously pushed the origins of the manufacturing revolution well back into the eighteenth century, the new "chronology of improvement now makes a strong case for the close interdependence of agriculture and manufacturing, with the springs of much manufacturing improvement to be found in the early dynamism of the agricultural sector."

At the very least, then, understanding the American Industrial Revolution requires that we examine American industry's colonial agricultural roots. But we also need to look at how farm practice changed during the era of the American Revolution and into the nineteenth century if we are to link agricultural innovation to industrial development. Nor can we limit our attention to the farm activities of the late colonial era. The new scholarship on Britain certainly raises the possibility that the initial British settlers of any given region engaged in agricultural innovation from the outset. Many of their activities paralleled, even when they did not precisely reenact, those of progressive agriculturalists who remained at home. But the innovativeness of colonists who undertook such activities as clearing forests and planting maize has generally escaped notice because farmers undertook these novel tasks from the start of colonial agricultural history, making the new practices appear either "natural" or "necessary." They were neither. The relative ease with which colonists adopted new practices simply reflects that these novel tasks entailed relatively straight-forward translations of new British agricultural strategies to the colonial situation.

In the absence of significant scholarly attention to common agricultural practice, I concluded that, before I could begin to document change in early American agricultural technology, analyze its origins, or link it to manufacturing, I needed to find out what American farmers and farm wives had done and how they had done it from the beginnings of settlement to the mid-nineteenth century. In other words, I had somehow to catch a glimpse of all those red wheelbarrows and white chickens. Understanding anything else about early American technology ultimately depended upon seeing those.

After reaching such a disconcerting conclusion, I made several strategic decisions that converted an impossible task into a manageable one. First, I acknowledged that there is no such thing as a representative colonial farm, farm community, or farm region. Indeed, I will argue later that attempting to find a typical farm family and a standard array of farm tools misstates the problem in a way that inevitably misleads us.

I focused on the mid-Atlantic region because it was the only major region where industry and agriculture flourished side by side and because the mid-Atlantic's emphasis on mixed livestock and grain farming set the patten for much later American agriculture. The Middle Colonies qualify as the quintessential American region in other respects as well. As Frederick Jackson Turner noted nearly a century ago, the region "mediated between New England and the South, and the East and West," and "it had a wide mixture of nationalities, a varied society, the mixed town and country system of local government, a varied economic life, many religious sects." Insofar as these factors influenced agricultural technique, the mid-Atlantic region represents the best microcosm of early American farm practice. Yet, the mid-Atlantic has received far less scholarly attention than has either New England or the South.

Given the rich diversity of the region, five counties warranted close examination. Each country both shares features with and differs from the others. Thus, comparing data from the various counties should indicate which of several relevant

factors—length of settlement, ethnic composition, access to markets, relative affluence, and natural endowment, for example—offer the best explanation of particular
agricultural patterns. Examining several counties simultaneously should also provide a built-in reminder that there were many "right" answers to the question of how
best to farm, a useful corrective to the biases of both secondary literature and the
writings of early American agricultural reformers. Limiting my choice of counties to
New Jersey and Pennsylvania also kept manageable the number of different curren-
cies and the various legal parameters to be considered. At the same time, my choices
were likely to disclose technological differences associated with the westward
course of settlement, an aspect of colonial agriculture that has received far less attention than have North-South differences.

Burlington County, New Jersey, offers a case of very early settlement, beginning
roughly in the last quarter of the seventeenth century. Close to Philadelphia and to
good water transportation, it represents nearly ideal access to a rapidly growing urban
market. It also exemplifies a heavily British population with strong Quaker influence.
By the nineteenth century, Burlington should illustrate farming practice in a region that
rusticated, for its growth slowed early. By contrast, Hunterdon County, New Jersey, the
county just north of Burlington in West Jersey, shows a rapid transition from frontier
to settled farming region. Initial settlement lagged about two generations behind that
of Burlington, but during the second quarter of the eighteenth century Hunterdon's
population came to equal and then to surpass that of its neighbor to the south. Hunterdon also differed from Burlington in its significant Dutch and substantial German
population, although British and New England influences were also prominent. Like
Burlington, the county sent crops by water to Philadelphia, but its northern reaches
also traded with New York.

Moving west, York and Adams counties in south central Pennsylvania exemplify
a mid-eighteenth-century frontier, a rich natural endowment, and a highly mobile
population that went on to shape the southern back-country as well as the near Midwest. Adams, where Gettysburg is situated, was formed out of York in 1800. Settlement of the combined eighteenth-century country began about a generation after that
of Hunterdon. Like Hunterdon, it attracted a large German population. Unlike Hunterdon, it drew an almost equally large Scotch-Irish contingent, concentrated especially
in the newer, western portions of York—those that became Adams County. York and
Adams counties also differed from counties to the east in their relatively poor market connections. Navigation on the lower Susquehanna was so poor as to render the
river an obstacle rather than a thoroughfare. Instead, as the Baltimore market developed in the late eighteenth century, York citizens petitioned for more roads to nearby
Maryland. Overland travel to Philadelphia took far longer, although Harrisburg and
Lancaster merchants served as convenient middlemen and attracted substantial York
commerce into Philadelphia's commercial orbit before the Revolution.

Located beyond the Appalachian Mountain barrier, Westmoreland County, Pennsylvania, was created on the eve of the Revolution and offers a chance to examine a
late-eighteenth-century frontier. After the Revolution, Westmoreland farmers clearly
perceived their situation as different from that of farmers to the east, at least judging
from their participation in the Whiskey Rebellion. In contrast to York and Adams,
Scotch-Irish settlers were a predominant early presence in Westmoreland, making
study of the county an opportunity to examine closely generalizations contrasting

their slovenly farming methods with those of their German-American contemporaries. Westmoreland also offers a case of dependence on western markets and on Ohio River—borne commerce.

Having selected five sample counties, my first task was to see whether their residents owned "red wheel barrows" and "white chickens." Without a clear image of what tools people commonly owned, I could not deduce what skills farm family members customarily possessed or determine whether agricultural practices were changing. Indeed, with roughly 80–90 percent of the colonial population engaged in agriculture, understanding the cultural and economic significance of an early American technology will entail viewing it within the context of agricultural technology. Since so much depends upon seeing those red wheelbarrows, I wanted to see as many of them as I could—to find a record that exists for enough individuals to capture the mundane technology of ordinary folk.

The record that forms the backbone of this study is the probate inventory, a document created, as the name suggests, when someone died. Probate inventories were not, as the name might suggest, limited to those with wills to probate. They exist for interstate as well as testate decedents. Briefly, inventories were, and are, intended to protect an estate's assets by providing a legal record of personal property ownership. (Real property was no usually listed in Pennsylvania and West Jersey probate inventories.) In some colonies and circumstances they were required whether or not the decedent had much personal property. For example, sometimes the law required an inventory whenever the decedent left minor children. Courts also ordered inventories when a potential heir or other interested party called for one. Those with no assets to protect clearly needed no inventories, so these documents miss the very poor. They do, however, report the assets of many men and women of modest means, and they are clearly more inclusive than other social history sources such as wills, travelers' accounts, account books, and diaries.

They are also far richer in technological detail. Indeed, the level of specificity often astonishes. Inventories distinguish weeding hoes from grubbing hoes, itemize goods of negligible value such as wooden trenchers, and list parts—plowshares, harrow teeth, and wagon covers—as well as, plows, harrows, and wagons. All told, then, inventories offer an unparalleled and essentially unutilized resource for historians of technology, both in the attentiveness to tools and in the coverage of the tool-owning population. They also exist continuously from early settlement through the mid-nineteenth century, unlike many social history records that either end or commence with the political transformations of late-eighteenth-century America.

Despite their many assets, like other historical documents, inventories will lead us astray unless we keep in mind why they were created. Otherwise, as one reads through probate inventories, the sense they convey of walking through the house and around the barnyard with the inventory takers can lull one into unwarranted confidence in a document's completeness. Inventories, as noted, were designed to protect an estate's personal property. But inventory takers certainly knew that not all assets needed equal protection. Obviously, listing assets such as cash or silverware afforded insurance against such valuables' disappearance into someone's pocket before settlement.

What is less obvious, until one begins reading wills, inventories, and administrators' accounts, is the need to protect much of the estate's personal property from disappearing into someone's stomach or into the woods. Joseph Wills, administrator of the estate of Daniel Wills of Burlington County, communicated this situation graphically when his 1729 accounts claimed credit for "two hogs appraised in the Inventory at 10/[shillings] Each[,] which either Strayd away with strange hogs or were Destroyd by Wolves or Dogs so that they never came to this Accomptants use"!

By contrast, other items were evidently deemed so secure that their absence from inventories does not necessarily spell rarity. Furniture attached to the walls of the house—built-in bedsteads or benches, for example—understandably seemed safe from depredations. In consequence, where featherbeds and other bedding are enumerated but bedsteads not listed, we cannot safely conclude that people were reduced to sleeping on the floor. Nor, of course, can we conclude that they were not.

More important, like all historical documents, inventories were shaped by prevailing gender assumptions. Legally, widows were entitled to a certain share of the property. Sometimes an inventory designates items as "belonging to the wito," to borrow a phrase from one York County inventory. Comparing such inventories with others is important in assessing whether local inventory takers tended to omit goods they assumed to be the widow's. Likewise, certain items were enumerated so rarely as to suggest that some property was commonly perceived as belonging to women, despite the formal legal assumption that a married woman's property belonged to her husband. For example, women's clothing appear almost exclusively in women's inventories; it is rarely listed in the estates of a woman's husband or father. Alternatively, some items associated with women may have been considered by male enumerators to be natural extensions of the woman or deemed so trivial because associated with women that they were not found worthy of enumeration in women's or men's estates. For example, I have found only eight needles and three thimbles in the more than 350 inventories I have examined closely thus far. Other items generally associated with women's work—poultry, for example—were also uncommon, if judged by inventories. Yet we know from other evidence, notably faunal remains in archaeological excavations, that, even in frontier Westmoreland, domestic fowl contributed substantially to the diet.

To generalize, then, our common practice of treating some documents as literary evidence, in which case they receive close reading and attention to nuance and to social construction, and of treating other documents as quantitative evidence, in which case we code them up and crunch out the numbers, entails a false dichotomy between literary and social scientific sources. Certainly inventories are both. They can, for example, be used to tell us that before the American Revolution a significant proportion of Burlington and Hunterdon County households—about 20–25 percent—owned slaves. But they can also be used to reveal something of slavery's meaning in the Quaker mid-Atlantic, if we note that Burlington inventory takers rather consistently listed slaves between the farm tools and the livestock.

Although part of my intention in quoting William's poem was to underscore the literary character of the historical enterprise, I do not minimize the importance of the quantitative. For example, I needed to devise a sampling strategy that would avoid aberrant years: times when events such as wars disrupted record keeping or times when epidemics or warfare made the population of decedents unusually young, for example. I found that I could best assure comparability among years if I used a fifteen-year interval in sampling. Starting with 1774, the last good pre-Revolutionary year, I moved forward in fifteen-year increments to 1849, a date chosen so as to conclude my study with results from the first full federal agricultural census, that of 1850. I got as close as possible to initial settlement by moving backward from 1774 in fifteen-year increments, collecting inventories as far back as records permitted.

This strategy has already generated a daunting array of information. My earliest sample comes from Burlington in 1714. Hunterdon supplies inventories beginning in 1729. York, founded in 1749, offers its earliest sample in 1759, and Westmoreland, organized in 1773, provides a small sample the following year. In order to ensure ample representation of inventories compiled in each season of the year and of assets left by various sorts of persons, I chose not to sample within years but to collect all inventories filed in each sample year. I have also chosen to retain virtually all of the original data.

The discussion that follows rests on a data base containing all of the eighteenth-century inventories for Burlington and Hunterdon, New Jersey, and for Westmoreland, Pennsylvania, and all of the York/Adams County inventories prior to 1789, about 350 inventories. That translates into an inventory data base of roughly twenty-six thousand records—individual inventory items, that is. The data I present here are drawn from a subset of 250 inventories chosen to include only individuals who were farmers and who owned at least some household goods.

Before exploring what these data suggest about early American agricultural technology, one final general question remains to be answered: What was early American agricultural technology? To date, restrictive definitions of technology have impeded the study of early farming technology. Accounts of colonial farming in particular regularly dismiss its technology as "primitive" and technological changes as "absent." Either characterization reflects an unfortunate tendency "to limit the definition of technology to those things which characterize the technology of our own time, such as machinery and prime movers," a definition that makes the nineteenth-century reaper seem to herald the dawn of American agricultural technology.

Fundamentally, historians' definitions of technology reflect the fact that we have written mostly about nineteenth- and twentieth-century technology and have given little thought to early modern technology or to farm technology generally. If suffices to say here that agricultural technology includes far more than machines, implements, and the knowledge of how to use them. At minimum it must also include the plants and animals that humans have developed, together with knowledge of plant and animal behavior; the methods of identifying land suited to particular purposes and of modifying and organizing that land; the construction methods, structures, and procedures devised for storing crops and housing livestock; and the knowledge of how to modify crops, land use patterns, and storage techniques to adapt to various climates. Under the household organization of labor that characterized early modern agriculture, the tools, skills, and knowledge employed in processing food, fiber, and other farm products—most of them widened by women—must also qualify as agricultural technology. Assuredly, the agricultural enterprise could not have functioned successfully without them. For purposes of this discussion, then, agricultural tools will include items such as pots, churns, stills, spinning wheels, maize, turnips, cattle, and sheep as well as implements such as plows, wagons, hoes, and axes.

What do probate records of such items allow us to conclude about tool ownership on early American farms? As suggested already, one very clear message is that there was no standard array of household and farm utensils that virtually all colonists owned or needed to own. That many individuals made do without plows, kettles, firearms, or Bibles reminds us, as we need always be reminded when we leave the era of modern technology, that the belief in "one best way" to perform a given task is an artifact of industrialized production. Indeed, the ability of modern households to own a standard array of tools reflects the existence of systems of transportation, communication, and manufacturing inconceivable in early modern societies. I stress the point because the history of technology has focused so narrowly on the recent period that aberrant features of industrial technology easily get read back into discussions of earlier eras.

Another conclusion warranted by these data is that eighteenth-century Americans were not technologically self-sufficient. Patterns of tool ownership imply extensive participation in the market. For example, only five inventories listed candle molds, and only about 5 percent enumerated tallow. A far larger proportion—24–40 percent—included candles or candle-holders, implying the acquisition of candles elsewhere. Likewise, although yard goods appears in most inventories, weaving equipment shows up in fewer than 5 percent of Burlington farm households. Even in more recently settled Hunterdon and York, where poorer transportation limited access to imported textiles and urban weavers, only about 15 percent of farm inventories generally listed looms. Where the prospect of acquiring textiles from Britain or from local population centers was extremely limited, as in the very remote settlements of late-eighteenth-century Westmoreland County or of York in 1759, the proportion of farm households prepared to weave still reached only 25 percent—hardly an impressive tally.

Eighteenth-century farmers not only purchased essential commodities such as cloth but also depended on mills or specialists to process much of what they grew. There is, for example, no evidence that any farmer owned tools to grind his own grain; and, except in frontier York with its exceptionally poor transportation facilities, most people who grew flax lacked both flax brakes to prepare the fiber, and many lacked hackles to comb it. More households owned spinning wheels, although only in York and in early Hunterdon did substantially more than half do so, a pattern probably indicative of the frontier population's relative youthfulness rather than of its relationship to the market. If eighteenth-century agricultural regions had been technologically self-sufficient, we might expect, at the very least, to find a region's ownership of spinning wheels to parallel its fiber production, but, except in York, the proportion of households owning sheep rather consistently outran the proportion prepared to spin wool. Indeed, in many years more Burlington decedents owned herds of sheep (twenty or more) than owned spinning wheels of any sort. Woolen wheel ownership exceeded the number of substantial sheep herds only in York and Westmoreland, where, given the persistence of wolves, large herds of sheep remained uncommon.

Similarly, tool ownership patterns clearly imply extensive wood-processing specialization. Remarkably, even common tasks such as firewood preparation entailed exchanges with outsiders. Throughout the eighteenth century three-quarters or more Hunterdon and Burlington households lacked mauls and wedges for splitting wood. Saws of various sorts and froes, for cleaving shingles, were even less common. As do the turning lathes listed in craftsmen's inventories, these data remind us that specialized production and employment long antedated American settlement. It is hardly surprising, then, that colonists presumed self-sufficiency to be unnecessary and, probably, undesirable. Certainly they quickly made it uncommon. The most dramatic case in point is that of frontier farmers, who generally distilled their grain into whiskey, a commodity whose high value relative to its bulk enabled it profitably to be transported long distances to market. Despite the relative cheapness of stills, most farmers relied on others to process their grain. Similarly, in eastern counties, where apple trees had had a chance to mature, most farmers depended on a small minority who owned cider mills.

Two additional aspects of tool ownership signal the market's mounting importance over the eighteenth century. First, early in the century Burlington farmers rarely (less than 15 percent of the time) owned wagons. Instead, between three-fifths and one-half of households had carts—relatively small, cheap, two-wheeled vehicles better designed for hauling small loads around the farm than for carrying crops to market. After midcentury, this pattern was reversed. About three-fifths to one-half of Burlington farmers came to own wagons, while cart ownership declined dramatically. At the same time, roughly two-thirds of Hunterdon farmers owned wagons, the greater proportion reflecting longer average overland distances to market. Even in York, where wagon trips to market were frequent, nearly two-fifths of households owned them. Only in remote Westmoreland did many farmers have to make do with pack saddles. During the same years, substantial proportions (from one-quarter to one-half) of farm households in each county came to own steelyards, signifying more frequent occasions to weigh goods for exchange.

Diverse patterns of tool ownership also reveal eighteenth-century mid-Atlantic farmers to have been a distinctly innovative lot. And, far from deriving from the romanticized jack-of-all-trades conjured up as part of the frontier subsistence myth, early American readiness to try new technology had several more mundane sources. First, it built on the common experience of the many colonists who came from a place—Britain—in the throes of an agricultural revolution. If we take differences in British and colonial circumstances into account, we find that land reorganization and reclamation, experimentation with and adoption of new crops, and increased attention to livestock husbandry engaged colonial yeomen as well as their British counterparts. Whereas the British brought new land into cultivation by adopting crop rotations suited to light, upland soil or by draining swamps or by irrigating meadows, early British Americans achieved the same outcome by acquiring the utterly alien skills needed to clear the continent's dense woodlands. And, like Englishmen at home who acquired their land reclamation technologies from their Dutch neighbors, mid-Atlantic English colonists developed forest destruction to a fine art by borrowing the technology of their Native American and Scandinavian predecessors and of their German contemporaries.

Among their tools, farmers' frequent ownership of axes best documents their openness to new land-making technology. Until relatively late in the eighteenth-century, for example, Burlington and Hunterdon County farmers were at least as likely to own axes as plows, and in York and Westmoreland they were far more likely to. Furthermore, despite the near certainty that most arrived from England without axes or tree-felling experience, a substantial proportion (one-quarter to one-third) of Burlington and Hunterdon decedents owned more than one axe.

Mid-Atlantic farmers also paralleled British agricultural revolutionaries in readily adopting new crops, such as Indian corn, listed rather consistently in 50–60 percent of inventories. The extent to which this formerly novel grain had achieved acceptance is best suggested by the evidence that almost all inventories after midcentury employ the words "wheat" or "rye" or "oats" to enumerate European grains; they reserve the word "corn" for maize. Indeed, so early and so thoroughly was Indian corn integrated into the mixed-farming regime brought by English colonists that one of the supreme ironies of eighteenth- and nineteenth-century agricultural history is apparent. The same reformers who praised English husbandmen for the willingness to experiment with new crops ignored the far more general adoption of maize by American farmers and, instead, derided them for their reluctance to grow turnips.

Also like their British contemporaries, mid-Atlantic farmers accorded particular attention to livestock husbandry. In every sample county, horses and cattle were far more common than plows or even axes for most of the century, and hay crops grew in frequency and value. Churn ownership suggests that farm women's work also shifted toward livestock husbandry. Burlington churn ownership increased to nearly one-fifth of estates by the late eighteenth century while in Hunterdon and York more than one-half and about two-thirds, respectively, of all inventories listed churns.

Repeated evidence that York County decedents more often employed progressive technology reflects the prominence of Germans in its population. But the case of German farmers' apparent progressiveness well illustrates that technological progress is always in the eye of the beholder. In fact, for German settlers the techniques that British farmers had recently adopted with so much fanfare represented established practice. So, for example, York farmers often owned tools for manuring: dung forks, dung hooks, and dung shovels appear in two-thirds of their inventories by 1774. By contrast, almost no Burlington farmers' inventories record any such implements. York farmers were also far more likely to wield cradles at harvesttime (20 percent of York farmer decedents versus, at most, 5–10 percent of Burlington farmers). And they generally owned hoes, indicative of more intensive cultivation (about 70–80 percent of York farmers' inventories versus about 30 percent of Burlington farmers' inventories during the same years). York's settlers often used those tools to cultivate potatoes and turnips (about 40 percent and 25 percent, respectively)—"the new root crops" from an English perspective. Farmers in York also employed far more winnowing fans (nearly one-third of York inventories listed them, versus only one Burlington inventory).

However commonplace German farmers may have found these technologies, viewed through British eyes they were innovative. It is all the more noteworthy, then, that by 1774 only about half of York farmers owning dung tools were German and even fewer potato growers were (about one-third). By contrast, fifteen years earlier, Germans had owned most dung tools (about three-fourths of them). In other words, tool ownership patterns show German agricultural technology diffusing earlier and more readily than most secondary scholarship has surmised.

Hunterdon County also had a substantial German population, and one derived from essentially the same sources as supplied York. But whereas York Germans arrived early in that county's history and generally predominated numerically, Hunterdon Germans arrived after their county's other principal ethnic groups and made up only a quarter of the population. As a result, techniques associated with German farming diffused far more selectively in Hunterdon. Where a technology proved well suited to established practice and could be introduced as a solitary innovation, German techniques fared well there. So, for example, winnowing fans became even more common there than in York (they appeared in about 35 percent of Hunterdon farm inventories). This adoption is hardly surprising, for they were clearly well suited to Hunterdon's late-eighteenth-century emphasis on wheat, a crop listed in 65–72 percent of farm inventories. Similarly, although at midcentury Hunterdon farmers, like their Burlington neighbors, rarely harvested with cradles, their increasing reliance on hay reinforced the increased presence of German exemplars to make cradle use more common in Hunterdon than in York. By 1789 two-fifths of Hunterdon farm inventories listed cradles, and only half of these are identifiable as German or Dutch. On the other hand, dung implements appear almost exclusively in German and Dutch inventories in Hunterdon, reflecting both the absence of evident soil depletion and the greater array of new behaviors dunging entailed.

Comparisons of York and Hunterdon can also help establish how much of York's apparent innovativeness derived from German influence and how much from the influence of the frontier. Again, data on tool ownership serve as useful corrective to the belief, pervasive in American popular culture, that frontier living meant being reduced to older, more primitive ways of doing things—a belief we readily incorporate into historical scholarship where evidence is absent. Tool ownership patterns indicate that, far from reverting to obsolete technology, frontiersmen generally brought the latest technology with them. For example, large, heavy, iron-reinforced, covered market wagons (from which the famed Conestoga was derived) showed up far more often in late-eighteenth-century York than in Hunterdon inventories of the same era. And most kettle-owning farm women in Westmoreland and York employed modern iron kettles, whereas traditional brass kettles continued longer in Hunterdon and, especially, Burlington.

Similarly, comparison of Burlington, Hunterdon, York, and Westmoreland inventories indicates that the technological commitments made by a region's pioneers could be hard to break. For example, over the eighteenth century, mid-Atlantic farmers followed a general European trend away from the use of oxen and toward the use of horses as draft animals. Thus, oxen were relatively common in early Burlington, showing up in more than one-quarter of inventories before 1730. By contrast, oxen appear in virtually no inventories in York, where most settlement occurred after midcentury. They are entirely absent from Westmoreland, settled even later. In Burlington, however, oxen represented established practice, and they remained relatively common even late in the century. Hunterdon, settled only a generation earlier than York, also relied heavily on horses from the outset, but a persistent minority used oxen late in the century—apparently Hunterdon immigrants from New England, an early and persistent ox-using region.

Frontier conditions also encouraged technological innovation more directly. Not surprisingly, all of the various rough woodworking tools appeared far more often in York than in Burlington or Hunterdon inventories. Likewise, specialized hoes were a feature of frontier agriculture. Most commonly, inventories distinguished between grubbing hoes and weeding hoes. Such distinctions were especially common in York, ten times more common than in Burlington inventories. Widespread ownership of both weeding and grubbing hoes certainly made sense under frontier conditions. Corn, an ideal crop on new land, generally received hoe cultivation—hence the weeding hoe—and new land also required farmers to use hoes to grub out roots, stones, and other debris.

Frontier and German influence intersected somewhat differently to shape food-processing technology. One of the more striking technological differences between German and British settlers was that Germans were accustomed to cook and heat with stoves, whereas the British relied on open hearth cookery and heating. Like many German technologies, stoves eventually became the British American's modern technology, but there is less evidence of their colonial diffusion. In English Burlington, for example, despite ready access to stoves in nearby Philadelphia, only one stove was enumerated in any eighteenth-century inventory. Rather, food preparation methods appear to have been highly resistant to change, a pattern anthropologists have often ascribed to the deep-seated cultural conditioning of dietary preferences. A look at the technology involved suggests instead that the domestic craftswomen who prepared most meals understandably resisted adopting new tools that threatened their hard-won proficiencies, altered the quality of the work experience, and would have required them to learn a new repertoire of skills.

Domestic tool ownership patterns in York support this interpretation. As a frontier community with a very poor transportation system, York was a difficult place to obtain a stove. Nonetheless, nearly half of York's German decedents had managed to acquire stoves by the 1770s (about 20 percent of all inventories). Even more striking is the suggestion implicit in York's domestic tool ownership pattern that German farm wives who lacked stoves merely tolerated fireplace cooking as a temporary expedient. Trammels, elaborate contrivances for hanging and adjusting pots over the fire, are absent from York inventories although they appear often in Burlington ones. Instead, York mistresses relied on simple pothooks. For varying the heat they applied, they placed their pots on pot racks designed to elevate pots and frying pans over coals on the hearth. Not only did this cooking method come closer to replicating stove cooking, but also pot racks served as complements to legless cooking vessels—vessels one would prefer to retain or purchase if one expected ultimately to acquire a stove.

By contrast, Hunterdon County domestic tool ownership patterns suggest how farm women came to adopt new technology. Although more favorably situated to acquire stoves, few Hunterdon decedents owned them (about 10 percent of inventories). Nor did Hunterdon Germans show a preference for pot racks (fewer than 10 percent of inventories enumerated pot racks, even fewer than in Burlington); county farm wives of all ethnic groups employed trammels. Essentially, this very different behavior reflects differences in the timing of German settlement. As relative latecomers, Hunterdon Germans generally moved into existing houses—houses that embodied a preference for fireplace cooking. Moreover, Hunterdon Germans tended to be poorer than those who could afford the longer trek and greater farm-making investment required in York. Most probably arrived without pots and pans and acquired kitchen utensils from craftsmen accustomed to supplying Hunterdon's established British settlers.

Ethnic differences in food processing are also manifest in the distribution of specialized tubs between York and Burlington. With one exception all of the powdering tubs—tubs used to preserve meat by salting—appear in Burlington inventories. By contrast, all of the pickling tubs show up in York inventories, evidence of a divergent meat preservation tradition. Cabbages and implements for processing cabbage are, likewise, limited almost exclusively to York and Hunterdon German inventories. In sum, the distribution of food processing implements in eighteenth-century inventories hints at a larger, historically invisible array of technologies: the skills and knowledge essential to transforming crops into food.

Although we can glimpse only obliquely the skills and knowledge that constituted most of colonial agricultural technology, inventories offer a rather direct look at the material component of that technology: the tools, livestock, and plants that early Americans commonly employed. This preliminary account of several hundred such documents demonstrates how productive of new and revised understandings of early agricultural practice the actual evidence of tool ownership can be. Looking at farmers' possessions reveals that there existed no standard array of implements farmers and farm wives owned or needed to own; it shows the belief in "one best way" to perform a task to be a historical artifact, an intellectual by-product of industrial society that we inadvertently project onto the preindustrial past.

Certainly, colonial farm households tools show a diversity that we deem uncommon in the world we inhabit. In part this diversity reflected the considerable and growing involvement of farmers and farm wives in networks of exchange—with one another and with the local representatives of distant producers. In part the diversity reveals selective adoption from the varied menu of innovations that American farmers employed virtually from the start of settlement; land-clearing and woodworking tools, new field and garden crops, and the various creatures, structures, and implements that embodied a growing commitment to livestock husbandry. And, whereas the ethnic diversity of the colonial population may have introduced much of this technological diversity, close examination of late-eighteenth-century tool ownership discloses extensive cross-cultural borrowing, especially in regions where ethnic diversity began early. Inventories also reveal diversity emerging from the diverse times at which counties were settled. Technological patterns established early evidently continued to influence local farmers' and farm wives' technological options. Given the continuous westward course of settlement, then, temporal diversity gradually assumed a geographic manifestation.

These preliminary observations about early American tool ownership carry obvious implications for the large question with which I began: What accounts for America's sudden, rapid, and comparatively successful early nineteenth-century industrialization? They suggest that the wellsprings of American willingness and ability to innovate were mundane rather than mythic, endemic rather than heroic. Judging from these data, the sources of early American technological innovation—and, by extension, America's early industrialization—should sound familiar to American historians: the rise of a market economy, the selective transfer of European culture, the social consequences of ethnic diversity, and the significance of the frontier. These are themes to which students of the American past perennially recur.

If these themes also best elucidate our early technological history, then "so much depends" on closely scrutinizing the small technologies found on early American farms—much more than a new portrait of early tool use. If, as these preliminary findings suggest, traditional historical themes will play a predominant role in explaining America's technological history, historians of technology will have to question the wisdom of their increasing specialization and separation from the larger historical profession. More than most historians, we should recognize and avoid the high cost of unnecessarily reinventing the wheel. Likewise, once early American historians recognize their perennial concerns as having great relevance to understanding the problem of technological innovation, they may wonder at their former willingness to delegate study of this crucial issue to historians of technology. Like all contemporary Americans, early American historians should recognize and avoid the high potential costs of leaving technology solely to the technology experts. Finally, if early American technological diversity helped precipitate America's remarkable nineteenth-century technological innovativeness, the findings discussed above hold a moral for us, early American historians and historians of technology alike. Studies of early American technology need all of our various approaches; scholarly innovation thrives best when a field's cultivators know there is no "one best way" to farm.

🔺🔺 F U R T H E R   R E A D I N G

Boydston, Jean. *Home and Work: Housework, Wages, and the Ideology of Labor in the Early Republic* (New York: Oxford University Press, 1990).

Cummings, Abbott Lowell. *The Framed Houses of Massachusetts Bay, 1625–1725* (Cambridge, MA: Harvard University Press, 1976).

Hindle, Brooke. *Material Culture of the Wooden Age* (Tarrytown, NY: Sleepy Hollow Press, 1981).

Littlefield, Daniel C. *Rice and Slaves: Ethnicity and the Slave Trade in Colonial South Carolina* (Baton Rouge: Louisiana State University Press, 1981).

McCusker, John J. and Russell R. Menard. *The Economy of British America, 1607–1789* (Chapel Hill, NC: University of North Carolina Press, 1985).

Mintz, Sidney. *Sweetness and Power: The Place of Sugar in Modern History* (New York: Viking, 1986).

St. George, Robert Blair. *Material Life in America, 1600–1860* (Boston: Northeastern University Press, 1988).

Silver, Timothy, *A New Face in the Countryside: Indians, Colonists, and Slaves in the South Atlantic Forests, 1500–1800* (Cambridge, England: Cambridge University Press, 1990).

Ulrich, Laurel Thatcher. *Good Wives: Image and Reality in the Lives of Women in Northern New England, 1650–1750* (New York: Knopf, 1982).

CHAPTER
4

The Debate over Manufactures in the Early Republic, 1785–1820

It is difficult now to appreciate the extent to which society, politics, and life in general were locally oriented two hunderd years ago. When people spoke of "my country," as Thomas Jefferson and others did, they more often than not were refer-ring to their home state or even to their hometown or county than to the United States. In Jefferson's America, one's neighborhood was one's world.

Local loyalties and institutions served relatively well in colonial America. As adjuncts of the British empire, each colony dealt directly with the king's ministers in England. Since the hub of the colonial system was London, relatively little need existed for intercolony compacts. All that changed during the 1770s. After their war for independence and eventual separation from England, the thirteen original states sought a means of addressing common problems related to defense, trade, and foreign affairs. The first attempt at establishing a national government with a written consti-tution took place during the Revolutionary War with the Articles of Confederation. Ratified in 1781, the Confederation government was authorized to conduct foreign affairs, make treaties, manage Indian affairs, coin money, establish a postal system, and declare war. However, it was constrained by its inability to levy taxes or regulate commerce. These two powers, which resided with each of the "free and sovereign" states, became the Confederation's greatest weakness. In 1787, a new constitution was drafted that removed these constraints and tied the individual states much closer to the federal government. The new constitution went into effect with the election of George Washington in 1789 as the first "president" of the "United States."

Of the many public policy issues Washington's administration encountered during his two terms in office (1879–1797), none proved more critical than defining the role the new federal government should play in fostering manufacturing. The exclusion of American merchants from key British markets coupled with tensions generated in Europe as a result of the French Revolution (1789) meant that Europe was no longer a reliable source for key goods. This was particularly true of certain military stores, such as gunpowder and firearms. These considerations, coupled with a growing popular feeling that the United States could never be completely independent of Great Britain and other European powers until it achieved economic independence, ignited a protracted, and often heated, debate over the future of manufacturing in America.

At issue were the imposition of tariffs to protect American manufacturers from foreign competition, the issuance of bounties to encourage certain types of manufacturing, the passage of outright nonimportation laws for various European manufactured goods, and the establishment of a patent system to encourage and secure the rights of inventors. The patent issue was resolved with the establishment of the U.S. Patent Office in 1790. But the other three questions remained serious bones of contention for the next seventy years. The tarriff question led, in 1832, to a constitutional crisis over whether an individual state (South Carolina) had the right to declare null and void a federal tariff law that did not serve its interests. Some thirty years later, similar declarations by eleven southern states following the election of Abraham Lincoln would lead to civil war.

From the outset, key members of Washington's cabinet were divided over the issue of manufacturing. The chief protagonists were Secretary of Treasury Alexander Hamilton, ostensibly the administration's leading proponent of manufacturing, and Secretary of State Thomas Jefferson, considered by many the foremost spokesman for agricultural interests. At issue were fundamental questions pertaining not just to manufacturing and technology but also to cultural and moral predispositions as well as to the conduct of foreign affairs. How did Jefferson's position on manufacturing differ from Hamilton's? To what extent did their respective backgrounds and local political roots influence their policy positions? In the long run, whose ideas—if anyone's—exercised lasting influence? To what extent did national political debate influence technological change?

𝐴𝐴 D O C U M E N T S

The first selection comes from Thomas Jefferson's *Notes on Virginia.* First published in England in 1785, this book argued against the establishment of large-scale factory manufacturers in America and in support of an entirely agrarian regime. In the second selection, Philadelphian Tench Coxe, a Philadelphia merchant, sought to counter Jefferson's accusation that urban factories would lead to "degeneracy," eventually threatening the very existence of the American republic. In Coxe's view, manufacturing would have the opposite effect, strengthening the moral fabric of society while ensuring national prosperity.

Coxe's influence is reflected in the third selection, Alexander Hamilton's 1791 "Report on Manufactures." Although indicative of Hamilton's skill as an economic planner, the report failed to generate sufficient congressional support. Nonetheless, it marked the beginning of the formulation of government policy toward manufacturing and became the foundation on which later advocates of American industrial expansion based their arguments.

Faced with military challenges to the Unted States posed by European powers during and after his presidency, Thomas Jefferson seemed to change his views about the need for developing extensive home industries. Or did he? The next selection comprises letters written by Jefferson between 1795 and 1816. They bear careful comparison with his earlier statements published in the *Notes on Virginia.*

The final selection comes from Dr. Thomas Cooper, a South Carolinian. Cooper had once been a strong proponent of manufacturing, but, like many individuals from the plantation South (John C. Calhoun, for example), his views changed as upward adjustments of the tariff began to threaten planter interests. Cooper's rhetoric about the moral implications of manufacturing is reminiscent of Jefferson's *Notes on Virginia*. Interestingly, his vitriolic attack on "proud and wealthy capitalists" and the "dreadful curse" of their machinery anticipates later critiques of industrial capitalism, most notably those of Karl Marx and Friederich Engels.

Thomas Jefferson's "Notes on Virginia" (Excerpts), 1785

The present state of manufactures, commerce, interior and exterior trade?

We never had an interior trade of any importance. Our exterior commerce has suffered very much from the beginning of the present contest. During this time we have manufactured within our families the most necessary articles of cloathing. Those of cotton will bear some comparison with the same kinds of manufacture in Europe; but those of wool, flax and hemp are very coarse, unslightly, and unpleasant: and such is our attachment to agriculture, and such our preference for foreign manufactures, that be it wise or unwise, our people will certainly return as soon as they can, to the raising raw materials, and exchanging them for finer manufactures than they are able to execute themselves.

The political œconomists of Europe have established it as a principle that every state should endeavour to manufacture for itself: and this principle, like many others, we transfer to America, without calculating the difference of circumstance which should often produce a difference of result. In Europe the lands are either cultivated, or locked up against the cultivator. Manufacture must therefore be resorted to of necessity not of choice, to support the surplus of their people. But we have an immensity of land courting the industry of the husbandman. It is best then that all our citizens should be employed in its improvement, or that one half should be called off from that to exercise manufactures and handicraft arts for the other? Those who labour in the earth are the chosen people of God, if ever he had a chosen people, whose breasts he has made his peculiar deposit for substantial and genuine virtue. It is the focus in which he keeps alive that sacred fire, which otherwise might escape from the face of the earth. Corruption of morals in the mass of cultivators is a phaenomenon of which no age nor nation has furnished an example. It is the mark set on those, who not looking up to heaven, to their own soil and industry, as does the husbandman, for their subsistence, depend for it on the casualties and caprice of customers. Dependance begets subservience and venality, suffocates the germ of virtue, and prepares fit tools for the designs of ambition. This, the natural progress and consequence of the arts, has sometimes perhaps been retarded by accidental circumstances: but, generally speaking, the proportion which the aggregate of the other classes of citizens bears in any state to that of its husbandmen, is the proportion of its unsound to its healthy parts, and is a good-enough behavior barometer whereby to measure its degree of corruption. While we have land to labour then, let us never wish to see our citizens occurpied at a work-bench, or twirling a distaff. Carpenters,

From Thomas Jefferson, "Notes on Virginia," in Michael B. Folsom and Steven B. Lubar, eds., *The Philosophy of Manufactures* (Cambridge, MA: MIT Press, 1982), pp. 16–17.

masons, smiths, are wanting in husbandry: but, for the general operations of manufacture, let our work-shops remain in Europe. It is better to carry provisions and materials to workmen there, than bring them to the provisions and materials, and with them their manners and principles. The loss by the transportation of commodities across the Atlantic will be made up in happiness and permanence of government. The mobs of great cities add just so much to the support of pure government, as sores do to the strength of the human body. It is the manners and spirit of a people which preserve a republic in vigour. A degeneracy in these is a canker which soon eats to the heart of its laws and constitution.

Tench Coxe Speaks for Factories, 1787

Providence has bestowed upon the United States of America means of happiness, as great and numerous, as are enjoyed by any country in the world. A soil fruitful and diversified—a healthful climate—mighty rivers and adjacent seas abounding with fish are the great advantages for which we are indebted to a beneficent creator. Agriculture, manufactures and commerce, naturally arising from these sources, afford to our industrious citizens certain subsistence and innumerable opportunities of acquiring wealth. To arrange our affairs in salutary and well digested system, by which the fruits of industry, in every line, may be most easily attained, and the possession of property and the blessings of liberty may be completely secured—these are the important objects, that should engross our present attention. The interests of commerce and the establishment of a just and effective government are already committed to the care of THE AUGUST BODY now sitting in our capital.—The importance of agriculture has long since recommended it to the patronage of numerous associations, and the attention of all the legislatures—but manufactures, at least in Pennsylvania, have had but a few unconnected friends, till sound policy and public spirit gave a late, but auspicious birth, to this Society.

The situation of American before the revolution was very unfavorable to the objects of this institution. . . . But as long as we remained in our colonial situation, our progress was very low, and indeed the necessity of attention to manufactures was not so urgent, as it has become since our assuming an independent station. The employment of those, whom the decline of navigation has deprived of their usual occupations—the consumption of the encreasing produce of our lands and fisheries, and the certainty of supplies in the time of war are weighty reasons for establishing new manufactories now, which existed but in a small degree, or not at all, before the revolution.

While we readily admit, that in taking measures to promote the objects of this Society, nothing should be attempted, which may injure our agricultural interests, they being undoubtedly the most important, we must observe in justice to ourselves, that very many of our citizens, who are expert at manufactures and the useful arts, are entirely unacquainted with rural affairs, unequal to the expenses of a new settlement; and many we may believe, will come among us invited to our shores from

From Michael B. Folsom and Steven B. Lubar, eds., *The Philosophy of Manufactures* (Cambridge, MA: MIT Press, 1982), pp. 33–62.

foreign countries, by the blessings of liberty, civil and religious. We may venture to assert too, that more profit to the individual and riches to the nation will be derived from some manufactures, which promote agriculture, than from any species of cultivations whatever. . . .

Let us endeavor first to disencumber manufactures of the objections, that appear against them, the principal of which are, the high rate of labor, which involves the price of provisions—the want of a sufficient number of hands on any terms,—the scarcity and dearness of raw materials—want of skill in the business itself and its unfavorable effects on the health of the people.

Factories which can be carried on by watermills, windmills, fire, horses and machines ingeniously contrived, are not burdened with any heavy expence of boarding, lodging, cloathing and paying workmen, and they multiply the force of hands to a great extent without taking our people from agriculture. By wind and water machines we can make pig and bar iron, nail rods, tire, sheet-iron, sheet-cooper and sheet-brass, anchors, meal of all kinds, gunpowder, writing, printing and hanging paper, snuff, linseed oil, boards, plank and scantling; and they assist us in finishing scythes, sickles and woolen cloths. Strange as it may appear they also card, spin and weave by water in the European factories. Bleaching and tanning must not be omitted, while we are speaking of the usefulness of water.

By fire we conduct our breweries, distilleries, salt, and potash works, sugar houses, potteries, casting and steel furnaces, works for animal and vegetable oils and refining drugs. Steam mills have not yet been adopted in America, but we shall probably see them after a short time in New-England and other places, where there are few mill seats and in this and other great towns of the United States. The city of Philadelphia, by adopting the use of them, might make a saving of above five *percent.* on all the grain brought hither by water, which is afterwards manufactured into meal, and they might be usefully applied to many other valuable purposes. . . .

Machines ingeniously constructed, will give us immense assistance.—The cotton and silk manufacturers in Europe are possessed of some, that are invaluable to them. One instance I have had precisely ascertained, which employs a few hundreds of women and children, and performs the work of 12000 carders, spinners and winders. They have been so curiously improved of late years, as to weave the most complicated manufactures. In short, combinations of machines with fire and water have already performed much more than was formerly expected from them by the most visionary enthusiast on the subject. Perhaps I may be too sanguine, but they appear to me fraught with immense advantages to us, and full of danger to the manufacturing nations of Europe; for should they continue to use and improve them, as they have heretofore done, their people must be driven to us for want of employment, and if, on the other hand, they should return to manual labor, we shall underwork them by these invaluable engines. We may certainly borrow some of their inventions and others of the same nature we may strike out ourselves; for on the subject of mechanism America may justly pride herself. Every combination of machinery may be expected from a country, A NATIVE SON of which, reaching this inestimable object at its highest point, has epitomized the motions of the spheres, that roll throughout the universe.*

---

*David Rittenhouse, Esq. of Pennsylvania.

The lovers of mankind, supported by experienced physicians, and the opinions of enlightened politicians, have objected to manufactures as unfavorable to the health of the people. Giving to this humane and important consideration its full weight, it furnishes an equal argument against several other occupations, by which we obtain our comforts and promote our agriculture. The [planting] business for instance— reclaiming marshes—clearing swamps—the culture of rice and indigo and some other employments, are even more fatal to those, who are engaged in them. But this objection is urged principally against carding, spinning and weaving, which were formerly manual and sedentary occupations. Our plan, as we have already shewn, is not to pursue those modes, for we are sensible, that our people must not be diverted from thier farms. *Horses, and the potent elements of fire and water, aided by the faculties of the human mind (except in a few healthful instances) are to be our daily labourers.* After giving immediate relief to the industrious poor, these unhurtful means will be pursued and will procure us private wealth and national prosperity.

Emigration from Europe will also relieve and assist us. The blessings of civil and religious liberty in America, and the oppressions of most foreign governments, the want of employment at home and the expectations of profit here, curiosity, domestic unhappiness, civil wars and various other circumstances will bring many manufacturers to this assylum for mankind. Ours will be their industry and what is of still more consequence ours will be their skill. Interest and necessity, with such instructors, will teach us quickly. In the late century the manufactures of France were next to none; they are now worth millions to her yearly. Those of England have been more improved within the last twelve years, than in the preceding fifty. At the peace of 1762, the useful arts and manufactures were scarcely known in America. How great has been their progress since, unaided, undirected and discouraged. Countenanced by your patronage and promoted by your assistance, what may they not be 'ere such another space of time shall elapse. . . .

We must carefully examine the conduct of other countries in order to possess ourselves of their methods of encouraging manufactories and pursue such of them, as apply to our own situation, so far is it may be in our power. . . . Premiums for useful inventions and improvements, whether Foreign or American, for the best experiments in any unknown matter, and for the largest quantity of any valuable raw material must have an excellent effect. . . . The state might with great convenience enable an enlightened Society, established for the purpose, to offer liberal rewards in land for a number of objects of this nature. Our funds of that kind are considerable and almost dormant. An unsettled tract of a thousand acres, as it may be paid for at this time, yields very little money to the state. By offering these premiums for useful inventions to any citizen of the Union, or to any foreigner, who would become a citizen, we might often acquire in the man a compensation for the land, independent of the merit which gave it to him. . . .

It might answer an useful purpose, if a committee of this society should have it in charge to visit every ship arriving with passengers from any foreign country, in order to enquire what persons they may have on board capable of constructing useful machines, qualified to carry on manufactures, or coming among us with a view to that kind of employment. It would be a great relief and encouragement to those friendless people in a land of strangers, and would fix many among us whom little difficulties might incline to return.

Extreme poverty and idleness in the citizens of a free government will ever produce vicious habits and disobedience to the laws, and must render the people fit instruments for the dangerous purposes of ambitious men. In this light the employment of our poor in manufactures, who cannot find other honest means of a subsistence, is of the utmost consequence. A man oppressed by extreme want is prepared for all evil, and the idler is ever prone to wickedness, while the habits of industry, filling the mind with honest thoughts, and requiring the time for better purposes, do not leave leisure for mediating or executing mischief.

An extravagant and wasteful use of foreign manufactures, has been too just a charge against the people of America, since the close of the war. They have been so cheap, so plenty and so easily obtained on credit, that the consumption of them has been absolutely wanton. To such an excess has it been carried, that the importation of the finer kinds of coat, vest and sleeve buttons, buckles, broaches, breastpins, and other trinkets into this port only, is supposed to have amounted in a single year to ten thousand pounds sterling, which cost the wearers above 60,000 dollars. This lamentable evil has suggested to many enlightened minds a wish for sumptuary regulations, and even for an unchanging national dress suitable to the climate, and the other circumstances of the country. A more general use of such manufactures as we can make ourselves, would wean us from the folly we have just now spoken of and would produce, in a safe way, some of the best effects of sumptuary laws. Our dresses, furniture and carriages would be fashionable, because they were American and proper in our situation, not because they were foreign, shewy or expensive. Our farmers, to their great honor and advantage, have been long in the excellent œconomical practice of domestic manufactures for their own use, at least in many parts of the union. It is chiefly in the towns that this madness for foreign finery rages and destroys—There unfortunately the disorder is epidemical. It behoves us to consider our untimely passion for European luxuries as a malignant and alarming symptom, threatening convulsions and dissolution to the political body. Let us hasten then to apply the most effectual remedies, ere the disease becomes inveterate, lest unhappily we should find it incurable.

I cannot conclude this address, gentlemen, without taking notice of *the very favorable and prodigious effects upon the landed interest,* which may result from manufactures. The breweries of Philadelphia in their present infant state require forty thousand bushels of barley annually, and when the stock on hand of English beer shall be consumed, will call for a much larger quantity. Could the use of malt liquors be more generally introduced, it would be, for many reasons, a most fortunate circumstance. Without insisting on the pernicious effects of distilled liquors, it is sufficient for our present purpose to observe, that a thousand hogsheads of rum and brandy, mixt with water for common use, will make us much strong drink as will require 120,000 bushels of grain to make an equivalent quantity of beer, besides the horses, fuel, hops, and other articles of the country, which a brewery employs. The fruits of the earth and the productions of nature in America are also required by various other manufacturers, whom you will remember without enumeration. . . . So great are the benefits to the landed interest, which are derived from them, that we may venture to assert without apprehension of mistake, that the value of American productions annually applied to their various uses, as just now stated, without including the manufacturers of flour, lumber and bar-iron, is double the aggregate amount of all our exports in the most plentiful year with which Providence has even blessed this fruitful country.—How valuable is this market for our encreasing product—How clearly does it evince the importance of our present plan. But we may venture to proceed a step further—Without manufactures the progress of agriculture must be arrested on the frontiers of Pennsylvania. Though we have a country practicable for roads, our western counties are yet unable to support them, and too remote perhaps to use land carriage of the most easy kind. . . . The inhabitants of the fertile tracts adjacent to the waters of the Ohio, Potowmack and Susquehannah, besides the cultivation of grain must extend their views immediately to pasturage and grazing and even to manufactures. Foreign trade will never take off the fruits of their labor in their native state. They must manufacture first for their own consumption, and when the advantages of their mighty waters shall be no longer suspended, they must become the great factory of American raw materials for the United States. Their resources in wood and water are very great, their treasures in coal are almost peculiar. . . .

How numerous and important then, do the benefits appear, which may be expected from this salutary design! It will consume our native productions now encreasing to super-abundance—it will improve our agriculture and teach us to explore the fossil and vegetable kingdoms, into which few researches have heretofore been made—it will accelerate the improvement of our internal navigation and bring into action the dormant powers of nature and the elements—it will lead us once more into the paths of virtue by restoring frugality and industry, those potent antidotes to the vices of mankind and will give us real independence by rescuing us from the tyranny of foreign fashions, and the destructive torrent of luxury.

Should these blessed consequences ensure, those severe restrictions of the European nations, which have already impelled us to visit the distant regions of the eastern hemisphere, defeating the schemes of short-sighted politicans will prove, through the wisdom and goodness of Providence, the means of our POLITICAL SALVATION.

Alexander Hamilton's "Report on Manufactures," 1791

The expediency of encouraging manufactures in the United States, which was not long since deemed very questionable, appears at this time to be pretty generally admitted. The embarrassments, which have obstructed the progress of our external trade, have led to serious reflections on the necessity of enlarging the sphere of our domestic commerce: the restrictive regulations, which in foreign markets abridge the vent of the increasing surplus of our Agricultural produce, serve to beget an earnest desire, that a more extensive demand for that surplus may be created at home: And the complete success, which has rewarded manufacturing enterprise, in some valuable branches, conspiring with the promising symptoms, which attend some less mature essays, in others, justify a hope, that the obstacles to the growth of this species of industry are less formidable than they were apprehended to be, and that it is not difficult to find, in its further extension, a full indemnification for any external disadvantages, which are or may be experienced, as well as an accession of resources, favorable to national independence and safety. . . .

From Jacob E. Brooke, *The Reports of Alexander Hamilton* (New York: Harper & Row, 1964), pp. 115–116, 127–128, 136, 141–144, 146–147, 149–150, 159, 161–162, 165, 166–177, 202–205.

. . . [M]anufacturing establishments not only occasion a positive augmentation of the Produce and Revenue of the Society, but . . . they contribute essentially to rendering them greater than they could possibly be, without such establishments. These circumstances are—

1. The division of labour.
2. An extension of the use of Machinery.
3. Additional employment to classes of the community not ordinarily engaged in the business.
4. The promoting of emigration from foreign Countries.
5. The furnishing greater scope for the diversity of talents and dispositions which discriminate men from each other.
6. The affording a more ample and various field for enterprize.
7. The creating in some instances a new, and securing in all, a more certain and steady demand for the surplus produce of the soil.

Each of these circumstances has a considerable influence upon the total mass of industrious effort in a community. Together, they add to it a degree of energy and effect, which are not easily conceived. . . .

. . . [I]t is the interest of nations to diversify the industrious pursuits of the individuals who compose them—that the establishment of manufactures is calculated not only to increase the general stock of useful and productive labour; but even to improve the state of Agriculture in particular, certainly to advance the interests of those who are engaged in it. . . .

. . . [T]he greatest obstacle of all to the successful prosecution of a new branch of industry in a country, in which it was before unknown, consists, as far as the instances apply, in the bounties premiums and other aids which are granted, in a variety of cases, by the nations, in which the establishments to be imitated are previously introduced. It is well known . . . that certain nations grant bounties on the exportation of particular commodities, to enable their own workmen to undersell and supplant all competitors in the countries to which those commodities are sent. Hence the undertakers of a new manufacture have to contend not only with the natural disadvantages of a new undertaking, but with the gratuities and remunerations which other governments bestow. To be enabled to contend with success, it is evident that the interference and aid of their own governments are indispensable. . . .

The objections to the pursuit of manufactures in the United States . . . represent an impracticability of success, arising from three causes—scarcity of hands—dearness of labour—want of capital.

The two first circumstances, are to a certain extent real, and, within due limits, ought to be admitted as obstacles to the success of manufacturing enterprise in the United States. But there are various considerations, which lessen their force, and tend to afford an assurance that they are not sufficient to prevent the advantageous prosecution of many very useful and extensive manufactories.

With regard to scarcity of hands, . . . great use . . . can be made of women and children; on which point a very pregnant and instructive fact has been mentioned— the vast extension given by late improvements to the employment of Machines, which substituting the Agency of fire and water, had prodigiously lessened the necessity of manual labour . . .

As to the dearness of labour (another of the obstacles alleged) this has relation principally to two circumstances, one that which has been just discussed, or the scarcity of hands; the other, the greatness of profits.

As far as it is a consequence of the scarcity of hands, it is mitigated by all the considerations which have been adduced as lessening that deficiency.

. . . [I]t is also evident that the effect of the degree of disparity, which does truly exist, is diminished in proportion to the use which can be made of machinery. . . .

The supposed want of Capital for the prosecution of manufactures in the United States, is the most indefinite of the objections. . . .

The following considerations are of a nature to remove all inquietude on the score of the want of Capital.

The introduction of Banks, as has been shown on another occasion has a powerful tendency to extend the active Capital of a Country. Experience of the Utility of these Institutions is multiplying them in the United States. It is probable that they will be established wherever they can exist with advantage; and wherever they can be supported, if administered with prudence, they will add new energies to all pecuniary operations.

The aid of foreign Capital may safely, and, with considerable latitude, be taken into calculation. Its instrumentality has been long experienced in our external commerce; and it has begun to be felt in various other modes. Not only our funds, but our Agriculture, and other internal improvements, have been animated by it. It has already in a few instances extended even to our manufactures. . . .

But while there are Circumstances sufficiently strong to authorize a considerable degree of reliance on the aid of foreign Capital towards the attainment of the object in view, it is satisfactory to have good grounds of assurance, that there are domestic resources of themselves adequate to it. It happens, that there is a species of Capital, actually existing within the United States, which relieves from all inquietude on the score of want of Capital. This is the funded Debt. . . .

Public Funds answer the purpose of Capital, from the estimation in which they are usually held by Monied men, and consequently from the Ease and dispatch with which they can be turned into money. This capacity for prompt convertibility into money causes a transfer of stock to be in a great number of Cases equivalent to a payment in coin. . . .

Hence in a sound and settled state of the public funds, a man possessed of a sum in them can embrace any scheme of business, which offers, with as much confidence as if he were possessed of an equal sum in Coin.

This operation of public funds as capital is too obvious to be denied. . . .

There seems to be a moral certainty, that the trade of a country which is both manufacturing and Agricultural will be more lucrative and prosperous than that of a Country, which is merely Agricultural. . . .

. . . [T]here is always a higher probability of a favorable balance of Trade, in regard to countries in which manufactures founded on the basis of a thriving Agriculture flourish, than in regard to those, which are confined wholly or almost wholly to Agriculture. . . .

Not only the wealth, but the independence and security of a Country, appear to be materially connected with the prosperity of manufactures. Every nation, with a view of those great objects, ought to endeavour to possess within itself all the essentials of national supply. These comprise the means of *Subsistence, habitation, clothing,* and *defence.*

The possession of these is necessary to the perfection of the body politic; to the safety as well as to the welfare of the society. . . . The extreme embarrassments of the United States during the late War, from an incapacity of supplying themselves, are still matters of keen recollection: A future war might be expected again to exemplify the mischiefs and dangers of a situation to which that incapacity is still in too great a degree applicable, unless changed by timely and vigorous exertion. . . .

If then, it satisfactorily appears, that it is the Interest of the United states, generally, to encourage manufactures, it merits particular attention, that there are circumstances which Render the present a critical moment for entering, with Zeal upon the important business. . . .

In order to [form] a better judgment of the Means proper to be resorted to by the United states [to encourage manufacturing], it will be of use to Advert to those which have been employed with success in other Countries. The principal of these are—

    I. Protecting duties—or duties on those foreign articles which are the rivals of the domestic ones intended to be encouraged . . .
    II. Prohibitions of rival articles, or duties equivalent to prohibitions . . .
    III. Prohibitions of the exportation of the materials of manufactures . . .
    IV. Pecuniary bounties . . .
    V. Premiums . . .
    VI. The exemption of the materials of manufactures from duty . . .
    VII. Drawbacks of the duties which are imposed on the materials of manufactures . . .
    VIII. The encouragement of new inventions and discoveries, at home, and of the introduction into the United states of such as may have been made in other countries; particularly those which related to machinery . . .
    IX. Judicious regulations for the inspection of manufactured commodities . . .
    X. The facilitating of pecuniary remittances from place to place . . .
    XI. The facilitating of the transportation of commodities. . . .

There is little room to hope, that the progress of manufactures, will so equally keep pace with the progress of population, as to prevent, even, a gradual augmentation of the product of the duties on imported articles.

. . . It is evident, at first glance, that they will not only be adequate to this, but will yield a considerable surplus.

This surplus will serve:

First. To constitute a fund for paying the bounties which shall have been decreed.

Secondly. To constitute a fund for the operations of a Board to be established for promoting Arts, Agriculture, Manufactures and Commerce. Of this institution, different intimations have been given, in the course of this report. An outline of a plan for it shall now be submitted.

Let a certain annual sum, be set apart, and placed under the management of Commissioners, not less than three, to consist of certain Officers of the Government and their Successors in Office.

Let these Commissioners be empowered to apply the fund confided to them to defray the expenses of the emigration of Artists and Manufacturers in particular branches of extraordinary importance—to induce the prosecution and introduction of useful discoveries, inventions, and improvements, by proportionate rewards, judiciously held out and applied—to encourage by premiums both honorable and lucrative the exertions of individuals, and of classes, in relation to the several objects they are charged with promoting—and to afford such other aids to those objects as may be generally designated by law. . . .

There is reason to believe that the progress of particular manufactures has been much retarded by the want of skilful workmen. And it often happens, that the capitals employed are not equal to the purposes of bringing from abroad workmen of a superior kind. Here, in cases worthy of it, the auxiliary agency of Government would, in all probability, be useful. There are also valuable workmen in every branch, who are prevented from emigrating solely by the want of means. Occassional aids to such persons properly administered might be a source of valuable acquisitions to the country. . . .

The great use which may be made of a fund of this nature, to procure and import foreign improvements is particularly obvious. Among these, the articles of machines would form a most important item.

The operation and utility of premiums have been adverted to; together with the advantages which have resulted from their dispensation, under the direction of certain public and private societies. Of this some experience has been had, in the instance of the Pennsylvania Society for Promotion of Manufactures and useful Arts; but the funds of that association have been too contracted to produce more than a very small portion of the good to which the principles of it would have led. It may confidently be affirmed that there is scarcely any thing which has been devised, better calculated to excite a general spirit of improvement than the institutions of this nature. They are truly invaluable.

In countries where there is great private wealth, much may be effected by the voluntary contributions of patriotic individuals; but in a community situated like that of the United States, the public purse must supply the deficiency of private resource. In what can it be so useful, as in prompting and improving the efforts of industry?

Thomas Jefferson, Manufacturer (Correspondence), 1795–1816

To M. de Meusnier

Monticello, Virginia, Apr. 29, '95.

In our private pursuits it is a great advantage that every honest employment is deemed honorable. I am myself a nail-maker. On returning home after an absence of ten years, I found my farms so much deranged that I saw evidently they would be a burden to me instead of a support till I could regenerate them; & consequently that it was necessary for me to find some other resource in the meantime. . . . I now employ a dozen little boys from 10. to 16, years of age, overlooking all the details of their business myself & drawing from it a profit on which I can get along till I can

From Michael B. Folsom and Steven B. Lubar, eds., *The Philosophy of Manufactures* (Cambridge, MA: MIT Press, 1992), pp. 24–30; and A. Whitney Griswold, *Jefferson's Agraian Democracy* (Lexington, MA: D. C. Heath, 1971), pp. 49–50.

put my farms into a course of yielding profit. My new trade of nail-making is to me in this country what an additional title of nobility or the ensigns of a new order are in Europe.

To Archibald Stuart

Monticello, Jan. 3, '96.

Dear Sir,

I troubled you once before on the subject of my nails, and must trouble you once more. . . . I set out with refusing to retail, expecting the merchants of my neighborhood and the upper country would have given a preference to my supplies, because delivered *here* at the *Richmond whole prices,* and at hand to be called for in small parcels, so that they need not to keep large sums invested in that article & lying dead on their hands. The importing merchants however decline taking them from a principle of suppressing every effort towards domestic manufacture, & the merchants who purchase here being much under the influence of the importers, take their nails from them with their other goods. I have determined therefore to establish deposits of my nails to be retailed at Milton, Charlottesville, Staunton, Wormester, & Warren. . . . It is tolerably certain that the moment my deposit opens there will be an entire stoppage to the sale of all imported nails, for a body can *retail* them in the upper country at the Richmond *wholesale* prices, advanced only 5 to 10 percent. and as I mean to employ only one person in each place to retail, it will be of some advantage to the merchant who will undertake it, to have the entire monopoly of the nail business, & so draw to his store every one who wants nails. . . .

To Mr. Lithson

Washington, January 4, 1805.

Dear Sir,

Your favor of December 4th has been duly received. Mr. Duane informed me that he meant to publish a new edition of the Notes on Virginia, and I had in contemplation some particular alterations which would require little time to make. My occupations by no means permit me at this time to revise the text, and make those changes in it which I should now do. I should in that case certainly qualify several expressions in the nineteenth chapter, which have been construed differently from what they were intended. I had under my eye, when writing, the manufacturers of the great cities in the old countries, at the time present, with whom the want of food and clothing necessary to sustain life, has begotten a depravity of morals, a dependence and corruption, which renders them an undesirable accession to a country whose morals are sound. My expressions looked forward to the time when our own great cities would get into the same state. But they have been quoted as if meant for the present time here. As yet our manufacturers are as much at their ease, as independent and moral as our agricultural inhabitants, and they will continue so as long as there are vacant lands for them to resort to; because whenever it shall be attempted by the other classes to reduce them to the minimum of subsistence, they will quit their trades and go to laboring the earth. A first question is, whether it is desirable for us to receive at present the dissolute and demoralized handicraftsmen of the old cities of Europe? A second and more difficult one is, when even good handicraftsmen arrive here, is it better for them to set up their trade, or go to the culture of the earth? Whether their labor in their trade is worth more than their labor on the soil, increased by the creative energies of the earth? Had I time to revise that chapter, this question should be discussed, and other views of the subject taken, which are presented by the wonderful changes which have taken place here since 1781, when the Notes on Virginia were written. Perhaps when I retire, I may amuse myself with a serious review of this work; at present it is out of the question. Accept my salutations and good wishes.

To Colonel David Humphreys

Washington, January 20, 1809.

Sir,

. . . Knowing most of my own State, I can affirm with confidence that were free intercourse opened again tomorrow, she would never again import one-half of the coarse goods which she has done down to the date of the edicts. These will be made in our families. For finer goods we must resort to the larger manufacturies established in the towns. Some jealousy of this spirit of manufacture seems excited among commerical men. It would have been as just when we first began to make our own ploughs and hoes. They have certainly lost the profit of bringing these from a foreign country. My idea is that we should encourage home manufactures to the extent of our own consumption of everything of which we raise the raw material. I do not think it fair in the ship-owners to say we ought not to make our own axes, nails, etc., here, that they may have the benefit of carrying the iron to Europe, and bringing back the axes, nails, etc. Our agriculture will still afford surplus produce enough to employ a due proportion of navigation. Wishing every possible success to your undertaking, as well for your personal as the public benefit, I salute you with assurance of great esteem and respect.

To John Adams

Monticello, January 21, 1812.

Dear Sir,

I thank you before hand (for they are not yet arrived) for the specimens of homespun you have been so kind as to forward me by post. I doubt not their excellence, knowing how far you are advanced in these things in your quarter. Here we do little in the fine way, but in coarse and middling goods a great deal. Every family in the country is a manufactory within itself, and is very generally able to make within itself all the stouter and middling stuffs for its own clothing and household use. We consider a sheep for every person in the family as sufficient to clothe it, in addition to the cotton, hemp and flax which we raise ourselves. For fine stuff we shall depend on your northern manufactories. Of these, that is to say, of company establishments, we have none. We use little machinery. The spinning jenny, and loom with the flying shuttle, can be managed in a family; but nothing more complicated. The economy and thriftiness resulting from our household manufactures are such that they will never again be laid aside; and nothing more salutary for us has ever happened than the British obstructions to our demands for their manufactures. Restore free intercourse when they will, their commerce with us will have totally changed its form, and the articles we shall in future want from them will not exceed their own consumption of our produce.

To Thaddeus Kosciusko

June 28, 1812.

Our manufacturers are now nearly on a footing with those of England. She has not a single improvement which we do not possess, and many of them better adapted by ourselves to our ordinary use. We have reduced the large and expensive machinery for most things to the compass of a private family, and every family of any size is now getting machines on a small scale for their household purposes. Quoting myself as an example, and I am much behind many others in this business, my household manufactures are just getting into operation on the scale of a carding machine costing $60 only, which may be worked by a girl to twelve years old, a spinning machine, which may be made for $10, carrying 6 spindles for wool, to be worked by a girl also, another which can be made for $25, carrying 12 spindles for cotton, and a loom, with a flying shuttle, weaving its twenty yards a day. I need 2,000 yards of linen, cotton and woolen yearly, to clothe my family, which this machinery, costing $150 only, and worked by two women and two girls, will more than furnish. For fine goods there are numerous establishments at work in the large cities, and many more daily growing up; and of merinos we have some thousands. . . . [N]othing is more certain than that, come peace when it will, we shall never again go to England for a shilling where we have gone for a dollar's worth. Instead of applying to her manufacturers there, they must starve or come here to be employed. . . .

To James Ronaldson

Monticello, January 12, 1813.

Household manufacture is taking deep root with us. I have a carding machine, two spinning machines, and looms with the flying shuttle in full operation for clothing my own family; and I verily believe that by the next winter this State will not need a yard of imported coarse or middling clothing. I think we have already a sheep for every inhabitant, which will suffice for clothing, and one-third more, which a single year will add, will furnish blanketing.

To John Melish

Monticello, January 13, 1813.

I had no conception that manufacturers had made such progress [in the Western states] and particularly of the number of carding and spinning machines dispersed through the whole country. We are but beginning here to have them in our private families. Small spinning jennies of from half a dozen to twenty spindles, will soon, however, make their way into the humblest cottages, as well as the richest houses; and nothing is more certain, than that the coarse and middling clothing for our families, will forever hereafter continue to be made within ourselves. I have hitherto myself depended entirely on foreign manufactures; but I have now thirty-five spindles agoing, a hand carding machine, and looms with the flying shuttle, for the supply of my own farms, which will never be relinquished in my time. The continuance of the war will fix the habit generally, and out of the evils of impressment and of the orders of council a great blessing for us will grow. I have not formerly been an advocate for great manufactories. I doubted whether our labor, employed in agriculture, and aided by the spontaneous energies of the earth, would not procure us more than we could make ourselves of other necessaries. But other considerations entering into the question, have settled my doubts.

To Benjamin Austin

January 9, 1816.

You tell me I am quoted by those who wish to continue our dependence on England for manufactures. There was a time when I might have been so quoted with more candor, but within the thirty years which have since elapsed, how are circumstances changed! We were then in peace. Our independent place among the nations was acknowledged. A commerce which offered the raw material in exchange for the same material after receiving the last touch of industry, was worthy of welcome to all nations. It was expected that those especially to whom manufacturing industry was important, would cherish the friendship of such customers by every favor, by every inducement, and particularly cultivate their peace by every act of justice and friendship. Under this prospect the question seemed legitimate, whether, with such an immensity of unimproved land, courting the hand of husbandry, the industry of agriculture, or that of manufactures, would add most to the national wealth? And the doubt was entertained on this consideration chiefly, that to the labor of the husbandman a vast addition is made by the spontaneous energies of the earth on which it is employed: for one grain of wheat committed to the earth, she renders twenty, thirty, and even fifty fold, whereas to the labor of the manufacturer nothing is added. Pounds of flax, in his hands, yield, on the contrary, but pennyweights of lace. This exchange, too, laborious as it might seem, what a field did it promise for the occupations of the ocean; what a nursery for that class of citizens who were to exercise and maintain our equal rights on that element? This was the state of things in 1785, when the "Notes on Virginia" were first printed; when, the ocean being open to all nations, and their common right in it acknowledged and exercised under regulations sanctioned by the assent and usage of all, it was thought that the doubt might claim some consideration. But who in 1785 could foresee the rapid depravity which was to render the close of that century the disgrace of the history of man? Who could have imagined that the two most distinguished in the rank of nations, for science and civilization, would have suddenly descended from that honorable eminence, and setting at defiance all those moral laws established by the Author of nature between nation and nation, as between man and man, would cover earth and sea with robberies and piracies, merely because strong enough to do it with temporal impunity; and that under this disbandment of nations from social order, we should have been despoiled of a thousand ships, and have thousands of our citizens reduced to Algerine slavery. Yet all this has taken place. . . . Compare this state of things with that of '85, and say whether an opinion founded in the circumstances of that day can be fairly applied to those of the present. We have experienced what we did not then believe, that there exists both profligacy and power enough to exclude us from the field of interchange with other nations: that to be independent for the comforts of life we must fabricate them ourselves. We must now place the manufacturer by the side of the agriculturist. The former question is suppressed, or rather assumes a new form. Shall we make our own comforts, or go without them, at the will of a foreign nation? He, therefore, who is now against domestic manufacture, must be for reducing us either to dependence on that foreign nation, or to be clothed in skins, and to live like wild beasts in dens and caverns. I am not one of these; experience has taught me that manufactures are now as necessary to our independence as to our comfort. . . .

Thomas Cooper Against Factories, 1823

To take advantage of machinery.—If capital, employed in commerce, bring 15 per cent. and capital, employed in machinery, bring 15 per cent. there is nothing gained by converting the one into the other.

Oh, but a cotton mill will perform the work of a thousand hands—Will it so? What then, if it brings me no higher than common profit? But it will bring much greater profit—Will it so? Then so many people will have cotton mills, that in a year or two, the profit will decrease to the common level, and I shall be no gainer.

The machinery of England, is, in many instances, a dreadful curse to that country; and the British manufacturing system would be so to this. The works usually go night and day, one set of boys and girls go to bed, as another set get up to work. The health, the manners, the morals, are all corrupted. They work not for themselves, but for the capitalist who employs them: they are employed on the calculation of how small a sum will subsist a human creature: they are machines, as much so as the spindles they superintend: hence they are not calculated to turn readily, from one occupation to another: they are the most discontented, the most ignorant, the most turbulent of the British population. The whole system tends to increase the wealth of a few capitalists, at the expense of the health, life, morals, and happiness of the wretches who labour for them. I would rather see treatises on the sources of national happiness, than national wealth. We want in this happy country, no increase of proud and wealthy capitalists, whose fortunes have accumulated by such means. It is not the careful, skilful superintendant of his own business, living frugally, but plentifully on reasonable profits, who expresses discontent at the present state of things—no, it is the would-be great man, anxious to acquire wealth speedily, by means of an extorted monopoly, who is most forward in petitioning, for an increase of prohibitory duties. Neither the prophecies, the promises, or the statements of these men, are to be trusted. They may pledge themselves to any thing, for they know they cannot be called on to redeem it. They calculate the imposition will last their time. Well meaning and good men, have been over persuaded by the bold assertions of those who are intrusted; and we stand now actually on the very brink of the precipice to which they have urged us. It is impossible to shut our eyes to the wonderful superiority in permanence of capital invested in agriculture, over capital invested in machinery.

From Michael B. Folsom and Steven B. Lubar, eds., *The Philosophy of Manufactures* (Cambridge, MA: MIT Press, 1982), pp. 255–257.

⚰ E S S A Y S

If Jefferson condoned but never fully embraced the factory system, Tench Coxe clearly did. The first selection, from Leo Marx's *The Machine in the Garden,* discusses Coxe's pivotal role in shaping public opinion about the benefits of factory manufacturing. While Jefferson worried that the factory system would erode moral virtue, as he believed it had in England, Coxe maintained that the special qualities of the American environment would cleanse the factory and make it a place where the poor—especially widows and children—could earn a living, and at the same time learn "correct habits" of industry, honesty, and thrift. Since "virtue" was thought to be essential to the survival of the republic, Coxe's argument appealed to policymaking elites. What might the practical benefits of factory labor have been to the merchants whom Coxe spoke for? Coxe had an uncanny ability to muster empirical evidence in favor of his argument and, most important of all, to cast it "in the idiom of the dominant [agrarian] ideology."*

Alexander Hamilton is often depicted as the architect of America's industrial revo-lution. Yet the second selection, from John R. Nelson's *Liberty and Property,* claims that Hamilton's role as a policymaker has not only been overstated but completely misunderstood. Arguing contrary to traditional scholarship, Nelson holds that "Hamilton was not an advocate of American manufacturing." What mattered most to him were fiscal affairs, particularly stabilizing the nation's credit and paying off the national debt. Manufacturing assumed a secondary status in Hamilton's list of priorities because he needed the support of wealthy merchants and bankers to carry out his fiscal program. He consequently devised government policies that favored mercantile interests over those of manufacturers, a case in point being his opposition to protective tariffs. Nelson argues that the first real support for manufacturing came not from Hamilton's Federalist party but from Thomas Jefferson's Republicans, particularly Jefferson's close associates, James Madison and Secretary of the Treasury Albert Gallatin.

What role did government policy play in the development of manufacturing in the nineteenth-century America? Can any one party or policy be given credit for inaugurating the industrial revolution in America? What energized the process of industrialization? Were there viable alternatives?

The Machine

LEO MARX

It did not occur to Jefferson that the factory system was a necessary feature of tech-nological progress. In 1786, the year after the first printing of *Notes on Virginia,* with its plea that America let its workshops remain in Europe, Jefferson was in England. This was a moment, as [Matthew] Boulton put it in a letter to his collaborator, James Watt, when the population seemed to have gone "steam-mill mad." At Blackfriar's Bridge, near London, there was a new mill powered by Boulton and Watt engines which was generally considered one of the mechanical wonders of the age, and Jefferson went to see it. He was delighted. "I could write you volumes," he said in a letter to Charles Thomson afterward, "on the improvements . . . made and making here in the arts." Of course Jefferson's passion for utilitarian improvement, gadgets,

---

*Leo Marx, *The Machine in the Garden* (London: Oxford University Press, 1964), p. 151.

From Leo Marx, *The Machine in the Garden* (London: Oxford University Press, 1964), pp. 149–169.

and labor-saving devices of all kinds is familiar to anyone who has read his letters or visited Monticello. But in England at this time the new technology was visibly related to the new factory system, and one therefore might have expected to hear Jefferson sound another, less enthusiastic, note. But not so. He singles out the steam mill as deserving of particular notice because, he says, it is "simple, great, and likely to have extensive consequences." And he is not thinking about consequences only in England.

> I hear you are applying this same agent in America to navigate boats, and I have little doubt but that it will be applied generally to machines, so as to supercede the use of water ponds, and of course to lay open all the streams for navigation. We know that steam is one of the most powerful engines we can employ; and in America fuel is abundant.

Today Jefferson's attitude is bound to seem curious. Why, we cannot help asking, does he fail to connect the new machinery with Soho [Bolton and Watt's Works] and the transformation of England into a vast workshop? Why does he want the latest, most powerful machines imported to America if he would have factories and cities kept in Europe?

Part of the answer is that Jefferson's attitude reflects American economic realities. At the time industrialization scarcely had begun in America. Native manufactures were primitive. The war had stimulated production, to be sure, but chiefly in the form of household industry. In America there was nothing comparable to Soho, nor would there be for a long time. True, ritual gestures toward the "promotion" of manufactures often had been made, notably by Benjamin Franklin, but even he assumed that industry, as compared with agriculture, would be of trivial significance. All reliable opinion supported this view. In *The Wealth of Nations (1776)*, the work of political economy to which the age deferred beyond all others, Adam Smith had warned Americans that it would be folly to direct capital into manufactures. Everyone repeated his sensible argument. During the war, especially, the British delighted in reminding their difficult cousins that, even if they won political independence, they could count upon protracted economic subservience. Edmund Burke popularized this idea, and the Earl of Sheffield summarized it with an incontrovertible body of facts and figures in his *Observations on the Commerce of the United States (1783)*. An advocate of a tough policy toward America, Sheffield demonstrated the Republic's helplessness. No matter how oppressive a policy the British followed, he said, there was no danger of provoking serious competition from America. The book was widely read, going through six editions by 1791, and it helped to establish the idea that America's economic development would be unusual, if not unique. Not that many people were disposed to quarrel with Sheffield. Most American statesmen accepted his seemingly flawless case. "I say," John Adams had written to Franklin in 1780, "that America will not make manufactures enough for her own consumption these thousand years."

Under the circumstances, there was nothing farfetched about the prophecy. What made it plausible was not so much the absence of factories and machines, it was the geo-political situation of the country. One has only to recall how small an area had been occupied by 1786; most of the continent was unsettled and, for that matter, unexplored; nine out of ten Americans lived on farms; land was cheap, if not free, and capital was scarce. To be sure, political independence had removed Parliament's legal prohibitions against colonial manufactures, but it is doubtful whether they had made much difference. Geography had been more effective than any laws could have been in blocking manufactures, and it still seemed to present overwhelming obstacles. The most formidable was simply the presence of the land itself—that "immensity of land courting the industry of the husbandman" which encouraged Jefferson in the hope that (the war being over) his countrymen would gladly revert to their former dependence on England. The availability of land worked against manufactures in two ways: it provided an inducement to agriculture, and it dispersed the people over an area too large to be a satisfactory market for manufactures. It is not enough, therefore, to think of the landscape at this time merely as an emblem of agrarian sentiments; it is a perpetual reminder of American differences, a visual token of circumstances which guarantee that the nation's workshops will remain in Europe. But workshops, to Jefferson, are one thing and machines another. It is no accident that his enthusiasm is aroused by a mechanized grist mill—a piece of machinery peculiarly suited to a rural society.

Quite apart from the state of the American economy, however, there are compelling reasons for Jefferson's failure to see the new machines as a threat to his rural ideal. For one thing, the very notion of "technology" as an agent of change scarcely existed. (It was not until 1829 that Jacob Bigelow, a Harvard professor, coined the word itself.) Although many features of what we now call industrialism already were visible, neither the word nor the concept of a totally new way of life was available. Today our view of history is so deeply colored by an appreciation, if not awe, of technology as an agent of change that it is not easy to imagine Jefferson's state of mind as he inspects the powerful engines at Blackfriar's Bridge. Curiously enough, his very devotion to the principles of the Enlightenment obscures his perception of causal relations we now take for granted. Assuming that knowledge inescapably is power for good, he cannot imagine that a genuine advance in science or the arts, such as the new steam engine, could entail consequences as deplorable as factory cities.

From Jefferson's perspective, the machine is a token of that liberation of the human spirit to be realized by the young American Republic; the factory system, on the other hand, is but feudal oppression in a slightly modified form. Once the machine is removed from the dark, crowded, grimy cities of Europe, he assumes that it will blend harmoniously into the open countryside of his native land. He envisages it turning millwheels, moving ships up rivers, and, all in all, helping to transform a wilderness into a society of the middle landscape. At bottom it is the intensity of his belief in the land, as a locus of both economic and moral value, which prevents him from seeing what the machine portends for America. . . .

By this time, however, there were some Americans—not many—whose predilections enabled them to foresee what Jefferson could not. The most astute was Tench Coxe, an ambitious, young Philadelphia merchant who was disturbed by the unhappy state into which American affairs had fallen by the end of the Revolutionary War. Although only thirty-one, Coxe already had made a name for himself as a capable spokesman for the nascent manufacturing interest. Later he was to be Alexander Hamilton's assistant in the Treasury, where he would play an important part in drawing up the *Report on Manufactures* of 1791. . . .

In September 1786, just a few months after Jefferson's visit to the mill at Blackfriar's Bridge, Coxe attended the Annapolis meeting on commercial regulations which in turn led to the calling of the Constitutional Convention of 1787. By the following summer his anxiety about the deterioration of the economy of the young Republic had deepened. He was convinced that nothing less than the "salvation of the country" rested upon the delegates who were assembling to write, as it turned out, the Constitution of the United States. Although not a delegate himself, Coxe made his ideas known to the Convention. On May 11, three days before the scheduled meeting, he addressed the Society for Political Enquiries at the home of Benjamin Franklin. Some fifty leading citizens belonged to the organization, which met every two weeks to discuss topics of general interest. Later Coxe saw to it that his speech (*An Enquiry into the principles, on which a commercial system for the United States of America should be founded . . .* [and] *some political observations connected with the subject)* was published and "inscribed to the members of the convention." Then again, on August 9th, while the Convention still was in session, he elaborated upon his theme. At the request of Dr. Benjamin Rush, the president, he gave the inaugural address at the organizing meeting of the Pennsylvania Society for the Encouragement of Manufactures and the Useful Arts. Taken together, these two speeches outline the case for industrialization as a means of realizing the ideal of the middle landscape.

Like most of the official delegates to the Convention, Coxe argues for a stronger, more centralized government with power to enforce uniform economic policies. On the political side, accordingly, he expounds the standard doctrine of the capitalist and nationalist groups. But Coxe is more interested than most in long-range economic goals. Convinced that political independence ultimately will require greater economic self-sufficiency, he insists upon the need for a "balanced economy" and thus, above all, for native manufactures. Without them the young nation's prosperity and its security always will be precarious. At the outset, then, he runs head on into the whole body of respectable economic theory that denies the feasibility of American manufactures. His problem, he admits, is to "disencumber" the case for manufactures of the usual objections: *"the high rate of labour, . . . the want of a sufficient number of hands . . . ,—the scarcity and dearness of raw materials—want of skill* in the business itself and *its unfavorable effects on the health of the people."* Impressive as they are, all of these objections may be disposed of, according to Coxe, by one new fact under the sun. It is so new that he does not even have a name for it, but he is certain that it will make all the difference, and so he says:

> Factories which can be carried on by water-mills, wind-mills, fire, horses and machines ingeniously contrived are not burdened with any heavy expense of boarding, lodging, clothing and paying workmen, and they supply the force of hands to a great extent without taking our people from agriculture. By wind and water machines we can make pig and bar iron, nail rods, tire, sheet-iron, sheet-copper, sheet-brass, anchors, meal of all kinds, gun-powder . . .

And so on. Describing the incredible productive power of machines and factories, Coxe becomes excited; a note of wonder and prophecy gets into his sober discourse:

> Strange as it may appear they also card, spin and even weave, it is said, by water in the European factories.

> Steam mills have not yet been adopted in America, but we shall probably see them after a short time. . . .

Machines ingeniously constructed, will give us immense assistance.—The cotton and silk manufacturers in Europe are possessed of some, that are invaluable to them. Several instances have been ascertained, in which a few hundreds of women and children perform the work of thousands of carders, spinners and winders.

The cumulative effect of all this is to undermine most prevailing expectations about the future American economy. Once the new technology is brought into the picture, Coxe is saying, the prospect changes completely. Indeed—and this is the crux no one else seems to have recognized —the very factors usually cited as inhibiting to the nation's growth, such as the scarcity of labor, then will become stimulants. Paradoxically, the extraordinary abundance of land in America is what lends a unique significance to the machine. Coxe knows that the practical, conservative men in his audience will suspect him of being a "visionary enthusiast," but he cannot restrain himself. So inspired is he by the changes to be wrought by machines that he is not satisfied merely to reject the idea of the young Republic's subservience to Europe:

> . . . combinations of machines with fire and water have already accomplished much more than was formerly expected from them by the most visionary enthusiast on the subject. Perhaps I may be too sanguine, but they appear to me fraught with immense advantages to us, and not a little dangerous to the manufacturing nations of Europe; for should they continue to save and improve them, as they have heretofore done, their people may be driven to us for want of employment, and if, on the other hand, they should return to manual labour, we may underwork them by these invaluable engines.

To appreciate Coxe's prescience it is necessary to recall how conjectural these ideas were in the summer of 1787. Although machine production was becoming an accepted fact of life in England, it was little more than an idea in America. But this is not to suggest that Coxe was the only American drawn to the possibility. In the small but influential group of "friends of American manufactures" who made up the new Philadelphia society there were a number of men who had expressed one or the other of Coxe's thoughts on the subject. In 1787, moreover, Matthew Carey had founded a new journal, *The American Museum,* which took the same general line. Besides, it is misleading to stress the backwardness of native manufactures. Beneath the surface of economic life the colonies had accumulated a rich fund of technical knowledge and skill, soon to be revealed in the achievements of inventors like Evans, Fitch, Whitney, and Fulton. When all of these allowances have been made, however, the fact remains that it was Coxe who first gathered these scattered impulses and ideas into a prophetic vision of machine technology as the fulcrum of national power.

But for Coxe the machine is the instrument and not in itself the true source of America's future power. If anything, he exaggerates its European identity, and he frankly advocates certain devious methods of wresting the secrets of technological power from the Old World. At the time the British were attempting, by strict regulations, to prevent any plans or new engines of production or skilled machines from leaving the country. As countermeasures, Coxe and his colleagues advertised for technicians; they offered special bonuses to those who would emigrate—a policy notably successful in the well-known case of Samuel Slater; they also attempted to smuggle machines packed in false crates out of England, and the British foreign service was alerted to intercept these illicit cargoes; for a time, in fact, the Americans and the British played an elaborate game of technological espionage and counterespionage.

Although Coxe led the campaign to import the new methods, he was intelligent enough not to conceive of American power as emerging from technology *per se,* but rather from the peculiar affinities between the machine and the New World setting in its entirety: geographical, political, social, and, in our sense of the word, cultural.

In his 1787 speeches Coxe displays a striking sensitivity to the prevalence of rural pieties. He tactfully defers to agriculture as the "great leading interest" and repeatedly insists upon the subordinate rôle of manufactures. By employing workers unsuited to farming and thereby helping to develop a home market, he argues, the factory system will benefit agriculture. He anticipates all of the stock protectionist arguments of the next century. Farmers and planters, he says, are the "bulwark of the nation," and their pre-eminence will grow with the "settlement of our waste lands." In his references to the wilderness, incidentally, there is not a trace of primitivism or literary sentimentality. Unimproved land, he says, is "vacant"—a "waste." When discussing the middle landscape, moreover, he adopts the familiar pastoral attitudes. Of course, he says, "rural life promotes health and morality by its active nature, and by keeping our people from the luxuries and vices of the towns." To allay the fears of Jeffersonians, he relies chiefly upon the "safety valve" argument. After all, "the states are possessed of millions of vacant acres . . . that court the cultivator's hand," so how can anyone question the "great superiority of agriculture over all the rest [of the economic interests] combined'? It is impossible to tell how much of this is the calculated strategy of a "gladiator of the quill"—as William Maclay referred to Coxe—and how much he really believed.

At any rate, instead of denying that the economic supremacy of agriculture ultimately inheres in the close relation between farmers and the soil (as Hamilton is tempted to do in the *Report on Manufactures* four years later), Coxe ingeniously contrives an equivalent argument for manufacturing. Building factories, he claims, is necessary to fulfill imperatives embedded in the terrain. "Unless business of this kind is carried on," he says, "certain great *natural powers* of the country will remain inactive and useless. Our numerous mill seats . . . would be given by Providence in vain." (Throughout Coxe is at pains to break down the association of manufactures with the "artificial" as against the alleged "naturalness" of a rural life.) Describing the policy to be inferred from the presence of numerous mill seats, he continues:

> If properly improved, they will save us an immense expence for the wages, provisions, cloathing and lodging of workmen, without diverting the people from their farms—Fire, as well as water, affords . . . a fund of assistance, that cannot lie unused without an evident neglect of our best interests. Breweries, . . . distilleries, . . . casting and steel furnaces . . . are carried on by this powerful element. . . . 'Tis probable also that a frequent use of steam engines will add greatly to this class of factories.

Nowhere is Coxe's genius as a propagandist more evident than in the way he depicts the aims of American society as emanating from geography. He presents his program of economic development as part of a grand topographical design. Not only the abundance of resources but the breadth of the ocean supports his case for developing native manufactures. In fact, America is better suited to the purpose than Europe. With the aplomb of a public relations expert, he turns the standard symbols of the pastoral myth to his own uses. The "clear air and powerful sun of America" will give producers of linens and cottons a distinct advantage over their overseas competitors when it comes to bleaching because, he says, the "European process by drugs and machines impairs the strength." (Although this apparent slur on machines may seem inconsistent, it fits the Coxean formula—the notion that machines merely bring out powers latent in the environment. Thus textile production is more "naturally" suited to America than to Europe.) As for the alleged immorality and ill-health of factory workers, Americans need not be concerned about that. He says that the objection to manufactures as "unfavourable to the health" is urged principally against the production of textiles which *"formerly* were entirely manual and sedentary occupations." The use of machine power erases that old objection.

At this point Coxe anticipates what was to become a central theme in the ideology of American industrialism: the capacity of the New World environment to "purify" the system. Just as the American sun is a more potent bleaching agent, so the entire social climate of the new Republic will cleanse the factory system of its unfortunate feudal residues. Later this idea also would ease Jefferson's mind: in 1805, recalling his diatribe against manufactures in Query XIX, [see the excerpt from *"Notes on Virginia"* on page 105], he explains to a correspondent that in the 1780's he had been thinking about workers "of the great cities in the old countries . . . with whom the want of food and clothing . . . [had] begotten a depravity of morals, a dependence and corruption" he had no wish to see repeated in America. But now, he observes, American "manufacturers are as much at their ease, as independent and moral as our agricultural inhabitants, and they will continue so as long as there are vacant lands for them to resort to. . . ." Later variants of this refrain would be heard from European visitors, many of whom would develop the contrast between the pure, apple-cheeked farm girls in American mills (the "nuns of Lowell" in Chevalier's resonant phrase) and their pathetic European counterparts. Ironically, the sentiment rests at bottom upon the idea that the factory system, when transferred to America, is redeemed by contact with "nature" and the rural way of life it is destined to supplant.

But to return to Tench Coxe in 1787. In addition to his foresight and the subtlety with which he adapts his program to rural values, what is most impressive about his thought is his responsiveness to the topographical and, indeed, "mythic" quality of the dominant ethos. He fully appreciates the function of the landscape as a master image embodying American hopes. At a decisive point in his first speech, accordingly, he offers by way of summary "to draw a picture of our country, as it would really exist under the operation of a system of national laws formed upon these principles." What follows is a geo-political landscape painting:

> In *the foreground* we should find the mass of our citizens—the cultivators (and what is happily for us in most instances the same thing) the independent proprietors of the soil. Every wheel would appear in motion that could carry forward the interests of this great body of our people, and bring into action the inherent powers of the country. . . . *On one side* we should see our manufactures encouraging the tillers of the earth. . . . Commerce, *on the other hand* . . . would come forward with offers to range through foreign climates in search of . . . supplies . . . which nature has not given us at home. . . .

Coxe has no difficulty blending factories and machines into the rural scene. Combining the best of art with the best of nature, the picture matches the pastoral ideal of the middle landscape.

As a frame for his whole program, Coxe begins his second speech of 1787 by invoking the American moral geography:

> Providence has bestowed upon the United States of America means of happiness, as great and numerous, as are enjoyed by any country in the world. A soil fruitful and diversified—a healthful climate—mighty rivers and adjacent seas abounding with fish are the great advantages for which we are indebted to a beneficent creator. Agriculture, manufactures and commerce, naturally arising from these sources, afford to our industrious citizens certain subsistence and innumerable opportunities of acquiring wealth.

In arguing for the development of machine power, Coxe depicts it as "naturally arising," like agriculture, from the divine purpose invested in the New World landscape. To Matthew Boulton steam engines represented simple, stark power, but Coxe understands that it is wise to represent the machine to Americans as another natural "means of happiness" decreed by the Creator in his design of the continent. So far from conceding that there might be anything alien or "artificial" about mechanization, he insists that it is inherent in "nature," both geographic and human. On the "subject of mechanism," he says, "America may justly pride herself. Every combination of machinery may be expected from a country, A NATIVE SON of which, reaching this inestimable object at its highest point, has epitomized the motions of the spheres, that roll throughout the universe."

With this deft allusion to David Rittenhouse and his orrery, Coxe brings his celebration of the machine in its New World setting to a climax. By reminding his audience of the famous orrery, a miniature planetarium which had won the Pennsylvania scientist international fame, he enlists the immense prestige of Newtonian mechanics in support of his economic program. The orrery is an ingenious replica of the universe: when the clockwork machinery turns, the heavenly bodies revolve in their orbits, music plays, and dials move indicating the hour, the day of the month, and the year. Here, Coxe implies, is a visual and auditory display of the same harmonious plan which has provided America with endless resources for manufactures. If a colonial farmer's son can "epitomize" the ultimate laws of nature—the very music of the spheres—then imagine what Americans will accomplish when they apply the same principles to their entire national enterprise!* At this point the impressive, Miltonic reach and grandeur of Coxe's rhetoric imparts a metaphysical sanction to his vision of American economic development. As he describes the situation in 1787, the momentous achievements of science, the political movement to establish the new American Republic and the forthcoming use of machine power in production all belong to the same encouraging flow of history. They are all signs of a progressive unfolding of the structural principles of the universe—the laws of "mechanism."

There are few words whose shifting connotations register the revolution in thought and feeling we call the "romantic movement" more clearly than "mechanism." Once the influence of Wordsworth, Coleridge, and Carlyle had been felt in America, no writer (whether sympathetic with them or not) would find it possible to use "mechanism" in the unself-conscious, honorific sense in which Coxe uses it. His entire argument for what we would call industrialization rests on the assumption that celestial mechanics, the orrery, the new engines of production, even the factory system—all embody the same ultimate laws of nature. What is more, and this is perhaps the

---

*As if sharing Coxe's sentiments, incidentally, the new Society for the Encouragement of Manufactures and the Useful Arts proceeded to elect Rittenhouse to its vice-presidency.

most difficult attitude to grasp in retrospect, it is the same "mechanism" to which we respond, aesthetically, in the presence of the natural landscape. The identification of visual nature with the celestial "machine" is difficult to grasp because of our own feeling, learned from the romantics, that "organic" nature is the opposite of things "mechanical." But it is impossible to appreciate the dominant American attitude toward technology if we project this sense of contradiction too far back into the past. . . .

The speeches of Tench Coxe in the summer of 1787 prefigure the emergence of the machine as an American cultural symbol, that is, a token of meaning and value recognized by a large part of the population. By 1851, when Walt Whitman tells the Brooklyn Art Union that the United States had become a nation "of whom the steam engine is no bad symbol," he assumes that his audience knows what he is talking about. Needless to say, a collective image of this kind gathers meanings gradually, over a long period, and it is impossible to fix upon any single moment when it comes into being. Besides, it invariably combines a traditional meaning and a new, specific, local or topical reference. The garden image brings together a universal Edenic myth and a particular set of American goals and aspirations. So with the machine. What is most fascinating about the speeches of Tench Coxe is that in them we witness the virtual discovery of the symbolic properties of the machine image—its capacity to embrace a whole spectrum of meanings ranging from a specific class of objects at one end to an abstract metaphor of value at the other.

To Coxe the new and most exciting implication of "machine" is technological. In the summer of 1787 the possibilities of the latest technological innovations were just beginning to take hold of the American imagination. While the Constitutional Convention was in session, as it happens, "Mad" John Fitch managed, after inconceivable trials and tribulations, to propel a steam-powered vessel against the current of the Delaware River. When some of the delegates went down to the waterfront to inspect this remarkable invention, what they saw was another instance of, in Coxe's language, the power of mechanism. The existence of this kind of machine leads him to an optimistic view of the Republic's future, and there can be no doubt that in his mind the development of steam power and the business of the Constitutional Convention are aspects of the same grand enterprise. They both represent a release of power through seizure of the underlying principles of nature. The universe is a "mechanism." At the abstract end of the spectrum, then, the symbol of the machine incorporates a whole metaphysical system. It often has been noted that the dominant structural metaphor of the Constitution is that of a self-regulating machine, like the orrery or the steam engine; it establishes a system of "checks and balances" among three distinct, yet delicately synchronized, branches of government.

Between the two extremes, the machine as concrete object and the machine as root metaphor of being, Coxe identifies the power of "mechanism" with a specific economic faction. He is an avowed spokesman for the manufacturing interest. He and his associates in the Pennsylvania delegation are chiefly concerned about the kind of power to be generated by the national government's authority to enforce uniform economic laws, protect patents, and establish tariffs. Running through much of what they had to say is an inchoate sense of the vast transformation of life to be accomplished through what we should call economic development or industrialization. "The time is not distant," said Gouverneur Morris at one point in the debates, "when this Country will abound with mechanics & manufacturers who will receive their bread from their employers." But this is a rare example; the vocabulary at the command of Coxe, Morris, and their friends was inadequate to express their full sense of the power to be released through the combined agencies of commerce, science, technology, and republican institutions. To speak of it as "manufacturing" power hardly sufficed, particularly in view of the fact that the word still carried much of its pre-industrial meaning, as in handicraft or household manufactures. Their vision had got ahead of their language.

Still, we can be sure about the widespread identification of the manufacturing interest, and the new Republic, and the new technology. On July 4, 1788, after the Constitution had been approved by the electorate, there were parades and pageants in many cities, and several featured displays of recent industrial progress. In Philadelphia, the new "manufacturing society" entered a float in the grand Federal Procession. It was thirty feet long and thirteen feet wide, and drawn by ten large bay horses. On board eleven men and women demonstrated the operation of the latest machinery used in textile manufacture—a spinning jenny, a carding machine, and a loom. A new American flag flew above the float, and to it was attached the motto: "May the Union Government Protect the Manufacturers of America." One hundred weavers marched behind the float carrying a banner inscribed, "May Government Protect us." Half a century later, when industrialization was well under way, the notion that 1789 marked the beginning of the process became something of a commonplace. The chief evil of the colonial situation, said Edward Everett in 1831, had been the "restraint" upon "the labor of the country," and "the first thought and effort of our fathers . . . [was to] encourage and protect the mechanical arts and manufactures. . . ."

Among other things, Everett had in mind the *Report on the Subject of Manufactures* which Alexander Hamilton, assisted by Tench Coxe, prepared for the Congress in 1791. This deservedly famous state paper reflects the unmistakable shift in attitudes toward manufactures that coincided with the formation of the new government. Only four years had passed since Coxe had expounded his ideas in Philadelphia, but Hamilton assumed that they had been widely accepted. "The expediency of encouraging manufactures in the United States," he says in the first sentence, "which was not long since deemed very questionable, appears at this time to be pretty generally admitted."

In many ways the *Report* goes far beyond Coxe's speeches; it is composed with a systematic rigor and comprehensiveness that makes his thought seem crude and impressionistic. But there is one respect in which Coxe's argument had been more subtle: it took into account, as the *Report* does not, the hold of the pastoral ideal upon the national consciousness. Although Hamilton begins with a routine effort to placate the agricultural interest, he is an undisguised advocate of continuing economic development. He offers no equivalent of Coxe's symbolic landscape, or his vague implication that, somehow, technology would help America reach a kind of pastoral stasis. In fact, he finally makes no rhetorical concessions to Jeffersonian hopes and fears. To support his argument for machine production, he describes the advantages of the "cotton-mill, invented in England, within the last twenty years . . ." in this blunt language:

> . . . all the different processes for spinning cotton, are performed by . . . machines, which are put in motion by water, and attended chiefly by women and children; and by a smaller number of persons, in the whole, than are requisite in the ordinary mode of spinning. And it is an advantage of great moment, that the operations of this mill continue with convenience, during the night as well as the day. The prodigious effect of such a machine is easily conceived. To this invention is to be attributed, essentially, the immense progress which has been so suddenly made in Great Britain, in the various fabrics of cotton.

Whether he fully intends to endorse it or not, Hamilton makes no effort to disclaim the chilling idea of putting women and children on the night shift in cotton mills. The passage exemplifies the tough, hard-boiled tone of the *Report*. Throughout Hamilton is forthright, unsentimental, logical, and clear. Taken as a whole, in fact, the *Report* is a blueprint for a society aimed at maximum productivity, not as an end in itself, but as the key to national wealth, self-sufficiency, and power. The power of the United States as a corporate entity is the ultimate goal; what Hamilton wants is the economy best suited to the establishment of America's supremacy among nations. There can be little doubt that Tench Coxe wanted much the same sort of society. Unlike Hamilton, however, Coxe saw the need to couch this aim in the language of the prevailing ideology. No matter what the economic behavior of his countrymen might seem to indicate, Coxe understood that they preferred not to acknowledge wealth and power as their goals. In this sense he was a subtler and more farsighted—if less candid—advocate of industrialization than Hamilton. He foresaw that Americans would be more likely to endorse the Hamiltonian program with enthusiasm if permitted to conceive of it as a means of fulfilling the pastoral ideal.

"Manufactures" Reconsidered

JOHN R. NELSON

Perhaps no other facet of Hamilton's political economy has been so greatly lauded as his advocacy of domestic manufacturing. There is a major problem in these expositions: the failure of their authors to integrate his Report on Manufactures and the Society for Establishing Useful Manufactures (SEUM) into the overall context of Hamilton's political economy and the circumstances under which he presented them. The question of Hamilton's relationship to manufactures involves three areas: the Report on Manufactures, the SEUM, and foreign economic policy, specifically commercial relations with Great Britain. . . . This third area involves the crucial issues of tariff rates, tonnage duties, and trade agreements with the chief competitor to domestic manufacturers, England. Of these areas, foreign economic policy is perhaps the most indicative of Hamilton's position on American manufactures. In the report and the SEUM, he evinced an ambivalence toward manufacturers that was transformed, under the pressures of the stock market, into active support for manufacturing in one form at least. In foreign policy, Hamilton acted in a manner unquestionably hostile to domestic manufacturers in that he surrendered by treaty America's ability to protect its manufactures from English imports. . . .

In 1791, Hamilton faced a highly protean security market on which rested his whole economic stabilization program. Speculation threatened his program by generating political opposition and fiscal instability. Constantly, he sought new ways to lessen market fluctuations and raise stock prices. In early April 1791, Hamilton decided on another means toward these ends, the Society for Establishing Useful Manufactures. Working closely with Tench Coxe, his assistant secretary, Hamilton seized on Coxe's long-standing scheme for a large manufacturing society. He chose

From John R. Nelson, *Liberty and Property,* pp. 37–43, 48, 50, 68–69, 72–73, 81–90. © 1987 The Johns Hopkins University Press. Reprinted by permission of The Johns Hopkins University Press.

a location in New Jersey near New York City, the center of stock speculation, and designed the financial apparatus for the society. His original proposal was for a capitalization of at least $500,000. Ninety percent of the SEUM stock would be subscribed in 6 percent government stock or bank stock and the remainder in 6 percent deferred stock. A foreign loan at 5.5 percent would then be obtained using the government and bank stock for collateral and interest payments.

Although Coxe sought a broad range of manufactures, including cotton, iron, glass, and wool, Hamilton narrowed it to cotton goods. He believed that "the operation must favour the holders of the public debt and Bank Stock by creating a new object for them, and taking large sums out of the market." With this in mind he wrote William Duer, future chairman of the society, "The more I considered the thing, the more I feel persuaded that it will equally promote the Interest of the Adventurers & of the public and will have an excellent effect on the Debt."

Involved in the final passage and execution of the national bank, Hamilton put aside the SEUM plan until August 1791. . . . [T]he bank . . . stimulated a long summer upswing in stock prices. In early August, the market faltered. Unchecked speculation had led Rufus King, a close ally, to write Hamilton of "mechanics deserting their shops, Shop keepers sending their goods to auction, and not a few of our merchants neglecting the regular & profitable commerce of the City." Although he believed some readjustment in prices useful in restoring sanity to the New York commercial community, Hamilton hoped desperately to preclude "a bubble," the "most formidable" of his "enemies." He instructed the local government broker, William Seton of the Bank of New York, "to keep the Stock from falling too low" by purchases, which, if at all possible, should aid "any Gentlemen who support the *funds*" not those "who *depress* them." Finally, he told Duer, the prince of the speculators and the great bull in the market, of his fervent hope that Duer could maintain the price of the bank stock against strong selling trends. "The acquisition of too much of it by foreigners will certainly be an evil." Hamilton feared the transfer of bank dividends abroad and the political repercussions of foreign ownership of the already controversial institution.

The moment appeared ripe to release SEUM's formal prospectus, and in late August Hamilton did so. In exalting the enterprise, the prospectus foreshadowed many of the arguments he would use in his Report on Manufactures. Women, children, immigrants, and machinery would mitigate the scarcity and cost of labor. Foreign and bank loans, secured by government stock, would supply needed capital. The initial capitalization would be $500,000 with the option, at the directors' discretion, of increasing it to $1 million. Naturally, all subscriptions to SEUM stock were required to be in government securities. As a "means of public prosperity and an instrument of profit to adventurers in the enterprise, it, at the same time, affords a prospect of an enhancement of the value of the debt; by giving it a new and additional employment and utility." Hamilton merely repeated the same justification he had included in his Report on a National Bank. SEUM, too, operated on the debt like a charm.

The stock market rose and continued its rise into the winter of 1791. New Jersey's legislature, weighted with investors and directors of the society, granted a charter of incorporation in late November. On the final day of the month Hamilton canceled a previously planned loan in Holland. "The prices of the public debt here," he explained to Short, render "it questionable whether it be any longer the interest of the United States to prosecute the idea of purchases [of stock] with monies borrowed at 5%." Prices were high enough to make any Treasury intervention in the market superfluous. Effective interest rates on the 6 percent stock neared 5.5 percent and were dropping. Then, as if to christen the SEUM three weeks after its legal birth, Hamilton presented his long overdue Report on Manufactures. More than a few were afflicted with postpartum blues.

. . . Jacob Cooke argues persuasively that "the SEUM was a practical demonstration of the arguments that would be included in the Report on Manufactures." Long ago Arthur H. Cole observed that "the state of domestic industry should not be looked upon as the occasion for Hamilton's advocacy of protection." His mind, as Cole further points out, was on new enterprise. Letters that Hamilton received from existing manufacturers pertaining to the report, as Cooke notes, "did not significantly influence" the final document. These are important points in assessing the report. These observations are consistent with the report itself, which revealed misapprehension of and an insensitivity toward the serious problems confronting American manufacturers. Hamilton directed the report toward the kind of men who would own and control the SEUM. . . .

To aid in an evaluation of the report, it is useful to compare it to an earlier draft prepared by Coxe. Significantly, Coxe's draft differed with Hamilton's final report in several major ways. In general, Hamilton expanded Coxe's defense of the utility of manufacturing while he tailored Coxe's concrete proposal to conform to the parameters of his stabilization program. Coxe's draft concentrated on developing a market in which domestic manufacturing could flourish. Unlike Hamilton, who depended to a great extent on existing financial intermediaries to provide capital for manufactures, Coxe mentioned the funding program and United States Bank only as stabilizers of an expanded circulating medium. Instead, he sought to stimulate investment in manufactures through the creation of a profitable market for domestically manufactured products. To create such a market, raw material costs would have to be reduced, an internal transportation system built, incentives offered to potential investors, and a tariff enacted for protection from foreign imports. Within such an environment manufacturers would expand their resources and profits and possibly attract capital from commerce and land speculation.

In a fundamental sense, a secure profitable market is an integral part of industrial development. Without access to such a market manufacturing could retain no substantial capital. No one would invest in nor long sustain ventures that promised no return. Thus, Coxe presented six proposals for securing that market for domestic manufacturers: a protective tariff on manufactured imports, outright prohibitions of some such imports, abolition of all duties on coastal trade, government construction of roads and canals, direct federal loans, and federal land grants to manufacturing entrepreneurs from a reserve of one-half million acres.

These were substantial proposals which, if implemented, would have provided a solid ground for American manufacturing. Coxe stressed the development of an internal market system to wean the domestic economy from foreign manufactures. The land grant proposal anticipated the chief method by which the government subsidized railroad construction in the latter half of the nineteenth century. During the 1790s, it was land that attracted foreign, especially Dutch, capital to the United States. Thus, if used as a premium, a land reserve promised to be a strong inducement for investment in manufactures. Yet, not only did Hamilton reject the land bounty; he also rejected or emasculated all of Coxe's proposals for stimulating manufacturing and attached himself instead to proposals that Coxe had rejected. A careful analysis of the report demonstrates Hamilton's selective revision of Coxe's draft.

In his report, Hamilton began with his renowned defense of manufacturing development and a systematic discussion of contemporary political economic theories. Although he attempted to demonstrate the interrelationship of agriculture and manufacturing, he neglected to deal at all with the problem that enlarged domestic manufactures would present to the political base of his stabilization program, merchants importing British manufactures, nor to the revenues those imports provided for his fiscal program. Unlike Coxe and other manufacturing advocates, who always strove to demonstrate the benefits manufacturing would bestow on most merchants, Hamilton did not confront this central issue. His neglect is comprehensive if one assumes that he planned no measures that would interfere with those merchants and the revenues their imports yielded. Indeed, the enterprise he had in mind was to be owned and directed by those merchant-creditors to the exclusion of existing manufacturers.

After the introductory remarks Hamilton began an analysis of domestic manufacturing. He discounted the complaints of the manufacturers—who had written of labor shortages, high wage rates, and capital deficiencies—on the grounds that they "are not sufficient to prevent the advantageous prosecution of many very useful and extensive manufactories." Historians have often interpreted Hamilton's optimism about manufactures, which permeates the report, as the great advocate of industrialization rallying his forces. But to American manufacturers, who were swamped by British imports, debts, and high labor costs, such optimism tended to undermine the urgency of their demands for aid. Another way of interpreting Hamilton's optimistic tone is that he was thinking not of the manufacturers, but of promoting the SEUM, whose backers possessed the capital and the political power to overcome, at least ephemerally, many of these difficulties.

In many respects, capital was the crucial issue. Adequate capital would allow manufacturers to purchase machines which would assuage labor shortages and generally expand their enterprises. But Hamilton's proposals for capital aid to manufacturers were dubious at best. Indeed, he seemed to have assumed that those interested in manufacturing had access to or already possessed the necessary capital. Such assumptions would be consistent with the report's orientation toward the SEUM.

Hamilton described three major capital resources for manufacturing: domestic banks, the funded debt, and foreign investment. The first resource promised to be of little use to manufacturers. The banks of the last quarter of the eighteenth century were basically a "clubbing together" of merchant capital to discount short-term notes during intravoyage periods. Bray Hammond observes that these banks "specialized in short term, self-extinguishing credit and exercised a function that was almost purely monetary." The average loan period was thirty to forty-five days. A manufacturer required long-term loans to acquire land, plant equipment, and skilled labor. To erect a factory, install machines, purchase materials, hire laborers, make products, and market them were not sixty-day operations. Manufacturers found it difficult, if not impossible, to obtain money from banks. Banks could not serve as a source of manufacturing capital, although, as Hamilton noted, they did facilitate commercial transactions and provide credit and, in effect, capital to merchants. Hamilton's orientation again appears to be toward the merchants, who invested in the SEUM and had access to bank loans, not the manufacturers.

Examined within its historical context the Report on Manufactures loses much of the superhistorical aura accorded to it in retrospective analyses. Like Hamilton's other reports, it was a polemic, however eloquent and portentous, and served a specific end: advancing the SEUM. He no more conceived of it as a grand plan for an industrial America than an advertising writer would consider his jingle a purely aesthetic endeavor. He hoped only to convince investors of the SEUM's viability and possibly induce some congressional legislation amenable to its prosperity. Indeed, Hamilton was so involved in the daily chore of running the Treasury and the fiscal program that it is virtually impossible to conceive of his putting aside the Bank of the United States, the security market problems, the SEUM, and the complex affairs of the sinking fund to pen a theoretical piece on manufactures without an intimate link to these overwhelming concerns. Only by yanking the report from its context can one impose on it the sorts of anachronistic visions so prevalent in historiography. . . .

Although Hamilton's funding program endured and his central banking system survived a decade of Republican rule, the society died before the conclusion of Washington's second term of office. The SEUM's failure was a result of incompetence in both conception and management. Manufactures were not the directors' field of business expertise. Even if successful, the SEUM would probably have produced the kind of industrial development broached in the southern Confederacy's wartime desperation or czarist Russia's equally unbalanced and government-franchised manufacturing enterprises. The SEUM so alienated public opinion that no manufacturing society was chartered for two years after its demise. Promotion of manufactures thus suffered. The society served as another rallying point used by the Republicans to organize the opposition of American manufacturers to Hamilton's policies. It became the symbol on which the frustration of those whom Joseph Davis labels the "class of small-scale producers" focused their wrath. The SEUM definitely alienated the small-scale manufacturers and their spokesmen. No doubt the interests of larger entrepreneurs were little helped by the repercussions of its ignominious collapse. . . .

In a sense the conflict [in 1790] between Hamilton and Jefferson [over Hamilton's policy of accommodation with England] was a struggle between the preservation of what was and the vision of what might be. Was the union, as it existed, capable of sustaining economic independence through commercial and territorial expansion without undermining the foundations of the union? This question was not susceptible to an academic answer—that is, no judgment could be made about which answer was "realistic" or which "idealistic." Only in practice and over time could any theory be proven valid or invalid. Jefferson worked to answer the question affirmatively, Hamilton to answer no. Success, not judgment, was the proof of this pudding.

. . . Hamilton supported "giving a free course to Trade" to preserve his "commercial" (i.e., fiscal) system. Operationally, this support meant acquiescence in existing foreign, chiefly British, restrictions on American trade. Jefferson, on the other hand, believed the government had "the obligation of effectuating *free markets*" for American goods. The distinction is crucial: "free trade" was not the same as "free markets." The sole means of "effectuating free markets" were commercial discrimination and reciprocity treaties. A nation that placed duties on American ships or goods had to be confronted by similar duties on its ships and goods in American ports.

Agreements could then be reached between the parties to reduce duties and open their respective markets on reciprocal terms. Simply giving a "free course to Trade" was tantamount to relinquishing the nation's sovereign power to promote its economic well-being.

Jefferson's foreign economic policy was twofold: commercial discrimination to "free" markets from restrictions on American trade and development of domestic industry to attain independence from closed markets. Ostensibly a universal foreign policy, in practice Jefferson's discrimination and domestic strategy was directed at Great Britain. England alone steadfastly refused to agree to reciprocal treaties with America. His strategy, then, demanded two countermoves: discriminate against English ships and products, and foster the development of an indigenous manufacturing base in America. The second move would serve to wean the United States from British manufactures *and* substitute a home market for those goods restricted in British and other European markets. He phrased it as an axiom: "If Europe will not let us carry our provisions to their manufactures we must endeavor to bring their manufactures to our provisions." It is of monumental importance to recognize that Jefferson's foreign policy mandated the development of domestic manufactures and that Hamilton's did not. Indeed, Hamilton's mandated the precise opposite: increased Anglo-American trade of raw materials for manufactured goods. As Merrill Peterson observes. "Ironically, the factories and workshops [Jefferson] had preferred to keep in Europe would the more likely result from his commercial system than from Hamilton's fiscal system." . . .

The distinction between opposition to political uses of the debt and opposition to commercial development is best illustrated in their [Jefferson and Madison's] response to the SEUM and the Report on Manufactures. Jefferson first heard of the SEUM in April 1791 when Tench Coxe sent him a copy of the plan and an explanatory letter. Informing him about a new manufactory accorded with Jefferson's known advocacy of domestic manufacturing. But a moment's perusal of the letter and plan immediately shifted Jefferson's attention from manufacturing to the debt, corruption, and speculation. The "mode of raising *the fund,*" Coxe wrote, "was obtained from the Secretary of the Treasury." Given the manufactory's location in New Jersey near the center of speculation, New York City, and the fact that it was subscribable only in federal stock, Jefferson discerned in it only a "new scheme . . . for bringing more paper to market by encouraging great manufacturing companies to form." Hamilton, he believed, was incubating another plot to satisfy "the appetite for gambling" and weaken further the capital resources available to "commerce, manufactures, buildings, & agriculture." Clearly, the basic issue for Jefferson was not large-scale factories versus household manufactures or industrialization versus independent yeomanry, but wasteful speculation versus productive uses of capital—uses that included manufacturing.

In response to Hamilton's Report on Manufactures, Jefferson and Madison focused their criticisms not on his advocacy of manufacturing but on his expansion of the general welfare provision of the Constitution. In the context of Hamilton's often expressed desire to increase federal powers beyond republican bounds and his informal aggrandizement of government support through the debt, they perceived in the report the subversion of the Constitution under the guise of aiding manufacturing. To meet this challenge publicly, Madison chose to confront federal support of manufactures per se as well as to oppose expansion of federal powers beyond those clearly prescribed in the Constitution.

From their perspective Hamilton's three main artifacts—the funding, the bank, and the SEUM—had become agents not of economic development but of political manipulation that enervated productive enterprise. Jefferson regretted his part in the assumption deal between Hamilton and Madison that fueled the speculation. The "gamblers" had won two successive victories in the bank and the SEUM. With the Report on Manufactures, there was no way of ascertaining the additionally damage that direct federal bounties to these speculators might inflict on the republic. Burned by their acquiescence in his fiscal program, they were shy of all Hamilton's plans. The promise of the Report on Public Credit had not been kept, as speculation waxed and production waned. Despite Hamilton's grandiose claims of commercial and industrial prosperity, the bank and the SEUM had merely incited the speculation further. Not ideological repugnance at industry and commerce, but the politicization of the debt, rampant speculation, and economic stagnation had led Madison and Jefferson to oppose Hamilton's plans for manufacturing and banking.

Nonetheless, if the acid test of support for America's economic independence was support for domestic manufacturing, Madison and Jefferson stood firm for protective tariffs and nonimportation; Hamilton vacillated according to the needs of his fiscal system. He acted sometimes with and sometimes against manufacturing, depending on the exigencies of the funding system, while Jefferson and Madison acted similarly, depending on the exigencies of economic independence. In the end it was not he but they who affirmed manufacturing because it came to be an essential condition of independence. It served no similar function in Hamilton's fiscal system; indeed, if anything, domestic manufacturing was a threat to importers and tariff revenues. . . .

The great issue in late-eighteenth-century America was national independence, both political and economic. Political independence came with the success of the Revolution, but the completion of independence was in substance an economic issue. Liberal thought held that a nation, like an individual, must be self-sufficient to be free and independent. Self-sufficiency meant autarky, but not in the sense of a commercially isolated entity, as early liberals conceived of China. Rather, it meant a national economy capable of sustaining political actions to maintain conditions for economic growth and prosperity. Foreign markets or territorial expansion might be integral to an expanding economy. In this respect, independence depended on external conditions. Such dependence, however, was only admissible insofar as the basic strength of the economy could secure through diplomacy or military coercion the external circumstances needed for domestic prosperity.

Great Britain was the class counterexample to China. Though her prosperity depended on world-wide commercial intercourse, England's military power secured its commerce and independence. Although its navy was the agency of independence, it was not the cause. "It is [Britain's] internal industry," Albert Gallatin explained in Congress, "and the protection afforded to manufacturers and commerce which have produced its wealth, that wealth had produced its immense commerce and has enabled them to support a powerful navy." In other words, political independence rested on comprehensive economic development. A strong economy provided the means to sustain growth, resist imperialism, and realize national independence.

America in the early 1790s had a strong agricultural base and a growing merchant marine. Britain's continuing effort to control American trade and markets threatened the expansion of agriculture and shipping. Both to provide an alternative home market and the means of defense, America required an industrial base. Manufacturing was a necessary ingredient to an independent economy capable of assuring the political power to enforce commercial interests in territory and independence. The greatest threat to independence was the economic hegemony of Great Britain's manufactures and navy. A syllogism of sorts developed out of this situation: national independence required breaking Britain's hold on the American economy; Britain's hold could be broken only by domestic manufacturing; thus, national independence required the development of manufacturing. And conversely, rapprochement with Britain meant neocolonial status for the United States. For these reasons, American manufacturers were a vital component in the political and economic struggles of the 1790s. Though relatively few, they were in symbol and fact that vanguard of an economically independent nation.

The manufacturing interest was heterogeneous in the late eighteenth century. Before the Revolution wage labor was relatively rare in domestic manufacturing, but population growth in the urban areas steadily eroded guildlike labor relations and made wage employment more common. The demographic changes and rapid economic expansion of the 1790s swelled the number of mechanics and workers and provided a labor pool for the new enterprises stimulated by the commercial expansion. The mechanic-manufacturer ranks became a critical urban political constituency whose support of the Constitution insured ratification and whose support of the Republicans would in 1800 put Jefferson in the White House.

Nomenclature is important, since it reveals an aspect of consciousness which indicates individual identification with larger socioeconomic groups. A mechanic or "manu-facturer" was one who worked with his hands in a nonagricultural endeavor. An entrepreneur could be subsumed under the terms "master mechanic" or "master manufacturer." In a very large enterprise the master mechanic might be only a foreman and the entrepreneur a manager in the more modern sense. Contemporaries also used "tradesman" to denote a manufacturer of a particular craft or trade. These broad categories subsumed the numerous crafts—coopers, cordwainers, ironmongers, ropemakers, sailmakers, shipwrights, and so forth. Nonetheless, when they organized or petitioned, these various crafts called themselves mechanics, tradesmen, and manufacturers. It is therefore not invalid to identify their shared consciousness as a manufacturing interest group.

By no means was there perfect correspondence among manufacturers. At least three major divisions existed among them: those involved in shipbuilding and outfitting, those in consumer goods, and those in household manufactures. Among these groups the consumer-goods producers were probably the largest. Most were protected from import competition by natural barriers: they produced customer-specific items or items unsuited to mass production, they were in the construction trades, or they were quasi-service-providers such as tailors, blacksmiths, and cobblers. These artisans were concerned largely with the general economic prosperity of their locale and were indirectly affected by commercial changes that affected their area's economy. Among those very directly affected by commerce, the largest were the maritime trades of shipbuilding and related support industries that congregated in and

around shipping centers. These manufacturers called themselves shipwrights, tradesmen, and manufacturers. The central thrust of their political demand in the 1790s
was a strong federal navigation law. They sought to encourage the use of American-
made ships in commerce and to counter the discrimination of foreign nations, particularly Great Britain, against American bottoms. . . .

For shipbuilders, navigation laws were tantamount to protective tariffs. . . . Not
surprisingly, these manufacturers supported Madison's proposals for discrimination
against British commerce.

Manufacturers of consumption goods that had to compete with imports pointed
out two salient problems: British imports and capital shortages. . . . [T]hese manufacturers looked toward federal tariffs to alleviate "the misfortune of a foreign intercourse" and unfetter America from the "commercial shackles which have so long
bound her." They produced glass, iron, linen, cotton cloth, woolens, hats, buttons,
leathers, and other products in direct competition with English imports. Though concentrated in the northern coastal states, they extended as far south as Carolina and as
far west as the Allegheny Mountains. Competition from imports harassed all these
manufacturers in several ways. The "price of all kinds of Manufactures," William
Williams of Connecticut observed, "are very much governed by that of imports." Connecticut "Hatters Complain that Foreign Importations Yet, very Much Injure the business here." Tanners and saddle-makers "suppose that the duty on imported Saddles is
not sufficiently high . . . [and] that the duty on tanned leather is too low." Rhode Island's
tanners, too, were harmed, "owing to the large Quantities of Leather imported from the
West Indies, the Duty on which is small." Across the Union, cloth, paper, button, and
glass manufacturers all repeated these demands for tariff protection from imports. And
whenever they specified a foreign competitor, that competitor was Great Britain.

British competition assumed a more invidious form in its use of credit and
agents in the American market. Moses Brown of Providence, a prominent merchant-
entrepreneur, explained: "British Agents have been Out in this and Other Manufacturing Towns with Large Quantities of Cotton Goods for Sale and strongly Solisiting
[sic] correspondence of people in the Mercantile Line to Receive their Goods at very
long Cre[dit] . . . doubtless for the Discouragement of the Manufactory here. The bate
[sic] has been too Eagerly taken by Our Merchants." Brown conceived of this practice in conspiratorial terms. The "Abilities of the Manufacturing Interest of Great
Britain to intercept the sale of Our Own Goods, at a price as low as theirs has been
heretofore sold by Our Importing Merchants, the Actual Combination of them . . .
forms a very great Discouragement of Men of Abilities to lay Out their Property in
Extending Manufactures."

The technique of these British agents was simple. American manufacturers were
plagued by cash shortages. They required prompt payment from retail merchants and
shopkeepers to finance raw materials, labor, capital replacement, and expansion.
British exporters, on the other hand, had huge credit reserves. They could discount
their commercial paper at any bank, as could their American counterparts. They gave
manufactures to retailers on consignment for extended periods and employed their
large cash reserves to carry on the trade while awaiting sales. Domestic manufacturers
lacked the resources to compete with this sort of credit extension. Thus, even if the
transportation costs and tariffs raised British goods to a price American producers
could match, the produce credit limitations often caused them to lose market outlets.

American manufacturers were strapped for capital. Banks of this era discounted only commercial paper and never lent on real property. Indeed, part of the reason importing merchants could offer good credit terms to retailers was precisely the support rendered by state banks and the Bank of the United States. The merchant-directors of these institutions would hardly consider lending money to domestic manufacturers in competition with their fellow importers and their own businesses. Finally, most venture capital, which might have been invested in manufactures, was absorbed by the omnipresent sponge of stock and land speculation. This situation led Peter Colt, a Connecticut arms manufacturer, to hope that "when the Active Stock of the Citizens shall no longer be embarked in paper Speculations, then we may expect to see part of it turned to the promoting & extending our manufactures & then those which languish and dwindle for want of being supported by proper Capitals may be expected to prosper & this Country freed from a disgraceful dependence on Europe for their ordinary cloathing." . . .

Most manufactories of consumption goods were smaller than shipbuilding industries. A few, however, employed over forty people in cotton textile production. One Massachusetts concern boasted sixteen hundred women and children in their "putting-out" workforce. Women and immigrants were the mainstay of the labor force in these and other industries. Surprisingly, one manufacturer reported skilled labor to be cheaper than in Britain, but he added that unskilled labor was much dearer. There was hope that child labor could compensate for unskilled adults. There was hope that child labor could compensate for unskilled adults. Another manufacturer noted that "poor children, who, while they are earning Something toward their subsistence, are prevented from contracting bad habits, and are introduced thereby to a Habit of Industry, by which we may hope to see them useful Members of Society." In addition to protective tariffs, these manufacturers requested government loans, contracts, and inspection of products to control quality. Significantly, northern manufacturers exported their goods to southern states and the West Indies. These exports included woolens, cotton cloth, iron, leather, furnishings, and several other items. This trade was substantial enough to induce Tench Coxe to attack the Jay Treaty publicly for its restrictions on manufactured exports to the West Indies.

Among the more vexing problems of political analysis in this era is the political affiliation of large manufacturers. Insofar as Coxe reflected the politics of these manufacturers, one can infer that at least some became Republicans. Jefferson had a close personal relationship with the munitions maker Pierre DuPont as well as a nascent political following among manufacturers in Brandywine Valley. Though apolitical, Eli Whitney also established an early rapport with Jefferson. Matthew Lyon, an iron manufacturer, became a Republican. There were others. Undoubtedly, the rising entrepreneurial character of the northern Republicans accorded with the interests of these manufacturers. Moreover, Republican banks often arose to provide credit and capital to groups excluded by Federalist institutions. "Farmers and Mechanics" banks, founded at the end of the 1790s, reflected in their nomenclature their economic orientation. During this period, however, state aid far outweighed federal support. Whatever the impact of national policies, a Federalist state legislature might find it politic to make loans available to manufacturers and assure, if not their political allegiance, at least their acquiescence. This road could be traveled both ways; Republicans might sway Federalist manufacturers with similar aid. . . . During the 1790s the evidence of large manufacturer support for Republicans is scattered and ambiguous.

The most common manufactures in this period were household. Homespun clothing and household goods were the products of farm women providing necessities for themselves and their families. They produced their own because they lacked either the money or the access to commercial manufactures. Protective tariffs, therefore, would have little impact on their output. Still, many household producers mixed purchases of goods with homespun and could turn more toward one source than the other depending on price fluctuations. The principal interaction of farmers and manufacturers occurred in the curd processing of farm products into more marketable forms: tobacco into snuff, wheat into flour, grain into whiskey. These manufactures—and they were considered manufactures by all concerned—were widespread and important to the farm community, especially in the western areas of the nation.

Although farmers and manufacturers were connected materially in their exchange of consumption goods for farm produce, their strongest link was in this crude processing of farm produce for markets. Farmers often doubled as distillers. Regardless of its narrow application, the federal excise on liquor was seen by all as a tax on manufactures. Hamilton defended it as such; distillers and farmers attacked it as such. . . .

One perceives a small-producer consciousness in all these groups of manufacturers, a consciousness, created during the Revolution and shared by many small farmers. While the manufacturers found government excise tax levies repugnant, they sought aid, protection, and recognition from the great men of Philadelphia. They were democratic, for in democracy lay their hopes for an impact on government policies. They were nationalistic, for their prosperity depended on a strong and independent economy. They were the progeny of the "Spirit of '76" born in the General Societies of Mechanics and Tradesmen. Their small-producer consciousness ultimately found a home in the Republican party as the events of the 1790s again transformed collective thought into political action.

. . . The breakdown of the manufacturers' alliance with Hamilton and the Federalists began with a tension implicit in the constitutional coalition. Hamilton oriented his program to large merchants and speculators, the centerpiece of his support. His tariff proposals were deemed inadequate by the goods producers in shipbuilding and nonshipbuilding industries. Shipbuilders thought federal navigation laws an insufficient counterbalance to British regulations. Rampant speculation in securities pressed all manufacturers for capital at reasonable interest rates. Hamilton's program engendered this speculation and proved incapable of controlling it. Above all loomed the British, their imports, their ships, their credit, their American correspondents. More than the excise, antipathy to Great Britain brought together the disparate manufacturers. Such antipathy boded ill for a man who believed a connection with Britain to be in [the] best interests of America.

After the conflict over the issue of tariff and navigation laws, a major rupture occurred between Hamilton and manufacturers as a result of the SEUM. Most of the other societies for promoting manufacturers disseminated technical information and offered prizes for new machinery or loans to manufactures. The SEUM did not. On the contrary, it was a quasi-public corporation engendered by wealthy speculators and aided by the New Jersey legislature. The SEUM offered nothing but competition to existing producers. Although a few manufacturers expressed interest in the project, speculation and mismanagement soon disenchanted them. Other manufacturers raised a hue and cry over this "political monster" as a creature of speculation sapping the foundation of industry.

George Logan, who ran the gamut from president of the German town Society for Promoting Domestic Manufacturing through Democratic Society organizer to Republican senator, attacked the SEUM as a monopoly constructed for the speculators. "Should this scheme take place," he warned, "a valuable class of citizens, *personally engaged* in useful manufactures, will be sacrificed to the wealthy few." Logan held up the society as symbolic of the government's orientation toward wealth and privilege in its laws and programs. Finally, he made the inevitable connection to British efforts to suppress American manufactures. "Had the Court of Britain," he harangued, "pensioned a number of men in America, to effect the ruin of the infant manufactures of our country, they could not have adopted a scheme better calculated to answer that purpose, than the scheme of DUER and HAMILTON." . . .

The "panic" [stock market crash] of March 1792, which wounded the SEUM mortally, further strained Hamilton's relations with urban manufacturers. In New York the manufacturers were already angered by the Federalist-controlled assembly's rejection of their petition for incorporation of their General Society. The collapse of the market destroyed Duer and ruined many tradesmen who had lent him money. Hamilton's efforts through his urban allies to control the stock speculation and commercial expansion only exacerbated tensions between the manufacturer-mechanic interest and the Federalist leadership. The subsequent recession and tight money weakened Federalist support among manufacturers. The scene was repeated in Maryland and other areas affected by the market's collapse. As yet, however, no event had crystallized manufacturers into organized opposition against Hamilton's program. Then England and France went to war.

In part the excise, in part sympathy with France and opposition to England, but principally the sense among manufacturers, mechanics, small farmers, merchants trading outside the British empire, and others that those administering the government were abrogating their interests led to the formation of the Democratic Societies in 1793. Though specific in their economic demands, the societies recaptured part of the Revolutionary spirit and a strong sense that the government had grown away from many of its citizens. They became a lobby for a more democratic republic. This ideological stance flowed naturally from the members' perception that their economic interests were not adequately considered in policy decisions. Economic growth, the profits from stock speculation, and heavy immigration increased both the wealth and the poverty in the seaport cities. Federalists sought to impose their policies and politics on manufacturers and mechanics. The manufacturers and mechanics concluded that the government was unrepresentative and, owning to its solicitude of large merchant-creditors and Great Britain, aristocratic as well. The Democratic Societies, as Eugene Link observes, "rolled up mass opposition to the antidemocratic tendencies of the period."

From Charleston to Boston, in the cities and the hinterlands, societies were organized. A typical society was led by merchants and master manufacturers. Its rank and file consisted chiefly of mechanics and manufacturers, with significant elements of the farm community and a sprinkling of seamen, lawyers, and physicians. Proportions varied with location. Many Irish, Scotch, and German immigrants entered the societies. Opposition to British economic hegemony and ideological kinship with France's revolutionaries welded the members together. The corollary to anglophobic sentiments was strong advocacy of domestic manufactures. Organizations of manufacturers and mechanics shared membership and goals with the Democratic Societies. In virtual concert they demanded an end to the liquor excise, resistance to Britain, protection for manufactures and American-made ships, and an end to the Treasury Department's alliance with the rentiers. In essence, they sought to restructure radically Hamilton's stabilization program.

The societies' leadership was perhaps the most significant and striking political alliance of the 1790s: merchants trading outside the British empire and manufacturers. In New York City's society the presidents included David Gelston and James Nicholson. Both were very wealthy merchants; Nicholson was Gallatin's father-in-law. Among the leaders of Philadelphia's society was John Swanwick, another prosperous merchant. The majority of established merchants shunned the societies, yet, in numbers too large to be ignored and with wealth equal to the Federalist grandees, merchants assumed key positions in the Democratic Societies of the nation's cities.

The political activities of the societies peaked between 1794 and 1795, with the Whiskey Rebellion and British commercial depredations serving as rallying points for this activism. The societies, however, did not survive concerted Federalist efforts to destroy them. Washington's condemnation and the links to armed rebellion imputed to the societies by their critics were blows from which they could not recover. Despite an ephemeral existence, they demonstrated that manufacturers and mechanics were not alone in their dissension and foreshadowed the coalition of merchants, farmers, and manufacturers that would constitute the Republican party after 1795. Finally, the societies revealed that the economic concerns of significant groups of citizens could translate into an activist commercial program opposed to Hamilton's. The key elements of this program were opposition to British economic hegemony in any form, support of domestic manufactures, and advocacy of world trade restricted only by choice. With the passing of the Democratic Societies, many merchants, mechanics, and manufacturers throughout America looked toward the nascent Republican party to continue the battle for these goals.

FURTHER READING

Banning, Lance. *The Jeffersonian Persuasion: Evolution of a Party Ideology* (Ithaca, NY: Cornell University Press, 1978).

Baxter, Maurice G. *Henry Clay and the American System* (Lexington, KY: University Press of Kentucky, 1995).

Cole, Arthur H., ed., *Industrial and Commercial Correspondence of Alexander Hamilton* (New York: A. M. Kelley, 1968).

Cooke, Jacob E. *Tench Coxe and the Early Republic* (Chapel Hill, NC: University of North Carolina Press, 1978).

Folsom, Michael B., and Steven D. Lubar, eds., *The Philosophy of Manufactures: Early Debates over Industrialization in the United States* (Cambridge, MA: The MIT Press, 1982).

Goodrich, Carter, ed., *The Government and the Economy: 1783–1861* (Indianapolis, IN: Bobbs-Merrill Co., 1967).

Kasson, John F., *Civilizing the Machine: Technology and Republican Values in America, 1776–1900* (New York: Grossman Publishers, 1976).

Kulik, Gary, Roger Parks, and Theodore Z. Penn, eds., *The New England Mill Village, 1790–1860* (Cambridge, MA: The MIT Press, 1982).

McCoy, Drew R. *The Elusive Republic: Political Economy in Jeffersonian America* (Chapel Hill, NC: University of North Carolina Press, 1980).

Nelson, John R., Jr. *Liberty and Property: Political Economy and Policymaking in the New Nation, 1789–1812* (Baltimore, MD: The Johns Hopkins University Press, 1987).

CHAPTER
5

Inside Factory Systems,
1820–1885

⚶

Unlike the two great political upheavals of the eighteenth century, the American Revolution (1776–1783) and the French Revolution (1789–1799), the industrial revolution was so gradual and incremental that some question the appropriateness of calling it a "revolution" at all. But certain changes that began in late eighteenth-century England and continued in the early nineteenth-century United States were of such overarching importance that historians have long felt the need for a dramatic descriptive term. These changes included a shift from hand to machine production, the application of water and steam power to machinery, the organization of production in larger shops and factories, the introduction of speedier methods of communicating at long distances, and the invention of new, more regimented and bureaucratic methods of managing the people—men, women, and children—who worked in the new shops and factories. This chapter will focus on the last of these phenomena, the various new (and some arguably not so new) production regimes that working Americans encountered in the age of "industrial revolution."

Not everyone involved in the production of goods in the early nineteenth century worked within large factory complexes. Most manufactures remained relatively small throughout the nineteenth century, employing fewer than fifteen or twenty workers, and survived by finding niches in the marketplace for specialty products. Often these smaller enterprises clustered around larger factory-scale operations, providing goods and services that the latter found either unprofitable or bothersome to produce. After the War of 1812, for example, the U.S. Armory at Springfield, Massachusetts (a facility that employed about two hundred workers), frequently contracted with nearby forges and machine shops for various types of millwork and machinery as well as the actual components used in the assembly of its major product, military muskets. Local textile mills often did the same, supporting a number of small-scale manufacturing operations in the vicinity at the very time that they were increasingly moving toward mass production standards.

Many American artisans and workers—particularly white northern men—enthusiastically embraced mechanization and participated in the invention and development of new mechanical technologies. But even this group did not necessarily embrace the factory system. Even during the early years of industrial development,

*when factory work seemed somewhat novel and held out the promise for greater
personal prosperity, both men and women frequently balked at rules and regulations
that governed their lives after they entered the factory gate. Free African Americans
were excluded from most factories, although a growing minority of slaves became
involved in nonagricultural capitalist production as the nineteenth century progressed.*

*Some scholars of the nineteenth-century factory system have held that it made
more goods available at lower prices to more people and strengthened popular faith
in the United States as a land of promise, increase, and democracy. Others argue
that factories not only increased production but redistributed it, actively subverted
the democratic dreams of male artisans, economically marginalized women, and
perpetuated southern agricultural slavery. The equitable distribution of factory-made
goods and the perpetuation of democracy, they argue, were not intrinsic features of
factory-based capitalism and its remarkable new machines, but had to be continually,
often bitterly, fought for, always with mixed results. Whatever one's position on the
efficacy of factory production, the contrast between commonly held ideas of personal
freedom (some of which were codified in the U.S. Constitution) and the governance
of the work environments most nineteenth-century Americans found themselves in
was striking. It remains striking today. How was this contrast mediated?*

*Was regimentation inevitable under factory systems? What prompted factory
masters to establish rules and regulations in the first place? What alternatives, if
any, existed in nineteenth-century America? What issues seemed most problematic
to working people? What were the similarities and differences between factory work
in the North and industrial slavery in the South?*

⚶ DOCUMENTS

The first document reprints the rules and regulations governing workers at the
Matteawan Company textile mill near Newburgh, New York. It typifies the sorts of
work rules factory masters promulgated during the early nineteenth century.

The next two selections were written by young women (using the pen names
"Almira" and "Amelia") who worked in the textile mills in Lowell, Massachusetts, during the early 1840s. Although both voice criticism of the factory system, they come to
different conclusions about their work experiences and whether they would recommend
factory work to others. Almira's criticism is perhaps more muted because the piece was
published in a company-sponsored organ, *The Lowell Offering*. As a member of one
of the country's first women's unions, the Female Labor Reform Association, Amelia
presents a more militant view of mill owners and their policies.

The fourth selection focuses on one of the earliest industries to manufacture a
complex precision instrument for a large consumer market, and one of the few metalworking industries to employ large numbers of women. Cheap, machine-made pocket
watches first appeared in the United States during the 1860s at the American Watch
Company (later the Waltham Watch Company) in Waltham, Massachusetts. The
document not only contrasts European and American manufacturing methods but
reveals how gender biases were built into American production.

The fifth selection comes from the public sector of the American manufacturing
economy during the early 1840s and consists of three letters. On March 21, 1842, the
work force at the U.S. Armory at Harpers Ferry, Virginia (now West Virginia) walked
off their jobs and subsequently sent a delegation to Washington to protest the superintendent's installation of a clock and the imposition of a ten-hour day. Upon presenting

their complaints to President John Tyler, the armorers were promised that they could return to their posts without fear of retribution, but that "they must go home and hammer out their own salvation." In the first two letters, the military superintendent at Harpers Ferry, Major Henry K. Craig, reports the outbreak to his military superior in Washington, chief of the Army Ordnance Department, Colonel George Talcott. In the third letter Colonel Talcott responds to an inquiry made by Secretary of War John C. Spencer concerning the imposition of "military rules" on the civilian labor force at Harper's Ferry. His letter sheds light on key issues igniting labor-management disputes in the early industrial era—many of which continue to this day.

The sixth selection is from the autobiography of Frederick Douglass, a former slave who became a leading abolitionist during the antebellum period. Douglass's sojourn as an apprentice caulker in a Baltimore shipyard during the mid-1830s testifies to the racism and open hostility that slaves as well as free blacks encountered whenever they worked alongside free white workers. As the writings of Almira and Amelia attest, white factory workers in the North often referred to themselves as "slaves," but that did not necessarily mean that they opposed the enslavement of blacks. White racism toward black workers continued long after the Civil War and was especially rampant in trade unions. Why was this so?

Rules and Regulations of the Matteawan Company, 1846

No person will be admitted into the yard during working hours, except on business, without permission of an agent. At all other times, the watchmen will be invested with full control.

The work bell will be rung three minutes, and tolled five minutes; at the expiration of which, every person is expected to be at their work, and every entrance closed, except through the office, which will at all times be open during the working hours of the factory.

No person employed in the manufacturing departments can be permitted to leave their work without permission from their overseer. All others employed in and about the factory are requested to give notice to the agent or superintendent, if they wish to be absent from their work.

No talking can be permitted among the hands in any of the working departments, except on subjects relating to their work.

No spirituous liquors, smoking, or any kind of amusement, will be allowed in the workshops or yards.

Those who take jobs will be considered as overseers of the persons employed by them, and subject to these rules.

Should there exist among any of the persons employed, an idea of oppression on the part of the company, they are requested to make the same known in an honorable manner, that such grievances, if really existing, may be promptly considered.

To convince the enemies of domestic manufactures that such establishments are not "sinks of vice and immorality," but, on the contrary, nurseries of morality, industry,

From "Manufacturing Industry of the State of New York," *Hunt's Merchants' Magazine* XV (Oct, 1846): 370–372. Reprinted in Carroll Pursell, *Readings in Technology and American Life* (New York: Oxford University Press, 1969).

and intelligence, a strictly moral conduct is required of every one. Self-respect, it is presumed, will induce every one to be as constant in attendance on some place of divine worship as circumstances will permit. Intemperance, or any gross impropriety of conduct, will cause an immediate discharge of the individual.

The agent and other members of the company are desirous of cultivating the most friendly feeling with the workmen in the establishment, believing that they are to rise or fall together. Therefore, to promote the interest and harmony of all, it is necessary there should be a strict observance of these rules and regulations.

"Almira" Weighs Discontent in the Lowell Textile Mills, 1841

"I will not stay in Lowell any longer; I am determined to give my notice this very day," said Ellen Collins, as the earliest bell was tolling to remind us of the hour for labor.

"Why, what is the matter, Ellen? It seems to me you have dreamed out an idea! Where do you think of going? and what for?"

"I am going home, where I shall not be obliged to rise so early in the morning, nor be dragged about by the ringing of a bell, nor confined in a close noisy room from morning till night. I will not stay here; I am determined to go home in a fortnight."

Such was our brief morning's conversation.

In the evening, as I sat alone, reading, my companions having gone out to public lectures or social meetings, Ellen entered. I saw that she still wore the same gloomy expression of countenance, which had been manifested in the morning; and I was disposed to remove from her mind the evil influence, by a plain common-sense conversation.

"And so, Ellen," said I, "you think it unpleasant to rise so early in the morning, and be confined in the noisy mill so many hours during the day. And I think so, too. All this, and much more, is very annoying, no doubt. But we must not forget that there are advantages, as well as disadvantages, in this employment, as in every other. If we expect to find all sun-shine and flowers in any station in life, we shall most surely be disappointed. We are very busily engaged during the day; but then we have the evening to ourselves, with no one to dictate to or control us. I have frequently heard you say, that you would not be confined to house-hold duties, and that you disliked the millinery business altogether, because you could not have your evenings, for leisure. You know that in Lowell we have schools, lectures, and meetings of every description, for moral and intellectual improvement."

"All that is very true," replied Ellen, "but if we were to attend every public institution, and every evening school which offers itself for our improvement, we might spend every farthing of our earnings, and even more. Then if sickness should overtake us, what are the probable consequences? Here we are, far from kindred and home; and if we have an empty purse, we shall be destitute of *friends* also."

"I do not think so, Ellen. I believe there is no place where there are so many advantages within the reach of the laboring class of people, as exist here; where there

From Benita Eisler, ed., *The Lowell Offering: Writings by New England Mill Women (1840–1845)* (Philadelphia: J. B. Lippincott, 1977), pp. 111–114.

is so much equality, so few aristocratic distinctions, and such good fellowship, as many be found in this community. A person has only to be honest, industrious, and moral, to secure the respect of the virtuous and good, though he may not be worth a dollar; while on the other hand, an immoral person, though he should possess wealth, is not respected."

"As to the morality of the place," returned Ellen, "I have no fault to find. I object to the constant hurry of every thing. We cannot have time to eat, drink or sleep; we have only thirty minutes, or at most three quarters of an hour, allowed us, to go from our work, partake of our food, and return to the noisy clatter of machinery. Up before day at the clang of the bell—and out of the mill by the clang of the bell—into the mill, and at work, in obedience to that ding-dong of a bell—just as though we were so many living machines. I will give my notice to-morrow: go, I will—I won't stay here and be a white slave."

"Ellen," said I, "do you remember what is said of the bee, that it gathers honey even in a poisonous flower? May we not, in like manner, if our hearts are rightly attuned, find many pleasures connected with our employment? Why is it, then, that you so obstinately look altogether on the dark side of a factory life? I think you thought differently while you were at home, on a visit, last summer—for you were glad to come back to the mill, in less than four weeks. Tell me, now—why were you so glad to return to the ringing of the bell, the clatter of the machinery, the early rising, the half-hour dinner, and so on?"

I saw that my discontented friend was not in a humour to give me an answer—and I therefore went on with my talk.

"You are fully aware, Ellen, that a country life does not exclude people from labor—to say nothing of the inferior privileges of attending public worship—that people have often to go a distance to meeting of any kind—that books cannot be so easily obtained as they can here—that you cannot always have just such society as you wish—that you"—

She interrupted me, by saying, "We have no bell, with its everlasting ding-dong."

"What difference does it make," said I, "whether you shall be awaked by a bell, or the noisy bustle of a farm-house? For, you know, farmers are generally up as early in the morning as we are obliged to rise."

"But then," said Ellen, "country people have none of the clattering of machinery constantly dinning in the ears."

"True," I replied, "but they have what is worse—and that is, a dull, lifeless silence all around them. The hens may cackle sometimes, and the geese gabble, and the pigs squeal"—

Ellen's hearty laugh interrupted my description—and presently we proceeded very pleasantly, to compare a country life, with a factory life in Lowell. Her scowl of discontent had departed, and she was prepared to consider the subject candidly. We agreed, that since we must work for a living, the mill, all things considered, is the most pleasant, and best calculated to promote our welfare; that we will work diligently during the hours of labor; improve our leisure to the best advantage, in the cultivation of the mind,—hoping thereby not only to increase our own pleasure, but also to add to the happiness of those around us.

Almira

"Amelia," Some of the Beauties of Our Factory System— Otherwise, Lowell Slavery, 1845

For the purpose of illustration, let us go with that light-hearted, joyous young girl who is about for the first time to leave the home of her childhood; that home around which clusters so many beautiful and holy associations, pleasant memories, and quiet joys; to leave, too, a mother's cheerful smile, a father's care and protection; and wend her way toward this far famed "city of spindles," this promised land of the imagination, in whose praise she has doubtless heard so much.

Let us trace her progress during her first year's residence, and see whether she indeed realizes those golden prospects which have been held out to her. Follow her now as she enters that large gloomy looking building—she is in search of employment, and has been told that she might here obtain an eligible situation. She is sadly wearied with her journey, and withal somewhat annoyed by the noise, confusion, and strange faces all around her. So, after a brief conversation with the overseer, she concludes to accept the first situation which offers; and reserving to herself a sufficient portion of time in which to obtain the necessary rest after her unwanted exertions, and the gratification of a stranger's curiosity regarding the place in which she is now to make her future home, she retires to her boarding house, to arrange matters as much to her mind as may be.

The intervening time passes rapidly away, and she soon finds herself once more within the confines of that close noisy apartment, and is forthwith installed in her new situation—first, however, premising that she has been sent to the Counting-room, and receives therefrom a Regulation paper, containing the rules by which she must be governed while in their employ; and lo! here is the beginning of mischief; for in addition to the tyrannous and oppressive rules which meet her astonished eyes, she finds herself compelled to remain for the space of twelve months in the very place she then occupies, however reasonable and just cause of complaint might be hers, or however strong the wish for dismission; thus, in fact constituting herself a slave, a very slave to the caprices of him for whom she labors. Several incidents coming to the knowledge of the writer, might be somewhat interesting in this connection, as tending to show the prejudicial influence exerted upon the interests of the operative by this unjust requisition. The first is of a lady who has been engaged as an operative for a number of years, and recently entered a weaving room on the Massachusetts Corporation; the overseer having assured her previous to her entrance, that she should realize the sum of $2,25 per week, exclusive of board; which she finding it impossible to do, appealed to the Counting-room for a line enabling her to engage elsewhere, but it was peremptorily refused.

The next is of a more general bearing, concerning quite a number of individuals employed on the Lawrence Corporation, where the owners have recently erected and put in motion a new mill, at the same time stopping one of the old, in which said persons were employed. Now as they did not voluntarily leave their situations, but were discharged therefrom on account of suspension of operations by the company; they

From *Factory Life as It Is: Factory Traits No. 1* (Lowell, MA: Female Labor Reform Association, 1845), pp. 4–7.

had an undoubted right to choose their own place of labor; and as the work in the new mill is vastly more laborious, and the wages less than can be obtained in many parts of the city, they signified their wish to go elsewhere, but are insolently told that they shall labor there or not at all; and will not be released until their year has expired, when if they can *possibly* find *no* further excuse for delay, they *may* deign to bestow upon them what is in common parlance termed, a "regular discharge;" thus enabling them to pass from one prison house to another. Concerning this precious document, it is only necessary to say, that it very precisely reminds one of that which the dealers in human flesh at the South are wont to give and receive as the transfer of one piece of property from one owner to another.

Now, reader, what think you? is not this the height of the beautiful? and are not we operatives an ungrateful set of creatures that we do not properly appreciate and be highly thankful for such unparalleled generosity on the part of our employers!

But to return to our foiling Maiden,—the next beautiful feature which she discovers in this *glorious* system is, the long number of hours which she is obliged to spend in the above named close, unwholesome apartment. It is not enough, that like the poor peasant of Ireland, or the Russian serf who labors from sun to sun, but during one half of the year, she must still continue to toil on, long after Nature's lamp has ceased to lend its aid—not will even this suffice to satisfy the grasping avarice of her employer; for she is also through the winter months required to rise, partake of her morning meal, and be at her station in the mill, while the sun is yet sleeping behind the eastern hills; thus working on an average, at least twelve hours and three fourths per day, exclusive of the time allotted for her hasty meals, which is in winter simply one half hour at noon,—in the spring is allowed the same at morn, and during the summer is added 15 minutes to the half hour at noon. Then too, when she is at last released from her wearisome day's toil, still may she not depart in peace. No! Her footsteps must be dogged to see that they do not stray beyond the corporation limits, and she *must*, whether she will or no, be subjected to the manifold inconveniences of a large crowded boarding-house, where too, the price paid for her accommodation is so utterly insignificant, that it will not ensure to her the common comforts of life; she is obliged to sleep in a small comfortless, half ventilated apartment containing some half a dozen occupants each; but no matter, *she is an operative*—it is all well enough for her; there is no "abuse" about it; no, indeed; so think our employers—but do we think so? Time will show. Here, too, comes up a case which strikingly illustrates the petty tyranny of the employer. A little girl, some 12 or 13 years of age, the daughter of a poor widow, dependent on her daily toil for a livelihood, worked on one of the Corporations, boarding with her mother; who dying left her to the care of an aunt, residing but a few steps from the Corporation—but the poor little creature all unqualified as she was, to provide for her own wants, was *compelled* to leave her home and the motherly care bestowed upon her, and enter one of those same large crowded boarding-houses. We do but give the facts in this case and they need no comment for every one *must* see the utter heartlessness which prompted such conduct toward a mere child.

Reader will you pronounce this a mere fancy sketch, written for the sake of effect? It is not so. It is a real picture of "Factory life;" nor is it one half so bad as might truthfully and justly have been drawn. But it has been asked, and doubtless will be again, why, if these evils are so aggravating, have they been so long and so peacefully borne? Ah! and why have they? It is a question well worthy of our consideration, and we would call upon every operative in *our* city, aye, throughout the length and breadth of the land to awake from the lethargy which has fallen upon them, and assert and maintain their rights. We call upon you for action—*united and immediate action.* But, says one, let us wait till we are stronger. In the language of one of old, we ask, when shall we be stronger? Will it be the next week, or the next year? Will it be when we are reduced to the servile condition of the poor operatives of England? for verily we shall be and that right soon, if matters be suffered to remain as they are. Says another, how shall we act? we are but one amongst a thousand, what shall we do that our influence may be felt in this vast multitude? We answer, there is in this city an Association called the Female Labor Reform Association, having for its professed object, the amelioration of the condition of the operative. Enrolled upon its records are the names of five hundred members—come then, and add thereto five hundred or rather five thousand more, and in the strength of our united influence we will soon show these *drivelling* cotton lords, this mushroom aristocracy of New England, who so arrogantly aspire to lord it over God's heritage, that our rights cannot be trampled upon with impunity; that we WILL not longer submit to that arbitrary power which has for the last ten years been so abundantly exercised over us.

One word ere we close, to the hardy independent yeomanry and mechanics, among the Granite Hills of New Hampshire, the woody forests of Maine, the cloud capped mountains of Vermont, and the busy, bustling towns of the old Bay State—ye! who have daughters and sisters toiling in those sickly prison-houses which are scattered far and wide over each of these States, we appeal to *you* for aid in this matter. Do you ask how that aid can be administered? We answer through the Ballot Box. Yes! if you have one spark of sympathy for our condition, carry it *there*, and see to it that you send to preside in the Councils of each Commonwealth, men who have hearts as well as heads, souls as well bodies; men who will watch zealously over the interests of the laborer in every department; who will protect him by the strong arm of the law from the encroachments of arbitrary power; who will see that he is not deprived of those rights and privileges which God and Nature have bestowed upon him—yes,

> From every rolling river,
>   From mountain, vale and plain,
> We call on you to deliver
>   Us, From the tyrant's chain:

And shall we call in vain! We trust not. More anon.

Amelia

Virginia Penny Contrasts European and American Watchmaking, 1863

A watch is said to consist of 992 pieces. . . . In Switzerland, families, for generation after generation, devote themselves to making particular parts of watches. Women have proved their ability to execute the most delicate parts. Twenty thousand Swiss

From Virginia Penny, *The Employments of Women: An Encyclopedia of Woman's Work* (Boston: Walker & Wise, 1863); pp. 242–245.

women earn a comfortable livelihood by watch making. They make the movements, but men mostly put them together. . . . A traveller states: "We see women at the head of some of the heaviest manufactories of Switzerland and France, particularly in the watch and jewelry line." In England, women have been until lately excluded from watch making by men, but some are now employed in one establishment in London and in several of the provincial towns. "There is a manufactory at Christchurch, England, where five hundred women are employed in making the interior chains for chronometers. They are preferred to men, on account of their being naturally more dexterous with their fingers, and therefore being found to require less training." From the November number of the *Knickerbocker* we quote: "All imported watches are made by hand, the American watches being the only ones made by machinery in a single establishment by connected and uniform processes. The Waltham watches have fewer parts and are more easily kept in order than any others; and are warranted for ten years by the manufacturers. They have over one hundred artisans employed, more than half of whom are women." The manufactory occupies a space more than half an acre in extent. Hand labor is cheaper in Europe than this country, but American watches are cheaper, because made by machinery. . . . A manufacturer of chronometers in Boston writes: . . . The principal objection to employing women is that they are very apt to marry just as they become skilful enough to be reliable; therefore, what does not require long apprenticeship or a great expense to learn, is most desirable for them. A good degree of intelligence is indispensable. The more, of course, the better." We would add to the requisites for a watchmaker, patience and ingenuity. The secretary of the American Watch Company at Waltham writes: "Women are employed at our factory. The employment is entirely healthy. We pay from $4 to $7 per week for intelligent girls, and women's average pay is $5. About half are paid by the piece. Men earn about double the wages of women, because, first, they do more difficult work, are more ingenious, more thoughtful and contriving, more reliant on themselves in matters of mechanics, are stronger, and therefore worth more, though not perhaps double, as an average; second, because it is the custom to pay women less than men for the same labor. Women and girls are paid from $2.50 to $4 per week during the first four months, while they are learning the particular part of our business we set them at. The requisites are a good common-school education, general intelligence, and quickness; light, small hands are best. The business is new to the country. We work every working day in the year, without detriment to the health of women, who seem to endure their labor as well as men. We work ten hours a day. . . . We employ seventy-five women out of two hundred hands, and because there are many parts of our work they can do *equally* well with men; but it is generally light and simple work, for which no high degree of mechanical skill is requisite. Nine tenths are American born. Our hands are all made perfectly comfortable in their labor. We employ female labor, where we can, as being cheaper; but we find women do not reach the posts where a high degree of skill is needed, as of course they do not those for which their strength is insufficient. They have abundant facilities for mental culture in the evenings. About half live with parents or relatives; the rest board, and pay from $2 to $3 a week, according to quality.

A Strike at Harper's Ferry (Correspondence), 1842

[Mar. 21, 1842]

Sir,

This morning most of the piece workers, and many of the day hands at the Musket Factory, marched in a body to the Rifle Works, and their numbers being increased by recruits from that establishment, they returned and assembled in the Arsenal Yard where one or more addresses were made by individuals of the league, after which they quietly departed to meet at some other place for the purpose of deliberation etc.

I was greatly surprised at this outbreak, not having had the slightest intimation that such matters were in agitation, nor do I yet know precisely the grounds of their complaints, though I believe they ostensibly, grew out of the late regulation requiring all workmen to conform to the hours for labour indicated by the Bell.

This affair having taken place at a moment when piece work is on the eve of being diminished for a time affords an opportunity of culling our ranks.

I suppose reason will be restored to the deluded portion of those who participated in the disorderly movement in the course of a day or two—I will then receive back such as it will be for the interest of the Government to employ.—Taking care to make examples of such of the instigators, and formenters of the outbreak as are within our reach.

There are some I am inclined to think who are beyond it.

H. K. Craig.

Sir,

Our workmen still hold off, and it is said intend to visit Washington in a body, having chartered a canal boat for the purpose; I am inclined to think they will not act so unwisely. There is no appearance of disorder, or tumult; and setting aside the impropriety of their conduct in quitting work, the behaviour of the workmen has been as correct as could be expected.

H. K. Craig.

Lt. Col. Talcott to Jno. C. Spencer, Ord. Office, May 17, 1842.

The Armory question may be explained by setting forth a few of the facts.

1st. There now is, and has been, a greater number of men employed than would be necessary to perform all the work, in case they labored with reasonable diligence ten hours a day.

2d. At all private manufactures the operatives are required to labor 12 hours & upwards per day, while at the Armories, only ten hours and at heavy forging only 7 to 8 hours labor are demanded.

From Ordnance Dept., Letters Received, Record Group 156, Records of the Office of the Chief of Ordnance, National Archives, Washington, DC.

3d. If the number now employed should labor ten hours a day—the annual appropriations, after providing the necessary materials, & tools,—would be entirely insufficient to pay the workmen, at present prices.

4th. The Regulations governing the workmen are <u>not</u> <u>changed</u>, they are <u>merely</u> <u>enforced</u>, every man being required to commence work at a fixed hour and labor during working hours—unless he finds it necessary to lose specific parts of a day, not less than a quarter being noted. The old practice of coming & going to suit the pleasure of each and working or playing—<u>in</u> hours or <u>out</u> of hours was an abuse formerly tolerated, but never sanctioned by regulations, & the pretext that <u>because</u> <u>men</u> <u>work</u> <u>by</u> <u>the</u> <u>piece</u>, they should be allowed to run machinery when they please & be absent whenever it suits their whim, finds no favor at private workshops nor can it be allowed where the work of one man depends on that done by another, for carrying on and keeping up all branches to a proper standard. The Master Armorer cannot keep all branches in a suitable state of advancement, unless he can rely on the quantity of work to be done by each man.

5th. The <u>real ground of opposition</u> to the present mode of supervision is well known to be this—The men have been paid high prices & were in the habit of working from 4 to 6 hours per day—& being absent whole days, or a week. At the end of a month their pay was generally the same in amount as if no absence had occurred.

They are now required to work full time and during fixed hours (according to old regulations) and the master of the Shop keeps a time account showing the time <u>actually</u> <u>spent</u> <u>in</u> <u>labor</u>. Here is the <u>great</u> <u>oppression</u> complained of. At the end of a month of <u>quantity</u> of <u>labor</u> <u>performed</u> for <u>product</u>, and the <u>time</u> during which it is effected are seen by a simple inspection of the Shop books. The degree of diligence used by each man is also known and hence results a knowledge of what is the <u>fair</u> <u>price</u> to be paid for <u>piece</u> <u>work</u>!!! The Armorers may attempt to disguise or hide the truth under a thousand clamors—but this is the <u>real</u> <u>cause</u> of their objections to a Military Superintendent. He enforces the Regulations which lay bare their secret practices (fraud—for I can use no better term). They can control a civil Supt. & have often done it! They have occasionally ousted one, and they have shot one.

It has long been considered a privilege to be employed at Springfield Armory and there are now about forty applications per week of first rate mechanics. It was formerly the custom for an Armorer to sell out his "chance" as it was called when he chose to do so—$100 dolls. have been paid for a "chance" to blow & strike in the Smithy and 200, 250 & even 300 dollars have been paid for "chances" in various branches at the Armory!!!

We say to the Armorers—here are our Regulations, if you will not abide by them—go elsewhere—for we know that as many good or better workmen can be had at any moment. They answer—no, we will not leave the armory. We insist on working for the United States and will fix our own terms!!! This is practically the fact & all private manufacturers at the North complain of the high prices paid at the Armories for <u>mechanical</u> skill of no great pretensions. Indeed, since the introduction of so many new machinery—very little skill is required to use them—a young man from the plough who had never used a tool in a workshop entered the armory in Feby. 1841— He now earns at present prices sixty dollars a month!! The subject can be extended almost indefinitely but I will stop.

G. Talcott.

Beaten in a Baltimore Shipyard, 1835

FREDERICK DOUGLASS

Thus, after an absence of three years and one month, I was once more permitted to return to my old home at Baltimore. . . .

In a few weeks after I went to Baltimore, Master Hugh hired me to Mr. William Gardner, an extensive ship-builder, on Fell's Point. I was put there to learn how to calk. It, however, proved a very unfavorable place for the accomplishment of this object. Mr. Gardner was engaged that spring in building two large man-of-war brigs, professedly for the Mexican government. The vessels were to be launched in the July of that year, and in failure thereof, Mr. Gardner was to lose a considerable sum; so that when I entered, all was hurry. There was no time to learn any thing. Every man had to do that which he knew how to do. In entering the shipyard, my orders from Mr. Gardner were to do whatever the carpenters commanded me to do. This was placing me at the beck and call of about seventy-five men. I was to regard all these as masters. Their word was to be my law. My situation was a most trying one. At times I needed a dozen pair of hands. I was called a dozen ways in the space of a single minute. Three or four voices would strike my ear at the same moment. It was—"Fred., come help me to cant this timber here."—"Fred., come carry this timber yonder."—"Fred., bring that roller here."—"Fred., go get a fresh can of water."—"Fred., come help me saw off the end of this timber."—"Fred., go quick, and get the crowbar."—"Fred., hold on the end of this fall."—"Fred., go to the blacksmith's shop, and get a new punch."—"Hurra, Fred.! run and bring me a cold chisel."—"I say, Fred., bear a hand, and get up a fire as quick as lightning under that steambox."—"Halloo, nigger! come, turn this grindstone."—"Come, come! move, move! and *bowse* this timber forward."—"I say, darky, blast your eyes, why don't you heat up some pitch?"—"Halloo! halloo! halloo!" (Three voices at the same time.) "Come here!—Go there!—Hold on where you are! Damn you, if you move, I'll knock your brains out!"

This was my school for eight months; and I might have remained there longer, but for a most horrid fight I had with four of the white apprentices, in which my left eye was nearly knocked out, and I was horribly mangled in other respects. The facts in the case were these: Until a very little while after I went there, white and black ship-carpenters worked side by side, and no one seemed to see any impropriety in it. All hands seemed to be very well satisfied. Many of the black carpenters were freemen. Things seemed to be going on very well. All at once, the white carpenters knocked off, and said they would not work with free colored workmen. Their reason for this, as alleged, was, that if free colored carpenters were encouraged, they would soon take the trade into their own hands, and poor white men would be thrown out of employment. They therefore felt called upon at once to put a stop to it. And, taking advantage of Mr. Gardner's necessities, they broke off, swearing they would work no longer, unless he would discharge his black carpenters. Now, though this did not extend to me in form, it did reach me in fact. My fellow-apprentices very soon began to feel it degrading to them to work with me. They began to put on airs,

Frederick Douglass, *Narrative of the Life of Frederick Douglass, An American Slave* (1845; New York: New American Library, 1967) pp. 99–104.

and talk about the "niggers" taking the country, saying we all ought to be killed; and, being encouraged by the journeymen, they commenced making my condition as hard as they could, by hectoring me around, and sometimes striking me. I, of course, kept the vow I made after the fight with Mr. Covey, and struck back again, regardless of consequences; and while I kept them from combining, I succeeded very well; for I could whip the whole of them, taking them separately. They, however, at length combined, and came upon me, armed with sticks, stones, and heavy handspikes. One came in front with a half brick. There was one at each side of me, and one behind me. While I was attending to those in front, and on either side, the one behind ran up with the handspike, and struck me a heavy blow upon the head. It stunned me. I fell, and with this they all ran upon me, and fell to beating me with their fists. I let them lay on for a while, gathering strength. In an instant, I gave a sudden surge, and rose to my hands and knees. Just as I did that, one of their number gave me, with his heavy boot, a powerful kick in the left eye. My eyeball seemed to have burst. When they saw my eye closed, and badly swollen, they left me. With this I seized the handspike, and for a time pursued them. But here the carpenters interfered, and I thought I might as well give it up. It was impossible to stand my hand against so many. All this took place in sight of not less than fifty white ship-carpenters, and not one interposed a friendly word; but some cried, "Kill the damned nigger! Kill him! kill him! He struck a white person." I found my only chance for life was in flight. I succeeded in getting away without an additional blow, and barely so; for to strike a white man is death by Lynch law,—and that was the law in Mr. Gardner's ship-yard; nor is there much of any other out of Mr. Gardner's ship-yard.

I went directly home, and told the story of my wrongs to Master Hugh; and I am happy to say of him, irreligious as he was, his conduct was heavenly, compared with that of his brother Thomas under similar circumstances. He listened attentively to my narration of the circumstances leading to the savage outrage, and gave many proofs of his strong indignation at it. The heart of my once overkind mistress was again melted into pity. My puffed-out eye and blood-covered face moved her to tears. She took a chair by me, washed the blood from my face, and, with a mother's tenderness, bound up my head, covering the wounded eye with a lean piece of fresh beef. It was almost compensation for my suffering to witness, once more, a manifestation of kindness from this, my once affectionate old mistress. Master Hugh was very much enraged. He gave expression to his feelings by pouring out curses upon the heads of those who did the deed. As soon as I got a little the better of my bruises, he took me with him to Esquire Watson's, on Bond Street, to see what could be done about the matter. Mr. Watson inquired who saw the assault committed. Master Hugh told him it was done in Mr. Gardner's ship-yard, at midday, where there were a large company of men at work. "As to that," he said, "the deed was done, and there was no question as to who did it." His answer was, he could do nothing in the case, unless some white man would come forward and testify. He could issue no warrant on my word. If I had been killed in the presence of a thousand colored people, their testimony combined would have been insufficient to have arrested one of the murderers. Master Hugh, for once, was compelled to say this state of things was too bad. Of course, it was impossible to get any white man to volunteer his testimony in my behalf, and against the white young men. Even those who may have sympathized with me were not prepared to do this. It required a degree of courage unknown to them to do so; for just at that time, the slightest manifestation of humanity toward a colored person was denounced as abolitionism, and that name subjected its bearer to frightful liabilities. The watchwords of the bloody-minded in that region, and in those days, were, "Damn the abolitionists!" and "Damn the niggers!" There was nothing done, and probably nothing would have been done if I had been killed. Such was, and such remains, the state of things in the Christian city of Baltimore.

Master Hugh, finding he could get no redress, refused to let me go back again to Mr. Gardner. He kept me himself, and his wife dressed my wound till I was again restored to health. He then took me into the ship-yard of which he was foreman, in the employment of Mr. Walter Price. There I was immediately set to calking, and very soon learned the art of using my mallet and irons. In the course of one year from the time I left Mr. Gardner's. I was able to command the highest wages given to the most experienced calkers. I was now of some importance to my master. I was bringing him from six to seven dollars per week. I sometimes brought him nine dollars per week: my wages were a dollar and a half a day. After learning how to calk, I sought my own employment, made my own contracts, and collected the money which I earned. My pathway became much more smooth than before; my condition was now much more comfortable. When I could get no calking to do; I did nothing. During these leisure times, those old notions about freedom would steal over me again. When in Mr. Gardner's employment, I was kept in such a perpetual whirl of excitement, I could think of nothing, scarcely, but my life; and in thinking of my life, I almost forgot my liberty. I have observed this in my experience of slavery,—that whenever my condition was improved, instead of its increasing my contentment, it only increased my desire to be free, and set me to thinking of plans to gain my freedom. I have found that, to make a contented slave, it is necessary to make a thoughtless one. It is necessary to darken his moral and mental vision, and, as far as possible, to annihilate the power of reason. He must be able to detect no inconsistencies in slavery; he must be made to feel that slavery is right; and he can be brought to that only when he ceases to be a man.

I was now getting, as I have said, one dollar and fifty cents per day. I contracted for it; I earned it; it was paid to me; it was rightfully my own; yet, upon each returning Saturday night, I was compelled to deliver every cent of that money to Master Hugh. And why? Not because he earned it,—not because he had any hand in earning it,—not because I owed it to him,—nor because he possessed the slightest shadow of a right to it; but solely because he had the power to compel me to give it up. The right of the grim-visaged pirate upon the high seas is exactly the same.

E S S A Y S

During the first half of the twentieth century, and indeed well into the 1970s, scholars interested in the history of technology paid relatively little attention to what transpired inside mills, factories, and other industrial settings. There were exceptions, such as Louis C. Hunter's perceptive treatment of steamboats and their factorylike environments in *Steamboats on Western Rivers*. By and large, however, historical research focused primarily on "who's first" questions of invention, development, and technology transfer.

An emphasis on the sources of invention and economic growth ruled the day mainly because engineers and economic historians (many of them economists) were the earliest scholars to take a serious interest in the history of technology. Quite naturally, the questions they posed reflected the interest of their professions. Readers learned much about the exploits of inventors, engineers and industrial leaders and how they built modern America. Conspicuously absent were the day-to-day experiences of working people and the roles they played in industrial enterprises.

The following essays represent attempts to right the balance by integrating the history of workers with the history of technology. The first selection, from Judith McGaw's *Most Wonderful Machine,* addresses the relationship between mechanization and work in the papermaking industry of Berkshire County, Massachusetts. In addition to noting the impact of mechanization on the health of workers and the pace of their work, McGaw discusses the gendering of technology within the industry's labor system. She argues that men's work tended to become mechanized while women's work did not.

The second essay, from Charles Dew's *Bond of Iron,* examines industrial slavery through the ironmaking operations of William Weaver at Buffalo Forge near Lexington, Virginia. Close scrutiny of Weaver's record books allows Dew to reconstruct the daily lives and labors of Weaver's slaves and so provide intimate details seldom available to historians. Dew argues that the possession of essential skills by slaves like Sam Williams and "Tooler" gave them a certain ability to ameliorate their condition, something that fieldworkers (the vast bulk of southern slaves) did not have.

The final essay, by Merritt Roe Smith, seeks some common patterns between free and industrial slave labor and finds them in the ways industrial workers accommodated to regimentation through the practice of on-the-job pacing, as well as in their communal activities outside the factory gate. Although outright violence occasionally flared within and around industrial workplaces, all three authors recognize—and emphasize—the daily, often covert resistances and reciprocal practices that existed between masters and workers in antebellum America.

Gender and Papermaking

JUDITH A. MCGAW

Several thousand men worked in the Berkshire paper industry between 1827 and 1885. Of necessity I have relied primarily on statistical summaries to identify who comprised the work force and how its composition changed over time. By itself, however, such an approach cannot answer the question "Who were the workers?" It automatically excludes from consideration salient but nonquantifiable characteristics. One of these—workers' pride—deserves special notice at the outset, because it pervades workers' correspondence and memoirs and should influence the interpretation we place on the quantitative evidence that follows. It was expressed most directly by Alfred Hoxie in 1930 as he recalled his fellow employees in the 1880s:

> The old paper makers took a lot of pride in their work. If a man was a machine tender, he thought of course he was the big fellow in the paper business. Best paid job, and most skilled man. The loft man—[I] was a loft man. He took pride in that. They had learned their trade, and it was a matter of pride to them.

From Judith A. McGaw, *Most Wonderful Machine* (Princeton, NJ: Princeton University Press, 1987), pp. 282–283, 289, 296–297, 304–305, 309–311, 317–318, 322–324, 334, 337–353, 368–369.

Hoxie's recollection might be suspect as filtered through the haze of memory, but the same message reverberates in contemporary workers' correspondence. Writing from Bridgeport, Connecticut, in 1849, Charles Barnes informed the Cranes:

> I thank you for the offer which you have made me, but I must now decline accepting it, and as you have another person engaged to fill the place designed for me, I trust it will not be much of a disappointment to you that I refuse to accept.
>
> As to the other situation you mention, at Ballstown Springs [Ballston Spa] I would say that I consider it no compliment to be tendered such a one, under J.G. [the mill's sometimes drunken superintendent], a being with more tongue than conscience. It would be beneath the dignity of any man with a mind sensitive to attempted injuries, and that too without the least provocation.

Thirty years later, despite diminished prospects for advancement, A. M. Martin's letter from Holyoke sounds the same note of pride:

> Mr. S. R. Wagg informs me that you are in want of a first class machine tender and I having a good experience of 14 years on machine I think I could suit you in every respect. I do not get drunk and neglect my work and can say that I neither chew tobacco or drink rum. I am now to work for the Crocker Mfg. Co. Have been for the last year. One thing I will say two is that in changing orders I do not change as most machine tenders do at random or guess work but use figures to [do] it and there by know just what my machine is making per hour and also being very corect to weight in changing and starting on difrent orders. Can furnish you any amount of the best recomends in the hand. Should you feel like giving me a trial pleas state wages and if steady work etc. My object in changing is to better my self[.]

Writing from the same town two years later, Edward Breck expressed the same sentiment more succinctly: "This sheet I write on was made by my self." . . .

Mill owners . . . visited the mill, yard, engine room, and machine shop, . . . maintaining familiarity with all of the skills their diversified work force possessed. Their increasingly generalized knowledge contrasted sharply with their workmen's growing specialization. The divergence was especially noteworthy between owners and skilled paper workers, those workmen with whom owners had once held much in common. . . . [B]y 1885 most paper workmen no longer designated themselves "paper maker," the traditional term signifying training and expertise in all phases of paper manufacture. Only a small group of retirees used the term in preference to any other. Instead, over four-fifths (80.4 percent) of those specifying paper-making occupations identified themselves as possessing more specialized skills and knowledge. Paper workmen listed themselves as "machine tender," "back tender," "engineer," "finisher," "assistant finisher," "foreman of the drying room," "superintendent of the rag room," and so forth.

Workers' letters convey the same sense of specialization. Almost all asked for a specific job and those mentioning two positions usually indicated a preference. When enumerating their qualifications, workers listed their experience at a particular task far more often than any other trait. Some were even more specific, such as William P. Phair, writing in 1852, who had "attended Cylinder Machines on course paper"; James Lovell, who heard of a machine-tending position in 1870 and explained, "I have not been used to Cylinder Machines, but thinking it might be for the Fordrinier I concluded to write you"; or Walter R. Brooks, applying in 1872, who noted his expertise at bank note paper making. Those few who claimed the broad experience of "a paper maker by trade" or "a regular bred paper maker" were atypical, such as Mr. Grady, an old man when he sought work in 1847, and Peter Sulivan, a newly arrived Englishman writing in 1881. More common were unemployed individuals who noted their special skills, but expressed willingness to perform other tasks. For example, Joseph Carroll wrote in 1871: "I am used to engines & finishing, but am not particular to making myself generally useful in the line of papermaking. I am just from England and am desirous of obtaining a situation as soon as possible."

. . . [I]nventors and developers of new machines most successfully replicated the manual skills of male employees: vatmen, couchers, layboys, loftmen, sizers, and some finishers, such as rulers. Thus, we might expect that, for men at least, mechanization altered paper mill work adversely. In some respects it did. Accelerating the trends that had originated in the hard-pressed hand mills of the 1820s, the adoption of new and improved machines subjected workmen to a more hectic pace, longer hours, and periodic unemployment. Moreover, unlike earlier paper makers, machine tenders and many of their fellow male employees risked being killed or maimed. Added to the workers' increased specialization and diminished prospects of social mobility, these changes further differentiated the work experience of worker and owner, in this case clearly to the detriment of the worker.

Yet we should not exaggerate the degradation of paper mill work in the wake of mechanization. As noted above, the men who tended paper mill machinery were highly skilled, proud, and often greatly in demand. During prosperous times especially, they capitalized on these attributes to bargain for steady work, more healthful conditions, higher wages, and promotion to supervisory positions. Also, most had only infrequent supervision, so that they could exercise some measure of control over their work. In addition, we should recall that employers had substantial incentives to eliminate or minimize the principal sources of unemployment: low water, equipment failure, fire, and depressed paper markets. And owners spent enough time in the mills to be aware of the hardships associated with long hours, dangerous machines, and unhealthful workplaces, so they generally improved conditions as they found themselves more economically secure. Of course, economic circumstances fluctuated with the business cycle and differed among firms, and so did working conditions.

The worker's situation also varied with his position, so that to visualize men's experience of mechanization, we must first look at the tasks they came to perform. Although machines most often assumed men's traditional paper-making tasks, they did not alter the terms of the sexual division of labor that had prevailed in the unmechanized industry. The new or modified work that men performed around machines bore fundamental similarities to the hand operations the machines superseded. Men continued to hold positions requiring long training, strength, or initiative, and jobs conferring prestige or authority. Mechanization multiplied workers' output, changed their specific duties and transformed their working conditions, but it did not free mill owners from their dependence on workmen's skills and judgment.

. . . Machines did not replace workers, reduce their level of skill, or subdivide their tasks. Rather, as intended, mechanization multiplied the output of the limited number of skilled workmen. Eventually, by reducing paper's cost and abetting its more general use, mechanization also multiplied jobs for skilled paper workers, jobs filled by men trained while performing less skilled tasks such as backtender, engineer's assistant, duster or bleach boiler attendant, and trimmer man. Of the new, non-paper-making positions added by enlarged mills, skilled occupations such as bookkeeper, carpenter, steam engineer, and machinist employed about as many men as did unskilled jobs such as ditch digger, teamster, and night watchman.

Although mechanization did not entail any profound redefinition of paper mill tasks, it did transform the conditions of work. . . . [W]hether or not they tended paper-making machines, all workmen experienced unprecedented pressure to keep the mill's expensive machinery fully employed. The result was a more hectic, less flexible work pace, the most pervasive and permanent deleterious effect of mechanization. Less common and shorter-lived indications that machine production affected paper mill work adversely were longer work days, periodic unemployment, and more dangerous and unpleasant surroundings. Skilled male workers experienced most of this deterioration in working conditions. . . .

Mechanization had a more direct impact on the atmosphere and safety of the workplace, especially affecting the industry's most skilled workers. In the early years, the odor of lard oil, the principal lubricant, and the smoke of kerosene or coal oil lanterns fouled the air over the long hours that unventilated machine rooms operated. Water evaporated from the paper on the machine and dryers and condensed on the cooler walls and ceilings. Some mills lined machine room ceilings with heated oils to reduce condensation, but others remained so damp that one worker seeking employment with Z. M. Crane explained. "My object in leaving this place is on account of the Room in which I work, it is verry wet and is ingering my health." After quoting his wages he concluded, "you see my wages is good—But money will not purches health." Engineers also endured wet working conditions, while rag room workers breathed in air filled with dust and lint from dusters and rag cutters.

In later years improved ventilation, heating, hoods over the machines, better lubricants, and gas lightning alleviated these problems. Mill owners also improved the cleanliness of their establishments. For example, in 1871 a *Scientific American* reporter found H. D. Cone's Housatonic mill so clean that he thought of "carefully removing all dust from his shoes before entering." Similarly, in their 1879 renovation of the Colt mill, Z. M. and J. B. Crane invested in improved sanitation by installing urinals, water closets, and copper-bottomed basins.

By contrast, nothing could be done to still the deafening noise that Fourdriniers and more numerous beaters brought to the mills' machine rooms and engine rooms. The many moving parts of paper-making machines forced machine tenders to shout when they needed to be heard over the continuous clash of metal against metal, a sharp contrast to the quiet conversation and easy jests the vat room had permitted. Louder talk had prevailed in early beater rooms as engineers seeking diversion raised their voices over the rumble of the rag engine, but as mills added more and larger engines, the thunder of the beaters reduced engine room conversation to a minimum. Also, while the rising tumult of their surroundings effectively isolated skilled male employees from life outside the mill's walls, machines incorporated more tasks and became more automated, making men's work more solitary.

The noise, isolation, dust, odor, and dampness of mechanized mills impaired workers' health and affected the quality of their working lives gradually and undramatically, attracting little contemporary comment. By contrast, the dangers of the new machines were highly visible. Any reader of the local press learned repeatedly of their destructiveness of workers' lives and limbs. For example, in its first fifteen years (1857–71) the *Valley Gleaner* of Lee reported fifty-four paper workers injured on the job, eight of them fatally. Because men performed most mechanized work, almost all accident victims (87 percent) and all but one of those killed were men. Over two-thirds of these accidents were directly attributable to machine production, while the remainder involved construction workers and teamsters, whose work increased as mechanized mills grew and prospered.

Workers had to exercise particular care around the flying shafts and belts that transmitted power throughout the mechanized portions of the mill. The majority of fatalities and the second largest number of injuries occurred when the transmission system caught men's clothing or arms and they were drawn in and crushed, or thrown across the room. Accidents involving paper-making machines, rag cutters, and machine shop tools caused fewer fatalities, but affected more workers, most of whom lost fingers, hands, or arms. Boiler explosions and escaping steam injured the rest. In the worst instances, high-pressure steam scalded workers in one case fatally, while the force of explosions and flying debris cut and bruised others, including one man who was blown out a window by the blast of an exploding bleach boiler. By the 1870s and 1880s machine makers advertised safety features on cutters and trimmers, and experience with steam boilers made explosions uncommon, but the mill's principal machine and its transmission system remained hazardous. In sum, mechanization had transformed paper making from a relatively safe craft to a relatively dangerous industry. . . .

The absence of evident class consciousness is not surprising given the limited and gradual change in the relative status and comparative activities of workers and owners. Unlike industries in which factories superseded self-employed craftsmen or household manufacture, paper making had always taken place in mills that some men owned and in which others collected wages. Mechanization did not alter this situation; instead, emergent distinction in the tasks and prospects of employer and employed constituted changes in degree rather than in kind. For example, owners came to spend more time in the office and on the road, but they still learned paper-making in the mills and maintained familiarity with the workers and their work. Similarly, before the Civil War some workers still advanced to ownership and owners frequently failed and became employees. After the war workers continued to become owners, although those who bought Berkshire mills failed or held small working interests, and the numbers and ultimate fates of those who bought mills outside the county are difficult to ascertain. Moreover, mechanized paper making entailed long hours for owners as well as workers and subjected both entrepreneurs and employees to the uncertainties of a boom-and-bust economy.

Simultaneously, the introduction of machines forged new bonds between worker and owner as they shared responsibility for mechanization. Workers built, installed, operated, and repaired machines, usually supervised by other employees. In the process workers helped shape the equipment, organization, and operating methods of mechanized mills. For example, in the early 1850s skilled employees J. D. Gibbons and T. T. Chapin authored many of the letters relaying technical information from L. M. Crane's Saratoga and Ballston Spa mills to his brothers in Dalton. The correspondence documents especially the continuous expertise workmen contributed to developing procedures for processing stock and adding new chemicals. Mechanical invention occurred more sporadically, but between July 1857 and October 1858 the *Valley Gleaner* reported four improvements made by Platner & Smith's workmen: a "letter copying press of a large and unique pattern, which . . . reflects great credit upon the maker . . . an apprentice . . . named William Jenne"; "a new and simple apparatus for handling paper for trimming," which increased output by one-third and cost only half as much as a conventional press; Robert McAlpine's "very simple and excellent device for raising and lowering the pens" on the ruling machine; and a mechanism for grinding the paper-making machine's seven-foot cutter knives "so that any number of knives may be ground exactly alike, thus saving very much, both of labor and the wear of knives," "invented and built by those ingenious mechanics. Messrs. A. and W. Palmer." Workers also abetted and shaped mechanization when training additional workers, sometimes acting as mentors to future mill owners. For example, Byron Weston acknowledged that when Saugerties paper worker James McDonald taught him how to beat stock, he "laid the basis . . . which has enabled [me] to be a manufacturer of the finest grade of paper made in this country." Workers who moved from mill to mill as many increasingly did, helped disseminate and standardize the new technology, exerting an influence that complemented mill owners' visits and correspondence. . . .

. . . In accord with the relatively clear, distinct, and rigid notions of masculine and feminine behavior that emerged in nineteenth-century America, workers viewed themselves first and foremost as men and, thus, as the mill owners' equals, an attitude that made personal negotiation more appropriate than collective bargaining. The refrain of a poem quoted in a twentieth-century publication devoted to early paper-making history and lore expresses this attitude succinctly: "Business is business, but men are men." Similarly, workers' memoirs humorously recount mill owners' foibles and the pranks workers and owners played on one another, emphasizing that owners were fellow men, not remote or superior beings.

The egalitarian implications of shared manliness were underscored during the years of paper industry mechanization by Jacksonian rhetoric and the achievement of manhood suffrage. That some contemporary workers achieved ownership, while some owners reverted to the status of employee conveyed the same message. By the 1860s, 1870s, and 1880s, widely shared masculine experience on Civil War battlefields had reinforced this sense of shared manhood and had helped certify Irish workmen as equals.

Workers' sense of manliness helps account for the absence of protest against the new dangers of the workplace. One suggestive anecdote comes from the lore of the paper industry and involves Nosey Hill.

> It used to be said that one would never be a good machine tender until his fingers had been nipped in the calenders. However true this may be, "Nosey" had little sympathy for his backtenders when they were nipped in this manner. When asked whether he had ever been nipped, "Nosey" promptly answered. "Sure, but I never made a fuss about it. Why I had my arm drawn into a calender up to the elbow once, but I just took it calmly and when the rolls started jumping I jerked my arm out and went along about my business."

As usual, Nosey embodies common experience in exaggerated form. The tale's message—that injury forms an inevitable part of learning, which real men bear with fortitude—simply expresses contemporary notions of manhood, notions that were reiterated and glorified locally in commemorations of Civil War battlefield bravery.

At the same time, the dangers men encountered outside the mills must have minimized their sense that paper mill dangers were unusual or unavoidable. Horses injured far more local citizens than did paper machinery, and local newspapers reported frequent railroad and steamship accidents, including the death of thirty-six-year-old paper worker John Quirk, killed after he boarded the wrong train and fell between cars while searching for the conductor.

Equality based on shared masculinity also helps explain the absence of evidence that Berkshire paper workers acted collectively as adversaries of the mill owners, in contrast to reported organization or spontaneous and sporadic group protest in county industries employing larger numbers of less skilled workers. The skill and small size of the paper mill's male work force apparently enabled workers to keep protest individualized, to express grievances man to man. A few extant letters depict such interactions, although most took place face to face and left no record. Writing to the Cranes in 1857, the father of one of their workers lodged the following protest: "my Boy says that you have paid three Dollars of his wages out to Charles Whitcom[.] if you pay eny mony out for me with out my orders You will pay it again if i can make you[.] you have no rite to pay out my mony without my orders[.]" In a similar tone, James Wells castigated Marshal Crane in 1865 as not having "acted manley by me" when employing him in a different mill and at different hours than they had originally negotiated.

Because owners varied in their personalities, the outcome of individualized protest depended on the man being approached; thus, workers probably exercised most control over their circumstances when they decided to apply to a particular man. Many workers indicated the importance they placed on their choice of employer when they listed who they worked for, rather than their occupation, in the county directory. . . .

I am inclined to believe that, favored by growing numbers and greater local longevity, workers who valued security and pride in a job well done came to exert far greater influence in Berkshire mill towns than those who valued power or affluence. Their expertise with machines, preference for sobriety, and rough sense of equality with the owners left them with few regrets over industrialization and few grievances that they could not express openly. For those anxious to risk seeking greater independence or adventure, the mill doors swung both ways and opened on a variety of paths. Such was not the case for their female co-workers. Their tale remains to be told. . . .

Turning our attention from male to female paper workers, we seem to enter another world, a world cut off from the dynamic arena where male workers and owners wrestled with the problems and opportunities of mechanization. In 1885 most women working in paper factories performed tasks identical to those of women in preindustrial paper mills, and the few who tended machines did essentially similar work, seated alongside the mill's smallest and least efficient mechanisms. Women continued to earn far less than men and encountered few of the novel risks and arduous conditions associated with men's mechanized work. For most, apparently, labor outside the home continued to be a transitory stage, peripheral to the domestic and maternal vocations that earned them social approbation. All told outward appearances imply that earlier notions of women's work exerted such profound influences as to preclude technological change making any significant difference where female paper workers were concerned.

As in preindustrial paper mills, most women could be found laboring in the predominantly female rag rooms and finishing rooms of mechanized mills. The largest number still worked at rag processing, where they either sorted rags by color, fabric, and condition or cut them to open seams, remove fasteners and damaged portions, and reduce the rags to small, uniform squares. Mechanization altered only the number of workers and the distribution of rag room work. The development of more standardized rag grades reduced the relative demand for sorters, especially in fine paper mills. Simultaneously, mechanized mills' greatly augmented fiber consumption made more work for cutters, an increase offset only belatedly and partially by the use of mechanical rag cutters and nonrag fiber.

For most of the nineteenth century, rag rooms remained technologically primitive. Rag sorting involved manual manipulation and visual discrimination. . . . Rag cutters employed the same simple hand tools as women had used in Berkshire's original mill. Melville has left us a graphic account of these women's tools and tasks. In the rag room there "stood rows of girls. Before each was vertically thrust up a long, glittering scythe. . . . The curve of the scythe, and its having no snath to it, made it look exactly like a sword. To and fro, across the sharp edge, the girls forever dragged long strips of rags, washed white, picked from baskets at one side; thus ripping asunder every seam, and converting the tatters almost into lint. . . . [Occasionally] the girls, dropping their rags, plied each a whetstone up and down the swordblade."

Nor did mechanization alter the pace of women's rag room work. Because mill owners depended on women's care in sorting and cutting rags for their paper's quality, they did not press for greater individual output. The women worked under a modified piece-rate system in which they cut or sorted a specified number of pounds to earn a day's pay and received added compensation for "over work." Expected productivity depended on the quality of the rags and did not increase with mechanization. . . .

Tedious but unhurried manual labor also engaged most other finishing room women. Female workers continued to count paper by hand, a task unchanged by mechanization save for there being more paper to count and more women busily counting it. As with other feminine tasks, quantitative standards derived from qualitative concerns. At Crane & Co.'s Government Mill, which made currency, bond, and bank note paper, counts had to be precise and verified by a second counter. There, an average pair of female counters turned out forty thousand sheets per day. Counts of letter and ledger paper could be less accurate and need not be verified, so that each worker had sole responsibility for somewhat more paper. Finishing room women also folded paper by hand, using wooden blocks as guides. Like other traditional feminine tasks, the work required dexterity and care, but not long training.

The same attributes characterized the few new jobs women performed around machines. As noted earlier, men adjusted and maintained finishing room machines. Women simply sat alongside the mechanisms, feeding in paper or withdrawing the finished product. Most of these women—those tending platers, calenders, and ruling machines—worked in pairs, one woman placing paper in the machine and the other removing it. Perhaps, as Melville described, they obtained "some small variety to the monotony" by occasionally changing places. Smaller stamping and envelope machines required only one attendant, each generally working beside similarly employed women. Apparently, as mechanization created new jobs, owners simply assigned women to those that resembled traditional women's work: those that were monotonous and interruptible, requiring neither long training nor initiative.

The few short-lived jobs women performed in the machine room conform to the same pattern. Before mechanical layboys were perfected, women tended the cutter end of the machine, removing and stacking the sheets by hand. Such work must have appeared perfectly appropriate to women who had performed and continued to perform the same tasks in dry lofts. As long as loft drying persisted, women continued the traditional, repetitive work of hanging sheets to dry and jogging dry stacks to even the edges.

The relative uniformity of women's paper mill jobs is confirmed by their letters of application. They were much less likely than men to request a particular job or to cite their prior experience. Reflecting the limited training required, a few mentioned their lack of paper mill experience, in sharp contrast to male applicants. Owners' letters offering women employment also depict women's tasks as interchangeable. Byron Weston, for example, offered Mary and Sarah Hall work on the calender and the ruling machine, but noted, "We think we can keep you busy at the work we name but want to feel at liberty to ask you to change to other work when we have not enough of the kind you work at generally." Similarly, he told Lydia Smith, "We will give you a good chance, either at finishing & stamping, on the calender or ruling machine. We want you as an extra hand & to do anything in the finishing room. . . ."

Profound continuity despite mechanization also characterized female paper workers' wages, hours, and working conditions. Women continued to earn substantially less than their male co-workers and to lack the unskilled man's expectation of acquiring skills that commanded considerably higher incomes. . . . Statewide data collected in 1885 . . . show 70 percent of paper mill women earning less than $6 a week, whereas only 5 percent of male paper workers earned so little. The majority of men earned $6 to $10 a week, but almost as many, 43 percent, earned more than $10. By contrast, only 1 percent of the women earned more than $10, probably by far exceeding standard piecework requirements."

At the same time, because women's work was not tied to the pace of the machine, women's hours, unlike men's did not increase, come to require shift or night work, or lose their earlier flexibility. Most women routinely accomplished one and a half times the required day's work so that some came to work fewer than the traditional eleven hours even in the early years of mechanization, when female workers were greatly in demand. Most Berkshire paper mill women obtained a ten-hour day long before an 1874 Massachusetts legislative decree mandated a ten-hour limit for female employees. In fact, state commissioners studying the problem in 1865 found that women at the Hurlbut Paper Company worked only nine hours. Thereafter, Saturday work gradually declined to a half day. By 1885 one-quarter of the state's paper mills assured all female workers less than ten hours daily. Some women further curtailed their work hours by taking advantage of the piecework system. In the 1880s married women left Crane's mill two hours early.

Likewise, women's working conditions remained much like those of preindustrial workers. Separated from the mill's heavy machinery, they worked in comparative quiet, permitting conversation to relieve the tedium of their work. Moreover, unlike men's increasingly solitary jobs, all women worked in groups, in pairs, or alongside other women, so that conversation remained possible. Their separate workrooms kept women away from most new workplace hazards. Men suffered nearly seven times the reported injuries and all but one of the fatalities. And of the few accidents involving women, nearly half occurred when women ventured out of their workrooms and came too close to revolving shafts.

This is not to say that women's work entailed no risks, only that the dangers changed little with mechanization and either remained invisible to contemporaries or were deemed too trivial to report. As Melville observed, "The [rag room] air swam with fine, poisonous particles, which from all sides darted, subtilely, as motes in sunbeams, into the lungs." In addition to risking respiratory disease, at least two women apparently contracted smallpox from infected rags before mills began providing vaccination. Rag room women, especially newcomers, must have cut their hands; paper cuts were certainly ubiquitous among finishing room workers; and long-time paper sorters sometimes snapped tendons after years of rotating their wrists through the same motion. Mechanization increased the number of women at risk, but may have decreased the percentage seriously affected because women, like men, worked shorter average stints in mechanized mills.

As in preindustrial mills, women's tenure in mechanized mills was briefer than men's suggesting that women continued to give employment a secondary place in their lives. Census takers in 1880 compiled substantial evidence that women worked temporarily, before marriage, and near home. The preponderant female worker was young, single, and lived under parental supervision. Girls under the age of twenty-one made up 41 percent of the mills' female work force, 64 percent of the women remained unmarried, and 46 percent lived with one or both parents. Time book data during the years of mechanization substantiate the impression that most women viewed their work as temporary. At Crane's mill single women averaged less than a year's employment between 1834 and 1848, and only slightly over a year between 1863 and 1876. Single females put in slightly longer average stints at L. L. Brown's mill, but there, too, they were the mill's least persistent workers.

These characteristics of paper mill women and their work typify the vast majority of nineteenth-century women, whose history is "a tale of continuity despite superficial change." For virtually all wage-earning women, "sex-segregated labor markets, the assumption that female workers are transient, and the persistence of lower pay for women encouraged the conceptualization of 'women's work' according to preexisting sex-role stereotypes and permitted the continued employment of women in less mechanized or industrialized occupations. . . . Even when machines or the emergence of new industries created apparently novel jobs, employers consistently assigned women to jobs that were relatively monotonous and did not call for rapt attention, were interruptible and easily resumed, and were not visibly hazardous," jobs like those of preindustrial women. Moreover, the characteristics of female employees' tasks made their work essentially the same as that of the majority of nineteenth-century women: wives and mothers performing housework. In fact, the largest groups of female employees labored as domestic servants and needlewomen, performing tasks identical to those of unpaid wives and mothers.

The striking absence of mechanization from homes and most other feminized workplaces underscores the uniformity of women's work throughout industrializing America. That women usually performed unmechanized work encouraged demeaning generalizations in the mechanically innovative nineteenth century. Contrasting apparent continuities in women's manual labor with dramatic changes in men's mechanized jobs, contemporaries readily concluded that God or nature had assigned women their work and that society could not or should not alter it. Such assertions minimized the novel functions of women's traditional tasks in their new technological context, obscuring women's contributions to mechanization. Placing women in technological history requires that we set their work in the context of technological innovation. . . .

Paper mills provide a valuable perspective on the role of women's work in a mechanizing society because rag rooms and finishing rooms were visibly connected to the sites of men's technologically innovative work, unlike contemporary homes, laundresses' kitchens, seamstresses' garrets, and most other feminized work locales. Contrasts between men's and women's work in paper mills reveal why women retained their traditional tasks and how those tasks contributed to mechanization. Whereas machines took over craftsmen's skilled occupations in paper mills, women's apparently simpler jobs proved difficult or impossible to mechanize. Yet women's unmechanized work compensated for and abetted mechanization; it assured machine-made paper a market by maintaining its quality. As a result, mechanizing mills grew increasingly dependent on their female employees. Moreover, by remaining relatively unspecialized, female workers gave mill owners considerable flexibility in their employment, a valuable asset as the employment of specialized male workers and expensive papermaking machines reduced flexibility elsewhere in the mills.

Nonetheless, woman's traditional, quality-oriented, unspecialized work earned diminished recognition as Americans came to value progress, quantitative increases in productivity, and specialized skills. The sharpened contrasts between men's and women's paper mill work strengthened traditional assumptions that women lacked skill and did not deserve high wages, beliefs reinforced by women's analogous activities in homes and other feminized work sites. As men grew less experienced in comparable work, employers and supervisors readily accepted that women's skills and financial needs were inferior to men's and greatly benefited from their society's elaboration of those beliefs. Judging from paper mills, then, it appears no coincidence that the doctrine of separate spheres emerged to minimize women's skills and economic importance at the very time that mechanization actually made their work more critical. The obvious serviceability in paper mills of new beliefs about women helps identify women's substantial contributions to industrial mechanization through their labor in the more separate feminine sphere: the home.

Women continued to perform their traditional preindustrial tasks in mechanized paper mills primarily because . . . machine builders did not and probably could not devise commercially viable mechanical alternatives. In particular, the sorting of rags and the inspection of finished paper entailed visual discrimination not replicable by machines and only partially superseded in twentieth-century mills by electronic scanning devices. Similarly, although machines were devised to reduce rags to relatively uniform pieces, mechanical rag cutters could not open seams, remove fasteners, or eliminate damaged portions, tasks for which female rag cutters relied on their eyes as well as their hands.

Women's work around finishing room machines underscores the limitations of nineteenth-century mechanization. Although machines successfully imitated the manual labor of ruling or stamping, the precise placement of sheet after sheet of paper, a task involving hand-eye coordination, evidently eluded consistent mechanical replication. Judging from the substantial costs attributable to paper broken or damaged by finishing room machines, the capacity to handle dry paper without wrinkling or tearing some sheets also proved difficult to build into machines. This accounts for women's retention to remove paper from machines, feed it into calenders, fold it manually, and even its edges after stacking it. Likewise, while it is possible to conceive of mechanical paper counters, it is hard to imagine a machine operating much more rapidly than hand counters but not damaging sheets so as to require further sorting. Only modern electronic technology has produced such an efficient mechanism suggesting that the hand-eye coordination characterizing the female paper counter's work had no acceptable mechanical analog. . . .

In helping to establish and maintain the quality of machine-made goods, paper mill women performed an essential function, one shared by women in other mechanizing industries. Without these women's labors, mechanization might well have been delayed or prolonged by more limited markets for the machines' augmented output. This is not to dispute the general contention that Americans mechanized more readily than the English because Americans more readily accepted inferior machine-made commodities. It is certainly conceivable that, given paper mills' reliance on business markets, maintaining traditional standards figured more prominently in the paper industry than in industries producing consumer goods. But quality is relative, not absolute. Like late nineteenth-century newsprint mills, all industries encountered some market-imposed standards of acceptable product quality and these standards probably declined only gradually as mechanization progressively opened new markets by lowering prices. The role of paper mill women, therefore, suggests that nineteenth-century female industrial employees, although disproportionately concentrated in unmechanized finishing and inspection jobs, made a substantial contribution to mechanization, and one that has been minimized by simply comparing the American emphasis on price and quantity to the British concern with quality. By performing unimpressive manual operations, women successfully enforced standards and applied finishing touches that maintained and created markets for the products of mechanized industry.

Women also helped mill owners adjust output to the unpredictable fluctuations of nineteenth-century markets, for demand was fickle as well as selective. Publishers and paper wholesalers could not usually predict customer response to new commodities such as specialized periodicals, books by American authors, or tinted stationery. In filling rush orders, coping with the business cycle, and tailoring production to meet varying demand for various products, mill owners could rely on the willingness and ability of their female workers to alter their tasks and modify their work schedules. Initially, flexible female workers especially helped unspecialized mills balance out finishing work that varied with the product. Later, women's flexibility continued to be an asset because it compensated in part for the specialization and inflexible schedules of men and machines.

As noted above, employers sought women who would "work at anything in the finishing room" so as to keep them fully employed when demand flagged for the products of one specialized machine. Unlike men, women were expected to move back and forth between various tasks no matter how long they had been employed. . . .

As new technology came to require periodic shutdowns for repairs and maintenance, employers could also more readily reduce female than male employment, thus helping to lower the costs associated with unpredictable technology. When mills stopped for repairs, female workers were simply told to stay home, sometimes for weeks at a time, whereas male employees continued to work and receive wages. Routine maintenance also curtailed women's employment. For example, rag room women at L. L. Brown's mill lost two days in May 1858 while other workers were "Washing up for Spring."

Mill owners' flexibility in their employment of women reflected the comparative ease with which women learned paper mill work and transferred their skills from one mill to another. Employers revealed their expectation that almost any woman could do the work by issuing frequent general newspaper advertisements for female workers, whereas they relied almost exclusively on informal informational networks to select appropriately skilled men. The rag room work and paper sorting that engaged most female laborers was also the work most quickly mastered. Of the seventy women's jobs advertised in the *Valley Gleaner* from 1860 through 1874, fifty-six fell into these categories, and none of these advertisements cited skill or experience as a requirement. A few finishing room tasks involved somewhat more training, thus a few advertisements and workers' letters of application mentioned experience. But women mastered even these jobs with relative ease allowing mill owners to make do with inexperienced women. For example, calender work took the longest to learn, but when Crane & Co. sought an experienced woman, Ballston Spa mill superintendent Fred Thompson found that the only skilled woman available was a widow who anticipated child-care problems if she moved to Dalton. Rather than offer the widow special inducements to come, as owners often did for male workers, Thompson suggested, "There is lots of Yankee girls about here—but none at liberty that understands the Callenders but it would not take very long to learn on Collar Paper—so I think perhaps it would be better to send you a girl than the widow."

Women also adjusted quickly to differences between mills, whereas even highly skilled men needed time to acquire familiarity with the idiosyncrasies of individual paper-making machines and rag engines. As a result, mill owners could meet short-term demand for female workers through arrangements with fellow manufacturers. Crane family correspondence frequently mentions "girls" sent from Dalton to the New York state mills operated by Crane and Laflin family members, or women brought to Dalton from New York state. Similarly, Byron Weston inquired of May & Rogers: "Can you send us a good girl finisher & one paper sorter for 2 or 3 weeks? Three of our girls are out, sick, & the work is getting very much behind." Evidently the practice was common, for Weston promised, "If you can send only the finisher & will do it we will try & reciprocate." He sent similar requests to Carson Brothers, Platner & Smith, and the Union Paper Company. Such work, at employers' convenience, contributed to single women's brief average tenure, especially during the early years of mechanization, when mill owners coped with very unpredictable markets. For example, Weston was "very much obliged for the favor" when Sarah Hall filled in for three days on his ruling machine. She had evidently come some distance, for Weston supplied temporary boardinghouse accommodations.

The ease with which large numbers of women learned papermaking tasks, exchanged one task for another, and adjusted to different mills helped confirm the impression conveyed by emergent differences between men's and women's work: that women's work was unskilled, natural, and God-given. From the mill owners' perspective the work was justly designated "unskilled" because it required little mill training and no formal education. Yet the evidence that machines could not replicate women's work and that mill owners benefited from the relatively low wages such work commanded should caution us not to accept at face value mill owners' assessments of their female employees' skills. Comparison of women's "unskilled" paper mill work with women's domestic labor indicates that housework, a new nineteenth-century feminine occupation, ensured all women substantial training in useful manufacturing skills and served to minimize the value of those skills.

As we have seen, female paper workers, like most female employees, performed tasks that required care and attentiveness, despite the monotony of the work. Had their attention lapsed frequently, they would not have fulfilled their function: maintaining quality. Yet the work itself had so little inherent interest that constant alertness must have been difficult to maintain. Indeed, the only apparent stimulation women experienced on the job came from their simultaneous conversation with other women. It seems likely, then, that conversation not only made the work bearable, but also contributed to alert workmanship. One twentieth-century superintendent acknowledged as much when he concluded from an attempt to employ male paper sorters that men could not do the job because they could not work fast enough while talking. . . .

While less remunerative than textile mill work, paper mill work attracted wives and female household heads because it best suited women with children and homes to care for. Paper mill jobs offered two great advantages: flexible hours and safety. As noted earlier, most paper mill women had comparatively short hours by contemporary standards, whereas a number of textile mills employed women longer than ten hours even after legislative prohibition. Lacking housekeeping assistance, wives and widows sorely needed the extra weekday and Saturday hours that paper mills assured all female employees. By choosing to process rags or sort paper, occupations that permitted the adept worker to leave early, a woman could further shorten her hours. Women with unsupervised infants and preschool children must have willingly accepted the lower pay in order to leave work early. At least some mothers also left the rag rooms and finishing rooms several hours early so as to supervise children returning from school, a substantial boon for those with all children between the ages of five and ten, about one-seventh of working wives and widows.

In addition, paper mills accommodated women whose family responsibilities occasioned periodic work interruptions. For example, Elizabeth Wharfield began working at the Cranes' mill in 1846, shortly after her daughter's birth, but left work for several months in 1848. Perhaps she lost her babysitter or her sick toddler required special motherly care. The following year Charlotte Tifeny, who had left work to be with her brother, informed the Cranes, "I would like to come back." She evidently expected reemployment for she wrote in late September and told the Cranes, "I would like an anser beefore cattle show."

Married women especially availed themselves of the opportunity to leave the mills and return. Between 1863 and 1876 nearly half of the Cranes' married female employees left work for at least a month, averaging five months away before returning. Over the same period, only one-fifth of the unmarried women interrupted their employment. Recurrent work interruptions also occurred most frequently among married women. At the Cranes' mill between 1863 and 1876, married women took two or more sustained work breaks over three times more often than did single women. L. L. Brown's time book showed a similar pattern. And timekeepers' records missed additional married women who left one mill and returned to work for a different employer. For example, Mrs. Hutchens of Cheshire had worked as a paper sorter, probably for L. L. Brown, but applied to the Cranes in 1864 when she wanted renewed employment after spending "some months in taking care of a sick friend."

Paper-making technology permitted women's flexible schedules. Women's shorter hours reflected the technical feasibility of ending women's workdays without shutting down the machines. Likewise, women's ability to leave and return periodically rested on the greater awareness of individual needs that a less labor-intensive industry permitted. . . . [I]n 1880 paper mills averaged 67 workers, about half of them women. By contrast, cotton mills employed an average of 137, about half female, and woolen mills averaged 147, about two-fifths female. Merely in planning, then, paper mills had an easier time accommodating married women's special needs.

Slave Ironworkers in Virginia

CHARLES DEW

. . . By 1860, William Weaver owned sixty-six slaves: twenty-eight adult men, fifteen women, fourteen boys, and nine girls. His core forge crew in that year had all grown to manhood at Buffalo Forge: Sam Williams, master refiner; Henry Towles, refinery underhand; Tooler, Jr., chaffery hammerman; Harry Hunt, Jr., chaffery underhand; and Henry Matthews, forge carpenter. All these men had served their apprenticeship at Buffalo Forge, and often they had trained alongside their own fathers. All belonged to families that had an impressive history of turning out highly skilled artisans.

Assembling a full crew of skilled forgemen and maintaining their number as death and injury thinned the ranks of his original force were formidable challenges for Weaver. These were not, however, the ultimate challenges he faced as a southern ironmaster. Even more imposing was the task of motivating these slaves to work, and work well, at the art—for that is what it was—of ironmaking.

Weaver, of course, had considerable coercive power at his disposal. He could punish any recalcitrant or troublesome slave, but if he had relied on the whip to achieve satisfactory levels of production, his career as a Virginia ironmaker would have been very short-lived indeed. Excessive use of force certainly would have backfired, and a whipping administered to a skilled slave would, at minimum, leave the man sore and incapable of work. It would probably leave him seething with anger as well and looking for ways to get back at the master. Acts of industrial sabotage could be accomplished with relative ease around a forge. To cite only one example, the huge wooden beams that supported the 500- to 600-pound cast-iron hammerheads in the forge—"helves" was the name given to these beams—occasionally broke in the normal course of operations and had to be replaced. The forge would shut down for at least a day, sometimes more, while the forge carpenter installed a new helve. Weaver's forgemen could break these helves intentionally whenever they wished, and who could say whether it was or was not deliberate? Another alternative would be for the slave to burn the forge down. On any working day, live charcoal was there to do the job. The slaves, in short, were in a position to do considerable physical and

From Charles Dew, *Bond of Iron* (New York: Norton, 1994), pp. 107–109, 120–121, 173–175, 180–185, 262–267, 274–280.

financial damage to Weaver's interests, even if they limited their activities to passive forms of resistance like work slowdowns or slipshod performance of their duties. Not surprisingly, there is no indication that Weaver ever whipped one of his slave forge workers at any time during his forty years in the Valley.

A far greater threat to the slaves was the possibility of sale. Even skilled slaves who tried to run away or who carried their resistance beyond Weaver's level of toleration could be turned over to slave traders and readily sold. Yet no ironmaster would want to part with a trained slave ironworker. . . . Buying or training an immediate replacement would be difficult, if not impossible, and trying to hire skilled slave forge workers was, as Weaver well knew, both uncertain and expensive. It was far better, from Weaver's point of view, to avoid the use of physical coercion to the fullest extent possible and to turn to a weapon like the sale of a slave only in the most extreme circumstances.

The alternative to force was positive incentive. From his earliest days in Virginia, Weaver paid slaves who did extra work. Weaver's artisans had a daily or weekly task to perform, but he compensated them either in cash or in goods from his store at Buffalo Forge, for anything they turned out over and above the required amount. Payment for "overwork," as this system was called, was a common practice at slave-manned manufacturing establishments throughout the antebellum South, and it was a feature of the labor regimen at southern ironworks as early as the mid-eighteenth century. The task for slave refiners at Buffalo Forge, and everywhere else in the Valley, was [to manufacture] a ton and a half of anchonies [a forged piece of wrought iron] per week for a forge worked in the customary fashion—two-handed by a master refiner and his underhand. . . .

The unchanging nature of these tasks over time suggests that both master and slave regarded them as a traditional standard. . . . The whole intent of the task system was to encourage slaves to produce a set amount of output in a given time and then to work beyond that minimum point in order to earn compensation for themselves. . . .

Weaver generally got what he most wanted and needed from his slave force—a sufficient quantity of high-quality iron produced at a cost that allowed him to earn a profit on his sizable investment in land, ironworks, and labor in Virginia. Weaver could have been a slaveowner without the extensive use of the overwork system, but he could not have been the successful ironmaster that he was—the master of Buffalo Forge—without it.

The slaves, as always, got much less out of the bargain. Only one, Ben Gilmore, seems to have gotten what slaves universally in the South wanted above all else, a chance at freedom. But they did earn recognition and limited reward, they gained considerable protection for themselves and their families against sale and abuse, and they secured the chance to do something tangible to improve their own lives and the lives of those they loved. Considering the limits imposed by the always degrading and frequently brutal system of southern bondage, these were not insignificant achievements. . . .

Sam Williams, Jr., spent the first eight years of his life at Etna Furnace. . . .

. . . Sam and his brothers did not at first carry their father's last name; they were entered on Weaver's books as "Sam Etna," "Washington Etna," and "Charles Etna." The reason seems clear. The "Etna" designation clearly identified the boys as coming from that portion of the "Wilson negroes" born at Etna Furnace and previously held by Thomas Mayburry. It was easier for the clerks to write "Sam Etna" than "Sam Williams, Jr.," and if you identified the oldest brother in this way, why not do it for the younger ones as well? Washington was nine years old at the time of the division, Charles seven or eight. Like Sam, both of these boys would later take their places as ironworkers in Weaver's forge. And Sam would eventually reclaim his father's name, although it took a long time—sixteen years—before "Sam Etna" became "Sam Williams" on the pages of the time books and ledgers kept at Buffalo Forge. . . .

Young Sam Williams's first duties for Weaver were primarily agricultural. . . . There is no indication that he did any ironworking during his initial twelve months with Weaver. But Sam came from "a family that produces good mechanics," as Weaver liked to say, and Weaver was probably waiting for Sam to reach his full growth. In 1838, when Sam was eighteen, he began his training as a forgeman. . . .

Weaver undoubtedly had Sam go down to the forge and watch the black refiners and hammermen at their jobs before deciding whether he wanted to apprentice to one of the master workmen. This was Weaver's usual practice, and there is no reason to suspect that he did things differently this time. Sam's father had suffered eye injuries in the forge, and that might have given young Sam pause, but he also would have been well aware of the advantages forge work would bring him. In making himself indispensable to Weaver's ironmaking operations, he would be gaining a significant amount of influence over his own fate. There was no sure guarantee against punishment or sale; like all southern masters, Weaver could do pretty much what he wished in the way of punishment, and if he should fall deeply into debt or die suddenly, his slave force could be dispersed by either sale or the division of his estate. Barring that sort of catastrophe, however, Sam would be in a much stronger bargaining position as a skilled ironworker than in any other occupation at Buffalo Forge. If he trained as a refiner and showed an aptitude for the work, he would have talents Weaver would need for many years into the future. There was, of course, another advantage as well. Of all the slaves used by Weaver in various agricultural and industrial pursuits, the forgemen were in the best position to earn substantial sums for themselves through their overwork. . . .

The things Sam Williams did with his overwork earnings in the 1840s and 1850s tell us a good deal about this man and his attitudes and priorities. He supplemented Weaver's standard rations of pork and cornmeal with regular purchases of flour, sugar, coffee, and molasses, and he frequently bought cloth for [his wife] Nancy to sew into garments for the family. His overwork kept him, and perhaps Nancy as well supplied with tobacco. And his gifts to various members of his family continued. His mother received fifty pounds of flour from him in February 1845, and he gave his father a pound of coffee in April 1846—to cite two instances where the items were specifically mentioned in the records as going to his parents. Nancy, as might be expected, received a number of presents: a pair of buckskin gloves at Christmas in 1848; a shawl in May 1849; and a very expensive—$12—gift of fabric in October 1851 that included silk and four yards of "Bolt Clothe." One of Sam's special purchases for his children that is clearly identified in his account came in 1853. On June 22 of that year, he spent $1.75 for "8 ¾ yds [cloth] for Annie for Bedspread." His daughter Ann turned ten in 1853, and the bedspread may well have been a birthday present for her.

Sam also bought items of apparel for himself during the mid-1840s. There was nothing that could match his blue baptismal coat, but he bought a pair of "Fine shoes" for $2.50 and a "Summer Coat" for $4.50 in May 1845, probably to wear when he attended church services in Lexington. He added "1 Fine Hat," priced at $4, to his wardrobe the following November.

The most fascinating item that he acquired during these years were the articles of furniture he bought for the cabin that he, Nancy, and the girls shared. His major Christmas gift to the family in 1845 consisted of a table ($3) and a bedstead ($9), both of which he purchased at the Buffalo Forge store on Christmas Eve of that year. He added significantly to the cabin's furnishings six years later when he apparently attended an estate sale held in the neighborhood. In April 1851, he made two acquisitions "at Blackford's Sale": a set of chairs, for which he paid $7.25, and probably his most revealing purchase of the entire antebellum eras, "1 looking glass," priced at $1.75. . . .

. . . [T]here were other signs of pride as well, the most notable of which occurred in 1853.

Sam was thirty-three years old that year. He and Nancy had been married for thirteen years, they were raising their four girls, and he was a member of the Lexington Baptist Church. As the master refiner at Buffalo Forge, he was the most important single artisan in Weaver's employ. His overwork earnings exceeded those of any other hand on the place. If Weaver wanted to try a new brand of pig iron at the forge, it was up to Sam to make a couple of anchonies with the metal "to see how it worked." Sam's judgment determined whether Weaver would or would not place an order for the iron. Sam was also in charge of the annual slaughter of hogs at Buffalo Forge and was responsible for cutting up and salting the pork that served as the primary source of meat for almost all of Weaver's slaves. He and Nancy cultivated their own garden and corn lot, raised chickens and hogs, and regularly sold Weaver sweet potatoes, poultry, pork, and bacon, as well as the brooms Sam managed to find the spare time to make. When he was not pounding out anchonies at his refinery hammer, he was almost always engaged in some other type of productive labor: repairing the forge, cutting logs at Weaver's sawmill; driving a herd of cattle down from Bath Iron Works or over to Etna Furnace; working with the field hands at planting, fertilizing, and harvest times. It was time for Sam to get his own name back.

On the page in the Buffalo Forge "Negro Book" covering his work for the year 1853, his name appears two ways: as "Samuel Etna"and as "Sam Williams." On January 12 and 13, 1853, the clerk keeping the time book at the forge wrote: "Sam Williams & hands sowing plaster in the big field." Several days later, the clerk reverted to the old form. "Sam Etna & Hands sowing plaster," he wrote, and in June he noted that "Sam E" was among the five or six slaves who had come down with the mumps. But mistakes of this type became increasingly rare in the records kept at Buffalo Forge. As the year drew to a close, it was "Sam Williams" who drew $5 in cash against his overwork credit and bought 3¼ yards of expensive cassinette cloth for Nancy on Christmas Eve. Four days later when all hands went to work cutting blocks of ice from the pond behind the forge dam to fill Weaver's icehouse, it was "Sam Williams" who received a day's wage and a whiskey ration for his part in seeing this project through to completion. And when his overwork account was totaled up at the end of 1853 and his expenditures ($36.58) were subtracted from his earnings ($63.50, for more than twelve tons of overwork during the year), his credit balance of $26.92 was posted on a new ledger page carrying only one name, "Samuel Williams." From this point on, as far as the records were concerned, he was almost always identified as "Sam Williams." His father was "Sam Williams Senior." . . .

Nancy Williams had a savings account, too, and in her own name. Since she was in charge of the dairy operations at Buffalo Forge and did a good deal of housework at Weaver's residence, she clearly had opportunities to earn overwork pay in her own right. Without the house accounts it is impossible to say exactly how she made all of this money, but we can identify some of the things that resulted in payments to her. Weaver sometimes noted in his cashbooks why certain sums were paid out, and occasionally these entries show Nancy as the recipient. During the 1850s, she received money for raising calves, for a stone pitcher she sold Weaver, and for indigo she grew in her garden. She was given money on one occasion to buy starch, which indicates that she was ironing at Weaver's residence. And she also kept her own hogs at Buffalo Forge which were weighed, slaughtered, and put up in the smokehouse in her name when hog-killing time arrived. Some of this meat could have been sold to Weaver. By these means other forms of overwork we unfortunately cannot identify, she had managed to accumulate savings that were fully two-thirds the size of her husband's. Between them, Sam and Nancy Williams had $153.27 in cash in 1856, the 1992 equivalent of approximately $2,500.

What were they saving for? No evidence exists to show that Weaver had given them the right to buy their own freedom or that of their children, so self-purchase apparently was not the reason. The fact that they were saving at all suggests that they felt their material standard of living was adequate to the family needs; if it had not been, they probably would have spent much more than they did on various food items and cloth, and they would not have sold Weaver items like chickens, pork, and sweet potatoes if they had needed them for their own table. The most logical explanation for their extraordinary, and substantial, bank accounts would seem to be that they both had extra overwork funds and they simply put their money in a safe place where it would earn interest for them. The safest place they could find was apparently the Lexington savings bank. . . .

The picture that emerges from this story of two slaves with savings accounts is by no means a simple one. On the surface, one might be tempted to argue that Sam and Nancy Williams simply swallowed more of the bait Weaver offered to induce his black laborers to work like slaves and that their behavior indicated a placid acceptance of their status and condition. Since they had to complete their required tasks before they could start earning money for themselves, they obviously were turning out a considerable amount of work for their master. Yet they were doing a great deal for themselves as well, and for their children. They were improving the material conditions under which all of them could live and they were protecting themselves against the fearful threat that hung over them all—the breakup of the family through sale. Weaver would be very reluctant indeed to part with workers like this man and woman, who meant so much to the smooth running, and the success, of his iron-making and farming activities. Nor would he want to run the risks he would face if he tried to sell Sam and Nancy's daughters off Buffalo Forge. . . .

. . . Sam had seen his family broken once before. It had been over twenty years since Thomas Mayburry had taken Sam's grandmother and three of her children away, but there was no way Sam could forget that event. Now, with [his daughter] Betty's new baby, Sam Williams had even more reason to do whatever he could to shelter his family and try to protect all of them—his mother, his father, his wife, his children, and his grandchild—from the worst aspects of the slave regime. . . .

The celebratory dinner on August 6 marked the completion of only part of the harvest season at Buffalo Forge in 1850. The crops of wheat, oats, rye, and hay were all in, but the fields and fields of corn were still ripening in the late summer sun. That harvest would begin in September, and winter wheat would be planted from mid-September to early October. By the second week in October, the field hands would finish sowing the wheat crop and turn their attention to planting the rye that would be harvested the following year.

The week that began on Monday, October 10, was a beautiful one in the Valley. Clear, cool days followed one after another, ideal weather for outdoor work. Plow gangs moved through the fields every day that week as the soil was prepared for the rye crop, and sowing began on Thursday, October 13. Garland Thompson, Jr., delivered his daily load of charcoal to the forge, and Sam Williams and Henry Towles were at their refinery hammer as usual, Monday through Saturday. As dusk fell on Saturday, October 15, Brady could look back on the week's work with satisfaction.

Late Saturday night, a heavy frost spread over the Valley. There was a sharp chill in the air as the Buffalo Forge community awoke to a day of rest on Sunday, October 16. That same day, 175 miles to the north, a band of abolitionists led by John Brown launched their attack on the United States arsenal and armory located at Harper's Ferry, Virginia. . . .

Something akin to panic swept over much of the South in the wake of John Brown's raid, and the Valley of Virginia was no exception. Lexington's two weekly papers, the Whiggish *Gazette* and the Democratic *Valley Star,* carried full reports of the attack on the government installations at Harper's Ferry and published highly emotional editorials the following week. . . .

The law moved swiftly in the case of John Brown. His one-day trial for treason at Charlestown, Virginia, on November 2 concluded with the judge declaring that no reasonable doubt existed as to his guilt. His execution by public hanging was scheduled for Friday, December 2, 1859.

The month prior to Brown's execution was filled with wild rumors in Virginia of armed attacks on the border, of fanatical attempts to rescue Brown, and of abolitionist plots to kidnap prominent citizens and members of their families and hold them as hostages for Brown's release. The Richmond *Enquirer,* in an editorial reprinted in the *Gazette,* urged the citizens of the commonwealth to arm themselves and organize "as patrols and guards, and as volunteer videttes."

This was the mood among whites in the Valley as preparations began for a double wedding in the slave community at Buffalo Forge. Caroline Williams, the seventeen-year-old daughter of Sam and Nancy Williams, and Andrew Reid, a slave teamster belonging to Jacob Fuller of Lexington, were hoping to get married. So were fifteen-year-old Amy Banks, the daughter of Warder and Frances Banks, and James Carter. . . . The process, as was always the case when one of Weaver's slaves wanted to marry off the property, could not go forward without the consent of the masters. . . .

. . . A double wedding, with both grooms coming from off the property, meant a large gathering of slaves; and the timing—the day after John Brown was hanged—was undoubtedly the reason a distinctly unwelcome group of uninvited guests turned up at Buffalo Forge that day. On Saturday, December 3, the Rockbridge County slave patrol came calling.

Fear of possible slave rebellion was commonplace in the South in the aftermath of Brown's attack on Harper's Ferry, and whites argued that the only way to prevent such uprisings was through an overwhelming show of force and the immediate suppression of the slightest hint of insurrectionary activity. . . . We do not know what, if anything, Weavers' slaves said about John Brown, but one of them apparently said or did something the patrol did not like. The hated "paddyrollers," as the blacks called them, left Buffalo Forge after the wedding party broke up on Saturday, but they were back the next day.

Overnight the temperature plunged and the first snow of the season fell at Buffalo Forge. Sunday dawned bright and clear, one of those magnificent early-winter days in the Valley when the air is crisp and fresh and the cloudless sky forms a stunning contrast to the snow-covered Blue Ridge. The tranquility of this December day was soon shattered by the clatter of horses' hooves as the slave patrol rode up the hill to Weaver's house. Perhaps a snide remark had been directed their way the day before and had festered in the patrollers' minds during the night. Maybe it was nothing more than rumors of some loose talk among the slaves at the forge. It did not take much to set off the paddyrollers in the overheated atmosphere brought on by John Brown's raid. Whatever the reason, their return visit resulted in an ugly incident. The patrol singled out Henry Towles for punishment; the twenty-three-year-old forge hand was taken out, stripped and whipped. Towles did not return to work until December 15, eleven days after the beating administered by the Rockbridge County patrol.

The whipping of Henry Towles, one of Weaver's most dependable forge hands, was a stark reminder of a basic fact of life at Buffalo Forge. The black workers there, no matter how skilled, were still no more than chattel in the eyes of the law, a piece of human personal property subject to the disciplinary whims of the master and regularly constituted county authorities. Whether Weaver concurred in the patrol's decision to whip Towles is unknown; he probably could not have stopped them even if he wanted to. White repression of suspected slave insurrectionary activity during the 1850s was often vicious and brutal, and the whipping of Henry Towles was only one incident among many carried out by panic-stricken southern whites during the late antebellum era. This mindset was probably best summed up in an editorial that appeared in a Tennessee newspaper in 1856 when slave ironworkers along the Tennessee and Cumberland rivers were supposedly preparing to "rise," as the expression went, against the white population:

> The crimes contemplated should be atoned for precisely as though those crimes had been attempted and consummated. Fearful and terrible examples should be made, and if need be, the fag(g)ot and flame should be brought into requisition to show these deluded maniacs the fierceness and the vigor, the swiftness and completeness of the white man's vengeance. Let a terrible example be made in every neighborhood where the crime can be established, and if necessary, let every tree in the country bend with negro meat. Temporizing in such cases as this, is utter madness. We must strike terror, and make a lasting impression, for only in such a course can we find the guaranties [sic] of future security. . . .

Two striking examples of slave resistance occurred at Buffalo Forge in the summer of 1860. One involved a twenty-eight-year-old field hand named William Green. The other involved Sam Williams.

In December 1854, Henry McCormick had attended the sale at Mount Torry Furnace in Augusta County where part of the property belonging to the estate of Matthew Bryan was being auctioned. McCormick had made two purchases for Weaver at this sale: a six-mile team, wagon, and gear which he bought for $587.75; and "Boy William Bot @ Mt Torry about 21 years of age" for whom he paid $975.00. Weaver knew the slave William Green quite well. He had gone to work as a hireling at Buffalo Forge in the spring of 1854, and Weaver undoubtedly gave his friend McCormick instructions to buy the slave when William was returned to Mount Torry in time for the sale scheduled to take place at the end of the year. Weaver's purchase of this slave was probably prompted by something more than his desire to acquire another prime hand. Among William Green's overwork purchases at Buffalo Forge in 1854 was a "Dress for Matilda," for which he paid $2. This was a gift for his wife, and his wife was Matilda Thompson, a daughter of Garland Thompson, Sr. She was also the young woman Weaver had given to James Davidson's nine-year-old daughter Mary in 1849, when Matilda was seventeen. Four years later, in 1853, Matilda Thompson and William Green were married. The children born to Matilda in the ensuing years grew up in the Davidson household in Lexington.

William worked at Buffalo Forge during 1855 and for part of the next year. In the summer of 1856, he was sent over to Etna, and he served as a furnace hand there until the spring of 1857. At this point, James Davidson appears to have hired him so that he could be near Matilda and their children. William moved to the Davidson home in Lexington, and things seemed to go reasonably well for a while. But in the summer of 1859, an incident occurred there which placed his status as one of Davidson's servants in grave jeopardy.

On August 2, 1859, James Davidson wrote a detailed letter to Weaver in which he described an altercation which had taken place the previous evening between Williams and one of James Davidson's sons, Greenlee Davidson. This letter is a remarkable document on many grounds and deserves to be cited in full:

> Greenlee had a difficulty with William last night, and he [William] went off, saying that he would go down to you.
>
> About 11 oclock last night, Greenlee left the office & I remained, engaged writing. When he got home, he found William lying in the wood yard, very drunk—indeed drunker than usual. He endeavored to get him up into the kitchen. He replied impudently, as he has often done to me, *when drunk.* Greenlee became foolish excited at the ravings of a drunken man & threatened to whip him up. But neither he nor Matilda could get him up. Greenlee came into the house & William followed him, calling for me. He gave more impudence & threatened Greenlee, when he struck William with the shovel a severe blow. They sent for me and I met them coming up—Greenlee on his way for an officer. I met William. He yielded to me. I took him back—but he would not go to bed & said he would go to you.
>
> I should not trouble you with this. But I wish you to speak *positively & firmly* to William or he will be of no more account to me. I told him if he went off I would never send for him—nor will I. When sober, he attends to my business well, but when drunk, as he often is, he is more impudent & unmanageable. Dont let him or any one at home but Brady know I have written this as it will prejudice the warnings & commands you

may give him. You know how to talk to him & manage him & can now teach him a lesson. Greenlee was indiscreet in saying any thing to a drunken man, & he regrets now he
had any thing to do with him and would now wish to leave me to manage him in my own
(way.) His drunkenness will in the end cause me to part company with him. On account
of his wife & children, this would be painful to me. If William would say to Greenlee,
that he was drunk and did not know what he was doing, Greenlee would be kinder to him
than ever. You might say so to him, in your own way. I shall never *coax* him again. He
suits me well, & if he would keep sober would always have a good home. Keep this
to yourself.

On August 5, Brady wrote a brief note to Davidson informing him that Weaver
had received his letter but that "Bill," as Weaver generally called him, had not arrived
at Buffalo Forge, nor had they heard of him. "I hope he has returned home ere this,"
Brady added.

If William did return to the Davidson home in Lexington, he did not remain
there long. By early September, he was back at Etna working as a furnace hand and
doing a job for which he was paid an allowance of $4 per month. . . .

William Green seems to have been a man who kept a tremendous amount of
anger and rage bottled up inside. When his self-control was weakened by alcohol,
however, his fury broke forth, and he placed both himself and his family at risk.
There is no way to know if he was willing to apologize to Greenlee Davidson and
return hat in hand to the Davidson household, but chances are he was not. That was
probably why he was working at Etna in September 1859. . . .

Over the years, Brady had grown accustomed to the steady work habits of his
refinery forgemen. Tooler and Harry Hunt, Jr., might be something less than reliable,
but Sam Williams and Henry Towles were almost invariably pounding out anchonies
unless the forge was flooded or down for repairs or the water was low or one of the
men was truly sick or injured. But both Sam and Henry had their own ideas about
when they had worked long enough and hard enough to deserve a break, and the
summer of 1860 was such a time.

The two men manned their forge through some very warm days at the beginning
of July, but by the middle of the month they had obviously had enough. Henry said
he was too ill to work on Wednesday, July 18, and Brady apparently believed him.
"Henry Towles sick," he recorded in his journal. Jim Garland was brought in to
relieve Henry, and he and Sam put in a full day together. The next day, the temperature reached 100 degrees at one o'clock in the afternoon, and the heat in the forge
must have been stifling. Henry did not show up for work that day, either. "Henry
Towles sick i.e. loafing" was Brady's assessment. Sam and Jim Garland continued
to work, so the forge had its supply of anchonies that day, but Sam was working
under very trying conditions, and no one knew it better than he. Sam and Jim finished out the week, however, with "Henry Towles loafing" both Friday and Saturday.

On Monday, July 23, it was Sam's turn, and he may not even have made a pretense of being sick. Henry returned to work that day; he could handle Sam's job,
with Jim Garland's help. Sam was now "loafing," according to Brady, and he stayed
out "loafing" the entire week. At the end of Sam's first week of rest, a period when
the heat in the Valley had been particularly oppressive, Tooler and Harry Hunt, Jr.,
also took matters into their own hands. On Saturday, July 28, they carried out an act
of industrial sabotage: "Tooler & Harry drew a few pounds & then broke down to

loaf," Brady wrote. A point of diminishing returns had obviously been reached, and Brady decided about the middle of the day that there was no sense fighting it any longer: "All hands had a ½ [day] holiday." From Weaver's and Brady's vantage point, Saturday, July 28, had been an exceedingly difficult day. The slaves undoubtedly took just the opposite view.

Sam's vacation was not over yet, however. He did not go back to work for three more weeks. From Monday, July 30, to Saturday, August 18, Brady regularly noted that Sam was "loafing" each day. He did not return to his post at the refinery forge until Monday, August 20. He had been off the job *four* full weeks.

Sam returned to work as if nothing had happened. . . .

What this fascinating incident suggests is that Sam was fully aware of the power he possessed and the quite distinct limits of that power. He knew that his skills were critically important to his master and that this gave him a considerable amount of leverage in his dealings with Weaver and Brady. In his view, he deserved some time off, and he chose the hot, muggy dog days of July and August 1860 to take it. It was probably no accident that he did not leave his forge until Henry Towles returned. This kept the situation from assuming potentially dangerous and threatening dimensions. Since they were off one at a time, Jim Garland could come in to spell each one of them temporarily, and forge operations could continue. Ironmaking would not grind to a complete and costly stop because Henry was feigning illness and Sam was "loafing" back at his cabin. Thus Weaver and Brady would not be backed into a corner where they would be forced to crack down on their two refinery hands. Sam knew just how far he could go with his resistance, and he was careful to keep the situation under control.

At the same time, he had enough pride in himself to insist, through his actions, that there was a line beyond which he would not allow himself to be pushed. Months of steady labor, followed by forge work in temperatures reaching 100 degrees, comprised a step over that line. He took off for a month, and there were certainly risks attendant in that. But they would probably be manageable risks, and that was the way things turned out. By tolerating his absence, Weaver and Brady tacitly recognized that Sam had the power to force reasonable, limited, and temporary changes in his work regimen; they also silently acknowledged that, in a certain sense, he was justified in what he was doing. . . .

Sam Williams won this confrontation, probably because of who he was and because his challenge to the system was guarded and oblique and had a limited objective—rest from work. William Green's case was quite a different matter. William's wife, Matilda, came out from Lexington in early July to help her sister through childbirth. Eliza Thompson King was expecting a baby, and Matilda was at Buffalo Forge on July 7, 1860, when Hannah, as Wilson and Eliza named their new daughter, was born. Whether Matilda's presence at Buffalo Forge had any impact on her husband's subsequent course of action is unknown, but William's anger at living apart from his wife and children may well have been heightened by her visit. Early in the morning on Friday, July 27, William ran away from Buffalo Forge. The next day, July 28, was the day Tooler and Harry Hunt, Jr., sabotaged the forge and Brady gave all hands half the day off. Sam Williams was in the midst of his month-long absence from work at this time.

Weaver wasted little time in sending an experienced party in pursuit of William. James E. Carson, the Augusta County slave trader, was given the job of hunting the runaway down. With William's wife and children back in Lexington, his capture was only a matter of time. On Tuesday, August 7, Carson brought "Bill Greenlee," as he was generally referred to in Weaver's records, back to Buffalo Forge in shackles. "Carson . . . to dinner," Brady wrote in his journal. "Sold Bill Greenlee." The price was $1,150. . . .

If, as seems likely, William was indeed sold to a Lexington buyer in 1860, he was extremely fortunate. The week he was captured, the Lexington *Gazette* carried Carson's advertisement stating that he wished to buy "500 likely YOUNG NEGROES of both sexes, for the Southern market, for which I will pay the highest market prices in cash."

Carson's appearance at Buffalo Forge on Tuesday, August 7, seems to have had no affect on Sam Williams. Weaver's master refiner had been "loafing" for two weeks when Carson brought William Green back, and if Sam were going to be intimidated into returning to work, the slave trader's visit should have done it. But Sam stayed off the job the remainder of that week and all of the next. His month-long absence from the finery clearly was not enough to convince Weaver that he should part with his most valuable forgeman.

William Green, in his late twenties and a "prime hand" in the language of the slave trade, was, from the perspective of Weaver's labor needs, still only a furnace and agricultural worker. Even more important, his defiance of the slave regime was open and direct and had an objective that no slaveholder could tolerate—freedom. Not surprisingly, Weaver brought the full force of the system swiftly and brutally down on him. The example of the unsuccessful runaway's being taken off in chains was immediately before the eyes of Sam Williams and every other slave at Buffalo Forge, and that was undoubtedly the way Weaver wanted it. Even Sam's status as a master refiner probably would not have protected him if he had carried his resistance as far as William Green took his.

William's attempt to escape and Sam's much more limited protest raise one of the ultimate questions about American slavery. What, in fact, was the better part of valor for a slave? Should one fight, confront, resist openly, run away, do everything one could to bring the system down? Or should one maneuver as best one could within the system, stay with one's family and try to help and comfort them, and attempt to carve out the best possible life, despite the physical and psychological confines of enslavement? These were questions each slave had to decide; they were not easily answered then and they are not easily answered now.

The Political Economy of Pacing

MERRITT ROE SMITH

The possession of tools and skills stands at the center of any discussion of the Industrial Revolution. Numerous scholars have noted that one important consequence of mechanized industrial production was that increasing numbers of workers no longer

From Merritt Roe Smith, "Industry, Technology, and the 'Labor Question' in 19th-Century America: Seeking Synthesis," *Technology and Culture*, Vol. 32, No. 3, July 1991, Chicago: The University of Chicago Press, 1991: 558–569. Copyright © 1992 by The Society for the History of Technology. Reprinted by permission.

owned their own tools. As factories, railroads, and other capital-intensive systems came to the fore, handicraft methods receded. Expensive banks of specialized machinery became the tools for the job and stood far beyond the reach of most ordinary mechanics. Skill, so the argument went, was being "built into" the machines. While recent research has challenged certain aspects of this notion, the fact remains that the decline of individual tool ownership had significant social and economic ramifications. In effect, it meant that people found themselves working for employers who owned the tools of production and who insisted on dictating how, when, and where the work should be executed. Given the fact that the earliest recruits came to mills, factories, and other large industrial enterprises from small, often family-owned enterprises (i.e., shops and farms), it is not surprising that tensions arose. The question of who should control production became a fundamental point of contention in the 19th-century industrial world. This was the "contested terrain" that social historians have written so much about.

The issue seemed clear enough to captains of industry. After all, they possessed the capital and felt that, by legal right, they should decide how it should be deployed. The position of workers, on the other hand, was more ambiguous. With them the control question involved matters of degree. Much depended on one's bargaining power, and bargaining power depended on a number of things, including gender, age, ethnic and religious background, skill, experience, and, not least of all, market demand. Since they experienced lesser social standing and possess fewer marketable skills, women and children benefited least under the industrial system. Oftentimes they were given menial but presumable "safe" jobs in mills and paid a pittance. By and large, they had little power and little to say about how things got done. Men, especially crafted-trained artisans, on the other hand, possessed more marketable skills and, not surprisingly, exercised greater influence in their shop-floor relations with owners and supervisors. Many of them, in fact, owned their own hand tools, although that sort of tool ownership assumed less importance in the age of precision machinery. Their skill represented their source of power. Knowing the "secrets" of a trade gave them a certain degree of leverage with employers. Consequently, they stood to lose more under the factory system because self-acting machinery, divisions of labor, piecework payments, and the like tended to alter the circumstances of production. Any shift in technique—managerial or technical—constituted not only a shift in knowledge but also a shift in shop-floor power. The installation of a new machine or the reorganization of a job changed the character of production and almost always meant that adjustments in the deployment and pay of labor would follow. The process of negotiating these adjustments and coming to terms with employers on the shop floor provided one of the great ongoing dramas of 19th-century industrialization. Workers, like managers, had to be vigilant.

As the new social history reveals, the forms these contests for control took varied from industry to industry and from community to community. Strikes and other types of open confrontation provide the most visible manifestations of struggle. But . . . they occurred sporadically in some communities and hardly at all in others. Consequently, they do not provide a very accurate picture of what was actually going on in industrial society. Far more revealing are the day-to-day interactions that took place between workers and managers. In these seemingly mundane affairs we find complex, subtle relationships that blend deference with defiance and suggest action among equals as well as an emerging sense of class differentiation. As one writer put it, "a 'we-they' comprehension of things" was beginning to emerge on both sides.

When one scrutinizes social relations in early industrial communities, it becomes increasingly apparent that workers as well as capitalists made choices. Several historians have described these relations as give-and-take situations in which workers and managers continually sparred with one another over wages, hours, and working conditions. Writing about the small textile villages that dotted the New England countryside, Jonathan Prude observes that "employees in local manufactories persistently blended obedience and deference with efforts to push back against the men and rules governing them." "Indeed," he continues, "the tugs back and forth between managers and operatives over work discipline, and the compromises that consequently developed, represent a crucial unfolding motif in the antebellum history of textile factories."

Although Prude limits his observations to small and medium-size textile-mill communities in New England, a large body of evidence indicates that much the same thing was going on elsewhere. Even in the repressive slave economy of the South, industrial slaves negotiated with their masters about where they would or would not work. Fearing runaways, slipshod work, and sabotage, neither masters nor employers particularly wished to force slaves to work where they did not want to reside. As a result, historian Charles Dew argues, "the central tendency" at industrial ironworks throughout the antebellum South "was for slavery to function more through mutual accommodation than outright repression." A code of mutuality prevailed as slaves exercised considerable influence in getting whites to adjust their labor practices. In his study of industrial slavery, Ronald Lewis describes the process as a three-way relationship: "Slaves pushed just hard enough to win additional advantages, gain some life-space, and yet remain within acceptable (if unspoken) bounds. On the other hand, employers yielded without losing ultimate control, while slaveowners attempted to protect and profit from their property at the same time. By initiating, and then manipulating, this triangular push-and-pull of self-interest, blacks gained a degree of influence over the nature of their daily existence." Given the heavy demand for and short supply of slaves during the pre-Civil War years, a certain degree of leverage existed between masters and industrial slaves. "The result," Lewis concludes, "was a system not of absolute power, but one which involved a complex interplay between the ironmaster, the slaveowner, and the slave himself.

Nineteenth-century industrial workers doubtless accommodated themselves to new technologies and stricter regimens, but they did so selectively and, one might add, on their own terms. Accommodation did not necessarily mean assent. A case in point concerns the promulgation of work rules in 19th-century industrial establishments. One might ask: To what extent did employers actually enforce their regulations and to what extent did workers obey them? At Lowell's Hamilton Manufacturing Company the record is clear. Between 1826 and 1839, the company agent discharged 603 workers—mostly weavers—and fined many others. The reasons given for the firings ranged from "poor work performance" (46.6 percent of the dismissals) to absenteeism and other forms of unacceptable behavior (including theft, disobedience, lying, striking, nonpayment of debts, and foul language). Yet, even though a no-nonsense attitude existed at the Hamilton Company and doubtless other large mills of its type, their labor policies proved to be atypical.

At other industrial establishments far looser regimens prevailed. Judging from the owner's complaints, for example, it is clear that workers often skirted the rules at the Du Pont gunpowder yards along the Brandywine. Trying to get powder workers to curtail their drinking habits or to leave their smoking materials outside the company gate was, to use an old British expression, like trying to put a deer in a harness—that is, next to impossible. Owners and managers might promulgate rules, but workers more often than not chose when, where, and how to abide by them. By and large, this attitude pervaded the country's working population—in Philadelphia, in Cincinnati, in Springfield, Massachusetts, in Troy, New York, in Harpers Ferry and Richmond, Virginia, in rural towns and villages and on the nation's burgeoning railway system. The work process, in short, involved all sorts of reciprocal relationships. Owners and superintendents might lower piece rates and attempt to increase the pace and load of production, but workers knew how to circumvent these measures. There was more than one way to skin the proverbial cat. What they could not bargain for, they often controlled through on-the-job behavior.

No better example of selective accommodation can be cited than the long-standing practice of pacing. Most industrial workers in the iron, machine, shoe, and textile trades received piece-rate rather then day wages by the 1830s. Because factory masters tended to lower piece rates with a relatively short period after introducing new techniques, workers quite naturally attempted to maintain the existing rate by deliberately restricting production. This practice, of course, placed them in constant tension with their employers.

Pacing or "soldiering," as Frederick W. Taylor would later call it, took many forms. Working to collectively define "stints," taking unauthorized breaks to have a smoke, go to the john, share a cup of whiskey, or purchase cakes being hawked outside the mill gate by a local baker, looking for missing tools, sharpening and repairing other tools, and reading newspapers while at work are common examples of pacing. At the federally owned Springfield and Harpers Ferry armories, for example, the practice had become particularly pervasive by the 1840s. "I cannot shut my eyes on what is passing before them," an exasperated senior army ordinance officer wrote to the secretary of war in August 1841. "I have frequently been at the [Springfield] shops and witnessed the truth of what had been reported to me. In one branch of labor, every man finishes his days work by *ten o'clock* in the morning. In others, they complete it in the first half of the day. A very limited number work over *five* hours, and probably none so long a time as *seven* hours a day when engaged in 'piecework.' The fact is they earn all the money they want, or all that they dare suffer to appear on the payroll, by working only a moderate portion of each day. . . . What would be the fate of a *private* manufactory where the operatives were allowed to fix their own wages and privileges?" the officer asked.

A subsequent civilian investigatory commission that visited the Springfield armory confirmed the ordnance officer's accusation and added further substance to the charges. Two points received particular emphasis in their final report to the secretary of war. "First," the commissioners observed, "it appears that men have been [absent] from their shops several days in a month, and yet have been able to earn from $50 to $60; and it was the opinion of the inspectors that, at some branches, from $70 to $100 per month might be earned by a mechanic working ten hours a day." "For example," the report continued, "one man worked fourteen days, and turned in $41 worth of work; two others, who were absent two weeks, or certainly ten working days turned in work, respectively, to the amount of $44 and $49. It also appears that one many who was absent an entire month, yet turned in work to the amount of $30, which work was doubtless executed by another individual, who himself received full wages. There appears to be no reason to doubt that a workman, on some of the branches, may be absent one-fourth of his time, and yet make up a full month's work, without laboring longer than ten hours a day." By carefully pacing themselves and, at times, even taking on another's tasks, workers at the Springfield armory were able to maintain their wages and at the same time reduce the length of the work day.

The second point in the commission's report came to the heart of the pacing issue. "It appears," they concluded, "that an opinion prevails among the workmen that their monthly earnings ought not to appear too large on the pay-roll; and, to avoid such a result, work is transferred from one to another, or kept back at the end of the month; and this has been done with the knowledge of the inspectors, though in direct violation of the regulations of the armory. These facts show a general loose-ness in the management of the armory, which could not exist in a private, and ought not to be permitted in a public establishment." In the commissioners' view, workers and overseers had established a silent code at Springfield that dominated the produc-tion process and flew in the face of established rules and authority.

Pacing and worker absenteeism may have been particularly blatant at the national armories, but the commissioners were certainly mistaken when they reported that such practices "could not exist" in the private sector. Virtually every industrial estab-lishment in America—textile mills, machine shops, foundries, rolling mills, railroads, shoe factories—experienced the problem of pacing in one form or another. To be sure, practices varied from one place to another, but the ultimate result remained the same. Faced with the introduction of new technologies and consequently with the threat of subsequent stretch-outs or wage cuts, workers sought to control the pace and dura-tion of their labor. At the Lukens rolling mill in Coatesville, Pennsylvania, it was the ironworkers, not the owners, who determined how many heats constituted a fair day's labor. Even at the closely monitored textile mills of Lowell, pacing occurred. Although they did not exercise the degree of shop-floor control that skilled metal-workers did, mill workers nonetheless found ways to circumvent the system by "spelling" one another at their banks of machines and, on occasion, even absenting themselves from the mill. They also found ways to relax and goof off without their employers' knowledge.

Indeed, the so-called labor question and its association with pacing had become so pervasive in America by the 1880's that industrial "reformers" like Frederick W. Taylor (who, by the way, came at the end rather than the beginning of a long line of systematizers) set out to break labor's control of the shop floor by prescribing various standardized procedures popularly known as "scientific management." It is significant that the first recommendation made by the commissioners who visited the Springfield armory in 1841 emphasized that "the superintendent should be a man of science, well acquainted with the best models of the musket, versed in the construction and opera-tion of machinery, educated in the habits of punctuality and order, and accustomed to control and direct the labor of others." Taylor could not have put it better when he published *The Principles of Scientific Management* seventy years later.

Although generally overlooked by historians, pacing proved to be a critical variable in the 19th-century workers' world. Indeed, it appears that a correlation exists between the extent to which pacing occurred in industrial establishments and the degree of tension that existed between workers and managers. A deeper understanding of the practice may also help to explain why people in some trades tended to resort to political protest more readily than others during the late 19th-century. Skilled machinists, like the armorers at Springfield, were militant about their rights and privileges, to be sure. But they rarely exhibited radical political tendencies. Increasingly "sweated" trades like shoemaking, ready-made clothing, and anthracite mining, on the other hand, operated in markets where piece rates relentlessly drove the work process and ruthless competition pressed wages and workers to the breaking point. Workers caught in such webs of oppression had little recourse other than to turn to radical forms of protest and politics.

Considered at a broader level, the pacing phenomenon points to an aspect of industrial life that lay beyond the purview of employers and thus beyond the reach of their paternalistic systems. As owners and overseers well understood, pacing represented a group rather than an individual response to the conditions of industrial employment and as such, was closely related to communal values and feelings. Its effectiveness depended on the cooperation not only of workers themselves but also of their families, friends, neighbors, and acquaintances—virtually the entire working community. That they succeeded in disguising the practice, perpetuating it, and keeping it beyond the effective grasp of employers testifies to the resilience and power of their separate community cultures—cultures that often came in contact with well-to-do owners and managers yet nonetheless stood apart from them. While these cultures could not stop the intrusions of paternalistic employers, they could deflect them and lessen their impact. Pacing thus represented a quintessential expression of labor values that derived as much—perhaps more—from the village and neighborhood cultures in which workers lived as they did from their places of employment.

Whether they resided in rural mill villages, company towns, or urban neighborhoods, workers had their own interests and forms of expression and perpetuated ways of life that stood apart from their sources of employment. The existence of such interests and forms of expression, in fact, made industrial life more tolerable. Work and community life were related, to be sure, but clear demarcations existed between the workplace and the home. Such demarcations served an important purpose because they enabled workers to separate their personal lives from the often-suffocating commands and constraints they experienced on the job.

Numerous activities point to another, more valued realm of life beyond the employer's gate. The fact that workers frequently absented themselves from their industrial labors to hunt and fish, drink and carouse, visit friends and relatives farm, tend gardens, and do various household chores attests to the value they paced on these personal, more intimate aspects of life. Although employers tended to interpret such activities as evidence of laziness, unreliability, dishonesty, and ungratefulness, such was rarely the case. Hunting, fishing, gardening, and farming, for example, often proved absolutely necessary for workers, for without the produce that came from these undertakings their families would have been deprived of basic dietary needs.

Yet, in an equally fundamental sense, workers did these things because they were familiar and customary. People did not simply abandon old habits and traditions on entering industrial employment. Indeed, they clung to them and often elevated them to idealized levels in order to maintain a sense of identity with the past—the world they had lost—as they encountered new and unfamiliar changes. Such ways of thinking and acting helped workers accommodate the new industrial order while trying to preserve older ways they valued. To view absenteeism and pacing solely as expressions of worker protest and alienation is to overlook the inherent complexities of what they experienced and misconstrue why they responded to change the way they did.

In many communities religious life counted for much among working people. A revealing example is the contingent of Irish Catholics who labored at the Du Pont gunpowder mills near Wilmington, Delaware. Given their ethnic background and rather well-defined insularity from other groups in the area, these people well illustrate the point that industrial working families had a way of life beyond the boss's grasp.

Du Pont's Catholic families never felt completely comfortable about sending their children to the Brandywine Manufacturers' Sunday School (1817–1840s), and on more than one occasion they expressed their reservations on the subject. As much as they may have respected the du Pont daughters who operated the school, they never fully trusted them because the du Ponts were Protestants who held different theological views. In fact, some Irish families refused to send their children to the manufacturers' school. Ever fearful that their children would be exposed to heretical teachings, they pressed for the establishment of a Catholic school in St. Joseph's parish. It is not surprising that, once the parish school opened, enrollments at the Brandywine Manufacturers' Sunday School declined. The very existence of St. Joseph's church and school and the presence of its highly respected pastor as a social leader in the Irish community reminded the du Ponts that their workers had their own quite separate spheres of devotion and interaction apart from their place of employment. They earned a living at the mills, but they did not necessarily orient their lives around them. The same generally held true for working communities throughout the United States.

Given the extent of intermarriage among working families in 19th-century America, extended kinship and friendship networks constituted the very heart of early industrial communities. The special bonds that characterized these networks defined a community's inner life and governed its dynamics. Numerous scholars have noted how often workers used family metaphors to describe the close relationships that existed in their communities. Just as in other small towns, rural areas, and urban neighborhoods, people depended on one another and indeed expected kin and friends to help them out in times of need. Those who failed to live up to these expectations placed themselves in jeopardy. For in addition to being poorly thought of and perhaps even publicly scolded, they would be shunned when they needed comfort and support.

Examples of the centrality of kinship in the workplace abound. People often found employment through the influence of family members. Once on the job, newcomers frequently worked alongside kin and soon developed a sense of the boundary conditions that affected their situation and governed what they could or could not do. Through such contacts workers learned various skills, shortcuts, and tricks of the trade, including covert practices that dictated the pace of work on the shop floor.

When workers, young or old, experienced trouble with their bosses, kinsmen often interceded to mediate and clear up the difficulty. In countless ways, family members served as helpmates and guides to the uninitiated. Indeed, part of the learning process involved playing practical jokes on newcomers as a way of orienting them to work customs, teaching them their place in the pecking order among co-workers, chastising them for transgressions and reminding them of the need for group loyalty and solidarity. While often associated with good-natured fun, pranking also served a very serious social purpose.

If anything, family bonds proved even stronger outside the workplace. Although much remains to be learned about the dynamics of family and communal life, contemporary scholarship is beginning to acknowledge the critical roles played by women in industrial communities. Women, of course, were among the earliest recruits to the factory system. Yet while thousands of women found industrial employment, countless others stayed home to raise families, take in boarders, do outwork for merchant-manufacturers, and perform numerous other chores. Clearly, the coming of mechanized industry meant more, not less, work for these women as they struggled to find niches for themselves and their families in new social settings. The experience, as demanding as it was, doubtless led to certain tensions along gender lines in industrial households. Yet, by virtue of their steady presence in the community, women became virtual bulwarks in its daily affairs while helping to preserve older customs. Through a "porch culture" of visiting and gossip, they kept abreast of what was going on with neighbors and kin and, once alerted to problems, performed many acts of kindness (with the expectation, of course, that the same would be done for them if the need arose). When relatives or neighbors became ill and could not work, local women voluntarily stepped in and cared for them and their children. When a family did not have enough to eat or perhaps had too much of one item and not enough of another, neighboring women took them food and shared what they had. When someone died, they prepared them for burial, kept vigil, and provided the grieving family with baked goods and the like. These and other neighborly acts did as much as anything to foster a sense of closeness and strengthen common bonds among working people in industrial communities.

Although men also participated in these acts of helping and sharing, their presence is not as evident as that of women. The interesting thing, of course, is that these traits were not unique to people living in industrial communities. They could be found in rural areas and small towns throughout 19th-century America and, in fact, were transplanted when people moved to industrial locations. As with so much of industrial society, custom proved to be one of the buoys to which people clung as they confronted the present and contemplated the sea changes in their lives. Workers and their families found strength and solace in tradition, just as engineers and masters relied on it to guide them in designing the new technologies of the machine age.

F U R T H E R   R E A D I N G

Dublin, Thomas. *Women at Work: The Transformation of Work and Community in Lowell, Massachusetts, 1826–1860* (New York: Columbia University Press, 1979).
Gordon, Robert B., and Patrick M. Malone. *The Texture of Industry: An Archaeological View of the Industrialization of North America* (New York: Oxford University Press, 1994).

Hindle, Brooke, and Steven Lubar. *Engines of Change: The American Industrial Revolution, 1790–1860* (Washington, DC: Smithsonian Press, 1986).

Hunter, Louis C. *A History of Industrial Power in the United States, 1780–1930,* Vol. I: *Water Power* (1979) and Vol. II: *Steam Power* (Charlottesville: University of Virginia Press, 1985).

Jeremy, David J. *Transatlantic Industrial Revolution: The Diffusion of Textile Technologies Between Britain and America, 1790–1830s* (Cambridge, MA: The MIT Press, 1981).

Macauley, David. *Mill* (Boston: Houghton Mifflin, 1983).

Scranton, Philip. *Proprietary Capitalism: The Textile Manufacture at Philadelphia, 1800–1885* (New York: Cambridge University Press, 1983).

Smith, Merritt Roe. *Harpers Ferry Armory and the New Technology* (Ithaca, NY: Cornell University Press, 1977).

Wallace, Anthony F.C. *Rockdale: The Growth of an Industrial Village in the Early Industrial Revolution* (New York: Knopf, 1978).

"Second Nature": Steam, Space, and a New World Order, 1840–1900

Americans readily sensed the volatility of steam applied to manufacturing. As new reorderings of human and machine, male and female, labor and capital, country and city, factories always held the potential of social disruption. From the eighteenth to the twentieth centuries, a wide and conflicting range of languages was available to describe mills and their machinery. Unreflective celebration was hard to muster except in wartime.

But steam applied to transportation was constructed, at least initially, as free of moral ambiguities. The locomotive seemed not only an innocent machine but a new species of animal—the "Iron Horse." It moved; it had personality. It was made the central character in a drama between Americans and "space," or "man" and "nature." The railroad gave new embodiment to the old Western project of "overcoming natural obstacles," gospel in the expansive farming culture of the United States. The English origins of the technology were easily forgotten, as American railroads became known as "engines of democracy."

The railroads' role in the more mundane relations among Americans was, at first, obscure. Most writers believed trains would somehow bind people together. This goal of binding together what some saw as a dangerously large and diverse republic was first assigned to canals, later to trains. But by 1860, the cleavage between North and South was nowhere expressed more clearly than in maps of American railroad mileage. "Union" came through war, not railroads.

By the 1870s the political realities of living and working within the world's largest railroad grid began to weigh heavily on many Americans. Western farmers and other groups economically marginalized by the railroads sought to wrest control of this unprecedentedly large and powerful technological system from its private owners, or at least subject it to public regulation. The results were modest. Labor militancy raged through the railroad system in the late nineteenth century. Around 1911 the term efficiency was introduced into public discourse as part of another political campaign to influence railroad behavior.

The Populist and Progressive–era railroad debates centered around who would control the system. Few suggested that the technological system itself was mistaken or flawed. In contrast to language about factories, Americans had developed no critical vocabulary for machines that moved through space. The train—like the later automobile, airplane, and rocket—remained the dazzling, even romantic end of an always troubled techno-industrial regime. Locomotives and steamships became the ornaments not only of this industrial system but of national identity. As Michael Adas points out in his selection, they even became enmeshed in the most invidious of all cultural distinctions—race.

△△ D O C U M E N T S

The first two selections appeared in *Hunt's Merchants' Magazine* in 1840 and 1846, when railroads were still new and surprising. "Railroads of the United States," written anonymously, and "The Moral Influence of Steam" by Charles Fraser are typical of the enthusiastic treatment given the new technology in antebellum journals and newspapers. The third passage, from *Scientific American* (1847), describes American railroad engineers in Russia. It proposes a link—which would continue to be made in other contexts—between technology and democracy.

The fourth and fifth articles were written by the editor of the *Technologist,* a journal for engineers and architects, in 1870 and 1871. The transcontinental railroad system was by then a reality, the North had won its war for union, and, in the first selection, the editor outlines what he sees as the next technical and social challenge. Note the close mixture of different language styles, objects, and metaphors—the railroad, civilization, the scientific phenomenon of crystallization, progress, race, and the education of engineers. In the second selection the same editor, in the course of arguing with a missionary, suggests large projects that the railroad might still accomplish.

The sixth and seventh selections are statements by Native Americans, previously published in *Native American Testimony.* Old Lady Horse of the Kiowa tribe relates a folktale about buffalo, soldiers, and railroads, which is also about the fate of her people. Next, Chief Plenty Coups of the Crow describes a journey he made from Montana to Washington, DC, in 1880 to meet the president of the United States. The trip was mostly by railroad, and the conversation with the president was mostly about railroads.

"... gorgeous scenes of oriental fiction," 1840

In order to judge of the advantages to the republic, of land and water communication by steam, we need only to look back at the condition of the country in this respect before that agent was introduced. We had at that time the same spirit of enterprise, the same power of production, the same wide agricultural and mineral territory, the same large cities, acting as places of deposit and shipment, as well as the feeders for the interior, the same rivers and lakes, coursing like the veins of the human system through the whole frame of the country; but what advantages did they then present, compared with those which they now afford? The vessels which were accustomed to ply from port to port in the interior, locked up by ice a considerable portion of the year, even when navigation was free, were dependent upon the capricious chances of the wind, and although carrying valuable freights, which were required to be brought rapidly into market, were obliged to moor with sails reefed, in some safe bay, until a propitious breeze urged them towards their havens. Upon the land, the means of transportation, if more certain, were also as slow. The lumbering wagon bearing its heavy loads, was seen jolting its victims as it toiled up hills and over tiresome roads. . . . The population at remote points, were kept in ignorance of passing events both at home and abroad, until a long time after they had happened; of events too, which, had they been known, might have exercised an important bearing upon their interests and happiness. The whole country was manacled as with chains, to struggle on against the obstacles which nature ever throws in the path of human industry, as trials of the soul.

Let us contrast that state of things with the present improved condition of the means of intercommunication. Upon the land and the water, upon the surfaces of all our wide rivers and lakes, and upon our hills and valleys, we see the smoke of the steamship, and hear the clattering of the railroad car, rushing through the waves against wind and tide, propelling huge fabrics with amazing speed, or drawing their splendid saloons almost with the rapidity of lightning along their iron tracks. It seems indeed as if our own age is destined to realize the gorgeous scenes of oriental fiction, their floating palaces wafted along by melodious music, with banners streaming from their mirrored walls, their flying dragons rushing through the air, who counted time and space as nothing. We have moved palaces on the water and the land, saloons with gilded columns, carpeted with the costly fabrics of foreign looms, adorned with mirrors and paintings and rich tapestry, and dragged along by dragons of mightier power, with iron muscles that never tire, breathing smoke and flame through their blackened lungs, feeding upon wood and water, outrunning the race horse in their motion, yet without animal life, carrying forward huge bulks as if they were gossamer, making locomotion not a labor, but a luxury, producing companionship among communities in distant points, increasing intelligence, intercourse, union, and productive wealth. Not contented with scattering its trophies upon the land and the internal waters of the world, these iron monsters have made their path across the ocean, and drive their gorgeous palaces from the old world to the new, bearing to New York or Boston the fresh flowers which twelve days previous, were culled in the gardens of London or Liverpool. These are the triumphs of our own age, the laurels of mechanical philosophy, of untrammelled mind, and a liberal commerce!

. . . We believe that the steam engine, upon land, is to be one of the most valuable agents of the present age, because it is swifter than the greyhound, and powerful as a thousand horses; because it has no passions and no motives; because it is guided by its directors; because it runs and never tires; because it may be applied to so many uses, and expanded to any strength. We believe that it is to be the great moral agent in bringing the world into neighborhood; and the human mind, in the various parts of the globe, into contact, and, ultimately, into concurrent action. By approximating different nations, we believe that it is to increase intelligence; and, by consequence, advance the benevolent enterprises of the day. By augmenting the destructive power of men, we believe that it is designed to dull the edge of war, and plant perennial bowers of the olive branch upon fields which have been fattened by the blood of millions. We believe that its direct consequence will be to increase the influence of men, and their virtue, in the same proportion that it diffuses light; that it will advance the coming age, as it has already advanced the past, for the distance of centuries, an age which is destined to be an age of more expanded benevolence; that it will rush over the mountains which, "interposed, make enemies of nations;" batter down their narrow prejudices, and cause them to regard each other as members of one common family, designed to be confederated in bonds of benevolent action, for one common end; that it will compress the globe into one third its present space, and quintuple the practical and effective power of man, both in providing for himself luxuries, and in accumulating wealth, and doing good.

    . . . We behold it on the great American lakes, which have been but recently rescued from the dominion of the savage; and on those of Scotland, Switzerland, and Ireland. It drags the manufactures of Birmingham to the British metropolis; starts from within sight of the castle at Edinburgh; ploughs the waves of Constantinople, and moves its paddles through the waters of the Pacific. We see it upon the Red sea, the Black sea, and the Baltic; on the echoing rivers of the west, upon whose borders the savage and the wild beast yet retain a divided monarchy; and beneath the soft and sunny skies of an Italian clime, whose banks are rich with the sculptured and marble ruins of ancient art. We see it tossed, with its huge fabrics, by the great surges of the Atlantic, grappling with the winter tempest, under stormy and scowling skies; and gliding with the beauty of the barge of Cleopatra, by green and flowery banks, and along transparent waters, to the village haven. . . .

    When this enormous power of steam moves along the land, the horses and the cattle, which before toiled along the dusty road, are turned out to feed; the mechanic drops the plane, the hammer, and the saw, and bids machinery do his work: when it plies its wheels upon the waters, the shallop reefs its white sails. . . .

    The sensation, now scarcely worn off, in which we are first borne away by the railroad car is not easy to describe. We feel as if a new power had been called into existence, and that we were ushered into a new era of human progress. The beauty of the long trains of coaches, in size and decoration like the parlor, rushing over plain and through valley, the trim round barrel of the engine, which seems too small to drag so ponderous a bulk, the long iron arms which project from its furnace, in shape like the legs of a grasshopper, the bright polished wheels, the short black hissing pipe, the bounding speed of the car, when its propelling force is increased, strike us with amazement. Nor is the distant view of the railroad car less to be admired. At a distance, we behold it upon the landscape, dragging its linked trains with a motion entirely distinct from any thing else, a motion neither rolling or creeping but gliding along its iron track like some new land-monster different from any other species, as strange as the sea-serpent of Nahant, or a Kraken upon the coast of Norway!

    . . . The peculiar importance of the system of railroads to the United States, in a political point of view, can scarcely be overrated. Our broad commonwealth extending over so wide a surface, and with a population so various in their origin and diverse in their objects, must necessarily have distinct local views and principles, were they separated from the other parts in intercourse and trade. By the introduction of the system of railroads, rapid vehicles of communication are established between the several parts of the country, motives are furnished for travel, and ample means for the transportation of merchandise are provided. The great bulk of the people, who by the constitution are invested with the political power of the nation, circulating, as they do, through the different parts of the country, are thus made acquainted with the interests and feelings of the others, and must be blind if they do not perceive that the commercial fortunes and fate of each section is depending in a great measure upon the prosperity of the whole, for markets are provided in one section for the productions of each, producing, as they do, different *material,* which are required in the other parts of the country. Thus the political mind of the nation becomes liberalized, the republic is bound together by interests of trade and commerce, and railroads stand as iron bars running from state to state, which encircle the republic, and bind together the interests of the Union!

The Moral Influence of Steam (Excerpt), 1846

CHARLES FRASER

. . . The United States . . . recovering from the effects of a recent war, found herself in the possession of incalculable resources, which were, comparatively, unavailable to her. Her lands were fertile, her population growing and industrious. But the length of her great rivers and the strength of their currents, denied to the agriculturist and the merchant the benefit of a reciprocal trade. The boats that went down the Mississippi could not return, but were broke up, and sold for what their materials would bring in New Orleans.

Then, again, our confederacy embraced every variety of soil, climate, and habit. Indeed, its basis was a concession of conflicting interests and prejudices. Many of its members were so widely separated from each other, as to be strangers to friendly or social intercourse. To harmonize such discordant elements, and to produce a union of sentiment at all analogous to the political union they possessed, was scarcely within the reach of legislation. Something was wanting to give a practical effect to the prominent theory of our government. The philanthropist regarded it as the last experiment of rational freedom, and trembled for the result. But an agent was at hand to bring everything into harmonious co-operation, to vanquish every obstacle, to crown all enterprise, to subdue prejudice, and to unite every part of our land in rapid and friendly communication; and that was *steam.* Itself the parent of other, and, perhaps, more important discoveries, it has promoted a spirit of practical investigation, as wide as the field that invites it. There are features in the *magnetic telegraph* that cannot belie its kindred. It is the eldest born of a great family which shall spring up to bless future generations. . . . [W]hat is to be its ultimate influence on the moral condition of man? Is he to be altogether relieved from the necessity of corporeal exertion, and to be permitted to enjoy the blessings of life without the price of labor? . . . Will he be insured against the cravings of idleness, the languor of repose and apathy, in short, will he be happier for "the golden secret, the sought '*kalon*' found?" But the reply is, that he will then have time for the cultivation and advancement of the higher qualities of his nature; . . . that he who now tills the earth or delves the mine, will labor only for the improvement of those faculties which he has in common with the most intelligent of his race. . . . But such speculations (for speculations they are, and visionary, too,)

From Charles Fraser, "The Moral Influence of Steam," *Hunt's Merchants' Magazine* XIV (June 1846): 499–575.

would lead us into a maze of difficulty. Let us then pass to such views of the subject as are of more immediate and tangible interest.

1st. The abridgment of human labor to the extent we have seen, has certainly had the most disastrous effects in manufacturing countries. It has overthrown one of the great barriers against licentiousness, which is employment. It has strengthened the line of separation between the higher and lower classes of society; it has increased political discontent; it has weakened attachment to country, and forced the unhappy sufferers to expatriation, as their only refuge. Again the accelerated action which steam gives to commerce, appears to have imparted a feverish and unhealthy rapidity to all its operations, and to have produced a restlessness unfavorable to the ordinary habits of business, and the staid maxims of prudence and reflection. Speculation, hazardous adventure, fictitious and borrowed capital, all take place of that old-fashioned plain dealing which once looked to a fortune as the reward of a *life* of thrift and regularity. May we not attribute much of that moral delinquency, which, of late years, has been so rife in our country, to that eagerness after gain which, looking only at its object, becomes indifferent to the means of attaining it?

Another objection, too much underrated, is the destruction of life and property occasioned by steam; an objection to which the navigation of the American waters has been peculiarly exposed. There is scarce a river or sound, or, indeed, any part of our extensive coast, that has not been the scene of fatal disaster. . . .

These are, certainly, deplorable evils. But what great revolution was ever unaccompanied by evil? Every sudden change in the policy and condition of society, must be convulsive; and when we reflect that it is not upon one or two nations, only, but upon the whole civilized world, that this change is now in progress; when we see industry diverted from its ancient channels by a new and unexpected agent; when we see the productiveness of time multiplied fifty fold, and the impediments of distance vanishing, and its limits contracted to a span before this formidable and triumphant engine: when we see it spreading civilization to the remotest corners of the earth, transplanting and naturalizing the literature of one country into another, and replenishing the garners of one people with the harvest of another's intellectual labors; indeed, when we regard the whole framework of society through a medium that magnifies its proportions to so gigantic a scale, can we be so far intoxicated with the prospect as to forget the frailty of human nature, and to expect neither moral nor physical evil from the operation of causes capable of producing such incalculable results? . . . Indeed, when we connect the whole subject with the future prospects and destiny of men and of nations, when we think of the mighty revolutions to be accomplished in the moral and physical relations of society, of the change to be wrought throughout the world by this all-subduing agent, the mind is overwhelmed and lost, as if in the contemplation of endless time, or immeasurable space.

. . . [O]ught we not to glory in the privilege of being in the very midst of an influence so potent and pervading, and, withal, so benign; of being ourselves its subjects, seeing, hearing, and feeling it at every turn? And shall we be wanting in gratitude to the Giver of all good for bestowing on our generation what has been withheld from all that have preceded it, and make no effort to become worthy of so signal a distinction? Let it be remembered that steam, expansive as it is, and capable of such wonderful effects, is but the vapor of a simple element discovered and applied by the ingenuity of man, and, therefore, obedient to the control of his will. *His* is the responsibility for its abuse as an agent, a responsibility which would be aggravated in proportion to his knowledge of the happy results it is capable of producing.

If the steam-ship, as we have been endeavoring to show, is emphatically the off-spring of peace, and, above all other human contrivances, calculated to spread the tidings of good-will amongst men, and to make them—

> "Live brother-like, in amity combined,
> And unsuspicious faith,"

how ought the philanthropist to grieve at finding it converted into an engine of of-fensive war, calculated to aggravate its horrors, and to make it more sanguinary and desolating! But far be the day when steam shall be used as an engine of destruc-tion—when that which has hitherto been the harbinger of peace, shall be converted into a weapon to enforce the *law of violence*. . . . If that beautiful moral fabric which is rising in grandeur before an admiring world, should be assailed by its own archi-tect, its ornaments mutilated, and its proportions destroyed, where, ever, can be found the master-hand to restore it?

The *Scientific American* on Railroads and Russian Peasants, 1847

If we now turn our eyes to the North of Europe, we behold still greater triumphs of American genius and enterprise. There, in the heart of the Russian Empire—the most mighty of earth's despotic dominions, we behold a few American mechanics engaged in undertakings which will, in our opinion, exert an influence upon the fu-ture destinies of the North of Europe and Asia, portentous with glorious results. Under the superintendence of Major Whistler, there are now about 30,000 Russians, building railroads, and under the superintendence of Messrs. Harrison, Winans and Eastwick there are about 2000 occupied in building machinery. Two hundred loco-motives, 5000 trucks and 70 passenger cars are to be completed by 1849, and then across the Steppes of the Volga and through the Passes of the Ural mountains, will yet roll the swift American locomotive, pealing notes of nobler victories than those of the reddest warfare—the triumphs of American mechanical genius. Who knows now what great and good influence in the cause of Freedom and Reform is exercised by the mingling of our mechanics with the peasantry of the Russian empire.—Who knows but in a few years the now Russian serf, may stand a freeman at his own cot-tage door, and as he beholds the locomotive fleeting past, will take off his cap, kneel and bless God that the Mechanics of Washington's land were permitted to scatter the seeds of social freedom in benighted Russia.

". . . to float upon this tide" (Editorial), 1870

It is not many years since two-thirds of the territory of the United States, though nominally under the control of our Government, were actually in the possession of the bison and the Indian. But to-day this savage dominion is passing away. From

From *Scientific American* (September 4, 1847): 397.
From *The Technologist* 1:1 (February 1870): 1–2.

the outposts of civilization on both sides of the continent, a slender line has been projected, and on either side of this line the forces of civilization are producing a rapid crystallization that must soon fill the whole continent, just as we have seen a slender thread of crystals shoot across a huge mass of liquid, and become a line of innumerable centres, from which fresh crystallizing influences proceeded, until the whole liquid seemed to be converted into an aggregation of brilliant and beautiful forms.

A marked feature of the present age is co-operation and the division of labor— features due in a great measure to the higher civilization that we have attained. Fifty years ago, the pioneer went out into the wilderness with his axe and his rifle as his sole companions, and, building for himself a home, relied upon his own resources for the supply of all his wants. To-day, this may be possible, but it is hardly desirable, and competition on the part of others who appreciate the advantages conferred by the powerful agencies that have been developed within the last few years places all such Robinson Crusoe-like attempts at an overwhelming disadvantage. The day of log-houses and corduroy roads is in a measure past. He who attempts to found a village, and fails to secure the assistance of good architects, will hardly succeed in attracting the best class of settlers to his new colony; while, on the other hand, the farmer who wanders to a distance from the works of the engineer may succeed in raising good crops, but will hardly succeed in making them available in a pecuniary sense. The most pressing of our requirements, therefore, is a large increase in the number of engineers, architects, and educated superintendents of technological processes, and this want will be rendered still more apparent, if we consider the great additions which are being made to the lower grades of our laboring population by the influx of foreigners; for, whatever view we may take of emigration in general, and Chinese labor in particular, it is very obvious that we might as well attempt to oppose the advance of the tides of the ocean as to oppose the human tide that the superior attractions of our country will draw to our shores. Our only hope of escape from being overwhelmed lies in our ability to float upon this tide, instead of being sunk beneath it. The battle between muscle and brain will be waged as fiercely in the ranks of labor, as ever was the battle of caste between the feudal aristocracy and their vassals; and it is not difficult to predict the result. He who depends upon mere muscle for success, whether in the field of agriculture or the mechanic arts, will go to the wall as surely as the serfs of old went down before their steel-clad lords; and, if we are to hold our own in this country, it must be by so educating ourselves that we may be competent to direct and superintend the unskilled labor that is soon to be thrown on the market.

Railroads and Missionaries (Editorial), 1871

It is always to be regretted when any of the advocates either of religion or science, attempt to place these two in opposition to each other. It was therefore with considerable pain that we read, in a report of a speech made by him, on the occasion of the departure of some lady-missionaries to Japan, that Dr. Howard Crosby openly

---

From *The Technologist* (July 1871): 188.

expresses the hope that "the day is not far distant when money, instead of being used for the arts, sciences, and railroad schemes, will flow freely for the conversion of the world." Of the accuracy of the report we have no doubt, since it is taken from our able and trustworthy contemporary, *The New York Observer*. We had hoped that there could not have been found in the land a clergyman of prominence who could give utterance to such an illiberal sentiment. Had it not been for the arts and sciences of which Dr. Crosby speaks so contemptuously, where would the missionaries be at the present time? The truth is, that printing-presses, railroads, steamboats, telegraphs, and the inventions at which he sneers, have done more to diffuse a knowledge of the gospel than all that their illiberal depreciators have ever achieved. It is by the agency of railroads, and railroads alone, that Mormonism will be broken up, that India will be civilized and Christianized, and that massacres will be rendered impossible in China. No sensible man will deny that the distribution of the Bible is the most efficient means of advancing Christianity that has ever been devised. Where would this work have been if it had not been for the printing-press, the type-foundry, the electrotype, the stereotype, paper-making, and a thousand other things that all depend upon the arts and sciences? The missionary, the engineer, and the scientist are brothers and co-workers. Science owes much to the missionary; the latter has often found the engineer, with his level and transit, the best and most efficient of pioneers. To create jealously and ill feeling between them is the work of the Devil.

"The Buffalo Go": Old Lady Horse Tells a Folktale

Everything the Kiowas had came from the buffalo. Their tipis were made of buffalo hides, so were their clothes and moccasins. They ate buffalo meat. Their containers were made of hide, or of bladders or stomachs. The buffalo were the life of the Kiowas.

Most of all, the buffalo was part of the Kiowa religion. A white buffalo calf must be sacrificed in the Sun Dance. The priests used parts of the buffalo to make their prayers when they healed people or when they sang to the powers above.

So, when the white men wanted to build railroads, or when they wanted to farm or raise cattle, the buffalo still protected the Kiowas. They tore up the railroad tracks and the gardens. They chased the cattle off the ranges. The buffalo loved their people as much as the Kiowas loved them.

There was war between the buffalo and the white men. The white men built forts in the Kiowa country, and the woolly-headed buffalo soldiers [the Ninth and Tenth Cavalries, made up of black troops] shot the buffalo as fast as they could, but the buffalo kept coming on, coming on, even into the post cemetery at Fort Sill. Soldiers were not enough to hold them back.

Then the white men hired hunters to do nothing but kill the buffalo. Up and down the plains those men ranged, shooting sometimes as many as a hundred buffalo a day. Behind them came the skinners with their wagons. They piled the hides and bones into the wagons until they were full, and then took their loads to the new railroad stations that were being built, to be shipped east to the market. Sometimes there would be a pile of bones as high as a man, stretching a mile along the railroad track.

From Peter Nabakov, ed., *Native American Testimony* (New York: Viking Press, 1991), pp. 174–175.

The buffalo saw that their day was over. They could protect their people no longer. Sadly, the last remnant of the great herd gathered in council, and decided what they would do.

The Kiowas were camped on the north side of Mount Scott, those of them who were still free to camp. One young woman got up very early in the morning. The dawn mist was still rising from Medicine Creek, and as she looked across the water, peering through the haze, she saw the last buffalo herd appear like a spirit dream.

Straight to Mount Scott the leader of the herd walked. Behind him came the cows and their calves, and the few young males who had survived. As the woman watched, the face of the mountain opened.

Inside Mount Scott the world was green and fresh, as it had been when she was a small girl. The rivers ran clear, not red. The wild plums were in blossom, chasing the red buds up the inside slopes. Into this world of beauty the buffalo walked, never to be seen again.

Plenty Coups Travels to Washington (Memoir), 1880

They said they were going to take me to Washington. I though it over for a while. I thought it was a wise thing. I told them I would go. This was my first trip east. I also told them that I wanted some other chiefs to go with me. I asked Two-Belly. At first he didn't want to go, but finally he said he would. The others were Old Crow, Pretty Eagle, Long Elk, and Medicine Crow. Three white men also accompanied us: A. M. Quivey, Tom Stewart, and J. R. Keller.

It was during the spring. There was no railroad yet in our country, and we had to travel by stagecoach which carried a light at night. We traveled in two coaches. Snow was still lying on the ground. We set out from the old agency, near Flesh Scraper Mountain. The horses were relayed, but we had no rest during these changes of horses. We traveled toward Butte [Montana], which took us four nights and five days. The further we came into the mountains, the deeper lay the snow. At Butte we rested for the first time. We slept a whole day and night. And I combed my hair for the first time since leaving our camp.

Early the next morning we were told to dress quickly and eat. The teams were ready and we traveled down the mountain, following Flathead River. Again we were delayed. We continued until we came close to another mountain, and we saw an Indian driving some horses. We called him to us. He was a Bannock. We asked him where the Bannocks were. He told us that they were on the other side of the mountain, in the valley. He also told us that their chief, Comes Out of the Grease, had gone to Washington. . . .

Early the next morning we took a sweatbath with the Bannocks. They told us that the road from their camp to the next station was hard and rough, and that it was better to travel by daytime. At that station, however, we should see the Fast Wagon [train]. They described it as a big black horse with his belly nearly touching the ground. This horse had a big bell on his back. He ran so fast that everytime he stopped, he puffed.

From Peter Nabakov, ed., *Native American Testimony* (New York: Viking Press, 1991), pp. 140–144.

We left about noon and came to a big barn after dark where we slept. Early the next morning we started again and found the snow deep. Soon it started to rain which made the roads even worse. It was again after dark before we stopped at a dugout town, where they were building the railroad. Here we had supper. A white man with us pointed to a clock and told us that when the hands should be in a certain position we should start again. We did not know what he meant. Next morning we were awakened, took our bundles, and were taken to the train. We walked into the cars and sat down. We placed our bundles on shelves and looked out of the window. The train followed the river. Through the windows we could see many horses, game, and mountains. Stewart, who was traveling with us, acted as interpreter. We arrived at the Bannock Agency, and many Indians were there. As soon as the train stopped, we wanted to get off, but we were told to stay. That black horse was panting so hard that the bell on his neck was ringing.

We thought the train journey was grand. I realized, however, that it was not a horse that pulled it, and I wondered what made it go so fast. Birds would fly along outside our windows. They were swift, but before long we outdistanced them.

We had often been told that the Sioux were a numerous tribe. But it seemed to me that the Bannock was even larger. We halted at a junction, and another train passed going in a different direction. I saw a lake with a mountain rising from its center. We saw many white man's places, and passed many freshly skinned elk and buffalo carcasses. . . .

We came to a big forest and passed it and finally we arrived at the Missouri. Here we met a white man called Wood Frost who had been our agent. He invited us to dinner and gave us some red paint and shells. We had not even finished our meal when we had to leave for the train. We crossed the Missouri and were told that we were going to Chicago.

It was the first time that I had seen so many white people together. It was strange to see so many tall black houses. Here we left the train. There was a big lake and we spent much time there watching the ice bump against the shore and break into pieces. It was the biggest ice breakup I had ever seen, and the waves were very high.

There was more travel by train and finally we arrived in Washington. Here wagons were ready waiting for us. They took us to our lodging, and we were told to sleep until the next morning when we should be taken to President Hayes. The next day we were escorted to the President, who shook hands with us and told us that he was glad to see us. The President said that he had sent for us to talk concerning the future of our people. He said that he wanted us to send our children to school and that they would build a house and barn for each of us. He wanted us to learn how to farm. He said they were going to build a railroad through the Yellowstone Valley, but that they wanted us to make peace with the other tribes in our part of the country.

My companions told me to make some reply so I said that we were also glad to see him and that we wished to speak with him too. I said that he had asked us to do many things, but that before we could give him our answer, we would like time to talk it over among ourselves. The President gave us two days to consider his requests. Two days later we returned and again met with him. I said that we agreed to send our children to school and to let the Government build houses for us. I said that as far as stopping the fighting with other tribes, we wanted to fight them for about two more years and then we would reconsider this question. I added that we did not want a railroad built through our country because it was our hunting ground.

When we said this, the President kept us in Washington for over a month. We had several conferences with him in which he tried to overrule our objections, but he failed. The President suggested giving us another hunting ground, in North Dakota, but I refused because we did not wish to leave our country. When the President asked my reasons I said that in North Dakota the mountains are low and that I wanted to live where the mountains are high and where they are many springs of fresh water.

Then the President asked how we had treated the soldiers, and I said that we had been friendly to them. When their horses' feet were sore, so were ours. When they had to drink alkali, we shared their misfortune. When they suffered, we suffered, and I said we would continue to have friendly relations. Then the President said that he would grant our request to remain in the country where we lived, but that in return he expected us to let them build a railroad through the valley of the Yellowstone.

I said that when I returned to my people I would talk with them and hear their objections. I said then he could send us one of his servants and we would hold a council with him and he would tell the President of the results.

We were in Washington a long time. I became anxious to return home and see my people again. The President told us that we could return home in two Sundays. Although we dreaded the long journey, we were glad. When the day arrived, we again walked into the cars and traveled for a long time. It was late summer when we finally reached home, but the trees were still in full leaf.

Soon after we returned, we had a conference with the railroad and Government officials. We finally agreed to let them build the railroad through our country, and they agreed to give us free transportation. This was done at first, but soon this agreement was not lived up to and since then we have had to pay for our own transportation. A few years later the Government began to build homes for the Crows on the Big Horn River. I then went to Pryor [the westernmost town on the Crow India reservation]. I donated the use of four head of horses and had a log house built on the land where I live today.

𝄴 E S S A Y S

In the first essay, from *Nature's Metropolis,* author William Cronon places railroads in a landscape of developing capitalism centered on the new city of Chicago, where they interact with the technologies constituting the meatpacking industry. Elsewhere in his book, Cronon argues that the railroad was part of a "second nature" white Americans superimposed on the "first nature" discovered at the confluence of the eastern woodlands, the Great Lakes, and the Great Plains—the site of Chicago. Even Cronon's "first nature" was not static, nor was it just "nature." It included the buffalo-hunting culture of the Plains tribes, dependent on horses brought to the Americas by sixteenth-century Spaniards.

As Americans invaded the Great Plains, European powers conducted a related project—colonialism—on a worldwide scale. While Cronon focuses on the reordering, or "commodification," of nature, the second essay, from Michael Adas's *Machines as the Measure of Men,* discusses how the peoples of the world came to be reordered, or classified, using the language of Western science and technology. Does Adas's discussion of European racialist doctrines apply to nineteenth-century America as well, or was American racism constructed differently? What is the relationship, if any, between technology and "nature" in Cronon's essay, and technology and "race" in Adas's? Are machines still the "measure of men" and women at the end of the millennium?

Annihilating Space: Meat

WILLIAM CRONON

Although in retrospect the significance of Chicago's nineteenth-century grain elevators and lumberyards seems undeniable, visitors to the city in the years following the Civil War often failed to recognize their import. . . .

The same could hardly be said of that other great institution where western nature met the Chicago market: the stockyards. . . .

A New Zealand tourist told of having shown an American visitor one of his nation's great natural wonders, the geysers at Rotorua, only to have the American, unimpressed, remark, "Well, I guess, stranger, you would reckon it a grander sight to see a man standing to his waist in blood sticking pigs. We do that in my country." Although the New Zealander had been taken aback by this remark, which appeared "at the time a leap from the sublime to the ridiculous," he decided after finally visiting the Chicago stockyards for himself that the American "was quite right. It was a wonderful sight, and almost true to the letter."

Others might be no less impressed, but also feel appalled that the taking of animal life could have become so indifferent, so efficient, so calculating and cold-blooded. The stockyards might be "of vast importance and of astounding dimensions," one such visitor admitted, but "the whole business [is] a most unpleasant one, destitute of all semblance of picturesqueness, and tainted with cruelty and brutality." A person could visit the grain elevators and lumberyards without pondering their meaning, but such equanimity seemed somehow less appropriate at the stockyards. Rudyard Kipling was appalled at what he found there, and even more appalled by the apparent indifference of some of the visitors. He described one young woman who looked on quite coolly, standing "in a patch of sunlight, the red blood under her shoes, the vivid carcasses tacked round her, a bullock bleeding its life away not six feet away from her, and the death factory roaring all round her. She looked curiously, with hard, bold eyes, and was not ashamed." Her indifference seemed to Kipling the most frightening thing he saw at the stockyards, and made him worry about the effect of so mechanical a killing house on the human soul. As Upton Sinclair would remark in the most famous passage ever written about the place, "One could not stand and watch very long without becoming philosophical, without beginning to deal in symbols and similes, and to hear the hog-squeal of the universe." Kipling's young woman to the contrary, few who heard that squeal, or who saw the vast industrial landscape devoted to its exploitation, could avoid wondering what it might signify about animals, death, and the proper human relationship to both.

From William Cronon, "Annihilating Space: Meat," in *Nature's Metropolis* (New York: W. W. Norton & Co., 1991), pp. 207–259.

Chicago merchants had been dealing in hog squeals for decades before the Union Stock Yard opened for business on Christmas Day in 1865. . . .

For years, shippers had driven their animals through crowded streets to reach one of several small stockyards scattered in various districts in the southern parts of the city. . . .

. . . Although most stockyards were initially located on prairie land just outside the built-up area of the city, they were soon surrounded by houses and factories that limited their expansion and cut off their original supply of hay and grazing land. The congestion of city streets inconvenienced drovers, endangered pedestrians, and injured animals; worse, it also broke up the Chicago market, making it difficult for buyers and sellers to compare the prices being offered in different yards. Financial reporters for the city's newspapers had trouble gathering information about price movements, and the inaccuracy of the resulting reports compounded the difficulties of those in the trade. The problem grew steadily during the 1850s and reached crisis proportions in the early years of the Civil War, when the Union army's demand for provisions led Chicago to surpass Cincinnati as the largest meat-packer in the world. By the mid-1860s, as an early Chicago historian described it, "centralization was urgently demanded, as a means of competition, from both buyers and sellers."

The railroads would provide the means to escape these problems and transform Chicago's role in the meat trade. The solution—a single unified stockyard that would concentrate the city's livestock business at one location—was proposed in the fall of 1864, when Chicago's nine largest railroads, in conjunction with members of the Chicago Pork Packers' Association, issued a prospectus for what they called the Union Stock Yard and Transit Company. Capitalized at nearly a million dollars, the new company purchased a half square mile of land in the town of Lake, just south of the Chicago city limits in the open prairie lying west of Halsted Street. Four miles from city center, it seemed far enough away to avoid being overtaken by urban growth at least for the immediate future. The chief engineer of the Chicago and Alton Railroad drew up plans for the site, and construction began on June 1, 1865. . . .

A visitor standing atop Hough House [a hotel] and taking in the sights of what Chicagoans were fond of calling "THE GREAT BOVINE CITY OF THE WORLD" could hardly fail to be impressed that this vast network of rails and fences had only one purpose: to assemble the animal products of the Great West, transmute them into their most marketable form, and speed them on their way to dinner tables around the world. The economic miracle of the stockyard had much in common with that of the grain elevator. It concentrated an abundant but scattered natural resource to create a new kind of commodity. For cattle, this meant traveling east by rail in heretofore unheard-of-numbers while still alive, since beef packing was not at first a major activity at the Chicago stockyards. For pigs, it meant passing through the "disassembly line"—pioneered in Cincinnati but perfected in Chicago—that divided animals into their most minute constituent parts so that the greatest possible profit from their sale could be gained. In each case, the fundamental process remained the same: moving animals ever further in their passage from pulsing flesh to dead commodity.

At the stockyards, this economic alchemy was accomplished in a yellow limestone structure located next to the hotel. Known as the Exchange Building, it contained a bank that during the 1860s regularly handled up to half a million dollars worth of transactions each day, as well as telegraph facilities that gathered meat prices and livestock news from every corner of the globe. Its most important feature, though, was the great hall where dealers conducted their daily business in much the same way as the grain traders at the Board of Trade. As one New Yorker described it, "In this elegant Exchange room two classes of cattle men meet,—those who collect the cattle from the prairie States,—Texas, Missouri, Kansas, Illinois, Iowa, Wisconsin, Minnesota,—and those who distribute the cattle among the Eastern cities."

Here, then, was the whole point of the stockyard, the ultimate meeting place of country and city, West and East, producer and consumer—of animals and their killers. Its polished wood surfaces and plush upholstery offered an odd contrast to the wet muck and noisy, fecund air in the pens just outside its doors. The Exchange Building seemed somehow at a distance from the animals in whose flesh it dealt, as if to deny the bloody consequences of the transactions that went on within it. For some, this was a sign of civilization, whereby "a repulsive and barbarizing business is lifted out of the mire, and rendered clean, easy, respectable, and pleasant." Those who handled the animals in their pens had little to do with those who bought and sold them, and vice versa. "The controlling minds"—the large traders and meatpackers—were thereby "left free to work at the arithmetic and book-keeping of the business," undisturbed by manure or blood or the screams of dying animals. . . .

Chicago and the lands lying several hundred miles to its west had originally been covered by plants of the tallgrass prairie: wild rye, slough grass, switch grass, the bluestems, and others. Growing in the lush abundance of a well-watered land, grasses like the big bluestem could rise to over six feet in height—so high, the artist George Catlin reported, that he and his companions were "obliged to stand erect in our stirrups, in order to look over its waving tops," as they rode through it. . . .

The tallgrass prairie of the upper Mississippi Valley would vanish during the years of Chicago's greatest growth, to be replaced by some of the most fertile farmlands in the world. The rise of agricultural markets in Chicago and elsewhere meant that wheat and especially corn would become the new artificial dominants of the old prairie ecosystem. As the railroads fingered their way beyond the eastern margins of the Great Plains, agricultural settlement of the grasslands increased its pace, almost exploding with the completion of the first transcontinentals in the late 1860s and early 1870s. . . .

. . . The mixed and shortgrass prairies would prove to be wonderful rangeland for domesticated grazing animals, a fact already evident from the vast herds of wild grazers that had long made homes there. An English visitor in the 1860s offered an accurate prophecy when he wrote, "Nothing short of violence or special legislation can prevent the plains from continuing to be forever that which under nature's farming they have ever been—the feeding ground for mighty flocks, the cattle pasture of the world." But if livestock was to become the new foundation for agriculture on the High Plains, would-be settlers and ranchers had to alter the earlier landscape of the region. In particular, they had to confine or eliminate its original human and animal inhabitants.

Among the latter, none was more astounding in its abundance than the American bison. At the beginning of the nineteenth century, the plains had been home to a bison population numbering upward of twenty, thirty, or even forty million animals. So numerous were they that they significantly modified their habitat, shifting the species composition of grasslands toward shorter and more resilient species (especially the well-named buffalo grass) that could best withstand heavy grazing. The bison lived in scattered herds of fifty to two hundred individuals, that in a desultory and almost random way, migrated north and south with the seasons, and hither and yon between burned and unburned prairie, in search of fresh grass for forage. During the late summer, these small herds congregated for what was called the "running season," when bulls challenged each other for territorial mating rights. When assembled in this way, the great mass of animals became an awe-inspiring sight for all who witnessed it, indisputable proof that the grasslands were an extraordinarily productive environment for grazers. . . .

So numerous were the enormous shaggy beasts that travelers found themselves groping for verbal images to describe them adequately. They were like fish in the sea, an army in battle, a biblical plague of locusts, a robe that clothed the prairies in all directions to the horizon. Perhaps the most common observation, made by many before and after Catlin, was that the animals literally changed the color of the landscape, "blackening the whole surface of the country." They seemed, as the Reverend Robert Rundle said in the borrowed words of Milton, "in numbers—numberless." When William J. Hays sought to record the vast scale of a stampeding herd in a painting he made while visiting the plains in 1860, eastern critics attacked him for his exaggeration and want of accuracy. Yet those who had seen the great herds for themselves could testify that Hays had gotten his image exactly right.

Hays produced his painting at almost the last possible moment he could have made it from life. The bison were already doomed. Their numbers, like those of the beaver and other North American fur-bearing mammals, began to dwindle as soon as the market economy placed a price on their skins. In the early years, that price was measured in liquor, firearms, and other trade goods sought most actively by Plains Indian tribes. As early as the 1830s, Catlin heard tell of a party of six hundred Sioux warriors in the Dakota country who had exchanged fourteen hundred fresh buffalo tongues for "a few gallons of whiskey"; somewhere nearby, fourteen hundred carcasses presumably lay unused and rotting in the summer sun. During the first half of the nineteenth century, Plains tribes began to consider the bison an object of trade as much as of subsistence. A market in robes sprang up in the East to encourage such ventures. At the same time, fur traders and U.S. Army posts grew to rely on the animals for food. The great herds came under increasing pressure, and their numbers began to decline.

But the real collapse of the bison population did not come until after the Civil War. With the arrival of the Union Pacific in Nebraska and Wyoming during the 1860s, followed a few years later by the Kansas Pacific farther south, the railroads drove a knife into the heart of buffalo country. As everywhere else, trains introduced easier, faster travel into territory that had formerly been much less accessible. They made market demand more effective as the cost of transportation fell. . . . Suddenly it became possible for market and sport hunters alike to reach the herds with little effort, shipping back robes and tongues and occasionally trophy heads as the only valuable parts of the animals they killed. Sport hunters in particular enjoyed the practice of firing into the animals without ever leaving their trains. As they neared a herd, passengers flung open the windows of their cars, pointed their breechloaders, and fired at random into the frightened beasts. Dozens might die in a few minutes, and rot where they fell after the train disappeared without stopping.

Then, disastrously, in 1870 Philadelphia tanners perfected techniques for turning bison hides into a supple and attractive leather. The next year, all hell broke loose. Commercial hunting outfits—"pot-hunters"—descended on the plains in greater numbers than ever before, shipping back hundreds of thousands of skins to eastern manufacturers. So great was their enthusiasm and so little their skill that three to five animals died for every robe that eventually made the rail journey back east. "Every man," wrote Richard Dodge, an army officer who witnessed the height of the slaughter, "wanted to shoot; no man wanted to do the other work. Buffalo were slaughtered without sense or discretion, and oftentimes left to rot with the hides on." Now that the dead animals were a more reliable source of cash, such waste made less economic sense, and so merchants soon organized more professional hunting parties. A typical outfit came to consist of four men: a shooter, two skinners, and a cook who was also responsible for stretching hides and taking care of camp. They were supported by a growing network of depots and smokehouses that served as gathering stations where merchants assembled their stock for shipment to Omaha, St. Louis, Chicago, and finally the great leather manufacturers in Philadelphia and especially New York.

The bison had once had few predators. As a herding animal, it instinctively responded to attack either by standing its ground or stampeding. Both behaviors proved lethal in the face of market hunters carrying guns. . . . Such shooting was hardly hunting at all; it was almost literally like working in a slaughterhouse, and the plains soon gained the appearance of a vast, nightmarish abattoir. "Where there were myriads of buffalo the year before," Dodge wrote, "there were now myriads of carcasses. The air was foul with sickening stench, and the vast plain, which only a short twelvemonth before teemed with animal life, was a dead, solitary, putrid desert."

The result was just what George Catlin had prophesied forty years earlier: "the ranks must be thinned, and the race exterminated, of this noble animal, and the Indians of the great plains left without the means of supporting life. . . ." Dodge's image was more poetic but no less accurate. "The buffalo," he wrote, "melted away like snow before a summer's sun." Within four years of the appearance of the railroads and a market in tannable hides, well over four million bison died on the southern plains alone. In Kansas, the slaughter reached its peak between 1870 and 1873, and then collapsed. . . .

. . . As the bison disappeared, the Great Plains Indian tribes found their subsistence more and more threatened. Custer's defeat at the Little Bighorn may have been the climatic event in Plains Indian resistance to the American invasion, but it was the last stand of a people whose ecological homeland had nearly vanished. The Indian wars of the 1870s took place in the shadow of hunger and starvation occasioned by the loss of the animals on which Indian economies and cultures had been relying for generations. Sitting Bull and his followers may have won their great battle, but they lost the war to defend their earlier way of life. Henceforth, they would have to find new lives for themselves without the great herds to sustain them. . . .

Like that of many other places, the old market geography of the grasslands was transformed by the railroad. At the end of the war, construction crews for the Kansas Pacific began to work their way out into the buffalo country of the southern plains, surveying a line west from St. Louis and Kansas City into the heart of the mixed-grass prairie. As the hunters set about their bloody work with the bison, other entrepreneurs began to speculate about how best to solve the transportation problem of the Texas longhorns. Somewhere along the route of the new line it ought to be possible, as one such entrepreneur explained, "to establish a market whereat the Southern drover and Northern buyer would meet upon an equal footing.

Just such a place came into being at Abilene, Kansas. Starting its existence as "a very small, dead place, consisting of about one dozen log huts," Abilene began its brief time of glory in 1867 when an Illinois livestock dealer named Joseph G. McCoy purchased 250 acres and established a stockyard near the rail depot there. Texas cattlemen had already learned of the railroad's westward extension but had been uncertain about where best to meet it. McCoy gave them their answer. He developed and promoted an old trading route, the Chisholm Trail, as the best corridor for bringing livestock north. It ended in Abilene. Cattle began to arrive there by August, and the first twenty-car shipment of animals left the city on September 5. Their destination, predictably enough, was Chicago.

The great cattle drives of the 1860s, 1870s, and 1880s are among the best known and most romantic of American frontier icons. The classic image is that of cowboys on horseback working to round up scattered cattle, assembling great herds of hundreds or even a thousand or more animals before urging the bellowing mass forward. The lonely life of the trail has entered American mythology by way of folk songs, dime novels, and western films as a series of familiar moments: the long march across windswept prairies, the potential disaster of river crossings and thunderstorms, the ever present threat of stampedes, the smell of beans and salt pork cooking over open campfires, the uneasy quiet of the night watch. The cowboy rapidly emerged as the new nomad of the Great Plains, driving and trailing his herds along the same paths that bison and Indians had followed just a few years before. But wherever he did his work, however remote the landscapes he called home, his essential task remained the same: bringing the fatted herd to market. The cowboy was the agent who tied [the] livestock-raising zone to its metropolitan market. Far from being a loner or rugged individualist, he was a wageworker whose task was to ship meat to the cities—above all, to Chicago. . . .

For cattle that had grown fat on the grasses of the High Plains and the corn of the Iowa feedlots, Chicago was the end of the line. It was the place, more than any other, where animals went to die. In the grimy brick buildings that sprang up beside the great stockyard, death itself took a new form.

The actual task of killing was not the biggest problem Chicagoans had to solve as they faced the thousands of animals that poured into the stockyard. Killing was a relatively simple matter—a blow to the head, a knife to the throat—complicated only by how much one cared about the pain or terror animals felt in dying. The real problem was what to do with animals once they were dead, for unless people intervened at once they soon went the way of all flesh. Decay was the great enemy of the meatpacker, wasting an investment in fatted hogs and steers far more quickly than the animals lost weight on a long drive. . . .

Aside from the differences between beef and pork as meats the animals from which they came—being quite unlike each other in size, shape, and temperament—lent themselves to different kinds of marketing. Cattle, with their long legs, large size, and easygoing nature, did not generally object to being driven. If well handled, they could walk hundreds of miles without losing so much weight that they became unprofitable to sell. Hogs, on the other hand, were smaller, closer to the ground, and more ill-willed toward their keepers. Their bad humor made them so hard to drive to market that drovers sometimes stitched shut the eyelids of particularly obstreperous animals. Once blinded in this way, they could still keep to the road by following their companions, but were less inclined to make havoc. Hogs lost weight quickly while on the road, and this too made it unprofitable to drive them very far. . . .

Frontier farmers raised hogs as their great residual crop. Unlike cattle, pigs were perfectly willing to fend for themselves even in the earliest days of settlement, whether in prairie or in woodland. Often allowed to run wild, they grazed, ate acorns, foraged in cornfields, and consumed any household garbage not being put to other uses. From the perspective of a farm family struggling to establish itself in a new location, they were wonderfully productive animals, converting grain to meat with two or three times the efficiency of cattle or sheep. A hog contained considerably more usable meat and fat as a proportion of its body weight than a steer. Moreover, a sow could start reproducing when only a year old, whereas a cow did not become fertile until sometime in its third year. A sow dropped her litter of several piglets after only four months gestation, whereas cows took nine months to produce only a single calf (or occasionally two). As a result, pigs multiplied at a much greater rate. Their prodigious meat-making powers meant that once farmers had harvested their corn crop, pigs (along with whisky) were generally the most compact and valuable way of bringing it to market. Farmers tried hard to gauge the ratio of pork prices to corn prices, and fed corn to their pigs whenever it seemed the most profitable course to follow. As one nineteenth-century commentator put it, "The hog eats the corn, and Europe eats the Hog. Corn thus becomes incarnate; for what is a hog, but fifteen or twenty bushels of corn on four legs?" . . .

Just as Buffalo had invented the grain elevator that would revolutionize Chicago's grain trade, Cincinnati pioneered the manufacturing techniques that would transform Chicago meat-packing. The enormous number of pigs that filled Cincinnati's streets each fall, and the urgent need to stop the clock of their decay, led the city's packers to develop new ways of organizing the traditional process of butchering. The earliest step toward mechanization was a large horizontal wheel from which dead pigs hung. As it rotated, workers at the eight points of its compass cleaned and gutted the animals in eight separate steps before sending them off to a storage room for cooling. Once cold, they were taken to tables where master butchers systematically cut them into pieces to be packed and marketed. Cincinnati packers later supplemented the wheel with an overhead rail which carried pigs through each step of the butchering process, and with multistoried packing plants in which animals and carcasses moved by the force of gravity from station to station. The most powerful description remains that of [Frederick Law] Olmsted:

> We entered an immense low-ceiled room and followed a vista of dead swine, upon their backs, their paws stretching mutely toward heaven. Walking down to the vanishing point, we found there a sort of human chopping-machine where the hogs were converted into commercial pork. A plank table, two men to lift and turn, two to wield the cleavers, were its component parts. No iron cog-wheels could work with more regular motion. Plump falls the hog upon the table, chop, chop; chop, chop; chop, chop, fall the cleavers. All is over. But, before you can say so, plump, chop, chop; chop, chop; chop, chop, sounds again. . . . Amazed beyond all expectation at the celerity, we took out our watches and

counted thirty-five seconds, from the moment when one hog touched the table until the next occupied its place.

The whole system came to be called the disassembly line and was among the most important forerunners of the mass production techniques that swept American industry in the century to come. In relation to what would soon happen at Chicago, several key facts stand out about Cincinnati. One was that the disassembly line's chief innovation depended much more on the minute division of human labor than on new mechanical technologies. Chicago would go much further with mechanization, but ultimately the organic irregularities that made each animal unique also made human eyes and human hands indispensable for most of the packing process. The division of labor allowed packers to accelerate the rate at which workers handled hogs, and led to specialized ways of dealing with each constituent body part. The enormous volume of animals meant that even body parts that had formerly been wasted now became commercial products: lard, glue, brushes, candles, soaps. Because of such economies, Cincinnati packers in the 1840s could pay seven to ten cents more per hog than packers in other places. But the very rivers that had brought Cincinnati its flood of pork also tied it to the same seasonality that governed the activities of . . . other lesser packers. Even Porkopolis did most of its work in the winter, leaving its immense capital plant idle for the rest of the year. The natural cold that could slow death's decay still held ultimate sway over production.

Chicago merchants had conducted a substantial meat trade even before the coming of the railroad, but they did not come close to the Ohio city in total volume. At the start of the 1850s, Chicago packed 20,000 hogs, compared with Cincinnati's 334,000. Chicago pork packing was still largely the domain of the general merchant. . . . Then, as the railroads extended their network west, they worked their transforming magic. Chicago's western hinterland grew, bringing ever greater quantities of live hogs and chilled carcasses to the city's merchants. Interior communities could now ship their animals eastward via Chicago rather than southward via the river towns. Cincinnati's rivers had brought it more pork than any other American city, but the trade had reached its natural limits by midcentury; Chicago, on the other hand, was just beginning to grow. . . .

By creating vast pork hinterland that extended all the way across the corn region of Illinois and Iowa, the railroads gave Chicago economies of scale that even Cincinnati could not match. Borrowing a lesson from the river town, Chicago packers abandoned the simple warehouses that had sufficed in earlier days. They constructed elaborate factories designed to slaughter animals and move them past a long chain of workers, each of whom helped disassemble a small part of the carcass into its constituent parts. During the Civil War decade, Chicago firms invested immense sums in specialized buildings, steam engines, and other equipment that enabled them to handle an even larger number of animals. . . .

Capital investment on such a scale underscored the seasonal problems of pork packing as an industry. During the first decade of rail-based packing in Chicago, the vast majority of the city's pork receipts occurred during November, December, and January. Although a trickle of live hogs continued to arrive during the rest of the year, they were slaughtered mainly for fresh consumption within Chicago itself. Few if any animals were packed, for warm temperatures made that impractical. Inefficient use of capital was the seemingly unavoidable result. Half a million dollars in buildings and equipment might pay handsomely for themselves during the early months of winter when they processed the immense stream of carcasses and live hogs that flooded into Chicago from western farmlands. But for the rest of the year, capital plant sat idle, earning little or no return for its owners. This was the trade-off between the simple warehouse facilities that hinterland merchants . . . used for their packing and the more specialized factories of Chicago pork packers. Specialization yielded greater meat output from each pig and each human worker, but only by employing equipment that was useless for other purposes during warm seasons, when the meat trade fell off. Seasonal fluctuation meant using capital inefficiently.

Faced with this problem, Chicago pork packers took the obvious step: they began to consider ways of manipulating the seasons of the year. If only winter temperatures could somehow be stored for use during the hot Illinois summers, expensive capital plant need not sit idle. The railroads provided the means for performing even this improbable feat. Merchants in the East had for half a century been cutting ice from ponds near cities like Boston and New York to supply the urban demand for refrigeration. Stored in insulated warehouses and delivered by wagon to commercial and residential customers, ice was traded locally by land and over great distances by sea, so Boston ice merchants could supply the West Indies and American South as well as their own city. But ice was a large-bulk, low-value commodity and had to await the coming of the railroad before it could travel far by land. Chicago was again in the right place at the right time: rail-shipped ice became available at just the moment that rail-shipped hogs began to pose problems. . . .

Farmers could now count on finding a year-round market in Chicago for their corn-fattened pigs—because the city's packing plants never closed. Access to the Chicago market changed the agricultural calendar, spreading pork production across the entire year. Ice and rails together enabled Chicago to pack an ever larger share of the western hog supply; by 1882, its peak year, the city processed nearly half the Midwest's total urban output. The railroads, by carrying hogs to the city even when older modes of transportation proved impassable, had helped Chicago break the wheel of the seasons. The packers had learned to store the winter.

Although the ice trade undoubtedly increased the volume of pork packing in Chicago, its effect on the city's beef market was revolutionary. Because American consumers preferred their steaks fresh, the cattle that railroads brought to Chicago from as far away as Texas, New Mexico, and Montana did not generally end their journey in the city. Initially, most steers at the Union Stockyard, aside from the fraction destined for dinner tables in Chicago itself, were transferred to eastbound railroads and sent to butchers in New York and other cities. As late as 1871, less than 4 percent of the cattle that arrived in Chicago were packed there, those few being shipped mainly to England and imperial outposts like India. Packing as an industry relied almost entirely on pigs, not cattle.

Pork packers used ice to do artificially in summer what cold air had done naturally in winter: cure carcasses before actually preserving them with salt. But Americans' preference for unsalted beef suggested to a few packers an alternative way to use ice. If one could butcher cattle in Chicago and then ship them in refrigerated form to eastern markets, beef packing might become a more profitable activity. Chilling beef in Chicago was easy enough, given the infrastructure already devoted to the ice trade for pork packing. The problem was how to keep meat cold once it began its eastbound journey. The earliest solution was that of George H. Hammond, a Detroit packer who in about 1868 used a special refrigerated railroad car—an icebox on wheels originally designed for fruit shipments—to send sixteen thousand pounds of beef to Boston. . . .

The refrigerated railroad car, like the grain elevator, was a simple piece of technology with extraordinary far-reaching implications. The most obvious was the steep growth in Chicago beef packing that began in the mid-1870s. In 1883–84, the number of cattle slaughtered in Chicago surpassed the number shipped east for the first time; henceforth, "meat-packing" would replace "pork packing" as the name of the industry. The packers themselves attributed their success to the new technology. "The refrigerator car," announced Swift and Company in a later brochure, "is one of the vehicles on which the packing industry has ridden to greatness." . . .

. . . [T]he refrigerated car bore [an] important resemblance to the grain elevator. Both partitioned a natural material—a steer or a bushel of wheat—into a multitude of standardized commodities, each with a different price, each with a different market. No. 1 spring wheat found customers different from no. 2's. The same was true of different animals raised at different locations, and even of the different parts of a single animal. Chicago's No. 1 cattle were the corn-fed animals raised in Illinois, Iowa, Kentucky, and Indiana. They produced the fattest and most desirable meats and went to "first-class customers," swank urban hotels, and the discriminating English buyers in Liverpool. No. 2 cattle were from Colorado and Montana and were the heaviest and best tasting of the western range animals. No. 3 cattle were the common Texas longhorns and went mainly to domestic markets that were not so selective in their tastes. Different supply areas in the West became linked to customers of different classes in different regions, even in different countries.

Beef and pork did not develop formal grading systems in the same way that grain did at the Chicago Board of Trade (though a futures market in pork did emerge). Live animals varied too much in weight and quality to be traded as completely abstract commodities at the stockyard. Unlike buyers of grain, livestock purchasers continued to examine individual animals before offering prices for them. Standardization happened later, after a sale was complete and animals had entered the packing plant. Then, their transmutation into commodities went even further, since a single living creature could be divided into literally hundreds of different products. Whereas the local butcher in a city or small town had little choice but to sell the parts of an animal to nearby customers for whatever they were willing to pay, the Chicago packers could amass body parts and ship them wherever they would bring the best price. Profits from one body part could help subsidize the sales of other parts, giving the Chicago firms an enormous competitive advantage. When a carload of dressed beef arrived in an area, it could contain only the cuts of meat most likely to sell there, with none of the other material local butchers had to try to sell.

The real genius of the refrigerator car had more to do with marketing that with technology. The proof of this came when customers examined the cuts of meat [butcher and entrepreneur Gustavus] Swift offered for sale. Traditional butchers, especially wholesale ones, kept few if any samples of their final products on display for customers. The bulk of their meats hung as carcasses in a cooler and were cut to order. Swift's insight was to realize that customers (including retail butchers) would buy more meat, doing so essentially on impulse, if a variety of different products met their eyes when they walked into a shop. The most important of those products from Swift's point of view were cuts like the plate and chuck and round, which were not ordinarily as desirable as ribs or loins. If one could sell parts such as these at favorable prices, one would get maximum profits from the animal as a whole. The best way to accomplish this goal was to cut meat cosmetically into the most attractive possible pieces and display them to best advantage, an idea Swift had first tried in his Massachusetts butcher shops. Now he applied it to dressed beef, urging his agents to "cut it up and scatter the pieces," for "the more you cut, the more you sell." The strategy showed real insight into consumer psychology, and Swift's competitors soon adopted it as well.

Shrewd marketing and low prices had precisely their intended effect. Once customers overcame their initial reluctance, they sought Chicago dressed beef whenever they could get their hands on it. And yet this at first was harder to do than one might think, for both they and the packers faced formidable adversaries. Dressed beef profoundly disrupted the traditional American beef trade. The opportunity it represented for Chicago packers seriously threatened others in the trade: livestock shippers, eastern packers, wholesale butchers, and, not least, the railroads themselves. Its effects paralleled changes already going on in Chicago's grain and lumber markets. Dressed beef vastly extended the geographical reach of Chicago' market, enabling one city to transform the economic landscape of a broad region, rearranging its environment according to the dictates of capital. Dressed beef went beyond grain and lumber in proliferating the logic of the market, for people in the East felt some of its greatest effects as much as people in the West. Dressed beef brought the entire nation—and Great Britain as well—into Chicago's hinterland.

Perhaps the most serious hurdle that Swift and the other dressed beef firms faced came from the very institution that had made their success possible in the first place: the railroads. The transport companies did not welcome refrigerated beef with open arms. They had long tried to move livestock as far as possible by rail, and had invested a great deal of capital toward that end. They had built immense stockyards not just in Chicago but throughout the country, especially in the northeastern cities where butchers ordered large shipments of western cattle for local slaughter. Those stockyards would become worthless if the dressed beef companies managed to shift most slaughtering to Chicago. Livestock shippers were among the railroads' biggest and most favored customers, served by a vast fleet of cattle cars in which the roads had invested hundreds of thousands of dollars. Such cars were more flexible than the new refrigerator cars, since they could easily carry eastern manufactured goods on their return journey and avoid the cost of traveling empty. This was one reason why the roads refused to furnish the Chicago packers with refrigerated cars, calling them "speculative." Swift and the others had to build and operate their own cars on the model of the express companies, which had been running fast freight cars on contract with the railroads since the Civil War.

From the railroads' perspective, livestock was a bulkier, heavier load than dressed beef. All other things being equal, live animals intrinsically generated more freight charges than meat—which was, after all, why dressed beef had a competitive advantage over them. Faced with protecting their investment, and with their classic problem of fixed capital costs in a competitive economic environment, the roads tried to support livestock shippers who could guarantee them a large and reliable volume of freight traffic. . . .

Ironically, the railroads' efforts to concentrate the livestock trade at Chicago also created conditions that encouraged the development of the dressed beef industry there. The city's prices, facilities, and handling charges had all made it the obvious location when Hammond, Swift, and Armour had been deciding where to set up operations. . . . But this did not prevent the railroads from responding to dressed beef with a kind of passive resistance. They refused to provide capital equipment in the form of refrigerator cars and icing stations. They were reluctant to guarantee a steady volume of traffic or the rapid handling that was essential to iced shipments. They set rates that put dressed beef at a disadvantage against live shipments, charging it at the traditional rate for barreled beef, which was about three times higher than that for livestock. Although they could not forbid dressed beef shipments entirely, they did what they could to make them inconvenient and unprofitable.

Fortunately for Swift, there was one eastern railroad with no significant interest in live animal shipments: the Grand Trunk. Saddled with the longest and most northern of cross-country routes, the Grand Trunk skirted the Canadian shores of Lakes Erie and Ontario before connecting with American railroads near Montreal to reach the Boston and New York markets. Because its line was so much more circuitous than those of its competitors, and because cattle required constant feeding and watering while they traveled, the Grand Trunk had never succeeded as a livestock carrier. Locked out of the highly profitable American meat trade, its managers were delighted when Swift approached them about carrying dressed beef. Travel distance mattered little for chilled meat so long as ice was available along the way—and on that score the Grand Trunk's colder northern route wa a positive advantage. The railroad quickly became the leading carrier of Chicago dressed beef. . . .

The collapse of the older system [of shipping live animals] affected no one more than wholesale butchers in eastern states from Ohio to New England. Their ordinary habit had been to buy livestock from local farmers or from Chicago itself, slaughtering the animals and selling cuts of meat to retail butchers and their final customers. Shrewd marketer that he was, Swift realized that it would be better to have the wholesale butchers as allies than an enemies, so in many towns he approached the leading butcher—usually a person of considerable means—about becoming a partner in the dressed beef business. Those who agreed took a one-third interest in the local trade, while Swift and his brother took the remaining two-thirds. In this way, he and the other Chicago firms linked their business to an already existing trade network and source of local capital, and encouraged wholesale butchers of live animals to become wholesale distributors of dressed beef.

In many communities, butchers refused to handle Chicago dressed beef, claiming that the product was unsanitary and that no customer should buy meat that had been killed a week or more before. One butcher, when approached by an agent of Nelson Morris about introducing dressed beef to the Pittsburgh area, replied, "I sell no beef unless I see it killed." The wholesale butchers believed that only live animals could be safely inspected for disease, and feared the loss of their traditional role slaughtering all meat sold in a particular community. Most lacked the icehouse facilities to store large quantities of chilled beef, and were unwilling or unable to invest the capital needed to acquire refrigeration technology for themselves.

When a Chicago packer appeared in a new town offering to sell dressed beef, local butchers often formed an organization to fight the incursion. Members agreed not to deal with the packers and put signs in their windows saying, "No Chicago dressed meat sold here." By 1887, opposition had become widespread enough that butchers met in a nationwide convention to create the Butchers' National Protective Association, with the express purpose of defending themselves against Chicago dressed beef. Stating that their only object was the public good, they declared their intention to "secure the highest sanitary condition" for food by fighting "diseased, tainted, or otherwise unwholesome meat. . . . In the butchers' eyes, dressed beef represented disease, monopoly, and tyranny.

But it was a losing battle. When the packers encountered such resistance, they quickly moved to break open the local market. A company agent might appear at the local railroad depot with a carload of beef—nicknamed a peddler car—and sell it as cut-rate prices directly off the tracks. The more permanent approach was to build a refrigerated warehouse in town, called a branch house. From it, the packers sold meat to all comers at whatever price it took to gain a foothold in the market. . . .

The Chicago packers were ruthless competitors, and had little compunction about selling dressed beef at whatever price would bring customers. They had good reasons for this. Their product was perishable and had to be sold quickly before it spoiled. If potential customers were prejudiced against dressed beef, the only way to convince them otherwise was to use bargain prices to get them to try it for themselves. Since chilled beef required expensive capital equipment for refrigeration, the unwillingness of local jobbers to handle it meant that the packing firm had to set up its own branch house to sell the product at all. Swift's motto was "If you're going to lose money, lose it. But don't let 'em nose you out." Market share was the paramount concern, and the packers were willing to do almost anything to gain it. They sold meat below its cost of production to break the resistance of local butchers, raising their prices once they had succeeded in entering the market. In this, they gained considerable price flexibility from the disassembly line itself, since they could recover losses on some cuts and body parts with the profits from others. The same was true geographically: with the proceeds from a successful struggle in one town, they could move on to the next. The sheer scale of their production, the reach of their marketing activities, and their accumulated capital made it impossible for any local butcher to withstand them. A Pennsylvania butcher described the experience of those who tried by declaring "We are working for glory now. We do not work for any profit. I can give you that straight." . . .

Like the progressive reformers who followed them, the packers worshiped at the altar of efficiency, seeking to conserve economic resources by making a war on waste. This was their most important break with the past. Chicago pork packers in the 1850s had relatively limited options in utilizing the nonmeat portions of the animals they killed. They could boil them down into tallow and lard, which a number of firms used for making candles, soap, and other products. They could feed packing wastes to scavenger pigs, practicing an early form of recycling in which pig flesh people were unwilling to eat was reconverted into pig flesh they were willing to eat. But whatever was left sooner or later made its way as refuse into the Chicago River. The stench that hung over the South Branch and the filthy ice harvested from it were clear signs of its pollution. Decaying organic matter, whether in the form of packing wastes, manure, or raw human sewage, was the chief water supply problem the city faced by midcentury. Seeing it as a threat to health and comfort alike, Chicagoans were trying to do something about it as early as the 1850s. . . .

Since industrial wastes produced pollution wherever one threw them away, [one] solution might be to avoid throwing them out in the first place. If the packers could devise ways of using meat-packing refuse for productive purposes, it would cease to be waste at all. The refuse would pollute the river less, and—better still— turn a tidy profit for its owner. "There was a time," remembered Philip Armour at the end of the century, "when many parts of cattle were wasted, and the health of the city injured by the refuse. Now, by adopting the best known methods, nothing is wasted, and buttons, fertilizer, glue, and other things are made cheaper and better for the world in general, out of material that was before a waste and a menace."

As the packers pushed the disassembly line toward its fullest possible develop- ment, they turned what had been a single creature—a hog or a steer— into dozens and then hundreds of commodities. In the new chemical research laboratories that the packers installed during the 1880s and 1890s, older by-products like lard and tallow were joined by more exotic items like oleomargarine, bouillon, brushes, combs, gut strings, stearin, pepsin, and even canned pork and beans. One visitor described the output of the plants as follows:

> Everything—without particularizing too closely—every single thing that appertains to a slaughtered beef is sold and put to use. The horns become the horn of commerce; the straight lengths of leg bone go to the cutlery-makers and others; the entrails become sausage-casings; their contents make fertilizing material; the livers, hearts, tongues, and tails, and the stomachs, that become tripe, all are sold over the butchers' counters of the nation; the knuckle-bones are ground up into bone-meal for various uses; the blood is dried and sold as a powder for commercial purposes; the bladders are dried and sold to druggists, tobacconists, and others; the fat goes into oleomargarine, and from the hoofs and feet and other parts come glue and oil and fertilizing ingredients.

The portion of any single animal that might go into one of these by-products was very small. More than half of a steer's bodyweight became dressed beef, but less that 1 percent of it became glue or dried blood or neat's foot oil. No ordinary butcher could afford the capital investment needed to deal in such small quantities, and so waste was inevitable when traditional methods were used. Not so for the packers. Because they dealt in enormous numbers of animals and because they could search out customers anywhere in the world, they were able to find specialized markets for even the most minute of body parts. By-products became an ever more important source of packers' profits. Armour estimated that a 1,260-pound steer purchased in Chicago for $40.95 would produce 710 pounds of dressed beef. When sold in New York at an average price of 5 and ⅜ cents per pound, this beef would earn only $38.17—a clear loss even without deducting production and transport costs. Only by selling by-products could the packers turn this losing transaction into a profitable one. Indeed, the income from such sales was crucial in enabling the packers to lower dressed beef prices far below those of ordinary butchers. As Swift and Armour saw it, they earned their profits on the margin largely from things that butchers threw away.

The rise of the by-products industry had several other implications. For one, it undoubtedly changed the rate and character of pollution entering the Chicago River from the packing plants. Packingtown remained one of the smelliest and most envi- ronmentally degraded neighborhoods in all of Chicago, and the water that flowed from its sewers was extraordinarily foul. Upton Sinclair could still describe Bubbly

Creek in 1906 as "a great open sewer a hundred or two feet wide" in which grease and chemicals underwent "all sorts of strange transformations," so it was "constantly in motion, as if huge fish were feeding in it, or great leviathans were disporting themselves in its depths." Visitors and residents assaulted by the smell of the place could hardly have believed that it represented any kind of improvement over the past, but in a sense it did. Compared with those of an ordinary butcher's slaughterhouse, the packers' wastes constituted a smaller share of the animals they killed. They might be more concentrated and no less dangerous, but their total volume had grown less quickly than the total production of the plants.

Rather more sinister was the packers' increasing ability to sell products which customers would never have purchased, let alone eaten, in their original form. By shrewdly manipulating bone and offal and even spoiled meat in myriad ways, Chicago companies could convert them not just into salable commodities but into substances which had all the appearance of human food. It seems unlikely that anyone objected to the idea that waste hair be turned into brushes, dried blood into fertilizer, bones into buttons, cartilage into glue. But people were more suspicious about the packers' sometime practice of marketing mixed, altered, or adulterated products as pure food. One butcher complained about having to sell his own kettle-rendered lard in competition with lower-priced packinghouse product that was "as solid as a rock; it looks white; but is a compound of cotton-seed oil, stearine, etc." Although vegetable shortening and oleomargarine were "unnatural" products, they would gain steady ground in the American market and diet, however much traditionalists like this butcher might oppose them. Dairy farmers in Wisconsin tried to discourage oleomargarine consumption in that state well past the middle of the twentieth century, even as most Americans quite happily traded butter for its cheaper alternative.

But other manufactured foods seemed less benign even to people who ate oleo without a second thought. Most drew the line when packers took otherwise inedible materials—or spoiled, diseased, or tainted meats—and altered them so that they would appear to be ordinary, healthy food. Dressed beef was always open to the suspicion that it had been cut from diseased cattle, and processed meats were most suspect of all. Bologna sausage became the great waste disposal product because it could hide such a multitude of sins. Once ground up and combined with spices and potato flour, all manner of body parts could go into it: inferior meats that drew lower prices on the open market, meat from diseased cattle, meat that had spoiled and begun to smell, sweepings from other production processes, even sawdust and dirt. . . . Public fears about the health hazards of dressed beef and its by-products did not finally explode until 1906, when Upton Sinclair published his muckraking novel *The Jungle* and Congress passed the Meat Inspection and Pure Food and Drug Acts, which subsequently imposed much stricter inspection standards on the packers and their products.

Waste, then, was one of the symbolic paradoxes of meat-packing in Chicago. For those like Upton Sinclair who saw in the city all that was most evil in capitalism, Packingtown represented the decline of corporate morality and the end of an earlier, more familiar and trustworthy way of life. . . . "Under the system of rigid economy which the packers enforced," wrote Sinclair, "there were some jobs that it only paid to do once in a long time, and among these was the cleaning out of the waste barrels." . . . Public health was not alone in being jeopardized by such perfidy. The packers drove honest butchers out of business with their deceitful products, so that in the end there would be nothing left but the Big Four and their foul meats. The Chicago packers had wasted honesty and community alike in their single-minded drive to extract every last penny from the wretched animals that walked through their doors. The tyranny of monopoly, and the public revolt against it, would be their final legacy.

And yet such a description was surely not the whole truth, if it was truth at all Armour was right: his profits, like those of the other packers, came because he managed to save what others threw away. He had built his empire on waste. This seemed akin to making something out of nothing, which was surely not such a bad thing to do. Writing a decade and a half after the Vest Committee, another government investigation was more willing to acknowledge the public benefits that had accompanied what the earlier committee had seen as the "artificial and abnormal centralization" of Chicago's markets. "The margins between prices of stock and prices of meats," the later committee wrote,

> have been kept during recent years, by reason of the thorough utilization of by-products, at a point lower than would have been possible under the methods of slaughtering and packing which prevailed thirty or more years ago. By virtue of the economics secured in the handling of former wastes, and in other ways, the development of huge packing establishments has beyond question been beneficial to cattle raisers and meat consumers.

Because of the Chicago packers, ranchers in Wyoming and feedlot farmers in Iowa regularly found a reliable market for their animals, and on average received better prices for the animals they sold there. At the same time and for the same reason, Americans of all classes found a greater variety of more and better meats on their tables, purchased on average at lower prices than ever before. Seen in this light, the packers' "rigid system of economy" seemed a very good thing indeed. . . .

[The packers] had [made many meats available year-round at lower prices] by creating immense, vertically integrated corporations capable of exercising managerial control over the food of many nations on a scale never before seen in the history of the world. Nothing in Chicago at the end of the nineteenth century better symbolized the city's profoundly transformed relationship to the natural world than its gigantic meat-packing corporations. Although they joined the Board of Trade and the lumberyards in guidebooks that sought to impress visitors with the ways in which Chicago stood first among cities, the packers in fact represented the city's greatest break with nature and the past. At the Board of Trade, hundreds of grain traders vied with each other to profit from the sale of wheat and corn drawn from Chicago's broad western hinterland, but none of them could control the market for long. A handful of meat-packers, on the other hand, could do just that. By managing supply and demand, they effectively rearranged the meat trade of the entire world. Ranchers on the plains, feedlot farmers on the prairies, butchers in the cities, and meat eaters the world over increasingly inhabited a system in which the packers called most of the important shots. "A few enterprising men at Chicago," wrote the Vest committee, "engaged in the packing and dressed beef business, are able through their enormous capital to centralize and control the beef business at the point."

However impressive individuals like Swift or Armour might be, their real achievement was to create immense impersonal organizations, hierarchically structured and operated by an army of managers and workers, that would long outlive their founders. No one person was essential to such enterprises. The very scale on which they operated made them increasingly susceptible to the same abstract logic which the railroads had first discovered in the balance sheets. Fixed costs meant an inescapable need to service debt. Unused capital—whether in the form of equipment, employees, or raw materials—meant waste. Waste meant inefficiency, and inefficiency in a competitive economic environment could all too easily mean death. It must be eliminated with every strategy and device that managerial ingenuity could muster against it. Summer must be made to seem like winter so that the great factories could continue their work all year. Death's hand must be stayed to extend by hundreds and thousands of miles the distance between the place where an animal died and the place where people finally ate it. Prices must be standardized so that markets in distant places would fluctuate together if they fluctuated at all. An industry that had formerly done its work in thousands of small butcher shops around the country must be rationalized to bring it under the control of a few expert managers using the most modern and scientific techniques. The world must become Chicago's hinterland.

The combined effect of these many managerial strategies was to make meat seem less a product of first nature and more a product of human artifice. With the concentration of packing at Chicago, meat came increasingly to seem an urban product. Cows and cowboys might be symbols of a rugged natural life on the western range, but beef and pork were commodities of the city. Formerly, a person could not easily have forgotten that pork and beef were the creation of an intricate, symbiotic partnership between animals and human beings. One was not likely to forget that pigs and cattle had died so that people might eat, for one saw them grazing in familiar pastures, and regularly visited the barnyards and a butcher shops where they gave up their lives in the service of one's daily meal. In a world of farms and small towns, the ties between field, pasture, butcher shop and dinner table were everywhere apparent, constant reminders of the relationships that sustained one's own life. In a world of ranches, packing plants, and refrigerator cars, most such connections vanished from easy view.

The packing plants distanced their customers most of all from the act of killing. Those who visited the great slaughterhouses came away with vivid memories of death. Rudyard Kipling described being impressed much more by the "slaying" he saw in Chicago than by the "dissecting." "They were so excessively alive, these pigs," he wrote. "And then they were so excessively dead, and the man in the dripping, clammy, hot passage did not seem to care, and ere the blood of such an one had ceased to foam on the floor, such another, and four friends with him, had shrieked and died." The more people became accustomed to the attractively cut, carefully wrapped, cunningly displayed packages that Swift had introduced to the trade, the more easily they could fail to remember that their purchase had once pulsed and breathed with a life much like their own. As time went on, fewer of those who ate meat could say that they had ever seen the living creature whose flesh they were chewing; fewer still could say they had actually killed the animal themselves. In the packers' world, it was easy not to remember that eating was a moral act inextricably bound to killing. Such was the second nature that a corporate order had imposed on the American landscape. Forgetfulness was among the least noticed and most important of its by-products.

The packers' triumph was to further the commodification of meat, to alienate still more its ties to the lives and ecosystems that had ultimately created it. Transmuted by the packing plants into countless shape-shifting forms, an animal's body might fill human stomachs, protect human feet, fasten human clothes, fertilize human gardens, wash human hands, play human music—do so many amazing things. The sheer variety of these new standardized uses testified to the packers' ingenuity in their war on waste, but in them the animal also died a second death. Severed from the form in which it had lived, severed from the act that had killed it, it vanished from human memory as one of nature's creatures. Its ties to the earth receded, and in forgetting the animal's life one also forgot the grasses and the prairie skies and the departed bison herds of a landscape that seemed more and more remote in space and time. The grasslands were so distant from the lives of those who bought what the packers sold that one hardly thought of the prairie or the plains while making one's purchase, any more than one thought about Packingtown, with its Bubbly Creek and its stinking air. Meat was a neatly wrapped package one bought at the market. Nature did not have much to do with it.

There was a final irony in this for Chicago itself. The new corporate order, by linking and integrating the products of so many ecosystems and communities, obscured the very connections it helped create. Its tendency was to break free from space altogether, managing its activities with organizational charts that stressed function rather than geography. The traditional butcher shop had belonged very much to its particular place, bound to customers in the immediate neighborhood and farmers in the surrounding countryside. The packing companies had none of these ties, not even to the place that had nurtured their own birth. By the 1880s, their managers could already see that Chicago's advantages—its transportation facilities, its concentrated market, its closeness to western supplies of cattle—were by no means unique. Conditions at the Union Stockyards were crowded, there was little room for expansion, and the city was not as close to the chief grazing regions of the country as were certain other cities that lay still farther to the west. The sensible thing to do was not to invest more capital in Chicago but to set up new plants that could take advantage of more favorable conditions elsewhere.

All the major Chicago packers saw the logic of this analysis; it was, after all, the logic of capital. Swift's behavior was typical of the group. In 1888, he built an entirely new packing plant, replicating his operations at Chicago, in Kansas City, Missouri. Because it was well suited to handle the livestock output of the southern plains but did not have good rail connections with areas farther north, he built another new plant at Omaha just two years later. East St. Louis received a Swift factory in 1892 and St. Joseph in 1896. Swift and other Chicago packers invested increasing amounts of capital in these new operations, and so the major cities of the Great Plains began to rival Chicago for primacy in the cattle trade. By the end of the century, Omaha was butchering nearly a third as many steers as Chicago was, while Kansas City was packing more than half of the lakeside city's total volume.

It was the beginning of the end. Chicago retained its primacy, but had lost the quality that had made its nineteenth-century experience so remarkable. Its growth had stopped. Its production of pork and beef flattened out from the 1880s forward, while other cities surged to accommodate new packing facilities and output. Chicago continued for the next half century to handle an immense number of animals, never fewer than thirteen million per year, but its relative share declined as the industry continued its steady westward movement onto the plains. The rise of the diesel truck eventually undermined the technological tendency toward centralization that the railroads had promoted, until finally Chicago lost its earlier advantages altogether. By the 1930s, the output of the stockyards was in steady decline; by 1960, all the major packers had shut down their Chicago factories. Ten years later, the stockyards finally closed altogether. The familiar odor of manure vanished, and the strange silence of abandonment fell over the old animal pens. Grass began to grow again amid the ruins.

The whole point of corporate meat-packing had been to systematize the market in animal flesh—to liberate it from nature and geography. Chicago had been the place to accomplish that feat, but the industry the city fostered ultimately exercised its independence even from the great Union Stockyard itself. Corporate headquarters might remain for a time in Chicago, directing vast networks for the production and distribution of food and other commodities, but they ultimately had only the most marginal reasons for preferring one location to another. Once within the corporate system, places lost their particularity and became functional abstractions on organizational charts. Geography no longer mattered very much except as a problem in management: time had conspired with capital to annihilate space. The cattle might still graze amid forgotten buffalo wallows in central Montana, and the hogs might still devour their feedlot corn in Iowa, but from the corporate point of view they could just as well have been anywhere else. Abstract, standardized, and fungible, their lives were governed as much by the nature of capital as by the nature that gave them life. It was perhaps nothing more than simple justice that the city which had remade them in this way should be subject to the same alchemy. In losing control of its corporate meat-packing hinterland, Chicago's stockyard fulfilled the logic of its own birth.

Machines as the Measure of Men

MICHAEL ADAS

As industry spread, locomotives increased in speed and comfort, inventions multiplied, and European scientists probed ever more deeply into the workings of nature, Europeans translated their material superiority into global hegemony. Industrialized nations—first Great Britain and later France, Germany, and the United States—flooded African and Asian markets with cheap machine-made consumer goods, ranging from cotton textiles to kerosene lamps. The great advances in weapons design and production that accompanied the process of industrialization permitted the Europeans to subdue forcibly any overseas peoples who resisted their efforts to trade, convert, or explore. When combined with military forces which, well before the Industrial Revolution, had achieved clear superiority in discipline and organization, mass-produced weapons, railway and telegraph lines, and iron-clad steamships made it possible for the Europeans to conquer and rule directly—or defeat and control through indigenous surrogates—virtually all African and Asian peoples. Each year between 1871 and 1914 the European imperialist powers added an area the size of France to their empires.

But it was not the conquests themselves that most impressed European observers (victory had become rather routine, despite temporary reverses such as those the

From Michael Adas, *Machines as the Measure of Men* (Ithaca, NY: Cornell University Press, 1989), pp. 143–147, 151–153, 195–197, 204–205, 214, 223, 231–233, 362–365.

French suffered in the 1880s in Vietnam); it was the relatively low cost and the growing ease of colonial conquest. Though only small forces and not always the most advanced weapons were committed to colonial wars, conflict with the Europeans meant that African warriors or the banner armies of China were subjected, as D. A. Low points out, to "vastly greater, more lethal demonstrations of force than any which [they] had experienced from any quarter in the past." An operation such as the destruction of large flotillas of Chinese war junks by small squadrons of British men-of-war or the annihilation of thousands of determined Mahdist warriors at Omdurman served to bolster the consensus among European thinkers, politicians, and colonial administrators that they had earned the right (and duty) to be the "lords of humankind."

As the evidence of their material achievement multiplied and pervaded all aspects of life in industrializing societies, Europeans and (increasingly) Americans grew more and more conscious of the uniqueness and, they believed, the superiority of Western civilization. Those involved in the colonies and intellectuals who dealt with colonial issues came to view scientific and technological achievements not only as the key attributes that set Europe off from all other civilizations, past and present, but as the most meaningful gauges by which non-Western societies might be evaluated, classified, and ranked. Science and technology were often conflated as criteria for comparison, rather than treated as distinct endeavors, as they had tended to be in earlier centuries. In addition, generalized assertions of superiority or inferiority supplanted the detailed descriptions of individual tools or particular ideas which had been characteristic of earlier accounts of overseas cultures. This shift reflected a growing sense on the part of overseas observers that African and Asian peoples had little to offer Europe in techniques of production and extraction or in insights into the workings of the natural world. Increasingly industrialized European (and North American) cultures *as a whole* were seen to be a separate class, distinct from all others. The polarities were numerous and obvious: metal versus wood; machine versus human or animal power; science versus superstition and myth; synthetic versus organic; progressive versus stagnant. All aspects of culture could be linked to these polarities, to the fundamental dichotomy between industrial and preindustrial societies. Beggars, for example, who had once wandered in great bands throughout France and England and whose sparse numbers in China and Africa had once been noted with approbation by European observers, now scandalized visitors to the "Orient" and the "Dark Continent." As numerous travelers recounted on arriving in a non-Western port (which increasingly meant a colonized area), the very tempo of speech and motion slowed noticeably and even the spatial arrangement of the material environment altered disconcertingly.

Most nineteenth-century observers mixed nontechnological or nonscientific gauges—systems of government, ethical codes, treatment of women, religious practices, and so on—with assessments of African and Asian material mastery. As the century passed, however, colonial administrators and missionaries, travelers and social commentators increasingly stressed technological and scientific standards as the most reliable basis for comparisons between societies and civilizations. In an age when what were held to be "scientific" proofs were increasingly demanded of those engaged in the study of natural history and social development, material achievement and anatomical measurements proved irresistible gauges of human capacity and worth. Mechanical principles and mathematical propositions could be tested;

bridges, machines, and head sizes could be measured and rated for efficiency. Thus, unlike earlier gauges by which the Europeans compared societies, those favored in the nineteenth century were believed to be amenable to empirical verification and were especially suited to the late Victorian penchant for "statistical reductiveness."

Improved and cheaper techniques for mass printing, advances in graphics and statistical enumeration, and (from the middle of the century) developments in photography all reinforced the preference for evaluative criteria that were tangible and testable. Empirical observation and "objective" evaluation appeared to elevate comparisons between Europeans and African and Asian peoples to the realm of "demonstrated truths," which John Seeley—one of the great champions of late nineteenth-century British imperial expansion—viewed as the main source of the greatness of Western civilization. . . .

Because nineteenth-century Europeans believed that machines, skull size, or ideas about the configuration of the solar system were culturally neutral facts, evaluative criteria based on science and technology appeared to be the least tainted by subjective bias. Blatantly narcissistic gauges of the worth of non-European peoples—skin color, fashions in or lack of clothing—receded in importance; measurements of cranial capacity, estimates of railway mileage, and the capacity for work, discipline, and marking time became the decisive criteria by which Europeans judged other cultures and celebrated the superiority of their own. The fact that these criteria were as culturebound as earlier gauges and even more loaded in favor of the industrializing West was grasped by only a handful of intellectuals who continued to value the achievements of non-Western peoples. . . .

Perhaps no more striking illustrations of the importance of technological superiority as a justification for imperial dominance can be found than in Mary Kingsley's recollection of the sense of pride and reassurance that Britain's industrial technology gave her as she explored the rainforests and savannas of west Africa. Kingsley was one of the most intrepid and independent-minded of nineteenth-century travelers, and her works are studied today mainly because of her sincere and, at the time, rather rare admiration for African beliefs and customs. Yet however strong her defense of African peoples and cultures, she made no secret of her conviction that the British were superior and that technological accomplishment was the best test of their superiority:

> All I can say, that when I come back from a spell in Africa, the thing that makes me proud of being one of the English is not the manners or customs up here, certainly not the houses or the climate; but it is the thing embodied in a great railway engine. I once came home on a ship with an Englishman who had been in South West Africa for seven unbroken years; he was sane, and in his right mind. But no sooner did we get ashore at Liverpool, than he rushed at and threw his arms round a postman, to the official's embarrassment and surprise. Well, that is just how I feel about the first magnificent bit of machinery I come across; it is the manifestation of the superiority of my race.

. . . Even those who questioned the validity of science and technology as gauges of human worth admitted that they had dominated British attitudes toward colonized peoples. Though Rudyard Kipling retreated late in life into a rural refuge free of telephones and other modern contrivances, for decades his stories and poems had celebrated the technical skills, assertiveness, and commitment to hard work that had made the British rulers of more than a quarter of the globe. . . . Even Dean William Inge, who emerged as one of the leading critics of England's industrial order in the first decades of the twentieth century, readily acknowledged that nineteenth-century Englishmen routinely equated material achievement with civilized advance. Writing in the shambles that the Great War had made of European societies, Inge mused on the Victorians' reasoning that if they could travel sixty miles per hour by train, they must be five times more civilized than non-Europeans who could do at best twelve miles per hour by nonmechanized transport.

The current of hostility to industry and capitalist values was stronger in France than in England, so much so that some economic historians have seen these attitudes and the French attachment to handicraft production as major reasons for France's late industrialization relative to its cross-channel rival. France's slower and less extensive industrialization may also account for the fact that most French writers adhered more than the invention-conscious British to the eighteenth-century preference for scientific rather than technological gauges of human worth, though the two were often blended. Gustave Le Bon and Arthur de Gobineau, for example, who did much to shape nineteenth-century thinking on racism and attitudes toward non-Western cultures, found much to criticize in industrial Europe. But both viewed peoples of European stock as racially superior to all others and cited the white or Aryan race's achievements in science and, to a lesser extent, technology as clear proof of the high level of civilization it had attained. . . .

In the late eighteenth century and the first decades of the nineteenth an awareness of European material mastery was confined to small numbers of educated travelers, colonial administrators, social theorists, and missionaries. As the pace of scientific discovery and technological innovation quickened in Europe and North America, while societies in other areas appeared to stagnate or break down, growing numbers of writers sought to determine the causes of Europe's unique transformation and the meaning of what they viewed as the failure of non-European peoples to initiate their own scientific and industrial revolutions. Through romantic novels or adventure stories, and especially in the popular press, the conclusions of phrenologists, social theorists, ethnographers, and storytellers such as Rudyard Kipling and Pierre Loti were disseminated widely among the middle and literate working classes. Often corrupted and vulgarized, invariably oversimplified and sensationalized, these ideas have played a major role from the nineteenth century to the present in shaping popular attitudes in Europe and North America toward African and Asian peoples and cultures. Notions of white supremacy and racial superiority, jingoistic slogans for imperialist expansion, and the vision of a dichotomous world divided between the progressive and the backward have all been rooted in the conclusions drawn by nineteenth-century thinkers from the fact that only peoples of European stock had initiated and carried through the scientific and industrial revolutions. . . .

The new sense of what it meant to be civilized and the conviction that only peoples of European descent measured up to standards appropriate to the industrial age owned much to the growing influence of "self-made" individuals in shaping European perceptions of non-Western peoples. James Mill, John Barrow, and Gustave Le Bon, for example, who played pivotal roles in shaping attitudes toward India and China and their respective societies, were from families of modest means and little status: Mill's father was a shoemaker, Barrow's a small landholder and agricultural laborer, and Le Bon's a provincial functionary. Each of these writers spent his early years far from the centers of political and intellectual life but was driven from an early age to rise above his modest origins and make his mark in society. Each aspired in particular to acceptance by the intellectual establishment of his respective society. Each sought acclaim as an authority: Mill on India and issue of political economy more generally; Barrow on China; Le Bon on a multitude of subjects from phrenology and mass psychology to India and Arabia.

Their schooling and professional careers made these men acutely aware of the sweeping scientific and technological transformations that were occurring in their respective societies. . . .

Common origins and ambitions, of course, did not necessarily produce common views, even on fundamental issues. Le Bon clearly thought both the Indians and the Arabs civilized and gifted in a number of areas, whereas Mill and Barrow continually referred to the Indians and Chinese as rude and barbaric. Le Bon also had much greater reservations than his British counterparts about the disruptive effects of the process of industrialization, as distinct from the benefits of invention and technological change more broadly. But whether or not there was consensus on which peoples measured up, or on the advantages and drawbacks of the particular course that technological change had taken in Europe, there was widespread agreement in this era on the criteria by which one could distinguish civilized from barbarian and savage cultures. This was particularly true among the parvenus who were the most explicit in applying the new standards and thus instrumental in promoting their growing acceptance. Evidence of scientific and technological accomplishment was no longer peripheral or regarded as symptomatic of more fundamental values and institutional arrangements. Machines and equations, or their absence, were themselves indicators of the level of development a given society had attained. Civilization was not a state; it was a process. Individuals who through education and hard work had risen above their modest family origins placed a high premium on improvement, a term that is ubiquitous in nineteenth-century writings on colonial areas. Change was not only good; it was essential for the civilized. Stagnation and decadence were associated with barbarians; "primitive" and poorly developed material culture with savages. The history of civilized peoples was a tale of progress, of continuous advance; that of barbarians, a dreary chronology of endless cycles of decline and recovery.

Nineteenth-century authors vied with each other to coin the most compelling labels to capture this contrast: J. R. Seeley offered "future" versus "past" societies; Charles Caldwell, "improving" versus "stationary"; Carl Carus, "day," "twilight," and "night" peoples; and there were many variations on the dichotomies of active and passive, male and female. As the century passed, these broad contrasts were refined. Specific attributes, associated with the scientific and industrial revolutions, came to be seen as characteristic of those who had achieved civilization. These ranged from ways of perceiving time and space to patterns of work and discipline. Unlike Le Bon, most European observers deemed peoples who lacked these qualities beyond the pale of civilization. If there was controversy, it focused on how to get non-Europeans to adopt civilized ways and the extent to which different peoples were capable of benefiting from the colonizers' civilizing mission. . . .

. . . Spokesmen for imperialist expansion argued that without Western science and technology there was no hope of improving the condition of the impoverished masses of China and India or of civilizing the "savages" of Africa. The more extreme advocates of European global hegemony, who adhered to a survival-of-the-fittest world view, went so far as to argue with Frederic W. Farrar that scientific and technological backwardness explained and justified the decimation or (in the case of the Tasmanians) the utter extermination of "primitive peoples" who had not "added one iota to the knowledge, the arts, the sciences, the manufactures, the morals of the world." But most imperialist spokesmen were content to rationalize the more unsavory aspects of colonial administration—such as demands for forced labor and the unregulated extraction of natural resources—as the inevitable consequences of the economic imbalance created by Europe's industrialization and the difficulty of diffusing Western technology among backward and suspicious peoples. The small numbers of Europeans who actually governed the colonized peoples relied on their superior technology not only for the communications and military clout that made the ongoing administration of vast areas possible but also for the assurance that they had the "right," even the "duty," to police, arbitrate disputes; demand tribute, and insist upon deference. The extent to which African and Asian peoples acquiesced to European domination out of respect for the colonizers' self-proclaimed technological superiority is hard to determine. But it is clear that the confidence—or arrogance—with which European administrators and missionaries set about the task of ruling and remaking the societies of Africa and Asia owed much to their sense of mechanical and scientific mastery.

. . . European colonizers assumed that it was both natural and mutually beneficial for advanced European societies to provide machines and manufactured goods in return for the primary products—foodstuffs, plant fibers, and minerals—exported from colonized areas and those such as China that had been "informally" divided into "spheres of influence" by the European powers. A revolution had been effected in global commercial exchanges. Europe and its North American offshoots, which had once been peripheral areas exporting mainly raw materials, had become the global centers for manufactured and finished goods, investment capital, and entrepreneurial and technical skills. India and China, which for millennia had been major sources of handicraft manufactures avidly sought in long-distance trade, were reduced to supplying cotton, tea, and raw silk to Euroamerican industries and consumers. Having set these changes in motion, the Europeans turned to transforming the very cultures of Africans and Asians to bring them into accord with modes of thought and behavior the colonizers deemed rational, efficient, and thus civilized. . . .

For many writers, the mastery of nature as manifested in scientific discovery and technological advancement was one of the most critical gauges of human achievement. In the early 1800s Julien Virey contrasted the Europeans, who were learning to control nature, with all non-Western peoples who, though they might have developed in some areas, had in this respect not risen above the level of savages. Ignorant of the workings of nature, prescientific and preindustrial peoples were subject to its every whim. Virey regarded those who lacked the desire to investigate the "source of life" and the "treasures of the earth" as little more than brutes, "mere cattle of the prairie." For Henry Thomas Buckle, who began his much noted *History of Civilization in England* in the 1850s, the "triumph of the mind over external agents" was the most meaningful measure of civilized development. . . .

Generalized assumptions about the correspondence between the mastery of nature and overall social development frequently influenced the judgments of European missionaries, travelers, and officials in the non-Western world. Often this measure of human worth was implicit in specific observations rather than a topic of elaborate discourse. Henry Drummond, for example, sought to illustrate the lowly state of the "half animal, half children" but "wholly savage" peoples who inhabited the interior of east Africa by noting that they had done little to reshape the environment in which they lived. He maintained that it never occurred to African peoples to push aside large stones that blocked well-traveled paths or even to remove trees that fell across the way. H. L. Duff also commented on the Africans' inclination to reroute a path rather than remove an obstacle. He could think of nothing that more vividly revealed the contrast between the European and African character than the image, on the one hand, of "the European engineer forcing with incredible toil his broad and certain way, stemming rivers, clearing marshes, shattering tons of earth and rock; and, on the other hand, the savage, careless of everything but the present, seeking only the readiest path and content to let a pebble baulk him rather than stoop to lift it." Charles Regismanset speculated that the Africans' refusal to remove natural obstacles was rooted in their fundamentally different perception of time and space: oblivious to the loss of time, not concerned to cover the shortest distance from one point to another, the Africans built roads that twisted and turned around trees rather than cutting a straight path through the forest growth. . . .

The assumptions that it was desirable for humans to master nature and that the scientifically minded and inventive Europeans were best at doing so led many authors to the conviction that it was the destiny and duty of the Europeans to expand into and develop regions occupied by less advanced peoples. The criticisms of earlier travelers to Africa, remarking on the inefficient exploitation of forest and mineral resources, often implied that if Europeans settled or controlled these areas, their resources could rapidly be harnessed to production for the world market. Similar arguments continued to be made by European observers throughout the nineteenth century. In fact, the growing demand for raw materials in industrializing areas in Europe and North America became (despite its neglect by writers on imperialist exploitation, such as Lenin, who placed unwarranted stress on the need to export Europe's surplus capital) one of the most frequently cited rationales for imperialist expansion into Africa, southeast Asia, and even heavily populated and extensively cultivated areas such as China. As Thomas Carlyle's highly charged 1840 essay "Chartism" make clear, the need to discover and exploit untapped resources was for many writers more than a mere pretext for European conquest and domination of other peoples; it was a moral obligation. Carlyle seethed with indignation over the widespread poverty and unemployment in England when overseas there existed "a world where Canadian Forests stand unfelled, boundless Plains and Prairies unbroken with the plough . . . green desert spaces never yet made white with corn; and to the overcrowded little western nook of Europe, our Terrestrial Planet, nine-tenths of it yet vacant or tenanted by nomades, is still crying, Come and till me, come and reap me!" Some decades later the French writer Edmond About exhorted the youth in Europe in the name of progress and higher civilization to migrate to the interior regions of Africa, Australia, and New Caledonia and make the resources of these areas available to Europeans who had the scientific knowledge and technical skills necessary to put them to productive use. . . .

More than any other technological innovation, the railway embodied the great material advances associated with the first Industrial Revolution and dramatized the gap which that process had created between the Europeans and all non-Western peoples. Powered by the steam engines that were the core invention of the industrial transformation, locomotives boldly exhibited the latest advances in metallurgy and machine-tooling. Running on tracks that reshaped the landscape across vast swaths of Europe and later the Americas, Africa, and Asia; crossing great bridges that were themselves marvels of engineering skill; serviced in railway yards whose sheds and mounds of coal became familiar features of urban centers around the world, railways were at once "the most characteristic and most efficient form of the new technic." "The railroad as a system," as Leo Marx has observed, "incorporated most of the essential features of the emerging industrial order: the substitution of metal for wood construction; mechanized motive power; vastly enlarged geographical scale; speed, rationality, impersonality, and an unprecedented emphasis on precise timing."

From the time of its introduction into England in the 1820s, the railroad was regarded as the "great wonder-worker of the age." In his biography of George Stephenson, whose engineering genius was responsible for the construction of the first successful commercial railway, Samuel Smiles reported that the Liverpool-Manchester line drew spectators from throughout the country. "To witness a railway train some five-and-twenty years ago," Smiles observed at midcentury, "was an event in one's life." In the decades after its introduction the railway became the most pervasive and compelling symbol of the new age. The laying of thousands and then tens of thousands of miles of tracks in the middle decades of the century was paralleled by the rapid growth in the number of travelers making use of trains. In England alone their numbers increased from five or six hundred per week in the late 1820s to nearly 360,000 per annum in 1871. No invention rivaled the railway in capturing the imagination of poets, novelists, and social commentators. . . .

When railways were introduced in North America in the 1830s and India in the 1850s, many European observers fixed upon them as the key symbol of the superiority, material as well as moral, that Western societies had attained over all others. The great engines and thousands of miles of tracks provided pervasive and dramatic evidence of European power and material mastery. Railways (and the steamboat in heavily forested, riverine areas such as that which provides the setting for Conrad's *Heart of Darkness*) made it possible for Europeans to open vast stretches of "hinterland" and "undeveloped wilderness" to colonization, settlement, and economic exploitation. Most of these areas had been little affected by European activities during the early centuries of expansion which, except in the New World, had been concentrated in coastal and island regions. Trains and steamboats led to more direct and effective European rule in such areas as India, Egypt, and Vietnam and furthered colonial expansion throughout much of Africa, southeast Asia, and Australia. Officials and their families could be stationed in interior districts and troops moved about quickly to places where the "natives" showed signs of unrest. Perhaps the most impressive use of the railway for troop movement was the construction in the late 1880s of four hundred miles of track across the Nubian desert from Wadi Halfa to the Blue Nile to transport and supply the expeditionary force led by Lord Kitchener against the Mahdist state in the Sudan. . . .

Because most of China was not ruled directly by European colonizers, and its preindustrial technological endowment was so impressive, there were significant differences between European approaches to the introduction of Western technology into the Qing empire and those adopted in India and Africa. In the minds of most European observers, the roles that Western machines and techniques could play in improving the condition of the Chinese people were also somewhat different from those envisioned for other areas. Through most of the early centuries of contact and roughly the first half of the nineteenth century, Europeans involved in China sought to induce the Chinese to adopt Western technology by demonstrating its superiority over the tools and machines the Chinese themselves possessed. For the most part this approach was frustrated by the stubborn refusal of the Chinese to realize, or at least to admit, that their technology was in fact inferior and that the adoption of Western innovations would be advantageous.

The Reverend Jacob Abbott vented some of these frustrations in his 1835 account of English relations with the Qing empire. Drawing on John Barrow's recollections, Abbott described in some detail the clocks, intricate firearms, and celestial machines that the Macartney mission had presented to the emperor and Qing officials in the hope of "forcing upon them a comparison [with] the highest efforts of the arts and sciences in their own country." Abbott surmised that this attempt at stimulating technological change through diplomatic channels was too subtle for the Chinese, who in their "self-conceit" saw not weapons and machines that were clearly superior to their own but tribute proffered by barbarians who had come from remote lands to honor their emperor. Within five years of Abbott's observations, the British, having lost patience with diplomacy and demonstration, resorted to warships and an expeditionary force to impress upon the Chinese the obvious fact of their technological superiority. The precipitant, of course, of the Opium War that resulted (as its name so graphically illustrates) was not the reluctance of the Chinese to import Western technology but their refusal to engage in commerce on terms that the British found consistent with their highly vaunted principles of free trade. In this instance, free trade meant that the Chinese must allow the importation of unlimited quantities of the Assamese opium that had disrupted the Qing economy and was sapping the strength of the military and the bureaucracy. . . .

In the 1870s the Protestant missionary Arthur Smith condemned Chinese resistance to the construction of railways near or through ancient cemeteries as the futile struggle of the forces of superstition and backwardness against the harbingers of the modern age. By this time, locomotives and Western machines were so regularly touted as instruments of China's salvation, that English art critic John Ruskin, who had little fondness for the industrial order, was moved to ridicule the faith that machines could civilize China. To do so, he related an incident that had occurred during his travels in the area around Shanghai:

> We were sailing on the river in a steam launch, which was making the air impure with its smoke, and whistling as steam launches are wont to do. The scene was appropriate to the conversation, for we were among a great forest of great junks—most quaint and picturesque they looked—so old-fashioned they seemed that Noah's Ark, had it been there, would have had a much more modern look about it. My friend to whom the launch belonged, and who is in the machinery line himself, gave his opinion. He began by giving a significant movement of his head in the direction of the uncouth-looking junks, and then pointing to his own craft with its engine, said he did not believe much in war (as a means of civilizing China); and the missionaries were not of much account. "This is the thing to

do it," he added, pointing to the launch; "let us get at them, with this sort of article, and steam at sixty pounds on the square inch; that would do it; that's the thing to civilize them—sixty pounds on the square inch."

Probably unaware of and certainly undaunted by Ruskin's barbs, the China helpers, who found growing number of Americans and Japanese in their ranks in the last decades of the century, laid more and more stress on the role of technology in China's regeneration. In a manner worthy of the modernization theorists a century later, James Wilson, a general in the United States Army, set forth the measures that he felt the Chinese had to take if they were to rescue their country from chaos and foreign conquest. They must, he argued, replace their "dry husks of worn-out philosophy" with Western scientific thinking and adopt Western approaches to practical problems. In addition, they must learn from Westerners how to build railroads, dig mines, produce iron and steel, and extract the untapped resources of their vast land. Wilson recommended the introduction of railways and steamships, above all other measures, to increase "human comfort" in China. These great inventions, he predicted, would teach the Chinese the means by which Westerners had learned to "annihilate" the obstacles of time and space and harness the forces of nature to human needs. . . .

. . . As early as 1890, when Japanese industrialization was just getting under way, no less imposing a figure than the French colonial theorist Paul Leroy-Beaulieu called for a new "Berlin Conference" on world economic affairs. He saw as the main task of such a gathering, to which both China and Japan would be invited, the integration of these emerging powers into a new global economic order. If these measures were not taken, he warned, the Japanese and Chinese, having mastered European techniques and machines, would show the "soft" Europeans just how much peoples who had not lost the zest for hard work could achieve.

As Leroy-Beaulieu's inclusion of China in his conference proposal suggests, European writers in this period saw dangers even greater than those already posed by Japan in the future spread of industrialization throughout Asia. Earlier complaints about the crudity of Chinese tools and the inefficiency of Chinese machines now took on new meaning. If modern tools were placed in the hands of China's hard-working and dexterous millions, what chance would European workers stand in the competition for market outlets? China's large surplus population meant an over-supply of labor and in turn, minimal labor costs and low prices for manufactured goods. Minimal living standards and labor demands also meant fewer strikes in China and India, at a time when work stoppages were a serious problem in industrialized Europe and the United States. Strikes by European workers would provide market opportunities that Asian producers were certain to exploit. For many late nineteenth-century writers, the rapid growth of a modern textile industry in India was an ominous portent of Europe's future economic decline. India, after all, was a British colony. But by the last decades of the century it was also a major competitor for textile markets within the subcontinent, in Britain's other colonial territories, and in England itself. These were clearly not the results the civilizing mission had been intended to produce; nor was the related possibility that a China with railways and modern arms might reassert its position as a great power.

There was not a little irony in the obsession of numerous European writers with competition from Asian laborers. Having for so long stressed the need to put the rest of the world to work, European colonizers now recoiled at the results of a mission's being fulfilled. As the Baron d'Estournelles de Constant's thoughtful 1896 essay "Le péril prochain" reveals, this was not the only contradiction in the civilizing mission that industrialization in Asia was bringing home to European thinkers. The acquisitive and energetic Japanese were relentlessly transforming inventions that had played central roles in Europe's rise to global hegemony, and had long been regarded as key symbols of European superiority, into weapons in an economic struggle that threatened to topple Europe from its position of global leadership. Cheap, mass-produced Japanese watches and clocks, he warned, were capturing the markets of the world, including those of Europe. Japanese businessmen and workers had not only mastered the new sense of time but had become more efficient and punctual than the Europeans themselves. Now they threatened to dominate production of the devices that were essential to the maintenance of the pace and discipline of industrial life. Even the railroads, which had been so vital to Europe's own industrial transformation and its overseas dominance, had become a double-edged sword. Building on a remark by the French essayist Joseph Renan, the Baron d'Estournelles observed that the same railway lines that carried European goods and troops out to the Far East could carry Japanese products and even soldiers back to Europe. In an interesting reversal of present-day patterns, he reported that English and American manufacturers were relocating their plants in Japan where labor was cheap and reliable, and government policies favorable. All these developments forced him to wonder whether Europeans would soon be left with anything other than ideas to export, whether the time had come when they must be content with the "noble role" of inventor or machines that would be used to enrich other peoples.

As Pierre Mille saw so clearly in 1905, Japan's successful industrialization ought to have put an end to the illusion that the Europeans' scientific and technological accomplishments provided empirical and incontestable proof of their racial superiority. A surprising number of Mille's contemporaries agreed. Jacques Novicov, who had little use for racial classifications of any kind, concluded that the industrial achievements of the Japanese demonstrated that they were the Europeans' equals. At the end of the Great War, when Japan's industrial and military might had again been demonstrated in fulfilling the terms of its 1902 alliance with Britain, Benjamin Kidd pronounced the Japanese nation the equal of any Western power. Two years later H. H. Johnston, who was fond of ranking the human races, placed Japan, alone of non-Western societies, with Great Britain, France, and the United States at the top of a scale that rated national development on the basis of standard of living, educational and sanitary practices, government efficiency, and level of agricultural and industrial production.

Though the concessions of such strident white supremacists as Johnston were indicative of the extent to which Japanese achievements had shaken racial ideology insofar as it was based on scientific and technological measures of ability, the Japanese found that they remained a target of popular racial prejudice. This point was driven home by their failure to win approval of an antiracist clause at Versailles in 1919, by the barriers erected against Japanese emigration to the United States and the British dominions before and after the Great War, and by continued racist slurs against them in both official circles and popular thinking in the interwar years and through World War II.

In addition, many writers who, like Mille, were considered authorities on colonial issues explicitly rejected his contention that Japan's industrialization demonstrated the unreliability of the technological and scientific standards of human worth. They dismissed the Japanese counterexample as an exception, pointing out that the Japanese were after all as different from other non-Western peoples as they were from the Europeans. They also argued that borrowing machines and imitating European manufacturing techniques were hardly proofs that the Japanese had the capacity to think scientifically or to invent new machines and methods of production. As Gustave Le Bon and numerous colonial theorists after him asserted, a Japanese student could garner every possible university degree, but he could never reason logically like a European, because that capacity came only through inheritance. The Japanese might have succeeded in adopting the outward forms of European civilization, but neither their basic beliefs nor their character had been transformed. Though the Europeans might be outproduced and undersold, they retained a unique capacity of invention and scientific discovery. They also remained morally superior to mere imitators like the Japanese—or so Le Bon and Saussure continued to argue. Their pronouncements were a good deal less convincing after four years of slaughter on the Western Front.

⚔ *F U R T H E R   R E A D I N G*

Chandler, Alfred. *The Visible Hand: The Managerial Revolution in American Business* (Cambridge, MA: Belknop Press, 1977).

Fogel, Robert. *Railroads and American Economic Growth* (Baltimore: Johns Hopkins University Press, 1964).

Giedion, Siegfried. *Mechanization Takes Command* (New York: Oxford University Press, 1948).

Headrick, Daniel. *The Tools of Empire* (New York: Oxford University Press, 1981).

Hunter, Louis. *Steamboats on Western Rivers* (1949).

Licht, Walter. *Working for the Railroad: The Organization of Work in the Nineteenth Century* (Princeton, NJ: Princeton University Press, 1983).

Mazlish, Bruce, ed. *The Railroad and the Space Program* (Boston: Technology Press, 1965).

Merchant, Carolyn. *The Death of Nature: Women, Ecology, and the Scientific Revolution* (San Francisco: Harper & Row, 1980).

Nye, David. *The American Technological Sublime* (Cambridge, MA: MIT Press, 1994).

Stilgoe, John R. *Common Landscape of America, 1580 to 1845* (New Haven: Yale University Press, 1982).

Twain, Mark. *A Connecticut Yankee in King Arthur's Court* (1889).

Telephony, 1872–1914

We speak of many modern technologies as objects or devices: "the automobile,"
"the telephone," etc. But these and other common objects are really the user-interface
of a system, or network, full of other objects, human beings, bits of "nature," and,
ultimately institutions, politicians, and laws. In tightly integrated networks, the
lines we usually construct between the technical, natural, and human tend to blur,
perhaps even disappear.

One device whose networked nature has always been apparent is the
telephone, the front part of the "telephone network," or the "telephone system."
Through most of the twentieth century this network/system was also a company:
American Telephone and Telegraph (AT&T), also called "the Bell System," or,
popularly, "Ma Bell." But the telephone did not follow a predictable trajectory as
it traveled from Alexander Bell to Ma Bell. What the telephone was, how it would
"work," and whom it would work for were issues often renegotiated during its
first forty years. This chapter traces the odd path of telephony from Bell's experiments through the development of long-distance calling and the creation of
telephone operators.

Network *and* system *are words historians of technology often grapple with.
The term* network, *preferred by Bruno Latour, suggests a certain flexibility: hetero-
genous elements joined together in often unpredictable ways, volatile and theoretically transformable.* System, *a term often used by Thomas Hughes (see previous
chapter) to describe similar phenomena, retains an air of direction and hegemony.
Hughes has described how electrical "systems" in the early twentieth century developed "momentum" by "incorporating" banks, government agencies, university
departments, dams, reservoirs, etc. The sound and associations of words are important both to historical actors struggling to define emergent technologies and to
historians seeking to imaginatively recreate their substance.*

The history of telephony was partly a negotiation over language (even
"hello" was the subject of contention). How did language shape and affect the
telephone's reception? If the telephone was a network or a system, where, exactly,
did it end? Were telephone users, for example, extraneous or were they in some
manner incorporated? What about the women who joined the network as telephone "operators"—how was this role negotiated? How did it change over time,
and why? How were gender and class inscribed within telegraphy and telephony?

⚸ D O C U M E N T S

In the first selection, from *Employments of Women* (1863), Virginia Penny describes the new field of telegraphy, then only a decade old, as a promising one for women. Thirty years later, Mrs. M. L. Rayne, writing in *What Can a Woman Do* (1893), visits the headquarters of the Western Union telegraph office in New York City and finds four hundred women employed as operators. The women are paid less than men performing the same work, for an interesting reason.

In the third article, published in the *Saturday Evening Post* in 1930, Katherine Schmitt recalls what it was like to be one of New York's City's first telephone operators. Her career began in 1882, more than ten years before Rayne visited Western Union.

The fourth selection, from a 1908 issue of *The American Telephone Journal*, is an actual set of rules for operating room employees. (The company is not identified.) The fifth set of short articles appeared in *The Telephone Review*, the in-house journal of the Bell System, and *The Telephone News*, in 1911–1914. They describe the standardization of switchboard work and the simultaneous portrayal of the telephone operator as heroine. Were these two phenomena related? The last two selections are telephone company advertisements. What does each suggest about the character of the telephone network?

A New Employment for Women, 1863

VIRGINIA PENNY

A new source of employment has been opened by the invention of the electric telegraph. Most of the telegraphing in England is done by women, and in the United States a number of ladies are employed as operators. . . . An English paper says: "Here women do the business better than men, because of the more undivided attention they pay to their duties; but considerable inconvenience is found to result from their ignorance of business terms, which causes them to make mistakes in the messages sent. However, a short course of previous instruction easily overcomes this impediment." We have been told that, in one telegraph office in London, several hundred women are employed. I hope the application of steam to the operations of the electric telegraph may not interfere with the entrance of women into the occupation. In New Lisbon, Ohio, a young woman was employed, a few years ago, as principal operator in a telegraph office, with the same salary received by the man who preceded her in that office. "I was told by her," writes my informant, "that several women were qualifying themselves, in Cleveland, for the same occupation." The ex-superintendent of a line writes: "I have long been persuaded that ultimately a large proportion of the telegraphists, employed exclusively for writing, would be females, both because of their usually reliable habits, their ability to abstract and concentrate thought upon their engagements, their greater patience and industry, and the economy of their wages. In offices where there is a large amount of business, and consequently, much intercommunication with customers, I have supposed the arrangement would be to have a clerk to receive and deliver communications, and the corps of operators and writers, composed exclusively of females, in an adjoining or upper

From Virginia Penny, *The Employments of Women: An Encyclopedia of Women's Work* (Boston: Walker, Wise, 1867), pp. 110–101.

room, apart from public inspection. And to this arrangement, I think, there is at this time very little to oppose, except the antagonism naturally felt by male operators, who see in it a loss of employment to themselves.

Mrs. Rayne Visits Western Union, 1893

At the headquarters of the Western Union Telegraph Company, on the northwest corner of Dey street and Broadway, New York City, more than four hundred young women are employed as operators, and in the branch office of the company through-out the country hundreds of others find an opportunity to earn a living. Many private offices, too, are served in similar fashion.

. . . The central office of the Western Union Telegraph Company is constantly educating young women for such work, although conducting no regular school, and more girls are prepared for the work there than can find positions. The girls who act as messengers in the vast operating rooms on the upper floors are continually pick-ing up professional information, and it is a favorite practice for any one of them to do a companion's work as well as her own a part of the day, thus leaving her com-rade free to practice herself in the use of the telegraphic instruments. These messen-gers receive from fifteen to twenty-five dollars a month, and when they have become skilled operators, from thirty to sixty-five dollars a month, the average salary of the skilled feminine operator being about five hundred per year. The highest salary of the male their operators is one hundred and ten dollars a month, and their average salary about seventy dollars.

Why this difference? Chiefly because a man's endurance is greater than a woman's, and because the men are liable to be called upon by night as well as by day. The best of the male operators will receive and transcribe a telegraphic message of fifteen hundred words in an hour; will transcribe it so legibly and carefully that it may be handed to the compositors of a newspaper in the shape in which it has left his hands. When the annual President's Message is in progress of being telegraphed from Washington to New York City, this dexterous feat of receiving and transcribing is by no means a rare one. But telegraph superintendents say that they do not call upon women to perform it, and do not expect such a service of them. "Considerable nerve" is required to execute this task—more "nerve" than a woman is supposed to have in reserve at any hour of the day or night. Comparatively few men, indeed can do it. . . .

For the women themselves the practice of telegraphy has certain simple and definite attractions. It does not soil their dresses; it does not keep them in a standing posture; it does not, they say, compromise them socially. A telegraph operator, they declare, has a social position not inferior to that of a teacher or governess. Some kinds of skilled work, they insist, are positively objectionable: "In a factory one's clothes are misused; in a store one can never sit down; in the kitchen of a private house one is only a servant, even though a *chef,*" and to regard these objections as merely senti-mental and unworthy of serious consideration would, they claim, be a mistake. At any rate, the pursuit of telegraphy is free from these inconveniences. Moreover, the young women operators at the Western Union Company's headquarters are treated by their

---

From M. L. Rayne, *What Can a Woman Do* (Petersburgh, NY: Eagle Publishing Co., 1893), pp. 136–140.

superintendent—a young woman very proficient in her profession—with sedulous courtesy. She addresses then, not familiarly by their Christian names, but by their surnames, with the prefix "Miss," and she insists upon their addressing one another in the same considerate fashion, except, of course, when one of them is speaking to an intimate friend.

Memoir of a Telephone Operator, 1930

KATHERINE M. SCHMITT

The autumn of 1882 I became an operator in the old Nassau exchange of what is now the New York Telephone Company. Few of my friends had ever seen a telephone, except as it was cartooned in the newspapers, and vaguely referred to my employment as something to do with "that newfangled invention—you know, the telephone."

Occasionally one of them would ask me, "Say, how does that thing work? Do you really talk through a wire?"

They actually pictured me tying wires together all day and shouting through them to the limit of lung capacity. Others were not even curious, for the telephone at that time was considered an impractical toy, receiving more ridicule than credulity from the public. . . .

When I came the fate of the telephone was still hanging in the balance. It was a temperamental child, afflicted with so many ailments that only a few visionaries thought it could live. I was one of those fortunate ones who helped nurse this child to maturity. I found the task so interesting that I remained with it until 1930.

I was just out of high school in Brooklyn, I didn't want to teach; teaching was prosaic, poorly paid and the profession was overcrowded. Few jobs were open to women then; even most stenographers were men; women employees in downtown New York were so scarce as to be conspicuous. The now ubiquitous young business woman had not yet contributed her share to the traffic jam of horse cars, hansom cabs and private carriages on lower Broadway. But I was young and adventurous. . . .

Our company—always part of the Bell System—was known at that time as the Metropolitan Telephone and Telegraph Company. It was a struggling concern barely three years old; we were poor, and our office looked it. It was heated by an old-fashioned coal stove in the center of the room which we stoked ourselves, and anyone swept out who had time to—the office boy, if we had one; the operator, if she was kind; or the manager, when not too busy with the complaints of peevish subscribers. Telephone wires were attached to the roof, so the exchange must be on the top story, as hot in summer as it was cold in winter. I remember one manager who used to try to reduce the summer temperature by sprinkling the floor with a watering can. . . .

There were only about 3000 telephones in old New York City then, as compared to almost 2,000,000 today; yet to make a local connection was an engineering feat. To hook up a Nassau number with one in Murray or Pearl involved all the thrills and hazards the radio fan experiences when he tries to tune in on London. It was fishing by wire instead of by air, and you had to be optimistic. With a little luck you got there, and the operator was as surprised as the subscriber.

From Katherine M. Schmitt, "I Was Your Old Hello Girl," *Saturday Evening Post* (July 12, 1930), p. 19.

My salary to begin with was ten dollars a month; my hours from 8:00 A.M. until 6:00 P.M., with time out for lunch when possible. When traffic was heavy, we operators forgot we were hungry, and we often worked twelve hours a day. . . . Even when we could avail ourselves of our half-hour lunch period, we girls seldom ate in a restaurant; we didn't like to be stared at. Besides, once a day was often enough to climb those interminable stairs; we either brought sandwiches from home or sent the office boy down with a basket to buy the most nourishing lunch available for fifteen cents.

All told, there were perhaps seventy-five operators in the city, including the night and day shifts, managers and switchmen. Those on the night shift were young men; in the 80's it was not proper for a woman to be seen unattended on the streets at night. But boys as operators proved complete and consistent failure. They were noisy, rude, impatient and talked back to subscribers, played tricks with the wires and on one another. As I listened to them I used to think that all the Indians had not yet left Manhattan. In short, nothing could be done with those boys, until, by common consent, they were abolished. . . .

There were no chief operators when I came. We supervised ourselves. The only one to keep order was the manager, who was only a young man himself, and the most harassed young man in the world. From time to time he would rise in wrath and read the constitution to us—rules and regulations of service and the proper tone of voice to use—but the fight would go on the next minute.

One evening as I was leaving, he said to me, "Miss Schmitt, aren't you well?"

"Yes," I replied in astonishment. "Why do you ask?"

"I haven't heard your voice all day. I was afraid you must be ill."

And he wasn't trying to be humorous.

Much of the time we were too busy for mischief. In rush hours the little white slips on which the numbers were filed would come falling like snowflakes on the table of the trunk operator, and it was a matter of pride to keep her lines cleared, just as the traffic policeman likes to keep things moving on the street. The work was not monotonous; it was fascinating. The telephone was as much a source of wonder to the operator as to the subscriber. I didn't know why things happened, but I knew my touch was magic. Ten hours a day I sat there, one arm half paralyzed from holding the receiver, performing miracles with my free hand—miracles I could not explain. A mere mechanical gesture, and lo two people miles apart were talking together as though in the same room. Why they could hear each other, the science behind the connection, was as mysterious as life itself, but as I asked questions I began to learn, and as the mystery cleared, the romance of it fired my imagination and made every day an adventure.

I remember, the first day I came to work, one girl in the office told me she had been with the company three years.

"Three years! Dear me, I'd hate to think I'd be here three years." I said.

Retribution certainly overtook me for those words. Fate plays queer tricks upon us. When, early in 1930, I retired from active service, nearly half a century had flown by, so fast I had scarcely noted its passage; and Mr. Bell's "impractical toy" had grown from an infant to a giant. But I am getting ahead of my story.

Those first years no one could afford a telephone except prosperous business men, who used it overtime to get their money's worth, for it was a expensive toy. It cost $240 a year to have a telephone in New York and $150 in Brooklyn, for all service was at a flat rate. The first New York telephone directory, issued in 1878, was a single sheet like an advertising handbill, listing 243 names—more exclusive than Mrs. Astor's carefully pruned 400—but without the same social distinction. By 1882 this list had grown to 3000 in round numbers, yet within two months I knew the name of every subscriber in our office. I still remember that Nassau 394 was "Lawrence Son & Gerrish," and we could call each individual subscriber by name as well as by number.

I shall never forget the awful moment when one of the girls shouted to me "You have cut Lazelle Daily off!"—her way of announcing I'd disconnected the druggist who was Nassau 110. And what a crime that was! I called him back and apologized profusely.

Subscribers were remarkably uncomplaining in view of the service they got and for this very reason, perhaps were inclined to be chatty with the operator. They were sociable, to say the least. One might introduce himself with "Hello, dearie; how are you today?" I remember another who used to say, "Hello, *cara.* You know '*cara*' means 'darling.'" In the most caressing tones; and of course they tried to make appointments to meet us. But interest was inclined to friendliness, and what talking there was between us was all in good spirit and not to the extent that business suffered. Besides, we operators were not vamps; we were just unsophisticated schoolgirls who lived at home with our parents—but where else could we live on ten dollars a month? You see, the telephone was a miracle then where now it is a commonplace fact; the operator was a person, where now she is a machine. The subscriber couldn't see her, but he could hear her voice, which made her a mystery, and the more alluring.

People used to say to me, "You must hear dreadful things over the telephone!"

But we didn't. In the first place, we were taught from the start not to listen in; in the second place, there wasn't time—traffic was too heavy. And I remember subscribers as cheery and pleasant all day long. Indeed, it was largely personal interest between subscriber and operator that kept us going in the pioneer days when we were just feeling our way.

Between us was a feeling of neighborliness that is not possible now. Once, while I was trouble operator, I sent a lineman to investigate trouble in a downtown bank. When he finished, the bank president asked him, "If your office wants you where will you be?" The lineman gave the number of his next call, and a few minutes later the big executive rang in, saying, "If you need your man, you can get in touch with him at Nassau 369."

There was always trouble in the old days. Our first task in the morning was to ring up every subscriber in the district with, "Good morning; this is the daily test. How do you hear me this morning?" . . .

The expert engineers who developed the art of telephony were only amateurs in those days, creating their own profession, struggling with brain-twisting problems which had never been encountered before. Whenever a new telephone line was needed, an overhead wire was strung up. Installations did not work smoothly. In most cases the ground was used for the return circuit—an unsatisfactory conductor. The wires themselves being of iron and poorly insulated, were only a degree better;

by induction they picked up every noise on the earth or above it. No one knew how to eliminate cross-talk; there sputtered out of the receiver a jangle or meaningless noises that might have been signals from Mars or some other sociable planet. . . .

But it is not the maze and mileage of cable with which my experience was concerned. My work was not outside with the engineers, but in the central office with the operators. Central-office management was working just as intensively with problems of operating as the engineers were working with problems of equipment. . . .

The first change took place with a mighty flourish. In 1888 the Cortlandt exchange was opened, consolidating five small exchanges. The old Nassau office was among those absorbed; it lost its identity. Without regret we moved from our noisy seventh-floor walk-up to an impressive building that held its own among the skyscrapers of that era. It was the company's first large building in New York, and it meant we were getting on. Within a few years Cortlandt was handling all the traffic of the downtown section.

Cortlandt at that time was reported to be the largest exchange in the world. Whereas Nassau had served 500 subscribers' lines, Cortlandt served 5000, and with far less expenditure of energy. The switchboard was not just a step but a gigantic stride toward efficiency. It ran around three sides of the room, comprising forty-three sections with three operators at each section. It was called a multiple switchboard because every subscriber's line was multiplied forty-three times. . . . The old trunk table where I had toiled was now a thing of the past. The switchmen who had lorded it over us for so many years had been promoted to operators. The dignity of this new title had repressed their savagery to the point where it broke out only occasionally, and that under provocation of orders from half a dozen operators at once. These orders were no longer shouted into space, but given over a call circuit.

The young man's only retort to this barrage was, "Aw, get off the circuit!" His spirit was not dead; it only smoldered.

One operator alone could now complete a local connection, where formerly it had required three. Only two were needed to complete a call with another exchange, where formerly it had required five. . . . The completion of a call was now a matter of seconds instead of minutes. . . .

. . . As growth continued and equipment improved, service had to keep step. The operator's manner had to be groomed; she was made more gentle and refined, quicker and more accurate; it was necessary to have some supervision of her ever-increasing forces. In 1896 a superintendent arranged for a central-office organization that provided a chief operator; I was asked to fill that position at Cortlandt. The responsibility of the chief operator is the training of her operating forces. . . . It is interesting that the system inaugurated at this time holds today, with but few changes.

The first years that followed saw the final exodus of the male operators. They were not discharged, but absorbed in other departments of the business as opportunity arose. No one shed a tear at seeing them pass forever from the central office. . . .

Heretofore the operator had learned her trade by the trial-and-error method. She sat at her board doing the best she could in a groping, hit-or-miss fashion. When she made a mistake, the supervisor told her why it had happened and, when she had a minute to spare, coached her on how it should be done. Or perhaps her more experienced neighbor operator lent her a helping hand; all were well-meaning, but blundering. But now the time had come when subscribers must be saved annoyances which were un-avoidable while the young lady at the switchboard was acquiring a telephone ear and familiarizing herself with her equipment.

For, however equipment may be perfected, telephone service, in its last analysis, depends on the operator. Much is expected of her. The subscriber is at his telephone because he is in a hurry. He does not see the operator at work; he only knows he wants an immediate connection; each second he waits is a minute long, each delay a personal affront. But the telephone has always aimed to please, to speak when spoken to—not bluntly but politely, and with pleasing brevity. The operator must now be made as nearly as possible a paragon of perfection, a kind of human machine, the exponent of speed and courtesy; a creature spirited enough to move like chain lightning, and with perfect accuracy; docile enough to deny herself the sweet privilege of the last word. She must assume that the subscriber is always right, and even when she knows he is not her only comeback must be: "Excuse it, please," in the same smiling voice.

Achievement of this ideal was the next problem that confronted the central office. Its solution was a school for the training of telephone operators, opened in 1902 in the old Gramercy Building at Eighteenth Street and Irving Place, and I was made its manager, responsible for the selection and initial training of every operator, in New York City. . . .

[The student operator] is . . . taught all the niceties of telephone etiquette, from the proper tone of voice to use to the proper attitude toward her work. It is impressed upon her that she is the personal representative of the telephone company, the one member of that vast family who comes in personal contact with the subscriber. From the moment she dons her operating set she is taught to get his viewpoint and never to lose sight of it. It is not difficult to teach her courtesy, for she likes the subscriber, finds him friendly and, in her anxiety to please, courtesy comes easily and naturally. And, because courtesy is contagious, the subscriber involuntarily responds to her cheerful phrases in the same pleasant tone of voice. . . .

The operator, whose role was never spectacular, has grown more and more incon-spicuous as service has been perfected and her voice has grown more gently modu-lated. Where once she was a free, untrammeled soul whose greatest asset was lung power and ability to make the switchmen behave, gradually her own identity has been lost in her very efficiency and the stereotyped but unfailingly cheerful phrases by which she is known. Today she is the one human touch in a service almost automatic. Now, with the installation of the dial system, she threatens to fade from the picture altogether.

Rules for Operating Room Employees, 1908

The handling of irregular calls is a branch of operating room work which, although a proper subject for rules which lay down definite principles, may require variations to be made to correspond to local conditions of business and sentiment.

Most operating men have devoted considerable thought to the handling of "regu-lar" calls and naturally so, as they form the larger proportion of the operators' work. No

---

From Kendall Weisiger, "Rules for Operating Room Employees," *The American Telephone Journal*, XVII:I (January 4, 1908).

less important, however, is the handling of irregular calls which, while causing a small percentage of the work, are none the less important. Almost any operator can handle a regular call and please the person who originates it, but the operator's real ability may be shown much better by the way in which the irregular calls are handled. . . .

Request for Time of Day.

—Should a subscriber ask for the time, say to him, for example. *"The time is four fifty-six."* . . .

Request for Operator's Name or Number.

—Should a subscriber ask for your name or number, say to him, *"I will give you my supervisor; ask her."* . . .

Request for Information About a Fire.

—If a subscriber asks, "Where is the fire?" say to him, *"We have no information about the fire."* Should this information not satisfy him, connect him with the information desk.

Should the information be given you by your supervisor, say to the inquiring subscriber, for example, *"The fire is at Smith's grocery on Market Street."* If he asks further questions, say to him, *"That is all the information we have received,"* and if the above does not satisfy him connect him with the information desk.

Request for Information About Ball Scores, Etc., Etc.

—Say to the calling subscriber, *"We do not get the returns."* Connect the subscriber with the information desk if he makes further inquiry.

Clippings from *The Telephone Review* and *The Telephone News* 1911–1914

Efficiency in Traffic Work [1911]

E. F. SHERWOOD

In order to determine whether a Traffic Department is efficiently managed, it is necessary to have some standard with which to compare the results obtained; without a standard of some sort, consciously or unconsciously assumed, it is impossible to come to any conclusion concerning efficiency. . . .

The principal items of the present standard of service of the New York Telephone Company are as follows:

From E. F. Sherwood, "Efficiency in Traffic Work," *The Telephone Review* (April 1911): 76–81; anonymous, "On Telephone Duty," *The Telephone Review* (October–November 1911): 244; "The Idle Hour," *The Telephone Review* (September 1912): 219; "Behind the Scenes," *The Telephone News* (January 1, 1914): 5.

Average time of answer by "A" operators	3–5 secs.
Average time of completing local connections	22. "
Average time of completing calling circuit trunk connections in the same city	28. "
Average time of disconnection	3–5 secs.
Average time of answer to supervisory signal	4–5 "
Per cent. of supervisory signals not answered in 10 seconds	15.
Per cent. of errors by operators	1.
Per cent. of irregularities by operators	15.

In considering the per cent. of irregularities, it should be borne in mind that the slightest departure from the rules laid down for the guidance of operators is counted as an irregularity—such as an answer of "Number" instead of "Number, please?" a hurried repetition of a call, etc. It has been suggested that the standard for errors and irregularities should be zero. Such a standard would be proper if we were not obliged to depend upon human beings to operate our switchboards. With a constantly changing force of operators whose average length of service is somewhat less than three years, we must expect a reasonable percentage of errors and irregularities. It has been repeatedly proved that pressure persistently exerted to reduce irregularities below a reasonable point produces irritation and a feeling of discouragement which lead to an increase in irregularities rather than a decrease. . . .

. . . [I]t is easy to understand why the public should be upset by even a comparatively slight decrease in the efficiency of the service. The telephone has tremendously increased the capacity of men to transact business, and as a time saving and labor saving device has, during the last twenty years revolutionized the methods of conducting business. It has also materially affected social usages, and in a large measure the invitation by telephone to dine or to join a theatre party has taken the place of the formal written invitation. . . . We should bear in mind that while the public is fair-minded when we can present and argue our case, yet it is impatient with failure and is not inclined to accept excuses gracefully. . . .

On the other hand, it has been repeatedly demonstrated that the public will respond quickly and liberally to an increase in efficiency. . . .

In the first place, the traffic engineering work plays a very important part. The switchboards must be so designed and constructed that the overloading of operators, which produces poor service, and the underloading of operators, which produces extravagance and waste, are avoided as far as possible. . . .

A very heavy burden of responsibility rests upon those who select and train the student operators who are constantly being added to the operating forces. The standard of eligibility must be high in order that those who are in the slightest degree physically or mentally unfit, or those who have defects of temperament, may be excluded. A successful operator must be mentally alert and in all respects must be much above the average young woman. The standard of the New York Telephone Company is such that only about 10 per cent. of those who apply pass the examination and are accepted. . . .

The education of an operator does not cease . . . when she graduates from the School, and it may be said that her real education begins when she commences to handle calls at a regular central office switchboard. . . . She must learn to think rapidly and to eliminate any lag between mental conception and action. . . . It may be said of the telephone operator that "She who hesitates is lost." If she cannot overcome the habit of hesitating when an opportunity to pass a call occurs, she is in the position of one who meets a person in the street and dances around while trying to make up his mind as to whether he should go to the right or to the left. If this occurs in the middle of a busy street he is in danger of being run over by an automobile or a truck. The operator who hesitates is in danger of being "run over" by her subscribers. The knack of passing calls over a busy calling circuit without loss of time and without making a nuisance of one's self to other operators is one which is not easy to acquire. If you do not think that this is so, try it. You will find that dodging automobiles and trucks is a mild form of pastime by comparison. . . .

I also wish to say to the members of the Traffic Department that eternal vigilance is the price of our jobs. In order to "make good" we must be animated by a spirit of restless dissatisfaction, this dissatisfaction being expressed, not by carping criticism and irritating fault-finding with those reporting to us, but by exhibiting an optimistic faith in our ability to make progress and to come nearer our ideals. Beware of any feeling of complete satisfaction with past results. If you are ever tempted to put your feet on your desk and say that the job is about finished and with very little assistance will run itself hereafter, promptly consult the physician in whom you have the most confidence. Such an idea may be interpreted as a symptom of mental disorder. One of the charms of telephone work lies in the unlimited field of opportunity for development which it offers: not only the development of the art and of the business, but the development and improvement of ourselves in the study and solution of its problems.

On Telephone Duty [1911]

The A. T. & T. Company has recently issued an attractive and most timely pamphlet bearing the above title, and consisting of thirty-two pages with illustrations.

The introduction reads as follows:

THE GIRL AT THE SWITCHBOARD.

The best telephone service demands human intelligence at the switchboard.

The Bell telephone operator is frequently called upon to act quickly in an emergency.

The situation frequently calls for coolness and courage.

Crises arise which call for self-reliance and initiative on the part of the operator: occasions when prompt and intelligent action is demanded.

The following instances gleaned from the columns of the daily press and from other sources, are records of the unselfish devotion, the splendid courage, and the keen intelligence of the loyal and devoted army of Bell telephone workers.

The illustrations are pictures of thirty-four Bell Telephone operators whose acts are recorded in the booklet.

This piece of literature does more than it purports to do. For example, the case is cited of Miss Rose Coppinger, as told by the Arkansas *Gazette.* Miss Coppinger, a telephone operator at the Pioneer Telephone Company's Exchange at Webbers Falls, Okla., "remained at her post until the last, summoning assistance from rural districts," while the business section of the town was wiped out by fire, and by her heroism probably averted the destruction of the whole village. "She was carried from the building in a wet blanket," is the terse comment of the newspaper.

Just imagine what would have happened—

If this had been an automatic system, instead of the Bell with a brave and intelligent operator:

If this had been an "independent" local company, instead of the Bell with lines everywhere;

If the farmers in the "rural districts" had had their own "independent" system instead of being connected with the Bell.

Incidents of fire and flood, of robbery and murder, and of accident are set forth in such array as not only to reflect the highest credit upon the telephone operators, but to show how indispensable they are in rendering service of the greatest value to the subscribers; not only to demonstrate the benefits of telephone connections to those who needed the help of others, but how it might be of equal or greater value to all if occasion should arise; not only the value of telephone service, but the importance of universal Bell Telephone service.

More instances than these will occur to any casual observer of events, and our canvassers for new business would do well to take advantage of such cases to support their arguments.

Protection [1912]

"Women who are alone in a flat all day take many precautions to insure safety," a gas collector said. "One way that I learned the other day made me feel rather foolish. When I went into the kitchen to read the meter the mistress of the flat stepped to the telephone and said:

"'It's all right, Central. It's only the gas man.'

"Of course she was under no obligations to explain that cryptic allusion to myself, but she did it voluntarily.

"'Every time the doorbell rings when I am here alone,' she said, 'I take the receiver off the hook and leave the telephone open before I go to the door, so that if I should have occasion to scream they could hear me at headquarters and send somebody to my assistance.'

"To utilize the telephone company as a private detective bureau struck me as nervy, but I have since learned that a lot of lone women resort to that plan with satisfaction to all concerned."—*N. Y. Times.*

[1914]

"I suppose that means," laughed the business man, "that the ding-a-ling of the telephone bell in my office really means 'Come-running, come-running.'"

"At least," said the Superintendent, "it is one of the many things which prove the wonderful importance of the public's coöperation; and a telephone service of the fullest satisfaction is made possible not alone by the army of employees, but the greater army of telephone users. You, as the public, by answering promptly, by the practice of the telephone smile, by reporting a service difficulty at the time it occurs, help to round out the fullest measure of service value. It is this coöperation which may make or mar any public service, and perhaps nowhere as in the art of telephony is advancement so dependent upon the appreciation and help which the public accords the Company in the solution of its problems."

The New York Telephone Company vs. "Hello" (Advertisement), 1911

Courtesy Between Telephone Users

Would you rush into an office or up to the door of a residence and blurt out "Hello! Hello! Who am I talking to?" and then, when you received a reply, follow up your wild, discourteous salutation with "I don't want you; get out of my way. I want to talk with Mr. Jones." Would you? That is merely a sample of the impolite and impatient conversations that the telephone transmits many times a day.

There is a most agreeable mode of beginning a telephone conversation which many people are now adopting, because it saves useless words and is, at the same time, courteous and direct. It runs thus:

The telephone bell rings, and the person answering it says: "Morton & Company, Mr. Baker speaking." The person calling then says" "Mr. Wood, of Curtis & Sons, wishes to talk with Mr. White."

When Mr. White picks up the receiver, he knows Mr. Wood is on the other end of the line, and without any unnecessary and undignified "Hello's," he at once greets him with the refreshingly courteous salutation: "Good morning, Mr. Wood." That savors of the genial handshake that Mr. Wood would have received had he called in person upon Mr. White.

Undoubtedly there would be a far higher degree of telephone courtesy, particularly in the way of reasonable consideration for the operators, if the "face-to-face" idea were more generally held in mind. The fact that a line of wire and two shining instruments separate you from the person with whom you are talking, takes none of the sting out of unkind words.

Telephone courtesy means answering the telephone as quickly as possible when the bell rings—not keeping the "caller" waiting until one gets good and ready to answer. Telephone courtesy, on party lines, means being polite when some one else unintentionally breaks in—not snapping, "Get off the line; I'm using it."

In a word, it is obviously true that that which is the correct thing to do in a face-to-face conversation, is also correct in a telephone conversation, and anyone has but to apply the rules of courtesy, prescribed long years before the telephone was first thought of, to know the proper manners for telephone usage.

Be forbearing, considerate and courteous. Do over the telephone as you would do face to face.

From an article in the *Telephone Engineer,* by Frank J. Wisse.

NEW YORK TELEPHONE CO.

From *The Telephone Review (1911).*

"In the Bell Democracy" (Advertisement), 1911

In the Bell Democracy

Membership in the telephone democracy of the Bell System means equal opportunity for every man, no matter who he is or where he is.

Each member of this Bell democracy has the same chance of communication, limited only by the distance the voice can be carried.

However remote, whether in the adobe house on the Rio Grande, on the Montana sheep ranch or in the isolated New England farm house, the Bell telephone is an open doorway to the Universal Bell System.

From each Bell outpost run lines that connect it with the central office—that nerve center of the local system.

Long distance and toll lines connect these nerve centers and furnish clear tracks for telephone talk throughout the land.

12,000,000 miles of wire are the highways over which 20,000,000 telephone talks are carried daily.

The Bell System binds together the social and business activities of a people in a shoulder-to-shoulder march of progress.

AMERICAN TELEPHONE AND TELEGRAPH COMPANY
AND ASSOCIATED COMPANIES

One Policy   *One System*   *Universal Service*

𝕬𝕬 E S S A Y S

In the first essay, from *The Telephone Book,* Avital Ronell makes a close reading of the autobiography of Thomas Watson, Alexander Graham Bell's famous collaborator. Watson, an electrician, was also interested in spiritualism. Ronell suggests that it was not so clear, in the mid-1870s, to which world the telephone belonged.

In the second essay, Venus Green relates how women were recruited as telephone operators and explains why they continued to run switchboards long after automation had become technically feasible. Telephone companies had complex ideas not only about what a telephone operator should do, but what she should be.

In the last essay, Bruno Latour traces a crucial episode in the making of the Bell System—the creation of long-distance calling. Latour has argued that the distinctions we maintain among science, technology, and society are mere conventions—that engineers and scientists create all three when they construct machines and technological systems of wide influence.

These three essays successively question the boundaries between science and the occult, between technology and people, and between science, technology, and society. Were these distinctions important to those most intimately engaged in the development of telephony? Did the "stakes" in the maintaining or the blurring of these boundaries depend on where one was located in the network? Was there something about modern communications technologies, like the telephone, that invited boundaries to be arranged in new ways?

From *The Telephone Review* (1911).

Watson, I Need You

AVITAL RONELL

. . . Watson always presents the telephone as something that speaks, as if by occult force. His perception of electricity rarely strays from its homeland in the occult, or what in contemporary California bookstores is classified as metaphysics. A member of the Society of Psychical Research, Watson could claim with dignity before any telephone was ever erected: "a faint, elongated glow a little brighter than the sunlight on the grass . . . Was it a personal emanation? . . . The columnar halo followed me!" He was already himself attuned to the ghost within.

. . . The circuit of telephony begins, should a circuit be subsumable under a notion of beginning, on July 16,1872: "We 'had a spirit circle' at Phillips' house with 'strong manifestations.'" The vampiric citational marks probably refer to the official rhetoric of spiritualism that also could be found in the journal to which Watson subscribed, *The Banner of Light*. Yet, they should not relativize the effect of the real, for Watson claims to be talking real ghosts. It all begins modestly enough, with sound manifestations introduced via the fingertips indexing the body prints from where future calls are to come. The dialogics of strong manifestations takes shape spontaneously.

> These were at first entirely table tippings and rappings, from the merest ticks to loud knocks. Phillips and I sat at the table with our finger tips on its upper surface, and asked questions of the spirits, who instantly responded by three knocks or table tips for "yes" and two for "no" . . . The movements of the table varied greatly. Sometimes it rose gently from the floor with its top level and was lowered just as softly, and sometimes it jumped up quickly and was slammed down. More often it would be tipped up on two legs sometimes gently, sometimes forcibly and on several occasions when the table was tipped in this way, I sat on the high side and felt it as firm as if it were resting on the floor.

. . . The fact that the site for these sittings goes under the name of Salem has not escaped you. Male witchery got by, switching to electric cable systems that would carry the name of scientific experiment in the most original sense of a meeting scheduled between cognition, peril, and risk. . . . The telephonic seed, remember, was planted in Salem. After a few of these sittings I decided there was nothing electric about the doings (writes Watson), "but they seemed so supernatural. I accepted the 'disembodied spirit' theory of their cause. I determined, however, from the start that I had no power to produce the phenomena. From or through Phillips alone they all came." Watson had no power to produce; they all came from or through the conduit reserves of the other. We were so interested in the wonderful nightly occurrences, he continues, "that we had a sitting nearly every night the first week, some of them at my house, where they were quite as strong as at the other house." A third man joins the circle: Phillips and I and another young man, John Raymond, afterwards mayor of Salem, were the sole participants and all three of us soon became firm believers in spiritualism. We read the spiritualist paper, *Banner of Light*. From this paper they learn about slate writing and at their next meeting ghostly teletyping becomes de rigueur. Henceforth the ghosts will participate in a new grammatology of the mystic writing pad:

From Avital Ronell, *The Telephone Book* (Lincoln, NE: University of Nebraska Press, 1989), pp. 246–248, 251–252, 255–267.

My old school slate, with a short piece of pencil on its upper surface was placed on Phillips' hand which he then reached under the table. Instantly the pencil began to write briskly with the dash of a fluent penman, and, when Phillips took the slate from under the table, there was unmistakable writing on it!

. . . Working on underwater explosives, Watson's wondering what is next to come. The next exploding mine was to be Alexander Graham Bell:

> One day early in 1874 when I was hard at work for Mr. Farmer on his apparatus for exploding submarine mines by electricity and wondering what was coming next, there came rushing out of the office door and through the shop to my workbench a tall, slender, quick-motioned young man with a pale face, black side-whiskers and drooping mustache, big nose and high, sloping forehead crowned with bushy jetblack hair. It was Alexander Graham Bell, a young professor in Boston University, who I then saw for the first time. He also was living in Salem, where he tutored the deaf child of Thomas Sanders, and came in to Boston practically every day.

Bell had broken down the rudimentary discipline of the shop "by coming directly to me," like a projectile. He rushes into the subjectless space to make direct contact with Watson; Watson is struck with particular force by the way the other breaks into a space of anonymity. Watson recreates this scene by explaining that the workers in the back never knew for whom they were at work, under whose command they were building technology. "To make my work on his apparatus more intelligent, Bell explained them to me at once. They were, he said, a transmitter and a receiver of his 'harmonic telegraph.' . . . The principle on which his telegraph worked has the same sympathetic vibration which sets a piano-string or organ-reed vibrating, when its own note is sounded near it." Regarding Bell's invention using instead of air an intermittent current of electricity over the wire, Watson does not neglect to assert, "his apparatus was very simple." . . .

Running his direct line to Watson, Bell leaves no doubt as to the sympathetic vibrations which flared in the primal transmission that Watson received. Not only was the apparatus very simple, "The operation was also very simple." The problem with this very simple apparatus regulated by equally simple operational methods was that when Bell tried to send several telegraphic messages simultaneously (this possibility is in what the harmonic telegraph consisted), "they did not work as well as they theoretically ought." Bell explains that "the receivers would not always pick out the right messages." Eventually he aimed at the autograph telegraph, an apparatus for telegraphing facsimile writing and pictures, which was a use Bell wanted to make of his harmonic telegraph when he got it perfected. So prior to the autograph telegraph, they are two, Watson, Bell, and the imperfect theory—busted because the receivers could not pick out the right messages. . . .

> Bell had another fascination for me: he was a pianist, the first I had ever known. To play the piano had always seemed to me the peak of human accomplishment. It seemed so occult and inexplicable that I asked Bell one evening, when he was playing on his boarding-house piano, if it was necessary to hit the keys exactly in order to play a piece or would striking them anywhere in certain vicinities of the keyboard answer the purpose? My respect for the art was deepened when he said the precise key had to be struck every time. The possibility of my ever learning the art, which had been one of my secret aspirations, faded at this revelation of its unexpected difficulties.

While this avowal produces an impression of unparalleled naiveté, which we have no intention of perturbing, it situates the scientific compulsion in a band way above the technosphere in which one would perhaps falsely hope to locate the mind of an inventor. It seems rather clear that for Watson "the peak of human accomplishment" supersedes the strictly human in a manner that appears neatly paradoxical. If piano playing flags the summit of human doing for Watson, then he supposes it to rise above the experiential strains to a suprasensory realm of sheer occult projection. The piano calls music. The hand, while instrumental, remains incidental. The somewhat scientific exactitude with which a melodious piece of artwork is made (hitting the right key, picking the right message) stuns the spiritualist, leaving him commensurately dispirited. The register of organized sound had seemed occult to Watson, and inexplicable.

The stupefying revelation concerning the piano can be viewed as crucial to the extent that the very next chapter enters the space of mutual collaboration by hitting the key on Bell's contraptions, named instruments ("I worked away his instruments."). In a similar vein, pitched to the same grand image, the desire to telegraph sound belongs to "an apparatus with a multitude of tuned strings, reeds and other vibrating things, all of steel or iron combined with many magnets. It was as big, perhaps, as an upright piano." And for the duration of their work on what someone could be tempted to classify according to a strictly "scientific" taxonomy, Watson abides the ghosts he had long ago conjured: "The apparatus sometimes seemed to me to be possessed by something supernatural, but I never thought the supernatural being was strictly angelic when it operated so perversely." By this reference Watson means the telegraph, which Bell was having trouble improving, allowing that some recognizable brand of Salem intervention, not quite angelic, created circumstances which were "messing up his telegraph." Regardless of what forces participated in the labor of inventing the telephone, Watson consistently organizes its facticity around a shared concept of art and science, laying the primary emphasis on the conception that takes place in the history of a pure idea:

> History gives us many illustrations of the transforming power of an idea, but Bell's conception of a speech-shaped electric current ranks among the most notable of them. The conception itself was the great thing and any mechanism embodying it, even the very first form that was discovered, is of minor importance. If Bell had never found the apparatus for which he was searching his name should have been immortalized. My realization of this has always made me very modest over my contributions to the art of telephony. I knew other electricians who could have done my work with Bell as well as I did it, but here was only one Bell with his big idea.

Watson's reading of the telephone as pure idea ought not to be overlooked in haste. For, unlike other "great things," the telephone did not come into being as an effort of some demand or generally articulated desire. It was the cause of the effects which nowadays places it strangely in the locus of effect. It was not the culmination of a teleological movement, a finality, science's response to an audible demand. The telephone was a private, an imaginary, and a somewhat more perverse conception than you would allow. At these moments of its analysis, Watson takes a step back, diminishing himself to the spot of an electrician who wired and set up the instruments of an unpinnable "mad," that is to say, art-bound scientist. Yet, we have seen the very special currency on which the marginal electrician operates; it is not wrong to suppose that the two men pooled their ghostly resources. . . . The telephone was conceived as their baby. They hasten to advance its infancy, eager to have their child talk:

> I made every part of that first famous telephone with my own hands, but I must confess my prophetic powers, if I had any, were not in operation that day. Not for a moment did I realize what a tremendously important piece of work I was doing. No vision of the giant that new-born babe was to be in a few years came to me as I hurried to get it ready to talk. I am sorry I was too busy at lathe and bench to do any dreaming for it would make a pretty story if I could record that I foresaw the great things to come and was stimulated by them to extra exertions. But there was nothing of the kind; I rushed the work because I was mightily interested in the invention and wanted to hear it talk.

No time for dreaming or projection, Watson's want is articulated as "I wanted to hear it talk." When it does begin to talk, its primal sounds are conceived as a birth cry, brought to light by Bell and Watson. At the moment of giving birth, the couple has to change positions in order to get it right. They are already a telephone, but they still need to fit into the right position—the one receiving, the other disseminating and repeating the effort. This sort of harmonic relationship, like the telegraph that initiated it, needs practice: the first trial of the new telephone has Bell listening in the attic with the receiver reed pressed against his ear, while Watson talks into the telephone.

> But alas, shout my loudest. Bell could not hear the faintest sound. We changed places, I listened in the attic while Bell talked into the telephone downstairs. Then, I could unmistakably hear the tones of his voice and almost catch a word now and then . . . We tried every way we could think of to make the telephone talk better that night but soon the parchment of its drumhead became softened by our breath and the reed breaking away from it put the telephone out of commission until repairs had been made.

Eventually, 109 Court Street, Boston, gave birth to their instrument:

> I was sitting at the window nearest Hanover Street when I plucked the reed of that harmonic telegraph transmitter and made the twang that has never stopped vibrating. Bell was at the other window when he heard the faint sound in his receiver which was the birth-cry of the telephone. . . .

Bringing up baby is another matter for the pair. They have to take it on tours with them, staging countless performances to calm mass epistemological anxiety: no one can believe their ears. To have their ears believe this extraordinary protégé, the public has to see it talk with their own eyes. Watson and Bell assume their parental task: "Getting that famous first sentence through the telephone seemed to exorcise some of the tantalizing imps that always pester the babyhood of a new invention as infantile disease do a human baby, and a few weeks later the telephone was talking so fluently you did not have to repeat what you said more than a half a dozen time.'"

Like Heidegger and K. of *The Castle,* Mr. Watson has an ear for the silence that the telephone was capable of speaking. "This early silence in a telephone circuit," he writes, "gave an opportunity for listening to stray electric currents that cannot be easily had to-day. I used to spend hours at night in the laboratory listening to the many strange noises in the telephone and speculating as to their cause." His sonic speculations disclose the atonal symphony of random noise:

> One of the most common sounds was a snap, followed by a grating sound that lasted two or three seconds before it faded into silence, and another was like the chirping of a

bird. My theory at this time was that the currents causing these sounds came from explosions on the sun or that they were signals from another planet. They were mystic
enough to suggest the latter explanation but I never detected any regularity in them that
might indicate they were intelligible signals.

If the apocalypse is supposed to reveal itself as unbearable sound, breaking the universal eardrum, then Watson's ear is already probing remote planetary explosions. At
this level of supraglobal listening, he claims a unique status for himself. "I don't believe any one has ever studied these noises on a grounded telephone line since that
time," he writes, adding, "I, perhaps, may claim to be the first person who ever listened
to static currents." . . .

The telephone worked the night shift. Watson early noticed "that the telephone
talked better nights and Sundays than it did during the busy hours of week days, although our laboratory, being on a side street, was always fairly quiet. . . . At night or
on Sunday, the diminution of city sounds gave the telephone a much better chance
to be heard." Thus ends the ninth chapter of the autobiography. Its final sentence
speaks of giving the telephone a chance to be heard, as if it had to defend itself
against some silent reproach or well-known accusation. . . .

Before you know it "and about six weeks after I signed the contract Bell decided
his baby had grown big enough to go out doors and prattle over a real telegraph line,
instead of gurgling between two rooms" and two grown men. For Watson this entails
some sacrifice, for "up to that time I had been living in Salem with my father and
mother, going back and forth on the train every day, but now it became necessary for
me to live in Boston." . . .

In passing, I will note for the benefit of the superstitious that the laboratory room
was numbered 13, which in this case at least did not bring bad luck." More or less laying aside the harmonic and autograph telegraphs they now "concentrated almost entirely on speech transmission." The parts were few—the electromagnet and its coils,
the diaphragm, and the mouthpiece, with either a battery or a permanent steel magnet
to excite the electromagnet. The diaphragm typically causes a number of problems,
bringing back the intensity of an original human body on which to work. To an impressive degree—this will become clear in the Bell section—the table in Room 13
also served as something of an operating table for the reanimation of corpses. Watson
works on partial-object corpses; he was charged with constructing several telephones,
"down to a minute affair I made from the internal bones and drum of a real human ear
that Dr. Clarence Blake, the well-known aurist, gave to Bell—of course, after his
patient had finished with it. They all worked, even the real ear telephone, which was,
however, the poorest of the lot. We finally decided on a diaphragm of iron of the same
size and thickness as is used to-day." Nevertheless, the ancestor of the telephone you
are used to using remains the remains of a real human ear.

It is small wonder that Watson will essay in a subsequent chapter to fend off
charges of the occult adherency that the telephone supposedly represented. Somehow
the telephone will have to be disconnected from its ghostly origin, which Watson's
tome tries to suppress, halfheartedly, only in the final chapters. For Watson never en-
gages an oppositional logic that would ground a purity of scientific inquiry at the
price of a fallen supernaturalism. The connections remain subtly intact as Watson
launches faint countercurrents to the ghostly origins of these technologies. As the
two were advancing toward a telephone that would both transmit and receive, they

still appeared to depend upon the paradigm of Watson's earlier séances, though this point is never made explicitly. One example to illustrate spooked circuitry may suffice: "I knew we were using the weakest current ever used for any practical purpose and that it was also of a very high intensity, for we had talked successfully through a circuit made up of a dozen persons clasping hands—a very great resistance. . . . These were some of my thoughts while I was manipulating things in every possible way, trying to make the telephone talk. . . . But it was useless, the thing was obstinately dumb." One night, the thing was no longer dumb. It was aroused from imperturbable slumber, and the first long-distance call was placed. But the call could not be verified. As in the case of a séance peopled with nonbelievers, Watson and Bell had to prove that the telephone actually had spoken, that this was not a rehearsed hallucination. Each began recording what was said at his end of the wire. "Then by putting the two records side by side he could prove to the doubters that the telephone could talk straight." The *Boston Advertiser* was to print the news of the first long-distance conversation the following morning. The first call travels between Kilby Street, Boston (Bell), and East Cambridge (Watson) on October 9. "These were telephones that would both transmit and receive."

There was a witness, rather literally appointed: the factory watchman. ("I let the watchman listen, but even then I think he felt it was some humbug. His relief at getting rid of me was evident when he let me out of the building towards morning to walk proudly back to Boston with the telephone, a bundle of wire and my tools under my arm wrapped in a newspaper." The first long-distance call bears recording. Here's what we have:

> I cut it [the relay] out with a piece of wire across its binding posts, rushed downstairs, followed at a much slower pace by the watchman, and listened at the telephone.
>
> It was no longer dumb! More loudly and distinctly than I ever had heard it talk between two rooms, Bell's voice was vibrating from it, shouting "Ahoy! Ahoy!" "Are you there?" "Do you hear me?" "What's the matter?" . . . Then began the first "long distance" telephone conversation the world has ever known. We recorded it word for word. The croakers made us do that. The common attitude toward any new thing is apt to be pessimistic for the average man thinks that what hasn't been done, can't be done. It was so with the telephone. It seemed a toy to most persons. Some of Bell's friends, although they had heard the thing talk at the laboratory were doubtful as to its practical value, and one of them of a scientific turn of mind told me that he didn't see how the telephone could be accurate enough for practical use for every spoken word has many delicate vibrations to be converted into electrical waves by the telephone and if some of them get lost the message cannot be intelligible.

. . . Ever since Watson had known Bell, he recounts, his habit of celebrating successful experiments by what he called a war dance was respected, and "I had got so expert at it that I could do it as well as he could. That night, when he got back to the laboratory, we forgot there were other people in the house and had a rejoicing that nearly resulted in a catastrophe."

The morning after: "after a sleepless night, as I started down the stairs to go to Williams' to build some more telephones, I saw our landlady waiting for me at her door with an acid expression on her face." The waiting woman at the end of the line, imaged in the liquefying anger of experimental elements her acid face about to have words. The naughty young man: "My conscience was troubling me and I felt something disagreeable was about to happen. My pretense of great haste did not work for she stopped me and said in an unpleasant voice, 'I don't know what you fellows are doing up in the attic but if you don't stop making so much noise nights and keeping my lodgers awake, you'll have to quit them rooms.' I couldn't say much to calm her. I assured her we would be more careful although for the life of me I didn't see how we could get along with any less noise than we had been making. I couldn't blame her finding fault. She wasn't at all scientific in her tastes and we were not prompt with our rent." This is the only time Watson invokes the prerogatives of scientific sensibility, in the key of aestetified taste, and we would not be wrong to suggest that he spits out the signifier with iron. The noise without which they would not be able to get along presumably resulted from the war dancing, as telephone connections were tried out in other spaces. . . .

The telephone was hardly a beloved or universally celebrated little monster. It inspired fear, playing on fresh forms of anxiety which were to be part of a new package deal of the invisible. This hardly replicates the way Watson puts it, yet he gives abundantly profiled clues to follow. It soon becomes clear that schizophrenia recognizes the telephone as its own, appropriating it as a microphone for the singular emission of its pain. Schizophrenia was magnetized by the telephone the way neurosis rapped on Freud's door. In a fundamental sense, we can say that the first outside call the telephone makes is to schizophrenia—a condition never wholly disconnected from the ever-doubling thing. Watson mounts his case slowly, describing the call of aberrancy first in terms of "embarrassment." Men in particular were uneasy about the thing. For instance: "It also interested me to see how many people were embarrassed when they used the telephone for the first time. One day a prominent lawyer tried the instruments with me. When he heard my voice in the telephone making some simple remark he could only answer after a long embarrassed pause, 'Rig a jig, and away we go.'" Regression takes hold, the call transfers the speaker to a partial object, a false self caught up in the entanglement of *fort/da*: away we go.

Watson defines essentially two kinds of men that visited the telephone. The first we have just listened to, away he went. The second returns us to a recurrent concern, the consummate knowledge of disconnection that connects the schizophrenic to things and machinery: "Men of quite another stamp from those I have mentioned occasionally." Though he is not necessarily playing *Carte postale,* you will note the self-addressed envelopes upon which these stamps are pressed. They go to the telephone laboratory like hypnotics mission-controlled toward their destination by unmarked signals. These men of another stamp arrive by letter, writing in secret codes of secret codes that would transform the telephone into a system of telepathically guided transferrals. "One day Mr. Hubbard received a letter from a man who wrote that he could put him on the track of a secret that would enable us to talk any distance without a wire." Mr. Hubbard, interested by this proposal, makes an appointment for the wireless man to meet Watson at the laboratory. Here goes their destinal encounter.

> At the appointed time a stout, unkempt man made his appearance. He glanced at the telephones lying around the benches but didn't take the least interest in them. He told me that the telephone was already a back number and if we would hire him he would show us how to telephone any distance without apparatus or wires. He looked as sane as most of the inventors I had worked with and I became interested. When I asked him what experiments he had made, he told me in a matter-of-fact tone that two prominent New York men, whose

names he knew but whom he had never seen, had managed surreptitiously to get his brain so connected with their circuit that they could talk with him at any hour of the day or night wherever he was and make all sorts of fiendish suggestions—even of murder. He didn't know just how they did it but their whole apparatus was inside his head and if I wanted to find out their secret I must take off the top of his skull and study the mechanism at work. For fifteen dollars a week, he said he would place himself entirely at my service to do whatever I please with him. Long before he finished his tale, I knew I was dealing with a crazy man. I didn't dare to turn down his proposition too abruptly for fear he might go on a rampage in that lonely attic so I excused myself from starting to dissect him at once on the ground of a pressing engagement and he went away promising to come again the next day. He didn't come again and the next time I heard of him (by phone, perhaps) he was in an insane asylum. Within the next year or two several men whose form of insanity made them hear voices which they attributed to the machinations of enemies, called at the laboratory or wrote to us for help, attracted by Bell's supposedly occult invention.

It was as if an unbeholdable, subliminal sign hung over the laboratory, bouncing signals for schizophrenics to phone home, for psychosis and auditory paranoia to settle down in the telephone. Watson retains the invisible headset telecommanding this man and those stamped in a similar way as part of the autobiography, which itself is a partial otobiography of the telephone; Watson hardly pushes this episode, whose repetitions he asserts, to some peripheral pocket of narrative disclosure. The call of the insane, who at first sight resemble the inventor, belongs to the fundamental history of the telephone, ingathering a "them" whose strict isolation and difference, as a guarantee of carceral alterity, I would not vouch for. Somewhere between an art and a science, the telephone still throws strangely stamped shadows off its primary invisibility. It divides itself among thing, apparatus, instrument, person, discourse, voice. Or rather, as a moment in onto-technology, does it not perhaps offer itself precisely as a nothing so that by putting off access to itself, abstaining or interdicting itself it might thereby come closer to being something or someone? . . .

. . . In November 1876 the telephone refused to cough up an intelligible sentence, "it didn't talk distinctly enough for practical use." Watson was getting desperate. So "one day in a fit of desperation, remembering my experience with the 'spirits' and being still of the belief that it really was spirits that did the table tipping and slate writing, I decided to consult a medium (without Bell's knowledge) and see if there was any help to be got from that source." Clearly, the ghosts have to be endeavored without Bell's knowledge, for Bell refuses to affiliate himself with this branch of telephonic epistemology. Watson, for his part, was reduced to tracking down a medium through newspaper announcements, having lost recourse to a mother of a best friend or any other familiar conductor of electric knowledge. "She gave me such rubbish I never afterwards tried to get the spirits to give the telephone a boost." This stands as the last recording of an attempt to levitate the telephone by means of outside mediums. From then on, they would be installed within the instrument.

. . . The telephone created agitation, doubt, and anxiety among those not specially stamped and delivered to the laboratory. "I don't believe any new invention to-day could stir the public so deeply as the telephone did then, surfeited as we have been with the many wonderful things that have since been invented." Bell presented the telephone first in the Salem lectures, followed by one in Providence, Rhode Island. Boston, New York, and the cities of New England soon followed. They were all given in the spring and summer of 1877. We detect to what extent Watson is still telling ghost stories.

I played an important part in Bell's lectures although I was always invisible to his audience, being stationed every evening at the distant end of a telegraph wire connecting with the hall, having in my charge apparatus to generate the various telephone phenomena Bell needed to illustrate his lectures. I had at the end of the line one of our loudest telephones especially adapted for the purpose, an electric organ on the principal of Bell's harmonic telegraph, a cornet player and sometimes a small brass band. But I was the star illustrator of Bell's lectures. My function was to prove to the audiences that the telephone could really talk, for which my two years of shouting into telephones of all sizes and shapes had fitted me admirably as it had developed in me a vocal power approximating that of a steam organ in a circus parade. I also had to do something else of importance for Bell's audience, called by courtesy, singing.

The invisible mouthpiece to Bell's audience, Watson would sing "Do Not Trust Him, Gentle Lady," which we should keep in mind as part of the repertoire of the telephone's early recitals. The inmixation of séance, dissimulation, music concert, magic show, scientific display, and operating theater prevails in the descriptive passages of Watson's invisible acts.

Professor Bell had by his side on the stage a telephone of the "big box variety we used at that time, and three or four others of the same type were suspended about the hall, all connected by means of a hired telegraph wire with the place where I was stationed, from five to twenty-five miles away." During the first part of his lecture Bell gave his audience the commonplace part of the show, organ playing, cornet music, the brass band, more of the same, "and then came the thrillers of the evening—my shouts and songs. I shouted such sentences as, 'Good evening,' 'How do you do?' 'What do you think of the telephone?' [this question being destined for us, here, now], which the audience could hear, although the words issued from the mouthpiece rather badly blurred by the defective talking powers of the telephones of that date." Then Watson would sing the songs he knew. "They were 'Hold the Fort,' 'Pull for the Shore' (I got these from Moody and Sankey who had just come to this country), 'Yankee Doodle,' 'Auld Lang Syne,' and a sentimental song I had learned somewhere called, 'Do Not Trust Him, Gentle Lady.' My singing was always a hit. The telephone obscured its defects and gave it a mystic touch. After each of my songs I would listen at my telephone for further directions from the lecturer and always felt the thrill of the artist when I heard the applause that showed me how much the audience appreciated my efforts. I was usually encored to the limit of my repertory." As performing artist, the telephone, like the schizo or a professor, speaks to a full house of anonymous listeners with unknowable identities.

Personal Service in the Bell System

VENUS GREEN

Technically unreliable equipment and usage by a skeptical public gave rise to the need for telephone switchboards, operators, and their services. During the telephone's first two years (1876–78), subscribers made their own connections by picking up the

From Venus Green, "The Decline of 'Personal Service' in the Bell System," *Technology and Culture:* October 1995, Vol. 36, No. 4, pp. 916–949. Copyright © 1995 by The Society for the History of Technology. Reprinted by permission of The University of Chicago Press.

phone and talking directly to the person called (usually signified by the number of rings). One wire connected each subscriber to the other, so there were as many wires as each subscriber had access to other people. Technicians invented exchange systems and switchboards so that all lines would come into a central office where they could be connected to other lines through a switchboard, eliminating all except one wire (or later a pair of wires) to the subscriber. Subscribers simply cranked up their magneto generators (used until common battery power became available) and waited for the operator. At the switchboards, operators performed various physical motions to connect the calls. Alone, however, these switchboard operations hardly convinced an incredulous public of the telephone's usefulness.

In its infancy, telephony competed with the telegraph as a method of communication, and telephone companies competed among themselves for hegemony over the entire business. The telephone industry realized that it would have to expand the functions of a telephone exchange beyond a simple connection. Even before the preference for female operators had been completely determined, telephone managers catered to the special needs of businessmen. In 1880, for example, the Metropolitan Telephone and Telegraph Company of New York City devoted an exchange of 58 Broadway almost exclusively to the service of "bankers and brokers" and one at 38 Whitehall Street to "produce and commission merchants." Specialized attention quickly developed into a profitable means of attracting new customers. Within the context of industrial expansion and competition, the meaning of telephone service changed from the simple notion of connecting two lines to providing an assortment of conveniences.

At the National Telephone Exchange Association meeting in April 1881, C. C. Haskins of the American District Telephone Company of Chicago presented a paper to executives from Bell and the independent telephone companies in which he defined "anything which may demand the service of the exchange instruments . . . as an auxiliary system; or at least *an auxiliary service.*" Auxiliary services provided by his company included "sending for a third party for the purpose of communication, the use of a messenger to convey a written message which has been transmitted by telephone, calling for police, the fire department, a carriage of physician" and the "summoning of a lawyer to attend a case in court." Exchange connections with a system of burglar alarms and a "*watch signal service,* by which a constant check (was) held over private watchmen in charge of property belonging to subscribers" could also be obtained. And, on a more individual level, "parties desiring to be called at an unusual hour in the day, either by telephone bell or by a messenger, have repeatedly availed themselves of this method for ensuring their engagements."

Other companies supplied "reserved seats for places of amusement" (i.e., theater tickets), notification of the precise time in Connecticut manufacturing communities, special lines for rural areas, and, for San Francisco's subscribers, an information bureau. Most Bell companies provided messenger service, news, racing results, time, weather, election results, football and baseball scores, and other auxiliary services at a minimum charge or none at all.

Some managers questioned the profitability of connecting fire alarm systems, but the majority agreed with W. H. Eckert of Cincinnati who drew attention to the long-range profits obtainable from the good public relations generated by auxiliary services. He stated: "We cannot afford to put ourselves in an awkward position as against the fire department or the insurance people. I have found that by making love to them I am making love to our profits in about the same proportion. It increases our subscribers and puts everybody on the side of the telephone." Consequently, managers expected the first operators, regardless of gender, to possess the necessary skills both to manipulate the switchboard and to stimulate goodwill among the subscribers.

Faced with competition and severe equipment problems, Bell executives quickly transformed auxiliary services into "personal service" as a means to capture and dominate the industry. For the Bell manager, "the personalization of the service (meant) . . . a service that is not only as nearly perfect technically as possible, but that is as pleasing as possible to the telephone user." In the early years, however, the imperfect equipment impeded connection services and the "pleasing" aspect became an important method of attracting new customers and soothing old ones frustrated by the constant technical problems. The pleasing aspect would transcend superficial niceties to give the subscriber service of substance. Personal service meant that each subscriber could immediately reach an operator who would accommodate his demands. And, equally significant, the subscribers would not be required to exert themselves a great deal to receive the service. Bell companies aimed to distinguish their services by offering businessmen attention similar to that given by domestic servants in the 19th-century home—efficient, confidential, and above all courteous.

In this era, executives believed that girls, socialized to defer on the basis of class, gender, and age, best qualified to give the kind of service Bell envisioned. Managers created a social and cultural relationship with the customers by employing young, single, native-born white women to cater to bourgeois concepts about servitude. Usually denied access to technologies, women, Marvin postulates, could have been hired only on the basis of these notions about class. It was necessary, she posits, "to make clear" that the "accommodating" telephone girl "was only a servant, not truly a member of the class to whose secrets she had access." Philadelphia managers, struck with this image of servitude, required operators "to wear a black uniform throughout summer and winter, with small, short, white aprons." . . .

The operator's role as a servant whose responsibility was to "satisfy" the "peculiarities" of each subscriber is also indicated by the Bell System's commitment to requiring the subscriber to work as little as possible when using the telephone. . . .

At their earliest meetings and conferences and in every form of company literature (instruction manuals, pamphlets, company newspapers and magazines, and circulars), telephone managers emphasized the importance of courtesy. As New York Telephone Traffic Manager J. L. Turner explained: "The words used by the operator are almost entirely prescribed in her rules. It is the voice expression, therefore, that she must supply in order to convey to the subscriber . . . the idea of pleasing and intelligent service as well as the mere courtesy of the operator." The operator should be "able to answer in such a manner that her subscriber immediately responds with a feeling of pleasure, whether expressed in so many words or not, 'Aha! There's my obliging operator. *She'll* give me what I want.'" If the operator could not oblige the subscriber, another emotion had to be communicated. When she said "Cortlandt 5-9-8-0 is *busy*" it would be with a sympathetic tone to convey "I am *sorry,* Mr. Smith, But I cannot give you what you want."

Customers rewarded many operators with letters of appreciation and gifts, while they punished others with complaints according to their perception of competence.

Pioneer operator Jessie Mix remembered that businessmen "used to send us boxes of candy and flowers and drop in to see us from time to time, and on occasions some of the livery stables, like Barker and Ransom's, would put a horse and carriage or sleigh at our disposal, and take the girls on a picnic." Another pioneer operator recalled that "boxes of candy, bottles of perfume, flowers, gloves, handkerchiefs, groceries and even turkeys were among the more common gifts." Eventually the telephone companies officially stopped this practice, yet it continued well into the 20th century in small towns, isolated communities, and even parts of some large cities.

But it is subscribers' complaints, rather than their generosity, that demonstrate more fully what they expected from the telephone exchange. With regard to call connecting, subscribers vigorously complained about slow pickups and disconnects, cutoffs, wrong numbers, false busies, no answers, and discourteous or impertinent behavior. . . .

However, subscribers resisted attempts to appease their grievances against structural and organizational changes that required work on their part. For example, they objected to having to re-call the operator whenever they reached a busy line or received no answer. They wanted telephone operators to call them back on busies and no answers long after the growth of telephone service and technological development had made this impractical. Subscribers also opposed calling by number instead of names. They did not want the responsibility of looking for numbers in the directory. Even though operators in larger exchanges had been instructed by the late 1880s to make connections by numbers only, subscribers continued to resist.

In 1902, for example, a *Boston Post* article criticized New England Telephone and Telegraph Company's rule about connecting by number only. Insisting that operators knew the most frequently called numbers anyway, the *Post* concluded that "the rule will break down of its own weight. It is easier for an operator to make the connection than to waste time arguing with the subscriber." As late as 1911, D. Lewis Dorroh, a lawyer from Greenville, South Carolina, sued Southern Bell Telephone and Telegraph Company over this issue. . . .

Dorroh and other subscribers' sense of entitlement had not only been encouraged by the company, it also had been nurtured by the operators. Frances Oberbeck, who began her telephone career in 1883 at St. Louis, explained that the early central office operators had "a general understanding that everyone was to do her best. We were all intensely loyal to the company." The pioneer operators encouraged subscribers to depend on them for services that exceeded call processing. Operators knew each customer by name, business, and personal needs. Some knew their customers' morning telephone routines so well they sequentially called each person the subscribers spoke with daily without being told to do so.

When businessmen placed phones in their homes, their wives often demanded a variety of domestic chores from the telephone operator. Occasionally, "mothers who wished to go out for afternoon tea or a meeting of the 'Dorcas Society' would leave their babies near the telephone with the receiver off, optimistically hoping that if the infant awoke . . . , it would cry and the operator . . . would call up the mother at the scene of the festivities." More frequently, the housewife would ask to have herself awakened from an afternoon nap. And when the housewife expected visitors who would not leave unless the telephone rang, she simply "prearranged calls from obliging operators." Bell System literature often boasted about the many domestic favors operators provided during the early days, and no evidence has been found to suggest that the operators objected to these menial tasks.

Indeed, operator's reminiscences record their willingness to go beyond the normal call of duty. Miss E. Newell of Stockton, California, recalled that operators adhered to the motto: "Give Service, no matter what happens!" There are accounts of heroism by operators who saved lives and property in situations which called for immediate, intelligent, and calm decision making. Operators halted robberies, attempted murders, and other crimes by quickly alerting the authorities. They saved hundreds of lives by calling doctors in acute medical situations and by alerting communities to impending dangers such as fires, floods, and hurricanes. Many operators lost their own lives by refusing to leave the switchboard before they warned everyone of an emergency. One famous story is that of Sarah J. Rooke of Folsom, New Mexico, who in August of 1908 remained at her switchboard notifying the village of an advancing flood until she was swept away. Neighbors found her body several miles below the village with "the headpiece, worn by telephone operators, still gripped [to] her ear." Operators sincerely felt the devotion and selflessness required to give personal service.

Women who put their "personal" in personal service thereby gave the Bell companies an edge against competitors. Bell managers used the idea of servitude as a marketing tool to expand their business. Bourgeois subscribers, accustomed to having servants, bought telephone service based on the expectation that operators would serve. And operators internalized these expectations and behaved accordingly. This cultural system resisted the change implicit in the dial system. As we shall see, the introduction of dial occurred when the most significant aspects of the subscribers' and the managers' cultural expectations regarding telephone service had nearly disintegrated.

Although imperfect in conception and implementation, the idea of automatic systems arose almost simultaneously with manual systems. M. D. Connolly, T. A. Connolly, and Thomas J. McTighe received the first patent for an automatic system in 1879, only a year after the first successful manual exchanges had been put into operation. This system never actually operated on a commercial scale, but it did establish a foundation for later work. Indeed, technicians patented and offered for sale more than eighty-six automatic systems, devices, and improvements between 1879 and 1898. Bell patent attorney Thomas D. Lockwood reviewed many of these new systems and approved the purchase of some as a safeguard against the future. Lockwood remained convinced, however, that automatic switching lacked any immediate value and that manual systems were inherently superior. Nonetheless, Bell executives, cognizant of the many claims made by inventors of automatic features, permitted their own engineers to work on various design projects for such features.

At first, Bell System engineers invented various types of automatics in an attempt to solve the high cost of providing service to small towns where there were not enough customers to justify the salary of an operator or even twenty-four-hour service. . . . At this time, Bell managers viewed automatic switching systems as temporary measures to provide service for thirty to forty-five subscribers. Such systems would inevitably be replaced by full manual systems when the number of subscribers exceeded these limits.

. . . Bell managers resisted automation because they were convinced that manual switching was technically superior and that an operator was needed to deliver high-quality personal service.

Not everyone, however, viewed depersonalization in negative terms. On the expiration of the Bell patents in 1894, independent companies hastily installed automatic exchanges to provide more formidable opposition to the Bell monopoly. In 1889 Almon B. Strowger (1839–1902), a schoolteacher turned undertaker who was reputedly angered by what he felt was too much personal contact, invented an automatic exchange for the elimination of operators. One version of the story claims that "he heard that one of his friends had died, and was very put out by the family's failure to turn to him to make the funeral arrangements. He conceived a strong animosity to telephone operators, suspecting them of having diverted the call of the bereaved family to one of his competitors, and he decided on a drastic remedy, to do away with telephone operators altogether." . . .

Since the first Strowger systems did not include dials, subscribers had to perform a number of operations to complete a call, pushing ones, tens, or hundreds buttons a specified number of times to register the number of the subscriber they wanted to call. Once the correct buttons had been pushed, the subscriber operated another button to ring the recipient. At the conclusion of the conversations, the subscriber pushed a button and hung up the receiver. Independents introduced dials in 1896, but the Bell System regarded the operation of dials as a considerable amount of work for the subscriber.

. . . Snubbed by the Bell System, Strowger allied with two other inventors to form what became the largest and most successful automatic telephone company and telephone equipment manufacturer in the United States, the Strowger Automatic Telephone Exchange. On November 3, 1892, the first commercial Strowger automatic exchange was installed at La Porte, Indiana. This system and its numerous improvements established the foundation for all automatic equipment of the step-by-step type.

Summarizing a report on the Romaine-Callender Automatic Exchange, Lockwood suggested to President Hudson that Bell "decline to identify . . . with the invention" because

> . . . the mechanism must be more costly than ordinary mechanism.
> . . . the said machine is inherently complex in the extreme.
>
> The increased complexity involves increased liability to get out of order, and this in turn makes the practically constant attendance of a skilled artisan a necessity.
>
> The strongest assertion made in behalf of the economy of such apparatus is that by its use, the operator may be dispensed with.
>
> But the operator is not a very costly appliance, considering that she brings to her work (theoretically at least) a modicum of human intelligence, and introduces elements conspicuous only by their absence in the automatic apparatus, to wit, elasticity of operation, the power of meeting irregular and chance contingencies, and the power of dealing with the public.

Most Bell System managers agreed with Lockwood that in exchange for the elimination of low-paid operators the first automatics entailed higher installation and maintenance costs due to the wages paid to skilled craftsmen, unreliable equipment, and limited types of services. Of course, "the power of dealing with the public" still concerned managers in 1893. While AT&T's long-distance, toll, and other services continued to require operators, independents could and did achieve savings because they operated few toll lines and provided no long-distance service. Economically, according to Lockwood, automatics were "no saving." . . .

Even without automatic switching, new machinery eroded many aspects of personal service. Aside from speeding up the operators' work pace and therefore increasing productivity, the introduction of various technical innovations significantly changed everything about operating, including the workday, training, discipline, and working conditions. One of the first noticeable changes was the gradual shift in operators' responsibilities. A typical operator in 1885 reported to work, made her morning tests by checking each subscriber's line, placed calls by name (even in New York City), called back on busy and no-answer calls, listened in on conversations to ensure that people were talking (disconnecting them if they were not), and performed innumerable personal services. Depending on the type of manual board used, each operator handled calls for fifty to 100 subscribers.

The major changes in operators' work resulted from breakthroughs in switchboard development. The introduction of the "multiple" switchboard during the latter 1880s and early 1890s led to growth in the number of subscribers but partially removed the possibility of operators knowing each subscriber by name. Multiple switchboards could place as many as 10,000 subscribers within the reach of each operator. The operator could connect each of 100 subscribers (whose names she did know and for whom she was directly responsible) to any of the 9,900 others. On the multiples, operators connected calls by number. Using numbers instead of names distanced the operator from the subscriber and signified one of the earliest retreats from personalized service. When common battery power displaced magnetic generators in the mid-1890s, it also lessened contact between the operator and the subscriber by eliminating the need for the morning tests.

. . . Despite the impact of these changes on personal service, however, an important distinction in managerial motives requires clarification.

In the 19th century, management's aims in switchboard development were more complex than simply increasing the operators' productivity. Depersonalization occurred as a by-product of Bell's efforts to use new technologies to defeat competition. New switchboards required different operating techniques that sometimes distanced the operator from the subscriber. In this sense, managers sought control over the workplace more for service stability than for higher operator productivity. With better switchboards, operators provided better service. In the 20th century, however, managers deliberately used scientific management techniques and technology to depersonalize operators' work and thereby increase their productivity. As before, depersonalization was economically motivated, but the impact on the subscribers and the operators was different. Ultimately, depersonalization led to the collapse of any cultural link between the subscribers and the operators.

. . . In 1902, the Bell System opened its first formal training school, where it indoctrinated operators with the expectations of a rationalized/scientifically managed work environment. Aside from instruction in the physical operation of the switchboard, operators learned a specific group of verbal phrases to be used with subscribers. Although courtesy remained a requirement, there could be no deviation from these phrases.

The degree to which the Bell System sought to establish preset terminology had been demonstrated in 1899 when New York Telephone's Western Division superintendent called the Yonkers manager's attention "to the rule prohibiting the use of the word 'hello!' for any purpose or at any time." The word was "not only meaningless," according to the superintendent, "it [was] confusing to subscribers" and also "cause[d] delay in the service. Operators were instructed to respond to subscribers by saying "number, please." This helped to diminish the friendly and spontaneous exchanges that had been so important in the first years of telephony.

Even if operators had been allowed to speak freely, they would not have said much because they were also placed under strict time limitations. AT&T expected operators to answer calls with 5 seconds, but they accepted 10 seconds as "a reasonable standard of service." New York Telephone and other associated companies, faced with an immensely higher traffic than the long-distance company, had established a more strict standard by 1911. New York Telephone required operators to answer or disconnect calls within an average of 3.5 seconds. . . .

Codification of methods for enforcing new procedures and the technologies for detecting deviations from the code developed rapidly after 1900. For example, AT&T's rigidly specific "Traffic Department Operating Instructions" dated November 1, 1910, were five times larger than the broad guidelines of the 1897 "Rules for the Government and Information of the Employees." And the No. 1 Relay switchboard, the main distributing frame, automatic call distribution, and service observing procedures enabled managers to supervise operators technically as well as physically. Kathering M. Schmitt, manager of the first telephone operating school, stated that the uniformity of equipment completed in New York by 1901 led to a "uniformity of operating practices" which in turn made possible uniform training of operators.

Depersonalization, however, did not occur in a uniform pattern. Even among managers of the largest exchanges, the concept of personal service declined slowly. In 1904, for example, Philadelphia operators still re-called subscribers on all "busy" and "no answer" responses. William R. Driver, a local manager, explained: "If a subscriber makes a call and we receive it and acknowledge it, we are then his agent or servant to see that it is completed. The idea of his having to give us his order two or three times before we complete it for him, is treating the public and the subscriber in a very discourteous and unkind way." As late as 1907, the president of the entire Bell System, F. P. Fish, reiterated AT&T's position on automatic switching: "It is clear to us that the Automatic System is not desirable. It simply throws upon the subscriber the work which should be done and which can be better done at the central office. It is no more 'secret' than the Manual System. . . . There are many objections to the Automatic System, which I am satisfied are conclusive against it as compared with the Manual System. Yet despite these objections to automatic systems the era of the friendly operator giving individualized attention and assorted information to subscribers was ending. . . .

. . . During the competitive era (1894–1914), the Bell System managers had many opportunities to voice their objections to total automation. In this period aggressive advertisements by independent telephone companies made extraordinary promises. The Automatic Telephone and Electric Company of Illinois, for example, claimed the following advantages: "Immediate connection with the number desired. . . . Entire absence of the frequent tedious delays occasioned by indifference of operators or inability to handle business as promptly as desired, and the equally frequent and un-satisfactory response to calls. 'They're busy.' . . . Absolute secrecy of conversation. . . . Continuous service, both day and night, . . . lower rental. . . . Perfect adaptability to the smallest towns and villages, as well as cities. . . . Impossibility of interruption or dis-connection during conversation. . . . [The independent phone companies' ads all] em-phasized the elimination of operators, reduced costs, and better transmission. . . .

Southern New England Telephone Company prepared a detailed brief against the Automatic Electric Company's campaign to win Connecticut over to automatic telephone service in 1904. . . .

As they attacked the independents . . . Southern New England managers clung to the necessity of having operators in the central office:

> The history of the manually operated switchboard abounds in instances where, in case of fire, assault and robbery, the manual operator has been able to summon assistance at all hours, day and night, and to bring to the aid of the subscriber, in such cases, the help of neighbors, of the police or of the fire department or of all of them together. . . .
>
> If there were no operator, and the automatic machinery at the subscriber's station and at the central office were employed, the would-be telephone user, who is oftentimes a mother or daughter or child, alone in the threatened household, would, in the excite-ment or danger of the moment, be unable to manipulate the automatic machinery and to do correctly all of the other things required before a call for help can be sent. This auto-matic system cannot be operated by the subscriber in the dark.

It is ironic that this argument was based on asserting the helplessness of females as it simultaneously affirmed the woman operator as the protector of the community at large.

Ma Bell's Road Trip

BRUNO LATOUR

As in Machiavelli's *Prince,* the progressive building up of an empire is a series of decisions about alliances: With whom can I collaborate? Whom should I write off? How can I make this one faithful? Is this other one reliable? Is this one a credible spokesperson? But what did not occur to Machiavelli is that these alliances can cut across the boundaries between human beings and "things." Every time an ally is abandoned, replacements need to be recruited; every time a sturdy link disrupts an alliance that would be useful, new elements should be brought in to break it apart and make use of the dismantled elements. These "machiavellian" strategies are made more visible when we follow scientists and engineers. Rather, we call "scientists" and "engineers" those subtle enough to include in the same repertoire of ploys human and non-human resources, thus increasing their margin for negotiation.

Take for instance the Bell Company. Telephone lines in the early days were able to carry a voice only a few kilometres. Beyond this limit the voice became garbled, full of static, inaudible. The message was corrupted and not transmitted. By "boosting" the

From Bruno Latour, *Science in Action* (Cambridge, MA: Harvard University Press, 1987), pp. 124–127, 130–121, 140, 142, 143.

signals every thirteen kilometres, the distance could be increased. In 1910, mechanical repeaters were invented to relay the message. But these costly and unreliable repeaters could be installed only on a few lines. The Bell Company was able to expand, but not very far, and certainly not through the desert, or the Great Plains of the United States where all sorts of small companies were thriving in the midst of complete chaos. Ma Bell, as it is nicknamed by Americans, was indeed in the business of linking people together, but with the mechanical repeater many people who might wish to pass through her network could not do so. An exhibition in San Francisco in 1913 offered Bell a challenge. What if we could link the West and the East Coast with one telephone line? Can you imagine that? A transcontinental line tying the US together and rendering Bell the indispensable go-between of a hundred million people, eliminating all the small companies? Alas, this is impossible because of the cost of the old repeater. It becomes the missing link in this new alliance planned between Ma Bell and everyone in the US. The project falls apart, becomes a dream. No transcontinental line for the time being. Better send your messages through the Post Office.

Jewett, one of the directors of Bell, looks for new possible alliances that will help the company out of its predicament. He remembers that he was taught by Millikan, when the latter was a young lecturer. Now a famous physicist, Millikan works on the electron, a new object at the time, that is slowly being built up in his laboratory. . . . One of the features of the electron is that it has little inertia. Jewett, who himself has a doctorate in physics, is ready for a little detour. Something which has no inertia loses little energy. Why not ask Millikan about a possible new repeater? Millikan's laboratory has nothing to offer, yet. Nothing ready for sale. No black box repeating long-distance messages cheaply and safely. What Millikan can do, however, is to lend Jewett a few of his best students, to whom Bell offers a well-equipped laboratory. At this point Millikan's physics is in part connected with Bell's fate, which is partly connected with the challenge of the San Francisco fair, according to a chain of translations. . . . Through a series of slight displacements, electrons, Bell, Millikan and the continental line are closer to one another than they were before. But it is still a mere juxtaposition. The Bell Company managers may soon realise that basic physics is good for physicists but not for businessmen; electrons may refuse to jump from one electrode of the new triodes to the next when the tension gets too high, and fill the vacuum with a blue cloud; the urge for a transcontinental line may no longer be felt by the Board of Directors.

This mere juxtaposition is transformed when Arnold, one of the recruited physicists, transforms a triode patented by another inventor. In a very high vacuum, even at very high tension, the slightest vibration at one end triggers a strong vibration at the other. A new object is then created through new trials in the newly opened laboratory: electrons that greatly amplify signals. This new electronic repeater is soon transformed into a black box by the collective work of Ma Bell, and incorporated as a routine piece of equipment in six locations along the 5500 kilometres of cable laid across the continent. In 1914, the transcontinental line, impossible with the other repeater, becomes real. Alexander Bell calls Mr. Watson, who is no longer downstairs but thousands of miles away. The Bell Company is now able to expand over the whole continent: consumers who had not before had the slightest interest in telephoning the other coast now routinely do so, passing through the Bell network and contributing to its expansion. . . . But the boundaries of physics have been transformed as well, from a few modestly equipped laboratories in universities to many well-endowed laboratories in industry; from now on many students could make a career in industrial physics. And Millikan? He has changed too, since many effects first stabilised in his lab are now routinely used along telephone lines, everywhere, thus providing his laboratory with a fantastic expansion. Something else has moved too. The electrons. The list of actions that defined their being has been dramatically increased when all these laboratories submitted them to new and unexpected trials. Domesticated electrons have been made to play a role in a convoluted alliance that allows the Bell Company to triumph over its rivals. In the end, each actor in this little story has been pushed out of its usual way and made to be different, because of the new alliances it has been forced to enter.

We, the laypeople, far away from the practice of science and the slow build-up of artefacts, have no idea of the versatility of the alliances scientists are ready to make. We keep nice clean boundaries that exclude 'irrelevant' elements: electrons have nothing to do with big business; microbes in laboratories have nothing to do with farms and cattle; Carnot's thermodynamics is infinitely far from submarines. And we are right. There is at first a vast distance between these elements; at the beginning they are indeed irrelevant. But "relevance" like everything else, can be *made*. How? By the series of translations I have sketched. When Jewett first fetches Millikan, the electrons are too feeble to have any easy connection with Ma Bell. At the end, inside the triode redesigned by Arnold, they reliably transmit Alexander Bell's order to Mr. Watson. The smaller companies might have thought that Ma Bell would never beat them since it was impossible to build a transcontinental line. This was counting *without* the electrons. By adding electrons and Millikan and his students and a new lab to the list of its allies, Ma Bell modifies the relations of forces. Where it was weak over longer distances, it is now stronger than anyone else.

We always feel it is important to decide *on the nature of the alliances*: are the elements human or non-human? Are they technical or scientific? Are they objective or subjective? Whereas the only question that really matters is the following: *is this new association weaker or stronger than that one.* . . .

The engineer's ability lies in multiplying the tricks that make each element interested in the working of the others. These elements may be freely chosen among human or non-human actors. . . .

It is now understandable why, since the beginning of this book, no distinction has been made between what is called a "scientific" fact and what is called a "technical" object or artefact. This division, although traditional and convenient, artificially cuts through the question of how to ally oneself to resist controversies. The problem of the builder of "fact" is the same as that of the builder of "objects": how to convince others, how to control their behaviour, how to gather sufficient resources in one place, how to have the claim or the object spread out in time and space. In both cases, it is others who have the power to transform the claim or the object into a durable whole. . . .

. . . *Understanding* what facts and machines are is the same task as understanding who the people are. If you describe the controlling elements that have been gathered together you will understand the groups which are controlled. Conversely, if you observe the new groups which are tied together, you will see how machines work and why facts are hard. The only question in common is to learn *which associations are stronger and which weaker.* We are never confronted with science, technology and society, but with a gamut of weaker and stronger associations. . . .

. . . [T]he reader may have noticed the shocking absence of the entities that traditionally make up Society. . . . [T]here has been not a word yet on social classes, on capitalism, on economic infrastructure, on big business, on gender, not a single discussion of culture, not even an allusion to the social impact of technology. This is not my fault. I suggested that we follow scientists and engineers at work and it turns out that *they do not know what society is made of,* any more than they know the nature of Nature beforehand. It is because they know about neither that they are so busy *trying out* new associations, creating an inside world in which to work, displacing interests, negotiating facts, reshuffling groups and recruiting new allies.

In their research work, they are never quite sure which association is going to hold and which one will give way. . . . There was nothing in the stable state of either Society or Nature that made an alliance of big business at Bell with electrons necessary or predictable. The Bell Company was deeply modified by its alliance with Millikan's physics, it was not the *same* Bell, but neither was it the same physics, the same Millikan nor, indeed, the same electrons. The versatility and the heterogeneity of the alliances is precisely what makes it possible for the researchers to get over the quandary of the fact-builder: how to interest people and to control their behaviour. When we study scientists and engineers at work, the only two questions that should not be raised are: What is Nature really like? What is Society really made of?

To raise these questions we have to wait until scientists and their allies—among whom social scientists should of course be included—have finished their work! Once the controversies have ended, then a stable state of Society, together with a stable rendering of the interests of its members, will emerge.

𝄞 *F U R T H E R   R E A D I N G*

Bernstein, Jeremy. *Three Degrees Above Zero: Bell Labs in the Information Age* (New York: G. Scribners, 1984).

Bruce, Robert V. *Bell: Alexander Graham Bell and the Conquest of Solitude* (Boston: Little, Brown, 1973).

Fishcer, Claude S. *America Calling: A Social History of the Telephone to 1940* (Berkeley, CA: University of California Press, 1992).

Israel, Paul, *From Machine Shop to Industrial Laboratory* (Baltimore: Johns Hopkins University Press, 1992).

Lipartito, Kenneth, "When Women Were Switches: Technology, Work, and Gender in the Telephone Industry, 1890–1920," *American Historical Review* 99 (1994).

Lubar, Steven, *InfoCulture* (Boston: Houghton Mifflin, 1993).

Martin, Michelle, *Hello Central?: Gender, Technology, and Culture in the Formation of Telephone Systems* (Montreal: McGill-Queen University Press, 1991).

Rakow, Lana F. *Gender on the Line: Women, the Telephone, and Community Life* (Urbana: University of Illinois Press, 1992).

Yates, JoAnne. *Control Through Communication: The Rise of System in American Management* (Baltimore: Johns Hopkins University Press, 1989).

CHAPTER 8

Inventing Efficiency: Scientific Management, ca 1900–1940

⋀⋀

The question of who should control the workplace, workers or employers, was one of the most hotly contested issues of the nineteenth century, and it remains so today. Although countless engineers and factory masters sought to "rationalize" the shop floor and exert greater management control, the name most frequently associated with such efforts is Frederick Winslow Taylor (1856–1916). Taylor grew up among Philadelphia's elite Quaker families. After briefly attending college, he withdrew to complete an apprenticeship as a patternmaker and machinist in 1878. Immediately afterward he went to work at the Midvale Steel Company. Owned by William Sellers, one of America's best-known machine tool builders and a close friend of Taylor's father, the Midvale works soon became a laboratory where the younger Taylor did some of his most innovative technical work. Among other things, he initiated a series of experiments on the development of self-hardening tool steels, an innovation that, when completed some twenty years later, revolutionized the design of machine tools and the speed at which they could operate.

During these years Taylor also became well acquainted with machine shop practices, including age-old customs by which machinists controlled the pace and duration of their work. "The shop," he later wrote, "was really run by the workers, and not by the bosses." His revulsion at worker control, coupled with his promotion to gang boss, prompted him to ask "Uncle William" Sellers "to spend some money in a careful, scientific study of the time required to do various kinds of work." His objective was to break soldiering and, through a series of strategic management changes, deliver fuller control to owners and their surrogates, industrial engineers.

Initial reaction to Taylor's system was mixed. Industrial unions, especially those that represented skilled workers, deplored it. But for some working women, scientific management seemed to promise more job opportunities at better wages. Engineers were initially divided. Perhaps because of the emphasis Taylor placed on its "scientific" aspect, academically trained engineers tended to be more favorably disposed than those trained on the shop floor. Division also existed among industrialists.

To some Taylor was a hero; to others he was a charlatan. Within military circles, however, Taylor's ideas met with approbation from the start. Long a proponent of system and uniformity, the U.S. Army Ordnance Department enthusiastically embraced Taylorism and introduced scientific management methods at the Rock Island, Illinois, and Watertown, Massachusetts, arsenals only to have them strongly opposed by arsenal workers. Strikes at these establishments in 1908 and 1911, coupled with vigorous lobbying by trade unions, eventually resulted in congressional prohibitions against time studies at all federal installations.

Taylor's most important alliance may have been cast in the worlds of law and politics. Boston attorney Louis D. Brandeis turned a floodlight on Taylorism when he argued, in 1910 and 1911, that instead of raising their rates, railroads could save a million dollars a day by adopting Taylor's methods. This caught the attention of journalists, and "scientific management"—a name newly coined for the system by Brandeis—achieved extraordinary public recognition. Taylor's emphasis on system, "rationality," "efficiency," and control captivated political and social reformers associated with the so-called Progressive movement of the early twentieth century. To many it seemed as if Taylor and his disciples had provided a magic formula. Middle-class reform—which had often been cast as good overcoming evil—became instead, in the words of one writer, "a technical question in which considerations of efficiency were important." Reformers would engineer society just as Taylor had engineered the workplace, by championing expert administration and active, interventionist initiatives at local, state, and eventually federal levels of government.

The heyday of Taylorism was relatively brief, occupying roughly the years between 1900 and America's entry into World War I in 1917. But the influence of scientific management extended well beyond the war years. It was built into the curricula of business schools and industrial and systems engineering programs at major universities. Although its most extreme political incarnation was the "technocracy" movement of the 1930s, the assumptions and language of scientific management became enmeshed in many types of twentieth-century "reform." Why did words and concepts initially used for machinery and machine processes come to have so large an influence on social and political concepts, and even on personal identity? What was considered "scientific" about Taylor's system? Given Taylor's belief that his system would lead to social harmony and prosperity, why were his ideas considered so threatening? How is technology related to management?

⚭ D O C U M E N T S

The first selection is from Frederick Taylor's *Principles of Scientific Management* (1911). Taylor claims that soldiering has a pernicious effect on productivity and advocates that management assert tighter control over the workplace.

Once publicized, Taylor's basic methods were widely applied. From laundry to janitorial work, no activity was too small or insignificant to be systematically studied and managed. The second selection, from Christine Frederick's *The New Housekeeping*, explains how a middle-class housewife could apply Taylor's ideas to the everyday details of cleaning, cooking, and child care. According to Frederick, the careful study and planning of one's household chores held the key to a "woman's liberation from drudgery."

Although Taylor and his disciples viewed scientific management as a means of bringing order and harmony to a disorderly world, union leaders like James O'Connell of the American Federation of Labor's International Association of Machinists considered it a serious threat. In the third selection, O'Connell voices his union's objections to Taylorism and urges his brothers to protest its introduction at government-owned arsenals. After striking against time studies at the Watertown Arsenal in 1911, arsenal workers submitted a petition (the fourth selection) to the secretary of war requesting that the Taylor system be discontinued.

The fifth selection, from 1937 textbook on scientific management, reports on a student project at the University of Iowa laundry.

In addition to formal resistance by unions, workers themselves sometimes resisted "efficiency experts" through ridicule. The sixth selection is a narrative by Henry Mitchell, a Penobscot Indian who worked at the Old Town Canoe Company in Old Town, Maine. The seventh is a "tall tale" about a character named "Highpockets" that made the rounds in Chicago during the 1930s. Although both stories point out the exploitative nature of Taylor's system, they also testify to the continued existence of what Taylor hoped to eliminate—a resilient shop-floor culture.

One of the most perceptive contemporary criticisms of scientific management came from a professor of political economy at Albion College in Michigan. In the eighth selection, Frank T. Carlton chides Taylor and his minions for their insensitive treatment of workers and, in effect, turns the tables by asking why they have not investigated the efficiency of the managers and corporations for whom they work. In Carlton's view, management as well as labor needed reform.

The Principles of Scientific Management, 1911

FREDERICK W. TAYLOR

President [Theodore] Roosevelt, in his address to the Governors at the White House, prophetically remarked that "The conservation of our national resources is only pre-liminary to the larger question of national efficiency."

The whole country at once recognized the importance of conserving our material resources and a large movement has been started which will be effective in accom-plishing this object. As yet, however, we have but vaguely appreciated the importance of "the larger question of increasing our national efficiency."

We can see our forests vanishing, our water-powers going to waste, our soil being carried by floods into the sea; and the end of our coal and our iron is in sight. But our larger wastes of human effort, which go on every day through such of our acts as are blundering, ill-directed, or inefficient, and which Mr. Roosevelt refers to as a lack of "national efficiency," are less visible, less tangible, and are but vaguely appreciated.

We can see and feel the waste of material things. Awkward, inefficient, or ill-directed movements of men, however, leave nothing visible or tangible behind them. Their appreciation calls for an act of memory, an effort of the imagination. And for this reason, even though our daily loss from this source is greater than from our waste of material things, the one has stirred us deeply, while the other has moved us but little.

As yet there has been no public agitation for "greater national efficiency," no meetings have been called to consider how this is to be brought about. And still there are signs that the need for greater efficiency is widely felt.

From Frederick W. Taylor, *The Principles of Scientific Management* (New York, W. W. Norton, 1967), pp. 5–7, 13–27, 36–39.

The search for better, for more competent men, from the presidents of our great companies down to our household servants, was never more vigorous than it is now. And more than ever before is the demand for competent men in excess of the supply.

What we are all looking for, however, is the ready-made, competent man; the man whom some one else has trained. It is only when we fully realize that our duty, as well as our opportunity, lies in systematically cooperating to train and to make this competent man, instead of in hunting for a man whom some one else has trained, that we shall be on the road to national efficiency.

In the past the prevailing idea has been well expressed in the saying that "Captains of industry are born, not made"; and the theory has been that if one could get the right man, methods could be safely left to him. In the future it will be appreciated that our leaders must be trained right as well as born right, and that no great man can (with the old system of personal management) hope to compete with a number of ordinary men who have been properly organized so as efficiently to cooperate.

In the past the man has been first; in the future the system must be first. This in no sense, however, implies that men are not needed. On the contrary, the first object of any good system must be that of developing first-class men; and under systematic management the best man rises to the top more certainly and more rapidly than ever before.

This paper has been written:

First. To point out, through a series of simple illustrations, the great loss which the whole country is suffering through inefficiency in almost all of our daily acts.

Second. To try to convince the reader that the remedy for this inefficiency lies in systematic management, rather than in searching for some unusual or extraordinary man.

Third. To prove that the best management is a true science, resting upon clearly defined laws, rules, and principles, as a foundation. And further to show that the fundamental principles of scientific management are applicable to all kinds of human activities, from our simplest individual acts to the work of our great corporations, which call for the most elaborate cooperation. And, briefly, through a series of illustrations, to convince the reader that whenever these principles are correctly applied, results must follow which are truly astounding. . . .

These principles appear to be so self-evident that many men may think it almost childish to state them. Let us, however, turn to the facts, as they actually exist in this country and in England. The English and American peoples are the greatest sportsmen in the world. Whenever an American workman plays baseball, or an English workman plays cricket, it is safe to say that he strains every nerve to secure victory for his side. He does his very best to make the largest possible number of runs. The universal sentiment is so strong that any man who fails to give out all there is in him in sport is branded as a "quitter," and treated with contempt by those who are around him.

When the same workman returns to work on the following day, instead of using every effort to turn out the largest possible amount of work, in a majority of the cases this man deliberately plans to do as little as he safely can—to turn out far less work than he is well able to do—in many instances to do not more than one-third to one-half of a proper day's work. And in fact if he were to do his best to turn out his largest possible day's work, he would be abused by his fellow-workers for so doing, even more than if he had proved himself a "quitter" in sport. Underworking,

that is, deliberately working slowly so as to avoid doing a full day's work, "soldiering,"
as it is called in this country, "hanging it out," as it is called in England, "ca canae," as
it is called in Scotland, is almost universal in industrial establishments, and prevails
also to a large extent in the building trades; and the writer asserts without fear of contradiction that this constitutes the greatest evil with which the working-people of both
England and America are now afflicted.

It will be shown later in this paper that doing away with slow working and
"soldiering" in all its forms and so arranging the relations between employer and
employé that each workman will work to his very best advantage and at his best
speed, accompanied by the intimate cooperation with the management and the help
(which the workman should receive) from the management, would result on the
average in nearly doubling the output of each man and each machine. What other
reforms, among those which are being discussed by these two nations, could do as
much toward promoting prosperity, toward the diminution of poverty, and the alle-
viation of suffering? . . .

This paper will attempt to show the enormous gains which would result from
the substitution by our workmen of scientific rule-of-thumb methods.

. . . The great majority of workmen still believe that if they were to work at their
best speed they would be doing a great injustice to the whole trade by throwing a lot
of men out of work, and yet the history of the development of each trade shows that
each improvement, whether it be the invention of a new machine or the introduction
of a better method, which results in increasing the productive capacity of the men in
the trade and cheapening the costs, instead of throwing men out of work make in the
end work for more men.

The cheapening of any article in common use almost immediately results in a
largely increased demand for that article. Take the case of shoes, for instance. The
introduction of machinery for doing every element of the work which was formerly
done by hand has resulted in making shoes at a fraction of their former labor cost,
and in selling them so cheap that now almost every man, woman, and child in the
working-classes buys one or two pairs of shoes per year, and wears shoes all the
time, whereas formerly each workman bought perhaps one pair of shoes every five
years, and went barefoot most of the time, wearing shoes only as a luxury or as a
matter of the sternest necessity. . . .

As engineers and managers, we are more intimately acquainted with these facts
than any other class in the community, and are therefore best fitted to lead in a movement to combat this fallacious idea by educating not only the workmen but the whole
of the country as to the true facts. And yet we are practically doing nothing in this
direction, and are leaving this field entirely in the hands of the labor agitators (many
of whom are misinformed and misguided), and of sentimentalists who are ignorant
as to actual working conditions. . . .

[Taylor quotes from a 1903 paper entitled "Shop Management.] "[L]oafing or
soldiering proceeds from two causes. First, from the natural instinct and tendency of
men to take it easy, which may be called natural soldiering. Second, from more
intricate second thought and reasoning caused by their relations with other men,
which may be called systematic soldiering.

"There is no question that the tendency of the average man (in all walks of life)
is toward working at a slow, easy gait, and that it is only after a good deal of thought

and observation on his part or as a result of example, conscience, or external pressure that he takes a more rapid pace.

"There are, of course, men of unusual energy, vitality, and ambition who naturally choose the fastest gait, who set up their own standards, and who work hard, even though it may be against their best interests. But these few uncommon men only serve by forming a contrast to emphasize the tendency of the average.

"This common tendency to 'take it easy' is greatly increased by bringing a number of men together on similar work and at a uniform standard rate of pay by the day.

"Under this plan the better men gradually but surely slow down their gait to that of the poorest and least efficient. When a naturally energetic man works for a few days beside a lazy one, the logic of the situation is unanswerable.

"'Why should I work hard when that lazy fellow gets the same pay that I do and does only half as much work?'

"A careful time study of men working under these conditions will disclose facts which are ludicrous as well as pitiable.

"To illustrate: The writer has timed a naturally energetic workman who, while going and coming from work, would walk at a speed of from three to four miles per hour, and not infrequently trot home after a day's work. On arriving at his work he would immediately slow down to a speed of about one mile an hour. When, for example, wheeling a loaded wheelbarrow, he would go at a good fast pace even up hill in order to be as short a time as possible under load, and immediately on the return walk slow down to a mile an hour, improving every opportunity for delay short of actually sitting down. In order to be sure not to do more than his lazy neighbor, he would actually tire himself in his effort to go slow.

"These men were working under a foreman of good reputation and highly thought of by his employer, who, when his attention was called to this state of things, answered: 'Well, I can keep them from sitting down, but the devil can't make them get a move on while they are at work.'

"The natural laziness of men is serious, but by far the greatest evil from which both workmen and employers are suffering is the *systematic soldiering* which is almost universal under all of the ordinary schemes of management and which results from a careful study on the part of the workmen of what will promote their best interests.

"The writer was much interested recently in hearing one small but experienced golf caddy boy of twelve explaining to a green caddy, who had shown special energy and interests, the necessity of going slow and lagging behind his man when he came up to the ball, showing him that since they were paid by the hour, the faster they went the less money they got, and finally telling him that if he went too fast the other boys would give him a licking.

"This represents a type of *systematic soldiering* which is not, however, very serious, since it is done with the knowledge of the employer, who can quite easily break it up if he wishes.

"The greater part of the *systematic soldiering,* however, is done by the men with the deliberate object of keeping their employers ignorant of how fast work can be done.

"So universal is soldiering for this purpose that hardly a competent workman can be found in a large establishment, whether he works by the day or on piece work, contract work, or under any of the ordinary systems, who does not devote a considerable part of his time to studying just how slow he can work and still convince his employer that he is going at a good pace. . . .

"Unfortunately for the character of the workman, soldiering involves a deliberate attempt to mislead and deceive his employer, and thus upright and straightforward workmen are compelled to become more or less hypocritical. The employer is soon looked upon as an antagonist, if not an enemy, and the mutual confidence which should exist between a leader and his men, the enthusiasm, the feeling that they are all working for the same end and will share in the results is entirely lacking." . . .

[C]onsiderable space will later in this paper be devoted to illustrating the great gain, both to employers and employés, which results from the substitution of scientific for rule-of-thumb methods in even the smallest details of the work of every trade. The enormous saving of time and therefore increase in the output which it is possible to effect through eliminating unnecessary motions and substituting fast for slow and inefficient motions for the men working in any of our trades can be fully realized only after one has personally seen the improvement which results from a thorough motion and time study, made by a competent man.

To explain briefly: owing to the fact that the workmen in all of our trades have been taught the details of their work by observation of those immediately around them, there are many different ways in common use for doing the same thing, perhaps forty, fifty, or a hundred ways of doing each act in each trade, and for the same reason there is a great variety in the implements used for each class of work. Now, among the various methods and implements used in each element of each trade there is always one method and one implement which is quicker and better than any of the rest. And this one best method and best implement can only be discovered or developed through a scientific study and analysis of all of the methods and implements in use, together with accurate, minute, motion and time study. This involves the gradual substitution of science for rule of thumb throughout the mechanic arts.

This paper will show that the underlying philosophy of all of the old systems of management in common use makes it imperative that each workman shall be left with the final responsibility for doing his job practically as he thinks best, with comparatively little help and advice from the management. And it will also show that because of this isolation of workmen, it is in most cases impossible for the men working under these systems to do their work in accordance with the rules and laws of a science or art. . . .

The body of this paper will make it clear that, to work according to scientific laws, the management must take over and perform much of the work which is now left to the men; almost every act of the workman should be preceded by one or more preparatory acts of the management which enable him to do his work better and quicker than he otherwise could. And each man should daily be taught by and receive the most friendly help from those who are over him, instead of being, at the one extreme, driven or coerced by his bosses, and at the other left to his own unaided devices.

This close, intimate, personal cooperation between the management and the men is of the essence of modern scientific or task management. . . .

It is the writer's judgment, then, that while much can be done and should be done by writing and talking toward educating not only workmen, but all classes in the community, as to the importance of obtaining the maximum output of each man and each machine, it is only through the adoption of modern scientific management that this great problem can be finally solved. . . . Under scientific management the "initiative" of the workmen (that is, their hard work, their good-will, and their ingenuity) is obtained with absolute uniformity and to a greater extent than is possible under the old system; and in addition to this improvement on the part of the men, the managers assume new burdens, new duties, and responsibilities never dreamed of in the past. The managers assume, for instance, the burden of gathering together all of the traditional knowledge which in the past has been possessed by the workmen and then of classifying, tabulating, and reducing this knowledge to rules, laws, and formulæ which are immensely helpful to the workmen in doing their daily work. In addition to developing a *science* in this way, the management take on . . . other types of duties which involve new and heavy burdens for themselves. . . .

. . . They scientifically select and then train, teach, and develop the workman, whereas in the past he chose his own work and trained himself as best he could. . . .

. . . There is an almost equal division of the work and the responsibility between the management and the workmen. The management take over all work for which they are better fitted than the workmen, while in the past almost all of the work and the greater part of the responsibility were thrown upon the men.

It is this combination of the initiative of the workmen, coupled with the new types of work done by the management, that makes scientific management so much more efficient than the old plan. . . .

Thus all of the planning which under the old system was done by the workman, as a result of his personal experience, must of necessity under the new system be done by the management in accordance with the laws of the science; because even if the workman was well suited to the development and use of scientific data, it would be physically impossible for him to work at his machine and at a desk at the same time. It is also clear that in most cases one type of man is needed to plan ahead and an entirely different type to execute the work.

The man in the planning room, whose specialty under scientific management is planning ahead, invariably finds that the work can be done better and more economically by a subdivision of the labor; each act of each mechanic, for example, should be preceded by various preparatory acts done by other men. And all of this involves, as we have said, "an almost equal division of the responsibility and the work between the management and the workman."

To summarize: Under the management of "initiative and incentive" practically the whole problem is "up to the workman," while under scientific management fully one-half of the problem is "up to the management."

Perhaps the most prominent single element in modern scientific management is the task idea. The work of every workman is fully planned out by the management at least one day in advance, and each man receives in most cases complete written instructions, describing in detail the task which he is to accomplish, as well as the means to be used in doing the work. And the work planned in advance in this way constitutes a task which is to be solved, as explained above, not by the workman alone, but in almost all cases by the joint effort of the workman and the management. This task specifies not only what is to be done but how it is to be done and the exact time allowed for doing it. And whenever the workman succeeds in doing his task right, and within the time limit specified, he receives an addition of from 30 per cent. to 100 per cent. to his ordinary wages. These tasks are carefully planned, so that both good and careful work are called for in their performance, but it should be distinctly understood that in no case is the workman called upon to work at a pace which would be injurious to his health. The task is always so regulated that the man who is well suited to his job will thrive while working at this rate during a long term of years and grow happier and more prosperous, instead of being overworked. Scientific management consists very largely in preparing for and carrying out these tasks.

The New Housekeeping, 1913

CHRISTINE FREDERICK

"George," I said, "that efficiency gospel is going to mean a great deal to modern housekeeping, in spite of some doubts I have. Do you know that I am going to work out those principles here in our home! I won't have you men doing all the great and noble things! I'm going to find out how these experts conduct investigations, and all about it, and then apply it to *my* factory, *my* business, *my* home."

The more I thought about it, the stronger hold the idea took upon me. Just a few days previous I had been reading an article by a prominent clubwoman who was solving the servant problem by substituting expensive household equipment in place of her three servants. Another review discussed the number of women who were living in apartments and boarding-houses, and who refused to shoulder the burdens of real homemaking. A third writer enlarged on the lack of youthful marriages, a lack which he claimed was due to the fact that young women of this era refuse to enter the drudgery of household tasks. On all sides it was the problem of the home, the problem of housekeeping and homemaking.

The home problem for the woman of wealth is simple: it is *solved.* Money, enough of it, will always buy service, just as it can procure the best in any other regard. The home problem for the women of the very poor is also fairly simple. The women of the poor themselves come from the class of servants. Their homemaking is far less complex, their tastes simple, and society demands no appearance-standard from them. Added to this, organized philanthropy *is* by every means teaching the women of the poor how to keep house in the most scientific, efficient manner. Settlements, domestic science classes, model kitchens and tenements, nursing stations, slum depots, charity boards, health boards, visiting nurses, night schools, and mission classes are teaching, *free,* the women of the poor how to transmute their old-world ignorance into the shining knowledge of the new hemisphere.

The problem, the real issue, confronts the *middle-class woman* of slight strength and still slighter means, and of whom society expects so much—the wives of ministers on small salary, wives of bank clerks, shoe salesmen, college professors, and young men in various businesses starting to make their way. They are refined, educated women, many with a college or business training. They have one or more babies to care for, and limited finances to meet the situation.

The soaring cost of living and the necessity for keeping up a fair standard of appearances obligatory on the middle class prevent any but the more than "average"

From Christine Frederick, *The New Housekeeping* (Garden City, NY: Doubleday, Page & Co, 1913), pp. 10–13, 17–21, 35–42, 79, 89, 99–101.

well-to-do from employing regular help. Among ten average families I know (scattered the country over) whose incomes range from $1,200 to $2,500 a year . . . only one family of the ten employs regular help. The others depend on intermittent cleaning and a woman to do the washing. It is this better class of refined but small-salary-family woman who becomes "all tired out," who never has any "time to herself," or who is forced to endure the slipshod methods of one retreating Lizzie after another because she cannot afford experienced help. . . .

After Mr. Watson's [an "efficiency expert" at her husband's company] talk on efficiency I began to consider this middle class—to which I belong—and whose difficulties I faced every day. . . .

[Watson said:] "If the housewife would only realize it, there is more expert advice being offered her free than is being offered any manufacturer. Take the pages in all the best publications devoted to the science of home management. The finest specialists and experts are retained by magazines to tell women how to care for babies, prepare foods, how to economize and how to make clothing. Both the booklets and the advertisements of various advertisers inform the housewife of new methods, recipes, devices, materials. The so-called 'Farmers' Bulletins' issued by the Department of Agriculture are many of them equal to a correspondence course in home economics, as for instance, 'Eggs and Their Uses as Food,' 'Economical Cuts of Meats,' which are sent free to any one on application. Perhaps you do not know how to use your oven properly. Large corporations like the gas company and others are only too glad to send a representative to tell you just how to use your stove, and inform you on other points. I learned the other day that it costs a certain sum an hour for the large burner, so much for the smaller burner, and so much for the little 'simmerer.' This exact knowledge should help one to save fuel. Demonstrators of other concerns, food and household shows, all act as 'competent counsel' to the housewife and homemaker.

"Then comes Standardized Operations, which includes the oft-mentioned 'motion study,'" Mr. Watson continued. "The homemaker takes countless steps and motions in every task, many of which are entirely avoidable. She may walk twenty feet to hang up the egg-beater; she may wash dishes in a way that wastes time and effort; or she lifts separately each piece of laundry from the basket at her feet, when the efficient thing would be to place the whole basket at her own level. Standardized conditions mean the right height of work-table, proper light, ventilation, and the correct tool for the purpose. In shops and factories where the experts have studied the manner in which work is done, and where, after repeated experiment, the one best method and best set of conditions has been determined, this best, shortest and most efficient way is written down so that all workers may read it. That is, the task is reduced to 'standard practice,' and the housekeeper can find countless tasks which she can reduce to standard practice, with a saving of effort, time, and vitality."

"What is this next point of 'Dispatching'?" I asked. "I know the best way to do a number of things, but I never can plan my work so as to get it done without interruption. I begin to cut out a waist, and the children want a drink and I have to stop and get it, and when I come back my pattern and goods are all upset, and I have almost forgotten what I was dong."

"There," laughed Mr. Watson, "is just where you need the principles of 'dispatching,' and 'scheduling.' Planning and arranging work come under these points.

For instance, a train starts from New York at 4 P.M., and arrives at Chicago the next morning at nine. The 'dispatching' consists in moving the train along so that it will reach every station at the right time. Applied to housework it would mean that there was a definite regular time for each task, so that each task was done at a certain time in relation to other tasks. You wouldn't cut out your waist unless you were sure you wouldn't be interrupted, you see.

"The 'Schedule' is the eighteen hours it takes the train to reach Chicago, and it is based on various trials and methods which enable it to make Chicago in just eighteen hours and no less. A housewife can find out her schedules for various tasks, how long it takes to make a cake, or clean the bathroom. Then, when she knows her schedule, she can more accurately plan or dispatch her work without fear of interruption." . . .

"And if the remaining principles of 'Discipline,' 'Fair Deal' and 'Efficiency Reward' could be carried out in the home," he concluded, "I venture to say that this whole awesome 'servant problem' would be solved. One of the remarkable things about scientific management is that there have been few, if any, strikes in the shops where its principles are in practice. The men remain because they are treated fairly, and their interests looked out for by the owner.

"Ninety per cent. of servant troubles are at bottom the fault of the mistress," Mr. Watson declared. "Now if a woman knew and applied scientifically the principle of 'fair play' her help wouldn't leave her, sick, in bed, as I have heard some maids have done. An efficient mistress would handle her help as scientifically as the manager of a big shop. She will use the principle of 'efficiency reward' with her helpers, and know how to secure from them that 'initiative.'" . . .

Even the simplest one-process tasks may be standardized. . . . One of the most common of tasks is to beat eggs, whip cream, or mix a cake batter. In each of these cases, the general way is to have the ingredients in a bowl, using the right hand to beat or manipulate the spoon or egg whip, while the left hand holds the bowl steady. We have become so accustomed to steadying a bowl in this way, with the left hand, that we can hardly believe such a method is extremely inefficient. It requires a strong and steady hold on the bowl to keep it at the proper slant or purchase for beating its contents. Why waste energy in keeping a utensil in place when we can easily clamp any bowl or glass churn to the table, and save the wasted motion of holding the utensil in place for the real task of beating or whipping? . . .

Another form of waste motion occurs in the bringing together of the proper ingredients, utensils and materials in one place, *before* the real task begins. The efficiency engineers who study conditions in factories watch a man at work. They note how much time it takes him to do the actual work. They time him on how long it takes him to bring his tools together, and how long it takes him to put the finished work away.

Supposing it should take a man ten minutes to do a piece of work. If he does it in ten minutes, he will have an efficiency of approximately 100 per cent. But if it takes him four unnecessary minutes to bring his tools together, or to lay his work away, his efficiency will be lowered to 71 per cent. The whole aim, of course, is to have the efficiency of the worker as near 100 per cent. as possible.

I know dozens of women who would be graded 100 per cent. on the actual time they take in making a cake, or doing other tasks: but they waste motion—and hence time—bringing utensils and materials together before they begin the actual task;

instead of grouping flour and flavouring, baking-powder, eggs and sugar all on the table at once, they beat the egg then stop and get the sugar, then reach for the flavouring, and possibly have to go for the forgotten cup of milk in the icebox.

Another most important cause of waste motion in the kitchen is poor arrangement of utensils, not only with regard to a particular task, but with regard to all tasks, and other equipment. This is a point given great emphasis by efficiency engineers. Whole factories have been remodelled so that the machines could be in a right position, not only for the individual worker, but in right relation to other equipment and processes of the factory. . . .

In shops and factories the efficiency engineers make "time studies" of the work of the men, down to the fraction of a second, and on these studies the wages of the men are determined. Such detail is not needed in the house, but the object of our standardization in the home also is to find out the shortest, or more properly the average, time it takes us to perform any given task. When I know how long it takes me to do some of my common tasks, I can the better plan my entire work along "schedule" lines.

Here is a list of some of the common tasks I do, and how long each requires, working under "standard" conditions:

Task	*Time required*
Baby's bath.	15 minutes
Working bread (3 operations)	12 minutes
Mix layer cake	10 minutes
Ice layer cake	5 minutes
Salad dressing.	15 minutes
Pudding or dessert	12–15 minutes
Dust, brush up five small rooms daily	30 minutes
Mix pan of muffins.	6 minutes
Mix pan of biscuit.	8 minutes
Make pie.	10–12 minutes
Polish silver	40 minutes
Clean bathroom	20 minutes

A last cause of waste motion is the use of the inefficient or wrong tool. I have often used a chopping bowl and knife, and it took me seven minutes to chop one pound of cooked meat. The person using a chopping knife raises and lowers his knife as he chops, and half the time he is not chopping meat, but air. Now with a meat chopper of family size I can grind three pounds of meat in one minute. That is because I am grinding meat all the time, and air none of the time, and because there is no wasted motion of raised and lowered arm fifty times or more.

It is very often true that an improved labour-saver or household device is able to standardize work better than any method. This is true of a chopper, of a vacuum cleaner, which takes the place of both broom and duster, of a gas or electric iron, which saves the repeated motion of changing irons, and of other equipment. But too many women put over-emphasis on the tool and too little on themselves. If a woman is inefficient, how can she use a tool except in an inefficient way? I believe strongly that woman's liberation from drudgery lies not so much in tools as in her own improved methods of work. . . .

For instance, in improving my method of dishwashing, I did buy several small tools to render the work more efficient. But was that the main factor in making the work easier, and causing it to require less time? The important thing was *the way* the dishes were handled, the position of the sink, the height of the sink, the method of sorting, etc. . . .

I have not dwelt on the devices that use electricity. It is true that electricity has transformed our whole modern life, and many people look to the electrically equipped home as a solution of the servantless household. I am enthusiastic in favor of electric equipment, but from observation I have found it is, as yet, too expensive to supplant hand power in the operations of devices in the home. It is also true that while city dwellers have come to believe in the prevalence of the electric button, electricity is actually in use by only a fraction of our population. Until current can be supplied at a cheaper rate per kilo than at present, I feel it cannot be a great factor in reducing household expense, especially for a large or moderate size family. . . .

Some of my friends laugh at what they call my "schedule babies," because their hours for sleep and food and play are quite regular. But the fact remains that babies are not such a care as some women make of them. Most normally healthy babies can be trained easily to regular habits. My babies, on "schedule" feedings, have awakened at the very minute by the clock! And, trained as mine are to go to bed early, I can hardly keep them awake later than the regular hour. Much of the excitement and fuss from so-called "restless" children is due not so much to the children as to the mothers themselves and *their* irregular habits. . . .

Some women may also say that because I do sewing and other tasks in this apparently formal manner, that I am reducing them to bare mechanical processes, and robbing them of their beauty and that "home touch" which has been praised for ages. That is just what I do not do. I put into them all the inspiration and love which any task must receive to be other than mere factory work. So many women say, "I don't want to run my home like an office or a factory. I want it to be a *home.* I hate system and methods, and all this efficiency idea seems to be too mechanical and formal for me to follow."

But these same women and hosts of others are continually talking about home drudgery. If they have been doing all these home tasks all these centuries in such a beautiful and poetic way, why is it that women are fleeing from housework into professions and outside work? Why are they living lazily in coöperative apartments, eating delicatessen meals, and refusing to assume the burdens of motherhood?

"Motherliness" and "hominess" in the past usually have meant drudgery. True and better homemaking will come from a higher realization of the tremendous possibilities of the homemaker who uses scientific methods instead of rule-of-thumb. If housework is drudgery to a woman it is only because that woman refuses to accept the efficient methods and improved equipment offered her on every hand. It is just as stimulating to bake a sponge cake on a six-minute schedule as it is to monotonously address envelopes for three hours in a downtown office.

A Trade Unionist Attacks Taylorism, 1911

JAMES O'CONNELL

Affiliated with the American Federation of Labor.
International Association of Machinists,
Office of International President,

404–407 McGill Building, Washington, D.C., April 26, 1911.

Official circular No. 12.

To the order everywhere, greeting:

It has been the purpose of the grand lodge in the past to raise a warning voice whenever dangers have arisen which would affect our craft, and to point the way to safety. Through the efforts of our organization the machinists' trade has been raised to a higher level, as far as wages and conditions of labor are concerned, than otherwise would have obtained.

Wherever a high-paid class of labor exists by reason of organization and skill combined it has had the effect of stimulating the inventive genius of employers to find ways to eliminating skill and with it the high-priced mechanic and substituting common laborers with corresponding low wages.

The latest danger, and the one we propose to deal with in this letter, is the so-called Taylor system of shop management. Mr. Taylor, the originator of this system, is a former master mechanic of the Midvale Steel Co., Philadelphia, Pa., and is well qualified by disposition and education to undertake to undermine our trade. His system is very insidious in the process of installation and operation, it being his plan to install it slowly, and by a process of selecting workmen, he will have it in full operation in a shop in the time it takes him to select a body of docile, nonresisting workmen.

Mr. Taylor's system, as applied to the machinist trade, in brief, is as follows:

1. Instead of having a general foreman in a shop, he has four specialized shop foremen, each of whom performs a specified part of a foreman's job. They are called the "speed boss," "gang boss," "repair boss," and "inspector boss." These jobs are given out as plums to machinists who are willing to act as pacemakers.

2. Instead of machinists using their judgment in doing their work, Mr. Taylor has a "planning department," which furnishes the machinist with an "instruction card" similar to a drawing, telling him exactly what feeds, speeds, tools, and machines to use; how to hold the work, etc., leaving nothing to the workman's judgment. This eliminates skill and common laborers are used.

3. Instead of relying on the honor of the machinists, together with the watchfulness of the foreman as a means of getting a fair day's work from the men, Mr. Taylor holds a stop watch on the best workman while working fast, and leaves out the time on all such movements as he thinks is unnecessary. The result forms a standard for a

From Clarence B. Thompson, *Scientific Management: A Collection of the More Significant Articles Describing the Taylor System of Management* (Cambridge, MA: Harvard University Press, 1914), pp. 783–785.

day's work. To get a man to work at a terrific pace is his method. He solves it something like this:

(a) Offering a bonus for reaching this maximum.

(b) Standardizing the movements of a workman, thus making an automaton of him.

(c) Fining the workman all the way from 1 cent to $60.

(d) Discharging all who fail to reach the maximum pace after a trial.

(e) Discharging the dissatisfied workman, and keeping those who will do as they are told.

(f) Offering the foreman a bonus to keep the men spurred up to the top speed.

(g) Installing piece work with a differential rate per piece, thus: If the maximum day's work is 10 pieces, and the workman many get, say, 35 cents a piece, or $3.50 per day, if he succeeds in completing the entire task. If, however, he fails to finish 10 pieces, even if he misses this limit by only a fraction of 1 piece, he gets only 25 cents a piece, or less than $2.50 per day. This gives a tremendous incentive to a man to exert himself to the utmost.

4. Instead of collective bargaining, Mr. Taylor insists upon individual agreement, and any insistence on organized labor methods will result in discharge.

Wherever this system has been tried it has resulted either in labor trouble and failure to install the system, or it has destroyed the labor organization and reduced the men to virtual slavery, and low wages, and has engendered such an air of suspicion among the men that each man regards every other man as a possible traitor and spy.

The present effort on the part of Mr. Taylor is to have his system installed in the Government arsenals and navy yards. He has been so successful that the War Department has decided to give his system a trial. This would give his methods a tremendous advertisement, and only be a short time until all private manufacturers throughout the country would adopt his system, since, with the public, the Government has the reputation of being a good employer. This is but another instance in which a good reputation is exploited for a despicable purpose. We do not know what motives the War Department has in the matter, but we do know that this proposed staggering blow at labor must be met by determined resistance.

The installation of the Taylor system throughout the country means one of two things, *i. e.,* either the machinists will succeed in destroying the usefulness of this system through resistance, or it will mean the wiping out of our trade and organization, with the accompanying low wages, life-destroying hard work, long hours, and intolerable conditions generally.

It is manifestly impossible in a short letter to explain the Taylor system satisfactorily, but let this letter serve as a warning to you to prepare for the struggle. . . .

We trust that you will be impressed with the importance of this matter, and will see the impending danger. Act quickly.

Yours fraternally,

JAS. O'CONNELL,
International President, International
Association of Machinists.

Arsenal Workers Strike, 1913

Watertown Arsenal, June 17, 1913.

Hon. Lindley M. Garrison,
Secretary of War, Washington, D.C.

DEAR SIR;—We, the undersigned, employees of the Government, representing 349 of a total of 373 hands employed in the various departments as indicated hereon, respectfully petition that the Taylor system, now in operation at this Arsenal, be immediately discontinued for the reasons as hereinafter set forth.

We object to the use of the Stop Watch, as it is used a means of speeding men up to a point beyond their normal capacity. It is humiliating and savors too much of the slave driver.

A comparison of the record of serious accidents occurring in the works since the introduction of the Stop Watch Premium System will convince the most skeptical that it is dangerous to limb and life, and we claim that a large percentage of these accidents are the direct result of the driving system in vogue at this Plant.

We believe that this System, instead of producing what was claimed it would produce—high wages to employees, with a low cost of production has worked exactly opposite inasmuch as the investigation into the wages paid (outside of premium) will show that there has been no material increase in wages, while the cost of production has been increased to such an extent that large deficits are being reported on nearly every job of any consequence that is done at this Arsenal.

The number of non-productive employees in proportion to the productive employees who are necessary to carry out the details of the System, has been largely responsible in the great increase in overhead expense, which in many cases, has resulted in the Government being unable to compete with outside concerns and has resulted in contracts being placed with outside parties to do work which the Arsenal is equipped to do and which, under normal conditions, could be done at a cost considerably under that charged by the Contractor securing the work. For instance, it has become the practice to let large contracts for manufacturing patterns, which the Arsenal is equipped to manufacture and could manufacture at a figure considerably below that charged by outside concerns; the quality of work being considered were it not burdened by an excessive overhead charge which must be carried to pay an abnormal non-productive force of employees.

We cite the above case to show that there is ground for our belief that the continuance of this System would finally eventuate in closing this Arsenal as a manufacturing Plant.

A large corps of inspectors are kept busy examining and rejecting material, and the number of pieces rejected since the Premium System was inaugurated has increased by a large percentage. The number of parts rejected since the System was installed will run well into the thousands.

From Clarence B. Thompson, *Scientific Management: A Collection of the More Significant Articles Describing the Taylor System of Management* (Cambridge, MA: Harvard University Press, 1914), 745–747.

The effect of this System here has been to create a feeling of distrust between the employees and the management; it has destroyed every vestige of coöperation between the workmen and the foremen collectively, and has produced a condition of unhappiness throughout the whole works.

For the reasons as stated above as well as many others which we will not trouble with at this time, we respectfully pray that you, as head of the War Department, take such immediate steps as will effectually remove this System from Watertown Arsenal and restore the workmen to a condition similar to that enjoyed by other artisans and laborers in the public service as well as in most private manufacturing plants.

We also respectfully petition that the records as obtained by means of stop watch observation be removed from this Arsenal or destroyed altogether as they do not represent the normal time in which given work should be accomplished, but rather they are the product of the "speed up" System which has resulted in accidents, inferior work and numerous abuses such as no American Citizen should be called upon to endure.

In conclusion let it be understood that the signatures of this petition were not obtained by coercion or unfair means and each individual signing this petition, does so of his own free will and accord.

Respectfully submitted,

Maurice W. Bowen
Chairman Representative Committee
23 Charles St., Auburndale, Mass.

Signed by 51 molders and helpers; 25 pattern makers, carpenters, and painters; 17 blacksmiths and helpers; 53 yard laboring men; 88 machinists and helpers, assembling department; 88 machinists and helpers.

An Engineering Student Instructs A Laundress, 1939

The University of Iowa Laundry processes over four million pounds of laundry per year. This includes laundry from the university hospitals, dormitories, and dining rooms.

. . . Roscoe C. Richards undertook to improve the method as a project in an industrial engineering course. . . .

The production rate on finishing fairly simple nurses' uniforms was 15 uniforms per hour using the old method. When the improved method was used, the operator could finish 25 per hour, an increase in output of 66 per cent.

The following reasons account for this increase in output:

1. Fewer lays were required to do the same work.
2. The distance that the iron was carried was reduced from 63 feet to 16 feet per uniform.

From Ralph Barnes, *Motion and Time Study: Design and Measurement of Work* (New York: John Wiley and Sons, 1963), pp. 198–199.

3. The distance the operator walked was reduced from 18 feet to 6 feet per uniform.
4. The operator was trained in the correct dampening and ironing methods, eliminating patting and excessive drying time.
5. A cordless iron was used, and a definite place was provided for the iron when not in actual use.

Indian Canoe Makers vs. An Efficiency Expert, 1938

HENRY MITCHELL

Henry Mitchell was born in 1884 on the Penobscot Indian Reservation on Indian Island, Maine. He worked for years in the Old Town Canoe Company factory before he was laid off. "I went to the manager, but it was no use. When a man gets to be over fifty they toss him out in favor of a younger man. This is the machine age, and I suppose employers think that young men can keep pace with machines better'n older men."

I don't remember exactly when the Old Town Canoe Company was started. Al Wickett was the superintendent in the canoe shop when I went to work there. We went to work at six-thirty in the morning and worked a ten-hour day. They introduced a piecework system about the year I went to work and although the hours were long, we made good pay. Thirty-six to forty dollars a week. That was too good to last, of course, and after five years of it they began to cut the pay. It was really Sam Gray's [the owner's] fault but we always blamed the French Canadians. They came in here by the carload. Sam knew he could get them for less money and he did. A lot of the Indians lost their jobs, but, of course, he had to keep some of us. There was a picture of an Indian on the outside of their catalogue, and the book told about how the patient Indian craftsmen constructed the successors to their birch-bark canoes. Sightseers used to come in and sometimes one of the women would say, "Oh, I want to see the Indians." Sam would lead them around to where a few of us were working and say, "Here are a few of them right here. We would never be able to run this place without them, I assure you."

Sam put Brown, the efficiency man, in here. He was a young fellow, just out of college, telling old canoe-makers how to go about their work. It was funny but Sam never got around to the point where he could see the joke. Brown was responsible for some worthwhile innovations here: he recommended blowers for the basement and ventilators and exhaust fans in the color room. But any dumbbell could have told Sam about the need for those things long before Brown came here. Sam should have known about it himself.

After Brown got through turning things upside down everywhere else, he got around to Hymie's room, the filling room. They used to fill a canoe and let it dry slowly for four or five days longer. That, of course, was as it should be. However, Brown must have been reading up on ceramics, for he says to Hymie, "Have some drying bins put in here. Ten days to dry a canoe is unheard of! We've got to speed it up a lot!" They

---

From Ann Banks, ed., *First Person America* (New York: Knopf, 1980), pp. 75–76.

got the bins built and all fitted up with steam pipes, and they shoved the canoes in. It took only four hours to dry them in the bins. There was some talk about Sam appointing Brown general manager and handing him a few blocks of shares.

They got a big order of five hundred canoes from Macy's that year and they broke all records of getting them out. It was all due to the drying bins that Brown thought up. About two months after the last canoe was shipped, they commenced to come back. They had warped and cracked ribs and splintered gunwales. Some of them had places where big gobs of paint a foot across had dropped off. There was 275 came back out of 500.

Sam, I guess, was sorry that the old custom of burning people at the stake had died out among the Indians, or he would have turned Brown over to us with orders to give him the works. As it was—laws being what they are—the best he could do was fire Brown without ceremony.

Highpockets, A Taylorist Folktale, 1930s

NELSON ALGREN

Highpockets was an efficiency expert's dream, an imaginary factory worker who bent every muscle toward helping the company. Nelson Algren's story about the perfect, tractable employee is a proletarian version of the traditional tall tale, a form invented by members of the Chicago Writer's Project. Algren, who had already published Somebody in Boots, *was one of the major contributors to an unpublished manuscript of Chicago industrial folklore. The best of these tales were intended for a FWP [Federal Works Project] collection,* A Tall Chance to Work, *which was never published.*

When Highpockets first came into the mill room, he was walking like a man stepping over cornstalks. We knew he was a hillbilly from way back at the fork of the crick. Them guys raised on pumpkins and yaller crick water is anxious to work and get ahead; a jitney looks as big as a grindstone to them.

The time-study man had made it hard enough on us before Highpockets came, but afterwards—oh, man!—afterwards, it was hell on wheels. The time-study man, that mother-robbing creeper that watches you from behind dolly trucks and stock boxes, he's always trying to figger a way to get more work out of you at the same pay. He'll even ask you if they ain't some way you could do a little more than you are. He never expects you should say yes, and that's why it almost knocked him off the Christmas tree when Highpockets told him he reckoned he could do a sight more than he was. He was tending a milling machine that worked pretty fast, but it only took one hand.

Next thing we know, by Jesus, the time-study man was having the millwright put in another milling machine for Highpockets' left hand and be damned if he didn't turn out twice as much work as before. The time-study man has got real fond of him

From Ann Banks, ed., *First Person America* (New York: Knopf, 1980), pp. 90–92.

by this time, and hangs around watching and admiring him. Trouble is, he started in on the rest of us, wanting we should do something about them idle left hands of ours.

Still, the time-study man ain't satisfied with Highpockets' work, because that cornfield canary is so husky it looks like he ain't taxing his strength a particle. Next, there's a block-and-tackle business fastened to Highpockets' right leg, and he's pulling stock pans off one conveyor onto another slick as you please. He's happy as a meadowlark in a plowed field of fat worms, and by quitting time he's as fresh as a daisy and skittish as a yearling bull.

"Take it easy, buddy, f' Christ's sake," we say to Highpockets every time we pass by him on the way to the can or water cooler. We say it low, so's the time-study man won't catch on, but might as well talk to an eight-wheeler that's lost her airbrakes on a downhill grade. These cornfield canaries ain't got sense enough to pound sand in a rat-hole or pour water out of a boot when it's got full directions printed on the heel.

It goes from bad to worse, with next a band fastened to Highpockets' left leg, and be damned if he ain't jerking empty fender hooks off another conveyor and piling them in a dolly box, neat as apple pie.

It looks bad for us, that's the God's truth, and beginning to look worse. The time-study man goes around saying: "He's true blue. He's the kind of man that get ahead, got the company's interest at heart. Yes, sir, that kind of man *gets* somewhere around this plant. You birds that get full as ticks every night, booming and whoring around and coming in here next morning half-crocked, you get your hands in the company's pockets halfway to your elbows."

We thought Highpockets was speeded to full steam finally, because he's got a little bar in his teeth and with this he's jerking his head back and forth and this runs a brush back and forth over new stock coming in and knocks the dust off it. He's finished, we said, he *can't* do no more. He's doing all he can, and that's all a little red bull can do, boys. He's going like a blind dog in a meathouse, and it's REACH (right hand) REACH (left hand) KICK (right leg) KICK (left leg) PULL (teeth), REACH REACH KICK KICK PULL. He goes so fast you can't see him for steam.

"He's true blue! He's true blue! The kind of man that gets somewhere in this plant," the time-study man says, as he wiggles back and forth in tune with High-pockets' motions and whispers something in his ear. We know he's asking him if they ain't lost motion somewhere. This time we feel swell because about all Highpockets can really say is: "Gee, you got me there, boss, I give up."

All of us keep going at the same old merry-go-round, but we cock an ear to hear what Highpockets has got to say. This time the time-study man's got him where the wool is tight.

The sweat is falling off him like Niagara Falls. Here he goes, lickety-split, never misses a stroke: REACH REACH KICK KICK PULL REACH REACH KICK KICK PULL REACH REACH KICK KICK PULL. . . .

He was true blue, that cornfield canary was, and a credit to the human race. The kind of a man that *gets* somewhere in this plant. He grins game as a fighting cock and chirps right out loud:

"Sure, if you want to stick a broom someplace, I think I could be sweeping the floor!"

A Political Scientist on Scientific Management, 1914

FRANK T. CARLTON

Efficiency programs are attracting much attention in this country, at the present time, because nearly all of the great expanse of land found within the borders of the United States has been taken up and the vast natural resources of the nation have been tapped. We are entering a period of diminishing returns; and a period in which increasing attention will be directed toward small economies that were not considered worthy of notice a generation ago. "The cream has been skimmed off the pan of our natural resources." Also, factory legislation, laws as to hours of labor, and the activity of labor organizations are tending to raise the level of wages and to increase the expense of operating a business. As a consequence, employers are being stimulated to adopt more efficient methods.

Many indications point to the conclusion that modern industrial nations are passing over the threshold of a new era in industrial and social progress. We are about to enter upon a period marked by the rapid increase in the use of machinery and of carefully planned methods of doing work. . . . The term "industrial revolution" has heretofore been applied to the rapid adoption of new tools and machines.

"Social invention" is to be typical of the epoch just ahead. . . .

Scientific management or efficiency engineering is concerned with two somewhat interrelated matters. The first is efficient systematization of the work in a given factory from the engineering or the mechanical point of view. . . . The second factor is psychological in its nature; it relates to the effective methods of "energizing" the workers by providing potent incentives and by stimulating interest in the work. . . . Efficient methods of doing work will sooner or later displace less efficient methods just as, for example, the steamboat has displaced the sailboat, the automobile is displacing the horse upon the streets of our cities, and the giant drop-hammer has displaced the village blacksmith. The transformation may be retarded; but the constant pressure of economic forces will finally break down all opposition.

But the second portion of the program of the efficiency engineer cannot be forced through. It cannot be secured by coercion; it can be effectively carried out only when the wage-earners harmoniously coöperate with the managers in working out the proposed plan. The fundamental problem of efficiency engineering centers around the treatment of the wage-earners. . . . The pioneer and leading exponent of efficiency engineering, Mr. F. W. Taylor, writes: "This close, intimate, personal coöperation between the management and the men is of the essence of modern scientific or task management." And Harrington Emerson asserts that to "establish rational work standards for men requires, indeed, motion and time studies of all operations, but it requires in addition all the skill of the planning manager, all the skill of the physician, of the humanitarian, of the physiologist; it requires infinite knowledge directed, guided, and restrained by hope, faith, and compassion."

From Frank T. Carlton, "Scientific Management and the Wage-Earner," in *Scientific Management: A Collection of the More Significant Articles Describing the Taylor System of Management* (Cambridge, MA: Harvard University Press, 1914), pp. 720–726.

In theory, according to its advocates, scientific management stands for increased productive capacity without increased effort; it aims to do away with lost motion and useless movements. It means maximum results with a minimum of effort; it does not mean "frenzied production." Now, these objects are certainly worthy of approval; and, consequently, opposition to efficiency engineering must arise because of the methods employed in carrying out the policy. Our attention evidently must be directed toward this pertinent inquiry: How, then, can this "close, intimate, personal coöperation," of which Mr. Taylor speaks, be secured? . . .

The wage-earner is today insistently demanding that a portion of his share in the advantages accruing from the introduction of improved machinery and of scientific management be given to him in the form of a shorter working-day. His conception of a desirable form of society in the twentieth century is not one in which a certain number of individuals work at high speed during a long working-day but one in which all work during a short working-day. There are, obviously, at least two alternative methods which may be pursued in producing a given quota of economic goods and services: a small number of men may be employed for a long working-day or a larger number for a shorter working-day. From the standpoint of the wage-earner observing a large and apparently growing army of unemployed, the second alternative is by no means repulsive. His ideal is not necessarily maximum productivity per worker per day; but a condition in which work and recreation are blended for each and every individual. And, if economics is "the reasoned activity of a people tending toward the satisfaction of its needs," shall the economist confidently assert that the wage-earner's ideal is one worthy only of contemptuous rejection?

If scientific management has great possibilities, the effect of its introduction may not be unlike that caused by the displacement of the hand tool by the machine. Not only may increased production be anticipated, but also the displacement of workers, temporary unemployment for many, and a multitude of industrial evils which accompany every important readjustment in the sphere of industry. The introduction of scientific management bids fair to cause "another intensive, resistless reordering of industrial life." And the wage-earner, with his skill as his sole capital, with only a small savings account or none, and with a family to provide for, is justified in manifesting alarm. . . .

The model workman, from the standpoint of the typical efficiency engineer, is the vigorous man who freely expends all of his surplus energy during working-hours and who utilizes his non-working-hours only for recuperation and preparation for another day's work. It is not the purpose of efficiency engineering to allow the worker to depart from the door of the factory at night with more than a minimum of surplus energy for recreation, for family life, for civic duties, or for trade-union activities. In short I find little in the actual program of efficiency engineering which indicates that the wage-earner is to be given opportunity for individual development—and I have not overlooked the various paternalistic endeavors classified as welfare work. A human machine rather than a man is the "model workman." I also find little, or more accurately nothing, in Mr. Taylor's book which indicates that he appreciates or sympathizes with the viewpoint of the wage-earner.

Mr. Taylor informs us that a long series of experiments has shown that an increase in wages up to 60 per cent beyond the wages usually paid has a good effect upon the men. But, "on the other hand, when they receive much more than a 60 per cent increase in wages, many of them will work irregularly and tend to become more or less shiftless, extravagant, and dissipated. Our experiments showed, in other words, that it does not do for most men to get rich too fast." But what of the efficiency of the corporation which receives large increases in its rate of profits? How do such increases affect the alertness of the managers, the adoption of improved methods, machines, and safety appliances? Can the workers or the consumers afford to allow an employing corporation to increase its rate of profits? If so, how rapidly and how much? This is an unworked field of efficiency engineering. And our efficiency engineers are not enthusiastically interested in investigations of this sort.

𝄪 E S S A Y S

In the first selection, Sudhir Kakar points to the novel features of Taylorism and places them in a larger national and international context. He concludes that few people criticized Taylor's goals. Rather, differences arose over the means he used to achieve greater productivity.

Thomas P. Hughes looks at Taylor himself in the second selection. For Hughes the modern industrial world is best understood from the perspective of large technological systems. Taylor, according to Hughes, was the first to contend that systems included human and organizational components as well as artifacts. Taking this idea to extreme conclusions, yet imagining himself to stand "between" capital and labor, Taylor could never understand the hostility his system elicited from workers and labor leaders.

Although scientific management extracted control from male craft workers, it greatly increased opportunities for professionals and their clerical assistants. Many new aspirants to both professional and clerical titles in this period were women. In the third selection, Sharon H. Strom looks at how some middle-class women embraced Taylor's ideas in the interest of cultivating equality in employment and the blurring of gender boundaries. One, Mary B. Gilson, passionately advocated and remolded Taylorism in the form of "personnel management." On both a personal and cultural level, was this a success?

Taylorism as an International Movement

SUDHIR KAKAR

Taylor's ideas have had an enormous influence on the industrial life of almost all countries. Many of his ideas are now looked upon as being so self-evident as to be part of normal industrial practice. The development of these ideas in relation to Taylor's personality and to the particular needs of his historical era has, however, for the most part been ignored.

Already in 1918, Taylor's system was taking on the trappings of an international movement independent of particular economic systems of political ideologies. In France, a circular of the Ministry of War, dated February 26, 1918, and signed by Georges Clemenceau, pointed out the imperative necessity of the study and application of methods of work according to the principles of "Taylorism" and ordered the

From Sudhir Kakar, *Frederick Taylor: A Study in Personality and Innovation* (Cambridge, MA: MIT Press, 1970), pp. 2–4, 188–191.

establishment in each plant of planning departments—a central feature of the Taylor system. The Ministry recommended that the heads of the plants make themselves familiar with Taylor's principal writings, including his magnum *opus, Principles of Scientific Management.* At the opposite end of the ideological spectrum, *Pravda,* in its issue of April 28, 1918, published an article of Lenin's on "The Immediate Tasks of the Soviet Government." Under the heading, "Raising the Productivity of Labour," Lenin wrote:

> We must raise the question of piece-work and apply and test it in practice; we must raise the question of applying much of what is scientific and progressive in the Taylor system; we must make wages correspond to the total amount of goods turned out, or to the amount of work done by the railways, the water transport system, etc., etc.
>
> The Russian is a bad worker compared with people in advanced countries. It could not be otherwise under the tsarist regime and in view of the persistence of the hangover from serfdom. The task that the Soviet government must set the people in all its scope is—learn to work. The Taylor system, the last word of capitalism in this respect, like all capitalist progress, is a combination of the refined brutality of bourgeois exploitation and a number of the greatest scientific achievements in the field of analysing mechanical motions during work, the elimination of superfluous and awkward motions, the elaboration of correct methods of work, the introduction of the best system of accounting and control, etc. The Soviet Republic must at all costs adopt all that is valuable in the achievements of science and technology in this field. The possibility of building socialism depends exactly upon our success in combining the Soviet power and the Soviet organisation of administration which the up-to-date achievements of capitalism. We must organise in Russia the study and teaching of the Taylor system and systematically try it out and adapt it to our own ends.

The fact that both a conservative bourgeois regime in France and a revolutionary regime in Russia propagated Taylor's system should not be a surprising one. To them, Taylor's work was a part of technology with its implications of *universality and neutrality.* What Taylor had done was to extend, or rather to enlarge, the concept of technology, which had hitherto been restricted to mechanical and chemical—in other words, nonhuman—processes. His effort was to bring human work and the organization of work into the realm of technology.

Taylor's system was directed to the following ends:

1. Standardizing work, which meant the determination of the "one best way" of working; and
2. Controlling so extensively and intensively as to provide for the maintenance of all these standards.

The implications of Taylor's work thus go beyond mere industrial management technique to the broader issues of the very nature of *work* and *control.* And his work becomes increasingly relevant to the philosophical-ethical complex of problems subsumed under the heading technology and society (or, in popular terms, the relationship of man and machine) which today is so much in the center of discussion all over the world.

Taylor was thus the founder of a system that stated the relationship of man—workers and managers—to the new technology. To him, "scientific management" was completely free of value judgments; it was simply the discovery of technological imperatives as they applied to men at work. The only implicit moral "commandment" was that of increasing productivity. Persons or groups of persons, workers, management, owners of capital who transgressed against this law were all equally sinners. It is no wonder that he was attacked from all sides. His statement of the relationship between men and technology seemed to leave everyone unfree, stirring up anxieties at a deeper, unconscious, psychic level. For if a man is to maintain his own particular individuality in the midst of other individualities, there are certain prerogatives he cannot afford to lose—he would fight against the perceived danger of such a loss with all the resources at his command, conscious and unconscious, collective and individual. Some of these prerogatives have been called a sense of *wholeness,* a sense of *centrality* in time and space, and a sense of *freedom of choice.*

In the new, regimented work patterns, Taylor's system, with its goal of increased productivity, seemed to deck technology with the mantle of determinism and thus to threaten one of the essential prerogatives; *freedom of choice.* The comparison of him with Darwin now seems to become at least more understandable, for Darwin, of course, threatened another prerogative: a sense of *centrality* in time and space. . . .

From a historical standpoint, Taylor's enduring importance would seem to derive from his leadership in the introduction of the scientific method into the area of work. Indeed, the development and spread—not to mention the popularization—of scientific method is the most characteristic innovation of the nineteenth century. As Alfred North Whitehead put it, "The greatest invention of the nineteenth century was the invention of the method of invention." Reasoned application of the method seemed to certify progress, to ensure that henceforth progress would not have to depend on the chance cropping up of infrequent genius or sporadic superhuman will, but that ordinary men, armed thus, could with methodical patience, systematically and predictably mine the deeper veins of knowledge—in science, in technology, as well as in general scholarship. Taylor's application of the scientific method to work, and in particular to industrial work, thus meant a revolutionary change, with subtle but devastating implications, from amateurism to professionalism in factory organization and management. The rise of a new profession, industrial engineering, and a host of new managerial functions is only the most obvious manifestation of this revolution. . . .

To a very great extent, Taylor is responsible for the managerial philosophy that prevails today, which can be summed up as follows: To increase productivity, 1. break the work process into the smallest possible components; 2. fit jobs into structures that clearly emphasize the duties and boundaries of each job rather than its part in the total process; 3. wherever possible use individual or small group monetary incentive system, gearing pay to the output; 4. subtract skill and responsibility from the job to make them functions of management. . . .

[A]rguments with Taylorism have to do with the matter of means; with Taylor's ends there is no quarrel. All who reject Taylor's system for its ignorance or depreciation of the social and psychological dimensions of work gear their arguments and justify their cases with reference to a common goal—increased productivity. The concept of increased productivity has become the lodestar of modern work, replacing such concepts as morality, expiation of sin, individual self-realization, aesthetic fulfillment, and community well-being that, singly or together, defined and guided work in other historical epochs. Efficiency, with which Taylor's name is primarily associated—this efficiency, expressed in measurable, quantifiable terms—has thus already become a core element of the new technological identity.

The System Must Be First

THOMAS HUGHES

[W]e reflect too little about the influences and patterns of a world organized into great technological systems. Usually we mistakenly associate modern technology not with systems but with such objects as the electric light, radio and television, the airplane, the automobile, the computer, and nuclear missiles. To associate modern technology solely with individual machines and devices is to overlook deeper currents of modern technology that gathered strength and direction during the half-century after Thomas Edison established his invention factory at Menlo Park. Today machines such as the automobile and the airplane are omnipresent. Because they are mechanical and physical, they are not too difficult to comprehend. Machines like these, however, are usually merely components in highly organized and controlled technological systems. Such systems are difficult to comprehend, because they also include complex components, such as people and organizations, and because they often consist of physical components, such as the chemical and electrical, other than the mechanical. Large systems—energy, production, communication, and transportation—compose the essence of modern technology. . . .

. . . In seeking the creators of modern industrial America, we must consider the system builders as well as the independent inventors and the industrial scientists.

Henry Ford's production system remains the best known of the large technological systems maturing in the interwar years. Contemporaries then usually perceived it as a mechanical production system with machine tools and assembly lines. But Ford's system also included blast furnaces to make iron, railroads to convey raw materials, mines from which these came, highly organized factories functioning as if they were a single machine, and highly developed financial, managerial, labor, and sales organizations. . . .

Electrical light-and-power systems, such as those managed and financed by the system-building utility magnate Samuel Insull of Chicago, incorporated not only dynamos, incandescent lamps, and transmission lines, but hydroelectric dams, control or load-dispatching centers, utility companies, consulting-engineering firms, and brokerage houses, as well. When Ford placed a mechanical assembly line in motion, the public was greatly impressed, but electrical systems transmitted their production units too rapidly to perceive: 186,000 miles per second, the speed of light. . . .

Of the American system builders, none took on a more difficult and controversial task than Frederick Winslow Taylor. Ford directed his ordering-and-controlling drive primarily to production machines; Insull focused his on ensuring the large and steady flow of electrical power; Taylor tried to systematize workers as if they were components of machines. Ford's image was of a factory functioning as a machine;

From Thomas Hughes, *American Genesis* (New York: Viking, 1989), pp. 184–203.

Insull envisaged a network or circuit of interacting electrical and organizational components; and Taylor imagined a machine in which the mechanical and human parts were virtually indistinguishable. Idealistic, even eccentric, in his commitment to the proposition that efficiency would benefit all Americans, Taylor proved naïve in his judgments about complex human values and motives. In the history of Taylorism we find an early and highly significant case of people reacting against the system builders and their production systems, a reaction widespread today among those who fear being co-opted by "the system." . . .

Taylor was not the first to advocate a so-called scientific approach to management, but the enthusiasm and dedication, bordering on obsession, with which he gave himself to spreading his views on management, his forceful personality, and his highly unusual and erratic career filled with failure as well as success have left a strong, indelible impression on his contemporaries and succeeding generations. More than a half-century after his death, many persons in Europe, the Soviet Union, and the United States continue to label scientific management "Taylorism." Labor-union leaders and radicals then and now find Taylor convenient to attack as a symbol of a despised system of labor organization and control. In the early decades of this century, Europeans and Russians adopted "Taylorism" as the catchword for the much-admired and -imitated American system of industrial management and mass production. The publication in 1911 of Taylor's *Principles of Scientific Management* remains a landmark in the history of management-labor relations. Within two years of publication, it had been translated into French, German, Dutch, Swedish, Russian, Italian, Spanish, and Japanese. In his novel *The Big Money* (1936), John Dos Passos gave a sketch of Taylor, along with ones of Edison, Ford, Insull, and a few others, because he believed that they expressed the spirit of their era. Dos Passos noted that Taylor never smoked or drank tea, coffee, or liquor, but found comparable stimulation in solving problems of efficiency and production. For him, production was the end-all, whether it be armor plate for battleships, or needles, ball bearings or lightning rods.

Taylor's fundamental concept and guiding principle was to design a system of production involving both men and machines that would be as efficient as a well-designed, well-oiled machine. He said, "in the past, the man has been first; in the future the system must be first," a remark that did not sit well then with workers and their trade-union leaders and that today still rankles those who feel oppressed by technology. He asked managers to do for the production system as a whole what inventors and engineers had done in the nineteenth century for machines and processes. Highly efficient machines required highly efficient functionally related labor. When several Taylor disciples, including later U.S. Supreme Court Justice Louis D. Brandeis, sought a name for Taylor's management system, they considered "Functional Management," before deciding on "Scientific Management." Taylor and his followers unfeelingly compared an inefficient worker to a poorly designed machine member.

Taylor developed his principles of management during his work as a machinist and then as a foreman in the Midvale Steel Company of Philadelphia. . . .

Worker soldiering, variously called "stalling," "quota restriction," "goldbricking" by Americans, *Bremsen* by Germans, and "hanging it out" or "Ca'canny" by the English and Scots, greatly offended Taylor's sense of efficiency. Having concluded that workers, especially the skilled machinists, were the major industrially inefficient enclave remaining after the great wave of nineteenth-century mechanization, Taylor proposed to eliminate "soldiering." He later wrote that "the greater part of systematic soldiering . . . is done by the men with the deliberate object of keeping their employers ignorant of how fast work can be done." The machinists at Midvale, for example, were on a "piecework" schedule, so they were determined that the owners not learn that more pieces could be turned out per hour and therefore demand an increase in the number of pieces required. They did not trust the owners to maintain the piece rate and allow the workers, if they exerted themselves, to take home more pay. The workers believed that the increased effort would become the norm for the owners. We can only conjecture about the natural rhythm and reasonableness of the pace that the workers maintained over the long duration; Taylor believed that they were soldiering. Nevertheless, he also showed that he was determined that the diligent worker be rewarded with a share of the income from more efficient and increased production. To his consternation, he later found that management and the owners also soldiered when it came time to share the increased income. Taylor was no close student of human nature; his approach was, as he described it, scientific.

After being put in charge of the machinists working at the lathes, Taylor set out to end soldiering among them. His friends began to fear for his safety. As Taylor recalled, the men came to him and said, "Now, Fred, you are not going to be a damn piecework hog, are you?" To which he replied, "If you fellows mean you are afraid I am going to try to get a larger output from these lathes," then "Yes; I do propose to get more work out." The piecework fight was on, lasting for three years at Midvale. Friends begged Taylor to stop walking home alone late at night through deserted streets, but he said that they could shoot and be damned and that, if attacked, he would not stick to the rules, but resort to biting, gouging, and brickbats. At congressional hearings in 1912—about thirty years later—he insisted:

> I want to call your attention, gentlemen, to the bitterness that was stirred up in this fight before the men finally gave in, to the meaness of it. . . . I did not have any bitterness against any particular man or men. Practically all of those men were my friends, and many of them are still my friends. . . . My sympathies were with workmen, and my duty lay to the people by whom I was employed.

In his search for the one best way of working, of deciding how and how fast a lathe operator should work, he used a method that he considered scientific. He believed values and opinions of neither workers nor managers influenced his objective, scientific approach. Beginning in 1882, first he, then an assistant began using a stopwatch to do time studies of worker's motions. Timing was not a new practice, but Taylor did not simply time the way the men worked: he broke down complex sequences of motions into what he believed to be the elementary ones and then timed these as performed by workers whom he considered efficient in their movements. Having done this analysis, he synthesized the efficiently executed component motions into a new set of complex sequences that he insisted must become the norm. He added time for unavoidable delays, minor accidents, inexperience, and rest. The result was a detailed set of instructions for the worker and a determination of time required for the work to be efficiently performed. This determined the piecework rate; bonuses were to be paid for faster work, penalties for slower. He thus denied the individual worker the freedom to use his body and his tools as he chose.

Taylor stressed that the time studies, with their accompanying analysis and synthesis, did not alone constitute scientific management. He realized and insisted that, for the work to be efficiently performed, the conditions of work had to be reorganized. He called for better-designed tools and became known for his near-fixation about the design of shovels. He ordered the planning and careful management of materials handling so that workers would have the materials at hand where and when needed. Often, he found, men and machines stood idle because of bottlenecks in complex manufacturing processes. Taylor even attended to lighting, heating, and toilet facilities. Seeing inanimate machines and men together as a single machine, he also looked for ways in which the inanimate ones failed. Believing that machine tools could also be driven faster, he invented a new chromium-tungsten steel for cutting tools that greatly increased their speed. As we would expect, he did not leave decisions about even the cutting speed of the machine tool or the depth of the cut to the subjective judgment of the machinist. In his book *On the Art of Cutting Metals* (New York, 1907), he described his thousands of experiments that extended over twenty-six years.

As a system builder seeking control and order, Taylor was not content to redesign machines, men, and their relationship; he was set upon the reorganization of the entire workplace or factory as a machine for production. Stimulated by his example, individuals with special education, training, and skill contributed to the establishment of "the new factory system." To understand this achievement, we need to consider the way in which the work process was carried out in many machine shops, engineering works, and factories before Taylor's reforms. After the concern received an order, copies specifying the product and quantity to be made were sent to the foremen. They carried most of the responsibility for the production process. Once draftsmen had prepared detailed drawings, foremen in the machine shop, the foundry, pattern-making shop, and forge determined the various component parts needed, ordered the raw materials, and wrote out job cards for the machinists. The machinists then collected drawings, raw materials, and tools, and planned the way in which the job for a particular component part would be done. When the machinists had completed the particular job, they reported to the foreman for another. The foremen had overall supervision, but there was little scheduling and, therefore, little planned coordination of the various jobs. Components sometimes reached the assembly point, or erecting shop, haphazardly. Because of lack of planning, scheduling, and close monitoring of the progress of work, raw materials were often not on hand. How the workmen might then use their time is not clear, but proponents of Taylorism leave the impression that they were idle.

Taylor found the disorder and lack of control unbearably inefficient and declared war on traditional methods responsible for these. His reform specified that an engineering division take away from the foremen overall responsibility for the preparation of drawings, the specification of components, and the ordering of raw materials. Upwardly mobile young graduates from the rising engineering schools were soon displacing their "fathers," the foremen. The planning department in the engineering division coordinated deliveries of materials, and the sequence in which component parts would be made. The planning department prepared detailed instructions about which machines would be used, the way in which machinists, pattern makers, and other workmen would make each part, and how long the job should take. Careful records were kept of the progress being made in the manufacture of each part, including materials used and time consumed. Unskilled workers moved materials and parts around shops so that they would be on hand where and when needed. By an elaborate set of instruction cards and reports, the planning department had an overall picture of the flow of parts throughout the shops, a flow that prevented the congestion of the work at particular machines and the idleness of other machines and workmen. The reports of worker time and materials consumed greatly facilitated cost accounting.

The complexity and holism of Taylor's approach was often ignored because of the widespread publicity given to some of his simplest and most easily reported and understood successes. Taylor often referred to the "story of Schmidt," who worked with the pig-iron gang at the Bethlehem Steel Corporation in Pennsylvania. When Taylor and his associates came to Bethlehem in 1897 to introduce their management techniques and piecework, they found the pig-iron gang moving on the average about twelve and a half tons per day. Each man had repeatedly to lift ninety-two pounds of iron and carry it up an inclined plant onto a railroad car. After careful inquiry into the character, habits, and ambition of each of the gang of seventy-five men, Taylor singled out a "little Pennsylvanian Dutchman who had been observed to trot backhome for a mile or so after his work in the evening about as fresh as he was when he came trotting down to work in the morning." After work he was building a little house for himself on a small plot of ground he had "succeeded' in buying. Taylor also found out that the "Dutchman" Henry Noll, whom Taylor identified as Schmidt, was exceedingly "close," or one who placed "very high value on the dollar." The Taylorites had found their man.

Taylor recalled the way he and Schmidt talked, a story that tells us more of Taylor's attitudes than of what actually transpired:

> "Schmidt, are you a high-priced man? . . . What I want to find out is whether you want to earn $1.85 a day or whether you are satisfied with $1.15, just the same as all those cheap fellows are getting?"
>
> "Did I vant $1.85 a day? Vas dot a high-priced man? Vell, yes, I vas a high-priced man."
>
> " . . . Well, if you are a high-priced man, you will load that pig iron on that car to-morrow for $1.85. You will do exactly as this man tells you to-morrow, from morning till night. When he tells you to pick up a pig, and walk, you pick it up and you walk, and when he tells you to sit down and rest, you sit down. . . . And what's more, no back talk."

Taylor found it prudent to add:

> This seems to be rather rough talk. And indeed it would be if applied to an educated mechanic or even intelligent laborer. With a man of the mentally sluggish type of Schmidt it is appropriate and not unkind, since it is effective in fixing his attention on high wages which he wants. . . .

Perhaps Taylor, the upper-middle-class Philadelphian, forgot that the Pennsylvania Dutchman was not so mentally sluggish that he could not save for land and build a house. Schmidt moved the forty-seven tons of pig that the Taylorites had decided should be the norm, instead of the former twelve and a half tons, and soon all the gang was moving the same and receiving sixty percent more pay than other workmen around them. We are not told whether Schmidt was still able to trot home and work on his house.

Numerous other examples of Taylor's methods increasing worker output and production abound, but there is also abundant evidence of failures. Ultimately his efforts at Bethlehem Steel exhausted him, and the head of the company summarily dismissed him. Taylor had come to the steel company with the full support of Joseph Wharton, a wealthy Philadelphian into whose hands the company had passed. Wharton wanted a piecework system installed in the six-thousand-man enterprise. Taylor warned that his system would be strongly opposed by all of the workmen, most of the foremen, and even a majority of the superintendents. Bold and determined, he forged relentlessly ahead, introducing a planning department and new administrative roles for the foremen. Instructions for routine were codified with time cards, work sheets, order slips, and so on. As worker resistance stiffened over several years, Taylor became rigid, even arbitrary, in dealing with labor and management. His achievements were impressive, but "as time went on, he exhibited a fighting spirit of an intensity almost pathological," an admirer wrote. Taylor's communications to the Bethlehem president were tactless and peremptory (he believed Wharton would shelter him). He complained of poor health and nervous strain. He thought that some of the major stockholders opposed him because he was cutting the labor force, and they were losing rents on the workers' houses. The curt note dismissing him came in April 1901.

Many workers were unwilling, especially the skilled ones, to give control of their bodies and their tools to the scientific managers, or, in short, to become components in a well-planned system. An increase in pay often did not compensate for their feeling of loss of autonomy. Taylor's scientific analysis did not take into account worker independence and pride in artful craftsmanship—even artful soldiering. Perhaps this was because Taylor, despite his years of experience on the shop floor, did not come from a blue-collar worker culture.

Samuel Gompers, a labor leader, said of Taylorism and similar philosophies of management:

> So, there you are, wage-workers in general, mere machines—considered industrially, of course. Hence, why should you not be standardized and your motion-power brought up to the highest possible perfection in all respects, including speeds? Not only your length, breadth, and thickness as a machine, but your grade of hardness, malleability, tractability, and general serviceability, can be ascertained, registered, and then employed as desirable. Science would thus get the most out of you before you are sent to the junkpile.

One of the most publicized setbacks for Taylorism took place at the Watertown Arsenal when Carl G. Barth, a prominent Taylor follower and a consultant on scientific management, tried to introduce the Taylor system. Serious trouble started in the foundry when one of Barth's associates began stopwatch-timing the men's work procedures. The skilled workers in the shop discovered that the man carrying out the study knew little about foundry practice. The foundrymen secretly made their own time study of the same work process and complained that the time specified by the "expert" was uninformed and represented an unrealistic speedup. The Watertown project was also flawed because Taylor's practice was to reorganize and standardize a shop before doing time-and-motion studies, and this had not been carried out at Watertown Arsenal. On the evening after the initiation of the stopwatch studies, the workers met informally and in a petition to the commanding officer of the arsenal they stated:

> The very unsatisfactory conditions which have prevailed in the foundry among the molders for the past week or more reached an acute stage this afternoon when a man was seen

to use a stop watch on one of the molders. This we believe to be the limit of our endurance. It is humiliating to us, who have always tried to give to the government the best that was in us. This method is un-American in principle, and we most respectfully request that you have it discontinued at once.

When stopwatch timing continued, the molders walked out on 11 August 1911.

Promised an investigation of the "unsatisfactory conditions," the molders returned to work after a week, but the publicity given a strike against the U.S. government intensified, fermenting union opposition to scientific management, specifically Taylorism, at Watertown and at another U.S. arsenal, at Rock, Illinois. August brought the formation of a special congressional committee of three to investigate scientific management in government establishments. The committee took extensive testimony from Taylor, among others. He became so exercised by hostile questions that his remarks had to be removed from the record. The report of the committee did not immediately call for any legislation. In 1914, however, Congress attached to appropriations bills the proviso that no time studies or related incentive payments should be carried out in government establishments, a prohibition that survived for over thirty years. Yet Taylorism involved, as we have seen, more than time studies and incentive payments, so work processes in government establishments continued to be systematically studied, analyzed, and changed in ways believed by management experts to be scientific.

Worn down by the never-ending opposition and conflict, Taylor moved in 1902 to a handsome house in the Chestnut Hill area of Philadelphia. He no longer accepted employment or consulting fees but announced that he was ready to advise freely those interested in Taylorism. . . .

Free from the confrontations in the workplace, Taylor dedicated himself to showing that his philosophy of management would ultimately promote harmony between management and labor. He argued that increasing production would increase wages and raise the national standard of living. His principles of scientific management struck responsive chords in a nation intent on ensuring economic democracy, or mass consumption, through mass production and also on conserving its natural resources. Taylor wrote that maximum prosperity could exist only as a result of maximum productivity. He believed that the elimination of wasted time and energy among workers would do more than socialism to diminish poverty and alleviate suffering.

Because of his firm belief that his method was objective, or scientific, he never fully comprehended the hostile opposition of aggressive, collective-bargaining labor-union leaders. He found the unions mostly standing "for war, for enmity," in contrast to scientific management, which stood for "peace and friendship." Nor could he countenance unenlightened and "hoggish" employers who either found his approach and his college-educated young followers unrealistic or were unwilling to share wholeheartedly with the workers the increased profits arising from scientific management. He considered the National Manufacturers Association a "fighting association," so he urged his friends in scientific management to cut all connections with it and its aggressive attitudes toward labor unions. Firmly persuaded that conflict and interest-group confrontations were unnatural, he awaited, not too patiently, the day when management and labor would realize, as he, that where the goal was increased productivity there were discoverable and applicable scientific laws governing work and workplace. Scientific managers were the experts who would apply the laws. He wrote:

> I cannot agree with you that there is a conflict in the interests of capital and labor. I firmly believe that their interests are strictly mutual, and that it is practicable to settle by careful scientific investigation the proper award that labor should receive for the work it renders.

Their interest was not only a mutual but a national one—production and democracy. Production and Democracy. Taylor's times were not ones of affluence for workers, so his means to the end of mass production, thereby raising living standards of the masses, seemed in accord with democratic principle. Within a few years, Vladimir Lenin argued that Taylor principles accorded with socialism, as well.

Taylor became nationally known when [Louis] Brandeis, the Boston "people's lawyer," argued in 1911 that scientific management, especially Taylorism, could save the nation's railroads so much money that the increased rates that the railroads were requesting from the Interstate Commerce Commission would not be needed. Since the rate hearings were well publicized, writers from newspapers and magazines descended on Taylor to find out about his system and then, at his suggestion, visited Philadelphia plants to see firsthand Taylorism in practice. The favorable publicity induced Taylor to write that "the interest now taken in scientific management is almost comparable to that which was aroused in the conservation of our natural resources by Roosevelt."

Taylor rightly associated his scientific management with the broader conservation movement that had attracted national interest and support during Theodore Roosevelt's terms as president, 1901–08. This progressive program for conservation focused on the preservation and efficient utilization of lands and resources. Like scientific management, it advocated that decisions about conservation be made scientifically by experts. Like Taylor, the progressive conservationists did not countenance as inevitable conflict of interests among ranchers, farmers, lumbermen, utilities, manufacturers, and others. To the contrary, they believed that such conflict was regressive, that it must be displaced by a scientific approach expected to bring harmonious and rational compromises in the general interest. This approach expressed a technological spirit spread by engineers, professional managers, and appliers of science, a belief that there was one best way. College-educated foresters, hydraulic engineers, agronomists should be, the progressives argued, the decision makers about resources; professional managers about the workplace.

Taylor and the growing number of his followers wrote books, published articles, gave lectures, and acted as consultants. He authorized C. G. Barth, H. K. Hathaway, Morris L. Cooke, and Henry L. Gantt to teach his system of management: "All others were operating on their own." Frank Gilbreth, among those who operated "on their own," became well known for his *A Primer of Scientific Management* (1914) and for the use he and his wife, Lillian Gilbreth, made of the motion-picture camera to prepare time-and-motion studies. Her contribution to scientific management has yet to be generally acknowledged. She, not her husband, had a Ph.D. degree in psychology (Brown University, 1915). Perhaps because of her study of psychology, she sensitively took into account complex worker characteristics. The Gilbreths' articles on scientific management show the influence of her concern that the worker should not be seen simply as a component in a Taylor system. After her husband's death, she continued her consulting work and served as a professor of industrial management at Purdue University.

Scientific Management, Gender, and Feminism

SHARON H. STROM

The office as we know it emerged at the turn of the twentieth century. The services it began to provide were indispensable to the managing of government, the dispensing of public utilities, the distribution of retail commodities, the production of manufactured goods, the exchange of money and the insuring of property and life. Its organizational form was increasingly hierarchial and bureaucratic. Its purpose was to integrate and facilitate the management of government and business through efficiency, account-ability, and precise record-keeping. Government reform and the growing reliance of the corporation on complex functions of cost accounting required the application of new systems of paperwork, computation production, and supervising techniques that came to be known loosely at "scientific management," a body of ideas first publicized by Frederick Winslow Taylor and other engineers in the decade before World War I. . . .

A new class of business professionals took up the application of scientific man-agement with missionary zeal. Perhaps because they were defensive about their rela-tively new claim to professional status, these professionals were particularly adamant about the masculine identity of their disciplines. Scientific management provided business professionals not only with a system of procedures but also with an ideolog-ical rationale for their own dominance. They saw the allocation of planning to man-agers and the rationalization of work as not only economic goals but also political goods; summarized as "efficiency," scientific management became an indisputable moral tenet of the early twentieth century.

Both male and female reformers in the Progressive period were often as attracted to Taylorism as were business professionals, and touted scientific management as a panacea for labor unrest, political corruption, and corporate irresponsibility. Women with feminist agendas saw in the even-handed execution of its methods a means of bringing sexual equality to the marketplace. Male business professionals more fre-quently used scientific management to promulgate what they perceived to be mas-culine values and modes of thought: scientific planning, an end to sentimentality, and the objectification of workers and materials. They saw themselves as forging new frontiers in a society whose old forms of male adventurism were about to end and pro-posed new expeditions for themselves along the corporate frontier of cost accounting, institution building, and managerial control. Conflicts between these ways of seeing and using scientific management emerged from differing positions of gender, profes-sionalism, and reform. . . .

When Frederick Winslow Taylor, an engineer, sought a new method of account-ing for his management techniques in the late nineteenth century he turned for advice to a leading railroad accountant. Taylor began to attack managerial problems on the factory floor in ways that were heavily dependent on both cost accounting and ad-ministrative reform. . . .

. . . Taylor and other scientific managers argued the institution of cost accounting and the paperwork it required could only work if a new administrative layer was

From Sharon Hartman Strom, *Beyond the Typewriter* (Chicago: University of Chicago Press, 1992), pp. 2–5, 25–26, 35, 68–70, 109–136, 152–154.

added; both bookkeeping and labor policies had to be taken out of the hands of the foremen and placed in the hands of the engineers and their assistants. The engineers would require an expanded clerical staff to handle the paperwork. As the contract system with foremen was eliminated and systematic management installed, Chandler observes, "a voucher system of accounts was introduced; times studies were carried out; route, time, cost and inspection clerks were employed; and the manager's staff was enlarged."

Systematic managers like Taylor . . . were trying to coordinate but also separate different aspects of management that had formerly been handled by foremen and book-keepers—purchasing, production control, inventory records, payroll, and pricing—by creating a series of administrative units or departments that had only existed in primitive forms in most businesses before 1890. These units required new kinds of office employees and records. While the engineer or administrator set up the system and gauged how well it was working, mid-level managers were needed to compile the information that would tell bosses what they wanted to know. And to keep the now far more detailed records that were required, new office staffs of clerks were essential. The coordination and management of these administrative systems was dependent upon the manufacture of paperwork, paperwork not required under the old order. By keeping better records management did two seemingly contradictory but really complementary things. It took administrative responsibilities away from the foreman and the bookkeeper ("centralizing" authority) as it delegated some of their mental responsibilities to subordinates like timekeepers and clerks ("decentralizing" authority). Management's overall purpose was to separate mental and manual work by extracting as much decision making as possible from production workers and transforming it into standardized tasks performed by clerks and managers. . . .

By 1912, then, the rhetoric of the accounting revolution had been formed. The scientific management movement, the emergence of the multidivisional corporation, the appearance of a growing and articulate class of professional experts, and the rising tide of government legislation requiring financial accountability had all contributed to the molding of that rhetoric. Its implementation on a material basis, however, was far from complete. That required a staggering new array of paperwork, computations, and hierarchy of office workers. Without fundamental changes in the organization of the office work force and its composition, the accounting revolution would not have been possible. . . .

Engineers, according to one historian, saw "their proposals as substitutes for progressive reforms, not as supplements to them." Their epithets for Progressive reformers included "utopist" and "dilletante," terminology frequently used in the past to question the sexual identity of male reformers. The business professions were not only careers, they were also masculine callings central to the maintenance of an orderly society. They would impose disciplined system on the chaos of capitalism so that the social and sexual order would be preserved. Even though women had helped to mediate social problems in earlier decades, they now needed to step aside or to confine themselves to assisting roles. . . .

. . . As Samuel Haber has observed, . . . "An efficient person was an effective person, and that characterization brought with it a long shadow of latent associations and predispositions; a turning toward hard work and away from feeling, toward discipline and away from sympathy, toward masculinity and away from femininity."

Many intellectuals of the Progressive period, including the founders of the business professions, sought to link their academic training and intellectual values to a masculine American tradition of heroism rooted in pragmatism, experimentation, and exploration, while rejecting pure idealism as inherently feminine and merely sentimental. Casting activities of the new professions in the heroic mold was critical to making them manly. What might be viewed by others as technical labor, paper-pushing, delegation of important tasks to others, and mere money-making had to be portrayed as adventurous, noble, and indispensable to the national purpose. Engineers and businessmen emphasized the ways in which they were pioneers conquering "new frontiers," subduing industrial disorder in much the same way their ancestors had "tamed" the wilderness. According to Arch W. Shaw, business publisher and early instructor at the Harvard Business School, "the manufacturer-merchant" had "become a pioneer on the frontier of human desires and needs." Louis Brandeis thought the best businessmen were pioneers breaking new paths that "will become the peopled highways." This posturing as pioneers, perhaps, reflected the same kind of crisis of masculinity and search for heroism found in the life of Theodore Roosevelt, whose affinity for both western-style adventure and engineers was well known. . . .

. . . George S. Morison, who spoke to fellow engineers at the American Society of Chemical Engineers in 1895, claimed that engineers "are the priests of material development, of the work which enables other men to enjoy the fruits of the great sources of power in Nature, and of the power of mind over matter. We are priests of the new epoch, without superstitions." E. E. Hunt, a self-proclaimed Taylor discipline and assistant to U. S. Secretary of Commerce (and engineer) Herbert Hoover, claimed in 1924 that "scientific management is becoming a part of our moral inheritance. Taylor has won a victory for the science of management which is no less overwhelming than Pasteur's victory for bacteriology." Taylor himself claimed that engineers could educate "not only the work men but the whole of the country as to the true facts." H. L. Gantt described the engineer as "a man of few opinions and many facts, few words and many deeds," who "should be accorded the leadership which is his proper place in our economic system." The necessity of maintaining the sexual purity of a profession that thought of itself as a priesthood was self-evident. . . .

Employment management, increasingly known as "personnel management" after World War I, appeared to be both more receptive to women and to catch their imaginations in ways which engineering and business administration had not. Although only a handful of women attended the national conference of the Employment Managers Association in 1917, more than a hundred did so in 1919, and by 1922 the Bureau of Vocational Information reported that employment management ranked sixth in frequency of requests for information from women on specific occupations. Advice books unequivocally endorsed personnel management as a suitable and stimulating career for ambitious women. It appeared true that at least one of the new business professions appealed to women, was suited to their supposed gender characteristics, and offered them real chances of employment.

The alleged gender characteristics of personnel management were wide-ranging. They reflected long-standing assumptions about women's "natural" propensity for such maternal tasks as domestic management and social work, and also emphasized modern professional women's interest in efficiency, the scientific method, and the ability to move comfortably among both sexes. The journalist Ida Tarbell focused on the traditional when she commented on women employment managers in 1920: "All the best practice proves the wisdom of bringing in women to deal with women. They know what to do in the case of headaches and crying spells. They know the springs to touch in order to turn a sulky and indifferent worker into a cheerful and interested one." But Mary G. Kiepe, employment manager at a meat-packing firm in Buffalo, omitted any reference to sentimentality and defined personnel management in modernist terms: "the necessity of conserving human beings and making them efficient; of applying to men what we are beginning to apply to things—principles of efficiency." . . .

The feminine and masculine sides of personnel management could be espoused by either sex; these were gendered traits of ideas and philosophies, not necessarily of individual sexes. Men and women contributed to the feminine aspect of personnel management, and both women and men sought to toughen the profession. In contrast to the more "masculine" business professions like business administration and engineering, personnel management purposely sought to incorporate an understanding of human behavior into the administration of capitalist enterprises. But most personnel managers emphasized that their methods were both systematic and profit-producing. Their expertise, they claimed, was just as integral to the proper functioning of scientific management as the other business disciplines.

In order to be heard by those who counted, personnel managers aligned themselves with the ideas of scientific management, the most powerful business and reform ethos of the period. Their simultaneous attempts to add "the human factor" to scientific management produced an intriguing mixture of both challenge and accommodation to capitalist and gender-based hierarchies. It also provoked some serious thinking about women's roles in the modern economic order. Were women to bring a feminine touch to the corporate enterprise, or should they present themselves as sex neutral professionals? How did feminist politics fit into humanized scientific management? The answers to these questions were not always so obvious.

The implications of personnel management for women should not be considered strictly by individual women's successes in rising with a reformist agenda. They were attracted to the discipline precisely because of its potential for reforming the traditional sexual division of labor. . . .

Personnel management emerged in the late teens from three occupations, all of which had reformist tendencies: psychology, vocational guidance, and welfare work. All three drew women into personnel management and allowed them to influence its development. The vocational guidance movement, which came out of social settlement work, college placement bureaus, and attempts to keep youngsters in high school, attracted women and gave them expertise in one aspect of early personnel work. College women's access to undergraduate and graduate training in psychology, particularly applied psychology, created a contingent of female psychological experts available to work as managers and researchers. As employers turned toward welfare departments to reduce labor turnover and to foster company loyalty, new managerial positions were created. Women often managed early welfare and employment departments in insurance companies, department stores, and factories where large numbers of women were employed. As these businesses expanded their functions to include personnel work, women welfare workers were in a position to move into personnel management.

The academic discipline of psychology, and its applied offshoots, particularly industrial psychology, provided personnel management with a theoretical framework. Vocational guidance added a progressive reform consciousness; welfare work supplied jobs in industry for both the ambitious and the reform-minded. . . .

Psychology immediately appealed to women as an academic discipline, and it was readily available to them by the turn of the century at co-educational institutions and women's colleges. Students preparing for "women's occupations" like education and social work often sought undergraduate training in psychology. The opening of more graduate programs at universities allowed women to seek advanced degrees in the field. By 1910 women could take graduate work in psychology at a wide variety of institutions, including Pennsylvania, Columbia, Yale, Clark, Cornell, Radcliffe, Bryn Mawr, and the universities of Chicago, California, and Wisconsin.

Feminist graduate students in psychology soon saw the possibility of using psychological research to challenge traditional ideas about women. The "greater variability" theory was especially detrimental to women's equal participation in politics, the academy, and nontraditional occupations; it argued that men's intelligence was more varied than that of women and therefore justified men's monopoly of important positions and occupations. Women's less varied intelligence suited them, not surprisingly, to domestic life, child-rearing, and the women's professions. John Dewey's student at the University of Chicago, Helen Bradford Thompson, conducted meticulous experiments to determine whether significant sex differences existed in men's and women's motor and mental performances. She found that there was a wide variation between the performance of individuals but hardly any important differences between those of women and men; sex was not a significant variable in performance. . . .

Whatever the attractions of the discipline, women took up psychology in ever greater numbers after 1910. By 1921, 20.4 percent of all the psychologists were women, a far higher proportion than in any other scientific field except nutrition. Of all doctorates awarded in psychology between 1920 and 1923 more than one-third went to women, and roughly 20 percent of the members of the American Psychological Association before World War II were women. But difficulty in obtaining academic positions continued, and many female psychologists gravitated toward applied psychology in business, government, and education.

Applied psychology, like engineering, was an amalgam of academic theory and hands-on experiments in the real world. . . . By 1910 business was approaching psychologists for help in developing employee selection tests, particularly for skilled machine clerks, telephone operators, and salespersons. . . .

The search for practical uses of psychology attracted women from the beginning. . . .

Standardized testing was the most eagerly sought-after application of psychology in the early twentieth century. . . . [M]ost of this testing, intentionally or not, was used to justify the status quo. Many psychologists turned to the testing of immigrants and blacks and, not surprisingly, produced results that bolstered middle-class, native-born white beliefs in the superiority of their own groups. Psychologists "found" that low intelligence, as measured by tests, could be correlated with darker skin, southern European backgrounds, or the "antisocial" behavior of the poor.

There is no evidence to suggest that women psychologists as a group were particularly immune to the elitist and racist biases of early testers. Liberal feminists were often committed to the notion that class hierarchies were both natural and desirable; what they wanted was a chance to prove the competence of women so that they could take their proper place in those hierarchies alongside the professional men who were already in control. When combined with the new field of vocational guidance, testing could validate channeling some boys and girls to vocational programs in high school and the sending of others, usually white and native-born, to college. Testing could make American society more efficient, and productive by sorting people according to their intelligence and talents into the occupations for which they were best suited. Vocational guidance and testing were pursued by many feminists and educators as at least partial solutions to American problems of inequality and class confrontation. Hierarchies based on "scientific placement" could be defended as reasonable forms of social organization. . . .

Vocational guidance was to become an important and influential strand of the expanding field of personnel management directly following the war. . . . [F]eminist educators were attracted to vocational guidance because it held out the possibility of putting people into positions on the basis of their training and merits rather than their family connections, race, sex, or appearance. It seemed a logical extension of the suffrage movement's attempts to promote equality in the public sphere. Vocational guidance remained one of the more marginal aspects of personnel management in business, but even on the periphery it could legitimize efforts to suit jobs to people and to develop internal promotion systems based on fair and reasonable criteria.

Another strain of personnel management came from early welfare work in business. Paternalistic factory owners first provided welfare services for employees in the nineteenth century. Welfare programs might have included one or more of a variety of services: bathhouses, company housing and stores, libraries, and lunchrooms. More systematic welfare programs appeared at the turn of the century. . . .

Firms that were installing highly rationalized assembly-line labor processes may also have been motivated by the realization that better-rested, fed, entertained, and exercised operatives would be more productive and efficient. H. J. Heinz, AT & T, General Electric, and Sears and Roebuck, all employers of large numbers of young women who performed repetitive tasks at a fast pace, systematically introduced welfare programs. . . . There were no reasons why such measures had to be incompatible with ruthless managerial methods; both National Cash Register and AT & T were so committed to the drive system that they eventually evoked employee resistance and strikes. . . .

Other factors spurred welfare programs as well. Interest in working conditions in reform circles and the public press during the Progressive period made employers anxious to prove to the general public that they could provide safe and pleasant jobs without government and union interference. Unions had made employers' dealings with male workers far more problematic. The growing numbers of clerical workers, managers, and salespersons in corporations created special work forces that, theoretically, needed to be treated differently from factory workers and from each other. In a period that still stressed the social propriety of separating the sexes, women clerks and factory workers needed spaces within plants and large office buildings where they could eat their meals, rest, and socialize away from men. Employers were also anxious to make certain that the lunch hour was taken with dispatch. The temptations to wander leisurely around town in search of food and to shop during the lunch hour often resulted in late employees, so providing lunch services on the premises gave employers more control.

It seemed logical to employers to put most of these burgeoning welfare programs in the hands of new kinds of managers. The YMCA offered instruction for "welfare secretaries" as early as 1904, and in 1905 Gertrude Beeks, in charge of a special welfare secretary consultation service for the National Civic Federation, claimed the status of "a new profession" for the welfare secretary. . . .

Although psychology, vocational guidance, and welfare work were all on the upswing in the teens, they remained suspect in business and engineering circles because of their "soft-hearted," effeminate overtones. On the other hand, those who were endeavoring to modernize managerial practice under the guise of Taylorism were finding that pure scientific management was almost too "hard-hearted" and required a human touch. Scientific managers began to argue after 1910 that their strategies should pay as much attention to "the human factor" as to rationalization, technology, and the techniques of cost accounting. The ruthlessness of earlier Taylorist methods, immediately understood by workers, had to be disguised by a smokescreen of incentives and manipulative management policies in order to gain employee consent.

Taylor had not foreseen this problem. He had assumed the implementation of "a fair wage for a fair day's work" would ensure cooperation from workers and be all that their employers need provide. Taylor and other scientific management engineers tended to view welfare workers as interfering busybodies. The early years of the century saw something of a standoff emerge between welfare managers and the Taylorites, with the scientific managers opposing welfare work as antiquated sentimentalism, and welfare managers perceiving the Taylorites as ruthless implementers of the drive system. But aspects of Taylorism anticipated both welfare work and personnel management: wresting employment and promotion powers from the foreman and placing them in the hands of management; studying in as detailed a way as possible the actual procedures of individual jobs with an eye to standardizing them; fixing wages according to a rational formula; and providing rest periods, decent working hours, proper tools, and good safety conditions to achieve maximum efficiency. But Taylor did not see any new discipline emerging to handle these functions. He thought most of them could be handled by engineers in a planning room close to the shop-floor and appears not to have envisioned the massive administrative and clerical "nonproductive" apparatus the new functions would require. His death in 1915 opened the door to wide-ranging modification of his ideas and conveniently allowed his disciplines to search his minimal body of written texts for endorsements of a wide array of schemes and positions he had probably never envisioned. Whether or not Taylor's plans were followed precisely, the enthusiasm for what was perceived to be his philosophy remained unbounded. After 1915, managers often sought credibility by claiming they were using "scientific management." Taylorite disciplines helped to create the impression that Taylor had provided the intellectual basis for personnel management and given it his blessing. . . .

. . . As long as it could be claimed that the methods in "other fields" paid off, that they increased efficiency, that they had been arrived at through a procedure vaguely resembling the scientific method, they could be stitched to the ever-growing patchwork quilt of scientific management.

More than a few women, some of them critics of the excessive of industrialism, others feminists or early personnel managers, were instrumental in assembling this quilt. Their interest in the faith of scientific management grew from several perceived affinities. Many women welfare workers and employment directors welcomed Taylorism because of the opportunity it gave them to appear to be tough-minded and efficient in their techniques and attitudes. Those who were feminists saw in Taylorism a chance to judge workers on the basis of aptitudes and productivity, and therefore saw an opening for more equal consideration of women. The ideology to scientific management, if applied justly, seemed to fit in well with the principles of vocational guidance; the workers should be suited to the job. Progressive reformers saw no necessary contradiction between protective legislation for women workers, trade union organization, less stressful working conditions, and the introduction of scientific management techniques. They believed that the "scientific" organization of production and machinery might eliminate seasonal work and overtime, reduce fatigue, provide higher wages, end conflict between managers and workers, and open opportunities to the talented. Taylor had eloquently promised as much. . . .

Mary Barnett Gilson was the most influential and articulate woman advocate of Taylorism. She laid out a coherent plan of scientific personnel management for a well-known business firm, argued that the new management techniques could further feminist goals, and tried to guarantee a place for women employment managers in the new system.

Gilson grew up in Pittsburgh, where her father was the editor of a religious newspaper, and she witnessed first-hand the effects of horrible working conditions in the Carnegie steel works. She remembers her college years at Wellesley as a time when she "floundered around," with the memorable exception of attending a stirring campus speech by social reformer Florence Kelley of the Consumers' League. Although Gilson thought that "most women who went to college in the nineties were serious in their vague hope to be of some use, not mere parasites," few options existed for executing this hope. She had no real interest in marrying and seemed to take pride in the fact that her red hair reminded her relatives of her "spinster great-aunt Jane." Teaching seemed the only possible career, and although one bold instructor suggested journalism, Gilson settled on library work in Pittsburgh, where she attempted to introduce books to slum children.

Having moved to Boston with a woman friend, Gilson took up training for department store girls at the Women's Educational and Industrial Union in 1910. Boston was the center of the developing vocational guidance movement. . . . Gilson decided to train . . . as one of the new vocational counselors at the Boston Trade School for Girls. "It was all new and exciting," she recalled, "We lived in hope that we could ultimately place all the round pegs in round holes and all the square pegs in square ones." But her work at the Trade School for Girls ultimately proved to be frustrating: "there was no really scientific method of detecting the motor-minded, so incomes, grades, the advice of teachers, and the will of parents were in essence the divining rods." After the schools provided guidance and training, the jobs offered to students were still low paying and working conditions unpleasant; most girls found positions in garment-making sweatshops. Vocational guidance alone was not enough.

Gilson was finally infused with a militant new sense of direction when Taylor came to Boston to give a series of lectures. "Those," she fervently recalled, "left me in the state of a person who has suddenly 'got religion.'" Here was the key to ameliorating the deplorable conditions of the working-class women she encountered and a way to carve out a niche beyond that of sentimental reformer for herself. . . . "[M]ore than anything else his stress on the responsibility of management impressed me. The time had come, [s]he said, when we should stop lecturing workers about their failures and duties *until* we had awakened management to its own responsibility for good workmanship."

Gilson was given an opportunity to do something with her new-found religion. In 1913 she was invited to become the service and employment director at Clothcraft Shops in Cleveland, a large garment factory that produced men's clothing and employed several thousand workers, nearly three-quarters of whom were women. Richard A. Feiss, the young works manager in an old family business, Joseph and Feiss Company, producer of the Clothcraft label for men's garments, had also been bitten by the bug of Taylorism. . . .

Feiss had done most of the things Taylor and other scientific manager engineers suggested. He had also established up-to-date welfare measures. But the "human factor" remained problematic. His firm was still plagued by typical employment woes of the garment industry: high labor turnover, tardiness and absenteeism, and seemingly untrainable workers, many of them non-English-speaking immigrants. Gilson was charged with systematizing employment and using welfare programs to create a more efficient and loyal labor force. Feiss gave her, evidently, a free hand in devising her system of management and made room for her feminist commitments too. . . .

For Gilson and Feiss, the most important key to happy workers and an efficient plant was proper placement; vocational guidance had moved from the school to the workplace. It was the special role of the employment manager to find the job best suited to the applicant and to draw on existing personnel as much as possible for positions beyond those of operatives. Feiss and Gilson both thought that effective placement, higher wages, internal promotion, and good welfare programs would undercut labor turnover, and did demonstrate turnover rates much lower than average for the garment industry. . . .

Gilson surely had an agenda that went beyond adding the human factor to Taylorism. For Gilson, good personnel work was also the key to issues of sexual equity in employment. She was offended by the discovery that recommendations for promotion from foremen were often the result of bribery or gifts. These had ominous implications in an establishment with male foremen and female operatives. She saw both the original application form and employee records, which were extraordinarily elaborate at Clothcraft, as a way of developing a pool of female labor from which promotions based on merit and aptitude could be made. The plant provided English classes and training programs for new positions. Factory operatives became forewoman, operatives moved into the office, and working-class women were trained as supervisors; Gilson also brought in college-educated women to be trained as executives. Given the proper set of wage inducements and promotion opportunities, Gilson argued, women made as reliable a set of employees as men. "All these women were competent and respected by management and workers," she claimed. "And all the predictions about high labor turnover among women and losing money training them did not come true. . . . The question of sex did not enter in when we were fine-combing our organization for able persons to take supervisory or other important positions. If a women was chosen she was held as responsible for capable performance as was a man."

Gilson firmly believed that women had the best chance of holding their own in a system based on performance and merit, as long as that system was sexually unbiased. She thought that holding workers directly accountable was the key to creating such a system. Using other criteria would win the circumstantial or subjective argument for men every time: "a profit-making system involves using the best available worker for a job and not employing a man because he has a sick wife or because he wants to pay a mortgage." Gilson was infuriated by such arguments. She had once heard an industrial relations man tell at a conference "how his firm attempted to discover who was 'worthy' of the best jobs. He said they found that one of the girls in their offices lived in a very nice apartment, and they decide she was not in need of promotion!" Women stood a better chance of gaining a place in industry by standing on their abilities and a system that judged workers completely on their merits. There were limits to Gilson's reforms in ending discrimination and opening opportunity, however. Although she rationalized wage rates and increased women's wages in general, women, were still paid about half as much as men, on average, at Clothcraft, and union protocol guaranteed that management would never make women operatives into cutters.

The service programs at Clothcraft were under Gilson's command as well. . . . By 1915 Clothcraft had an employee cafeteria, a medical department (which provided free eye examinations and eyeglasses), a thrift bank, recreation facilities, a factory orchestra and a choral club, and a branch of the Cleveland Public Library. Workers were encouraged to attend night school or continue their education.

Service programs were not confined to the factory; Gilson and her staff used an extensive system of home visits to root out tardiness and absences, inappropriate dress, poor health habits (including sleeping at night with the windows closed), and "causes of dissatisfaction." These visits, were, no doubt, both intrusive and maternalistic. But if Gilson's descriptions of them are analyzed more carefully, it is also clear that she saw them as an indispensable part of her feminist agenda. Reproving those who were tardy and absent had the same goal as a system that promoted piece rates and rapid, efficient production; it provided an atmosphere in which those who worked the hardest and were most able would be most rewarded. . . . Gilson was above all anxious to prove the critics of women workers wrong by demonstrating that women could take their jobs as seriously as men. And while she saw ending discrimination as one aspect of her campaign, she also saw creating new habits of industry and independence in her women workers as another. . . .

Gilson's plan for giving women more responsibility and self-confidence at Clothcraft depended on the cooperation of working-class women. Would they agree that every job, no matter how unimportant, was a test of women's reliability? Gilson's account of her days at Clothcraft was carefully tailored to prove the beneficence of scientific management. Low labor turnover at the plant probably indicated some degree of worker satisfaction with Gilson's policies and the better than average working conditions of Feiss's factory in Cleveland. But it is doubtful that women operatives always had the same goals Gilson did. It seems more likely that class perspective helped to shape feminist ambitions. Did women who looked forward to being married and having families want to assume the kind of rigorous self-accountability Gilson promoted if it meant giving up married life? Or were these largely the ideas of women managers, most of them single, like Gilson? Gilson's policies included the firing of women upon marriage. She claimed that married women were "as a rule irregular in attendance and burdened with household duties" and often had husbands whom they supported. But behind this policy was another idea of Gilson's: urging young women to postpone marriage to a later date. She claimed that the "unwritten" marriage law at Clothcraft had "materially lessened the early, precipitate marriages in our factory." She wanted women to become independent of fathers and husbands alike, not only because she thought they would be happier women, but also so that the sex of women could begin to prove its real worth.

Whatever the chord Gilson's ideas struck among women workers, her bid to offer managerial and executive positions to women generally fell on deaf ears at other corporations. . . .

During [World War I] and the months immediately following it, the recruitment of large numbers of women for responsible positions in industry brought Gilson's work at Clothcraft some notoriety. She used that public exposure to promote equal pay for equal work and access to promotions for women. . . .

Feminist demands for equal treatment and opportunity were converging with the development of modernized personnel systems, which also emphasized merit and an end to personal favoritism. Personnel departments were on their way toward "the systematic dispensation" of rewards and benefits. Such "bureaucratic control" characterizes the most modern corporate structures and tends to undermine labor discontent by creating segmented labor hierarchies whose tiers are allegedly based on rational criteria of education, training, experience, and merit. As Gilson's experiments demonstrated, the exclusion of women and people of color from upper-level jobs remained an irrational aspect of an increasingly rational system. "Rightly or wrongly," admitted a subcommittee of the Office Executives Division of the American Management Association in 1924, "most organizations . . . do not consider their female employees as timber for advancement in the same sense that the males employees are considered." The continuation of practices that denied promotion to certain categories of workers undermined the validity of rationalized personnel management. In future years the continued refusal of managers in both government and private industry to consider promoting people beyond certain levels because of race, sex, or religion would often spark resentment in bureaucratic organizations. The most articulate feminist critique of such policies developed in the civil services, where promises of internal promotion through examination and job review provided employees with a rationale for challenging discrimination. . . .

. . . The precarious alliance between Taylorism and Progressive reform, the labor shortages of the war, and the intervention of the federal government had allowed someone like Mary Gilson to voice her feminist and reformist views in the teens; in the 1920s these circumstances had changed.

Gilson's fate after 1920 is all too instructive. In a burst of enthusiasm Richard Feiss decided to build a new factory in Cleveland to house the anticipated gains in demand for men's clothing during World War I. But by the time the plant opened in

1921 the men's clothing industry suffered a headlong decline. Plunged into near financial ruin, Feiss suffered a nervous breakdown in 1924. He was forced out by company directors, who now suspected his progressive methods of putting the business in jeopardy. He and Gilson both left Clothcraft, and many of Gilson's programs were dismantled. In a swan-song appearance before the Taylor Society in 1924, Gilson outlined the contributions Taylorism had made to personnel management, but insisted that it had never really been implemented fairly with regard to women: "Many people have applied scientific management methods as far as 'the efficient use of men and materials' is concerned, but I have yet to be overwhelmed with many evidences of a broad and generous viewpoint concerning the efficient use of women in the matter of training and opportunity for advancement. A reservoir of pride and competence in workmanship has yet to be tapped when 'equal opportunity' becomes more than a pretty phrase."

Gilson left management and entered the academy. She wanted to study economics at Harvard, but was told by Dean Donham of the Harvard Business School that she would have to attend sex-segregated classes at Radcliffe; even more insulting, it seemed, was the rule that men could study in the library until 10 P.M. but women had to leave by 6. She did her Ph.D. work at Columbia instead. In the late 1920s she became an expert on the effects of unemployment, contributed to the growing support for government legislation to provide unemployment benefits for workers, and in 1931 joined the faculty at the University of Chicago. . . .

Gilson's unequivocal feminism is appealing to those in the present looking back at her work. But she and other scientific management enthusiasts of the teens and twenties, both women and men, had failed to see the darker possibilities of the drive to organize the human factor in the American workplace and how it might evolve when efficiency and cost accounting once again took the upper hand. Because profit-making was the ultimate goal of American business, and because male-dominated inner sanctums of business managed the implementation of that goal, most middle-class women would be as likely as working people to face exclusion. Without a feminist movement that came from below as well as from above, women like Gilson . . . were likely to be stranded on desert islands in a sea of male corporate culture.

⋈ *F U R T H E R   R E A D I N G*

Aitken, *Scientific Management in Action: Taylorism at Watertown Arsenal* (Princeton, NJ: Princeton University Press, 1960).

Banta, Martha. *Taylored Lives: Narrative Productions in the Age of Taylor, Veblen, and Ford* (Chicago: University of Chicago Press, 1993).

Copley, Frank B. *Frederick Winslow Taylor,* 2 vols. (New York: Harper, 1923).

Haber, Samuel. *Efficiency and Uplift: Scientific Management in the Progressive Era, 1890–1920* (Chicago: University of Chicago Press, 1964).

Jordon, John M. *Machine-Age Ideology: Social Engineering & American Liberalism, 1911–1939* (Chapel Hill, NC: University of North Carolina Press, 1994).

Kanigel, Robert, *The One Best Way: Frederick Winslow Taylor and the Enigma of Efficiency* (New York: Viking, 1997).

Layton, Edwin T. *The Revolt of the Engineers: Social Responsibility and the Engineering Profession* (Cleveland, OH: The Press of Case Western Reserve University, 1971).

Ford, Automobility, and Mass Production, 1908–1941

4A

Automobiles represent one of the key influences on twentieth-century American culture. Service stations, motels, drive-in theaters, drive-in banks, fast food chains, supermarkets, vast "auto miles" of new and used car dealerships, automotive parts stores, and shopping malls are obvious examples of the extended automotive system. The automobile provided an enormous stimulus to the petroleum, tire, machine tool, auto parts, and instruments industries. It also is associated with the growth of suburbs, consolidated school systems, and the deterioration of life in inner cities. Government established thousands of miles of new highways, the licensing of drivers, insurance regulations, public safety laws, policing, and gasoline taxes. In short, it appears that the automobile shaped American culture more than the other way around. But was this really the case? This chapter will approach the question by looking at Henry Ford (1863–1947), the Ford car, and the "mass production" system.

Although many individuals (the Duryea brothers, Ransom Olds, Albert Pope, Hiram Maxim, Henry Leland, the Dodge brothers, Charles Kettering, William Durant, and Alfred P. Sloan, to name a few) played roles in introducing automobiles to America, none proved more important or controversial than Ford. The Model T he introduced in 1908 was mass produced at very cheap prices ($950 in 1910; $290 in 1924) by combining precision techniques and new metalworking methods with continuous-flow assembly line processes. Ford inaugurated the "automobile age" by making available for the first time a car that many ordinary Americans could afford. He became a populist hero in the eyes of many contemporaries, who credited him with democratizing the marketplace and furthering the American dream. Yet a closer look at Ford—man, company, and machine—reveals all the division, hopes, enthusiasm, ugliness, and confusion that comprised early twentieth-century American society.

Why did Ford loom so large in America's pantheon of industrial heroes? Did price alone account for the widespread popularity of the Model T? How original was Ford's manufacturing system? How does the public image of Henry Ford as cultural hero square with his reputation as a no-nonsense captain of industry? Did Ford's drive to democratize the marketplace extend to his factories?

ꗸ *D O C U M E N T S*

The first selection reprints a well known *Encyclopedia Britannica* article on mass production ghostwritten for Ford by William Cameron. Second is an extract from Ford's autobiography that gives his view of the origins of the Model T and the assembly line, as well as the effect of repetitive labor on workers.

Ford's tendency to take the lion's share of the credit for the innovations introduced by his company is challenged in the third selection by Charles Sorensen. One of Ford's closest associates for nearly forty years, Sorensen admires Ford's leadership but credits others (including himself) for the key technical innovations.

The fourth selection, from Edmund Wilson's *American Earthquake,* describes the encounter of Bert, an English immigrant mechanic, with Ford's mass production system. Fifth is the personal narrative of a Russian Jew named Charles Madison, who worked at the Ford Motor Company at the height of the Model T era. Both are bluntly critical of Ford's labor policies and the ways that the company degraded and exploited employees. Yet their accounts also differ. Madison was an adolescent with relatively little experience when he entered the Ford plant, while Bert had worked at least seven years as a toolmaker in the British auto industry. Bert was well acquainted with shop customs, including pacing. Madison was a beginner. Their age difference may also explain their varying attitudes toward auto work. Bert feels victimized by his work experience and regrets coming to America. Madison, on the other hand, is more optimistic and sure of himself. Although he decries his servitude, he nonetheless retains a strong belief in the American dream.

Mass Production (Encyclopedia Article), 1926

The term mass production is used to describe the modern method by which great quantities of a single standardized commodity are manufactured. As commonly employed it is made to refer to the quantity produced, but its primary reference is to method. In several particulars the term is unsatisfactory. Mass production is not merely quantity production, for this may be had with none of the requisites of mass production. Nor is it merely machine production, which also may exist without any resemblance to mass production. Mass production is the focusing upon a manufacturing project of the principles of power accuracy, economy, system, continuity and speed. The interpretation of these principles, through studies of operation and machine development and their co-ordination, is the conspicuous task of management. And the normal result is a productive organisation that delivers in quantities a useful commodity of standard material, workmanship and design at minimum cost. The necessary, precedent condition of mass production is a capacity, latent or developed, of *mass consumption,* the ability to absorb large production. The two go together, and in the latter may be traced the reasons for the former. . . .

. . . What have been the effects of mass production on society?

(1) Beginning with management, where unquestionably mass production methods take their rise, there is a notable increase in industrial control, as distinguished from financial control. The engineer's point of view has gained the ascendancy and this trend will undoubtedly continue until finance becomes the handmaid instead of the

From *Encyclopaedia Britannica,* 14th ed., © 1929, 1930, by Encyclopaedia Britannica, Inc.

mistress of productive industry. Industrial control has been marked by a continuous refinement of standardization, which means the instant adoption of the better method to the exclusion of the old, in the interests of production. Financial control was not, in its heyday, marked by a tendency to make costly changes in the interests of the product. The economy of scrapping the old equipment immediately upon the invention of the better equipment was not so well understood. It was engineering control, entrenched in mass production methods, that brought in this new readiness to advance. In this way management has been kept close to the shop and has reduced the office to a clearing house for the shop. Managers and men have been brought into closer contact and understanding. Manufacturing has been reduced to greater single-ness of purpose.

(2) The effect of mass production on the product has been to give it the highest standard of quality ever attained in output of great quantities. Conditions of mass production require material of the best quality to pass successfully through the operations. The most accuracy must control all these operations. Every part must be produced to fit at once into the design for which it is made. In mass production there are no fitters. The presence of fitters indicates that the parts have been produced unfit for immediate placement in the design. In works of art and luxury this accuracy is achieved at the cost of careful handiwork. To introduce hand methods of obtaining accuracy into mass production would render mass production impossible with any reference to price-convenience. The standard quality of the product is guaranteed by the fact that machines are so constructed that a piece of work cannot go through them unless it exactly accords with specifications. If the work goes through the tools, it must be right. It will thus be seen that the burden of creation is on management in designing and selecting the material which is to be produced by the multiple processes utilised in mass production.

(3) The effect of mass production on mechanical science has been to create a wide variety of single-purpose machines which not only group similar operations and perform them in quantity, but also reproduce skill of hand to a marvellous degree. It is not so much the discovery of new principles as the new combination and application of old ones that mark this development. Under mass production the industry of machine making has increased out of all comparison with its previous history, and the constant designing of new machines is a part of the productive work of every great manufacturing institution.

(4) The effect of mass production on employees has been variously appraised. Whether the modern corporation is the destruction or salvation of arts and crafts, whether it narrows or broadens opportunity . . . must be determined by observable facts. A cardinal principle of mass production is that hard work, in the old physical sense of laborious burden-bearing, is wasteful. The physical load is lifted off men and placed on machines. The recurrent mental load is shifted from men in production to men in designing. As to the contention that machines thus become the masters of men, it may be said the machines have increased men's mastery of their environment, and that a generation which is ceaselessly scrapping its machines exhibits few indications of mechanical subjection.

The need for skilled artisans and creative genius is greater under mass production than without it. In entering the shops of the Ford Motor Company, for example, one passes through great departments of skilled mechanics who are not engaged in production, but in construction and maintenance of the machinery of production. Details of from 5,000 to 10,000 highly skilled artisans at strategic points throughout the shops were not commonly witnessed in the days preceding mass production. It has been debated whether there is less or more skills as a consequence of mass production. The present writer's opinion is that there is more. The common work of the world has always been done by unskilled labour, but the common work of the world in modern times in not as common as it was formerly. In almost every field of labour more knowledge and responsibility are required than a generation or two ago.

My Life and Work, 1929

HENRY FORD

From the day the first motor car appeared on the streets it had to me appeared to be a necessity. It was this knowledge and assurance that led me to build to the one end—a car that would meet the wants of the multitudes. All my efforts were then and still are turned to the production of one car—one model. And, year following year, the pressure was, and still is, to improve and refine and make better, with an increasing reduction in price. The universal car, had to have these attributes:

(1) Quality in material to give service in use. . . .

(2) Simplicity in operation—because the masses are not mechanics.

(3) Power in sufficient quantity.

(4) Absolute reliability—because of the varied uses to which the cars would be put and the variety of roads over which they would travel.

(5) Lightness. . . .

(6) Control—to hold its speed always in hand, calmly and safely meeting every emergency and contingency either in the crowded streets of the city or on dangerous roads. The planetary transmission of the Ford gave this control and anybody could work it. That is the "why" of the saying: "Anybody can drive a Ford." It can turn around almost anywhere. . . .

The design which I settled upon was called "Model T." The important feature of the new model—which, if it were accepted, as I thought it would be, I intended to make the only model and then start into real production—was its simplicity. There were but four constructional units in the car—the power plant, the frame, the front axle, and the rear axle. All of these were easily accessible and they were designed so that no special skill would be required for their repair or replacement. I believed then, although I said very little about it because of the novelty of the idea, that it ought to be possible to have parts so simple and so inexpensive that the menace of expensive hand repair work would be entirely eliminated. The parts could be made so cheaply that it would be less expensive to buy new ones than to have old ones repaired. They could be carried in hardware shops just as nails or bolts are carried. I thought that it was up to me as the designer to make the car so completely simple that no one could fail to understand it. . . .

From Henry Ford, *My Life and Work* (New York: Doubleday, Page, 1929), pp. 67–69, 72–73, 78–84, 103–107, 110–112.

Therefore in 1909 I announced one morning, without any previous warning, that in the future we were going to build only one model, that the model was going to be "Model T," and that the chassis would be exactly the same for all cars, and I remarked:

"Any customer can have a car painted any colour that he wants so long as it is black."

I cannot say that any one agreed with me. The selling people could not of course see the advantages that a single model would bring about in production. More than that, they did not particularly care. They thought that our production was good enough as it was and there was a very decided opinion that lowering the sales price would hurt sales, that the people who wanted quality would be driven away and that there would be none to replace them. There was very little conception of the motor industry. A motor car was still regarded as something in the way of a luxury. The manufacturers did a good deal to spread this idea. Some clever persons invented the name "pleasure car" and the advertising emphasized the pleasure features. The sales people had ground for their objections and particularly when I made the following announcement:

> I will build a motor car for the great multitude. It will be large enough for the family but small enough for the individual to run and care for. It will be constructed of the best materials, by the best men to be hired, after the simplest designs that modern engineering can devise. But it will be so low in price that no man making a good salary will be unable to own one—and enjoy with his family the blessing of hours of pleasure in God's great open spaces.

This announcement was received not without pleasure. The general comment was:

"If Ford does that he will be out of business in six months." . . .

The more economical methods of production did not begin all at once. They began gradually—just as we began gradually to make our own parts. "Model T" was the first motor that we made ourselves. The great economies began in assembling and then extended to other sections so that, while to-day we have skilled mechanics in plenty, they do not produce automobiles—they make it easy for others to produce them. Our skilled men are the tool makers, the experimental workmen, the machinists, and the pattern makers. They are as good as any men in the world—so good, indeed, that they should not be wasted in doing that which the machines they contrive can do better. The rank and file of men come to us unskilled; they learn their job within a few hours or a few days. If they do not learn within that time they will never be of any use to us. These men are, many of them, foreigners, and all that is required before they are taken on is that they should be potentially able to do enough work to pay the overhead charges on the floor space they occupy. They do not have to be able-bodied men. We have jobs that require great physical strength—although they are rapidly lessening; we have other jobs that require no strength whatsoever—jobs which, as far as strength is concerned, might be attended to by a child of three. . . .

A Ford car contains about five hundred thousand parts—that is counting screws, nuts, and all. Some of the parts are fairly bulky and others are almost the size of watch parts. In our first assembling we simply started to put a car together at a spot on the floor and workmen brought to it the parts as they were needed in exactly the same way that one builds a house. When we started to make parts it was natural to create a single department of the factory to make that part, but usually one workman performed all of the operations necessary on a small part. The rapid press of production made it necessary to devise plans of production that would avoid having the workers falling over one another. The undirected worker spends more of his time walking about for materials and tools than he does in working; he gets small pay because pedestrianism is not a highly paid line.

The first step forward in assembly came when we began taking the work to the men instead of the men to the work. We now have two general principles in all operations—that a man shall never have to take more than one step, if possibly it can be avoided, and that no man need ever stoop over.

The principles of assembly are these:

(1) Place the tools and the men in the sequence of the operation so that each component part shall travel the least possible distance while in the process of finishing.

(2) Use work slides or some other form of carrier so that when a workman completes his operation, he drops the part always in the same place—which place must always be the most convenient place to his hands—and if possible have gravity carry the part to the next workman for his operation.

(3) Use sliding assembling lines by which the parts to be assembled are delivered at convenient distances.

The net result of the application of these principles is the reduction of the necessity for thought on the part of the worker and the reduction of his movements to a minimum. He does as nearly as possible only one thing with only one movement. . . .

Along about April 1, 1913, we first tried the experiment of an assembly line. We tried it on assembling the fly-wheel magneto. We try everything in a little way first—we will rip out anything once we discover a better way, but we have to know absolutely that the new way is going to be better than the old before we do anything drastic.

I believe that this was the first moving line ever installed. The idea came in a general way from the overhead trolley that the Chicago packers use in dressing beef. We had previously assembled the fly-wheel magneto in the usual method. With one workman doing a complete job he could turn out from thirty-five to forty pieces in a nine-hour day, or about twenty minutes to an assembly. What he did alone was then spread into twenty-nine operations; that cut down the assembly time to thirteen minutes, ten seconds. Then we raised the height of the line eight inches—this was in 1914—and cut the time to seven minutes. Further experimenting with the speed that the work should move at cut the time down to five minutes. In short, the result is this: by the aid of scientific study one man is now able to do somewhat more than four did only a comparative few years ago. That line established the efficiency of the method and we now use it everywhere. The assembling of the motor, formerly done by one man, is now divided into eighty-four operations—those men do the work that three times their number formerly did. In a short time we tried out the plan on the chassis. . . .

. . . The speed of the moving work had to be carefully tried out; in the fly-wheel magneto we first had a speed of sixty inches per minute. That was too fast. Then we tried eighteen inches per minute. That was too slow. Finally we settled on forty-four inches per minute. The idea is that a man must not be hurried in his work—he must have every second necessary but not a single unnecessary second. We have worked out speeds for each assembly. . . . Some men do only one or two small operations, others do more. The man who places a part does not fasten it—the part may not be fully in place until after several operations later. The man who puts in a bolt does not put on the nut; the man who puts on the nut does not tighten it. . . .

We started assembling a motor car in a single factory. Then as we began to make parts, we began to departmentalize so that each department would do only one thing. As the factory is now organized each department makes only a single part or assembles a part. A department is a little factory in itself. The part comes into it as raw material or as a casting, goes through the sequence of machines and heat treatments, or whatever may be required, and leaves that department finished. . . . I did not know that such minute divisions would be possible; but as our production grew and departments multiplied, we actually changed from making automobiles to making parts. Then we found that we had made another new discovery, which was that by no means all of the parts had to be made in one factory. It was not really a discovery—it was something in the nature of going around in a circle to my first manufacturing when I bought the motors and probably ninety per cent. of the parts. . . . I hope that in the course of time the big Highland Park plant will be doing only one or two things. The casting has already been taken away from it and has gone to the River Rouge plant. . . .

Repetitive labour—the doing of one thing over and over again and always in the same way—is a terrifying prospect to a certain kind of mind. It is terrifying to me. I could not possibly do the same thing day in and day out, but to other minds, perhaps I might say to the majority of minds, repetitive operations hold no terrors. In fact, to some types of mind thought is absolutely appalling. To them the ideal job is one where the creative instinct need not be expressed. The jobs where it is necessary to put in mind as well as muscle have very few takers—we always need men who like a job because it is difficult. The average worker, I am sorry to say, wants a job in which he does not have to put forth much physical exertion—above all, he wants a job in which he does not have to think. Those who have what might be called the creative type of mind and who thoroughly abhor monotony are apt to imagine that all other minds are similarly restless and therefore to extend quite unwanted sympathy to the labouring man who day in and day out performs almost exactly the same operation. . . .

I have not been able to discover that repetitive labour injures a man in any way. I have been told by parlour experts that repetitive labour is soul- as well as body-destroying, but that has not been the result of our investigations. There was one case of a man who all day long did little but step on a treadle release. He thought that the motion was making him one-sided; the medical examination did not show that he had been affected but, of course, he was changed to another job that used a different set of muscles. In a few weeks he asked for his old job again. It would seem reasonable to imagine that going through the same set of motions daily for eight hours would produce an abnormal body, but we have never had a case of it. We shift men whenever they ask to be shifted and we should like regularly to change them—that would be entirely feasible if only the men would have it that way. They do not like changes which they do not themselves suggest. Some of the operations are undoubtedly monotonous—so monotonous that it seems scarcely possible that any man would care to continue long at the same job. Probably the most monotonous task in the whole factory is one in which a man picks up a gear with a steel hook; shakes it in a vat of oil, then turns it into a basket. The motion never varies. The gears come to him always in exactly the same place, he gives each one the same number of shakes, and he drops it into a basket which is always in the same place. No muscular energy is required, no intelligence is required. He does little more than wave his hands gently to and fro—the steel rod is so light. Yet the man on that job had been doing it for eight solid years. He has saved and invested his money until now he has about forty thousand dollars—and he stubbornly resists every attempt to force him into a better job!

The most thorough research has not brought out a single case of a man's mind being twisted or deadened by the work. The kind of mind that does not like repetitive work does not have to stay in it. The work in each department is classified according to its desirability and skill into Classes "A," "B," and "C," each class having anywhere from ten to thirty different operations. A man comes directly from the employment office to "Class C." As he gets better he goes into "Class B," and so on into "Class A," and out of "Class A" into tool making or some supervisory capacity. It is up to him to place himself. If he stays in production it is because he likes it.

In a previous chapter I noted that no one applying for work is refused on account of physical condition. . . . [The policy] carried with it the further condition that no one should be discharged on account of physical condition, except, of course, in the case of contagious disease. I think that if an industrial institution is to fill its whole rôle, it ought to be possible for a cross-section of its employees to show about the same proportions as a cross-section of a society in general. We have always with us the maimed and the halt. There is a most generous disposition to regard all of these people who are physically incapacitated for labour as a charge on society and to support them by charity. . . . [W]e have found it possible, among the great number of different tasks that must be performed somewhere in the company, to find an opening for almost any one and on the basis of production. The blind man or cripple can, in the particular place to which he is assigned, perform just as much work and receive exactly the same pay as a wholly able-bodied man would. We do not prefer cripples—but we have demonstrated that they can earn full wages. . . .

The discipline throughout the plant is rigid. There are no petty rules, and no rules the justice of which can reasonably be disputed. The injustice of arbitrary discharge is avoided by confining the right of discharge to the employment manager, and he rarely exercises it. The year 1919 is the last on which statistics were kept. In that year 30,155 changes occurred. Of those 10,334 were absent more than ten days without notice and therefore dropped. . . . Eighty-two women were discharged because their husbands were working—we do not employ married women whose husbands have jobs. . . .

We expect the men to do what they are told. The organization is so highly specialized and one part is so dependent upon another that we could not for a moment consider allowing men to have their own way. Without the most rigid discipline we would have the utmost confusion. I think it should not be otherwise in industry. The men are there to get the greatest possible amount of work done and to receive the highest possible pay. If each man were permitted to act in his own way, production would suffer and therefore pay would suffer. Any one who does not like to work in our way may always leave. The company's conduct toward the men is meant to be exact and impartial. It is naturally to the interest both of the foremen and of the department heads that the releases from their departments should be few. The workman has a full chance to tell his story if he has been unjustly treated—he has full recourse. Of course, it is inevitable that injustices occur. Men are not always fair with their fellow workmen. Defective human nature obstructs our good intentions now and then. The foreman does not always get the idea, or misapplies it—but the company's intentions are as I have stated, and we use every means to have them understood.

Inventing the Assembly Line (Memoir), 1956

CHARLES SORENSEN

We have seen how Model T slowly evolved. An equally slow evolution was the final assembly line, the last and most spectacular link in mass production. Both "just grew," like Topsy. But, whereas the car evolved from an idea, mass production evolved from a necessity; and it was long after it appeared that the idea and its principles were reduced to words. . . .

. . . Overhead conveyors were used in many industries, including our own. So was substitution of machine work for hand labor. Nor was orderly progress of the work anything particularly new; but it was new to us at Ford until . . . Walter Flanders showed us how to arrange our machine tools at the Mack Avenue and Piquette plants.

What was worked out at Ford was the practice of moving the work from one worker to another until it became a complete unit, then arranging the flow of these units at the right time and the right place to a moving final assembly line from which came a finished product. Regardless of earlier uses of some of these principles, the direct line of succession of mass production and its intensification into automation stems directly from what we worked out at Ford Motor Company between 1908 and 1913.

Henry Ford is generally regarded as the father of mass production. He was not. He was the sponsor of it. And later, in an article over his initials in the *Encyclopedia Britannica* and written, I believe, by Samuel Crowther, he gave what is still the clearest explanation of its principles. Another misconception is that the final assembly line originated in our Highland Park plant in the summer of 1913. It was born then, but it was conceived in July of 1908 at the Piquette Avenue plant and not with Model T but during the last months of Model N production.

The middle of April, 1908, six weeks after public announcement of plans for Model T, Walter Flanders resigned. I have already reported how Mr. Ford told Ed Martin and me to "go out and run the plant, and don't worry about titles." Ed, as plant superintendent, ran the production end. I was assistant plant superintendent and handled production development. This was a natural evolution from my pattern-making, which turned out wooden models of experimental new parts designs. . . .

As may be imagined, the job of putting the car together was a simpler one than handling the materials that had to be brought to it. Charlie Lewis, the youngest and most aggressive of our assembly foremen, and I tackled this problem. We gradually worked it out by bringing up only what we termed the fast-moving materials. The main bulky parts, like engines and axles, needed a lot of room. To give them that space, we left the smaller, more compact, light-handling material in a storage building on the northwest corner of the grounds. Then we arranged with the stock department to bring up at regular hours such divisions of material as we had marked out and packaged.

From Charles Sorenson, *My Forty Years with Ford* (New York: W. W. Norton, 1956), pp. 115–118, 128–132.

This simplification of handling cleaned things up materially. But at best, I did not like it. *It was then that the idea occurred to me that assembly would be easier, simpler, and faster if we moved that chassis along, beginning at one end of the plant with a frame and adding the axles and the wheels; then moving it past the stockroom, instead of moving the stockroom to the chassis.* I had Lewis arrange the materials on the floor so that what was needed at the start of assembly would be at that end of the building and the other parts would be along the line as we moved the chassis along. We spent every Sunday during July planning this. Then one Sunday morning, after the stock was laid out in this fashion, Lewis and I and a couple of helpers put together the first car, I'm sure, that was ever built on a moving line.

We did this simply by putting the frame on skids, hitching a towrope to the front end and pulling the frame along until axles and wheels were put on. Then we rolled the chassis along in notches to prove what could be done. . . .

The only ones in Ford Motor Company who looked at this crude assembly line idea were Mr. Ford, Wills, and Ed Martin. Mr. Ford, though skeptical, nevertheless encouraged the experiment. Martin and Wills doubted that an automobile could be built properly on the move. Wills was particularly hostile. That way of building cars, he said, would ruin the company. . . .

Henry Ford had no ideas on mass production. He wanted to build a lot of autos. He was determined but, like everyone else at that time, he didn't know how. In later years he was glorified as the originator of the mass production idea. Far from it; he just grew into it, like the rest of us. The essential tools and the final assembly line with its many integrated feeders resulted from an organization which was continually experimenting and improvising to get better production.

It became apparent that we should revamp the plant to cut down operation time in the different parts assemblies and speed up deliveries to the big ground-floor room where the cars were put together. It was for this purpose that I installed the first conveyer system. . . .

. . . Years later, in *My Life and Work,* a book which was written for him, Mr. Ford said that the conveyer-assembly idea occurred to him after watching the reverse process in packing houses, where hogs and steers were triced up by hind legs on an overhead conveyer and disassembled. This is a rationalization long after the event. Mr. Ford had nothing to do with originating, planning, and carrying out the assembly line. He encouraged the work, his vision to try unorthodox methods was an example to us; and in that there is glory enough for all. . . .

By August, 1913, all links in the chain of moving assembly lines were complete except the last and most spectacular one—the one we had first experimented with one Sunday morning just five years before. Again a towrope was hitched to a chassis, this time pulled by a capstan. Each part was attached to the moving chassis in order, from axles at the beginning to bodies at the end of the line. Some parts took longer to attach than others; so, to keep an even pull on the towrope, there must be differently spaced intervals between delivery of the parts along the line. This called for patient timing and rearrangement until the flow of parts and the speed and intervals along the assembly line meshed into a perfectly synchronized operation throughout all stages of production. Before the end of the year a power-driven assembly line was in operation, and New Year's saw three more installed. Ford mass production and a new era in industrial history had begun.

Today historians describe the part the Ford car played in the development of that era and in transforming American life. We see that now. But we didn't see it then; we weren't as smart as we have been credited with being. All that we were trying to do was to develop the Ford car.

The achievement came first. Then came logical expression of its principles and philosophy. Not until 1922 could Henry Ford explain it cogently: "Every piece of work in the shop moves; it may move on hooks on overhead chains going to assembly in the exact order in which the parts are required; it may travel on a moving platform, or it may go by gravity, but the points that there is no lifting or trucking of anything other than materials."

It has been said that this system has taken skill out of work. The answer is that by putting higher skill into planning, management, and tool building it is possible for skill to be enjoyed by the many who are not skilled. A million men working with their hands could never approximate the daily output of the Ford assembly line. There are not enough men on earth with skill in their hands to produce all the goods that the world needs.

When skill is build into machines and material flows continuously into those machines, two things are done at once. It has been made possible for unskilled workers to earn higher wages, and the products they turn out satisfy human wants that otherwise wouldn't be satisfied at all. Under this system man is not a slave to the machine, he is a slave without it. Machines do not eliminate jobs; they only make them easier— and create new ones.

Excerpt from "Detroit Motors"
from *The American Earthquake*

EDMUND WILSON

"It's not human—I could just bust when I talk about it—break the spirit of an elephant, it 'ud. I'd starve before I'd go back! They don't give ye no warnin'. Pick up your tools and get a clearance, the boss says—then they inspect your toolbox to see you're not takin' any of the company's tools—then ye report to the employment office with your time card and they give ye a clearance that says they 'cahn't use ye to further advahntage'—then ye're done. I've been laid off since last July. Sometimes they leave ye your badge, and then ye can't get a job anywhere else, because if ye try to, they call up Ford's and they tell 'em ye're still on the payroll, though ye're not workin' and not gettin' a cent. Then they can say they've still go so many men on the payroll. He's a wonder at the publicity, is Ford.

"In England they do things more leisurely-like. I was an auto and tool worker in Manchester from fourteen years old. I got six shillin's a week for seven years—till the War, then I went into the Royal Air Force—but I failed in the nerve test—I was a second-clahss air mechanic durin' the War. An ahnt of mine had been in the States and had seen the pawssibilities, and when she came back, she said, 'Bert, you're wastin' your time!'—so I came over in September, '23. They're ridin' for a fall in England— they've got their back to the wall—the vital industries are bein' bled away from 'em, and they cahn't do away with the dole, but if they stop it, they've got to face the music.

From Edmund Wilson, *The American Earthquake* (Doubleday, 1958), pp. 218–223.

There's young chaps there that have grown up on the dole, and now you cahn't make 'em work—when they're given a job they get fired on purpose. The government's between the devil and the deep sea. Take the bread away from the animals and they'll bite. The way they do things in England, it's a miracle how they ever come through!

"When I first came over, I worked at Fisher Bodies for three months. I took a three-shift job on production at the start rather than be walkin' around. But then I went to Ford's—like everybody else, I'd 'eard about Ford's wages. And you do get the wages. I got $5 a day for the first two months and $6 ahfter, for a year or so—then I ahsked for a raise and got forty cents more a day for two and a hahlf years—I never saw this $7 a day. But the wages are the only redeemin' feature. If he cut wages, they'd walk out on 'im. Ye get the wages, but ye sell your soul at Ford's—ye're worked like a slave all day, and when ye get out ye're too tired to do anything—ye go to sleep on the car comin' home. But as it is, once a Ford worker, always a Ford worker. Ye get lackadaisical, as they say in Lancashire—ye haven't got the guts to go. There's people who come to Ford's from the country, thinkin' they're goin' to make a little money— that they'll only work there a few years and then go back and be independent. And then they stay there forever—unless they get laid off. Ye've never got any security in your job. Finally they moved us out to the Rouge—we were the first people down there— we pioneered there when the machinery wasn't hardly nailed down. But when they began gettin' ready for Model A, production shut down and we were out of a job. I'd tried to get transferred, but they laid me off. Then I 'eard they were wantin' some diemakers—I'd never worked at die-making', but I said I'd 'ad five years at it and got a job, and I was in that department three years till I got laid off last July. I ahsked to be transferred and they laid me off. They'll lay ye off now for any reason or no reason.

"It's worse than the army, I tell ye—ye're badgered and victimized all the time. You get wise to the army after a while, but at Ford's ye never know where ye're at. One day ye can go down the aisle and the next day they'll tell ye to get the hell out of it. In one department, they'll ahsk ye why the hell ye haven't got gloves on and in another why the hell ye're wearin' them. If ye're wearin' a clean apron, they'll throw oil on it, and if a machinist takes pride in 'is tools, they'll throw'em on the floor while he's out. The bosses are thick as treacle and they're always on your neck, because the man above is on their neck and Sorenson's on the neck of the whole lot— he's the man that pours the boiling oil down that old Henry makes. There's a man born a hundred years too late, a regular slave driver—the men tremble when they see Sorenson comin'. He used to be very brutal—he'd come through and slug the men. One day when they were movin' the plant he came through and found a man sittin' workin' on a box. 'Get up!' says Sorenson. 'Don't ye know ye can't sit down in here?' The man never moved and Sorenson kicked the box out from under 'im—and the man got up and bashed Sorenson one in the jaw. 'Go to hell!' he says. 'I don't work here—I'm workin' for the Edison Company!'

"Then ye only get fifteen minutes for lunch. The lunch wagon comes around— the ptomaine wagon, we call it. Ye pay fifteen cents for a damn big pile o' sawdust. And they let you buy some wonderful water that hasn't seen milk for a month. Sorenson owns stock in one of the lunch companies, I'm told. A man's food is in 'is neck when he starts workin'—it 'asn't got time to reach 'is stomach.

"A man checks 'is brains and 'is freedom at the door when he goes to work at Ford's. Some of those wops with their feet wet and no soles to their shoes are glad to get under a dry roof—but not for me! I'm tryin' to forget about it—it even makes me sick now every time I get on a car goin' west!"

This Englishman, whose name is Bert, lives with a man named Hendrickson, an American, who works for the Edison Company. Hendrickson gets thirty-five dollars a week for finding out what is wrong with dynamos and other machinery that doesn't work, but his interest in electricity does not stop with putting them back into running order. He had fitted up a little laboratory and study in the house where Bert and he board—hardly more than a narrow closet off the sitting-room, but with space enough for a blackboard, on which Hendrickson can chalk up his problems; a considerable technical library, including Whitehead's *Introduction to Mathematics,* and one work of pure literature, Montaigne's *Essays;* blueprints of Detroit transformers: intricate structures of long taut lines—here and there threading series of blocks or clusters of truncated carets—of an abstraction almost mathematical and with the beauty of mathematical diagrams; a little wash-closet turned into a dark room, in which he is able to make these blueprints for a third of what he would have to pay a photographer; a pile of original papers dealing with various problems, neatly bound up in blue folders; and photographs of Tesla and Steinmetz.

Hendrickson is a great admirer of Steinmetz. He has two photographs of him and thinks one of them particularly good. He explains that it was hard to get a picture of him on account of his being a humpback—he wouldn't be able to get into the country if he was to come over now, he adds. Hendrickson never actually saw Steinmetz, but he can tell you about the way he used to lecture almost as if he had heard him. Steinmetz used to talk without notes and unless he was stopped, would go on forever, but he was always so interested in what he was saying and made everything so clear to his hearers that he carried them all along with him and you were willing to keep on listening as long as he talked. Bert declares that Henderickson has the same gift.

In the next room, with its gray mottled wallpaper, its little prayer-meeting organ and its picture of Queen Victoria, the lady of the house, somewhat blowzy, is dozing among sheets of the Sunday paper, while her black-and-tan mongrel puppy disports itself on the carpet with a toilet-paper roll and a bone.

Bert has, in general, a great opinion of Henderickson's abilities and feels that he is being exploited by his superiors. He claims that the experts of the Edison Company get the credit for learned scientific papers for which Henderickson has furnished the material. In every organization, says Bert, one man owns the cart and another rides in it. But this doesn't seem to worry Hendrickson—he has no quarrel with the Edison Company. On the contrary, he takes a personal pride in the fact that Detroit can boast that it has more twenty-five-thousand-volt underground cables than any other city in the country. His face is permanently pocked and scarred with acid that was spilled on it some years ago, but this accident does not appear to have had any psychological effect on him. He is unceasingly preoccupied with the problems of electricity, and when for a few moments he has time on his hands, he sits down, no matter where he is, and immediately goes sound asleep.

It is plain that the British Bert is a maladjusted man not at home in America, unhappy between the middle and the working class; but Henderickson seems to inhabit a world that is homogeneous, in which classes do not exist because everybody in it is consecrated to the progress of electricity.

Henderickson is short on the practical side, and Bert on the theoretical. Henderickson can figure anything out and provide the mathematics, but Bert has to build it for him.

My Seven Years of Automotive Servitude (Memoir), 1980

CHARLES MADISON

As I wondered where I was to look for work, it occurred to me that only a block away, on Piquette and Beaubien, was the factory of the Ford Motor Company. I hurried over to Ford's employment office and applied for a job. On the application form I stated my age as eighteen, my experience as a drill press operator, and my request for fifteen cents an hour. The clerk asked me no questions after glancing over the sheet, gave me a brass check with a number, and told me to return the next morning at 6:30. I thanked him, hurried back for my pay envelope, and decided to celebrate by going to a cinema for ten cents.

In the spring of 1910 many of Ford's operations were being moved to a new mammoth plant in Highland Park facing Woodward Avenue. At the time of the move I applied to the foreman to let me operate a lathe, and he was good enough to let me do so. I was already familiar with its operation from close observance of those near me. My main reason for the request was that the lathe demanded greater skill to operate than other machines and therefore entitled the operator to a higher rate of pay. In my favor was my ability to read a micrometer, as the work often required accuracy to the thousandth of an inch when trimming the face of a gear. And, as I expected, my pay envelope soon indicated the payment of twenty cents an hour.

Although I was only fifteen, I began to consider myself a skilled machine operator, the highest paid worker below the class of toolmaker. If I were ambitious in that direction, I would have begun to study mathematics and other subjects needed by a toolmaker; but, without giving the matter deliberate thought, I knew I was not really interested in being a machinist. More and more I began to feel repelled by the dirt and grime and dullness which were inevitable in machine work. I also knew I could not aspire to office work in view of my limited education; nor did I then think I had any chance of going back to school.

One day it occurred to me that I might become a draftsman—an occupation that approached professional status and remuneration. I had previously learned to read blueprints of automobile parts, and knew they were prepared in the drafting room at one end of the building which had the appearance of an office.

After days of contemplation and soul searching I forced myself to approach the superintendent's office and told him of my ambition. He regarded me quizzically, and I wondered if he weren't amused by my stuttering. After asking me about my background and experience as a machine operator, and my assurance that I would attend night school to take the necessary courses, he nodded and gave me a note to the head of the drafting department.

From Charles Madison "My Seven Years of Automotive Servitude," *Michigan Quarterly Review* (Fall 1980–Winter 1981): 445–448.

The man to whom I applied—and I can still see his thinning hair and bulbous nose—seemed annoyed as he read the note. He told me he had no need of an apprentice, but since the superintendent requested it, he would take me in. I sensed that he did not like me, but I was too eager to get into the drafting room to let my pride get the better of me. So I thanked him, and said I would quit my job in the factory and come to him the following morning. I also discussed with him the courses I needed to take, and he suggested that I study algebra and drafting at the YMCA school. He then distressed me by informing me that an apprentice's pay was fifteen cents an hour. Tears came to my eyes as I pointed out that I had been getting twenty cents an hour and needed the money to help support my younger brothers. But he only said that I could return to the factory if I wished. I quickly figured that I must not give up the opportunity to better myself even though it meant a cut in my income, hopefully for a short time; also that with greater knowledge and experience I might in time be earning more than twenty cents an hour. Thus resolved, I meekly acquiesced. That evening I enrolled in the two suggested courses.

On my arrival the next morning, neatly dressed, I had to wait for some time before the man was free to see me. He took me into the blueprint room and began to show me how to place a drawing and blueprint paper together and place them in a revolving large glass tube lighted within and letting the two sheets emerge from the other side. The blueprint paper was then put in an acid vat, kept there for several minutes, and hung to dry. I saw at once that the lines and letters of the drawing appeared in white on the acid-wetted sheet. At first I was quite interested in seeing that the application of light and acid turned what seemed to me an ordinary blue sheet of paper into a useable blueprint. I also liked to see the strongly lighted large glass tube turning around and around, and I thought it was fun to place the blue sheet in the vat and then take it out with tongs and hang it on a laundry-like line. Soon I made numerous copies of each drawing, as requested, and began to recognize some of the blueprints I had used in the factory.

After a week of this work I quickly mastered the process, and my interest in it began to slacken. With my patience decreasing daily, after three weeks I asked to be transferred to the drafting room. My boss quickly informed me that I would have to remain six months in the blueprint room before I would be considered for the promotion. The news dismayed me. Bored with the work and feeling underpaid, I shuddered at the thought of having to wait more than five months before I could begin working on a drafting board. I felt that the course in mechanical drawing was fast equipping me to do professional drawing. Angered by the man's attitude and, as I realized, increasingly disillusioned by the mechanical nature of drafting, I told him I couldn't wait that long and was quitting. He made no effort to keep me.

I thought of returning to the lathe division to ask for my job back, but a sense of pride stopped me. That same day, reconciled to a return to machine work, I proceeded to the Dodge Brothers large new factory in Hamtramck, and obtained work at twenty-two cents an hour. What pleased me also was the more relaxed atmosphere in the machine shop. While at Ford, I, like other workers, was frequently timed by efficiency experts, a way of driving a worker to function at maximum speed, and a cause of constant tension. The Dodge foreman, on the other hand, expected me to work steadily and well, but snapped no whip of forced exertion.

Due to my YMCA courses and a speech clinic I attended the next year, my savings were very low, and the need of additional income gradually turned my attention to Ford's widely publicized policy of paying five dollars a day for eight hours of work. Publicity about Ford's largesse had brought thousands of men from all over the country to Highland Park. Reading about the brutal handling of these applicants and knowing of the slave-driving methods of the factory, I for a time fought back the temptation to seek work there. I liked the atmosphere at Dodge, even though it meant two more hours of work at almost half the pay. But the urge to earn more money was soon strong enough for me to yield to temptation.

One cold Monday morning I took the streetcar to Highland Park and hurried to the employment office. A long line of men was already waiting for the door to open. When it did, the crush to enter was fierce, but guards forced the men to keep in line and await their turn. Since many of them were without experience as machine or assembly operators, most of them were rejected in quick order. When my turn came, my experience as a lathe operator and my previous employment with the company impressed the interviewer and he hired me. Pleased with my success, I went to see the foreman at Dodge Brothers, and explained to him my need of additional income and told him of my gratitude for his friendly behavior toward me. He shook his head in regret, told me I'd be sorry, and generously stated that when I was ready to return he'd see what he could do for me.

I found the Ford plant greatly reorganized, and I was assigned to a lathe in a new section. The harried foreman told me that my operation had been timed by an efficiency expert to produce a certain number of finished parts per day. I timed myself to see what I could actually do, and realized that I might achieve the quota only if all went well and I worked without letup the entire eight hours. No allowance was made for lunch, toilet time, or tool sharpening. I refused to disallow necessary delays, although I managed to keep the machine going while munching my sandwich. When I failed to produce the assigned quota of finished parts, the foreman scolded me. The next day another efficiency timekeeper with a stopwatch was assigned to observe my work. After an hour of making notes as I worked he told the foreman I was too slow in placing the part in the machine and was making no effort to speed up. I defended myself as best I could, asserting that it was humanly impossible to keep up the expected pace. I was annoyed enough to accept dismissal without regret, but no action was taken against me. I continued to work at a fast pace, but made no real effort to produce the assigned quota.

I later concluded that the speedup policy was intended to get the maximum production out of the workers by requiring them to produce their operations at a high rate of speed without ever actually meeting the demanded quota. Much as I resented a policy I considered inhumane, I tried to resign myself to it in the hope of earning five dollars a day. I was therefore shocked and angered when my first pay envelope revealed that I was being paid twenty-five cents an hour or two dollars a day. When I questioned the foreman about this, he told be blandly that the arrangement was to begin paying five dollars a day only after a worker had been with the firm six months and had proved his ability to maintain his quota requirement. The unethical nature of this policy outraged me, and I told him I was quitting at once. Much as I wanted to earn the higher wage I refused to yield to the company's duplicity. The decision to quit gave me a feeling of pleasant relief, as if I had freed myself of an unpleasant burden.

Feeling sheepish, but in good spirits, I returned to the Dodge factory, admitted to the foreman that I had been a fool for leaving him, that the Ford lure was a mean deception, and that I would be grateful to get my job back. Even now I don't know why he was so friendly to me—so unlike the cold and crusty Ford foreman. But he not only agreed to take my back, but to put me on a newly established piecework system which enabled a speedy worker to earn more than his previous hourly wage.

I was glad to be back at my machine, and soon found it possible to earn three dollars or more daily without unduly forcing myself. It pleased me even more that, while I had felt too fatigued after leaving the Ford factory to do any serious reading or attend a play or concert (my urge toward intellectual cultivation was becoming my main interest), I was now able to indulge in such intellectual amenities. For some time thereafter the painful Ford interlude was a rancorous memory—a form of hell on earth that turned human beings into driven robots. I resented the thought that Ford publicists had made the company seem beneficent and imaginative when in fact the firm exploited its employees more ruthlessly than any of the other automobile firms, dominating their lives in ways that deprived them of privacy and individuality.

⋈ E S S A Y S

In the first essay, David Hounshell traces the roots of mass production to the earliest stages of American industrialization. Ford's system of production, he argues, was significantly different from anything that preceded it, marking an "entirely new epoch" in history of industrial capitalism.

In the second selection, Ronald Kline and Trevor Pinch look at how some Model T owners—especially farmers—modified the car for purposes not originally envisioned by the Ford Company. Users in effect became innovators, reshaping automobiles to suit various needs, interests, and identities. Even highly standardized artifacts like the Model T, Kline and Pinch argue, had "interpretative flexibility."

The third selection, from James Flink's *The Automobile Age,* focuses on Ford's work force. Like Charles Madison and the Englishman Bert, Flink finds much to criticize in Ford's labor policies. But he also finds more complex elements, such as the "five-dollar day." Ford also was one of the first major manufacturing companies to employ large numbers of African Americans, although racism dictated that they be given the dirtiest and most hazardous assembly line jobs.

Mass Production

DAVID A. HOUNSHELL

Mass production became the Great American art.
—Paul Mazur, *American Prosperity (1920)*

Since the 1920s the term "mass production" has become so deeply ingrained in our vocabulary and our thought that we seldom stop to ask how it arose and what lay behind its appearance. The purpose of this brief essay is to provide an overview of the development of mass production in America as a means of getting at these questions. In the first half of the nineteenth century, manufacturing in the United States developed

---

From David A. Hounshell, "Mass Production in American History, 1800–1932," *Polhem* 2 (1984): 1–28.

along such distinct lines that by the 1850s English observers came to speak of an "American system" of manufactures. Subsequently, the American system grew and changed in character so much that by the 1920s, the United States possessed the most prolific production technology the world has ever known. This was "mass production."

In 1925, the American editor of the *Encyclopaedia Britannica* wrote to Henry Ford asking him to submit an article on "Mass Production" for the three-volume supplement to the *Britannica,* the so-called 13th Edition. Apparently Ford's office, if not Ford himself, responded favorably and promptly set Ford's spokesman, William J. Cameron, to work on the article. Cameron consulted the company's chief production planner about how the "general reader" might comprehend the principles of mass production. When Cameron completed the article, he placed Henry Ford's name beneath it and sent it to the *Britannica's* New York office.

Although Cameron would later say that he "should be very much surprised to learn that [Henry Ford] read it," this article played a fundamental role in giving the phrase "mass production" a place in the English vocabulary. Even before the article appeared in the Britannica, the *New York Times* published it as a full-page, feature article in a Sunday edition. Under the banner, "Henry Ford Expounds Mass Production: Calls It the Focusing of the Principles of Power, Economy, Continuity and Speed," the article attracted the attention of a wide segment of the American population, especially since it also went through the wire service. While one can certainly wonder what led the *Britannica* editor to choose the term, mass production, there is little doubt that the ghost-written Ford article led to the widespread use of the term and its identification with the assembly line manufacturing techniques that were the hallmark of automobile production. Immediately, the article proved interesting enough to provoke a *Times* editorial. The term, which had not commonly appeared in reference works such as the *Reader's Guide to Periodic Literature* prior to the *Britannica Times* article, soon passed into general use in both popular and scholarly literature. After the appearance of "Mass Production," the previously popular expression, "Fordism," soon disappeared. The Ford article endowed mass production with a certain universality despite its ambiguity and its status as poor grammar.

Much more important than the story of how mass production entered the English vocabulary are the developments that lay behind the manufacturing system described in the article. Commenting in 1940 on Henry Ford and the *Britannica* article in his *Engines of Democracy,* Roger Burlingame raised the essential questions:

> With [Ford's] great one-man show moving toward a dictatorship of which any totalitarian leader might well be proud he was ready for what he calls [Mass] Production. [Mass] Production, Ford believes, had never existed in the world before. With the magnificent contempt of men immune to history, he disregards all predecessors: Whitney, Evans, Colt, Singer, McCormick, the whole chain of patient, laborious workers who wrought his assembly lines and all the ramifications of his processes out of the void of handicrafts. In a colossal blurb printed in the *Encyclopaedia Britannica* under the guise of an article on mass production, he writes: "In origin, mass production is American and recent; its notable appearance falls within the first decade of the 20th century," and devotes the remainder of the article and two full pages of half-tone plates to the Ford factory.

Burlingame was obviously contemptuous of the claims that mass production was a creation of the Ford Motor Company. Eli Whitney, Oliver Evans, Samuel Colt, Isaac Singer, and Cyrus McCormick, among others, he implied, provided essential building blocks for development at Ford. Burlingame was even more pointed when he later asked rhetorically, "What are those production methods in use today in every large automobile plant with scarcely any variation? They are simply the methods of Eli Whitney and Samuel Colt, improved, coordinated and applied with intelligent economy—economy in time, space, men, motion, money and material."

Since the establishment of the history of technology as an academic discipline in the United States, the assertions contained both in Ford's encyclopaedia article and in Burlingame's popular work have come under close study by a number of investigators. Indeed, the so-called "American system of manufactures," which describes the methods of Whitney, Colt, and the rest, has become one of the most productive areas of American scholarship in the history of technology, and there now exists a rich body of literature on this historical phenomenon. Portions of that new scholarship . . . indicate that the Ford article came much nearer the truth than did Burlingame and his followers. "[I]n origin," as the Ford piece suggested, "mass production is American and recent"—what Whitney et al., did in the nineteenth century was not true mass production. . . . [M]ass production differed in kind as well as in scale from the techniques referred to in the antebellum period as the American system of manufactures. This can be seen most clearly by first considering the American system itself.

Two decades of research on this topic have yielded a number of conclusions, particularly concerning a basic aspect of modern manufacturing, the interchangeability of parts. The symbolic kingpin of interchangeable parts production fell in 1960 when Robert S. Woodbury published his essay, "The Legend of Eli Whitney," in the first volume of *Technology and Culture*. Woodbury convincingly argued that the parts of Whitney's guns were not in fact constructed with interchangeable parts. In 1966, the artifactual research of Edwin A. Battison solidly confirmed Woodbury's more traditional, document-based research findings. Eugene S. Ferguson later wrote of Woodbury's pioneering article, "Except for Whitney's ability to sell an undeveloped idea, little remains of his title as father of mass production."

With Eli Whitney reinterpreted as a *promoter* rather than as a *pioneer* of machine-made interchangeable parts manufacture, it remained for Merritt Roe Smith to identify conclusively the personnel and the circumstances of this fundamental step in the development of mass production. Smith demonstrated that the United States Ordinance Department was the prime mover in bringing about machine-made interchangeable parts production of small arms. The national armory at Springfield, Massachusetts, played a major role in this process, especially as it tried to coordinate its operations with those of its sister armory at Harpers Ferry and John Hall's experimental rifle factory, also located in Harpers Ferry. While these federally owned arms plants occupied a central place in its efforts, the Ordnance Department also used contracts with private arms makers to further its aims. By specifying interchangeability in its contracts and by giving contractors access to techniques used in the national armories, the Ordinance Department contributed significantly to the growing sophistication of metalworking and woodworking (in the case of gunstock production) in the United States by the 1850s. British observers found these techniques sufficiently different from their own and alluded to them in expressions such as the "American system," the "American plan," and the "American principle."

Although British visitors to the United States in the 1850s, especially Joseph Whitworth and John Anderson, were impressed with every aspect of American manufacturing, small arms production received their most careful and detailed analysis. Certainly this was Anderson's job, for he had been sent to the United States to find out everything he could about small arms production and to purchase arms-making machinery for the Enfield Arsenal. In his report, Anderson indicated that the federal armory at Springfield had indeed achieved what the Ordnance Department had sought since its inception: true interchangeability of parts. Anderson and his committee went into Springfield's arsenal and randomly selected ten muskets, each made in a different year from 1844 to 1853. A workman then disassembled these muskets, and their parts were mixed together. According to Anderson, the committee then "requested the workman, whose duty it is to 'assemble' the arms, to put them together, which he did—the Committee handing him the parts, taken at hazard—with the use of a turn-screw only, and as quickly as though they had been English muskets whose parts had carefully been kept separate.

What Anderson was not likely to have known was the extraordinary sum of money that the Ordnance Department had expended over a forty or fifty year period, "[i]n order," as an Ordnance Officer wrote in 1819, "to attain this grand object of uniformity of parts." Nor was Anderson necessarily aware that the unit cost of Springfield small arms with interchangeable parts almost certainly was significantly higher than arms produced by more traditional methods. He should, however, have been aware that the Ordnance Department could annually turn out only a relatively small number of Springfield arms manufactured with interchangeable parts. Despite the high costs and limited output, Anderson pointed out that the special techniques used in the Springfield Armory as well as in some private armories could be applied almost universally in metalworking and woodworking establishments. In fact, by the time Anderson reached this conclusion, the application of those techniques in other industries was already under way.

The new manufacturing technology spread first to the production of a new consumer item, the sewing machine, and eventually it diffused into other areas, including consumer durables such as typewriters, bicycles, and eventually automobiles. Nathan Rosenberg has provided economic and technological historians with an excellent analysis of a major way in which this diffusion occurred. Rosenberg identified the American machine tool industry, which grew out of the small arms industry (notably the Colt armory and the firm of Robbins & Lawrence in Windsor, Vermont, and Hartford, Connecticut) as the key agent for introducing arms-making technology into the sewing machine industry, the bicycle industry, and the automobile industry. The makers of machine tools worked with manufacturers in various industries as they encountered and overcame production problems relating to the cutting, planing, boring, and shaping of metal parts. As each problem was solved, new knowledge went back into the machine tool firms, which then could be used for solving production problems in other industries. Rosenberg called this phenomenon "technological convergence." In many industries that worked with metal, the final products were vastly different in terms of the kinds of markets in which they were sold—the Springfield Armory, for example, "sold" its products to a single customer, the government, while sewing machines producers faced a widely scattered group of individual consumers.

Nevertheless, these products had *technological* things in common because their manufacture depended upon similar metalworking technique. These common needs "converged" at the point where the machine tool industry interacted with the firms that bought its machine tools.

Although he did not emphasize the point, Rosenberg recognized that individual mechanics played an equally important role in diffusing know-how as they moved from the firearms industry to sewing machine manufacture to bicycle production and even to automobile manufacture. Examples of such mechanics abound. Henry M. Leland is an obvious example: he worked at Springfield Armory, carried this knowledge to Brown & Sharpe Manufacturing Company when it was making both machine tools and Wilcox & Gibbs sewing machines, next created the Cadillac Motor Car Company and finally the Lincoln Motor Company.

But the process of diffusion was neither as smooth nor as simple as Rosenberg and others would have it. New research suggests that the factories of two of the giants of nineteenth century manufacturing, the Singer Manufacturing Company and the McCormick Harvesting Machine Company, were continually beset with production problems. Previously, many historians attributed the success of these two companies to their advanced production technology. But it now appears that a superior marketing strategy (including advertising and sales techniques and policies) proved to be the decisive factor. . . .

Joseph Woodworth, author of *American Tool Making and Interchangeable Manufacturing,* argued that the "manufacture of the bicycle . . . brought out the capabilities of the American mechanic as nothing else had ever done. It demonstrated to the world that he and his kind were capable of designing and making special machinery, tools, fixtures, and devices for economic manufacturing in a manner truly marvellous; and has led to the installation of the interchangeable system of manufacturing in a thousand and one shops when it was formerly thought to be impractical." Clearly the bicycle industry as a staging ground for the diffusion of armory practice cannot be overemphasized. Rosenberg's idea that the machine tool industry played a leading role in this diffusion applies even more clearly to the bicycle than to the sewing machine. The bicycle boom of the 1890s kept the machine tool industry in relatively good health during the serious depression that began in 1893, and it was accompanied by changes in production techniques.

Entirely new developments occurred in bicycle production—sheet metal stamping and electric resistance welding techniques. These new techniques rivalled in importance the diffusion of older metalworking technologies. During the 1890s, bicycle makers located principally but not exclusively in areas west of New England began to manufacture bicycles with many components (pedals, crank hangers, steering heads, joints, forks, hubs, etc.) made from sheet steel. Punch pressing or stamping operations were combined with the recent invention of electric resistance welding to produce parts at significantly lower costs. This technology would become fundamental to the automobile industry. . . .

Bicycle makers such as [Albert A.] Pope who used traditional armory-type production techniques looked with disdain at those who manufactured bicycles with parts made by the new techniques in pressing and stamping steel. An executive at the Columbia works [Pope's factory] called them cheap and nasty. Despite such views, the one manufacturer that outstripped Pope's production at the peak of the bicycle boom was the Western Wheel Works of Chicago, which made a "first class" bicycle out of pressed steel hubs, steering head, sprocket, frame joints, crank hanger, fork, seat, handlebar, and various brackets. Although not quite as expensive as the Columbia, the Western Wheel bicycle ranked high in the top price category among some 200 to 300 manufacturers. Production of this bicycle reached 70,000 in 1896, an output that was significantly less than that of the Ford Model T in 1912, the last full year of its pre-assembly line manufacture.

. . . In terms of production, it is only with the rise of the Ford Motor Company and its Model T that there clearly appears an approach to manufacture capable of handling an output of multi-component durables ranging into the millions each year.

Moreover, the rise of Ford marks an entirely new epoch in the manufacture of consumer durables in America. The Ford enterprise may well have been more responsible for the rise of "mass production," particularly for the attachment of the noun "mass" to the expression, than we have realized. Unlike Singer, McCormick, and Pope, Ford sought to manufacture the lowest priced automobile and to use continuing price reductions to produce ever greater demand. Ford designed the Model T to be a "car for the masses." Prior to the era of the Model T, the word "masses" had carried a largely negative connotation, but with such a clearly stated goal and his company's ability to achieve it, Ford recognized "the masses" as a legitimate and seemingly unlimited market for the most sophisticated consumer durable product of the early twentieth century. Whether Henry Ford envisioned "the masses" as the populace or 'lower orders' of late nineteenth parlance or merely as a large number of potential customers hardly matters, for the results were the same. Peter Drucker long ago maintained that Ford's work demonstrated for the first time that maximum profit could be achieved by maximizing production while minimizing cost. He added that "the essence of the mass-production process is the reversal of the conditions from which the theory of monopoly was deduced. The new assumptions constitute a veritable economic revolution." For Drucker, mass production was as much an economic doctrine as an approach to manufacture. For this reason if for no other, the work of the national armories, Singer, McCormick, Pope et al., differed substantially from Ford's. But Ford was able to initiate this new "economic revolution" because of advances in production technology, especially the assembly line.

Before the adoption of the revolutionary assembly line in 1913, Ford's production engineers had synthesized the two different approaches to manufacture that had prevailed in the bicycle era. On the other hand, Ford adopted the techniques of armory practice. All of the company's earliest employees recalled how ardently Henry Ford had supported efforts to improve precision in machining. Although he knew little about jig, fixture, and gauge techniques, Ford nevertheless became a champion of interchangeability within the Ford Motor Company, and he hired mechanics who knew what was required to achieve that goal. Certainly by 1913, most of the problems of interchangeable parts manufacture had been solved at Ford. In addition to armory practice, Ford adopted sheet steel punch and press work in an important way. Initially he contracted for stamping work with the John R. Keim Company in Buffalo, New York, which had been a major supplier of bicycle components. Soon after opening his new Highland Park factory in Detroit, however, Ford purchased the Keim plant and promptly moved its presses and other machines to the new factory. More and more Model T components were stamped out of sheet steel rather than being fabricated with traditional machining methods. Together, armory practice and sheet steel work equipped Ford with the capability to turn out virtually unlimited numbers of components. It remained for the assembly line to eliminate the remaining bottleneck—how to put these parts together.

The advent of line assembly at Ford Motor Company in 1913 is one of the most confused episodes in American history. . . . First, the assembly line, once it was first tried on April 1, 1913, came swiftly and with great force. Within eighteen months of the first experiments with moving line assembly, assembly lines were used in almost all sub-assemblies and in the most symbolic mass production operation of all, the final chassis assembly. Ford engineers witnessed productivity gains ranging from fifty percent to as much as ten times the output of static assembly methods. Allan Nevins quite correctly called the moving assembly line "a lever to move the world."

Secondly, there can be little doubt that Ford engineers received their inspiration for the moving assembly line from outside the metalworking industries. Henry Ford himself claimed that the idea derived from the "disassembly lines" of meatpackers in Chicago and Cincinnati. William Klann, a Ford deputy who was deeply involved in the innovation, agreed but noted that an equally important source of inspiration was flour milling technology as practiced in Minnesota. . . . Although there may have been a clear connection in the minds of Ford engineers between "flow production" and the moving assembly line, there is little justification for saying that the assembly line came directly from flour milling. The materials and processes of both were simply too different to support such a view.

The origins of the Ford assembly line are less important than its effect. While providing a clear solution to the problems of assembly, the line brought with it serious labor problems. Already, Ford's highly mechanized and subdivided manufacturing operations imposed severe demands on labor. Even more than previous manufacturing technologies, the assembly line implied that men, too, could be mechanized. Consequently during 1913 the Ford company saw its annual labor turnover soar to 380 percent and even higher. Henry Ford moved swiftly to stem this inherently inefficient turn-over rate. On January 5, 1914, he instituted what became known as the "five-dollar day." Although some historians have argued that this was a wage system that more than doubled the wages of "acceptable" workers, most recently the five-dollar day has been interpreted as a profit sharing plan whereby Ford shared excess profits with employees who were judged to be fit to handle such profits. In any case, the five-dollar day effectively doubled the earnings of Ford workers, and provided a tremendous incentive for workers to stay "on the line." With highly mechanized production, moving line assembly, high wages, and low prices on products, "Fordism" was born.

During the years between the birth of "Fordism" and the wide-spread appearance of the term, "mass production," the Ford Motor Company expanded its annual output of Model T's from 300,000 in 1914 to more than 2,000,000 in 1923. In an era when most prices were rising, those of the Model T dropped significantly—about sixty percent in current dollars. Throughout the Model T's life, Henry Ford opened his factories to technical journalists to write articles, series of articles, and books on the secrets of production at Ford Motor Company. Soon after the appearance of the first articles on the Ford assembly lines, other automobile companies began putting their cars together "on the line." Manufacturers of other consumer durables also followed suit. Ford's five-dollar day forced automakers in the Detroit vicinity to increase their wage scales. Because Ford secured more than fifty percent of the American automobile market by 1921, his actions had a notable impact on American industry.

Ford's work and the emulation of it on the part of other manufacturers led to the establishment of what could be called an "ethos of mass production" in America. The creation of this ethos marks a significant moment in the development of mass production and consumption in America. Certain segments of American society looked at Ford's and the entire automobile industry's ability to produce large quantities of goods at surprisingly low costs. When they did so, they wondered why, for example, housing, furniture, and even agriculture could not be approached in precisely the same manner in which Ford approached the automobile.

Consequently, during the years that the Model T was in production, movements arose within each of these industries to introduce mass production methods. In housing, an industry always looked upon as one of the most staid and pre-industrial of all, prefabrication efforts reached heights not achieved by the pioneers of prefabrication. Foster Gunnison, for example, strove to become the "Henry Ford of housing" by establishing a factory to turn out houses on a moving assembly line, and Gunnison was only one among many such entrepreneurs. Furniture production also saw the influence of Ford and the automobile industry. In the 1920's a large number of mechanical engineers in America banded together within the American Society of Mechanical Engineers in an effort to bring the woodworking industry into the twentieth century—into the century of mass production. Consequently, the ASME established in 1925 a Wood Industries Division, which served to focus the supposed great powers of mechanical engineering on all aspects of woodworking technology. In agriculture, Henry Ford himself argued that the problems of American agriculture could all be solved simply by adopting mass production techniques. Ford conducted experiments in this direction, but he was no more successful in agriculture than the mechanical engineers and housing fabricators were in bringing about mass production in their respective industries. One could argue, however, that today such an agricultural product as the hybrid tomato, bred to be picked, sorted, packaged, and transported by machinery, demonstrates that mass production methods have penetrated American agriculture. But in furniture and housing, there seems to be no equivalent to the hybrid tomato. . . .

. . . American furniture manufacturers continued to operate relatively small factories employing around 150 workers, annually turning out between 5,000 and 50,000 units. Beliefs that automotive production technology holds the key to abundance in all areas of consumption persist today. As recently as 1973, Richard Bender observed in his book on industrial building that "much of the problem of industrializing the building industry has grown out of the mistaken image of the automobile industry as a model." In many areas, the panacea of Fordism will continue to appeal to those who see in it solutions to difficult economic and social problems. The ethos of mass production, established largely by Ford, will die a hard death, if it ever disappears completely.

Yet the very timing of the rise of this ethos along with the appearance of the *Encyclopedia Britannica* article, "Mass Production," shows how full of paradox and irony history is. Although automotive America was rapidly growing in its consumption of everything under the sun and although Ford's achievements were known by all, mass production as Ford had made it and defined it was, for all intents and purposes, dead by 1926. Ford and his production experts had driven mass production into a deep cul-de-sac. American buyers had given up on the Ford Model T, and the Ford Motor Company watched its sales drop precipitously amid caustic criticism of its inability to accept and make changes. In mid-1927, Henry Ford himself finally gave up on the Model T after 15,000,000 of them had been produced. What followed in the changeover to the Model A was one of the most wrenching nightmares in American industrial history. Designing the new model, tooling up for its production, and achieving satisfactory production levels posed an array of unanticipated problems that led to a long delay in the Model A's introduction. In some respect, the Ford Motor Company never recovered from the effects of its first big changeover. Changes in consumers' tastes and gains in their disposable income made the Model T and the Model T idea obsolete. Automobile consumption in the late 1920s called for a new kind of mass production, a system which could accommodate frequent change and which was no longer wedded to the idea of maximum production at minimum cost. General Motors, not Ford, proved to be in tune with changes in American consumption with its explicit policy of "a car for every purpose and every purse," its unwritten policy of annual change, and its encouragement of "trading up" to a more expensive car. Ford learned painfully and at great cost that the times called for a new era, that of "flexible mass production."

The Great Depression dealt additional blows to Ford's version of mass production. With dramatic decreases in sales following the Great Crash, Ford and the entire industry began laying off workers. As a result, Detroit became known as the "beleaguered capital of mass production." Mass production had not prevented mass unemployment or, more properly, unemployment of the masses, but seemed rather to have exacerbated it. While overproduction had always posed problems for industrial economies, the high level of unemployment in the Great Depression made mass production an easy culprit for critics as they saw hundreds of thousands of men out of work in the Detroit area alone. Writing in the *New York Times* in 1931 Paul Mazur stressed that, "mass production has not proved itself to be an unmixed blessing; in the course of its onward march lie overproduction and the disastrous discontinuity of industry that comes as a consequence." Call it Fordism or mass production, it was nonetheless, "an alluring but false doctrine." Moreover, Mazur argued, "it is essential for business to realize that unquestioning devotion to mass production can [only] bring disaster.

Mazur's comments came in the wake of a previous *Times Magazine* article entitled, "Gandhi Dissects the Ford Idea." The article's author, Harold Callender, pitted Ford's doctrine of mass production against Mahatma Gandhi's notion that handicrafts, not mechanization, offered the solution to global problems of unemployment and hunger. The *Times Magazine* juxtaposed a photograph of an assembly line against one of a group of Indian hand spinners. Captions under the two photographs read as follows: "The Ford Formula for Happiness—A Mass-Production Line" and "The Gandi Formula for Happiness—A Group of Handicraft Spinners." While few would have agreed with the Gandhi formula, Americans in the depths of the Depression certainly seem to have concluded that developments in mass production had not been matched by the development of "mass consumption." As Mazur put it, "the power of production . . . has been so great that its products have multiplied at geometric rates . . . at the same time the power of consumption—even under the influence of stimuli damned as unsocial and tending toward profligacy [e.g., advertising and built-in obsolescence (frequent style changes)]—has expanded only at a comparatively slow arithmetic rate."

While Americans may have had doubts about the doctrine of mass production, they by no means were willing to scrap it in favor of the Gandhi formula. Already their desire for style and novelty, coupled with increased purchasing power in the 1920s, had forced even Henry Ford to change his system of mass production. When pushed by the Depression, the greater part of Americans looked for solutions in the sphere of "mass consumption." The 1930s witnessed the publication of an extensive amount of literature on the "economics of consumption." As history would have it, the prophets of mass production were proven at least temporarily correct as the United States pulled itself out of the Depression by the mass consumption of war material and, after the war, by the golden age of American consumption in the 1950s and 1960s.

The Social Construction of the Automobile in the Rural United States

RONALD KLINE AND TREVOR PINCH

SCOT [The Social Construction of Technology] emphasizes the "interpretative flexibility" of an artifact. Different social groups associate different meanings with artifacts leading to interpretative flexibility appearing over the artifact. The same artifact can mean different things to different social groups of users. For young men riding the bicycle for sporting purposes the high-wheeler meant the "macho machine" as opposed to the meaning given to it by women and elderly men who wanted to use the bike for transport. For this latter group . . . the high-wheeler was the "unsafe machine" (because of its habit of throwing people over the handle bars—known as "doing a header"). Such meanings can get embedded in new artifacts, and developmental paths can be traced which reinforce this meaning (e.g., placing even larger wheels on bicycles to enable them to go even faster). Interpretative flexibility, however, does not continue forever. "Closure" and stabilization occur, such that some artifacts appear to have fewer problems and become increasingly the dominant form of the technology. This, it should be noted, may not result in all rivals vanishing, and often two very different technologies can exist side by side (for example, jet planes and propeller planes). Also this process of closure and stabilization need not be final. New problems can emerge and interpretative flexibility may reappear. . . .

The first motor cars, like the bicycle before them, made a dramatic impression on rural American life. When they first appeared in the countryside in the early years of this century, driven by rich city folk out for a spin, they often met a hostile reception. Indeed, farmers joined small-town residents, suburbanites, and even irate city dwellers in many parts of the country in hurling such epithets as "red devil" and "devil wagon" at the dangerous, speeding car—names that soon symbolized the rising

From Ronald Kline and Trevor Pinch, "Users as Agents of Technological Change: The Social Construction of the Automobile in the Rural United States," *Technology and Culture,* October 1996. Copyright © 1996 by The Society for the History of Technology. Reprinted by permission of The University of Chicago Press.

clamor of rural protest. Motorists and automobile journals countered with the traditional antirural insults of "hayseed" and "rube," but also coined such new phrases as "autophobe" and "motorphobe" for all critics of the car—whether they lived in the city, town, or country. A group in St. Louis even defied the widespread opposition to "scorchers" in 1905 by calling themselves the Red Devil Automobile Club.

The main antagonism between farmers and the early car and its drivers seems to have stemmed from the dramatic effects which the cars had upon livestock. Horses reared at the car's noisy approach, often breaking away or upsetting buggies; chickens crossed the road for the last time. . . .

Many farm women complained that recklessly driven autos prevented them from driving their horse-drawn buggies on country roads. . . .

. . . Apart from the car's speed, many country folk were unimpressed with it as a means of transportation. It was a common sight to see farmers with their horses towing a car that had broken down or pulling a car out of muddy country roads—a source of income for some farmers and of moral satisfaction to those who despised the "devil wagon." Adding to the antagonism were the types of car drivers—urban, upper class—the farmers encountered. Another, later, source of criticism was the damage which the cars were thought capable of inflicting on the fabric of rural life. Farm people had built up a whole network of crucial institutions such as schools and churches based upon the transport system of the horse and buggy. The car with its much longer range threatened such institutions. Children could go to consolidated schools further away, other churches than the local one came within range. Worse, with the option of visiting friends or family in a nearby town for the day, or the other temptations which such a visit offered, why go to church at all?

The early antagonism was such that rural people resorted to both legal and illegal means to stop the influx of cars. Counties in West Virginia and Pennsylvania passed laws that banned autos; Vermont required a person to carry a red flag and walk ahead of the car. A flurry of legislation around 1908 required cars to slow down for horse-drawn vehicles, or stop if the horse appeared frightened. Lucrative "speed traps" also date from this period. Legislatures withheld support from road improvement schemes. The threat was perceived to be such that, as in the case of the bicycle, many farmers took the law into their own hands. The press reported numerous cases of farm men attacking motorists from 1902 to 1907, a period of widespread auto touring. Farmers shot a chauffeur in the back in Minnesota, stoned a motorist in Indiana, shot at a car passing a horse-drawn buggy in South Carolina, and assaulted a chauffeur in Wisconsin. New York farmers hit a motorist with a galvanized iron pail on Long Island, pushed a lawn mower into an auto's path, whipped a motorist for no apparent reason, and delayed a hill-climbing contest near Rochester by fighting with onlookers.

Farm men took these actions partly because they viewed country roads, which they built and maintained, in a proprietary manner. Yet many of them detested the "devil wagon" so much that they sabotaged their own roads to try and stop the growing menace. In 1905, Connecticut farmers spread a tire-cutting slag on roads (supposedly to fill in ruts!), and Minnesota farmers plowed up roads near Rochester. As late as 1909, Indiana farmers, tired of being awakened by revellers returning from a night of drinking in nearby roadhouses, weakened bridges and barricaded roads. In the same year, farmers near Sacramento, California, dug ditches across several roads and caught thirteen autos in their traps. Rural people booby-trapped other roads with an innovative assortment of rakes, saws, glass, tacks, and ropes or barbed wire strung across the road. Groups such as the Farmers' Anti-Automobile League near Evanston, Illinois, the Anti-Automobile Club of Grover, Missouri, and the Farmers' Protective Association in Harrison Township, Ohio, were formed to organize rural opposition to the car. The Illinois league had a twenty-member vigilante committee to mete out justice to reckless drivers.

In terms of SCOT we can say that these actions, termed an "anti-auto crusade" by one historian, showed the existence of an important relevant social group. For them the car was not the fond object of joy later encapsulated in such names as the "flivver" (so called apparently because the vibration of the car was considered to be good for the liver) or the "Tin Lizzie" (another nickname for the Model T)—it was the "Devil Wagon." Did this meaning of the car for this social group lead to a radical interpretive flexibility? The answer must be yes. By attempting to destroy cars directly and make roads impassible to cars, this social group was trying to affect perhaps in the most dramatic direct way possible the development of the artifact. If they had succeeded the car might have taken a very different form—it would have been a short distance city vehicle only. Railroads would have remained the main form of transportation to rural areas—modern America would look very different.

The anticar movement failed because of a combination of circumstances. Faced with the saturation of the urban luxury car market manufacturers developed a large rural market by producing more affordable cars designed to navigate country roads. The inexpensive Model T, to take the most successful example, sat high off the ground (also making repair easier) and had a high horsepower-to-weight ratio and a three-point suspension. The introduction of the Model T in late 1908 also came at a time of growing support for the car among farm leaders. The National Grange had passed a resolution that summer stating that the "motor vehicle is a permanent feature of modern life" and had a right to use rural roads. The Grange followed the lead of the influential Midwestern paper, *Wallace's Farmer,* which had begun to promote the gasoline automobile in January 1908 using the same methods it employed for any new technology it favored: advertisements, editorials, articles, and requests for readers' experiences. The paper's editor stated in February that "farmers have had their fun—and sometimes it was not fun, either—with the users of the automobile." Although farm people had justifiably "called it the rich man's plaything" and had sworn at it for disrupting rural life, they had begun to value cars and to buy them for themselves. The *Rural New Yorker,* a former critic of the automobile, started to promote it in 1909. *Wallace's Farmer* thought highly of two types of cars: the technologically out-of-date but inexpensive buggy car, whose high wheels cleared the hump in rutted country roads; and a touring car with a removable tonneau (backseat) that could be easily converted into a small truck. Manufacturers of both types flourished for a brief time, thus helping to introduce the automobile into the countryside. Roads were also improved. Gradually, the advantages of the car became all too clear-cut. The car promised to end the relative isolation of farm life. And the possible income to be derived from wealthy city people did not go unnoticed. Tourism thrived, as did repair shops. Farm men, many of whom had operated steam engines and stationary gasoline engines, were well-placed to become car users. As buggy cars, convertibles, and the Model T spread into rural areas, the anticar movement vanished. By 1920, in fact, the U.S. Census reported that a larger percentage of farm households owned an automobile than did nonfarm households (30 percent to 24 percent). Thus the radical meaning of car as "devil wagon" did not stabilize.

The main social groups of relevance to understanding the development of the rural car are manufacturers, farm men, and farm women. In studying a technology which had already stabilized in regard to its fundamental design—by 1909 the "large, front-engined, rear-drive automobile" of system Panhard—it is clear that one social group initially had more influence than any other in terms of giving a meaning to the artifact: the manufacturers. Because they produced the car, the automobile manufacturers exerted great influence on the form the technology initially took. But their position, although influential, was not overwhelmingly so. New manufacturers could (and did) produce new and different cars with different users in mind. Furthermore, although manufacturers may have inscribed a particular meaning to the artifact they were not able to control how that artifact was used once it got into the hands of the users. Users precisely as users can embed new meanings into the technology.

This happened with the adaptation of the car into rural life. As early as 1903, farm families started to define the car as more than a transportation device. In particular, they saw it as a general source of power. George Schmidt, a Kansas farmer, advised readers of the *Rural New Yorker* in 1903 "to block up the hind axle and run a belt over the one wheel of the automobile and around the wheel on a [corn] sheller, grinder, saw, pump, or any other machine that the engine is capable of running, and see how the farmer can save money and be in style with any city man." T. A. Pottinger, an Illinois farm man, wrote *Wallace's Farmer* in 1909 that the ideal farm car should have a detachable backseat, which could turn the vehicle into a small truck, and that it should be able to provide "light power, such as running a corn sheller, an ensilage cutter, or doing light grinding." The car was also used for domestic work, such as powering washing machines. . . . Although the car was sometimes used to assist in traditional "women's work" (e.g., by running the butter churn and cream separator), farm men—rather than farm women—more commonly used the car to provide stationary power, and mainly for "men's work"—that is, to run agricultural machinery. Corn shellers, water pumps, hay balers, fodder and ensilage cutters, wood saws, hay and grain hoists, cider presses, and corn grinders were all powered by the auto. A rancher even used a Cadillac to shear his sheep. A Maine farm man put a car to so many multiple usages in 1915 the tax assessors did not know whether they should classify the car as a pleasure vehicle or a piece of agriculture machinery. In addition to providing a stationary source of power, cars found a wide variety of unexpected uses in their mobile form. Farm men used them as snowmobiles, tractors, and agricultural transport vehicles. Indeed, it seems from the earliest days of the car's introduction onto farms that farmers were acutely aware of its potential, whether simply to transport fodder or to power a feed chopper. Adapting the auto to the myriad tasks of farm life was common enough practice that seven of twenty-three New York farm families who participated in a recent oral history project recalled that they or their neighbors had used the car as a hay rake, pickup truck, or power source. One farm man, eighty-eight-year-old Winfred Arnold, remembered that his neighbors used the car to power jobs around the farm, but he himself could afford to use stationary gasoline engines.

In these instances, rural users of the car have reintroduced what we would call "interpretative flexibility," but . . . this flexibility was not at the design stage. New meanings are being given to the car by the new emerging social group of users—in this case, technically competent farm men. To the urban user the car meant transport. For the rural users we have identified, the car, as well as being a form of transport, could be a farm tool, a stationary source of power, or part of a domestic technology, or perhaps all of these.

The remarkable interpretative flexibility of the rural car has a strong tie to the *structure* of gender relations between farm men and women. Most generalizations about social groups as large and culturally diverse as farm men and farm women are highly problematic, but gender relationships on farms during this period appear to have been fairly stable. As head of both farm and family in the 19th century, men were in a position to control the productive and reproductive labor necessary to sustain a large family and, increasingly, to farm on a commercial basis. By the turn of the century, farm women appear to have gained more control over their public and domestic lives as gender relations changed with "modernization," but many traditional sexual divisions of labor remained. On most family farms, men (husband, sons, and hired hands) performed what were regarded as the main income-producing activities in the field, barn, and machine shop; women (wife, daughters, and hired help) performed "supportive" tasks (from both men's and women's points of view) in the house, garden, and poultry shed. Men and women often shared tasks in the dairy. Although many farm women worked in the field at harvest time and at other periods of labor shortages, they usually viewed this economic function, as well as their income from selling vegetables, eggs, and dairy products, in terms of "helping out" the man in the field so that the farmstead could stand on its feet economically. For the same reason, women before World War II seem to have accepted the mechanization of "men's" jobs in the field before the mechanization of "their" work in the house, but not without some protest.

Within this flexible and historically variable gender *structure* were gender *identities* among farm men and women that help explain the social construction of the rural automobile. Many farm men, especially in the Midwest, saw themselves as proficient mechanics who could operate, maintain, repair, and redesign most machines on the farm, from steam engines and threshers in the field to water pumps in the kitchen. Although the social construction of masculinity has varied historically, competence in the operation and repair of machinery formed a defining element of masculinity (and thus gender identity) for many male groups in this period, including linotype operators, other craftsmen, small entrepreneurs, and farm men. Women might pump water, drive the horse and buggy to town, and occasionally operate field machinery, but men fixed a leaky pump, oiled and greased the buggy, and redesigned a hay binder to work over hilly ground. Technical competence helped to define their gender position as a form of masculinity and reinforced the rural gender system.

Consequently, the gasoline automobile, which was already *symbolically* inscribed for masculine use by Henry Ford and other manufacturers, came onto farmsteads headed, in general, by men partly because of their technical competence. Farm people usually viewed the early car as the latest highly sophisticated piece of farm machinery—and it generally became the province of men. Male and female access to the driver's seat varied widely in farm families. At one extreme, some women drove the car to the exclusion of men. Alice Guyer, an Indiana farm woman, recalled that her father "had trouble with them, and he just gave up the driving to my older sister." Bertha Pampel remembered that "my dad never did drive. My mother did all the driving." At the other extreme, some farm women who had been proficient with the horse and buggy never mastered the car and thus became more dependent on men and less technically competent. Laura Drake, another Indiana farm woman, recalled that her family had a car when she was growing up, "but we weren't allowed to touch it. Nobody touched that [car] but him [her father]. "At least two of the twenty-three families interviewed recently in New York said that a mother or daughter did not learn to drive.

A motor-wise farm woman was rare enough to be news. A New York woman told a reporter in 1915 that she was "thoroughly familiar with the machine," and then proceeded to fix a flat tire by vulcanizing it. In general, however, farm journals and oral histories indicate that farm men, rather than farm women, maintained, repaired, and tinkered with the new addition to the farmstead, especially because repair facilities were few and far between in this period. Although the average farm man was probably not an expert auto mechanic, most observers thought farm men could maintain and repair cars better than city men. The farm man's technical competence, rooted in his masculine identity, enabled him to reopen the black box of the car (by reinterpreting its function), jack up its rear wheels, and power all kinds of "men's" work on the farm and, less frequently, the "woman's" cream separator, water pump, or washing machine. . . . Our evidence overwhelmingly shows that farm men, not farm women, reconfigured the car in order to use it in an alternative manner. We have found only one exception—that of an independent "woman farmer" who used her car to pull a hay rake in 1918.

Farm men also converted the car from a passenger vehicle to a produce truck. Showing off further, they returned the car to its original configuration, as defined by the manufacturer, and either drove family members to town and church, or handed it over, in this more symbolically feminine form of usage, to women to operate— sometimes to go to town to get parts to repair field machinery.

The mutual interactions between the artifact, social groups, and intergroup power relations are clearly evident in this case. The gender identity of farm men, formed by defining it in contrast to the constructed femininity of farm women, enabled men to interpret the car flexibly and to socially construct it as a stationary power source. This social construction, in turn, reinforced technical competence as masculine, thus reinforcing farm men's gender identity vis-a-vis farm women. Thus gender not only shaped the motor car, but gender identities were also themselves in turn shaped by using the motor car.

How did farm women fare in this process? The evidence is not clear on this point. Some historians maintain that farm women gained independence by using the car to extend their sphere of influence and redefine their gender roles. By marketing their products more widely, they gained more economic power at home, and by using the car to visit friends and relatives, they were not tied so closely to the farmstead. Many contemporaries professed this view, especially such "modernizers" as home economists, editors of farm journals, and auto manufacturers who publicly espoused a Country Life ideology of saving the supposedly overworked farm woman. Many farm women praised the automobile. In response to muckraking concerns about the over-worked farm woman, "Mrs." Arthur Hewins in Massachusetts wrote in 1920 that the car reduced her workload. "In our 'Lizzie' I carry the milk three miles to the creamery every morning, Sundays included. . . . I have time to go for pleasure rides, and once or twice a week we go to the 'movies' in the nearest town, which is nine miles away."

Other historians argue that farm women travelled further, but stayed within their traditional, supportive gender roles when they shopped for domestic goods or went to town in an emergency to buy parts to fix the tractor. In this argument, using the car reinforced rural gender roles, as it had for suburban women. Does farm women's use of the car support historian Ruth Cowan's thesis of household technology lead-ing to "more work for mother"? Did the use of the car by full-time homeworkers on the farm tend to save the work of their helpers, promote a higher standard of living, and restructure work patterns, as it had for their sisters in the city and suburbs? We note first of all that the time-use studies that help support Cowan's thesis apply to farm women (in fact, the home economists who conducted the pre-1945 studies focussed on the "problem" of the overworked farm women). But these studies pro-vide much more information about time spent on household work than on using the automobile, and the farm women surveyed were probably atypically well-to-do and had adopted the urban domestic ideal to a great extent. Nevertheless, these 2,000 women, the vast majority of whose families owned automobiles, still worked a full week in the house, dairy, garden, and poultry pen.

An Ohio man's story of a farm woman and her car unwittingly provides one explanation of why the auto did not lead to more leisure. L. B. Pierce wrote the *Rural New Yorker* in 1919 that one morning, a farm woman cooked that night's dinner in a "fireless cooker" (an insulated box in which a boiled dinner could cook all day), drove forty-one miles to visit her daughter in Cleveland, shopped in the city in the afternoon, then drove home in time to put a late supper on the table from the fireless cooker. Before the family had a car, which the woman also used to run a butter and egg route, she would have had to skimp on her after-breakfast work and her husband would have had to get his own dinner. "After the car was bought she could wash the breakfast dishes, sweep the kitchen and then get to her customers as early as before, and generally get home in time to serve the dinner which the fireless cooker had been preparing in the basement." The car thus enabled this farm woman to do more work—to expand her egg business and still perform the tasks expected of her within the (expanded) sphere of "woman's work" on the farm, including shopping for bar-gains in the city and maintaining kinship ties.

The gender relations and associated meanings involved with the automobile in the countryside were quite stable over time compared with the other meanings of the car we have identified. The anticar meanings were obviously intense, but also transient, and disappeared for the most part when manufacturers introduced cars that were economical and met the criticism of the "anti's." Other social meanings, which defined the car as destroying the rural fabric of general stores, one-room schools, and local churches, eventually disappeared precisely because the countryside was trans-formed in the very manner feared by the critics. Between 1920 and 1940, the car had become a means to increase the radius of rural life to include larger towns, schools, and churches in the orbit of farm men and women.

In contrast, gender relations and associated meanings remained fairly stable. The interpretative flexibility of the early auto reinforced them, as we have seen. The auto's replacements for farm work, the truck and tractor, did not upset the gender structure either, even though women showed during World War I that they could drive a tractor, just like their sisters proved they could do factory work during the crisis. For instance, some urban women learned to drive and maintain tractors in the American Woman's Land Army—a voluntary organization that hired out "farmerette" squads to farms during the war—and farm women drove tractors at home to meet the "man-power" shortage. Yet when the war ended, farming by horse, car, or tractor was still considered to be primarily men's work. Gender relations were also not much affected by rural electrification, which—along with a general farm prosperity after World War II—enabled farm women to buy "urban" appliances like electric washing machines, ranges, irons, and refrigerators. Historian Katherine Jellison has argued that one result of this mechanization of housework, and an increased consumerism and the replacement of hired men by tractors after World War II, was to decrease women's work in the house, garden, poultry barn, and dairy, thus giving them the option of operating tractors in the field or using the auto to take a job in town. But the new technologies did not transform gender relations markedly since women were still viewed as "helping out," as supporting men's work on the farm. Indeed, Jellison's evidence indicates that country people wove these artifacts into the fabric of their society, that they shaped them within the flexible, yet durable, system of rural gender relations. . . .

Despite the increased availability of tractors, trucks, and gasoline engines, farm men and women owned many more automobiles than these technologies before World War II. Census data for the United States shows that automobiles were far and away the most popular form of inanimate power on the farm from 1920 to the war. A major reason was that during the agricultural economic crisis of the 1920s and 1930s, farm men and women preferred to use their autos, often purchased during the boom times of World War I, for multiple purposes like going to town, hauling produce, powering farm equipment, and even field work (for those who bought conversion kits or made their own). Large numbers of prosperous farms did, however, buy tractors, trucks, and gasoline engines. A survey of 538 well-to-do Minnesota farms in 1929 showed that over 90 percent of them had autos, two-thirds had stationary gasoline engines, nearly one-half had tractors, over one-third had electricity, and about one-third had trucks. The families used their autos almost equally for "farm" and "family" purposes, but the study did not mention any belt-power use of the car. The families made heavy use of tractors, gas engines, electric motors, and trucks to pull agricultural implements, provide belt power, and to haul farm products. More and more farms in the United States made these same technological choices after the federal government established a New Deal program in the 1930s that provided low-cost loans to purchase farm equipment. The program led to a large increase in the number of tractors on farms, thus helping to displace the rural auto as an all-purpose power source. . . .

It is clear that mutually constructed gender relationships and the transactional relationships between manufacturers, dealers, and buyers both constrained and enabled the design and usage of this technology. But the types of development processes we have identified sometimes followed paradoxical paths. Thus it was a masculinized gender position which enabled farm men to open up the black box of the car and for a time threaten the predominant meaning of the artifact. However, at the same time these new options reinforced predominant gender identities. For car manufacturers the new interpretative flexibility at first was a threat, but in the long run it helped to open up new and profitable markets as they and other manufacturers sold machines dedicated to each of the different usages we have identified. However, differentiation of usage and the creation of a new market is not always the response. The early attempts to manufacture an electric car for women failed and instead manufacturers adapted the gasoline car to make it more appealing to women (and men) users by inventing the electric starter and introducing the closed-in top and thereby created a larger market for an existing product. Thus the meaning of the car was changed in response to the social group of women, but whether the newly changed artifact significantly altered gender relations is, as historian Virginia Scharff shows, unlikely. However, the new (gasoline) car enabled different gender identities to be constructed. Women could do new sorts of things—it gave them a new freedom, and men did not have to be quite so manly (and risk life and limb cranking cars). Thus the meaning which using the technology gave to underlying gender identities shifted those identities somewhat.

. . . [W]e have attempted to show how artifacts and social groups are tied together during the course of technological development. We agree with recent scholars that users socially construct technology. Our approach has been to show how an explicit model of social construction can be used as a heuristic to tell a full story of users and technology. We have argued that such a story should examine the radical options for change and how other social groups respond to such options and thereby create new artifacts.

The interpretative flexibility we have described for the car disappeared by the early 1950s. Closure had occurred (once again) and farm people had stopped using their autos for grinding their grain, plowing their fields, or carrying their produce to town. Instead, they had begun to buy tractors and pickup trucks in large numbers— new artifacts that manufacturers developed partly in response to these novel interpretations of the car. The users, so easily overlooked in writing the story of technology, had made their mark.

Modern Times

JAMES J. FLINK

With the transfer of skills at Ford from men to specialized machines, the process that Harry Braverman had identified as the "degradation of work" turned highly skilled jobs into semiskilled and/or unskilled jobs. This revolutionized the workplace.

Fordism meant that neither physical strength nor the long apprenticeship required for becoming a competent craftsman were any longer prerequisites for industrial employment. The creativity and experience on the job that had been valued in the craftsman were considered liabilities in the assembly-line worker. "As to machinists, old-time, all-around men, perish the thought!" declared Horace Arnold and Fay

From James J. Flink, *The Automobile Age* (Cambridge, MA: MIT Press, 1988), pp. 117–128.

Faurote in 1915. "The Ford Motor Company has no use for experience, in the working ranks anyway. It desires and prefers machine tool operators who have nothing to unlearn, who have no theories of correct surface speeds for metal finishing, and will simply do what they are told to do, over and over again from bell-time to bell-time. The Ford help need not even be able bodied."

New opportunities for remunerative employment were opened to the . . . peasant from southern or eastern Europe, the black migrant to the northern city, the physically handicapped, and the educable mentally retarded. For the machine did not discriminate. . . . "Our employment office does not bar a man for anything he has previously done," boasted Ford. "He is equally acceptable whether he has been in Sing Sing or at Harvard and we do not even inquire from which place he has graduated. All that he needs is the desire to work."

The early Ford work force mirrored the ethnic character of Detroit, which at the turn of the century was essentially English and German. About half of Detroit's population in 1900 were native-born whites, the other half overwhelmingly immigrants from northern and western Europe.

The ethnic composition of the Ford work force changed dramatically with the coming of mass production. The first survey of the national origins of those workers, in November 1914, revealed that only 29 percent were American born and that two thirds were immigrants from southern and eastern Europe, with Poles (21 percent) and Russians (16 percent) being the largest ethnic groups. The Ford workers in this survey represented twenty-two national groups. Company announcements were printed in fourteen languages but invariably ended with the injunction, "Learn to Read English." Bilingual foremen were valued, and it became essential for straw bosses to learn how to say "hurry up" in several different languages. Native-born Caucasians were particularly underrepresented in unskilled and semiskilled jobs at Ford. As Nevins and Hill point out, "At the Ford plant the foundry workers, common laborers, drill press men, grinder operators, and other unskilled and semiskilled hands were likely to be Russians, Poles, Croats, Hungarians, or Italians; only the skilled employees were American, British, or German stock."

By 1919 the Ford Motor Company also employed hundreds of ex-convicts and 9,563 "substandard men"—a group that included amputees, the blind, deaf-mutes, epileptics, and about 1,000 tubercular employees. By 1923 Ford employed about 5,000 blacks, more than any other large American company and roughly half the number employed in the entire automobile industry.

Conditions on the assembly line were grudgingly accepted only by workers accustomed to even more repressive systems of labor or whose opportunities for employment elsewhere at a living wage were almost nil. Arnold and Faurote recognized that "the monotony of repetitive production can be alleviated only by a satisfactory wage-rate, and is, perhaps, much more easily endured by immigrants, whose home wage stood somewhere about 60 cents for 10 hours' work, than by native-born Americans." Indeed, one [of] the major reasons why mass-production techniques came to be innovated in the United States is that, in contrast with Europe, automobile manufacturers here could count on the availability of a large labor pool of unskilled, recently arrived, and as yet politically impotent peasants from the most socially and economically backward countries of Europe, and of blacks escaping from the oppressive socioeconomic conditions of the rural American South.

The demands of the assembly line put a premium on youth. Nevins and Hill relate that "the bosses had a natural liking for young, vigorous, quick men not past thirty-five. Experienced hands past that age, if they did not possess some indispensable skill were thus often the first to be dismissed and the last to be re-engaged." In their 1929 study, Robert and Helen Lynd tied mass production to the emergence of a cult of youth in the 1920s. Noting the trend toward employing younger men in Muncie, Indiana, factories, for example, the Lynds explained that "in modern machine production it is speed and endurance that are at a premium. A boy of nineteen may, after a few weeks of experience on a machine, turn out an amount of work greater than his father of forty-five."

"I have not been able to discover that repetitive labor injuries a man in any way," wrote Henry Ford. "Industry need not exact a human toll." Mass production shifted many backbreaking tasks from the worker to the machine, and Highland Park exemplified the clean, safe, well-lighted, and well-ventilated factory essential to efficient mass production. Nevertheless, a human toll was exacted, if only because mass production meant "the reduction of the necessity for thought on the part of the worker and the reduction of his movements to a minimum."

In the 1936 movie *Modern Times* Charlie Chaplin satirized the new breed of semiskilled worker created at Highland Park. Machines were closely spaced for optimal efficiency, and material was delivered to the worker at a waist-high level so that "wasted motion" was not expended in walking, reaching, stooping, or bending. The worker not only had to subordinate himself to the pace of the machine but also had to be able to withstand the boredom inevitable in repeating the same motions hour after hour. A fifteen-minute lunch break, which included time to use the rest room and to wash one's hands, was the only interruption of the fatiguing monotony of repetitive labor, the hypnotic trance that workers were lulled into by the rhythmic din of the machinery.

The precise coordination of the flow of assembly that mass production demanded meant a new ironclad discipline for industrial workers. "The organization is so highly specialized and one part is so dependent upon another that we could not for a moment consider allowing men to have their own way," Ford explained. "Without the most rigid discipline we would have the utmost confusion. I think it should not be otherwise in industry." Consequently, the easy camaraderie on the job that had been normal in American industry for unskilled as well as skilled workers was forbidden at Highland Park. Straw bosses and company "spotters"—another new element in the work force—enforced rules and regulations that forbade leaning against the machine, sitting, squatting, talking, whistling, or smoking on the job. Workers learned to communicate clandestinely without moving their lips in the "Ford whisper" and wore frozen expressions known as "Fordization of the face." There is not much personal contact," understated Ford. "The men do their work and go home—a factory is not a drawing room."

The impact of Fordism on the worker was debilitating. The individual became an anonymous, interchangeable robot who had little chance on the job to demonstrate his personal qualifications for upward mobility into the echelons of management. Thus, the American myth of unlimited individual social mobility, based on ability and the ideal of the self-made man, became a frustrating impossibility for the assembly-line worker. As the job became a treadmill to escape from rather than a calling in which to find fulfillment, leisure began to assume a new importance. The meaning of work, long sanctified in the Protestant Ethic, was reduced to monetary remuneration. The value of thrift and personal economy became questionable, too, as mass consumption became an inevitable corollary of mass production.

. . . The Ford Motor Company had from the beginning been an exemplary employer regarding monetary remuneration. Ford paid top wages, and early Ford labor practices in addition included bonuses, as well as educational, medical, and recreational programs. In 1905 every Ford worker received an incredibly generous Christmas bonus of $1,000. From 1908 through 1911 annual bonuses were paid of 5 percent of wages after one year's service, 7½ percent after two years, and 10 percent after three years. In 1911 the one- and two-year service bonuses were ended, but an "efficiency bonus" was added for salaried and supervisory personnel.

Despite the relatively high wages and bonus incentives paid at Ford, worker dissatisfaction was evident in unacceptable rates of labor productivity and labor turnover at the new Highland Park plant—"a new breed of factory," writes Stephen Meyer III, "with an entirely different pace and intensity of work even for unskilled workers. Like the peasants of the old world, Ford immigrant workers voted and voiced their opinions with their feet and abandoned the Highland Park factory in droves."

John R. Lee came to Ford with the 1911 acquisition of the John R. Keim Mills of Buffalo, New York, where he had been general manager. Lee became director of the Ford Employment Office. In the summer of 1913 he was asked to conduct an investigation to determine the causes of worker discontent and inefficiency at Highland Park. His report concluded that the chief causes were bad housing and home conditions, too long hours, too low wages, and arbitary treatment of workers by foremen and superintendents, who at that time had authority over hiring, firing, and advancement.

As a result of Lee's investigation, in October 1913 the Ford Motor Company instituted a comprehensive new labor program. Wages were increased an average of 15 percent. An Employees' Savings and Loan Association was formed so that workers could have a safe place to save and to borrow money at low rates when family emergencies occurred. Foremen were stripped of much of their authority in the management of the labor force as labor relations were centralized in a new Employment Department.

Probably the most significant of the Lee reforms was the rationalization of job skills and advancement within the Ford factory by a new skill-wage classification system that reorganized jobs into groups with similar levels of skill, and established a graded hierarchy of jobs from the least to the most skilled. This reduced the number of wage rates at Highland Park from sixty-nine to only eight, ranging from a high of 51 cents to a low of 23 cents an hour, for sixteen different levels of skill and competence. A worker received automatic increases as he reached specific standards of efficiency within a grade, and he was advanced to the next grade as his skill increased.

The significance of the Lee reforms was lost in the announcement of the five-dollar, eight-hour day by the Ford Motor Company on January 5, 1914. This plan roughly doubled for Ford's American workers the going rate of pay for industrial workers, and it shortened the work day by two hours as well. It had been foreshadowed on a far smaller scale at Ford-England's Trafford Park plant near Manchester. By paying his English employees the 1s. 3d. an hour, or £3 for a six-day,

48-hour week, in 1911, Ford had paid about twice the prevailing U.K. industrial wage, for a shorter work week.

The five-dollar minimum pay for a day's work was boldly conceived by Ford as a plan for sharing profits with his workers in advance of their being earned. "In accordance with Ford policy," writes Meyer, "wages were the 'earned' result of 'services and labor.' Profits were the conditional gift of the Ford Motor Company." Thus, only workers who met certain criteria established by Ford were entitled to a share of the profits. The normal wage rate of a laborer at Ford was $2.34 per day, for example, while his profit rate under the plan was $2.66. The profit rate was paid to him as an incentive for cooperating in increasing the efficiency of Ford production. Eligible workers were those who had been at Ford for six months or more and were either married men living with and taking good care of their families, single men over twenty-two years of age of proved thrifty habits, or men under twenty-two years of age and women who were the sole support of some next of kin. Almost 60 percent of the Ford workers qualified immediately, and within two years about 75 percent were included in the profit-sharing plan.

The Sociological Department was formed to check on the eligibility of Ford employees to participate in the Five-Dollar Day and to ensure that the profits shared with them were put to uses approved by Henry Ford. It was first headed by John R. Lee. He was succeeded in late 1915 by the Reverend Dr. Samuel S. Marquis, Ford's Episcopalian pastor, who changed its name to the Educational Department.

An initial staff of over 200 investigators, soon pared down to a permanent staff of 50, visited workers' homes gathering information and giving advice on the intimate details of the family budget, diet, living arrangements, recreation, social outlook, and morality. Americanization of the immigrant was enforced through mandatory classes in English. The worker who refused to learn English, rejected the advice of the investigator, gambled, drank excessively, or was found guilty of "any malicious practice derogatory to good physical manhood or moral character" was disqualified from the profit-sharing plan and put on probation. If he failed to reform within six months, he was discharged, and his profits accumulated under the plan were used for charity. Shockingly presumptuous, repressive, and paternalistic by today's standards, the policies of the Sociological/Educational Department reflected both the long-standing assumption of American businessmen that the employer had a right to interfere in the private lives of his employees and the most advanced theories of the social workers of the Progressive Era.

The Five-Dollar Day defied the conventional wisdom of classical economics, which called for paying wages at a subsistence level. Henry Ford implicitly acknowledged the validity of radical criticisms of income distribution under entrepreneurial capitalism when he told the Reverend Dr. Marquis that five dollars a day was "about the least a man with a family can live on these days." But Marquis knew that the five-dollar, eight-hour day "actually returned more dollars to [Henry Ford] than he gave out. It was unquestionably a shrewd and profitable stroke. To the credit of Mr. Ford be it said that he personally never maintained that his profit and bonus schemes were a means for distributing charity."

Ford's motives for introducing his radical profit-sharing plan undoubtedly were mixed. He recognized ahead of his fellow industrialists that the worker was also a consumer and that increasing workers' purchasing power would stimulate sales. He also wanted to stave off the organizing efforts of the radical International Workers of the World (IWW). His main concerns, however, were increasing labor productivity and stopping an incredibly costly rate of labor turnover at Highland Park. "When the [profit-sharing] plan went into effect, we had 14,000 employees and it had been necessary to hire at the rate of about 53,000 a year in order to keep a constant force of 14,000," recounted Ford in 1922. "In 1915 we had to hire only 6,508 men and the majority of these new men were taken on because of the growth of the business. With the old turnover of labor and the present force we should have to hire at the rate of nearly 200,000 men a year—which would be pretty nearly an impossible proposition." Ford asserted in 1922 that "the payment of high wages fortunately contributes to the low costs [of production] because the men become steadily more efficient on account of being relieved of outside worries. The payment of five dollars a day for an eight-hour day was one of the finest cost-cutting moves we ever made, and the six-dollar day [instituted at Ford in 1919] is cheaper than the five. How far this will go we do not know."

An estimated 15- to 20-percent increase in labor productivity at Highland Park in 1915 was attributed to the Five-Dollar Day. And with inauguration of the eight-hour day, Highland Park switched from running two shifts a day to three. The advertising and public-relations value alone was well more than the $5.8 million that the profit-sharing plan cost the Ford Motor Company during its first year of implementation. Henry Ford was roundly denounced as a "traitor to his class" by his fellow entrepreneurial capitalists, especially by his less efficient competitors in the automobile industry. The public response, on the other hand, was decidedly positive. "Nine-tenths of the newspaper comment was favorable, much of it almost ecstatic," write Nevins and Hill. "Industrialists, labor leaders, sociologists, ministers, politicians, all hailed the innovation in glowing terms."

. . . Although the eight-hour day and forty-eight-hour week quickly became the norm in American automobile factories, Henry Ford's doubling of the daily minimum pay stood for decades as an isolated example of self-interested benevolence. The strategy underlying the Ford profit-sharing plan did not become institutionalized in American industry until after World War II. Nor did the experiment in benevolent paternalism last longer than a few years at the Ford Motor Company. By 1918 the inflation of the World War I years had reduced the $5.00 minimum daily pay to only $2.80 in 1914 purchasing power, wiping out the workers' gains. . . . [T]he war also meant greatly reduced profit margins for Ford, and the company only survived the postwar recession by adopting stringent economy measures. As the 1920s wore on, as the Model T became outmoded and Ford's competitors became more efficient in production, the position of the Ford Motor Company in the automobile industry declined. Working conditions deteriorated with the speedup of the Ford assembly lines to meet the new competition. After the minimum daily pay of Ford workers was raised to $6.00 in January 1919, giving them $3.36 in 1914 purchasing power, there were no further advances in Ford wages until World War II. By the early 1920s $10.00 a day would have been necessary to match the $5.00 minimum pay of 1914. In 1925—Ford's pre–World War II high point in sales both in the United States and worldwide—the weekly earnings of Ford workers were $4.21 below the automobile industry average in the United States, although cutting the Ford work week to five days in 1926 reduced the gap to $1.37 by 1928.

The Educational Department folded and its records were burned after Samuel Marquis resigned as its head early in 1921. He later explained: "The old group of executives, who at times set justice and humanity above profits and production, were gone. With them, so it seemed to me, had gone an era of cooperation and good will in the company. There came to the front men whose theory was that men are more profitable to an industry when driven then led, that fear is a greater incentive to work than loyalty."

Ford benevolent paternalism had actually ended earlier. Over the course of World War I, the company's labor policies had undergone, as Meyer puts it, "a transition from a variant of welfare capitalism, which captured the mood of the Progressive Era, to a version of the American Plan, which typified the more recalcitrant employer attitudes of the twenties." Under the Espionage Act of 1917 and the Sedition Act of 1918, at Ford "more authoritarian and more repressive labor policies moved to the foreground. . . . Under extremely broad judicial interpretations, both of these laws were used to prosecute German, Austrian, and Hungarian immigrant workers, members of the IWW and the Socialist Party, and finally, any worker who voiced discontent with the war or American society."

The American Protective League (APL) was created as a "semiofficial auxiliary of the Justice Department," composed of some 250,000 volunteer "patriots" who were organized into a nationwide network of spies and informants in American industry. The Ford Educational Department coordinated the activities at Highland Park of about a hundred APL operatives, who were given access to the thousands of individual "records of investigation" maintained on employees under the Ford profit-sharing plan. Should an APL operative report suspicious statements or behavior by a Ford worker, his file would be pulled and a new record started containing an account of the incident. "This new record on the worker often passed into the hands of the Department of Justice, military intelligence officers, and local law enforcement officers," Meyer reports. Ford officials made high worker productivity a patriotic duty and considered any worker activity that retarded production to be, in Meyer's words, "a conscious and treasonable act of sabotage."

APL activities ostensibly ceased at Highland Park with the Armistice. However, under Alex Sparks in the Superintendent's Office, the Ford APL organization was converted in 1919 into a network of labor spies and informants whose mission was to thwart the organizing efforts of the Automobile Workers Union (AWU). Although all automobile manufacturers in the 1920s employed labor spies and informants to ferret out union organizers, the Ford Motor Company gained particular notoriety.

Citing the Ford Motor Company as the world's outstanding example of an industrial dictatorship, the *New York Times* on January 8, 1928, called Henry Ford "an industrial fascist—the Mussolini of Detroit." Probusiness *Fortune* magazine commented in December 1933 that it was well known in the automobile industry that "Mr. Ford's organization does show extreme evidence of being ruled primarily by fear of the job." Even Edsel was mercilessly bullied by the elder Ford, who thought his son too soft and held up as a model worthy of emulation Harry Bennett, an ex-pugilist with underworld connections. Bennett enforced discipline in the Ford plants as head of a gang of labor spies and thugs called the Ford Service Department. He came to be Henry Ford's most trusted associate and comrade after the Model A replaced the Model T in 1928 and production was shifted to the River Rouge plant.

From Edsel Ford on down, the Ford executives came to fear and despise Bennett as his influence grew, and by the mid-1930s Ford workers wondered whether Hitler had derived the idea for his Gestapo from Bennett's Ford Service. "As a rule, Ford's managers, having more to lose, came to watch their jobs more nervously than the men at the Rouge who swept the floor," relates Keith Sward. "On the lower tiers of the Ford organization, Ford Service gave rise to any number of unmistakable neuroses. These 'shop complaints' went all the way from mild states of anxiety to advanced nervous symptoms that were fit material for a psychopathic ward. Thus conditioned, the personality of any Ford employee was subjected to a process of subtle and profound degradation." Writing during the depths of the Great Depression, Jonathan Leonard, an early Ford debunker, declared, "Detroit is a city of hate and fear. And the major focus of that hatred and fear is the astonishing plant on the River Rouge." Leonard found almost all automobile factories in Detroit "horrifying and repellent to the last degree. But the Ford factory has the reputation of being by far the worst." The reason was that "over the Ford plant hangs the menace of the 'Service Department,' the spies and stool pigeons who report every action, every remark, every expression. . . . No one who works for Ford is safe from the spies—from the superintendents down to the poor creature who must clean a certain number of toilets an hour."

. . . With expansion into the Rouge plant and as labor relations deteriorated in the early 1920s, Ford hired more and more black workers. August Meier and Elliott Rudwick point out that Henry Ford was ambivalent in his attitude toward blacks: he believed that they were racially inferior and that the races should be segregated residentially and socially, but he also believed that blacks had constitutional rights to social justice and rights to decent housing, jobs, and economic security. He thought that the "superior" race was obligated "to give philanthropic service to subordinate races" and that "whenever blacks had received a fair chance their labor made them an asset to the community."

Blacks first began moving en masse into northern cities, including Detroit, to take advantage of the employment opportunities created by the World War I labor shortage. Packard became the first significant employer of blacks in the automobile industry, with 1,000 on its payroll in May 1917. Working in close association with the Detroit Urban League, Dodge also was a substantial early employer of blacks. In contrast, as late as January 1916 the Ford Motor Company had only 50 black employees in a work force of 32,702.

As fears of labor unrest and labor organization mounted in 1919, Ford rapidly expanded his recruitment of blacks and within a year became Detroit's leading employer of them. Ford's black workers were concentrated at the Rouge, where by 1926 they numbered 10,000 and constituted about 10 percent of the work force. Despite cutbacks in employment during the Depression, the number and proportion of black workers at the Rouge remained fairly constant—9,325 in 1937, constituting about 12 percent of the Rouge work force. This contrasts with 2,800 blacks constituting a mere 3 percent of the entire General Motors Michigan work force as late as 1941. By the outbreak of World War II Ford employed about two thirds of the blacks working in Detroit's automobile factories.

Recruitment was carried out through recommendations from Detroit's most prominent black citizens—particularly from the Reverend Robert L. Bradby, pastor of the Second Baptist Church, and Father Everard W. Daniel, pastor of St. Matthew's

Protestant Episcopal Church. Authority over black hiring, firing, disputes, and other matters was exercised by Donald J. Marshall, a former policeman and one of Father Daniel's parishioners, and Willis Ward, a black former football star at the University of Michigan. Marshall and Ward belonged to the Ford Service Department and reported directly to Harry Bennett and to Charles Sorensen. In effect, Ford had established a "Negro Department," with special procedures for black employees. And these procedures meant that black workers at Ford were under even more repressive scrutiny than white workers.

Although blacks employed in automobile factories earned relatively high wages in comparison with those employed in other industries, they tended to be concentrated in the most dangerous, dirty, and disagreeable jobs—chiefly in paint spraying and in foundry work. This was true at the Rouge, where fully 38 percent of the black workers were employed in the foundry and an additional 15.6 percent in the foundry machine shop, versus only 5.2 percent in motor manufacturing and assembly, 6 percent in chassis and parts manufacturing and assembly, and a minuscule 1 percent in the tool rooms. A white worker at the Rouge explained to an investigator, "Some jobs white folks will not do, so they have to take niggers in, particularly in duco work, spraying paint on car bodies. This soon kills a white man." Zaragosa Vargas demonstrates that although the relatively small number of Mexicans employed at the Rouge also were concentrated in the most disagreeable jobs, they were significantly less concentrated in them than were the blacks.

Nevertheless, Meier and Rudwick find that "Henry Ford was unique in the wide range of opportunities that he offered Negro blue-collar workers." Blacks could be found in all Ford production jobs working alongside whites. Ford had more black supervisory personnel than the rest of the industry combined. In a few instances black foremen were in charge of all-white crews. Blacks were admitted to apprenticeship schools only at Ford. And in 1924 James C. Price, an outstanding expert in abrasives and industrial diamonds, became the first black salaried employee at Ford. Meier and Rudwick cite the labor economist Herbert Northrup's conclusion that in the pre–World War II period Ford's black workers at the Rouge "came closer to job equality . . . than they did at any large enterprise . . . recorded in the literature." Significantly, however, this was true only at the Rouge. Outside the Detroit metropolitan area Ford employed blacks in menial jobs only, primarily as custodians.

The racist aspects of Henry Ford's unique treatment of his black workers were overlooked by Detroit's black community at a time when rabid Negrophobia was more characteristic of white employers than self-interested, benevolent paternalism. Black workers at Ford felt themselves superior and wore their company badges to church on Sunday. Black leadership, including the Detroit Urban League, praised Ford as a friend of the race who could do no wrong. "The income of Ford's black workers was the cornerstone for the prosperity of the black community's business and professional people," write Meier and Rudwick. "The latter, acutely aware of how much black Detroit's economic well-being and their own livelihood depended on the company, believed that what was best for Ford was best for the race."

Consequently, Ford's black workers remained amazingly loyal to him despite the repressive activities of the Ford Service Department, the degeneration of working conditions at the Rouge, and the existence of tokenism rather than true equality of opportunity in the Ford plants. They demonstrated this loyalty by remaining in the

River Rouge plant as strikebreakers during the 1941 strike that resulted in the unionization of the Ford Motor Company and the inauguration of a new era in Ford labor policy and labor-management relations.

⋀ *F U R T H E R   R E A D I N G*

Flink, James J. *America Adopts the Automobile, 1895–1910* (Cambridge, MA: The MIT Press, 1970).

Gartman, David. *Auto Slavery: The Labor Process in the American Automobile Industry, 1897–1950* (New Brunswick, NJ: Rutgers University Press, 1986).

Leslie, Stuart W. *Boss Kettering* (New York: Columbia University Press, 1983).

Lewis, David W. *The Public Image of Henry Ford* (Detroit, MI: Wayne State University Press, 1976).

Lichtenstein, Nelson, and Stephen Meyer, eds. *On the Line: Essays in the History of Auto Work* (Urbana, IL: University of Illinois Press, 1989).

McShane, Clay. *Down the Asphalt Path: American Cities and the Coming of the Automobile* (New York: Columbia University Press, 1994).

Meier, August, and Elliott Rudwick. *Black Detroit and the Rise of the UAW* (New York: Oxford University Press, 1979).

Meyer, Stephen, III. *The Five Dollar Day: Labor Management at the Ford Motor Company, 1908–1921* (Albany, NY: State University of New York Press, 1981).

Nevins, Allan, and Frank E. Hill. *Ford.* 3 vols. (New York: Charles Scribner & Sons, 1954–1962).

Rae, John B. *The Road and the Car in American Life* (Cambridge, MA: The MIT Press, 1971).

Scharff, Virginia. *Taking the Wheel: Women and the Coming of the Motor Age* (New York: The Free Press, 1991).

Wik, Reynold M. *Henry Ford and Grass Roots America* (Ann Arbor, MI: University of Michigan Press, 1972).

Toys Were Us: Invention and Technological Acculturation in Hobbyist Worlds, 1900–1940

卌

Studies of how nineteenth- and twentieth-century Americans were technically educated have traditionally focused on the "shop floor" or the university. In his book America by Design, *David Noble argues that college-level engineering education in the early twentieth century acculturated young males not only into a world of machines but also into the management of workers and other goals of corporate capitalism. Studies of the shop floor have focused on how the apprenticeship system passed knowledge from older to younger men, or how the often innovative culture of the machine shop was transferred to the "research lab"— most famously Thomas Edison's Menlo Park.*

Historians are just beginning to notice other important places where technical education, training, and acculturation took place. One spur to thinking has been the personal computer, initially developed not in shops or universities, but in houses and garages. Some of its inventors were acculturated into advanced technology in elementary school. Was this a fluke in the history of invention, or were houses, garages, and elementary schools important sites in earlier periods as well?

Other questions come from the history of sports and "leisure." Twentieth-century Americans increasingly, and passionately, used tools in nonwork settings. As Robert Post has shown, the sport/hobby of auto racing has induced scores of Americans to invest their time and fortunes in innovative "play" with technically sophisticated machines. Such studies raise questions about tool use in free and "unfree" time.

Feminist scholars, grappling with why and how modern technology has been gendered male, have also been exploring a wider variety of sites and issues. Nina Lerman, for example, has shown how vocational training in mid-nineteenth-century Philadelphia schools proceeded along separate tracks for boys, girls, whites, and African Americans. If childhood and adolescence are times of intense technical training, and the simultaneous inscription of gender, race, and class onto bodies, tools, and skills, they perhaps deserve closer historical attention.

This chapter focuses on the home world of American boys during the first half of the twentieth century—on the interrelation between innovation, technical acculturation, and play. It also contrasts this boys' world with that of men, and with the technical opportunities of girls. A related theme is the construction of the technological future, sometimes called "utopianism," but actually part of the reality of many technologies in their embryonic stage.

𝔸 DOCUMENTS

The first selection, from *The Century Magazine* (1902), was written by a newspaper editor in Newfoundland, where Guglielmo Marconi had just engineered transmission of the first transatlantic radio signals (December 1901). Marconi examined the proofs of the article "with great care" and wrote a brief introduction. It documents his thinking about who would be attracted to the technology and what further innovations he had to make to satisfy those groups.

The second series of articles appeared in the magazine *Electrician and Mechanic* between 1909 and 1913. This journal catered to boy hobbyists, who were then building and operating their own radio sets.

The third selection is the winning entry in an essay contest, sponsored by the Commonwealth Edison Company in 1917, entitled "How Electricity Effects Economy in the Home and Adds to the Happiness of the Family." The author was fifteen-year-old Fern Van Bramer of The Academy of Our Lady in Chicago, who won $50. The essay was printed in *Electric City Magazine.* The fourth selection is from a textbook on scientific management published in 1937. It reproduces the actual script used to train young girls for the assembly line at the Colonial Radio Corporation.

Marconi and His Transatlantic Signal, 1902

At the marine station on Signal Hill, at St. John's, Newfoundland on Thursday, December 12, 1901, at 12:30 p.m., Mr. Marconi received distinct and unmistakable electric signals, transmitted through space without wire or cable or other visible or tangible agency from his station at Poldhu near Penzance, in Cornwall, England. . . .

That Newfoundland enjoys the distinction of having been the theater of this unequaled scientific development, she owes to her advantageous geographical position, as the "half-way house" of the two hemispheres, the nearest point in America to the Old World. When the first Atlantic cable was laid, in 1858, Newfoundland was its natural western terminus. To-day, for the same reason, Marconi attempts his experiments here.

Guglielmo Marconi was born at Bologna, Italy, in 1875, his father being an Italian landed proprietor and his mother an Irish-woman, one of the Jameson family of Dublin, the well known whisky distillers. He was educated at Leghorn under Professor Rosa, and at Bologna under Professor Righi. While yet a youth, he was attracted to the study of electricity, and when only sixteen devoted himself to the development of wireless telegraphy, then in its embryonic stages. His connections

From P. T. McGrath, "Authoritative Account of Marconi's Work in Wireless Telegraphy," *The Century Magazine* (March 1902): 769–780.

being prosperous, he escaped the fate of most men of genius, who, from lack of wealth, are unable to give full play to their talents, and it is partly because of his having been in a position to conduct his experiments without resorting to the shifts and economics forced upon others that we find him, at this early age, a leader in this branch of electrical science.

Great though his latest feat has been, Mr. Marconi holds it to be small compared with his developing the practical working of his apparatus from two miles to two hundred and twenty-five. When he reached the two-mile limit he was balked for a long time, being unable to devise an apparatus which would manifest an observable activity for a greater distance. He was often discouraged almost to the point of despair, but he eventually overcame this difficulty, and after that it was plainer sailing. . . .

. . . [T]he electric waves created by Marconi's transmitter will, under ordinary circumstances, affect any number of receiving-stations which may be within range, by causing an electrical bobbing up and down in each of the perpendicular wires, and each such stations will receive the message transmitted.

This, it was realized, would minimize the value of the discovery as to its use in wartime, as the enemy would receive the news also; so a scheme was devised whereby the mast and wire were dispensed with and a parabolic copper reflector was substituted, by means of which waves could be sent out in a certain prescribed direction only. But this device, though suitable enough as far as it went, permitted of signaling for only about four miles, between points in sight of each other, and this deprived the main discovery of much of its value. The other waves influenced by this reflector were stopped by the curvature of the earth, whereas those projected by means of the "aërial" wire suspended from a mast were subject to no such limitations. To obviate this objection, Marconi has experimented with a view to syntonizing the transmitter with the receiver, so that messages destined for a particular station shall be received at that station and no other, unless the others happen to be in syntony or tune also. . . .

The instruments used on shipboard are of course much less powerful than those used for the transatlantic signaling, the output of the transmitter being only about one sixth of one horse-power, and they are all tuned to sympathy, that is, to the same wave-beat, so that, if in distress, the vessels may signal to each other. The instruments in land stations, each have a common and a special tune, so that the secrecy of commercial messages may be properly safeguarded. The tuning of the apparatus can be easily changed, however, so that in war-time the ships of each nation could work their own private code, so to speak. . . .

The system has been found of great service for naval purposes. It is installed on board thirty-seven British war-ships. In the late naval maneuvers its efficiency was demonstrated beyond question; signals were transmitted from ship to ship over a distance of one hundred and sixty miles, and the reports of the admirals commanding the rival fleets were strongly in its favor. . . . It will be of great value, also, in naval warfare, as an admiral can by its means maneuver ships hundreds of miles apart. It is applied most successfully at sea, where a virtually level surface is obtained; on land its value is diminished one half by the obstruction caused by the diversified physical features of the region it traverses. But it is easy to signal by it from hill to hill, and armies could speak to each other by its means from elevations, without enemies in the lowlands being aware of what they were doing. . . .

The grand scientific truth being demonstrated, Mr. Marconi now proposed to perfect the system so that it may be made applicable to commercial uses. It only requires increased power at Poldhu to transmit signals effective enough to actuate the recorder at the station at St. John's. Following upon that, additions to the same force will permit the electric energy to be projected to the uttermost ends of the earth. Mr. Marconi will build large stations at St. John's and Cape Cod of the same kind as that at Poldhu, and hopes within a few months to be able to transact commercial telegraph business across the Atlantic. He believes that at present his system is good for transmission over a thousand miles of land, and looks forward with confidence to ultimately signaling between England and India by this means. More amazing still, he is confident that he will be able to communicate between England and New Zealand direct, by way of Panama, the only land intervening being that narrow strip. Cecil Rhodes and he have already discussed "Marconigraphy" as a means of bringing together the vast distances of the South African continent, and the great empire-builder was much impressed with the idea.

In future, in military operations it will doubtless play a great part; for naval purposes it stands alone. In exploration it will find a place; it is already in use by the Belgian government in the Congo, and it may be extended to the arctic solitudes.

Clippings from *Electrician and Mechanic* magazine, 1909–1913

[October 1909]

. . . If one should take wireless up as a hobby, he should stick to it, as there is bound to be some trouble and aggravating failures before he gets the "hang" of it.

Some time ago, a friend of mine, being interested in electricity, but not understanding it to any great extent, decided that he would take up wireless telegraphy as a pastime. Not knowing enough about the subject to make his apparatus, he bought an outfit; one of these outfits that sell for $8 and $10, and consist of a small induction coil, coherer and relay. These outfits are just the kind to buy when beginning, but in the case of my friend,—he worked the outfit from one room to another in his home, instead of doing all kinds of "stunts" with it, such as seeing how far the transmitting and receiving radius was, and so on, and in about a week the novelty had worn out, and the apparatus was laid away. Now this is the case with many experimenters—they get discouraged if their first efforts are not crowned with success, like other amateurs they read of; others do not experiment enough to keep them interested, and consequently the novelty soon wears off. But returning to my friend again—he visited me some time later, and after being shown my station, which consists of all modern and up-to-date tuned apparatus, and after hearing messages come in from a long distance commercial station, his interest was reawakened, and he saw the real beauty of it. Instead of using his discarded instruments, he built himself a complete set of tuned instruments, patterned after my own, except the transformer and telephone receivers,

From S. Fulton Kerr, "Increasing the Efficiency of the Amateur's Wireless Equipment," *Electrician and Mechanic* (October 1909): 141.

which he found impossible to make. Today, he is one of the most enthusiastic wireless fiends I have ever seen.

Inasmuch as I have been studying wireless for a long time, I do not want other experimenters who may read this article to think that I am boastful, or in any way egotistical, in saying that I have the best equipped amateur station in the city in which I live, and it is no small city at that. It is a matter of pride with me to keep up with the procession, and if it were not that I had stuck to it from the beginning, I could not lay claim to the above fact.

[April 1910]
Washington, January 25.
Representative Ernest W. Roberts, who has pending a bill to regulate wireless telegraphy, has received some correspondence passing between officers of the United Wireless Telegraph Company of Boston, bitterly complaining of the activities of amateurs in and around the city. Some of these amateurs, it seems, "absolutely refuse to give way to the commercial stations."

Amateur station "R," owned by Ralph A. Wood, on Brentford Hall, Cambridge, is cited as continually calling ships, commercial and navy stations. Some of his language, it is claimed, is displeasing, and it is hinted that some of the commercial operators may find it necessary to settle the matter with Mr. Wood personally. . . .

Many organized wireless societies have in the past been organized to discourage such work, and their influence has been broadcast and tending to a betterment of conditions along this line of non-interference. In spite of this, there are those who will not affiliate with such organizations, and it is largely due to such persons that arbitrary rules must and surely will be put in effect in the near future.

[April 1910]
It is the solemn conviction of the aforesaid plaintiffs, expressed succinctly in the Commission Bill introduced by Mr. Roberts of Massachusetts, that the use of wireless telegraphy has assumed such proportions that legislation of a restrictive nature is not only advisable but imperative. The word USE would have been ABUSE if the intent of the sponsors of the bill had been truthfully stated. . . .

What is the situation? Precisely this: the navy, admittedly, cannot do its work as it should be done; the army is in a similar position; likewise the revenue service; and still likewise the commercial companies. That little word "Why?" naturally comes in here and the answer as naturally follows, "Because of continued and malicious interference by amateurs." Mr. Irrepressible Amateur argues that the government and the commercial companies have antiquated and inadequate equipments which should be replaced by up-to-date instruments. He also maintains that the operators of both navy and commercial stations are frequently to blame because they are ignorant (either through lack of training or interest in the work) of the capabilities of their own instruments. There is sense in both suggestions; but neither the members of Congress nor the directors of a wireless company can see much sense in the expenditure of

From *Electrician and Mechanics* (April 1910): 387.

From James M. Murdock, "The Wireless Situation," *Electrician and Mechanic* (April 1910): 380–381.

money to replace wireless equipment installed during the last five years. They see an easier way in the power of the law to restrict the field of the amateur and to arbitrarily remedy, for a time at least, the vexatiousness of inferior service.

The log-books offered as evidence of the necessity of restrictive legislation are interesting as disclosing the widespread activity of amateurs and experimenters in wireless science, and as presenting in a very strong way an issue which the defendant in the case seldom cares to consider, namely, a degree of malicious interference surprising to those who operate their apparatus with some regard for the rights of others. . . .

. . . [W]hat thinking person can feel any but the deepest pity for the poor, deluded amateur (mentioned in "The Nation") whose reason for breaking up the official work of a revenue cutter was merely to show that he had a stronger spark. . . . Of course there are operators in the navy and commercial service who take every occasion to "rag" the amateur, but that in itself constitutes no defense, and we should remember that now as always, discretion is the better part of valor.

[January 1913]

Principal Winthrop H. Lamb of the Freeman school has installed a wireless telegraph station at the school and will teach all they boys who wish to take the course the rudiments of wireless telegraphy. Mr. Lamb has had considerable experience with wireless telegraphy, and will supervise the work of the boys in this class. It is not expected that the course will equip the boys to be expert operators, but it is designed to give them an insight into a science which is deeply interesting and may prove profitable to the boys in after life.

[January 1913]

[O]n December 13 there goes into effect an act for the regulation of radio communication, whereby all wireless operators and all apparatus which work across State lines or can communicate with ships at sea are required to be licensed.

This act is one of the by-products of the Berlin international treaty, ratified in April by the Senate.

Examinations are being held at United States navy yards and army posts all over the country during this month. . . .

The fact that there are some 10,000 wireless stations, most of them amateur ones, around New York accounts in the minds of the examiners at the Brooklyn navy yard for the daily crush in their office. . . .

The veriest beginner amusing himself on a housetop in Flatbush by sending burning messages to his up-to-date friend in South Brooklyn is aware of the fact that he must get a second grade license right away if he wants to practice radio communication, or run the risk of having his precious paraphernalia pulled down by a stealthy inspector.

Anybody who wants a license must first go to the Custom House or to the electrical school at the navy yard and present an application, telling whether he knows anything about the Berlin International Radiotelegraphic Convention and regulations,

From *Electrician and Mechanic* (January 1913): 60.

From "Wireless Operators Rush to Get Licenses," *Electrician and Mechanic* (January 1913): 58.

the Continental and Morse telegraph codes, how much experience he has had and a dozen other things. Then he must let the examiner at the electrical school fire a lot of questions at him. His answers must be written ones, and they are corrected by the examiners under the supervision of the Department of Commerce and Labor. . . .

. . . [T]he beardless dabbler in sparks solemnly vows to cease troubling the air with his machinations when there are important messages flaring around the sky. . . .

One fact the officers have noticed with surprise during the kaleidoscopic comings and goings of applicants; that is, that there have been no women in the line.

One recalled yesterday, however, that when the wireless division of the Commercial Telegraphers Union of America was fighting the regulation bill last July, one of the chief objections mentioned was that the bill placed no bar upon the employment of women operators.

[January 1913]

"Amateur wireless operators [are] generally considered to be detrimental to the use of the wireless business," said H. C. Gawler, recently appointed supervisor of New England wireless stations. Mr. Gawler said that the amateurs did not cause interruptions of communications nearly as much as they are credited with doing, and that were it not for the amateurs, many of the best operators in the commercial fields would not have taken up wireless at all. From the extensive field of amateurs, the greater part of professional operators are selected.

In connection with interruptions Mr. Gawler said that many of the commercial ships themselves cause the disturbance that breaks the connection by the character of tuning waves from their own instruments. He also said that some of the amateur stations are more efficient and better equipped with more up-to-date instruments than are many of the commercial stations.

Mr. Gawler is given the entire New England district to look after. It is his duty to issue licenses to amateur operators who comply with the regulations regarding stations, operators and instruments.

[March 1913]

Every summer a large number of students in the various high schools and colleges throughout the country find very pleasant occupation as radio operators on the vessels engaged in coastwise trade. A large number of extra ships are put into service, or are changed from freighters to passengers ships during the summer months, causing accordingly a great demand for radio operators. In the past the supply has nearly always equaled the demand, oftentimes surpassing it, but things have a different aspect this year. The new wireless law makes the number of cases where it is necessary to employ radio operators far in excess of what it has been in the past. At the same time the law had placed many restrictions on the class of operators that may be employed. Many wireless amateurs throughout the country who are considering entering this occupation next summer are inquiring as to what they must know in order to obtain the necessary federal license.

From "Best Radio Operators Products of Amateur Field," *Electrician and Mechanic* (January 1913): 63.
From "Becoming a Commercial Radio Operator," *Electrician and Mechanic* (March 1913): 193.

How Electricity Effects Economy in the Home and Adds to the Happiness of the Family (Prizewinning Essay, 1917)

FERN VAN BRAMER

For some years the Commonwealth Edison Company has been steadily reducing the cost of electric power to the consumer and selling electrical home helps at moderate cost for small payments added to the monthly bills, so now the home of the working-man need no longer be a gloomy, unattractive domicile; indeed, for brightness and convenience, it may be on a plane with the home of the millionaire. . . .

A bright home is usually a happy home. Saloonkeepers and the owners of pool rooms and dance halls recognize the alluring power of bright lights. If more wives and mothers would only understand that money spent in beautifying their homes is the truest form of economy, fewer fathers and sons would be paying for the bright lights in unwholesome places. Some fathers are forced to return from work to dark, repel-lent homes. Such fathers too often take a walk after supper "down to the corner"— ah, the lights are burning brightly there! Far better for this family purse were the mother to treat herself to a few of the electrical home helps and burn a few kilowatts of electricity every evening.

How different in the home where things are done electrically: The father, return-ing from his day of toil, sees the well-lighted windows of his home and the happy faces of his children pressed against the pane eagerly watching for their daddy. Light floods the porch as the door is opened. Inside everything is warmth and cheer. The odor of hot biscuits, fresh from the electric oven, adds zest to his appetite. In the cheerful din-ing room, the mother, unwearied from her household duties because she uses elec-tricity in her work, takes a lively part in the conversation and joins in the merry laughter of the children. . . . Later the family gathers in the cozy living room, the older ones to read or chat, the younger ones to shout with joy over some electric toy. The in-structive merits of some of these toys is a feature not to be overlooked by parents who want to see their sons enter something better than "blind alley" jobs that lead nowhere.

Colonial Radio Saves Wasted Motion, 1934

The Colonial Radio Corporation is now successfully operating a school for training new assembly operators. All girls at the time of employment are given two to three days' training in a separate room under the supervision of a competent instructor.

The Classroom contains assembly benches with jigs, fixtures, hand tools, and the necessary parts and bins to handle such typical factory operations as screwdriver work, assembly and bench work with pliers, and soldering operations. Groups of 8 to 12, and never more than 15, are trained at a time. The girls are paid their regular base wage during the training period. At the beginning of the training period a simple

---

From Fern Van Bramer "How Electricity Effects Economy in the Home and Adds to the Happiness of the Family." *Electric City Magazine* (April 1917): 9.

From Ralph M. Barnes, *Motion and Time Study: Design and Measurement of Work,* New York: John Wiley and Sons. Copyright © 1937 by Ralph M. Barnes. Reprinted by permission of John Wiley & Sons, Inc.

explanation of the purpose of the course is given to the group. Extracts from this explanation are given below.

"As you are probably aware, the purpose of this class is to teach a better way of performing some of our more common assembly operations which involve such familiar parts as nuts, screws, lockwashers, wires, condenser, resistors, etc.

"All of us realize the fact that certain ways of doing a thing are better than others. It has been established that there is a best way of performing any given act, and we have also made the discovery, which most of you have probably known all along, that the best way is almost invariably, also, the easiest way. Haven't you found this to be the case in your experience?

"Just as you in your home attempt to find the best way of performing your household duties, so, in industry, were attempt to find the best way of doing the things required of us.

"It has been established that at least 25% of the motions used by the average employee in the average factory operations are wasted motions. These wasted motions are needless motions which contribute only one thing as far as the operator or the operation is concerned, and that is fatigue.

"Naturally you may ask—'What is the purpose of finding the best and easiest way of performing operations in the plant?' This can be stated briefly as follows:

"It is the desire on the part of Colonial to build a better radio set at a lower cost, without, however, requiring the expenditure of any more physical effort on the part of those of us directly engaged in building them.

"All of you realize the amount of work we have in our plant depends on the number of radio sets the Sales Organization of the Colonial Radio Company can sell. When you and I, and millions of other consumers, decide to buy a radio set, or any other merchandise, we always attempt to get the best product we can for the money we want to spend, and, if the best radio set we can buy for a given sum of money happens to be a Colonial radio, we will buy it. In other words, the welfare of the Colonial Radio Corporation and coincidentally in a large measure, all of us, depends on the ability of Colonial to build at least as good a set as any other manufacturer at the same or at a lower price."

After the above explanation has been made and any questions by members of the class have been discussed, the group is given a simple assembly operation to perform. An explanation is given of what the finished job must be like and then each person is allowed to do the task in any way that she wishes. Each girl is given a timer and pencil and paper to record the time for making ten assemblies.

She continues to do the task for an hour or so, recording the time for each set of ten assemblies.

Then an assembly fixture and improved bins are given to the operator. The proper arrangement of the work place is made and the girl is carefully instructed in the proper method of doing the work. An explanation is also given as to the principles of motion economy employed and why the new method is easier and faster than the old one.

After the girl understands how to do the task in the proper way, she again works for an hour or so timing herself for groups of ten pieces and recording the time as before.

The fact that the improved method saves time is obvious to her since she has set her own pace and read and recorded her own time. She is well aware that motion study is not a "speed up" but that it enables her to do more work with less fatigue.

After the new girl has worked on a simple assembly operation, she is given other jobs that are typical of those she will see in the factory and perhaps some of which she will work on after the training period is over.

Although the main purpose of school is to train new operators in the principles of motion economy, Colonial has found that the school also serves another very important function in that it shows the employees in a most convincing manner that improving methods of doing work is for their benefit as well as for the company and that actually the best way from a motion study angle is invariably the least fatiguing way and the most satisfactory way in every respect for the operator.

Incidentally, it requires approximately 50 per cent less time for a girl who has been through the training school to attain standard performance than for new girls going directly onto the production floor without the training.

During the past two years more than 700 girls have been trained in the manner described above.

∤∤ *E S S A Y S*

In the first essay, Susan Douglas describes an important development in the history of radio: the growth of a broadcasting culture among middle-class boys. These "amateur operators," influenced in part by utopian pronouncements on the possibilities of radio, constructed home radio sets and made important technical innovations in the course of play. But the very success of home wireless caused a literal "separation of the men from the boys" through legislation and licensing.

The second essay, by Ruth Oldenzeil, looks at hobbyist culture in a very different light. The boys who joined the Fischer Body Craftsman's Guild were not the young rebels of Douglas's story. According to Oldenzeil, they were General Motors "organization men" in the making.

What picture can we form of early twentieth-century boy hobbyists—and American culture in the same period—on the basis of Douglas's and Oldenzeil's essays (and the accompanying documents)? Are these the same boys viewed in different ways, or are they separate groups with dissimilar instincts? The two essays are set at different times and discuss different technologies—does this bear on their stories? Is class a factor? Do the authors have the same intention? Could their stories be told in different ways? What do the accounts tell us about girls?

Amateur Operators and American Broadcasting: Shaping the Future of Radio

SUSAN J. DOUGLAS

Radio both fitted into and extended Americans' notions of how the future would be made better, maybe even perfect, through technology. Not all technology was so embraced. The factory system, with its large, noisy, seemingly autonomous machines, had produced a range of complicated social problems that profoundly frustrated

From Susan J. Douglas, "Amateur Operators and American Broadcasting: Shaping the Future of Radio," in Joseph C. Lorn, ed. *Imaging Tomorrow: History, Technology, and the American Future* (Cambridge, MA: MIT Press, 1986), pp. 35–55.

most Americans. At the turn of the century, the American press was filled with self-congratulatory assessments of how far the country had come in 100 years, but just beneath that veneer of optimism was a deep anxiety about the dislocations and vulnerabilities that had accompanied industrialization. Radio was not only exempt from this anxiety, it was also meant to relieve it. Like certain other inventions, radio was seen as delivering society from a troubled present to a utopian future. What was it about radio that evoked both idealistic and fantastic visions of the future? What influence, if any, did these highly publicized and richly embellished predictions exert? Who, if anyone, believed them? Did they influence the course of broadcasting's early history? . . .

Reporters responded to wireless telegraphy with unprecedented awe. On December 15, 1901, when Marconi reported to the press that he had successfully transmitted the letter S from England to Newfoundland, he garnered bold front-page headlines and effusive praise. The press lionized the inventor-hero and compared him to Edison. Popular magazines set reporters to interview him and featured illustrated stories detailing in often melodramatic style the delays, doubts, and hardships that had preceded his success. With optimistic and excited rhetoric, these articles celebrated the new invention. "Our whole human existence is being transformed by electricity," observed the *North American Review*. "All must hope that every success will attend Marconi and the other daring adventurers who are exploring this comparatively unknown scientific region." Success was so important, continued the magazine, because no invention was "more pregnant with beneficial possibilities or calculated to be a more helpful factor in advancing the existing order of the world's life." *Current Literature* declared: "Probably no other modern scientific discovery has had to much romantic coloring about it as wireless telegraphy." Wireless held a special place in the American imagination precisely because it married idealism and adventure with science: "The essential idea belongs to the realms of romance, and from the day when the world heard with wonder, approaching almost incredulity, that a message had been flashed across the Atlantic . . . the wonder of the discovery has never decreased." Ray Stannard Baker, writing for *McClure's*, tried to transport his readers to this romance realm by putting them in Marconi's position: "Think for a moment of sitting here on the edge of North America and listening to communication sent *through space* across nearly 2000 miles of ocean from the edge of Europe! A cable, marvelous as it is, maintains a tangible and material connection between speaker and hearer; one can grasp its meaning. But here is nothing but space, a pole with a pendant wire on one side of a broad, curving ocean, an uncertain kite struggling in the air on the other—and thought passing between." *World's Work* asserted: "The triumph of Marconi remains one of the most remarkable and fruitful that have ever crowned the insight, patience, and courage of mankind."

Celebration quickly led to prediction. In contrast with the forecasts for other technologies, however, there were few, if any, forecasts of how wireless equipment would look or how it would change the American landscape. There were no speculations on wireless sets of the future, no fantastic drawings of modernistic equipment. Rather, the predictions focused on where the messages might go and on what wireless would do for society and for individuals. . . .

The introduction of wireless renewed hopes for the possibility of eventually securing world peace. *Popular Science Monthly* observed: "The nerves of the whole

world are, so to speak, being bound together, so that a touch in one country is transmitted instantly to a far-distant one." Implicit in this organic metaphor was the belief
that a world so physically connected would become a spiritual whole with common
interests and goals. The *New York Times* added: "Nothing so fosters and promotes a
mutual understanding and community of sentiment and interests as cheap, speedy
and convenient communication." Articles suggested that this technology could make
men more fraternal: with better communications available, misunderstandings could
be avoided. These visions suggested that machines, by themselves, could change history; the right invention could help people overcome human foibles and weaknesses,
particularly rivalry and suspicion brought on by isolation and lack of information.

The most stirring prophecies, however, envisioned individual rather than social
benefits. A sonnet published in the *Atlantic Monthly*, entitled simply "Wireless
Telegraphy," traced the flight of a word "over the wilds of ocean and of shore" until
it reached its intended destinations:

> Somewhere beyond the league-long silences.
> Somewhere across the spaces of the years.
> A heart will thrill to thee, a voice will bless,
> Love will awake and life be perfected!

Love and life would be "perfected" as wireless communication would ease loneliness
and isolation. The *New York Times* foresaw a time when "wireless telegraphy would
make a father on the old New England farm and his son in Seattle . . . neighbors—
perhaps by the use of their own private apparatus." *The Century Magazine*, reporting
"vastly greater things are predicted for the future" of wireless, offered this rather
poignant prophecy:

> . . . if a person wanted to call to a friend he knew not where, he would call in a very
> loud electromagnetic voice, heard by him who had the electromagnetic ear, silent to him
> who had it not. "Where are you?" he would say. A small reply would come "I am at the
> bottom of a coal mine, or crossing the Andes, or in the middle of the Atlantic." Or, per-
> haps in spite of all the calling, no reply would come, and the person would then know
> that his friend was dead. Think of what this would mean, of the calling which goes on
> every day from room to room of a house, and then think of that calling extending from
> pole to pole, not a noisy babble, but a call audible to him who wants to hear, and abso-
> lutely silent to all others. It would be almost like dreamland and ghostland, not the
> ghostland cultivated by a heated imagination, but a real communication from a distance
> based on true physical laws.

The rhetoric of this vision gets at the heart of what excited people about wireless. It
was the potential autonomy and spontaneity of such communication that gripped
Americans' imaginations. People could talk to whomever they wanted whenever
they wanted, no matter how much distance or how many obstacles intervened. This
technology would help them transcend the social and economic forces—particularly,
and ironically, industrialization—that had driven them apart.

America's population was in the midst of an accelerated shift from country to
city living, resulting in more frequent separation of family members and friends. To
communicate over distances, individuals could either write letters or go through corporate intermediaries. Using the networks operated by the Bell Company of Western
Union could be expensive, and privacy was compromised: both the telegraph and the

telephone relied on operators, who were, either by necessity or inclination, privy to the contents of the message. Wireless seemed to promise something different: instant communication, through "the air" free from both operators and fees. In addition, wireless seemed the technical equivalent of mental telepathy. Intelligence could pass between sender and receiver without tangible connection. Thus, to many, wireless bridged the chasm between science and metaphysics, between the known and the unknown, between actual achievement and limitless possibility. . . .

However, the enthusiasm of the press was not matched in either the corporate world or the armed services, for there was still a great discrepancy between present potential and predicted promise in the wireless field. The appealing predictions in the newspapers and magazines envisioned invisible, point-to-point connections between an unlimited number of senders and receivers. Implicit in these forecasts was the belief that there would be room for all potential users in "the air" and that these point-to-point conversations would be private. But in reality, Marconi and others were still struggling to eliminate interference between messages and ensure secrecy. These disadvantages, which inventors kept predicting would soon be corrected, explain the hesitancy of military and commercial clients to purchase wireless equipment. In addition, a combination of erratic equipment performance, poor marketing strategies, and corporate indifference or wariness about the potential value of wireless in general left the invention with no definite niche in the American marketplace. The two major communications companies, Western Union and American Telephone and Telegraph, concentrated on preserving the hegemony of their own systems and did not see any immediate advantage to acquiring and promoting the new technology. Only the most prestigious ocean liners, such as those of the Cunard line, installed wireless; smaller steamship companies were slow to adopt the invention. The American inventors Lee DeForest and Reginald Fessenden, who made the most significant technical contributions to American radio development, failed to find steady customers and a regular clientele. From a business standpoint, wireless was a failure.

Yet from 1906 to 1912, as American wireless companies were on the verge of or in fact declared bankruptcy, the United States experienced its first radio boom. Thousands of people, believing in a profitable future for the invention, bought hundreds of thousands of dollars' worth of stock in fledgling wireless companies. Others took even more decisive action and began to construct and use their own wireless stations. Thus, while the leaders of American corporate and bureaucratic institutions regarded the various prophecies with a skeptical eye, other individuals began translating vision into action. These Americans—primarily white middle-class boys and men who built their own stations in their bedrooms, attics, or garages—came to be known as the amateur operators, and by 1910 their use of wireless was being described in newspapers and magazines around the country. *The Outlook* outlined the emerging communications network:

> In the past two years another wireless system has been gradually developing, a system that has far outstripped all others in size and popularity. . . . Hundreds of schoolboys in every part of the country have taken to this most popular scientific fad, and, by copying the instruments used at the regular stations and constructing apparatus out of all kinds of electrical junk, have built wireless equipments that in some cases approach the naval stations in efficiency.

The amateurs were captivated by the idea of harnessing electrical technology to communicate with others, and were not deterred by lack of secrecy or interference. In fact, these features, considered such a disadvantage by institutional customers, increased the individual amateur's pool of potential contacts and the variety of information he could send and receive.

It is impossible to establish a causal relationship between the eager early predictions and these subsequent activities on the part of the amateurs. We cannot know how many wireless enthusiasts were inspired by what they read in newspapers or magazines. But we do know that there was a climate of enthusiasm, which the press reflected, embellished, and fanned. And we see the emergence of a widely dispersed group of individuals trying to accomplish what the journalistic visions had promised: communication over sometimes great distances with whomever else had a wireless set. The ways in which the amateurs came to use wireless—to contact strangers, to make friends, to provide communication during disasters, and to circumvent or antagonize private and governmental organizations—were enactments of the previously articulated visions.

The favorable social climate, though conducive to the development of the amateur wireless network, cannot fully explain the invention's proliferation. How were the amateurs able to master this particular technology? The first and most tangible development was the availability, starting in 1906, of the simple, inexpensive crystal set, a device that could, for some unexplained reasons, detect radio waves. Inventors did not understand how the crystal worked, but they knew that it was a sensitive, durable, inexpensive receiver that was simple to operate and required no replacement parts. At the time, how and why the crystal worked was not as important as its simplicity and its very low cost. (The crystal was placed between two copper contact points, which were adjustable so that the pressure could be regulated and the most sensitive portion of the mineral selected. To keep the contact as small as possible, often a thin wire, known popularly as the "catwhisker," was used.) The importance of the introduction of the crystal detector cannot be overemphasized. More than any other component, it contributed to the democratization of wireless, the concomitant wireless boom, and the radio boom of the 1920s.

The amateurs' ingenuity in converting a motley assortment of parts into working radio sets was impressive. With performance analogous to that of an expensive detector now available to them in the inexpensive crystal, the amateurs were prepared to improvise the rest of the wireless set. Before 1908 they had to, for very few companies sold equipment appropriate for home use. Also, one of the crucial components, the tuning coil, was not supposed to be available for sale because it was part of the patented Marconi system. As the boom continued, however, children's books, wireless manuals, magazines, and even the Boy Scout Manual offered diagrams and advice on radio construction. As one author instructed. "You see how many things I've used that you can find about the house." . . .

An unusual social phenomenon was emerging. A large radio audience was taking shape that, in its attitude and its involvement, was unlike traditionally passive audiences. [Francis] Collins summarized the development in (his children's book) *The Wireless Man*: "An audience of a hundred thousand boys all over the United States may be addressed almost every evening by wireless telegraph. Beyond doubt this is the largest audience in the world. No football or baseball crowd, no convention or conference, compares with it in size, nor gives closer attention to the business at hand." This was an active, committed, and participatory audience. Out of this camaraderie emerged more formal fraternities, the wireless clubs, which were organized all over America. By 1912, the *New York Times* estimated that 122 wireless clubs existed in America. Most of the club meetings took place "in the air" on a pre-arranged wavelength. The chairman called the meeting to order by sending out his call letters, and the members signified their attendance by answering with their own. During these meetings, the amateurs usually shared technical problems and solutions and drilled each other on transmission skills. A Chicago wireless club broadcast a "program" every evening "as a matter of practice for amateur operators in receiving." "The bulletin usually consisted of an article of some electrical or telegraphic interest . . . sometimes the program was varied by sending passages in foreign languages, to quicken the receiving ears of the amateur operators." . . .

What did the amateurs's ever-increasing activity in the airwaves portend? The emergence of the amateurs and their often unrestrained fervor influenced both the immediate and the long-range regulatory, technical, and social developments in broadcasting. As increasing numbers of amateurs took wireless communication into their own hands, their activities became a nuisance to wireless companies and the government. In contrast with the early visions, which suggested there would be room for all in "the air," it was sadly discovered that the spectrum could accommodate only so many transmitters in a given area, especially when many of the sending stations emitted highly damped waves from crude spark gaps. Experimenters also learned that point-to-point, directional signaling was, at the time, impossible to achieve. And while some of the amateurs were skilled operators, devoted to serious experimentation, others were novices who clogged the air-waves with inconsequential and slowly sent messages. Francis Hart, a wireless operator in New York City from 1907 to 1911, described the congestion in his log book: "The different kids around here raise an awful noise, all try to talk at once, call when anybody is in and never use any sense, half can't read 4 words a minute and sit calling everybody within 20 miles and can't hear 800 feet from another station." He commented on one amateur's conversations: "FH is a very good reader, but he tries to say too much at one time then the poor reader makes him repeat it and they keep that blooming business up for hours." As this sort of interference increased, so did "malicious" interference, which began to give the amateurs a bad reputation. Posing as military officials, some amateurs dispatched naval ships on fabricated missions. Navy operators received emergency messages warning them that a ship was sinking off the coast. After hours of searching in vain, receivers heard the truth: The supposedly foundering ship had just arrived safely in port. Navy operators at the Newport Naval Yard complained that amateurs sent them profane messages. Others reportedly argued with Navy operators over right-of-way in the air. *The Outlook* reported that during what Navy operators claimed was an emergency situation, amateurs refused to clear the air, "some of the amateurs even arguing with the Navy men over the ownership of the ether." In another instance, when a Boston amateur was told by a naval operator to "butt out," he reportedly made the following classic remark: "Say, you Navy people think you own the ether. Who ever heard of the Navy anyway? Beat it, you, beat it."

What had developed was the inevitable situation of too many people wanting access to the airwaves at the same time, with no guidelines for establishing priority.

Too many people had embraced the invention and its possibilities. During this era, before 1912, no spectrum allocation had occurred, and all operators—amateur, commercial, and naval—vied with each other for hegemony. Military lobbyists in Washington, citing safety at sea and national security as reasons, advocated legislation that would ban amateurs from transmitting over the then-preferred portion of the spectrum.

The amateurs could not accept that the Navy should suddenly step in and claim the airwaves for itself in the name of national security when the Navy had done little to develop or refine wireless. The amateurs asserted that they had much if not more right to transmit, because they had worked and experimented to earn that right. While the Navy relied on outdated apparatus and unskilled or disinterested operators, the amateurs claimed to promote technical progress and individual commitment. The airwaves were a national resource, a newly discovered environment, and the amateurs claimed that their early enthusiasm and their technical work had entitled them to a sizable portion of the territory. They asked where the Navy had been when they were translating vision into practice. Much as the nineteenth-century pioneers had obtained squatters' rights by cultivating the land on which they had settled, the amateurs had developed a proprietary attitude toward the airwaves they had been working for the past five years. They granted that there were a few outlaws in their midst, but they argued that the alleged violations did not justify the exclusion of all individual operators by the government.

Ultimately, the amateurs lost. During the *Titanic* disaster of April 1912, interference from amateur stations trying to relay as well as elicit news was so great that within four months the Congress banished their transmission to a portion of the spectrum then deemed useless: short waves. The Radio Act of 1912 also required that amateurs be licensed, and imposed fines for "malicious interference."

What impact, then, could a group of operators have on radio broadcasting who were, by 1912, banished to this etheric reservation? One scholar who has studied how Americans have managed the airwaves points out that "relatively deprived users" were "virtually forced to innovate spectrum-economizing, spectrum-developing technology. It was the amateurs, the recently deprived users, who would pioneer one of the biggest breakthroughs in radio: short-wave broadcasting. One of the more famous amateurs, Edwin Armstrong, developed the regenerative or feedback circuit, which amplified the often feeble signals coming in over the receiving antenna. Thus, the amateurs' technical contributions remained significant. Also, less creative amateurs, by reporting results to others, provided the more serious experimenters with valuable data on performance and results.

In the years after the Radio Act of 1912, the amateurs not only advanced radio technology but also anticipated broadcasting. Between 1910 and 1920, amateur stations began to broadcast music, speech, and even advertising. By 1917, amateurs were relaying messages not just regionally but from coast to coast, demonstrating the benefits of a national communications network. Some of the early amateur stations became commercial stations in the 1920s. Frank Conrad of Pittsburgh, a radio amateur and a Westinghouse employee, operated in his garage a small amateur station that is usually credited with inaugurating the broadcasting boom. In 1920, Conrad's station was moved to a portion of the Westinghouse plant and became KDKA. It was the amateurs who demonstrated that, in an increasingly atomized and impersonal society, the nascent broadcast audience was waiting to be brought together. Using the airwaves to inform, entertain, and connect the general public was, before 1920, still not in the corporate imagination. Institutions continued to view radio as merely a substitute for cables, a technology that would provide long-distance, point-to-point communications. The Radio Corporation of America, which was formed to establish an American-controlled international network, was compelled to reconsider its purpose and its goals shortly after its formation in 1919. The industry that would come to control radio broadcasting by the late 1920s had to respond to a way of using the airwaves pioneered by the amateurs.

In their fight to retain access to the preferred portion of the spectrum in 1912, the amateurs claimed to be surrogates for "the people," who, they declared were the rightful heirs to the spectrum. In congressional testimony and letters to magazines and newspapers, the amateurs insisted that individuals, not the Navy or big business, should determine how the airwaves were used. This democratic ideology, manifested both in rhetoric and in practice throughout the teens and the twenties, contributed to the legitimation of the public's claim to and stake in the air. The Communications Act of 1934, which established the Federal Communications Commission and required the licensing of all radio stations, mandated that these stations serve "the public interest, convenience, and necessity."

The turn-of-the-century predictions about radio's future applications had not come true. They had been based on a misunderstanding of how the invention worked, and they assumed that radio, by itself, could change the world. Yet even dreams that do not come true can have an effect. By encouraging and romanticizing the amateurs' hobby, these visions fostered experimentation among members of a subculture who had neither a corporate nor a political agenda. The predictions also articulated and reinforced the belief that this technology could and should be accessible to the greatest possible number of Americans.

Such dreams did not die in the 1920s. They were simply transformed to accommodate the new reality of institutional management. Radio was now indeed firmly embedded in a corporate grid, and the new visions of the 1920s, while still very enthusiastic, made concessions to this centralized control. Just as Frank Conrad's radio station moved from his garage to Westinghouse, so too did visions of radio's uses and benefits begin to reflect corporate agendas. In the 1920s there was little mention of world peace or of anyone's ability to track down a long-lost friend or relative halfway around the world. In fact, there were not many thousands of message senders, only a few. The theme of isolation was still central, but instead of the separation of one individual from another the predictions of the 1920s focused on certain individuals' separation from the mainstream of American culture. "All isolation can be destroyed," proclaimed Stanley Frost in a 1922 article entitled "Radio Dreams That Can Come True." Now radio had the potential to be a "tremendous civilizer" that would "spread culture everywhere" and bring "mutual understanding to all sections of the country, unifying our thoughts, ideals, and purposes, making us a strong and well-knit people." This audience would be passive: "We do not even have to get up and leave the place," exclaimed a *Collier's* contributor. "All we have to do is to press a button." Thus, through radio, Americans would not transcend the present or circumvent corporate networks. In fact they would be more closely tied to both. Visions and reality were merging.

Yet at least one vision of how radio would bring about a utopian future persisted. In the spring of 1919, Marconi announced that several of his radio stations were picking up very strong signals "seeming to come from beyond the earth." Nikola Tesla, another prominent inventor, believed these signals were coming from Mars. Articles in newspapers and magazines speculated about the signals and . . . asked "Can we radio a message to Mars?" *Illustrated World*, a magazine that popularized recent technical developments, urged that America try; only then would the Martians know that "their signals were being responded to, and that intelligent beings actually inhabit the earth." The writer then added: "We can imagine what excitement this would cause on Mars." But the most important reason for trying to contact Mars was to learn what it was assumed they must know about improving, even perfecting, the quality of life. As *Illustrated World* put it, "It is not unreasonable to believe that the whole world trend of our thoughts and civilization might change for the better." Martians would not only view our civilization with considerable detachment, but they would also presumably give us all the secret answers. Once again, through radio, we might be able to escape the institutions in which we found ourselves ensnared.

The idea of sending radio signals to Mars was in many ways the most revealing and poignant of the visions surrounding radio. It exposed a sense of isolation, insecurity, and dissatisfaction over things as they were. It revealed that, despite the failure of past predictions, many Americans were still inclined to view certain technologies as autonomous, as possessing superhuman or magical powers. This willingness to invest certain inventions with individual hopes and cultural aspirations has permitted the corporate sphere to exploit a range of technologies to profitable ends, but it has also led certain Americans, such as the amateur operators, to take technology into their own hands and in the process, profoundly influence the course of technical change.

Boys and Their Toys: The Fisher Body Craftsman's Guild, 1930–1968

RUTH OLDENZIEL

In 1931, an advertisement for the Fisher Body Craftsman's Guild in the *National Geographic* invited teenaged boys to participate in a model-making contest. It showed a boy offering a girl a miniature version of a "Napoleonic Coach"—an image that had been chosen as the emblem by the Fisher Body Company in 1922 to convey luxury, comfort and style. The Fisher Coach emblem had been created out of the coaches Napoleon I of France used for his wedding and for his coronation as Emperor. The Fisher Body firm, the organizer of the Guild, was the world's largest manufacturer of automobile bodies, and supplied principally for General Motors. The Fisher Body Craftsman' Guild aimed to train "the coming generation" and to secure "fine craftsmanship." Intended to appeal to boys of high school and college ages between 12 and 20, the ad portrays him as being fatherly: mature and responsible, ready to take his

From Ruth Oldenziel, "Boys and Their Toys: The Making of a Male Technical Domain and the Fisher Body Craftsman's Guild, 1930–1968," *Technology and Culture*, January 1997, v. 38, No. 1. Copyright © 1997 by The Society for the History of Technology. Reprinted by permission of The University of Chicago Press.

bride—a far cry from the boisterous bachelor or dare-devilling hotrodder. Opposite the Fisher boy stands a girl, positioned as the passive and grateful, but critical recipient of his Napoleonic Coach and suggesting the kind of future that such a gift seems to promise. The illustration implies that the Fisher boy is not only a builder of coaches, but also the builder of families and a secure future husband and breadwinner.

The Fisher Body Craftsmans' Guild (1930–1968), the organization that sponsored the ad, marks one of the most playful by-products of the very successful partnership between Fisher and cosponsor GM. At first glance, the Guild invites us to view the world of boys' toys hidden in attics, basements, barns, and backyards as whimsical, playful, and innocent, but a second reading reveals an intricate web of institutions that defined and maintained a male technical domain. The fascinating but now-forgotten history of the Guild suggests that the definition and production of male technical knowledge involved an extraordinary mobilization of organizational, economic and cultural resources. The Guild, "an educational foundation devoted to the development of handiwork and craftsmanship among boys of the North American continent," directly appealed to boys and relied for recruiting on the Boy Scouts, the YMCA and the public school system. Girls found themselves excluded as a matter of course.

This explicitly male technical domain came into existence at precisely the same time that "the consumer" became more and more explicitly gendered female, as scholars of consumer culture have argued. Through various means such as the "Body of Fisher" ad campaign, GM and the Fisher Body Company aligned their companies with women as their potential consumers. To consider a single example from many, the same Fisher Body Company that created the Craftsman's Guild ran an advertisement in *Life* Magazine in 1927 in which we find a different Fisher Girl, a flapper whose body sensuously replicates the curves of an automobile. Seen side by side, these two Fisher promotional campaigns exemplify the complementary ways in which we have come to portray men and women in their stereotypical relationships with the technological world—a world where men design systems and women use them; men engineer bridges and women cross them; men build cars and women ride in them; in short, a world in which men are considered the active producers and women the passive consumers of technology. Both ads point to a specific historical moment in which these roles were being articulated and shaped by GM and the Fisher Body Company. Considered in this light, the exclusion of girls from the Craftsman's Guild was not so much a culturally determined oversight as it was an expression of the need to shore up male identity boundaries in the new world of expanding consumerism.

The case study of the Fisher Body Craftsman's Guild also suggests that an exclusive focus on women's supposed failure in entering the field of engineering is insufficient for understanding how our stereotypical notions have come into being; it tends to put the burden of proof entirely on women and to blame them for their supposedly inadequate socialization, their lack of aspiration, and their want of masculine values. It also runs the risk of delineating gender as a analytical tool for historical research as merely an issue affecting women. An equally challenging question is why and how boys have come to love things technical, how boys have historically been socialized into technophiles, and how we have come to understand technical things as exclusively belonging to the field of engineering. The focus on the formation of boy culture is not to deny that women often face formidable barriers in entering the male domain of science and engineering; they have. The story of the Fisher Body Craftsman's Guild introduces one episode into the institutionalized ways in which boys, male teenagers and adult men have ben channeled into the domain designated as technical.

This article considers one side of the gendering process. The most substantial part focuses in detail on the male gendered codes in the Fisher Body Craftsmans' Guild and its miniature world of model cars to show how from the 1930s to the 1960s the Guild helped socialize Fisher boys as technophiles and sought to groom them as technical men ready to take their places as managers or engineers in GM's corporate world. If the first Guild's advertisement points to the making of a corporate male identity, the second ad suggests as the Fisher Company explained, that the making of the "technical," "hard," and "male" coded world of production has also been produced by and produced its opposite: a world of consumption coded as non-technical, soft, and female.

Between the 1920s and 1940s boys' toys developed into a booming consumer market. Wagons, sleds, scooters, bicycles, aeroplanes started to clutter boys' rooms, while chemistry and erector sets were sold because "every boy should be trained for leadership." Girls also acquired toys from their parents, of course, but theirs were less varied and not aimed to help smooth a career path. Toys were not only intended to amuse and entertain, but also "as socializing mechanisms, as educational devices, and as scaled down versions of the realities of the larger adult-dominated social world." Many toy companies such as the Gilbert Co., the Wolverine Co., or the Toy Tinkers, Inc. exploited the new passion, but none of these companies turned the play with toys into a totalizing experience as the Fisher Body Craftsman's Guild. Under the auspices of GM, the Guild combined the appeal of toys and the model-making tradition with corporate needs for training new personnel while crafting consumers' tastes.

The Annual Fisher Body Craftsman's Guild contest awarded a $5000 scholarship at an engineering school to the American or Canadian teenaged boy who managed to build the best miniature Napoleonic Coach (1931–1947) or car (1937–1968). One recruiting sign in 1930 read: "BOYS!! Enroll here in the FISHER BODY CRAFTS-MAN'S GUILD. No dues . . . no fees. An opportunity to earn your college education or one of the 980 other wonderful awards." The Guild sponsored the first continent-wide miniature coach contest in 1930 under the auspices of General Motors' Fisher Body—the division responsible for the design and production of GM automobile bodies from the 1920s on. When the Guild was founded, $5000 would buy eight Chevrolets or Fords, an average worker's income over three years; in 1940 Americans could buy a house for that price. With a college education perceived as an avenue for upward mobility, young men and their families could gain a great deal from participating in the Guild. GM's investment in the organization was not trivial either: beyond the $20,000 to $100,000 spent on actual awards, the company budgeted at least 20 times more for organizational expenses and publicity each year. Promotional literature boasted that the Guild had the largest membership of any young men's organization in the United States except for the Boy Scouts of America (established in 1910) and claimed that by 1960 over 8 million male teenagers between the ages 12 and 20 had participated in the Guild through national, state, and local contests and clubs. Whether these figures are trustworthy or not, it is clear that through its recruitment efforts alone the Guild influenced numbers of male adolescents much larger that the high school students who actually managed to finish and submit the complicated models to the competition each year.

If the stakes were high, so were the requirements. The teenaged boy who built a miniature coach or car had to be willing to invest an extraordinary amount of time, possess a large measure of patience, and acquire a high level of skill. The Guild's officials apparently realized that a completion of a coach would be extremely challenging without substantial corporate resources. Hence, they ensured that replicas would be prominently displayed in department stores windows and that color prints and scale drawings were printed in local newspapers and in the Guild's newsletters. To be sure, displays of the Fisher Coach served promotional purposes as well. Contest rules demanded that all parts be handmade, which necessitated the ability to build a miniature Napoleonic Coach (measuring $11 \times 6 \times 8$ inches) from scratch, to read complicated patterns, to draft accurately, carve wood painstakingly, work metal, paint, and make upholstery with utmost care. Boys of high school and college ages had to construct functioning mechanical parts: windows that could slide, steps that could be folded away, spoked wheels and cambered axles that could turn, and working leaf-spring suspension. The interior also needed painstaking attention to evoke the proper royal texture, while the coach's interior would feature lush upholstery, silk covers, rabbit fur carpets, and brocade curtains. Harking back to the time-consuming labor of craft traditions, the completion of a miniature Napoleonic coach to specification demanded an extraordinary amount of dedication and time—about 3 hours a day for over 10 months—not to mention the investment in materials.

The craft theme presented the organization with a full range of medieval symbols tailored to contemporary corporate needs. These were smoothly mixed with the most up-to-date technologies of the time: during the 1930s live radio broadcasts announced the winners to parents, family, friends, and neighbors; after World War II, airplanes carried the boys to GM's headquarters in Detroit for the festive four-day Fisher Body Convention. Here, GM officials staged events ranging from essay-writing contests to matches in swimming, golfing, and other athletic events in order to foster the boys' competitive spirit. Finally, the teenaged boys toured carefully selected industrial sites and GM laboratories that served as windows through which they could view their possible future in the corporations.

The evocation of the medieval theme found its culminating moment during the last day of the convention when the organization offered the contestants a banquet and an initiation rite at a candlelit table against a Gothic backdrop. Clad in medieval costumes, the state finalist entered into the corporate world as apprentices under the blare of trumpets. In 1939 Embury A. Hitchcock, a Guild judge and engineering educator, vividly portrayed the spirit of the ritual and showed how the ceremonies marked the transition from apprentice to master craftsman and from boyhood to manhood. He fondly recalled how "the light of flickering candles shows the ornate walls, the heavy-beamed ceilings, and shields and draperies much as they were in the guild halls of Brussels. . . . The trumpeteers, dressed in doublets, breeches, and buckled shoes . . . lead the procession of contestants, each man carrying his own coach. After the seating, a casement window on the second floor swings open and a representative of the master workmen of the guild days addresses the group on what is required in the way of long years of service to qualify as a craftsman." Most of all, the Guild succeeded in updating the old "Corporate" world of medieval guilds to modern times. Hitchcock described how—after the evocation of European Guild traditions—the medieval ornaments served as a backdrop for GM's American corporate modernity: "a picture of the modern boy, using power-driven tools in building his coach, shows the contrast between work in the Middle Ages and today." By deftly wedding medieval motifs to symbols of the modern age, then, the ritual not only trumpeted the past but also broadcast the future, reaching millions through radio shows, news bulletins, department store displays, photographs, short films and advertisements.

The Fisher Guild did more, however, than just update the medieval values of apprenticeship for the modern corporate world. As the Guild's ad suggested, the company sought to create a future generation of corporate workers while also expanding consumer markets for the future. During the Guild festivities organizers allotted time for shopping trips in downtown Detroit, suggesting that in the expanding consumer society men were no longer just breadwinners and producers but were also expected to take on new roles as consumers. At the same time, the Guild's advocates and GM officials explicitly encouraged Guild winners to seek GM jobs after graduation. During a 1931 radio broadcast announcing that year's winners, GM President Alfred Sloan Jr. extended "to all you boys the opportunity to become employees of the corporation as soon as your schooling is completed." During the depth of the Depression, this was a powerful message indeed.

Sloan's invitation was not a mere public relations ploy, for it was sustained by the corporation's active recruitment policy. As many participants later testified, the sumptuous banquet offered the teenagers easy access to key GM officials, and indeed the event was designed to encourage the boys to converse with men held up as successful role models and potential mentors. Local business leaders, GM chief designers and upper management, and the presidents and deans of major engineering colleges all fraternized with the contestants. GM's attention to the male teenagers went beyond fleeting moments of attention at banquets. By sponsoring a special Alumni Organization, the Guild held winners of past contests up as examples to others. Each year all members of this exclusive club were invited back to the banquets as guests of honor, giving GM ample opportunity to monitor their advances as they grew up. The Guild newsletter, *The Guildsman,* printed biographical narratives next to instructions on how to design the miniature coaches and cars. Working together, these narratives and technical instructions advised simultaneously on building perfect models and proper male character.

The corporation's recruiting efforts paid off handsomely: many of the winners later became chief designers and high-level managers at General Motors and elsewhere in the corporate world. In 1968, for example, 55 percent of the creative design staff at GM had been involved in Fisher Body's Guild while many other former contestants occupied key positions in other large corporations. . . .

The public narratives in the media stressed individual merit and preached "rugged competition," faithful as they were to the middle-class American ideal of the self-made man, but personal recollections suggest that the efforts were often collaborative. Many of the entrants seem to have come from the lower middle classes and small towns, and building the coaches and models fitted into the family economy and ambitions for upward mobility. After all, college education was the prize, a potential reward difficult to ignore for a teenaged boy and his family. In 1930, Raymond Doerr's father, for instance, allowed his son to postpone entry into the job market after high school graduation. Young Doerr lived off the family's income for about a year to devote all of his time to the competition. This family-induced decision indeed paid off, because Doerr won the 1931 competition. Other fathers assisted their sons with advice, tools, capital, or skills. Mothers helped with the complicated and elaborate work on the majestic upholstery that adorned the Napoleonic Coach. Myron Webb recalled that his mother "had at one time worked in a millinery shop designing and making hats and did beautiful handiwork. She did the sewing on the inside trim [of the Coach]." Brothers assisted by exchanging skills and sharing earlier experiences in the competition. The Pietruska brothers, Richard, Ronald and Michael, were all national winners, "needless to say we were very proud of our accomplishments, individually and as a family." Thus while the contest pushed a masculine identity of autonomy, individuality and honor in building the cars, actual practices suggest that model making was embedded in the family economy, in which family members shared their talent, capital, and time. Such pooling of family resources is perhaps not surprising given the promise of a scholarship, but it contrasted sharply with the Guild' representations of building proper male character as a lone, individual effort.

These family strategies developed in tandem with GM's search for personnel. The company sought to socialize male teenagers not only as future corporate employees, but also as breadwinners, and consumers. As one contemporary observer close to the automobile industry remarked, the goal of General Motors' sponsorship of the Guild "was to build good will, rather than to sell automobiles," but also considered "the boys' influence in automobile selling . . . a very powerful factor." In another appreciative assessment an advertising trade journal stated that the Guild served to whet the boys' appetite as prospective consumers. If this trade-literature assessment is correct, it is particularly significant that the Guild presented the boys in their new consumer roles as knowledgeable producers and builders—a portrayal that stood in marked contrast to the passive roles mapped out for girls in GM's advertisement campaign "Body by Fisher" initiated a few years earlier and the craft's recruiting literature during this period.

The Guild owed its remarkable success to more than the luster of banquets and the promise of substantial scholarships, however important they must have been in motivating the Fisher hopefuls. In an age of increasing marketing sophistication, the Guild's promoters succeeded particularly well because General Motors's organizational apparatus enabled the company to reach and recruit young men from across the United States, in a manner so convincing that the contest appeared to be an integral part of the life of the teenaged boy and his family. This was due both to GM's deft mobilization of leading economic, social, and cultural institutions to support the competition and to the intimate organizational parallels between the Guild and its corporate parent.

The organizational shape of the Fisher Body Guild's contest closely resembled General Motors's business organization and followed the company's strategy of multi-divisional management structure. In Sloan's formulation of the GM's corporate strategy, the company sought "decentralized operations through coordinated control." While centralized control played an important role, the Guild like its parent company invested in local economies and communities around the U.S. and Canada. By 1933, the Guild's organization had covered over 600 major cities and many more other communities. As is well known, GM's management approach contrasted with Ford's hierarchical and centrally-organized structure which sought to integrate production vertically. Ford and GM differed not only in their internal management structure but also in their views on the world outside the confines of their companies. For one, Sloan sought to manage the reproduction of skills and the succession of people through calculated and predictable bureaucratic means. Promoting the virtues of the "Organization Man" as the model of the new corporate worker, Sloan detested idiosyncratic personalities such as Ford's and Durant's [the founder of General Motors]. If the Ford company emphasized vertical and backward integration of production, Sloan's strategy stood out because it also crafted a consumer framework for GM's products by seeking to integrate both personnel and consumers forwardly into the organization in a more planned and organic fashion. GM's sophisticated advertising campaigns, such as the "Body by Fisher," represented one means of accomplishing that integration. The Guild represented another.

The Guild also marked an important alliance between the corporation and educational institutions. Its judging system, for example, cemented GM's collaboration with the educators by integrating the school system into its ranks. Teams of judges enlisted from local and national educational elites evaluated the models for faithfulness to the original and level of craftsmanship. On the national level, General Motors recruited a group of judges that reads like [a] roll call of . . . engineering's educational elite. In 1937, for example, six presidents of engineering schools and eight deans of engineering colleges participated. . . .

From the corporation's point of view the Guild's organization was powerful enough, but how did a boy get involved in such an institutional mobilization in 1930? How did the Guild succeed in becoming such an integral part of the life of the teenager and his family that he would be willing to spend at least three hours a day after school in the Guild? Based on information supplied by nearly 200 contestants, a composite biography emerges of how a boy got drafted smoothly into the Guild and learned to nurture his passion for cars as if it were his second nature. There were at least three all-male institutional settings where the teenage boy might be introduced to General Motor's Guild. The YMCA, which organized local Guild Chapters, provided the first avenue into the Guild; the Boy Scouts, which also participated in recruitment and integrated the contest into their merit badge program, was the second; and finally, the high school, where the vocational counselor's advice to participate often received further endorsement from the high-school principal's active support, offered a third entry way. GM secured the sponsorship of high school principals, rewarding that collaboration by presenting a trophy not only to the boy who had won the contest but also to the school he attended. To further wed these networks with the appropriate educational message, GM arranged for some 32 renowned athletes to narrate stories about enduring difficulties and overcoming initial failure on the path to ultimate success. Finally, GM organized promotional teams that visited 1,200 high schools each year. Some even visited the contestants at home.

Once introduced to the Guild and encouraged to participate in it, the teenager enrolled by submitting his name to the local Chevrolet, Buick, Oakland, Cadillac or Oldsmobile dealer in his area well in advance of the deadline; officials calculated that on average seven boys enrolled at each GM dealership throughout the country. After enrolling they received a membership card, a bronze Guild button, guide for their parents, a detailed manual with plans and instructions, and a quarterly newsletter called *The Guildsman* which counselled them on how to proceed and paraded previous winners who showed off their successful careers as additional trophies. To cap if off with a show of personal attention, members of the Guild received greeting cards wishing them a merry Christmas with the compliments of GM. In some cases the support was much more substantial than that: GM divisions such as Delco Remy in Anderson, IN, the Packard Electric Company, Mansfield Tool and Die Company, and the Fisher Body Plant in Hamilton, OH organized local guild clubs in their own communities under management supervision to help guide and encourage the boys making their models. . . .

The emerging social and economic network extended beyond the coalition between the corporation and the engineering education elite to include the active support of the media. More than 20 national and local newspapers participated in weaving these intricate social and economic networks together into a seamless web. Among several newspapers, the *Detroit News* directly sponsored the Guild by providing weekly instructions on how to plan, design, and build a model; other newspapers faithfully helped to build suspense by carrying accounts of deadlines, events, displays, or announcements of winners throughout the year. The Guild's advocates built the annual cycle of each contest in such a way that reports on the Fisher Body Craftsman's Guild appeared in the press monthly and sometimes even weekly.

In other words, the contest was as much about building media events and suspense as about building models and male character to which girls had no access. A photograph taken at the annual banquet in 1931 just moments before the winners were announced symbolizes these close parallels most graphically. The photograph shows rows of straight-backed boys identically clad in Guild attire: jacket, beret, tie, and pin. Facing the camera with similar expressions of suspense on their faces, each boy clings to his exact miniature replica of the Napoleonic Coach. We can read this 1931 photograph as a perfect rendition of the emerging male corporate ideal. The contest's demand for exact imitations of the original Coach model is neatly replicated in the demand for identical male character, something that would come to symbolize the ideal of the "Organization Man." As propagated so eloquently by Sloan, GM's corporate male ideal demanded patience, hard work, and a willingness to conform to the rules and regulations of a large organization, the very antithesis of the behavior associated with unpredictable and colorful personalities.

Many of the contest's features remained the same throughout the years, but over time organizers gradually introduced one important change. Until the outbreak of World War II, the contest required that entrants build a miniature replica of the coach featured in the Fisher Body logo, but after the war, the Guild's organizers decided to change this requirement—asking instead for an original design instead of the faithful imitation. This change occurred neither suddenly nor in straightforward fashion, but reflected the contradictions and challenges General Motors faced. If the "free model" design seemed a radical departure from the straightjacket of careful imitation of the craft as represented by the 1931 photograph, a closer look at the change also shows continuities between the values at work in the coach and in the free model contests and between the idealized nineteenth-century culture of production and the twentieth-century culture of consumption.

Why would an automotive giant such as GM and a body company such as Fisher sponsor an organization that harked back to the European Middle Ages and their craft traditions? Why would the Fisher company go at such extraordinary lengths to instill "craftsmanship" in a younger generation when automanufacturers changed their production methods so thoroughly? The premium put on skilled craftsmanship and endurance entailed a historic irony. At first glance, the Guild's emphasis on craft seemed at odds with the growing economic trend toward a Fordist mode of mass production that sought to eliminate workers and replace them with machinery.

The Fisher Body Guild celebrated the craft ideal and demanded undivided labor (the purchase of raw materials, tool making, design, execution, and finishing) at the same moment that production in the Fisher Body plants moved toward the assembly of parts by semi-skilled workers. Because of the extraordinary degree of difficulty, many teenagers who started the process never finished; others negotiated the craft challenge by competing year after year; some competed for as long as 7 consecutive years—from age 12 when they were first allowed to join the contest until the maximum age of 20 when they lost eligibility. The Guild's initial emphasis on craft as a path of male socialization disguised the emasculating nature of corporate America that produced it. The borrowings of Guild past attempted at recapturing and remaking a masculine culture in the context of twentieth century society looking for new resources. In time, the Guild evolved to fulfill the dual purpose—one concerned with the crafty imitation of existing models, the other based on the inspiration of new designs. This tension of near opposites reflected an often uncomfortable transition within the company and the automotive industry as a whole. The Guild expressed the contradictions, tensions, and solutions of GM's conflictual world of corporate culture that the Fisher family confronted as it moved into the corporation. As historian Roland Marchand has shown, many of the GM's corporate strategies during the 1920's not only had an "outward quest for prestigious familiarity" but also sought to promote internal loyalty and corporate centralization. The Guild and Fisher's promotional campaigns were no exception.

A thriving German-American family firm in Detroit during the second half of the nineteenth century, Fred Fisher and his six brothers swiftly built the firm into the world's largest manufacturer of automobile bodies when it began to mass produce closed bodies for various automobile companies during the first two decades of this century. Before the first World War, combustion-engine cars had been mainly associated with utilitarian farmers or upper-class male adventure and racing. Soon thereafter automotive design changed dramatically as manufacturers sought to broaden its appeal and market to include women. Closing the automobile's body on all sides did just that. For one, the automobile's closed body moved motoring away from an exclusively sporting, summer and leisure-time activity to a practical mode of transportation all year round, in all weather conditions. The Fisher brothers simultaneously stepped into and created this new market. "The Fishers kept their eyes on closed car possibilities from the start," one chronicler of the firm explained the Fishers' particular need for women as the company's market niche. "They saw that motoring would remain a summer sport until drivers and owners could be comfortable in the winter months. Women would never be really pleased with the automobile so long as their gowns and hats were at the mercy of wind and weather. After pressing these points on car manufacturers they were at last rewarded . . . for the first 'big order' for closed car bodies." Thanks to the closing of the car's body, the mass of middle-class and urban women could venture out on the road under all meteorological conditions. More importantly perhaps, the car's body became the selling point of the automobile as a whole over its technical specifications. The body of the car "is emphasized by thousands of successful automobile salesmen as an introduction to their selling effort and as an easy and sure way of having the buyer accept the entire car." In this technical and marketing transformation of the automobile, the Fisher Body Company played a critically important role as the world's largest producer of closed bodies and became the key company in GM's marketing strategy to beat Ford and other competitors.

Not only was the Fisher firm phenomenally successful in carving out a powerful new niche in the market, it also succeeded in making a smooth transition from a traditional, craft-oriented nineteenth-century family firm to a twentieth-century division of GM, despite rapid changes in product and modes of production this new market strategy entailed. The Fisher brothers, all seven of them, were brought into GM's managerial structure and without exception became leading corporate managers. At first the brothers successfully negotiated for their continuing control with General Motors. Holding on to their craft-inspired past and playing a crucial role in helping to bring about General Motors's success at styling, the Fisher clan moved into GM's managerial command during the 1930's. The Fisher company remained a family firm tightly embedded into the corporate structure; eventually, however, the brothers became the victims of their own success precisely because their very effective incorporation into the corporate structure rendered them obsolete.

The Fisher Body company's choice of the hand-made Napoleonic Coach as its logo serves as an illustration for the emblematic ways in which Fisher reworked the discontinuities and contradictions with the corporate world. Fisher company's Napoleonic Coach did not draw on an old family trademark, but represented an invented tradition. "This symbol" read an announcement in 1922, "will appear, from this time forward, on all finished products of the Fisher Body Corporation [and] records the care which the motor car manufacturer has exercised in providing your car with a body of the very best quality obtainable." The imperial coach harkened back to an old craft tradition and symbolized comfort and luxury—values believed to appeal to women in particular. Registered in 1922 and officially introduced as a trademark in 1923, the Napoleonic Coach logo began to circulate in the commercial and visual domain in 1926. That year also marked the Fisher company's incorporation in GM and the surrender of its autonomy as a coach-making firm. Ironically, the Napoleonic Coach—symbol and model for the Guild—represented the craft tradition that the Fisher family was about to lose to GM. The Napoleonic Coach perhaps breathed nostalgia for a Fisher that was long gone, but in the hands of GM it became less a symbol of the past than a malleable and invented tradition suitable for present and future use. The trademark proved so successful that the coach became a stand-in for GM's own logo well into the 1980s. Inside GM, the Fisher company and its Napoleonic logo mitigated the contradictions between the worlds of craft and of mass production; outside, they carved out a new market. The Fisher company's slogan "Body by Fisher" in advertisements, featuring the suggestive curves of the female body, sought to convey an image of beauty, elegance, luxury, and craftsmanship associated with European royalty, and held it as a promise to the newly emerging middle classes. Strictly speaking, of course, the European hand-crafted Napoleonic Coach was out of reach for the American middle classes, but the emperor's mass-produced coach by Fisher beckoned consumers to enter its fantasy world through the illusion of a custom-made body; something a Ford could not. Most importantly, the emphasis on comfort, luxury and safety aimed to appeal to women.

FURTHER READING

Aitken, Hugh G. J. *The Continuous Wave: Technology and American Radio, 1900–1932* (Princeton, NJ: Princeton University Press, 1985).

Corn, Joseph, ed. *Imagining Tomorrow* (Cambridge, MA: MIT Press, 1986).

Cowen, Ruth Schwartz. *More Work for Mother: The Ironies of Household Technology from the Open Hearth to the Microwave* (New York: Basic Books, 1983).

Douglas, Susan A. *Inventing American Broadcasting* (Baltimore: Johns Hopkins, 1987).

Noble, David F. *America by Design: Science, Technology, and the Rise of Corporate Capitalism* (New York: Knopf, 1977).

Nye, David E. *Electrifying America: Social Meanings of a New Technology, 1880–1940* (Cambridge, MA: MIT Press, 1990).

Post, Robert C. *High Performance: The Culture and Technology of Drag Racing, 1950–1990* (Baltimore: Johns Hopkins, 1994).

Marchand, Roland. *Advertising the American Dream: Making Way for Modernity* (Berkeley, CA: University of California Press, 1985).

Smulyan, Susan. *Selling Radio: The Commercialization of American Broadcasting, 1920–1934* (Washington, DC: Smithsonian, 1994).

Trescott, Martha Moore, ed. *Dynamos and Virgins Revisited: Women and Technological Change in History* (Metuchen, NJ: Scarecrow Press, 1979).

C H A P T E R
11

The Pest War: The Shifting Use and Meaning of Insecticides, 1940–1990

卅

DDT, the first of the modern insecticides, was one of the "secret weapons" contributing to Allied victory in World War II. The military used it for disease prevention. After 1945, DDT was released for civilian use, but under the banner of "war on insect enemies." By the 1950s, insecticide use had become linked to farming and food production, but in the early 1960s, DDT and other insecticides took on a radically new meaning—as poisons that were potentially destroying plant, animal, and human life, while having relatively little effect on insects. DDT was banned in the United States in 1972, but other powerful insecticides continued to be developed and used here and abroad. In Mexico and other developing countries, insecticides became bound up with "modernization" and international trade.

We have seen how technologies can change meanings, and meanings can change technologies. But the story of DDT, and chemical insecticides generally, presents an extreme and compelling case. The implications of believing or not believing claims about insecticides were presented as having enormous consequences—winning the war, feeding the planet, poisoning the planet, sustaining life or destroying it. The technological system, or network, in which insecticides were imbedded grew to be enormously complex: the U.S. government, large public and private research laboratories, small farmers, individual suburban homeowners, starving or disease-ridden people, birds, salmon, vegetables, and the soil. How one described this technological network—what elements were included or left out—or where one resided in the "food chain" became crucial to one's position on insecticide use.

The "pest war," as the insecticide project was described in a 1974 book, was also propelled by metaphor. The designation of particular insects as "pests" had a cultural dimension, as did the use of "war" and other military terms to frame how insecticides should be used. Increased food production in parts of Asia and Africa, associated with the rising use of insecticides, was called the "green revolution." Did these and other words affect how the technology—the network constructed around the chemical—actually developed? Is the history of insecticide use an aberration, or is it fundamentally the same as that of other successful technologies? What alternatives were (are) available to chemical insecticides? To what extent were the ideologies and assumptions of the pest war exorcised or replicated by "ecological" solutions in the 1970s and 1980s?

≠≠ D O C U M E N T S

The authors of nearly all the documents that follow were either scientists or claimed to be speaking in the name of science. Is there an objective "scientific voice" we can rely on to resolve this debate? Does science have an "inside" and an "outside"?

The first document is a press release by the Geigy Company, the Swiss-based developer of DDT, describing the chemical's early manufacture and use in World War II. The text, approved by U.S. army censors, was presented by Geigy at a press conference in May 1944. The second selection is from *Silent Spring* by Rachel Carson, a biologist with the U.S. Fish and Wildlife Service for sixteen years. First published in 1962, Carson's book became a bestseller and a landmark in public concern about insecticides. *Silent Spring* was not universally well received, however. In 1966, for example, it was criticized at length in the fourth selection, from *That We May Live,* by U.S. Congressman Jamie Whitten of Mississippi. The fifth document, from the textbook *The Pest War* (1974) reaffirms the importance of insecticides a decade after Carson's book.

The sixth selection, by computer scientists Roger Weinberg and Ronald Morgan of Kansas State University, is from a chapter entitled "Ecological Problems" in *Computers and the Problems of Society* (1972). It proposes that computers mediate between farmers and the world environment. The seventh selection is from an article by Dr. Rod MacRae et al., "Agricultural Science and Sustainable Agriculture," from the journal *Biological Agriculture and Horticulture* (1989), which presents the case for non–pesticide-based, or "sustainable," agriculture.

"Now It Can Be Told"
(Geigy Company Press Release), 1944

The True Story of DDT, Which Alleviated The Typhus Epidemic in Italy; Amazing Preventive Possibilities in Other Fields; Tremendous Benefits to Agriculture; Scientists Do 8 Years' Research in 2; End of Possibilities Not in Sight.

A chemical formula which lay dormant for almost seventy years in a dusty volume of "Berichte der Chemischen Gesellschaft" (the Reports of the German Chemical Society) has suddenly come to life as the progenitor of a spectacular series of insecticidal compositions that seem destined to achieve in preventive medicine an effectiveness already likened to that of penicillin and sulfa drugs in the curative field.

Apart from their sensational preventive properties, dramatically demonstrated in the Army's virtual conquest of typhus, the compositions, in results already attained and in hopes induced by current tests, encourage the belief that they will bring about an economic revolution in the field of agriculture by crops saved from the scourge of insect pests.

When the Geigy patent application was filed in Washington, the military authorities, having come upon a potential major weapon, clamped down a firm secrecy order which had prevented, until last summer, the revelation of any phase of the amazing developments involved. Now, Geigy Company Inc., New York, is able to disclose some of the major aspects of a remarkable discovery. . . .

. . . In 1939 the potato crop of Switzerland was seriously threatened by the imported (from America) Colorado Potato Beetle. Geigy made available to the Swiss entomologist, Dr. R. Wiesmann, a composition carrying the designation "Experiment #G1750" which was later called "Gesarol." Dr. Wiesmann conducted experiments in the Swiss Federal Experimental Agricultural Station at Waederswil and confirmed Geigy's results which culminated in the control of the destructive Potato Beetle. Shortages of the accepted insecticides, arsenates, pyrethrum and rotenone further encouraged the investigations which have revealed DDT compositions as the outstanding development in the insecticide field for many years. . . .

When the United States entered the War it became manifest that its uniformed men would be sent to all parts of the world, meeting the menace of typhus and other dread diseases in many infected areas. Geigy in Basle, aware it had the most effective enemy of typhus ever experienced in medical history, informed Major De Jonge, American Military Attache in Berne, in August, 1942, that Neocid, the lousicidal composition of DDT, had proved amazingly effective against the typhus carrying louse, and that it possessed incredible residual potency, an all important factor. . . .

From the materials submitted by Geigy to the U.S. Department of Agriculture, much excitement was created. . . . Thereafter, scores upon scores of the Bureau's experts undertook experiments in experimental stations all over the United States. . . .

ENTOMOLOGICAL INVESTIGATION CONTINUES AT A MADDENING PACE AND IT IS SAFE TO SAY THAT SCIENTIFIC DATA WHICH UNDER NORMAL CONDITIONS WOULD TAKE ALL OF EIGHT YEARS OF EFFORT TO COMPILE WILL BE AVAILABLE IN TWO YEARS. FEW WILL EVER KNOW WHAT SACRIFICES SCIENTISTS THROUGHOUT THIS COUNTRY HAVE MADE OF THEIR TIME AND EFFORT TO HAVE DDT COMPOSITIONS READY FOR THE ARMED FORCES AND THE PUBLIC. . . .

Geigy, in cooperation with the Cincinnati Chemical Works, was largely responsible for the louse powder which conquered the recent typhus epidemic in Naples and Cincinnati Chemical Works has been by far the largest producer of DDT up to this moment. . . .

Other compositions of DDT in emulsion form have been used to impregnate clothing. . . .

Walls and ceilings covered with a Gesarol spray remain deadly to flies for three months. Dairy cattle made nervous by flies have been quieted by sprayings of the compound, an important item when it is realized that a cow's milk productivity is lowered by a pestilence of flies—apart from sanitary considerations. Beef cattle similarly are benefitted. . . .

Tests on dogs and cats have shown that Neocid not only eradicates fleas but also affords subsequent protection for a long time. In ordinary domestic use, the composition has been most efficacious against moths, roaches, bedbugs, silverfish. Beds properly sprayed just once with a DDT composition continue to be 100%

effective even after 300 days against the bed-bug, the bane of some hospitals and institutions.

House owners may also be comforted by assurance of its deadliness to termites. . . .

. . . DDT compositions, Gesarol Sprays and Dusts, are successful against such garden pests as the Japanese Beetle, thrips, tomato fruit worm, plant lice and the three important cabbage worms. . . .

. . . Geigy believes that it has the support of the United States Department of Agriculture in predicting that the general commercial production of Gesarol, when the military needs have been accommodated, will open the way to what may be regarded as a revolution in the economy of agriculture and in the quantity of the world's food output. . . .

The toxicity of Gesarol and Neocid preparations to man and animals is still under investigation by the U.S. Public Health Service, the Food and Drug Administration and the Kettering Laboratory of Applied Physiology of the University of Cincinnati, the last mentioned research being sponsored by Geigy. Research goes on. Indeed, considerable research is still necessary to determine all the possible uses and ineptitudes of DDT compositions. The forms and methods of application, the rates of application and the dosages on specific plants and in specific climates must be settled. Research is proceeding as rapidly as good practice permits.

Enough has been revealed to indicate the possibility of wide application in agriculture, households and in preventive measures against disease-carrying insects to establish the DDT compositions as among the great scientific discoveries of our time.

MANY AUTHORITIES HAVE DECLARED THAT OUT OF THIS WAR HAVE COME THREE MOMENTOUS DISCOVERIES IN CURATIVE AND PREVENTIVE MEDICINE—PLASMA—PENICILLIN—and—DDT.

Eradicating The Japanese Beetle, 1962

RACHEL CARSON

Under the philosophy that now seems to guide our destinies, nothing must get in the way of the man with the spray gun. The incidental victims of his crusade against insects count as nothing; if robins, pheasants, raccoons, cats, or even livestock happen to inhabit the same bit of earth as the target insects and to be hit by the rain of insect-killing poisons no one must protest.

The citizen who wishes to make a fair judgment of the question of wildlife loss is today confronted with a dilemma. On the one hand conservationists and many wildlife biologists assert that the losses have been severe and in some cases even catastrophic. On the other hand the control agencies tend to deny flatly and categorically that such losses have occurred, or that they are of any importance if they have. Which view are we to accept?

The credibility of the witness is of first importance. The professional wildlife biologist on the scene is certainly best qualified to discover and interpret wildlife loss. The entomologist, whose specialty is insects, is not so qualified by training, and is not

From Rachel Carson, *Silent Spring* (Boston: Houghton Mifflin, 1962), pp. 83–89, 95, 141.

psychologically disposed to look for undesirable side effects of his control program. Yet it is the control men in state and federal governments—and of course the chemical manufacturers—who steadfastly deny the facts reported by the biologists and declare they see little evidence of harm to wildlife. Like the priest and the Levite in the biblical story, they choose to pass by on the other side and to see nothing. Even if we charitably explain their denials as due to the shortsightedness of the specialist and the man with an interest this does not mean we must accept them as qualified witnesses. . . .

During the fall of 1959 some 27,000 acres in southeastern Michigan, including numerous suburbs of Detroit, were heavily dusted from the air with pellets of aldrin, one of the most dangerous of all the chlorinated hydrocarbons. The program was conducted by the Michigan Department of Agriculture with the cooperation of the United States Department of Agriculture; its announced purpose was control of the Japanese beetle.

Little need was shown for this drastic and dangerous action. On the contrary, Walter P. Nickell, one of the best-known and best-informed naturalists in the state, who spends much of his time in the field with long periods in southern Michigan every summer, declared: "For more than thirty years, to my direct knowledge, the Japanese beetle has been present in the city of Detroit in small numbers. The numbers have not shown any appreciable increase in all this lapse of years. I have yet to see a single Japanese beetle [in 1959] other than the few caught in Government catch traps in Detroit . . . Everything is being kept so secret that I have not yet been able to obtain any information whatsoever to the effect that they have increased in numbers."

An official release by the state agency merely declared that the beetle had "put in its appearance" in the areas designated for the aerial attack upon it. Despite the lack of justification the program was launched, with the state providing the manpower and supervising the operation, the federal government providing equipment and additional men, and the communities paying for the insecticide.

The Japanese beetle, an insect accidentally imported into the United States, was discovered in New Jersey in 1916, when a few shiny beetles of a metallic green color were seen in a nursery near Riverton. The beetles, at first unrecognized, were finally identified as a common inhabitant of the main islands of Japan. Apparently they had entered the United States on nursery stock imported before restrictions were established in 1912.

From its original point of entrance the Japanese beetle has spread rather widely throughout many of the states east of the Mississippi, where conditions of temperature and rainfall are suitable for it. Each year some outward movement beyond the existing boundaries of its distribution usually takes place. In the eastern areas where the beetles have been longest established, attempts have been made to set up natural controls. Where this has been done, the beetle populations have been kept at relatively low levels, as many records attest.

Despite the record of reasonable control in eastern areas, the midwestern states now on the fringe of the beetle's range have launched an attack worthy of the most deadly enemy instead of only a moderately destructive insect, employing the most dangerous chemicals distributed in a manner that exposes large numbers of people, their domestic animals, and all wildlife to the poison intended for the beetle. As a result these Japanese beetle programs have caused shocking destruction of animal life and have exposed human beings to undeniable hazard. Sections of Michigan, Kentucky, Iowa, Indiana, Illinois, and Missouri are all experiencing a rain of chemicals in the name of beetle control.

The Michigan spraying was one of the first large-scale attacks on the Japanese beetle from the air. The choice of aldrin, one of the deadliest of all chemicals, was not determined by any peculiar suitability for Japanese beetle control, but simply by the wish to save money—aldrin was the cheapest of the compounds available. While the state in its official release to the press acknowledged that aldrin is a "poison," it implied that no harm could come to human beings in the heavily populated areas to which the chemical was applied. (The official answer to the query "What precautions should I take?" was "For you, none.") An official of the Federal Aviation Agency was later quoted in the local press to the effect that "this is a safe operation" and a representative to the Detroit Department of Parks and Recreation added his assurance that "the dust is harmless to humans and will not hurt plants or pets." One must assume that none of these officials had consulted the published and readily available reports of the United States Public Health Service, the Fish and Wildlife Service, and other evidence of the extremely poisonous nature of aldrin.

Acting under the Michigan pest control law which allows the state to spray indiscriminately without notifying or gaining permission of individual landowners, the low-lying planes began to fly over the Detroit area. The city authorities and the Federal Aviation Agency were immediately besieged by calls from worried citizens. After receiving nearly 800 calls in a single hour, the police begged radio and television stations and newspapers to "tell the watchers what they were seeing and advise them it was safe," according to the Detroit *News*. The Federal Aviation Agency's safety officer assured the public that "the planes are carefully supervised" and "are authorized to fly low." In a somewhat mistaken attempt to allay fears, he added that the planes had emergency valves that would allow them to dump their entire load instantaneously. This, fortunately, was not done, but as the planes went about their work the pellets of insecticide fell on beetles and humans alike, showers of "harmless" poison descending on people shopping or going to work and on children out from school for the lunch hour. Housewives swept the granules from porches and sidewalks, where they are said to have "looked like snow." As pointed out later by the Michigan Audubon Society, "In the spaces between shingles on roofs, in eavestroughs, in the cracks in bark and twigs, the little white pellets of aldrin-and-clay, no bigger than a pin head, were lodged by the millions . . . When the snow and rain came, every puddle became a possible death potion."

Within a few days after the dusting operation, the Detroit Audubon Society began receiving calls about the birds. According to the Society's secretary, Mrs. Ann Boyes, "The first indication that the people were concerned about the spray was a call I received on Sunday morning from a woman who reported that coming home from church she saw an alarming number of dead and dying birds. The spraying there had been done on Thursday. She said there were no birds at all flying in the area, that she had found at least a dozen [dead] in her backyard and that the neighbors had found dead squirrels." All other calls received by Mrs. Boyes that day reported "a great many dead birds and no live ones . . . People who had maintained bird feeders said there were no birds at all at their feeders." Birds picked up in a dying condition showed the typical symptoms of insecticide poisoning—tremoring, loss of ability to fly, paralysis, convulsions.

Nor were birds the only forms of life immediately affected. A local veterinarian reported that his office was full of clients with dogs and cats that had suddenly sickened. Cats, who so meticulously groom their coats and lick their paws, seemed to be most affected. Their illness took the form of severe diarrhea, vomiting, and convulsions. The only advice the veterinarian could give his clients was not to let the animals out unnecessarily, or to wash the paws promptly if they did so. (But the chlorinated hydrocarbons cannot be washed even from fruits or vegetables, so little protection could be expected from this measure.)

Despite the insistence of the City–County Health Commissioner that the birds must have been killed by "some other kind of spraying" and that the outbreak of throat and chest irritations that followed the exposure to aldrin must have been due to "something else," the local Health Department received a constant stream of complaints. A prominent Detroit internist was called upon to treat four of his patients within an hour after they had been exposed while watching the planes at work. All had similar symptoms: nausea, vomiting, chills, fever, extreme fatigue, and coughing.

The Detroit experience has been repeated in many other communities as pressure has mounted to combat the Japanese beetle with chemicals. At Blue Island, Illinois, hundreds of dead and dying birds were picked up. Data collected by birdbanders here suggest that 80 per cent of the songbirds were sacrificed. In Joliet, Illinois, some 3000 acres were treated with heptachlor in 1959. According to reports from a local sportsmen's club, the bird population within the treated area was "virtually wiped out." Dead rabbits, muskrats, opossums, and fish were also found in numbers, and one of the local schools made the collection of insecticide-poisoned birds a science project. . . .

These insecticides are not selective poisons; they do not single out the one species of which we desire to be rid. Each of them is used for the simple reason that it is a deadly poison. It therefore poisons all life with which it comes in contact: the cat beloved of some family, the farmer's cattle, the rabbit in the field, and the horned lark out of the sky. . . .

. . . Our attitude toward poisons has undergone a subtle change. Once they were kept in containers marked with skull and crossbones; the infrequent occasions of their use were marked with utmost care that they should come in contact with the target and with nothing else. With the development of the new organic insecticides and the abundance of surplus planes after the Second World War, all this was forgotten. Although today's poisons are more dangerous than any known before, they have amazingly become something to be showered down indiscriminately from the skies. Not only the target insect or plant, but anything—human or nonhuman—within range of the chemical fallout may know the sinister touch of the poison. Not only forests and cultivated fields are sprayed, but towns and cities as well.

"That We May Live"
A Congressman Responds to *Silent Spring,* 1966

JAMIE L. WHITTEN

Pesticides go through extraordinary tests for safety, and except for a rare allergic reaction, poisoning results only from a large exposure such as a suicide attempt or a major accident.

The extraordinary tests for safety that DDT underwent while it was being developed during World War II have generally been forgotten. Not only animals but human volunteers were fed the insecticide. Scientists from the Food and Drug Administration and the Public Health Service, working at the Department of Agriculture Laboratory at Orlando, Florida, gave a man a dose of 500 milligrams (mg) of DDT without ill effect. This was the equivalent of only about 17.5 thousandths of an ounce, but for a chemical of the insect-killing power of DDT it was quite a dose. Later the scientists gave the same man about 27 thousandths of an ounce, again without harm. . . .

On one point experts and would-be experts of every persuasion agree—there is a great need for more research. This is normal; it would be surprising if someone said there were no need for more research. The history of science shows that the process of finding the answers to questions always raises new questions that need to be answered. So under the impetus of *Silent Spring,* the report of the President's Science Advisory Committee, and the Ribicoff hearings, Congress has provided funds for greatly expanded research into the effects of pesticides. This research is under way. Many reports have yet to be published, but there is no indication at this writing that any results will be cause for alarm.

One type of study that was widely urged, for instance, was the "community study" to measure the average exposure to pesticides from people's total environment, not just their food supply. The Public Health Service began ten such studies in 1964, and Department of Agriculture monitoring operations are cooperating with them. Information on the presence of pesticides and the level of residues in people's bodies will be used to estimate the hazard from pesticide exposure. Many other new research projects are examining the effects of pesticides on animals and man. The result is sure to sharpen our knowledge of pesticides and how to use them safely. In the meantime, the knowledge and techniques we have seem quite adequate to protect the health of the nation's citizens.

One of the most effective voices in quieting the fears aroused by vague charges against pesticides has been that of Frederick J. Stare, professor and chairman of the Department of Nutrition, School of Public Health, Harvard University. A recent article by Dr. Stare, whose newspaper column is widely read, is worth reproducing . . . :

> The current hysteria about agricultural chemicals has seeped in under the doorsills of American homes.
>
> A woman recently said to me, "I feel like Lucretia Borgia every time I put dinner on the table. Am I poisoning my family?"

From Jamie L. Whitten, *That We May Live* (Princeton, NJ: Van Nostrand, 1966), pp. 83, 103–105, 109, 111, 133–141.

That concerned woman, interested primarily in the health and well-being of her family, deserves to have an end put to her confusion about agricultural chemicals, particularly pesticides. Her bafflement stems not from stupidity, but from the claims and counter-claims of self-appointed experts who usually don't know what they're talking about.

They are usually extrapolating to man some findings on birds, bees or fish, or the unfortunate result of some child inhaling or swallowing large quantities of some pesticide. Such findings just don't extend to the use of agricultural chemicals in growing, protecting or preserving of foods.

Let's set aside all arguments about how or why the current controversy started and concentate instead on letting facts speak for themselves.

One irrefutable fact the critics of pesticides have been unable to answer is this true statement: there is not one medically documented instance of ill health in man, not to mention death, that can be attributed to the proper use of pesticides, or even of their improper use as far as ill health from residues on foods. . . .

In spite of this lack of evidence, many people now have the impression that pesticides contaminate our food supply and are harmful, probably lethal. This gap between fact and fancy must be closed or we will do ourselves great harm by allowing disease and famine to rule the earth.

Are pesticides poison? Of course, that's why they work. They are poison to the insects, worms, rats, weeds and other pests against which they are directed. Because of strictly enforced regulations and tolerance levels, however, the hazard to man from pesticide residues on foods is almost nonexistent. They are dangerous if you handle them carelessly or leave them around where small fry may "play house" with them.

You can have full confidence in our foods. They are not full of poisons as some food faddists would have you believe. They are nutritious and the quality is much better than it was a generation ago.

Eat and enjoy them. . . .

My experience in the Yazoo–Mississippi River Delta region has convinced me that the birds there have actually benefited from the use of pesticides because mites, rodents, and other enemies of birds have been destroyed and because the cultivation of more and more land for grain crops has provided the birds with a plentiful food supply. The Delta, as I have described, is intensively treated with pesticides to fight the boll weevil and other pests. On a recent dove-shooting trip there, my companions and I saw literally thousands of birds and hundreds of sportsmen. At the end of the day many thousands of birds were still flying everywhere. . . .

Wildlife populations all over the nation are bigger and healthier than ever, not in spite of pesticides, but in many cases because of them. . . .

Perhaps Miss Carson's mainspring was the age-old desire we all share in varying degrees to recapture the days of one's youth—to be young again with all things as they were, when the sound of birds in springtime brought the keenest pleasure. Miss Carson pictures wonderfully the "good old days" when man was more in tune with other living things, when nature did not need to be controlled to the extent it does today to meet the needs of population growth and world leadership. In this practical world in which we live, however, we must be careful not to let sentiment and nostalgia blind us to the realistic requirements of modern society.

In the first chapter of *Silent Spring,* "Fable For Tomorrow," Miss Carson describes in beautiful and glowing language a delightful make-believe village in a rural setting "where life seemed to live in harmony with its surroundings." The chapter title itself should be sufficient to put an objective reader on notice as to the nature of her story.

Like many Americans, I grew up in such a small rural village. I, too, remember that the grass was green and the birds sang "sweet in the springtime." But my village has changed—mostly for the better. Regardless of sentiment and nostalgia, very few of us would want to return to the inconveniences of those earlier years. A comparison of my village as it was when I was a small boy with what it is today provides a striking example of the progress we have made through scientific discovery. I remember the "good old days," when to walk barefoot along a dusty country road, to drink cool water from a cistern filled with rain caught from the roof, to read lying flat on one's stomach before an open wood fire by the light of a coal oil (kerosene) lamp seemed to represent the utmost pleasure. Then I had time to listen to the singing of the birds. . . .

My village is one in which many people would like to live; but neither I nor they would want to go back to what it was. Above all, I would not want those who have been released from the farm by labor-saving chemicals, machinery, and electricity, who have moved to the city to provide telephones, automobiles, television sets and other consumer goods, to have to return and dig in the ground to grow food. I would much rather remember those "good old days" while watching television in a modern home, than go back to them with the reduced standard of living.

As I ponder over those "old days" I do remember that we burned on one side while nearly freezing on the other before that open fire. The sweltering heat of summer made it practically impossible to be comfortable. The dusty country road in summer covered us with dust on the shortest trip, and our car got "stuck in the mud" in other seasons.

A flyswatter had a short and hard life, and only a few miles away in the Delta or "bottom," mosquito netting was essential in summer. Really, it must have been my youth which made the "old days" seem so good. . . .

Miss Carson goes further in describing her village of fantasy when she says: "A strange blight came over the area. The people became sick . . . the birds were gone . . . the hens brooded but no chicks hatched . . . the roadsides, once so attractive, were lined with brown."

She then says that such a village does not exist but *might!* She should have known that such situations can and do exist in many places around the world. They exist largely in backward countries where man has not learned to make or to use the scientific weapons that have been developed to cope with disease and pestilence. These nations, almost without exception, have no chemical pesticides to fight insects and blight. . . .

Miss Carson had made a contribution to American literature. But she, along with Henry Thoreau and other essayists who have advocated a return to nature and "the simple life," must not lead us into substituting sentiment and nostalgia for scientific data and facts. . . .

I believe all must agree that *Silent Spring,* delightful reading that it is, certainly is not and was never claimed to be a scientific document nor an objective analysis of the chemical-human life relationship. Though we give to it our highest praise for its wonderful prose, for its timely warning, let us move it over from the non-fiction section of the library to the science-fiction section, while we review the facts—in order that we may continue to enjoy the abundant life.

The Pest War (Textbook Introduction), 1974

W. W. FLETCHER

The war against pests is a continuing one that man must fight to ensure his survival. Pests (in particular insects) are our major competitors on earth and for the hundreds of thousands of years of our existence they have kept our numbers low and on occasions they have threatened extinction. Throughout the ages man has lived at a bare subsistence level because of the onslaught of pests and the diseases they carry. It is only in comparatively recent times that this picture has begun to alter as, in certain parts of the world, we have gradually gained the upper hand over pests.

This war story describes some of the battles that have been fought and the continuing guerrilla warfare; the type of enemies we are facing and some of their manoeuvres for survival; the weapons that we have at our command ranging from the rather crude ones of the "bow and arrow" age of pest control to the sophisticated weapons of the present day, including a look into the future of some "secret weapons" that are in the trial stages; the gains that have been made; and some of the devastation which is a concomitant of war. As with all accounts of war there will be differences of opinion on the interpretation of results and situations; on the emphasis that should be laid on certain parts. This book does not claim to be a definitive account of pest control. It is written for the intelligent non-specialist in the field, who wants to know what the war is all about and the implications of it. It is also aimed at intending students of agriculture, horticulture, medicine, biological sciences; and should also serve as a useful introductory text for elementary courses in pest control in colleges and universities.

Indians, DDT, the Illiac IV: Computer Scientists Respond to the Environmental Crisis, 1971

ROGER WEINBERG AND RONALD MORGAN

Two basic religious concepts of the relationship between man and nature have influenced man's actions toward nature.

The first, appearing in both eastern religions and American (Indian) religions, is the oneness of man and nature. It led man to an inefficient but respectful use of his natural resources. . . .

A second contrasting concept, appearing in Judeo-Christian religion, is the duality of man and nature:

"Then God said, 'Let us make man in our image, after our likeness, and let them have dominion over the fish of the sea, and over the birds of the air, and over the cattle, and over all the earth and over every creeping thing that crawls upon the earth." (Genesis v. 10,27)

From W. W. Fletcher, *The Pest War* (New York: John Wiley, 1974), p. ix.

From Roger Weinberg and Ronald E. Morgan, "Ecological Problems," in *Computers and the Problems of Society* (Montvale, NJ: American Federation of Information Processing Societies, 1972), pp. 339–341, 349, 359, 364–380.

This second conception suggested that man would become an exploiter of nature. And he has exploited it during the 19th and 20th centuries in America, changing many productive Indian systems of life: the Oklahoma plains of the Kiowa, rich in grass and buffalo, into a dust bowl; the Washington salmon streams of the Haida into a sequence of DDT-poisoned reservoirs; the British Columbian Kootenay Lake of the Tlinglit, filled with fish, into a recipient for fertilizer. . . .

By 1971, however, man had also developed the computer, a constructive tool with which he could repair some of his past damage, prevent new damage, and even produce improvements in ecological systems. This tool could hold in its memory a model of a grassland, a salmon stream, a woodland pond, the earth's atmosphere, or even the cycling of elements among the animals and plants of the ocean and the land. It could present these models to man, who could then study and destroy the models instead of the actual systems. In so doing man could learn what to do, and what not to do with the real systems. . . .

With the advent of the electronic computer, accompanied by the concept of the ecosystem, man acquired the capability of simulating complex models of his environment and of analyzing both the model and the real world which it represents. . . .

By 1971 man has begun to use the computer to modify his environment to his liking. . . .

Some of these computers, the minicomputers, will be small and cheap, while others, the parallel processing ones, will be powerful and fast. The little minicomputers, smaller than a refrigerator, are binary computers with a selling price of from $4,000–$15,000. . . . Demand and mass production have already brought their cost down to $10,000 for a useful instrument with all necessary input and output (a teletypewriter is all a man needs). . . .

In the next few years, as the "computer on a chip" becomes a commercial reality, "general purpose" microcomputers will become an integral part of instruments, "modems," and terminals. . . .

As man uses his new technology to miniaturize computers, he will simultaneously use it to produce larger and more complex computers such as the Illiac IV. . . .

Proceeding one step further than the Illiac IV, man will use the computer utility, a network of facilities rather than a single computer, a network which the Illiac IV might be but one unit, a network of many memories and processors into which man can tap at any point for his information processing needs. . . .

With the utility, man is developing a system in which the tiny minicomputers with their sensors may serve as eyes, ears, and nose, receiving weather information at a remote Pacific island, partially processing it, passing it on to a larger, mainland computer which serves as a subunit of the brain. The mainlander considers the information it receives and passes on only important information to the gigantic main computer, which ponders the import of the information to the well being of man.

The utility can extend further, to include the moon and planets, transmitting information on waves through space, and enabling man to comprehend the orderly course of the universe.

Man, although only a small part of a large universe, still has the right to survive and to enjoy his life. He has, as Ehrlich (1968) points out, the right to: eat; eat meat; drink pure water; hunt and fish; view natural beauty; breathe clean air; and avoid pesticide poisoning. This impressive list, deceptively short and straightforward, implies planned terrestrial evolution with the big problems it poses philosophically, politically and economically. In order for the rights to have any meaning, man must understand and cope with these problems through social planning and action.

This will certainly entail limiting man's individual freedom. A Kansas farmer is no longer free to spray unlimited amounts of DDT on his wheat. But is his freedom limited? Freedom is illusory; it does not exist apart from society. . . .

Man obtains this leisure by constructing a society in which he controls the total system, human and nonhuman, in order to make each individual more productive in obtaining food and in avoiding danger. Societies use many norms to guide the formation of rules for control. . . . A Kansas farmer can have a terminal to the utility, at which he can ask on Monday, September 14, whether he can plant wheat next October. The computer may say yes, weather will be fine, and not too much wheat is being planted this year. The farmer tells the computer that he does plan to plant wheat. This information goes into a large data base. But the farmer is not committed. The next day he can change his mind, delete the wheat crop from the data base, and ask the computer whether he can plant sorghum. If the computer says he can, then he can tell it that his crop will be sorghum. By allowing rapid interaction between the data base and its users, the utility permits relatively free individual action while adhering to a firmly structured national policy.

Even though the farmer is free to change his mind, he must still obey the computer. If it tells him that too much sorghum is being planted, he cannot plant sorghum. But man is beginning to understand the advantage of limiting his freedom. . . .

The Illiac IV can be used for linear programming, a mathematical technique for allocating the use of limited resources to maximize or minimize a specified objective. A typical problem, under study at the University of Illinois, involves optimizing the output of the agricultural sector of the economy. The problem may involve regions ranging in size from a farm to an entire nation, the solution to a problem being the production of sufficient food to feed a population, or to export to starving nations. The resources which will be managed according to the solution of the problem will include land, labor, machinery, fertilizers, pesticides, herbicides, storage facilities and capital. The Illiac IV is large and fast enough to make feasible the solution of this large and complex problem. . . .

The systems will be useful to an untrained citizen who wants to know the best place for a fishpond, as well as to a sophisticated systems analyst who wants to know the best distribution of wheat fields for feeding starving nations. . . .

In order to [treat the cause of pollution], man should build a system of data acquisition, transmission, storage and processing, and usage. It will yield preventive or a priori controls over existing environmental systems. Unless the general public attitude changes more rapidly than in the past this goal may have to be accomplished through governmental coercion.

The concept of reorganizing the existing government agencies or creating new administrative bodies to better control science and technology is not new. . . .

The quantity of data necessary for the proper surveillance and monitoring of environmental systems will no doubt reach astronomical proportions. But of far greater importance is the quality and reliability of the data collected. The lack of a universal validation technique is compounded by absence of standardized methods, instruments and sampling techniques. The present diversities of purpose, measuring instruments, storage media and format, and analytical techniques make the purposeful integration of raw data an extremely difficult task. The centralization of such data collection, which is presently done by a hodge-podge of local, state, and federal governmental agencies, most of which are not part of the EPA, [Environmental Protection Agency] is going to become a necessity.

Once the raw data is uniformly stored in data banks a decision must be made as to how to make the most efficient use of it at the various levels in the governmental decision making hierarchy. Data generally takes three forms in any management information system: raw data, summarized data, and some form of indexing as to the kind and location of the data. The data, in one of the above forms, must be channelled upward from the local agency to the operating agency to the federal regulatory agency. . . .

If the data were to be stored geographically, it could either be kept at the regional level or at the operating level. At the present time the most logical configuration would seem to be a system utilizing the first method of data transmission with the raw data base increasing up to the operating level, where it could be stored in a categorical form. The data base could then be summarized at this level and sent upward to the appropriate federal regulatory agency in the Environmental Protection Agency, where it could be coordinated.

This coordination involves a jump to system design, a vast task requiring a team of experts from many disciplines. . . . [A]fter the data has been collected and stored at the operating level, interdisciplinary teams of experts from such fields as law, ecology, bioengineering, computer science, etc., should be assembled to decide which data is relevant and should be retrieved. In order to facilitate cooperation and understanding, the universities should begin to train multidisciplinarians at the doctoral level. There is a pressing need for sound ecological training with emphasis on new quantitative techniques. . . .

[T]raining programs should be based on concrete problems, with the interaction of faculty and students from different disciplines working together to find socially acceptable solutions. More specifically, the ecology students should receive a strong background in mathematical modeling and computer simulation. The present models will become larger and more realistic. The scope of these models will increase in detail, and interaction among more disciplines will be necessary in defining and developing them in order to help solve the rising ecological crisis. . . .

The federal regulatory agencies will be able to make recommendations, but without the proper legislation they will be powerless to enforce them. The present judicial system is simply not adapted to a technical civilization. . . .

Unfortunately it is not enough for the United States or any other single nation of the world to exercise environmental control. The global circulation of the air and ocean currents make it necessary that every nation of the world exercise some degree of pollution control. Senator Edmund Muskie has proposed that the United Nations be used as a fulcrum to expedite global monitoring of air, water and land pollutants. By forcing all the nations of the world to file a "detailed statement of intention and estimate of affects before undertaking any action capable of impairing the quality of the natural environment" the United Nations would have its first practical tool "to direct priorities, to avoid wasteful duplication, and to assure comprehensive action." . . .

In order to aid governments as they control society for its own good, the computer scientist must try to achieve the social goals he has set himself—intelligent and limited control of terrestrial evolution. . . .

Man was originally an insignificant hunting animal who had little impact on his environment. Compared to a 1971 urban commuter, he was free. He was free of a morning train schedule, and of the need to impress his boss at a golf course. He was free to establish his own schedule, and to run naked through the woods. He was also free to die before he was thirty-five, to suffer illness without medication, and to starve if a hunt did not net the requisite deer. For this primitive savage, "freedom is just another word for nothing left to lose." (From Me and Bobby McGee, song by Kris Kristofferson.)

Since these early beginnings man has developed powerful technologies that have been applied according to the rules of complex societies. These applications assured man more food and safety than he had ever enjoyed, but also destroyed whole races of animals and plants, segments of the landscape, and often even nations of people. Modern man must coordinate the restrictions imposed by his society in order to utilize the power conferred by his technology. On the one hand, he must compromise individual freedom in order to maximize the output of his world. On the other hand, he must encourage freedom so that society answers the needs of its members. The computer can aid in implementing individual freedom while preserving a unified plan of action.

Sustainable Agriculture, 1989

ROD J. MACRAE, STUART B. HILL, JOHN HENNING, AND GUY R. MEHUYS

Although many different descriptions of sustainable agriculture are available, the following one will be used as a starting point for this paper.

> Sustainable agriculture is a philosophy and system of farming based on a set of values that reflect heightened levels of awareness and empowerment. Efforts to ensure short-term viability are tested against long-term sustainability, and attention to the uniqueness of every operation is considered in relation to ecological and humanistic imperatives and global implications.
>
> It involves benign designs and management procedures that work with natural processes to conserve all resources, minimize waste and environmental impact, prevent problems and promote agroecosystem resilience, self-regulation, evolution and sustained production for the nourishment and fulfilment of all.
>
> In practice such systems have tended to avoid the use of synthetically compounded fertilizers, pesticides, growth regulators, and livestock feed additives, and instead rely upon crop rotations, crop residues, animal manures, cultivation, and mineral-bearing rocks to maintain soil fertility and productivity, and on natural, cultural and biological controls to control insects, weeds and other pests.

From R. J. MacRae, et al., "Agricultural Science and Sustainable Agriculture: A Review of the Existing Scientific Barriers to Sustainable Food Production and Potential Solutions," *Biological Agriculture and Horticulture* 6 (1989): 174–175, 207–208.

The potential of this approach, however, goes far beyond its present expression, which has largely been limited to the substitution of environmentally benign products and practices. More significant advances can be expected as a result of developments in the science and art of agroecosystem design and management.

Such a description includes farming systems variously referred to as organic, biological, ecological, agroecological, biodynamic, regenerative, alternative, natural, and permanent. . . .

Many of the new scientific methodologies are being performed by multidisciplinary teams that include people who are not professional scientists. The farmer, and other individuals who are directly involved in the food and agriculture system, are being recognized as having much to contribute to our understanding of ecological processes in agriculture. Farmer associations are being created to perform research. Some investigators even feel that most innovation in sustainable agriculture originates with the farmer. A study of organic farmers in the Midwest U.S.A. found that 62% of them were doing their own research. Brooks & Furtan (1985) have concluded that the higher the level of training and awareness, the more likely farmers are to do their own research, and by our definition, sustainable agriculture requires a high level of awareness. Some organizations have even produced manuals for lay scientists to encourage this interest in home-grown research. The potential value of lay science is reflected in the U.S. Congress O.T.A. [Office of Technology Assessment] (1985:5) conclusion that most innovative research is not taking place in the institutions normally associated with research activity.

Some scientists are already working directly with farmers. Known by many names (participatory research, farming systems research, on-farm research ethnoscience), each varying somewhat in approach, these methods have in common a belief that the practitioner has at least as much to contribute to the process of understanding biological systems as does the investigator. These approaches are also concerned with much more than the natural environment in which farming takes place. Sociocultural, economic, and political factors are all considered to be part of the investigation to obtain a more complete understanding of why certain agricultural practices work and others do not. The farmers' objectives as producers are critical to this understanding.

✠ *E S S A Y S*

In the first essay, Edmund Russell presents a detailed history of the development, testing, and early use of DDT during World War II. He cities evidence that certain scientists and military officials had deep concerns about this powerful chemical, but that this "complex" story had little effect on the "simple" story about DDT's benefits. In the second essay, Angus MacIntyre offers a "political economy" of insecticide use grounded in historical narratives about farmers, the economy, World War II, chemical companies, the U.S. Agriculture Department, research scientists, and southern congressmen. Rejecting the idea that insecticide use was a conspiracy orchestrated by chemical companies, he argues that American agriculture was predisposed to accept pesticides and that the chemicals became imbedded in an extensive web of interests.

The last selection is from Angus Wright's *The Death of Ramón González* (1990). Wright briefly describes the political economy of Mexico's Culiacán Valley and then traces a chain of events leading from American supermarkets to the use of a particularly dangerous chemical by valley growers in the late 1980s.

MacIntyre did not have access to Russell's evidence when he published his article. Would this knowledge have changed his conclusions, or are MacIntyre's and Russell's arguments complementary? What is Wrights's explanation of why dangerous technologies proliferate?

Testing Insecticides and Repellents in World War II

EDMUND P. RUSSELL III

This paper focuses on two stories about insecticide safety in World War II. One is the complex story. People in a bewildering variety of institutions conducted tests and made judgments on insecticide safety in World War II. They usually agreed and sometimes disagreed, but they shared a commitment to developing insecticides that would save lives in war. War conditions influenced their perception about what level of danger was acceptable. Many researchers distinguished between "military" and "civilian" criteria. Formerly classified documents reveal that researchers were very concerned about a wide variety of risks associated with insecticides, especially DDT, but that frightening information was often kept secret.

The other is the simple story. This story drew on the complex story, but it contrasted sharply with it. Whereas the complex story featured an ongoing struggle to compare risks and benefits, the simple story emphasized benefits. Risks had little role in public discussion until after a public image of DDT's safety was formed, and questions about safety were swamped by publicity of benefits.

These stories illustrate not only the influence of war on the development of technology, but on the way technology is understood. World War II offered incentives to conduct unprecedented research on insecticide safety before products were released to the public. War also created incentives to increase production and forecast wide civilian benefits. A direct result of this process was the lionization of DDT, which engendered public and professional enthusiasm for chemical control of insects after World War II. The environmental consequences of that enthusiasm were enormous.

This process also had cultural consequences. DDT passed into American iconography as a symbol of unforeseen effects. DDT was developed to save people from disease and starvation, the story goes, and no one knew its risks until the chemical was widely used. It is a good story, but flawed history. Many of the effects of insecticides that Rachel Carson excoriated in *Silent Spring* (1962) were known or suspected before DDT was released for public use at the end of World War II. The popularity of the "unforeseen consequences" version is a testament to the ability of powerful experiences to mold public understanding of technology. Fifty years after the simple story was first told, it still holds center stage.

A specific goal drove development of insecticides by the U.S. government in World War II: military victory. During World War I, louse-borne typhus had killed 2.5 million

From Edmund Russell, "Safe for Whom? Safe for What?: Testing Insecticides and Repellents in World War II" (paper presented at American Society for Environmental History, Pittsburgh, PA, March 4–7, 1993, and edited in November 1997).

people along the eastern front. Another insect-borne disease, malaria, had crippled French and British troops. As the United States mobilized for World War II, planners took these lessons to heart. By one estimate, half the American troops in malaria-infested areas would probably become casualties in the first mosquito season. Insecticides could contribute to victory by killing insects that transmitted typhus and malaria. . . .

In World War II, one of the services' most important allies was the Committee on Medical Research (CMR), an institution created to organize civilian research on military medicine. . . .

The Committee on Medical Research approached military medicine with the same pragmatism as military medical officers. Their commitment to military victory became clear when the committee decided to keep all medical advances secret. The committee, which included a number of medical doctors, reached this decision after some deliberation. They recognized that, as doctors, they were duty bound not to distinguish between friend and foe. However, they also recognized that a new prophylaxis against malaria, for example, might determine the outcome of the war. The committee decided that patriotic obligations overrode professional obligations.

Consequently, research for CMR was classified.

In 1941, the committee's Colonel James Simmons asked the U.S. Department of Agriculture's Bureau of Entomology and Plant Quarantine (BEPQ) to develop proposals to research insect repellents for mosquitoes and insecticides to kill lice. . . .

BEPQ decided to devote its laboratory in Orlando, Florida, to military projects for CMR. Investigations began in April 1942. Researchers in Orlando saw a distinction between their usual civilian research and their new military research. In their final report, researchers recalled: "Investigations that had been conducted prior to that time were largely for the purpose of developing methods of control for a limited number of species under conditions as they exist in peace time. The new type of mobile warfare required methods that could be applied under a variety of conditions and which would be effective against a wide range of insect species."

Not only did Orlando researchers seek technology suited for mobile warfare around the world, but they also needed to find something fast: "The problems were considered to be of an emergency nature and every effort was made to develop control methods within the shortest time possible." Finally, researchers emphasized pragmatism rather than perfection: "In order to develop practical control measures as quickly as possible all research was designed to obtain information that would be of immediate value in providing a satisfactory answer to a problem. Because of this approach, there was little opportunity to carry on studies of an academic or strictly fundamental nature."

At the urging of Colonel W. S. Stone of the surgeon general's office, the Orlando laboratory made louse powders its first priority. . . .

At the same time that researchers scrambled to find an effective lousicide, they also searched for an effective repellent to prevent bites by malaria-carrying mosquitoes. The National Research Council had been coordinating research by industry and foundations since 1940, but nothing satisfactory had been found. The urgency of the project led researchers to lower their standards for safety. National Carbon Company, for example, emphasized that the emergency called for evaluating insect repellents with different criteria from peacetime:

"To simplify our language we shall call a product for general public use a 'civilian repellent' and that for the military forces a 'military repellent.'

"Up to recently we were working on an improved civilian repellent. Now we are working on a military repellent. This shift in goals appears to have a profound effect on the choice of appropriate acceptance standards for some of the physiological tests.

"The alternative to the use of a civilian repellent is never worse than the discomfort of a harmless bite; while, with a military repellent, the alternative to its use may well be the bite of a dangerous insect with resulting prolonged or serious illness. The civilian repellent is merely a 'comfort' product. The military repellent is a disease prevention—sometimes almost a life or death, product. Clearly the military repellent does not call for such meticulous physiological acceptance standards if their adoption excludes an otherwise desirable product. . . .

"We are in a position right now where we must give heed to these general arguments. We are studying the properties of twenty new repellent chemicals whose dry repellent rating ranges from 125 to 265.

"To apply 'civilian' acceptance standards for Tests B and C, 'Primary Skin Irritation' and 'Human Skin Sensitization,' eliminates all but two or three chemicals and those remaining are of low rating. If on the other hand we apply 'military' acceptance standards we *retain* some 14 or 15 chemicals; eight of which have a rating of 200 or better.

"We now plan to use only the 'military' acceptance standards in rejecting products from further consideration." [Emphasis in original]. . . .

The army's concern about finding a product to protect soldiers from malaria immediately was well-grounded. From the surgeon general's point of view, 1942 was the beginning a "disastrous experience" with malaria. After the fall of Corregidor, a fortified island at the mouth of Manila Bay, American and Filipino troops retreated to Bataan, where they surrendered on 9 April 1942. A regimental surgeon described the dismal health of troops: "To give an accurate word-picture of conditions as they actually existed at the time immediately preceding the surrender of our forces on Bataan would tax the descriptive powers of a rhetorical genius, but in simple language, almost every man in Bataan was suffering, not only from the effects of prolonged starvation, but also from one or both of the acute infections that plagued us throughout the campaign, viz, dysentery and malaria." The *New York Times* trumpeted this failure of preventive medicine in a headline: "Troops on Bataan Routed by Malaria."

The experience on Bataan was not unique. In 1942, troops in Latin America suffered a malaria rate of 108.34 cases per 1,000 soldiers per year, compared to a worldwide rate for the U.S. Army of 7.18. In the China-Burma-India theater, the rate by June 1942 was 127. These numbers paled, however, compared to those in the South Pacific. The first malaria outbreak among allied troops occurred on Efate, a small island in the New Hebrides occupied in March 1942. By April, the malaria rate was 2,678 cases per 1,000 soldiers per annum. On Guadalcanal, the malaria rate was 1,664 per 1,000 per annum in October 1942, and 1,781 in November. Rates in some units were as high as 4,000 per 1,000 soldiers per annum. On average, every soldier in those hard-hit units came down with malaria four times a year. . . .

Just as supplies of insecticides became critical, a savior appeared in the form of a simple molecule called dichlorodiphenyltrichloroethane, or DDT. DDT, which looked so miraculous in 1943, had appeared utterly uninteresting in the United States just two years before. Geigy Company of Switzerland discovered DDT's insecticidal properties in 1939 and offered the substance to its U.S. subsidiary in 1941. The subsidiary declined to market it. DDT's only known use was for the Colorado potato beetle, which the subsidiary considered well-controlled with lead arsenate.

The demands of war led Geigy's parent company in Switzerland to try again. War opened a market for killing lice that had not existed before, led to free research and development by the United States government, and made synthetics attractive because imports of botanical insecticides were cut off. It also broke down barriers between BEPQ and industry. War-induced shortage of rotenone and pyrethrum had led the bureau to revise its policy on testing proprietary products. If a company presented sufficient evidence, the bureau would test insecticides for agricultural use. Plus, the Orlando laboratory tested every sample it could find, from whatever source and no matter how unproven, for military use. In October 1942, Geigy gave BEPQ some Swiss reports showing that DDT was not only efficacious against insects, but "relatively non-toxic to man and animals." It sent a sample of DDT (then known as Gesarol) on 3 November 1942.

The Orlando laboratory found DDT "had insecticidal properties possessed by no other synthetic organic chemical known at that time. The material showed a high degree of toxicity to lice, and the toxic action persisted for an unusually long time." The powder killed lice for at least three weeks, which was "the type of material we were looking for." In February 1943, the lab tested DDT on mosquito larvae. Researchers were thrilled to find that DDT killed *Anopheles* almost completely "at the extremely low concentration of 1 part of DDT to 100 million parts of water. . . . There was reason for real optimism: here was a material exactly 100 times as toxic to mosquito larvae as was phenothiazine, the most effective synthetic organic larvicide previously known." Further tests showed DDT was 25 times as effective as Paris green, the standard anopheline larvicide.

. . . Geigy officials said they could make DDT in the United States. Members of BEPQ and the Quartermaster Corps visited Geigy's plant in Norwood, Ohio, and "encouraged them to proceed as rapidly as possible with the production of DDT." Pilot plant production began in May 1943.

That same month BEPQ recommended, and the army adopted, DDT as a louse powder. . . .

Still unanswered, however, was the question of DDT's safety. No large-scale experiments on humans had been conducted, so planners accorded great weight to the experience of subjects and researchers in Orlando. A report from 11 May noted: "there are men at Orlando who have been in intermittent contact with neocid [DDT] (and some of whom have worn impregnated garments) for some three months, and who give no evidence of sensitization, or of toxic symptoms." Apparently referring to tests by the FDA, the report also said that DDT "is harmless if applied wet or dry for 24 hours to intact or abraded skin of rabbits."

Would solvents affect toxicity? M. I. Smith of the National Institute of Health undertook experiments focusing on absorption through the skin. In May 1943, he reported that painting 5% solution of DDT in kerosene on the shaved bellies of rabbits led to tremors and paralysis. Other experiments showed that 25% DDT solution in dibutyl phthalate killed rabbits.

Feeding tests also produced frightening results. The army's James Simmons later recalled, "The preliminary safety tests, made with full strength DDT, had been somewhat alarming. When eaten in relatively large amounts by guinea pigs, rabbits and other laboratory animals, it caused nervousness, convulsions or death, depending on the size of the dose." But the army was desperate for an insecticide, so, Simmons remembered, "in spite of the earlier rather startling toxicity reports we had asked our people to start a limited manufacturing program [of DDT.]" . . .

While researchers scrambled to assess toxicity, DDT production soared. Geigy expected to make 1000 pounds of DDT per week in May and 10,000 pounds a week in July, which roughly equaled the world production of pyrethrum. The army began contacting other firms to interest them in manufacturing DDT.

In July 1943, the National Research Council held a conference to review the status of insecticides and repellents. The FDA's H. O. Calvery reiterated that DDT killed test animals when ingested, but he felt that "the hazards must be weighed against the great advantages of the materials." Calvery accepted the use of DDT on clothing and in powder form for use against lice, because little DDT in those forms appeared to be absorbed. But DDT should not, Calvery warned, come into contact with skin when dissolved in solvents, because that would greatly facilitate absorption into the body. By this time, Geigy was producing enough DDT in Ohio to find its supply of materials (especially chloral hydrate) a bottleneck in production. The army asked the War Production Board to intervene to provide Geigy with more raw materials.

In August 1943, Calvery reported on DDT's chronic toxicity. Calvery rubbed rabbits with varying amounts of DDT ointments daily. . . .

Calvery's summary was grim: "DDT in solution is absorbed by the intact skin and is very toxic upon absorption. . . . Doses which do not cause death within the first week allow the animals to make an apparent recovery. However, such animals become subject to secondary infections and die from other causes due to lowered resistance. . . ."

At NIH [National Institute of Health], on the other hand, [Dr. P. A.] Neal's team was far less alarmed. Their inhalation studies found that species varied in their response. Mice often died, while monkeys "showed no signs or symptoms of any toxic action." Neal tested aerosols on two humans "without showing evidence of subjective or objective signs of Gesarol [DDT] poisoning." When Neal exposed dogs to "Massive Doses of Gesarol Dust," he found it "caused neither toxic effects nor definite pathological changes." He suggested that *the inhalation of fine Gesarol powder or the ingestion of powdered Gesarol without solvent is not as toxic as might be suspected* [emphasis in original]."

By October 1943, Neal and his colleagues were confident that DDT "posed no serious health hazards." While acknowledging DDT's "inherent toxicity," they concluded that Gesarol was safe when used as an aerosol, dust, or mist. In aerosol tests, only mice had shown symptoms of poisoning. DDT dusts seemed insoluble, plus particles were so large they lodged in the uppermost sections of the respiratory tract rather than in alveolar spaces. Finally, sprays were probably safe because they would expose people to "temporary and comparatively moderate exposure." Rabbits had survived smaller doses without showing signs of poisoning. The team warned, however, that "ingestion of massive doses of Gesarol will be toxic," and cautioned against "heavy contamination of food."

On 27 October 1943, Surgeon General Thomas Parran distributed the Neal team's report with his concurrence that DDT, in the forms tested, "offered no serious health hazards." The army's James Simmons exulted at this "final assurance that the material is not dangerous for use under the conditions which we had selected." . . .

Although the army had decided in May 1943 to adopt DDT louse powder, it had questions about solvent forms. Neal's report freed the army to use DDT for all insects, especially mosquitoes. Simmons "immediately started asking for a great expansion in production. This meant mobilizing the industrial manufacturers, with all of the complex legal machinery required to do so." The pressure to increase production was intense. Medical officers overseas fretted that DDT would not be available in time to stop typhus epidemics, which usually came in winter. In November, one officer complained, "[W]e have gone hook, line and sinker for D.D.T. for disinfestation of the civilian population in the Balkans and all militarily employed civilian labor, and it seems to me that our scheme is going to fall down very badly unless something can be done to get us the amounts wanted."

The rapid expansion of production came through just in time for DDT to play a role in one of the most famous events in the history of military medicine. During the winter of 1943–1944, typhus appeared in bombed-out Naples. Among other measures, Allied health organizations dusted over a million civilians with louse powder. They began with pyrethrum and rotenone powders, which broke the back of the epidemic. Then DDT powder arrived and permitted far wider dusting. This event marked the first time a typhus epidemic was halted in wintertime, and DDT received much of the credit. It was the new wonder weapon of public health. . . .

Until this time, strict secrecy had surrounded the insecticide projects. Now the army decided to go public. James Simmons, among others, began promising that DDT would solve civilian as well as military problems. For the first six months, news of DDT featured only its spectacular benefits with little hint of questions about its risks.

In December 1943, Simmons told the Associated Press that "The wartime development of effective repellents and insecticides will probably constitute the biggest contribution of military medicine to the civilian population after the war—a contribution even greater than blood plasma." He said a secret new insecticide "might be spread like a veneer on walls to make rooms fly-proof." . . .

In March 1944, the same month that the *Chicago Tribune* touted DDT as "harmless," the army summarized its knowledge about safety in a guide for soldiers. Its view was more complicated than the *Tribune*'s. DDT dust appeared to pose negligible risk, but "Since toxic doses of DDT can be absorbed through the skin from oil solutions, care must be taken to prevent continuous contact." It also noted that DDT should be kept away from food because "DDT is poisonous when ingested."

H. O. Calvery was especially concerned about chronic toxicity of DDT including the effects of small amounts eaten over long periods of time. On 30 May 1944, he reported: "Chronic and subacute feeding experiments show that small amounts of DDT in the diet will produce toxicity in small animals, and that the safe chronic level could be very low indeed. Chronic experiments extended over periods of time longer than 35 weeks will be necessary before chronic toxicity of this compound can be adequately assessed."

About the same time, the army approved release of publicity about DDT's remarkable powers that said little about safety tests. For example, the army gave permission for Geigy Company to issue a press release titled "NOW IT CAN BE TOLD." Its first ten pages were filled with news of DDT's development and benefits. On page eleven, one paragraph mentioned that the toxicity of DDT was under investigation at several institutions and that "Research is proceeding as rapidly as good practice permits." In context, it sounded as though there was little news about toxicity to report.

Within the chemical industry, however, rumors began to circulate about DDT's toxicity even while the army kept all reports classified. In July 1944, a trade journal reported that the National Research Council killed a report on DDT toxicity scheduled for an insecticide association meeting: "Enough data was presented in another paper, however, and in over-the-fence whispers, to indicate that there is a certain amount of fire behind the DDT toxicity smoke." One manufacturer was said to be labeling the product "poison."

Worries about toxicity concerns soon found print in more widely-read publications. In July 1944, the Surgeon General's Office was shaken by a report in the *Washington Post*. The article began, "DDT is dynamite for insects, but the Agriculture Department isn't sure some of its magic may not be harmful to man, beast and some insects such as the honey bee." The article said entomologists were worried that DDT might injure plants, and that DDT residues on fruits and vegetables would accumulate in people "to the point of eventual generous poisoning."

A member of the Surgeon General's Office telephoned W. E. Dove of BEPQ. Dove confirmed the concerns in the story while emphasizing that these were questions that needed to be answered. General Stanhope Bayne-Jones of the Preventive Medicine Service reflected that men using DDT dusts showed no sign of chronic poisoning. He noted, "Another statement made verbally by Dr. Dove to Col. Ahnfeldt—I am told— is that this 'scare' was thrown out to keep the farmers quiet while DDT is so scarce."

July 1944 was also the month that researchers began to publish their data on DDT toxicity in professional journals. M. I. Smith and two colleagues at NIH described DDT's effects on animal nerve cells, spinal cords, brains, muscles, kidneys, and especially livers in two articles in *Public Health Reports*.

Science News Letter took notice of the technical articles by Smith et al. It repeated their conclusion: "The toxicity of DDT combined with its cumulative action and absorbability from the skin places a definite health hazard on its use." . . .

Persistence, the trait that made DDT ideal as an insecticide, was also a source of concern. Looking ahead to possible uses of DDT in agriculture, *Science News Letter* said, "[S]cientists would like to know whether the liver or other organs may be seriously damaged by eating it on vegetables and fruits. The amount on each apple or tomato would be small, but in the course of a few years, quite a lot might accumulate in the body from such sources."

By this time, the public had been treated to more than six months of publicity stressing DDT's miraculous safety and efficacy. *Science News Letter* did not reach nearly so many people as did newsreels and newspapers, which had created images of DDT's safety that were not easily erased.

More publications soon followed. H. O. Calvery and his colleagues published their findings in a professional journal in August 1944. They noted that gross pathological changes were "not outstanding in any of the species studied" after being given DDT in various forms. Microscopic pathological changes, however, were common. In five pages of tables, they detailed symptoms for individual animals, with liver lesions being the most common. They warned that feeding experiments showed "small amounts of DDT in the diet will produce toxicity in experimental animals, and that the safe chronic levels would be very low indeed." They said that studies of longer duration would be needed to assess DDT's chronic toxicity.

Meanwhile, Neal found no reason to change his view that DDT was safe. To collect data on the effects of DDT on humans, his team chose to study three men who had been exposed to "extremely great" amounts of DDT while working at the Orlando laboratory. In physical examinations spread over four days, they found that "none of them present definite findings that can be attributed to the toxic action of DDT."

Calvery and Neal brought their results to the entomological community in November 1944, when they addressed the Entomological Society of Washington. Calvery summarized his position as, "More experimentation is needed before we will have clear and full understanding of DDT and the various formulations in which it may be used for insecticidal purposes." Neal, assessing aerosols, "concluded that despite the inherent toxicity, the use of DDT in one to five per cent solutions in 10 per cent cyclohexanone with 85 to 95 per cent 'Freon,' as aerosol, should offer no serious health hazards when used as an insecticide." In December 1944, the *American Journal of Public Health* announced "DDT CONSIDERED SAFE FOR INSECTICIDAL USE." It based its report on a November announcement by Neal. Calvery's concern about other formulations went unmentioned.

The army committee that oversaw insecticide development shared Neal's confidence. It reported in December 1944 that the "possibility of human intoxication was considered slight in the light of the widespread dissemination of instruction as to proper use." The committee did recognize that "an occasional case of intoxication may occur, in which event there is very little known as to effective antidotes."

Unfortunately, soldiers did not always use insecticides in the same manner as Neal. One of DDT's advantages was that it dissolved in almost any organic solvent. The army shipped concentrated DDT to theaters, where soldiers mixed it with whatever solvent was at hand. Although researchers focused their attention on DDT, solvents also posed a hazard. The army found "several cases which had both subjective and objective symptoms resulting from excessive exposure to the vapors or droplets of the solvents used for DDT."

A case in the China-India-Burma theater was typical. The commanding general sent a secret radiogram to Washington in July 1944 announcing that his troops had achieved good results in killing mites by impregnating clothing with DDT in acetylene tetrachloride solution. Impregnation was accomplished "by soaking clothing in a bucket of the solution, wringing out dry and evaporating the acetylene tetrachloride." General Stanhope Bayne-Jones of the Surgeon General's Office fired back this message: "Acetylene tetrachloride more properly known as tetrachlorethane is the most toxic of the halogenated organic solvents . . . this substance must not repeat not be used in open buckets as described . . . but must be employed in closed systems with special precautions to insure against exposure to fumes . . . recommend immediate survey of all pers[ons] who have engaged in process as you have described for signs of liver intoxication or acute central nervous system symptoms." In January 1945, the surgeon general's office suggested that DDT be dissolved in 80 octane gasoline to avoid "the toxicological complications encountered in the use of most solvents."

Although the army threw a tremendous effort into pushing the production of DDT, it expended far less on producing reports about toxicity. When someone in the office of Inter-American Affairs requested information on DDT's toxicity in January 1945, the army replied that it had "never published a comprehensive study" of DDT's safety.

As the end of the war neared and talk of civilian uses for DDT reached fever pitch, the Food and Drug Administration looked for effects of DDT that were of little concern for soldiers. One study, reported in August 1945, showed that DDT accumulated in [the] body fat of dogs. It also appeared in their milk.

The discussion so far has focused on toxicity to humans, which reflects the priority of the army and researchers throughout the war. But as DDT found use as a mosquito larvicide, researchers noticed that DDT could affect a variety of species. In March 1944, the army cautioned its soldiers: "DDT is a toxic agent[. W]hen used at rates recommended in oil or dust the toxic effect is limited to mosq. larvae [sic]. Other animal life that has come in contact with treated areas, such as fish, cattle, fowl, etc. has not been affected. However, if the dose is too heavy fish may be killed, and animals or men using this water for drinking purposes might ingest a toxic dose."

Reports of effects on non-target species tended to come not from medical doctors, who carried out some tests of DDT's efficacy in theaters. They generally came from entomologists and others with broader biological training. Leroy Christenson, an entomologist and captain in the Sanitary Corps, reported in January 1944: "A striking effect of DDT in pools where it was used was its toxicity to all other forms of macroscopic life. Usually the killing effect was a total one with small fish, crabs, and all types of immature insects such as dragon fly, damsel fly, and chironomid (midge) larvae being effected [sic]. Diesel oil without DDT had no ill effect on these types of animals." A British report commented on the same phenomenon: twenty four hours after spraying, researchers found dead prawns, fish, dragon flies, and caterpillars.

Orlando researchers pointed out these problems when they trained military personnel in the use of DDT. Edward S. Hopkins, a major in the Sanitary Corps who studied in Orlando, noted: "One ppm. of DDT emulsion admixed in the water of quiet pools will prevent larvae breeding for about a month. Higher dosage will be fatal to fish life and 2 ppm. is fatal to snakes, toads and frogs."

BEPQ personnel were also concerned about the effect of DDT on beneficial insects. Before World War II, bureau entomologists had stressed the importance of insect predators and parasites for keeping pest insects in check. They had even come to recognize that broad-spectrum insecticides could create pest problems, and DDT was a broad-spectrum insecticide without peer. Tests confirmed that DDT tended to kill most insects, not just target species. In fact, it sometimes killed beneficial parasites more readily than it killed pests. One study found a six-fold increase in aphid infestations in sugar cane plots dusted with DDT. Predators commonly attacked aphids in untreated plots, but they were absent from treated plots. Similarly, fruit trees sprayed with DDT became infested with mites and spiders after lady beetles were killed.

After conducting experiments in Panama, BEPQ's H. H. Stage and C. F. W. Muesebeck fretted, "Biological deserts may be produced by heavy treatments of DDT and these would be, of course, highly undesirable. In fact, any upset in the balance of nature is very apt to produce conditions unfavorable to the general welfare of the plants and animals present. If, for example, insects are eliminated from a large area, young birds may subsequently starve as the result." The bureau's F. C. Bishopp voiced a similar sentiment. "In connection with DDT over large areas, serious consideration must now be given beneficial insects, as well as other animal and plant life because areas devoid of life might be created by too generous and indiscriminate applications of DDT."

These concerns were not merely hypothetical. In its haste to deploy DDT, the army and navy sometimes rushed it to theaters before trained personnel or appropriate equipment were available. Field officers made do with whatever was at hand. A naval medical officer reported the effect of this policy on Espiritu Santo, an island in the New Hebrides: "The first DDT in the Pacific arrived on this island in April 1944. When the Naval Medical Research Unit # 2 arrived there in May it was found that large overdoses had been made and *complete destruction of plant and animal life had occurred* [emphasis added]."

The report from Espiritu Santo contrasted with most by military medical officers, which usually focused on DDT's effects on target species. (USDA entomologists, on the other hand, often mentioned DDT's effects on other species, especially insect predators and parasites.) The committee that coordinated the army's insect control activities succinctly stated its view: "From a military standpoint, it was pointed out that insects fall into two categories: (1) Primary importance; mosquitoes, mites, flies (houseflies and biting flies), lice, fleas and ticks, and (2) Secondary importance; roaches, bedbugs and ants." Beneficial insects and "the balance of nature" did not rise above the horizon. Rather, the army aimed to develop "a single easy method of DDT application to suit all circumstances." Two civilian collaborators summarized the approach: "The ideal treatment would be one which kills not only all adults [mosquitoes] in the treated area *at the time of treatment,* but also whose which migrate into that area *subsequently.* This means rendering the area more or less permanently toxic [emphasis in original]."

These sentiments, and a sudden enthusiasm for eradicating species of insects from the earth, shocked Ross Harrison, an eminent biologist. He "stated that as a naturalist he was appalled by the great number of doctors, soldiers, and scientists seeking means to eradicate insects. As an old zoologist he pleaded for caution and advised discrimination in the extermination of insects with DDT."

Colonel J. W. Scharff, a British malarialogist who praised the role of DDT in protecting troops from malaria, shared Harrison's shock: "As an entomologist and lover of nature, I believe that the use of aerial spraying with DDT should be reserved for serious military emergencies. DDT is such a crude and powerful weapon that I cannot help regarding the routine use of this material from the air with anything but horror and aversion."

Entomologists and malarialogists were not the only scientists concerned about DDT's unintended effects. In May 1945, Clarence Cottam of the Fish and Wildlife Service asked that DDT not be released for civilian use until the service could assess its effects on wildlife. That summer, the service conducted tests at Patuxent River Refuge in Maryland. It found "that at 5 lbs. of DDT per acre, 50 mg. DDT per sq. foot, the population of singing birds was drastically reduced soon after spraying, and that both top-feeding and bottom feeding fish are killed at as low an amount of DDT as 1/2 lb. per acre. . . .

Stage, Muesebeck, Bishopp, Harrison, Scharff, and Cottam voiced these concerns in classified meetings and reports. In public, the Department of Agriculture stressed the need to learn how to use this powerful chemical safely. In April 1945, it released a report saying: "Even if supplies were available, say entomologists, DDT insecticides could not be generally recommended at this time. Too little is yet known about the harm that DDT may do to beneficial insects, plants, soil, livestock, wildlife, or to consumers of fruit and vegetables containing DDT residues."

By this time, however, the image of DDT as a wonder weapon was firmly fixed. The Department of Agriculture complained that "Many farmers have been led to believe that DDT is a panacea for most of their insect problems." For those who saw insects as barriers to health, wealth, or comfort, non-target species were usually of secondary concern or irrelevant. DDT's reputation was so great that Paul Müller, the Swiss chemist who discovered DDT's insecticidal properties in 1939, received the Nobel Prize for Physiology or Medicine in 1948.

A select group of researchers had another concern about DDT during World War II that has apparently remained unknown until now. On 17 August 1944, Ludwik Gross, an army doctor at Camp Forrest in Tullahoma, Tennessee, sent a letter to the army surgeon general. Gross pointed out that DDT may "perhaps be capable of producing tumors in susceptible individuals. No reference to such a possibility, negative or otherwise, has thus far been made in reports on DDT hitherto issued. The possibility of carcinogenic action of DDT should, however, be considered before large scale application of this powerful new insecticide has been undertaken." . . .

By this time, the army was fully committed to DDT. Demand had recently soared when researchers in Orlando developed equipment to disperse DDT from airplanes. Now the army could send fast combat airplanes over the jungle before American troops landed, significantly reducing malaria hazards during invasions, and spray even larger areas afterward. The dream of preventing disease by rendering areas "permanently toxic" seemed within reach. This goal spurred yet another expansion of DDT production. In May 1944, the army estimated that it would need over 4 million pounds of DDT for aerial dispersal in 1945, in addition to some 17 million pounds to be dispersed by other methods.

A Political Economy of Agricultural
Pest Management to 1970

ANGUS MACINTYRE

This paper explores the question of why chemicals became the most widely used pest-suppression technique in American agriculture. In analyzes the major factors and historical trends that favored pesticide use during the period after their first appearance until 1970, but focuses mainly on the decades since World War II. The complex history of the American pesticide scene is not easily portrayed, nor is this intended as a comprehensive account. Indeed much empirical detail remains unpublished. . . .

A brief demonstration that we do use pesticides extensively is warranted before analyzing the reasons for [the] United States dependency upon synthetic chemicals to suppress destructive pests. Production and sales of pesticides grew steadily through the 1970s to a level exceeding half a billion pounds per annum. The economic value of these sales expended even more rapidly (due to increased oil prices), with average yearly increases of twenty percent between 1972 and 1977. Domestic pesticide sales now exceed one billion dollars annually. Further growth is anticipated. . . .

Farm production in America has long been a keenly competitive cash-cropping enterprise in which individuals take large financial risks and sometimes fail to make adequate returns on their investment. This single feature, more than any other, has predisposed farmers to adopt technological innovations that reduce production costs and insure their investments against the vicissitudes of nature. . . .

While pests existed throughout history and periodically caused localized famines, their economic significance grew by the turn of the century. This was due to the widespread adoption of monoculture, the associated decline in crop rotation practices, and the development of higher-yielding but more pest-susceptible crop varieties. Also, several particularly destructive foreign pests were introduced accidentally as world commerce spread. Not only did farm crops become more prone to pest outbreaks, markets became less tolerant of damaged produce. The expansion into distant markets necessitated shipment only of premium quality fruit and vegetables of maximum durability. This was due to fixed transportation costs, and increasing selectivity among competitively supplied urban buyers and consumers. Under these biological and market circumstances, continuing farm prosperity depended upon the ability to control pests. . . .

Because of technology-based productivity gains, United States agriculture became chronically prone to the economic trap in which the uncoordinated actions of many individuals leads to collective overproduction, market saturation, and plummeting prices. This happens because consumer demand for farm products has a low level of elasticity with respect to the quantity supplied. Climatic variation and new technology tended to compound these uncertainties, as did the major wars. While wars increased the demand for agricultural goods, they also created labor shortages and sudden declines in demand with cessation of hostilities. Generally, it was the larger, more heavily-capitalized farmers who survived these disruptive forces by

From Angus A. MacIntyre, Why Pesticides Received Extensive Use in America: A Political Economy of Pest Management to 1970," *National Resources Journal* 27:3 (Summer 1987): 534–577.

staying at the leading edge of technical developments and thus perpetually reaping the short-run income gains. Indeed, the relative cost of farm inputs in the United States has encouraged the substitution of technology, energy and land for human labor throughout this century. Government farm policies compounded the trend.

The extended agricultural depression, between the World Wars, saw the preceding factors and others operate in combination to drive thousands of small farmers from the land. When government intervened with price supports and acreage limitations in an effort to eliminate these destructive fluctuations, the result, once again, was to further encourage the use of technical innovations such as tractors, new plant varieties and fertilizer. By stabilizing farm incomes, price supports enabled larger farms to finance capital-intensive improvements that gave them an advantage over their labor-intensive neighbors. Moreover, with restrictions only on the number of acres planted, prosperous farmers shifted to a more intensive use of land, by substituting technologies such as hybrid seed, fertilizer irrigation, and pesticides. Thus, while price supports may have enabled marginal farms to persist for some years, governmental intercession ultimately contributed to continuing overproduction, economic dislocations and further concentration within the industry. This result occurred because larger farms with stabilized incomes could finance the purchase of their small, less-competitive neighbors.

Finally, few political jurisdictions were tempted to restrain the use of pesticides within their borders. Just as individual farmers had little choice in this matter, counties, states, and even nations relying heavily upon agriculture could not realistically restrict pesticide use. To have done so would have put their farmers at a competitive disadvantage vis-a-vis those in neighboring jurisdictions. . . .

Historically, farmers had difficulty establishing effective political organization. Such a group finally emerged following the Smith-Lever Act of 1914, which provided federal matching funds for the employment of county-level extension agents. The extension task, to transfer new research and technologies onto the farm, necessitated that the county agents develop and maintain a receptive audience. That audience turned out to be the technically progressive elements, which usually consisted of the larger and more prosperous farmers. Perceiving the benefits of government-sponsored research, those locally organized groups amalgamated statewide and then nationally in 1919 to form the American Farm Bureau Federation. Following this innocent beginning, a comfortable mutual relationship evolved as the Farm Bureau and various commodity groups lobbied for government subsidies to solve farm production problems. Meanwhile, the availability of government and industry funding created professional opportunities for research scientists, many of whom came both from farm backgrounds and service-oriented universities. It was a subtle process.

As others have pointed out, this research network soon aimed almost exclusively at surmounting the problems of *commercial* agriculture, where progressive farmers had access to the capital needed for adopting new technologies. Pest suppression was high on the list of research priorities particularly following WWII. Research on chemical methods thrived in this atmosphere of meeting the needs of a growing nation through service to commercial agriculture while other factors inhibited the development of nonchemical alternatives in pest management.

The chemical industry underwent a fundamental transition around WWII, as the production and use of pesticides increased dramatically. Insecticides first received intensive use at the end of the nineteenth century, but only on the most valuable crops. That first era in pesticide technology employed inorganic materials (predominantly copper sulfate and salts of arsenic) and plant extracts (such as pyrethrum and nicotine). Chemically simple or naturally occurring, these compounds were easily produced so a fragmented market emerged with many small, sometimes itinerant dealers, and farmers often mail ordered and mixed the materials themselves. Such conditions made it easy to bilk farmers with adulterated or useless chemicals. Fraud discouraged farmers from using pesticides . . . [and] it was not until WWII that the second era in pesticide technologies took hold. The war precipitated an intense USDA [United States Department of Agriculture] search for useful pesticides. When a Swiss chemical company unveiled DDT to U.S. officials, the new material was rapidly evaluated and recommended for disease control uses by the military. DDT was a dramatic technological success that was turned to public health and domestic agricultural uses soon after the war. It was cheaper and more effective than all existing methods. Thus, DDT and a few other synthetic organic pesticides quickly displaced earlier pest control practices, including the use of arsenical sprays.

The new products were sufficiently cheap and so effective as to stimulate their use against a wide variety of insects previously beyond the economic reach of chemical pest suppression. The corporate response to this lucrative market was rapid. Total production of DDT by U.S. firms increased from 10 million pounds in 1944 to more than 100 million pound in 1951. Over a similar period, between 1945 and 1953, manufacturers introduced some twenty-five new synthetic organic pesticides into commerce, among them some very effective herbicides. . . . [B]y 1950 the chemical industry had become large, product-diverse, and politically well organized. . . .

While estimates of research and development costs vary, they are high, and they are rising. Because of these costs, companies must capture large markets if product-lines are to remain profitable. Hence corporate research seeks chemicals with a broad spectrum of effectiveness. Narrowly-selective products do not usually recoup development costs because their sales are restricted to a few susceptible pests. Moreover, the cost of financing synthetic pesticide production may have reinforced the corporate predisposition for products likely to attract large markets through broad-spectrum activity. Two additional factors tended to exacerbate manufacturer preference for widely-active pesticides. Soon after the new chemicals were introduced, it became apparent than pests could develop genetic resistance to them. The threat of resistance implied that the useful life of any particular pesticide would be limited. This encouraged a strategy of competition by successive introduction of new chemicals—which, in turn, necessitated constant innovation and research. Again, research facilities could only be paid for through larger sales. And more recently, the growing stringency of required safety tests contributed further to the corporate emphasis on broad-spectrum pesticides by increasing the cost of licensing new products for the market.

While the search for broad-spectrum pesticides was certainly successful, their adverse social ramifications quietly mounted. Individual farmers were often confronted with competing products which, from their standpoint, were essentially indistinguishable. This feature, together with the need to educate users to the steady flow of new products, led manufacturers into extensive advertising campaigns and aggressive sales tactics. Most farmers received their information exclusively from the trade tabloids and directly from company representatives. All this competition in sales may have kept pesticide prices down, but low prices also encourage excessive use by the risk averse. Once the highly decentralized system of on-farm marketing was established it became possible (even necessary) for company salesmen to slip into promoting unnecessary and unsuitable uses. Given their personal experiences with crop failure, the fickle nature of their market, and their dependence upon credit financing, it was economically rational for individual farmers to resolve their doubts in favor of taking out insurance, in effect by applying pesticides more often than might be "strictly necessary."

New pesticides, more than many technical innovations, have benefits that are immediate and readily apparent while their costs are far less obvious and occur in the distant future. Their benefits are virtually known in advance since it is the prospect of profitable breakthroughs that motivates the haphazard search for effective new chemicals. On the other hand, the potential costs associated with adopting a technical innovation are often obscure during the initial stages of discovery, and may remain uncertain even after the technology had been in use for several years. Such temporal disparities in our accumulation of knowledge favor a presumption of using new technologies, especially in the case of pesticides where their costs are borne elsewhere (in time and space) by people other than the manufacture/farmer beneficiaries.

This general bias in the appearance of information was compounded by historical circumstances at the time second-generation pesticides were being developed. While evaluating DDT for military uses, the federal government was careful to assess the new chemical's safety. However, under the pressures of war including limited time, dwindling supplies of imported botanical pesticides, and the certainty of disease epidemics, those tests emphasized the acute, short-term toxicity to persons directly exposed. That truncated evaluation confirmed that the acute mammalian toxicity of DDT was indeed low, so the chemical was released for immediate military use. It was safe to apply, effective against a wide variety of pests, cheap, readily sprayable, and persistent. All of these qualities contributed to its substantial war-time successes against insect-borne disease. Extensive publicity portrayed DDT as one of the technologies that helped to win the war and this encouraged its rapid release to civilian uses. Although there were scientists who correctly viewed these gross manipulations of biological systems with skepticism, their protest was futile amid such popular acclaim and unprecedented technological optimism. DDT's early record was so impressive that many entomologists talked for the first time of eradicating the insect vectors of several important diseases.

The cautionary response against DDT was delayed further for a number of other reasons. At the time, pesticides could not be kept from the market place. The available legal recourse had evolved in response to the import restrictions sparked off by excessive arsenic residues. . . . Acting largely on the basis of its experience in setting arsenic residue levels, the Food and Drug Administration [FDA] in 1946 set the same threshold for DDT, as for arsenic, of 7 ppm in food products. The FDA also established a "zero tolerance" for DDT in milk, due to the importance of milk in the diet of infants and invalids.

These FDA regulatory actions were imposed swiftly. They seemed stringent at the time because DDT was believed to be considerably less toxic than lead arsenate, the notorious chemical it superceded. However, analogizing DDT to arsenic turned out to be seriously misleading. As we later found out, DDT's behavior in the environment was dissimilar and its toxic effects were novel. Arsenic salts left residues when sprayed directly onto food, but they were otherwise immobile in the environment, due to their insolubility. Moreover, arsenic residues could be removed from food by careful washing. DDT proved to be entirely different. As a synthetic organic, DDT is oil soluble so it is selectively incorporated into and retained by fatty tissues, which in turn, makes it highly mobile in the environment. DDT is also chemically persistent and thus likely to concentrate in organisms high on the food chain. When DDT was introduced, this chemical bio-concentration behavior was unknown, so it was unimaginable that DDT contamination would cause egg-shell thinning in some species of birds. Experience with first-generation pesticides had provided no basis on which to anticipate the problems with DDT and other synthesized chemicals. Indeed, the understandable but incorrect analogy between DDT and arsenic created a false sense of security and delayed the critical examination of DDT.

We simply did not understand the chronic adverse impacts of DDT. The necessarily truncated war-time testing had not adequately assessed the potential impacts of long-term, low-level exposure. Even with extensive use, these costs did not show immediately. Knowledge of DDT's effects evolved slowly, and then largely because of the independent development of more sensitive techniques in analytical chemistry which made it possible to detect and measure the minute levels of pesticide residue that had become dispersed widely beyond their sites of application. A thousand-fold increase in detection sensitivity made administrative and scientific nonsense of the FDA's "zero tolerance" for DDT in milk. Whereas residues had previously gone undetected, around 1960 it became increasingly apparent that wildlife contamination and human exposure were virtually universal. Only as the methods of detection improved could the science of toxicology evolve. Toxicology was not then sufficiently advanced to definitively assess the significance of DDT exposures. . . .

. . . In 1962, after successive improvements in instrumentation and years of investigation by concerned wildlife biologists, it was Rachel Carson who dramatically pointed to our woeful lack of knowledge. She called for systematic research on the environment and chronic health impacts of pesticide contamination. While expressions of public concern soon waned, Carson's lasting legacy was the private and federal research effort stimulated by the official reaction to *Silent Spring.* By the late-1960s DDT and a number of other synthetic pesticides were discovered to cause cancer in laboratory animals.

Only after three decades of extensive use had exposed all humans did the scientific case against DDT became reasonably clear. In sharp contrast, the initial deployment of that new technology had been a military necessity, an essential humanitarian act in the face of debilitating diseases and a continuing economic certainty for highly competitive agriculture. In hindsight, it is easy to argue that greater initial caution was warranted. Some people did. It must be remembered that our experience with post-WWII chemical technology has taught us what is now known and taken for granted. But once the chemical genie was unleashed, several factors operated against easy containment. It has taken time to translate knowledge about hazards into political action.

The law has difficulty staying abreast of rapid technological change where the costs cannot be anticipated, are slow to be manifested and ultimately remain uncertain.

While the adverse environmental and health effects of the organochlorine insecticides such as DDT were largely external to the farm setting, their heavy use eventually imposed other costs directly upon farmers who sprayed. The biological processes called forth by insecticide use have often necessitated that farmers subsequently make even larger and more frequent applications of these chemicals. . . . The net result of insecticide use has frequently been analogous to the process of drug addition [*sic*]: initial uses were followed by successively larger doses, then by troubled dependence, and eventually by some type of crisis. . . .

. . . When secondary pests began to appear, instead of abandoning insecticides, farmers became even more dependent on them in a treadmill effect. The dramatic successes initially offered by insecticides encouraged farmers to forego a variety of cultural practices that helped to suppress insect pests before the advent of effective, easily-applied chemicals. By coming to rely largely on chemical technology, agriculture made itself especially vulnerable to the failures of insecticides. The broad spectrum of activity that characterized the early synthetic insecticides meant that they killed both beneficial and harmful insects indiscriminately. Resurgent, or secondarily created pest outbreaks were then suppressed with more frequent and more massive applications. Abandonment of cultural practices and heavy reliance upon single, effective methods of pest control intensified the selective pressure, and thereby accelerated the onset of genetic resistance. Resistance was met by using different but equally indiscriminate pesticides. When those methods failed, various combinations of chemicals were used and so on.

The failure of broad-spectrum insecticides was another hidden cost of the technology, but unlike the uncertain risks inherent in widespread contamination, this cost was experienced primarily by the farmers themselves. For farmers who perceived the limitations of pesticides there was no simple escape, because the biological processes or resistance only compounded the economic tyranny of the treadmill in agricultural technology. Single farms contribute little to the onset of pesticide resistance, so individual farmers have little incentive to modify their pest control practices even though collectively their actions lead to declining profitability. Once entire regions of expansion monoculture had been disrupted in this manner, there was often no retreat at all for the individual (by now credit-dependent), except to switch to another (less-profitable) crop or to abandon farming altogether. Alternative methods were sought primarily when the failure of insecticides left insurmountable pest problems that literally threatened the economy of entire regions.

This biological treadmill effect was a conspicuous cause of our growing use of pesticides through the 1950s and the '60s, but it also precipitated a reassessment of the accepted practices. It has been suggested that internal failings of the technology ". . . were ultimately more important in forcing change" than the external protest over environmental contamination and health risks. It is not easy to disentangle these influences and determine their relative strengths. It is clear, however, that both worked toward the same effect, and the internal failure of pesticides eventually motivated some university entomologists, corporate farmers, and certain USDA officials to seek more sophisticated techniques of pest suppression. However, this shift in attitudes was far from unanimous. And even though genetic resistance is now seen as inevitable, chemical manufacturers have retained their commitment to large-market, broad-spectrum, pesticides—which still receive extensive use both within and outside the U.S.

When purchasing produce, consumers generally select the items they find most aesthetically pleasing. Other factors being equal, unblemished apples sell before those scarred by insects. And large, more colored oranges outsell their smaller pale rivals even though the latter may have superior flavor. Consumer behavior provides the basis for a series of formal and informal standards that effectively exclude much cosmetically imperfect produce from the market. Cosmetic imperfections involve superficial damage or alteration of external appearance that does not significantly affect the taste, nutritional value, or storability of produce. Farmers must comply with cosmetic standards or risk having their fruit, nuts, and vegetables rejected. With comparatively little bargaining power, growers respond by applying pesticides more frequently than they might otherwise choose. Thus our own fastidiousness as consumers is said to contribute substantially to pesticide usage. Doubtless there is much to the charge, but what little analysis there is on this question suggests that the causality is at least more complex, and may even be reversed to some extent.

. . . To protect consumers, the FDA maintains maximum allowable defect levels, which include tolerances for the presence of insect debris in processed food as it appears in the market. However, the food processing industry sets unofficial standards that are far more stringent. Processors frequently exceed the FDA standards by applying them to the raw produce as it comes from the farm, instead of the intended point of regulation—their own cleaned and processed output. Furthermore, processors often contract growers to provide produce that is virtually free of insects, weeds or pest damage, and they sometimes stipulate preventative spraying schedules. Condemnation of produce due to insect contamination is a ruinous prospect growers and processors can ill afford. When the processor exceeds federal standards farmers have no option but to comply.

As with fresh produce, however, the real driving force is likely to be competition within the food industry. Food packers and processors use quality standards to reduce their own need for wasteful cleaning and culling, and to restrict the quantity they must buy from contracted growers in high-yielding years. Thus, processors facing stiff competition shift costs back to the farmer to avoid being squeezed between their own fixed costs of processing and transportation, and the inelastic market demand for food. Processors also fear that consumers will turn to rival products (including increasingly available fresh produce) if cosmetically-damaged, or microscopically-defiled merchandise is encountered. As the industry complied with, and actually exceeded existing FDA standards, the regulators have only compounded matters by periodically increasing the stringency of their defect action levels so as not to lag too far behind industry performance. Hence, by regulating harmless insect debris to absurdly low levels, the federal government actively contributes to excessive pesticide use and thereby contravenes its other mandate—to minimize pesticide residues in food.

Cosmetic perfection in food is thus a logical outcome in our economic system, given the technical utility of pesticides, the relatively inflexible demand for food, and the strong tendency toward overproduction. However, it is in food advertising that the image of cosmetic perfection reaches it pinnacle, and presumably works its influence on consumer preferences. Only recently has our massive isolation from the land, and the advent of TV provided opportunities for food packers, processors and supermarkets to "create" demands that have little to do with fundamental nutritional qualities. It is not an inevitable human trait to desire visibly immaculate but less-than-wholesome food. This demand is a consequence of our technical capabilities and our urbanized capitalist system.

Whatever the complex origins of cosmetic standards, they have a number of adverse implications including greater reliance upon pesticides. Furthermore, the outward appearance of perfection, obtained through higher pesticide usage, implies an added, although inconspicuous, threat to health. Worse than elevating our dependence on pesticides, high cosmetic standards actively inhibit the use of alternative pest-suppression strategies. The omnipresent threat of crop-rejection due to a minimal presence of insects or their damage meant that farmers were understandably reluctant to utilize alternative controls, and it remained economic suicide for them to adopt these biological methods unilaterally. . . .

Unlike the second-generation pesticides which had many factors operating in their favor, alternative pest-suppression methods must surmount serious barriers to their initial discovery and scientific development, and then to their acceptance and use by farmers. The alternatives to relying solely on repeated applications of broad-spectrum synthetic pesticides are not easily characterized because they are diverse. They involve various combinations of techniques, among which are: biological control by naturally-occurring or artificially-augmented predators, parasites and diseases; cultural practices that interfere with pest survival and reproduction or facilitate biological controls; plant breeding for pest-resistance in crops; routine monitoring of insect populations in the field to allow minimally-disruptive and well-timed applications of conventional pesticides; and use of highly-specific, biologically-rational chemicals or processes that mimic the pest's own chemical signals and thereby pre-empt successful reproduction.

The common strategy is to rely simultaneously upon the careful integration of many different techniques, and not on one technique heavily enough to induce genetic resistance. The unifying objective is to suppress pest populations to levels just below their threshold for economic damage. Known as integrated pest management [IPM], this approach and its variants have proved extremely effective in many instances, and they almost always result in reductions of both pesticides use and the costs of agricultural production. Despite an impressive history of successes, and considerable potential for reducing pesticide use through new developments in IPM, by 1970 these alternatives remained a conceptual strategy more than a widely-applied method of control.

The development of these new pest control strategies was impeded by serious economic constraints stemming from biological and institutional sources. Each of the alternatives suffers from one or more of the following problems. First, IPM solutions usually apply to a narrow range of situations—often to a single pest species, region or crop. Such narrow applicability confines their potential market. Second, IPM programs necessitate detailed knowledge of the complex dynamics within entire agro-ecosystems and consideration of various techniques in combination, instead of relatively simple data on the susceptibility of single target species to a limited number of chemicals and doses. . . . Third, many IPM techniques involve living organisms and cultural practices that are not readily patented, thus further reducing the incentives for private research. . . .

Because they are highly-specific, knowledge-intensive, or nonpatentable, the IPM alternatives are logical candidates for public sector sponsorship. Indeed, most of the environmentally-benign alternatives already in existence emerged from land-grant colleges and USDA laboratories. . . . WWII seriously curtailed activity in this promising area. Hostilities closed down the search in foreign countries for bio-control agents. Wartime priorities redirected research, funding and personnel toward chemical techniques that promised immediate war-related pay-offs. Once the war intervened, other factors compounded the attrition. Broad-spectrum pesticides had proved so enormously successful that alternatives seemed entirely unnecessary, and research entomologists were understandably infatuated by the opportunities for funding and career development in chemical-related research. Moreover, the pesti-cide industry has never been enamored of government-subsidized research into tech-niques that would compete with chemical sales. Hence, funding for the biological control did not recover to pre-war levels until after 1950. Recovery began only after the belated appearance of problems associated with pesticide use—their external costs (environmental contamination, health hazards) and their internal failures (resurgence, pest creation, resistance). . . . IPM research finally received substantial federal funding early in the 1970s. Following an IPM development, the next serious barrier was convincing farmers to use such pesticide-sparing methods.

Farmers have been reluctant to adopt available IPM technology for several reasons. First, the economics of pest damage and crop protection are intrinsically un-certain. . . . Second, IPM approaches do not eliminate the pest species but maintain them at levels below their threshold for damage. The concept that previously ruinous pests should not be eradicated was unsettling for financially-extended farmers. Third, production loans and growers contracts frequently required pesticide applications. Fourth, cosmetic quality standards that call for produce virtually free of insects and pest damage discourage IPM strategies. Fifth, IPM occasionally requires cooperation between farmers because the technique is not interchangeable with chemical use on a small scale and because farmers cannot unilaterally defy informal grade standards for cosmetic perfection. Sixth, because IPM generally necessitates regular monitoring of insect populations, it implies both additional labor and expertise which farmers are sometimes reluctant to acquire. Finally, the complexity and subtlety of IPM means that education is extremely important, yet many of the channels open to farmers are saturated with news about chemical innovations—channels that are economically and ideologically inimical toward IPM.

. . . As Perkins observes, "Chemicals . . . provided the illusion of complete mas-tery over nature; spray and your enemy was dead, usually before your very eyes." . . . So long as chemicals remain effective, they alone are the pest suppression technique best suited to the political, social and philosophical underpinnings of our highly-competitive, capital-intensive, and individualistic form of agriculture. . . .

The public research establishment evolved in the service of commercial agricul-ture. The tremendous success and apparent safety of synthetic pesticides were soon bolstered in the following manner: farmers and pesticide manufacturers provided the

USDA and universities with political support for research on improved pesticide know-how. Congress funded research on pesticide effectiveness and explicitly discouraged critical research. Meanwhile publicly-funded and industry-contracted researchers developed their careers in this lucrative field, becoming experts on, and champions of chemicals designed to increase the productivity of agriculture "to feed a starving world." An important consequence of these mutually-agreeable interactions was an over commitment of research capability to the discovery, production, and application of chemical technology. Relatively few resources were expended to develop less-disruptive alternatives and even fewer to document the adverse impacts of pesticides. Funding independent from industry or government was virtually nonexistent. Within the land grant college establishment the narrow focus on chemical techniques was reinforced through training while the processes of academic peer review used in the funding, scrutiny and publication of research discouraged the expression of doubts about the beneficence of pesticide technology.

Occasionally these subtle peer pressures on scientific missions became so overt that political pressures were obviously being applied from outside the usual processes of academic review. Skeptical scientists have been harassed, and had their access to publishers threatened or blocked. National Academy committees have been stacked with production-oriented scientists. Government agencies have frustrated research efforts to evaluate the effectiveness of spray programs even when efficacy was in doubt. Research results critical of pesticides have been unreasonably delayed from public release. There has been serious fabrication of toxicity test data (including efforts to cover this up) by a private research facility that relied solely on industry-funded research explicitly intended to meet regulatory requirements. Only the blatant attempts at limiting the scope of conflict are detected while many more go unrecorded. Perhaps more important than all this deliberate obstruction, and certainly more continuous in effect, were the subtle and decentralized influences shaping the entire agricultural research agenda, and the sheer rate of pesticide innovation that continually swamped our limited capacity to assess adverse impacts which are far from obvious or certain. . . .

The American combination of congressional fragmentation, weak political parties, and delegation of law-writing authority to specialized committees has long maximized opportunities for blocking controversial legislation. Yet chairmen of legislative committees retained considerable informal power to oversee agencies within their jurisdiction. Unless there is some concerted showing of outside pressure for change, congressional committees often defined policy discreetly in collaboration with an administrative bureau and the organized interests deeply affected by its operations. These tripartite coalitions, or subgovernments, frequently have the autonomy to adopt and implement seriously biased policies (the agricultural research subsystem is a case in point). . . .

. . . When criticisms of pesticides began surfacing in the late 1950s, each of the agriculture committees effectively shielded and encouraged the USDA policy of unrestrained pesticide use. This was done by steadfastly blocking policy reforms responsive to emerging knowledge about the hazards and failures inherent in second-generation chemical technology.

The agriculture committees proved especially capable of maintaining their hegemony over pesticides from WWII through the early 1970s. Rural interests were

heavily over-represented in Congress until the Supreme Court ordered reappoint-
ment in 1964. Even after redistricting, conservative democrats from the rural South
continued to dominate the legislature, particularly the House of Representatives. In
particular Southerners controlled the entire agriculture jurisdiction in Congress, so
coalition building in agricultural price supports was dominated by cotton until 1973.

This predominance of conservative Southerners was significant for pesticide
policymaking for two reasons. First, cotton had long been a mainstay in the relatively undiversified Southern economy, and second, cotton production experienced
perhaps the worst case of pesticide addiction, escalating chemical use, and successive technological failures. "The production of cotton has utilized more pesticides
than any other single crop in the U.S. since about 1950." . . .

. . . Throughout the 1960's, the regulatory subgovernment responded to critics
with window-dressing but otherwise it refused to restrict pesticide use administra-
tively, and blocked proposals to amend FIFRA [the Federal Insecticide, Fungicide,
and Rodenticide Act, 1947] since all such bills were eventually referred to the agriculture committees. Congress has forcibly overridden its agriculture committees on
publicly visible and vulnerable matters, such as sugar and milk subsidies, but pesticide policymaking did not similarly suffer frontal confrontation or defeat. An important factor contributing to this continuing deference on pesticide policy, even in the
face of mounting technical evidence of policy failure, was the relative lack of public
concern or organized support for pesticide reform. . . .

Absent public concern and until recently, effective citizen groups, the impetus for
pesticide reforms has depended largely upon the initiative of private crusaders such
as Rachel Carson, and the civic-mindedness of non-elected officials. And due to the
subgovernment's tight control over the legislative agenda, virtually the only strategy
left to reformers was to *create* newsworthy incidents in the hope of generating enough
public concern to force elected officials from outside the pesticide power triangle into
this closed arena. . . . *Silent Spring* was the first plainly-written indictment of a technology previously considered humanity's salvation. Coincidentally, Senator Kefauver
made a dramatic media event of America's narrowly-averted thalidomide indifference
toward drug safety legislation. Notwithstanding that remarkable demonstration of the
potential for consumer politics, pesticide hazards failed to develop the popular appeal
of drug safety issues. Carson's charges were reviewed and cautiously vindicated by
the President's Science Advisory Committee which made sweeping recommendations to President Kennedy, who took no concerted actions. He had no desire to annoy
Southern democrats whose support was essential to making legislative progress on his
social priorities. Moreover, although the debate over pesticide risks was no longer a
closed, and strictly technical affair, public attention soon waned when civil rights,
JFK's assassination, the Great Society, and then Vietnam crowded onto the public
agenda. However, Carson had planted a seed but it did not germinate until seven years
later when DDT was implicated as cancer producing.

Pesticides, notably the adverse impacts of DDT and the Agent Orange herbicides,
regained national headlines in 1969 as a secondary concern within the popular environmental movement. Instead of visible pollution incidents, it was a rapid succession
of initiatives by outsiders that challenged the pesticide subgovernment. In that year the
National Cancer Institute announced that several pesticides including DDT caused
cancer in mice (thus shifting the existing emphasis on wildlife impacts to focus debate

squarely upon human health for the first time); the FDA seized large quantities of DDT-contaminated salmon; the General Accounting Office issued two devasting reports on pesticide policy; a non-agriculture House subcommittee held oversight hearings and then released its scathing reports; a private group called the Environmental Defense Fund attained considerable publicity in its Wisconsin trial against DDT; several states banned or restricted use of the chemical; and the Secretary of Health Education & Welfare's [HEW] Commission on Pesticides recommended phasing out all non-essential uses of DDT within two years. The USDA responded deviously to these pressures against DDT. It announced cancellations of almost all used of DDT but quietly retained the registration for cotton accounting for two-thirds of use. Try as they might, the few policy entrepreneurs focusing on pesticides could dislodge neither the USDA nor its congressional sovereigns. Even with these considerable efforts, public opinion reflected only the socially-conspicuous environmental problems—basically air and water pollution. So although public concern for environmental quality reached unprecedented levels, within that overall movement, pesticide hazards remained a stepchild seemingly unable to penetrate the pesticide subgovernment's defenses. Thus, agricultural committees could continue vetoing reform legislation, at a time when the White House and Congress were otherwise competing for credit over the more conspicuous environmental issues. . . .

. . . [S]tarting in the late 1960s, actors from outside the pesticide subgovernment began seeking avenues around some of these obstacles. An important consequence of the subgovernment's blockage and sparse expressions of public concern was that the agriculture committees were eventually circumvented by policy innovations from institutions outside the legislature: first, at the hands of a court; then in an executive re-organization, and ultimately by new administrations.

In response to litigation from EDF [Environmental Defense Fund], a federal judge completely reversed the USDA's interpretation of the pesticide statute by granting standing to citizens' groups and by shifting the burden of proof onto the manufacturer (1970–1971). Concurrently President Nixon transferred the pesticide jurisdiction away from the USDA into an Environmental Protection Agency in response to electoral competition over conspicuous air and water pollution problems (late 1970). New administrators were appointed who turned out to have responsive attitudes, different training, and a broader clientele. Consequently one partner in the original subgovernment had been drastically altered and the statute had been freshly reinterpreted.

The agriculture committees sought to regain their hegemony while amending FIFRA in 1972, but the result largely ratified the changes imposed earlier by judicial and executive outsiders. A number of new regulatory powers were delegated but the agriculture committees simultaneously provided themselves (and thus pesticide interests) with additional opportunities to intervene. EPA administrators, with little support, exerted tremendous initiative throughout the 1970s. They adopted stringent standards for pesticide registration which included a general presumption against cancer-causing chemicals. This was a significant accomplishment, particularly with respect to applications for the registration of new chemicals. However, severe resource constraints and pro-pesticide lobbying effectively stalled the retroactive implementation of EPA's anti-cancer innovation. While new products faced tough standards for the first time, little more than a handful of the 1,400 chemicals previously licensed were banned.

Meanwhile, farm use of pesticides increased by more than fifty percent during that decade of environmental regulation. Agricultural uses of herbicides increased from 207 million pounds in 1971 to 451 million pounds in 1982. Over that same period, however, the use of insecticides declined from 126 million pounds to 71 million pounds. Among the obvious contributions to this declining use of insecticides were the increasing incidence of insect resistance and technology failures, the large influx of federal funding for IPM research following 1970, and the consequent growth in practical applications of IPM by corporate agriculture since the mid-1970s. . . . Thus the biological, economic, technological, legal, and political forces that encouraged pesticide use have all been undergoing a gradual, if incomplete and uneven, metamorphosis. It remains to be seen how far and how rapidly the diminution in insecticide use will proceed, how successful IPM approaches have become, and whether herbicide use will continue to escalate.

Aerial Spraying in Mexico

ANGUS WRIGHT

The changes in Mexico associated with rising chemical dependence in agriculture are changes that must be understood by those north of the border. The exodus from the Mexican countryside and the explosive growth of the entire population, combined with a formerly dynamic but currently stagnating economy, are all intimately connected with the project of agricultural modernization. These things also mean two vital things to those who live in the United States. There will be a rapidly growing flow of Mexicans into the United States, and there will be insistent demands for radical political changes in Mexico of a kind that the government of the United States is likely to see as extremely threatening to the security of the United States. . . . [T]he combination of political change in Mexico and a migration of more Mexicans into the United States will present transcendently important and complicated challenges to the government and people of the United States. Surprisingly enough, the story of how pesticides came to be so badly abused in Mexico is a good place to begin in coming to an understanding of the nature of these challenges. . . .

The multimillion-dollar annual harvest of the Culiacán Valley includes so many vegetables for export to the United States that Culiacán alone accounts for about a third to a half of the tomatoes, cucumbers, bell peppers, summer squash, zucchini, eggplants, and chili peppers sold in the United States between December and May. Valley farmers also grow safflower for oil, sugarcane, alfalfa, wheat, soybeans, and corn. The Culiacán Valley and its continued productivity are always a central concern of investment bankers and government economists a thousand miles south in Mexico City. . . .

Culiacán has been strongly connected to the economy of the United States for a long time. Relatively small-scale irrigation projects built in the nineteenth century provided water for sugar, cotton, and fresh vegetable production. Seventy-five percent of the irrigated land was owned by U.S. firms before the Mexican Revolution of 1910.

From Angus Wright, *The Death of Ramón Gonzáles: The Modern Agriculture Dilemma* (Austin: University of Texas Press, 1990), pp. xvii, 11–12, 15–21.

The land laws of the 1917 Constitutions made such ownership illegal, but U.S. companies are still strongly present in Sinaloa. Some land is owned by *prestanombres,* name loaners, who provide a front for foreign owners. Most of the financing for the vegetable farms comes from U.S. firms—according to the head of the National Union of Vegetable Growers, about 90 percent. . . .

Battles for control of the land have been prolonged and bitter. The corruption of the Mexican land reform system makes it possible for large landholders to operate under the cover of legal forms intended for cooperative owners or small private landowners. Small landholders and peasant groups and communities have fought back, and landholders have retaliated through their own private security forces, *la guardia blanca,* with the help of the state and municipal police force at times. Through the 1960s and 1970s these conflicts were often violent, with land invasions by peasants, kidnappings, and murders. But the real control the large landholders have is their integration with the private and public credit institutions, their control over the market, and their ability to corrupt or intimidate agrarian reform officials. Through the exercise of these various forms of control, they have largely excluded true small holders and cooperative farms from the valley in violation of the spirit and often the letter of the agrarian reform legislation. The most frequent legal facade for these operations is to rent land from the legal small holders or cooperatives, but the fact and conditions of rental are completely determined by the large landholder, who uses corruption and the threat of force to obtain rental agreements from people who know from experience that if they do not cooperate, they cannot succeed as farmers in the face of the opposition of the large operators. The small holders and cooperative members "end up as wage labor peons working on their land." . . .

[In 1987, about 250,000 migrant workers came to the Culiacán Valley to plant, cultivate, and harvest the vegetables to be exported north. The workers lived in squalid camps, or *campamentos.*] . . . [I]n many important ways the conditions of the camps [on the large farms] were . . . hazardous to the farm workers. This was especially true because of a major change that had been made in the kind of pesticides most frequently used by the growers. Pesticides that presented one set of hazards had been replaced by other pesticides that brought equal or greater danger of a different kind. The implications of this transformation cannot be understood without a brief description of the characteristics of some of the most widely used pesticides.

One way of classifying chemical pesticides is according to the time it takes them to break down into other compounds once they are released into the environment. There are the *persistent* pesticides that have half-lives—the amount of time it takes for half the material to break down into something else—measured in months, years, or decades. Among these persistents are most of the chlorinated hydrocarbons such as DDT, BHC, Toxaphene, aldrin, dieldrin, endrin, chlordane, lindane, and many others. It was the persistents that were most widely used in Culiacán until the late 1970s and the early 1980s.

There is a second class of pesticides that are *nonpersistent,* with half-lives of hours, days, or weeks. . . . The nonpersistent pesticides began to replace the persistents in Culiacán beginning in the late 1970s. By 1983, the nonpersistents had become dominant.

The nonpersistent chemicals are, in general and with important exceptions, much more acutely toxic than the persistents. . . .

Although the persistent DDT has only 2 to 5 percent of the acute toxicity of the nonpersistent parathion, DDT is the chemical that has been much more widely banned or restricted. . . . A nonpersistent such as parathion, on the other hand, will be a much more severe problem at the time and in the place of its release, but its rapid decay presumably assures that its overall effect on the environment will be less lasting, less complex, and more easily managed. It is for this reason that environmentalists in particular have worked hardest to limit the use of the persistent pesticides, even though the nonpersistents are typically much more acutely toxic to humans and most animals. . . .

Between my first visit to the fields of Culiacán in 1980 and my later visits in 1983 and later, a major shift occurred in pesticide use patterns, from heavy use of the persistents to the substitution of the nonpersistents. . . . [P]ests were becoming strongly resistant to the persistents because the persistents had been used more commonly than the nonpersistents. The persistents are typically cheaper than the nonpersistents, which accounts for the fact that they were the group used most in the early decades of synthetic pesticide use. . . . With time, though, growers were forced to shift to the generally more expensive nonpersistent pesticides as resistance grew in target pest populations.

The second reason for shifting to the nonpersistents has to do with the political and public relations problems of Culiacán growers in relation to their markets in the United States. As the persistents, such as DDT and the "drins" (aldrin, dieldrin, endrin), were more and more heavily restricted in the United States and other highly developed countries due to concerns over their environmental effects and their possible role in long latency diseases such as cancer, journalists and other researchers noted that these chemicals were still being commonly used in Mexico and other Third World countries. Chemical companies were marketing the persistents even more aggressively in the Third World in order to recover investments lost in richer countries. . . .

. . . In a muckraking book called *The Circle of Poison* (1981), journalists Weir and Shapiro called public attention to the fact that consumers in the United States were eating pesticides that had been manufactured in the United States and Europe, exported to places like Mexico because the chemicals were no longer allowed in the country of manufacture, and imported back into the United States and Europe as residues on food. This image of a circle of poison captured the imagination of many consumers and the attention of national and state legislators. Residue inspection programs at the border were somewhat improved, some consumers turned away from imports, and the Culiacán growers became seriously concerned about the loss of markets in the United States.

Mexican growers talked to Mexican public officials, who in turn talked to their counterparts in the United States. Agencies in the two countries signed technical agreements for the exchange of information, and technical advisers from the U.S. agencies offered their services to Mexico under the terms of the agreements. Upon consultation, the judgment that many growers had made on their own took hold—if the growers would switch even more rapidly than they already were switching (as a response to resistance in pests) to the nonpersistent pesticides, they would run fewer risks of losing out to competing growers in other countries and in Florida. With the combined incentive of responding to pest resistance and concerns of consumers in the United States, the Culiacán growers made a decisive turn to the use of the non-persistent, very acutely toxic pesticides.

The logic of this shift was straightforward. Since the nonpersistents break down more rapidly, it would be easier to deliver vegetables to distant markets with low residue levels. Pesticides applied on crops would be largely decomposed by the time they reached the consumer. And since the nonpersistents were still largely permitted in the United States, any residue problems that did exist would not be different in kind from the residues encountered on domestic produce.

The trend toward the very acutely toxic nonpersistents in Culiacán had immediate and tragic consequences for farm workers. Most of the nonpersistent pesticides, as mentioned, are very acutely toxic. International, industry-supported standards require that anyone using such chemicals as parathion, methamidophos, guthion, phosdrin, or aldicarb should be thoroughly protected against contact with the poison through inhalation, ingestion, or skin absorption. In most cases, this means that people working with the chemical or working in fields recently sprayed with the substance should wear rubber shoes, a rubber apron or rubber coveralls, a hat, preferably of rubber or vinyl, and a mask or respirator.

In casual observation of hundreds of pesticide spray applications and systematic observation of fifty-two operations in the agricultural season of 1983–84, I never observed workers using any of this protective gear. In observation of ten spray operations in 1987, I observed one instance in which mixers using very acutely toxic materials were equipped with masks that they put on for a few minutes from time to time, and the pilot whose plane was spraying the mixture wore a respirator. In the other nine instances, foremen had made no provision for protective measures or gear. Even in the 1987 case of the mixers and pilot who had some protection, the pilot sprayed his highly toxic brew in a field only a few hundred yards from a *campamento* housing hundreds of people, and an old man and a young girl carrying a baby walked along the border of the field as it was being sprayed, with the material visibly drifting over them.

Although lack of proper gear is routine, it is certainly not the only abuse of safe pesticide use practices one observes in the fields of Culiacán. Growers have a choice of three different methods for pesticide application. They may order spraying by light aircraft, by tractor-drawn rigs, or by backpack spray rigs carried by individual workers, usually working in crews.

Aerial applicators operate in almost complete disregard for internationally recognized safety practices. In three instances, I observed aircraft spraying directly over crews of twenty to thirty workers—the sprays consisted of organophosphate insecticides mixed with copper and manganese-based fungicides. A television crew from CBS in Los Angeles filmed such an incident during the time I was doing fieldwork in Culiacán. A social worker employed by the growers' association told me, "We try to tell them how to protect themselves; to wear the proper gear, and to exhale when the plane passes over them in the field."

A common sight in Culiacán is a man standing at the edge of a field with an upraised flag, signalling to an approaching spray plane. The *bandalillero,* or flagman, is assigned the task of marking the boundary of the last pass taken by the pilot in spraying the field. Without such a moving marker, the pilot cannot determine where to fly without gaps and overlaps in the spray pattern. The flagman is sprayed dozens, even hundreds of times a day. Most flagmen run at the last minute to stay out of the thickest of the pesticide fog, but they nonetheless suffer heavy exposure. By universally recognized standards of safe practice, the *bandalillero* should be wearing a mask or respirator approved for use with the type of pesticides being used, and he should be well covered from head to foot in protective, impermeable gear. In observation of twenty-three *bandalilleros* at work in the Culiacán Valley, I never observed the use of any protective clothing other than a light cotton bandana worn across the face. . . .

Since the *campamentos* are in almost all cases surrounded on two, three, or four sides by fields running right up to the living areas, the lack of drift control means that everyone living in the camps is exposed to a variety of acutely toxic substances on a more or less regular basis, even in the case of children too young to work in the fields.

🜨 *F U R T H E R   R E A D I N G*

Dunlap, Thomas R. *DDT, Scientists, Citizens, and Public Policy* (Princeton, NJ: Princeton University Press, 1981).

Fitzgerald, Deborah. *The Business of Breeding* (Ithaca: Cornell University Press, 1990).

Graham, Frank. *The Dragon Hunters* (New York: E.P. Dutton, 1984).

Marco, Gino J., Robert M. Hollingsworth, and William Durham, eds. *Silent Spring Revisited* (Washington, DC: American Chemical Society, 1987).

McCormick, John. *The Global Environmental Movement* (New York: Wiley, 1995).

McPhee, John. *The Control of Nature* (New York: Farror, Straus, Giroux, 1989).

Pearse, Andre. *Seeds of Plenty, Seeds of Want* (Oxford, England: Clarendon Press, 1980).

White, Richard. *The Organic Machine: The Remaking of the Columbia River* (New York: Hill and Wang, 1995).

Worster, Donald, ed. *The Ends of the Earth: Perspectives on Modern Environmental History* (Cambridge, England: Cambridge University Press, 1988).

The Military-Industrial-University Complex, 1945–1990

╫

In American (and world) history, war and the preparations for it have had an extraordinary influence on technological change, industrialization, and economic development. In terms of scale and impact, however, World War II marked a dramatic departure in the application of science and engineering to military operations. The most famous example is the Manhattan Project, which resulted in atomic weapons and the devastation of Hiroshima and Nagasaki in 1945. But the massive wartime deployment of engineers and scientists also spawned a large array of new technologies, including radar, the proximity fuse, antibiotics, new chemical insecticides, analog and electronic digital computers, and the mass production of everything from tanks to paratrooper boots.

The institutional arrangements that fostered these technologies were equally unprecedented. Partly through the efforts of Vannevar Bush, an academician, engineer, and entrepreneur, a productive (and, as it turned out, lasting) alliance was forged during the war years among academic scientists, engineers, and the military. Research universities became integral components of what President Dwight Eisenhower would later describe as the "military-industrial complex." University involvement in the war effort influenced not only military-industrial matters but the shape of higher education in the postwar period.

In contrast to the Civil War, the Spanish-American War, and World War I, the United States did not completely demobilize with the defeat of the Axis powers in 1945. The close relationship that the federal government had forged with industry and academia during the war extended into the Cold War, an arrangement just as evident in the laboratories of Stanford and MIT as in the factories of General Electric and Boeing. Who were the architects of the new arrangement between industry, academia, and the military and what were their objectives? What effect did the new arrangement have on the kind of science and engineering that was supported in postwar America, and what were its implications for the larger political economy?

What controversies were generated by Eisenhower's identification of a "military-industrial complex" in America? How has the end of the Cold War altered the nature of the debate?

⋈ D O C U M E N T S

The first selection is from Vannevar Bush's 1945 report to President Harry Truman, entitled *Science—The Endless Frontier.* By associating science with the idea of the frontier, Bush touched on a legendary historical theme with patriotic and expansionist implications. He suggested that civilian—especially academic—engineers and scientists could contribute to American security and welfare. By calling for a permanent government institution (the National Research Foundation) to fund and coordinate scientific research, Bush's report laid the cornerstone for a federal science policy in the postwar era. In Bush's conception, science meant "big science." The fifty-year period that ended in 1990 with the breakup of the Soviet Union is frequently referred to as the "Vannevar Bush era" of American science and technology.

Bush's positive attitude contrasts with the somber note sounded in the second selection, from Eisenhower's 1961 farewell address. Why did Eisenhower, a war hero and a product of the American military establishment, feel compelled to voice concern over the so-called military-industrial complex and scientific-technological elite?

Although Eisenhower's warning was duly noted at the time, it did not become a subject of intense commentary and criticism until after the United States became embroiled in the war in Vietnam. One of the earliest and most outspoken critics of that conflict was Senator William Fulbright of Arkansas. In the third selection, Fulbright condemns the war and its corrosive effects while pointing to contract-hungry research universities as key components of the military-industrial complex.

The military-industrial complex had its defenders. One of the staunchest was Senator Barry Goldwater of Arizona. In the fourth selection, Goldwater explains why a large military establishment is necessary and criticized the Lyndon Johnson administration—especially Secretary of Defense Robert McNamara and his assistants (the so-called whiz kids)—for mishandling affairs at the Pentagon. In Goldwater's view, McNamara's "civilian complex," not the military, deserved the blame for whatever shortcomings existed at the Defense Department.

As has no other foreign conflict before it, the Vietnam War brought American society to a boiling point. Intense controversy arose over the social role of military institutions. Although critics continued to condemn the university community's involvement with the military long after the Vietnam War, other commentators saw advantages in maintaining the relationship. In the fifth selection, Westinghouse engineer C. A. Hudson describes military-industrial-university cooperation in developing computer-aided-manufacturing (CAM). The sixth selection, a 1983 article from *Newsweek,* links university and military research on supercomputers to the trade war with Japan.

In the last selection, Senator Jeff Bingaman of New Mexico and Admiral Bobby Inman single out the Department of Defense's Advanced Research Projects Agency (ARPA) as the most important sponsor of research in computer science and material science since the 1960s. Bingaman and Inman propose ARPA as a perfect instrument for creating a national technology base to serve both military and commercial needs in the post–cold war era.

Science—The Endless Frontier, 1945

VANNEVAR BUSH

We all know how much the new drug, penicillin, has meant to our grievously wounded men on the grim battlefronts of this war—the countless lives it has saved—the incalculable suffering which its use has prevented. Science and the great practical genius of this nation made this achievement possible.

Some of us know the vital role which radar has played in bringing the United Nations to victory over Nazi Germany and in driving the Japanese steadily back from their island bastions. Again it was painstaking scientific research over many years that made radar possible.

What we often forget are the millions of pay envelopes on a peacetime Saturday night which are filled because new products and new industries have provided jobs for countless Americans. Science made that possible, too.

In 1939 millions of people were employed in industries which did not even exist at the close of the last war—radio, air conditioning, rayon and other synthetic fibers, and plastics are examples of the products of these industries. But these things do not mark the end of progress—they are but the beginning if we make full use of our scientific resources. New manufacturing industries can be started and many older industries greatly strengthened and expanded if we continue to study nature's laws and apply new knowledge to practical purposes.

Great advances in agriculture are also based upon scientific research. Plants which are more resistant to disease and are adapted to short growing seasons, the prevention and cure of livestock diseases, the control of our insect enemies, better fertilizers, and improved agricultural practices, all stem from painstaking scientific research.

Advances in science when put to practical use mean more jobs, higher wages, shorter hours, more abundant crops, more leisure for recreation, for study, for learning how to live without the deadening drudgery which has been the burden of the common man for ages past. Advances in science will also bring higher standards of living, will lead to the prevention or cure of diseases, will promote conservation of our limited national resources, and will assure means of defense against aggression. But to achieve these objectives—to secure a high level of employment, to maintain a position of world leadership—the flow of new scientific knowledge must be both continuous and substantial. . . .

It has been basic United States policy that Government should foster the opening of new frontiers. It opened the seas to clipper ships and furnished land for pioneers. Although these frontiers have more or less disappeared, the frontier of science remains. It is in keeping with the American tradition—one which has made the United States great—that new frontiers shall be made accessible for development by all American citizens.

From Vannevar Bush, *Science—The Endless Frontier: A Report to the President* (Washington, DC: U.S. Government Printing Office, 1945), pp. 5–6, 12–14, 25–28.

Moreover, since health, well-being, and security are proper concerns of Government, scientific progress is, and must be, of vital interest to Government. Without scientific progress the national health would deteriorate; without scientific progress we could not hope for improvement in our standard of living or for an increased number of jobs for our citizens; and without scientific progress we could not have maintained our liberties against tyranny. . . .

From early days the Government has taken an active interest in scientific matters. During the nineteenth century the Coast and Geodetic Survey, the Naval Observatory, the Department of Agriculture, and the Geological Survey were established. Through the Land Grant College Acts the Government has supported research in state institutions for more than 80 years on a gradually increasing scale. Since 1900 a large number of scientific agencies have been established within the Federal Government, until in 1939 they numbered more than 40.

Much of the scientific research done by Government agencies is intermediate in character between the two types of work commonly referred to as basic and applied research. Almost all Government scientific work has ultimate practical objectives but, in many fields of broad national concern, it commonly involves long-term investigation of a fundamental nature. Generally speaking, the scientific agencies of Government are not so concerned with immediate practical objectives as are the laboratories of industry nor, on the other hand, are they as free to explore any natural phenomena without regard to possible economic applications as are the educational and private research institutions. Government scientific agencies have splendid records of achievement, but they are limited in function.

We have no national policy for science. The Government has only begun to utilize science in the nation's welfare. There is no body within the Government charged with formulating or executing a national science policy. There are no standing committees of the Congress devoted to this important subject. Science has been in the wings. It should be brought to the center of the stage—for in it lies much of our hope for the future. . . .

. . . But we must proceed with caution in carrying over the methods which work in wartime to the very different conditions of peace. We must remove the rigid controls which we have had to impose, and recover freedom of inquiry and that healthy competitive scientific spirit so necessary for expansion of the frontiers of scientific knowledge.

Scientific progress on a broad front results from the free play of free intellects, working on subjects of their own choice, in the manner dictated by their curiosity for exploration of the unknown. Freedom of inquiry must be preserved under any plan for Government support of science. . . .

In this war [World War II] it has become clear beyond all doubt that scientific research is absolutely essential to national security. The bitter and dangerous battle against the U-boat was a battle of scientific techniques—and our margin of success was dangerously small. The new eyes which radar supplied to our fighting forces quickly evoked the development of scientific countermeasures which could often blind them. This again represents the ever continuing battle of techniques. The V-1 attack on London was finally defeated by three devices developed during this war and used superbly in the field. V-2 was countered only by capture of the launching sites. . . .

There must be more—and more adequate—military research during peacetime. We cannot again rely on our allies to hold off the enemy while we struggle to catch up. Further, it is clear that only the Government can undertake military research; for it must be carried on in secret, much of it has no commercial value, and it is expensive. The obligation of Government to support research on military problems is inescapable.

Modern war requires the use of the most advanced scientific techniques. Many of the leaders in the development of radar are scientists who before the war had been exploring the nucleus of the atom. While there must be increased emphasis on science in the future training of officers for both the Army and Navy, such men cannot be expected to be specialists in scientific research. Therefore a professional partnership between the officers in the Services and civilian scientists is needed. . . .

One of our hopes is that after the war there will be full employment, and that the production of goods and services will serve to raise our standard of living. We do not know yet how we shall reach that goal, but it is certain that it can be achieved only by releasing the full creative and productive energies of the American people.

Surely we will not get there by standing still, merely by making the same things we made before and selling them at the same or higher prices. We will not get ahead in international trade unless we offer new and more attractive and cheaper products.

Where will these new products come from? How will we find ways to make better products at lower cost? The answer is clear. There must be a stream of new scientific knowledge to turn the wheels of private and public enterprise. There must be plenty of men and women trained in science and technology for upon them depend both the creation of new knowledge and its application to practical purposes.

More and better scientific research is essential to the achievement of our goal of full employment. . . .

Basic research is performed without thought of practical ends. It results in general knowledge and an understanding of nature and its laws. . . .

. . . It provides scientific capital. It creates the fund from which the practical applications of knowledge must be drawn. New products and new processes do not appear full-grown. They are founded on new principles and new conceptions, which in turn are painstakingly developed by research in the purest realms of science.

Today, it is truer than ever that basic research is the pacemaker of technological progress. In the nineteenth century, Yankee mechanical ingenuity, building largely upon the basic discoveries of European scientists, could greatly advance the technical arts. Now the situation is different.

A nation which depends upon others for its new basic scientific knowledge will be slow in its industrial progress and weak in its competitive position in world trade, regardless of its mechanical skill. . . .

Publicly and privately supported colleges and universities and the endowed research institutes must furnish both the new scientific knowledge and the trained research workers. These institutions are uniquely qualified by tradition and by their special characteristics to carry on basic research. They are charged with the responsibility of conserving the knowledge accumulated by the past, imparting that knowledge to students, and contributing new knowledge of all kinds. It is chiefly in these institutions that scientists may work in an atmosphere which is relatively free from the adverse pressure of convention, prejudice, or commercial necessity. At their best they provide the scientific worker with a strong sense of solidarity and security, as well as a substantial degree of personal intellectual freedom. All of these factors are of great importance in the development of new knowledge, since much of new knowledge is certain to arouse opposition because of its tendency to challenge current beliefs or practice.

Industry is generally inhibited by preconceived goals, by its own clearly defined standards, and by the constant pressure of commercial necessity. Satisfactory progress in basic science seldom occurs under conditions prevailing in the normal industrial laboratory. There are some notable exceptions, it is true, but even in such cases it is rarely possible to match the universities in respect to the freedom which is so important to scientific discovery. . . .

If the colleges, universities, and research institutes are to meet the rapidly increasing demands of industry and Government for new scientific knowledge, their basic research should be strengthened by use of public funds. . . .

There are within Government departments many groups whose interests are primarily those of scientific research. Notable examples are found within the Departments of Agriculture, Commerce, Interior, and the Federal Security Agency. These groups are concerned with science as collateral and peripheral to the major problems of those Departments. These groups should remain where they are, and continue to perform their present functions. . . .

By the same token these groups cannot be made the repository of the new and large responsibilities in science which belong to the Government and which the Government should accept. . . . [N]owhere in the governmental structure receiving its fund from Congress is there an agency adapted to supplementing the support of basic research in the universities, both in medicine and the natural sciences; adapted to supporting research on new weapons for both Services; or adapted to administering a program of science scholarships and fellowships.

A new agency should be established, therefore, by the Congress for th[is] purpose. Such an agency, moreover, should be an independent agency devoted to the support of scientific research and advanced scientific education alone. . . . Research is the exploration of the unknown and is necessarily speculative. It is inhibited by conventional approaches, traditions, and standards. It cannot be satisfactorily conducted in an atmosphere where it is gauged and tested by operating or production standards. Basic scientific research should not, therefore, be placed under an operating agency whose paramount concern is anything other than research. Research will always suffer when put in competition with operations. . . .

I am convinced that these new functions should be centered in one agency. Science is fundamentally a unitary thing. The number of independent agencies should be kept to a minimum. . . .

The agency to administer such funds should be composed of citizens selected only on the basis of their interest in and capacity to promote the work of the agency. They should be persons of broad interest in and understanding of the peculiarities of scientific research and education.

The agency should promote research through contracts or grants to organizations outside the Federal Government. It should not operate any laboratories of its own.

Support of basic research in the public and private colleges, universities, and research institutes must leave the internal control of policy, personnel, and the method and scope of the research to the institutions themselves. This is of the utmost importance. . . .

... [M]ilitary preparedness requires a permanent, independent, civilian-controlled organization, having close liaison with the Army and Navy, but with funds direct from Congress and the clear power to initiate military research which will supplement and strengthen that carried on directly under the control of the Army and Navy. As a temporary measure the National Academy of Sciences has established the Research Board for National Security at the request of the Secretary of War and the Secretary of the Navy. This is highly desirable in order that there may be no interruption in the relations between scientists and military men after the emergency wartime Office of Scientific Research and Development goes out of existence. The Congress is now considering legislation to provide funds for this Board by direct appropriation.

I believe that, as a permanent measure, it would be appropriate to add to the agency needed to perform the other functions recommended in this report the responsibilities for civilian-initiated and civilian-controlled military research. The function of such a civilian group would be primarily to conduct long-range scientific research on military problems—leaving to the Services research on the improvement of existing weapons.

Some research on military problems should be conducted, in time of peace as well as in war, by civilians independently of the military establishment. It is the primary responsibility of the Army and Navy to train the men, make available the weapons, and employ the strategy that will bring victory in combat. The Armed Services cannot be expected to be experts in all of the complicated fields which make it possible for a great nation to fight successfully in total war. There are certain kinds of research—such as research on the improvement of existing weapons—which can best be done within the military establishment. However, the job of long-range research involving application of the newest scientific discoveries to military needs should be the responsibility of those civilian scientists in the universities and in industry who are best trained to discharge it thoroughly and successfully. It is essential that both kinds of research go forward and that there be the closest liaison between the two groups.

Dwight Eisenhower's Farewell Address, 1961

We now stand ten years past the midpoint of a century that has witnessed four major wars among great nations. Three of these involved our own country. Despite these holocausts America is today the strongest, the most influential and most productive nation in the world. Understandably proud of this preeminence, we yet realize that America's leadership and prestige depend, not merely upon our unmatched material progress, riches and military strength, but on how we use our power in the interests of world peace and human betterment. . . .

Throughout America's adventure in free government, our basic purposes have been to keep the peace; to foster progress in human achievement, and to enhance liberty, dignity and integrity among people and among nations. To strive for less would

From Dwight, D. Eisenhower, "Farewell Radio and Television Address to the American People, January 17, 1961," *Public Papers of the President of the United States, Dwight D. Eisenhower, 1960–61* (Washington, DC: U.S. Government Printing Office, 1961), pp. 1035–1040.

be unworthy of a free and religious people. Any failure traceable to arrogance, or our lack of comprehension or readiness to sacrifice would inflict upon us grievous hurt both at home and abroad.

Progress toward these noble goals is persistently threatened by the conflict now engulfing the world. It commands our whole attention, absorbs our very beings. We face a hostile ideology—global in scope, atheistic in character, ruthless in purpose, and insidious in method. Unhappily the danger it poses promises to be of indefinite duration. To meet it successfully, there is called for, not so much the emotional and transitory sacrifices of crisis, but rather those which enable us to carry forward steadily, surely, and without complaint the burdens of a prolonged and complex struggle—with liberty the stake. . . .

Crises there will continue to be. In meeting them, whether foreign or domestic, great or small, there is a recurring temptation to feel that some spectacular and costly action could become the miraculous solution to all current difficulties. A huge increase in newer elements of our defense; development of unrealistic programs to cure every ill in agriculture; a dramatic expansion in basic and applied research—these and many other possibilities, each possibly promising in itself, may be suggested as the only way to the road we wish to travel.

But each proposal must be weighed in the light of a broader consideration: the need to maintain balance in and among national programs—balance between the private and the public economy, balance between cost and hoped for advantage—balance between the clearly necessary and the comfortably desirable; balance between our essential requirements as a nation and the duties imposed by the nation upon the individual; balance between actions of the moment and the national welfare of the future. Good judgment seeks balance and progress; lack of it eventually finds imbalance and frustration. . . .

A vital element in keeping the peace is our military establishment. Our arms must be mighty, ready for instant action, so that no potential aggressor may be tempted to risk his own destruction.

Our military organization today bears little relation to that known by any of my predecessors in peacetime, or indeed by the fighting men of World War II or Korea.

Until the latest of our world conflicts, the United States had no armaments industry. American makers of plowshares could, with time and as required, make swords as well. But now we can no longer risk emergency improvisation of national defense; we have been compelled to create a permanent armaments industry of vast proportions. Added to this, three and a half million men and women are directly engaged in the defense establishment. We annually spend on military security more than the net income of all United States corporations.

This conjunction of an immense military establishment and a large arms industry is new in the American experience. The total influence—economic, political, even spiritual—is felt in every city, every State [H]ouse, every office of the Federal government. We recognize the imperative need for this development. Yet we must not fail to comprehend its grave implications. Our toil, resources and livelihood are all involved; so is the very structure of our society.

In the councils of government, we must guard against the acquisition of unwarranted influence, whether sought or unsought, by the military-industrial complex. The potential for the disastrous rise of misplaced power exists and will persist.

We must never let the weight of this combination endanger our liberties or democratic processes. We should take nothing for granted. Only an alert and knowledgeable citizenry can compel the proper meshing of the huge industrial and military machinery of defense with our peaceful methods and goals, so that security and liberty may prosper together.

Akin to, and largely responsible for the sweeping changes in our industrial-military posture, has been the technological revolution during recent decades.

In this revolution, research has become central; it also becomes more formalized, complex, and costly. A steadily increasing share is conducted for, by, or at the direction of, the Federal government.

Today, the solitary inventor, tinkering in his shop, has been overshadowed by task forces of scientists in laboratories and testing fields. In the same fashion, the free university, historically the fountainhead of free ideas and scientific discovery, has experienced a revolution in the conduct of research. Partly because of the huge costs involved, a government contract becomes virtually a substitute for intellectual curiosity. For every old blackboard there are now hundreds of new electronic computers.

The prospect of domination of the nation's scholars by Federal employment, project allocations, and the power of money is ever present and is gravely to be regarded.

Yet, in holding scientific research and discovery in respect, as we should, we must also be alert to the equal and opposite danger that public policy could itself become the captive of a scientific technological elite.

It is the task of statesmanship to mold, to balance, and to integrate these and other forces, new and old, within the principles of our democratic system—ever aiming toward the supreme goals of our free society.

". . . the adherence of the professors," 1967

J. WILLIAM FULBRIGHT

Mr. President, today I resume my comments on the Vietnamese war and its far-ranging effects. In the first half of my statement I questioned the assumption on which the American war policy is based and suggested what seem to me to be the principal causes of the deep and widening division among the American people. Today I shall point to some of the destructive effects of the war upon our domestic life—to the growing militarization of the economy and the universities, to the deepening crisis of poverty and race, and to the underlying question of America's concept of herself, either as a traditional world empire as we seem to be becoming, or as an example of creative democracy, as we have traditionally regarded ourselves.

. . . While young dissenters plead for resurrection of the American promise, their elders continue to subvert it. As if it were something to be very proud of, it was announced not long ago that the war in Vietnam had created a million new jobs in the United States. Our country is becoming conditioned to permanent conflict. More

From *Congressional Record,* 90th Congress, 1st Session, December 13, 1967, vol. 113, pt. 27, pp. 36181–36184. Also reprinted in Herbert I. Schiller and Joseph D. Phillips, eds., *Super State: Readings in the Military-Industrial Complex* (Urbana, IL: University of Illinois Press, 1970), pp. 173–178.

and more our economy, our Government, and our universities are adapting themselves to the requirements of continuing war—total war, limited war, and cold war. The struggle against militarism into which we were drawn 26 years ago has become permanent, and for the sake of conducting it, we are making ourselves into a militarized society.

I do not think the military-industrial complex is the conspiratorial invention of a band of "merchants of death." One almost wishes that it were, because conspiracies can be exposed and dealt with. But the components of the new American militarism are too diverse, independent, and complex for it to be the product of a centrally directed conspiracy. It is rather the inevitable result of the creation of a huge, permanent military establishment, whose needs have given rise to a vast private defense industry tied to the Armed Forces by a natural bond of common interest. As the largest producer of goods and services in the United States, the industries and businesses that fill military orders will in the coming fiscal year pour some $45 billion into over 5,000 cities and towns where over 8 million Americans, counting members of the Armed Forces, comprising approximately 10 percent of the labor force, will earn their living from defense spending. Together all these industries and employees, drawing their income from the $75 billion defense budget, form a giant concentration of socialism in our otherwise free enterprise economy.

Unplanned though it was, this complex has become a major political force. It is the result rather than the cause of American military involvements around the world; but composed as it is of a vast number of citizens—not tycoons or "merchants of death" but ordinary, good American citizens—whose livelihood depends on defense production, the military-industrial complex has become an indirect force for the perpetuation of our global military commitments. This is not—and I emphasize "not"—because anyone favors war but because every one of us has a natural and proper desire to preserve the sources of his livelihood. For the defense worker this means preserving or obtaining some local factory or installation and obtaining new defense orders; for the labor union leader it mean jobs for his members at abnormally high wages; for the politician it means preserving the good will of his constituents by helping them to get what they want. Every time a new program, such as Mr. McNamara's $5 billion "thin" antiballistic missile system, is introduced, a powerful new constituency is created—a constituency that will strive mightily to protect the new program and, in the case of ABM, turn the "thin" system into a "thick" one, a movement already underway according to reports in the press. The constituency-building process is further advanced by the perspicacity of Defense officials and contractors in locating installations and plants in the districts of influential key Members of Congress.

In this natural way generals, industrialists, businessmen, labor leaders, workers, and politicians have joined together a military-industrial complex—a complex which, for all the inadvertency of its creation and the innocent intentions of its participants, has nonetheless become a powerful new force for the perpetuation of foreign military commitments, for the introduction and expansion of expensive weapons systems, and, as a result, for the militarization of large segments of our national life. Most interest groups are counterbalanced by other interest groups, but the defense complex is so much larger than any other that there is no effective counterweight to it except concern as to its impact on the part of some of our citizens and a few of our leaders, none of whom have material incentive to offer.

The universities might have formed an effective counterweight to the military-industrial complex by strengthening their emphasis on the traditional values of our democracy, but many of our leading universities have instead joined the monolith, adding greatly to its power and influence. Disappointing though it is, the adherence of the professors is not greatly surprising. No less than businessmen, workers, and politicians, professors like money and influence. Having traditionally been deprived of both, they have welcomed the contracts and consultantships offered by the Military Establishment.

The great majority of American professors are still teaching students and engaging in scholarly research, but some of the most famous of our academicians have set such activities aside in order to serve their government, especially those parts of the government which are primarily concerned with war.

The bonds between the Government and the universities are no more the results of a conspiracy than those between Government and business. They are an arrangement of convenience, providing the Government with politically usable knowledge and the universities with badly needed funds. Most of these funds go to large institutions which need them less than some smaller and less well-known ones, but they do on the whole make a contribution to higher learning, a contribution, however, which is purchased at a higher price.

That price is the surrender of independence, the neglect of teaching, and the distortion of scholarship. A university which has become accustomed to the inflow of government contract funds is likely to emphasize activities which will attract those funds. These, unfortunately, do not include teaching undergraduates and the kind of scholarship which, though it may contribute to the sum of human knowledge and to man's understanding of himself, is not salable to the Defense Department or the CIA. As Clark Kerr, former president of the University of California, expressed it: "The real problem is not one of Federal control but of Federal influence. A Federal agency offers a project. The university need not accept, but as a practical matter, it usually does. . . . Out of this reality have followed many of the consequences of Federal aid for the universities; and they have been substantial. That they are subtle, slowly cumulative and gentlemanly makes them all the more potent."

From what one hears the process of acquiring Government contracts is not always passive and gentlemanly.

"One of the dismal sights in American higher education"—writes Robert M. Rosenzweig, associate dean of the Stanford University graduate division—

> is that of administrators scrambling for contracts for work which does not emerge from the research or teaching interests of their faculty. The result of this unseemly enterprise is bound to be a faculty coerced or seduced into secondary lines of interests, on a frantic effort to secure nonfaculty personnel to meet the contractual obligations. Among the most puzzling aspects of such arrangements is the fact that Government agencies have permitted and even encouraged them. Not only are they harmful to the universities— which is not, of course, the Government's prime concern—but they insure that the Government will not get what it is presumably buying; namely, the intellectual and technical resources of the academic community. It is simply a bad bargain all the way around.

Commenting on these tendencies, a special report on government, the universities and international affairs, prepared for the U.S. Advisory Commission on International

Education and Cultural Affairs, points out that—"The eagerness of university administrations to undertake stylized, Government-financed projects has caused a decline in self-generated commitments to scholarly pursuits, has produced baneful effects on the academic mission of our universities, and has, in addition, brought forward some bitter complaints from the disappointed clients."

Among the baneful effects of the Government-university contract system the most damaging and corrupting are the neglect of the university's most important purpose, which is the education of its students, and the taking into the Government camp of scholars, especially those in the social sciences, who ought to be acting as responsible and independent critics of their Government's policies. The corrupting process is a subtle one: no one needs to censor, threaten, or give orders to contract scholars; without a word of warning or advice being uttered, it is simply understood that lucrative contracts are awarded not to those who question their Government's policies but to those who provide the Government with the tools and techniques it desires. The effect, in the words of the report to the Advisory Commission on International Education, is—"To suggest the possibility to a world—never adverse to prejudice—that academic honesty is no less marketable than a box of detergent on the grocery shelf."

The formation of a military-industrial complex, for all its baneful consequences, is the result of great numbers of people engaging in more or less normal commercial activities. The adherence of the universities, though no more the result of a plan or conspiracy, nonetheless involves something else: the neglect and if carried far enough the betrayal, of the university's fundamental reason for existence, which is the advancement of man's search for truth and happiness. It is for this purpose, and this purpose alone, that universities receive—and should receive—the community's support in the form of grants, loans and tax exemptions.

When the university turns away from its central purpose and makes itself an appendage to the Government, concerning itself with techniques rather than purposes, with expedients rather than ideals, dispensing conventional orthodoxy rather than new ideas, it is not only failing to meet its responsibilities to its students; it is betraying a public trust.

This betrayal is most keenly felt by the students, partly because it is they who are being denied the services of those who ought to be their teachers, they to whom knowledge is being dispensed wholesale in cavernous lecture halls, they who must wait weeks for brief audiences with important professors whose time is taken up by travel and research connected with Government contracts. For all these reasons the students feel themselves betrayed, but it is doubtful that any of these is the basic cause of the angry rebellions which have broken out on so many campuses.

It seems more likely that the basic cause of the great trouble in our universities is the student's discovery of corruption in the one place, besides perhaps the churches, which might have been supposed to be immune from the corruptions of our age. Having seen their country's traditional values degraded in the effort to attribute moral purpose to an immoral war, having seen their country's leaders caught in inconsistencies which are politely referred to as a "credibility gap," they now see their universities—the last citadels of moral and intellectual integrity—lending themselves to ulterior and expedient ends, and betraying their own fundamental purpose, which, in James Bryce's words, is to "reflect the spirit of the times without yielding to it."

"The so-called military-industrial complex," 1969

BARRY GOLDWATER

As a member of the Senate Armed Services Committee and as a member of the Senate Preparedness Subcommittee, I am greatly interested in the growing preoccupation of some groups and individuals these days with the so-called military-industrial complex in the United States. Indeed, if I were a psychologist, I might be tempted to the conclusion that the left wing in American politics has developed a "complex over a complex."

Judging from the view expressed by many of our public officials and commentators, the so-called military-industrial complex would seem to be responsible for almost all of the world's evils. Certainly a determined effort is under way to place at its doorstep almost full responsibility for the unfortunate war in Vietnam and the high cost of American defense. . . .

Let us take the military-industrial complex and examine it closely. What it amounts to is that we have a big military establishment, and we have a big industrial plant which helps to supply that establishment. This apparently constitutes a "complex." If so, I certainly can find nothing to criticize but much to be thankful for in its existence. Ask yourselves, for example, why we have a large, expensive military establishment and why we have a large and capable defense industry. The answer is simply this: We have huge worldwide responsibilities. We face tremendous worldwide challenges. In short, we urgently require both a big defense establishment and a big industrial capacity. Both are essential to our safety and to the preservation of freedom in a world fraught with totalitarian aggression.

Merely because our huge responsibilities necessitate the existence of a military-industrial complex does not automatically make that complex something we must fear or feel ashamed of. You might consider where we would be in any negotiations which might be entered into with the Soviet Union if we did not have a big military backed by a big industrial complex to support our arguments. You might wonder how we could possibly pretend to be interested in the freedom of smaller nations if the only military-industrial complex in the world was possessed by Communist Russia or Communist China.

Mr. President, in many respects I am reminded of the problem which confronted our nation in the early days of World War II. The madman Hitler was running rampant. Freedom was being trampled throughout all of Europe. Suddenly the United States found itself forced to fill the role of the "arsenal of democracy." This nation had to start from scratch and finally out-produce the combined efforts of the Axis powers. And we had to do it quickly. The very existence of freedom in the world as we knew it in the early 1940s depended on it. And how did we perform this miracle? Well, I'll tell you that we performed it with the help of an industrial giant called an integrated steel industry. Although this industry and others like it performed miracles of production at a time when the chips were down all over the world, it still was

From Senator Barry Goldwater, "Civilian Complex," Remarks by Senator Barry Goldwater of Arizona on the Senate Floor, April 15, 1969. Also reprinted in Carroll W. Pursell, Jr., *The Military-Industrial Complex* (New York: Harper & Row, 1972), pp. 264–270.

the subject of long and harassing investigation after the war because of its "bigness." Incredible as it seems, the very size of an industry which enabled us to defeat the Fascists' armies and remain free became the reason for investigation by liberals in the Congress during the immediate postwar period.

We never, Mr. President, seem to understand that size is not necessarily an evil. When the Russian *Sputnik* went up, this nation was deeply concerned. And that concern had to do with our inability at that time to duplicate the Soviet feat. Now that we have the industrial capacity to equal the Russians in space or in matters related to defense, there seems to be a nationwide effort to make us feel guilty.

What would the critics of the military-industrial complex have us do? Would they have us ignore the fact that progress occurs in the field of national defense as well as in the field of social sciences? Do they want us to turn back the clock, disband our military establishment and do away with our defense related industrial capacity? Mr. President, do these critics of what they term a military-industrial complex really want us to default on our worldwide responsibilities, turn our backs on aggression and slavery and develop a national policy of selfish isolation?

Rather than deploring the existence of a military-industrial complex, I say we should thank heavens for it. That complex gives us our protective shield. It is the bubble under which our nation thrives and prospers. It is the armor which is unfortunately required in a world divided.

For all those who rant and rave about the military-industrial complex, I ask this question: What would you replace it with?

What's more, I believe it is fair to inquire whether the name presently applied is inclusive enough. Consider the large number of scientists who contributed all of the fundamental research necessary to develop and build nuclear weapons and other products of today's defense industries. Viewing this, shouldn't we call it the "scientific-military-industrial complex." By the same token, don't forget the amount of research that has gone on in our colleges and universities in support of our defense-related projects. Maybe we should call it an "educational-scientific-military-industrial complex." Then, of course, the vast financing that goes into this effort certainly makes the economic community an integral part of any such complex. Now we have a name that runs like this: "An economic-educational-scientific-military-industrial complex."

What we are talking about, Mr. President, is an undertaking which grew up from necessity. It is the product of American initiative, incentive and genius responding to a huge global challenge. It is perhaps the most effective and efficient complex ever built to fill a worldwide function. Its ultimate aim is peace in our time regardless of the aggressive, militaristic image which the left wing is attempting to give it. . . .

As I have pointed out, many of the problems that are being encountered in the area of national defense today stem not so much from a military-industrial complex as they do from the mistakes and miscalculations of a "civilian complex" or perhaps I should say a "civilian-computer complex." My reference here, of course, is to the Pentagon hierarchy of young civilians (often referred to as the "whiz kids") which was erected during the McNamara era in the questionable name of "cost effectiveness." And this complex, Mr. President, was built in some measure to shut out the military voice in a large area of defense policy decision-making.

I suggest that the military-industrial complex is not the all-powerful structure that our liberal friends would have us believe. Certainly nobody can deny that this combination took a drubbing at the hands of Mr. McNamara and his civilian cadres during the past eight years.

If the military-industrial complex had been as strong and as cohesive as its critics would have us believe, it is entirely possible this nation and its taxpayers would not today be facing the need for rebuilding the defenses of freedom. I have already mentioned one example. The TFX decision which had proven to be such a costly fiasco was made by the civilian complex against the advice of experienced military men.

If the military-industrial complex had been the irresistible giant its critics describe, we would certainly today be better equipped. We would undoubtedly have a nuclear-powered navy adequate to the challenge presented by Soviet naval might. We would certainly have in the air—and not just on a drawing board—a manned, carry-on bomber. We would never have encountered the kind of shortages which cropped up in every area of the military as a result of the demands from Vietnam. There would have been no shortage of military helicopters. There would have been no shortage of trained helicopter pilots. There would have been no need to use outdated and faulty equipment. No concern ever would have arisen over whether our supply of bombs was sufficient to the task in Southeast Asia.

In conclusion, Mr. President, I want to point out that a very strong case can be made for the need for *a more powerful* military-industrial complex than we have had during the past eight years. At the very least, I wish to say that the employment practices of industries doing business with the Pentagon—practices which lead them to hire the most knowledgeable men to do their work—are no cause for shock. Nor are these practices dangerous to the American people.

I have great faith in the civilian leaders of our government and of our military services. I have no desire to see the voice of the military become all-powerful or even dominant in our national affairs. But I do believe that the military viewpoint must always be heard in the highest councils of our government in all matters directly affecting the protection and security of our nation.

Computers in Manufacturing

C. A. HUDSON

The author is Manager of Technology, Industry Automation Division, Westinghouse Electric.

While the U.S. remains among the most productive nations in the world, other industrialized countries are quickly closing the gap. . . .

In the U.S. the program to reverse this productivity pattern significantly must rely on the continued development of advanced technology and its application. Perhaps the most important element in this reliance on innovation is increased factory automation and a growing use of computers and microprocessor technology in manufacturing. Today, we are on the technological and sociological edge of a dramatic increase in the use of computers in our factories. . . .

Many computerized factory systems exist today as islands of automation. The immediate task of the scientific and technical communities is to use the increased

Excerpted with permission from C. A. Hudson, "Computers in Manufacturing," *Science*, February 12, 1982. Copyright 1982 American Association for the Advancement of Science.

power and simplicity of computers to link these elements into an integrated system. Making use of low-cost computer hardware to perform more and more jobs will make an integrated factory system economically viable. . . .

Advances in the two primary elements of factory computerization—computer-aided design (CAD) and computer-aided manufacturing (CAM)—will create a new industrial revolution. . . .

Computer-aided manufacturing has five main functions: tool design, machine control, process and materials planning, robotics, and factory management. . . .

Machine automation consists of a chain of increasingly sophisticated control techniques. At the lower end of the spectrum are fixed automation with relays or cams and programmable controllers, where relays have been replaced by electronics. Moving up the spectrum, numerical control (NC) refers to controlling a machine with prerecorded, numerically coded information to fabricate a part. In this case, the machine is hardwired and not readily reprogrammed. In computer numerical control (CNC) the machine is directly controlled by a mini-computer, which stores the machining instructions as software that is relatively easy to reprogram. Because of the computer control, CNC has the advantages of much higher storage capability and increased flexibility. Virtually all numerical control is computer-based. . . .

Factory management coordinates the operations of an entire plant. Factory management systems tie together individual machine tools, test stations, robots, and materials-handling systems into manufacturing cells and the cells into an integrated whole. An integrated CAM system of this sort is usually hierarchical, with microprocessors handling specific machining functions or robot operation, middle-level computers controlling the operation and work scheduling of one or more manufacturing cells, and a large central computer controlling the overall system.

Reliability is greatly improved by structuring the control system correctly. Local, distributed control (with defined responsibilities) reports up to a supervisory control that, in turn, is linked to a managerial computer. This parallels the structure of the typical industrial organization. . . .

Another major effort to integrate computer systems is an Air Force program called ICAM (integrated computer-aided manufacturing). This is a practical attempt to greatly shorten the time span for the implementation of compatible and standardized computer-manufacturing techniques and to provide a unified direction for industry. The ICAM program provides seed money for establishment, within private industry, of modular subsystems designed to computerize and tie together various phases of design, fabrication, and distribution processes and their associated management hierarchy. As appropriate, these mutually compatible modules will be combined to demonstrate a comprehensive control and management package capable of continual adjustment as production needs and the state of the art change. . . .

The ultimate goal in ICAM is the use of totally integrated manufacturing systems by industry in the completely automated factory. . . .

Robots can duplicate human manipulative skills with accuracy and precision. Their flexibility and versatility, as opposed to hard automation, make robots ideally suited to the kinds of small batch jobs that constitute the bulk of industry's manufacturing activity. Today, robots, are freeing people from jobs that present serious health hazards, are mundane, or are highly repetitive. In most cases their use is justified for non-economic reasons.

In the U.S. industry has been slow to adopt robotics. This reluctance appears to be due primarily to the large initial investment and the general availability of relatively inexpensive manual labor. Why install a $100,000 or $150,000 robot to perform a $25,000-a year job? . . .

This situation is changing. Robots are becoming more streamlined, and, when they are manufactured in large quantities, will rapidly decline in cost. . . . Equally important, system engineering, which represents as much as two-thirds of the cost of a robotic application, is being greatly reduced. It is not difficult to imagine that in a short time the cost of a typical robotic system will be paid back in one or two years. In the next decade the cost of a robot is likely to be down to $10,000 to $20,000, while skilled labor costs might easily be $25 or $30 an hour. When this economic threshold is reached, there will be a virtual flood of robotic applications.

When this happens, robots will play an important part in the totally integrated factory of the future. . . .

The Robotics Laboratory at Westinghouse is working on state-of-the-art applications in many of these areas. Systems and development engineers are working on the integration of controls, tooling, processes, computer, and other elements of the automated factory. Specialists in robotics are concentrating on developing and applying high-speed vision systems, tactile and force feedback sensors, high-performance electric servo systems, adaptable programmable assembly techniques and computer control, and artificial intelligence. . . .

In Japan, major advances are achieved through the efforts of the Ministry of International Trade and Industry (MITI). . . .

. . . The U.S. is one of the few major industrialized nations in the world without a significant coordinated industry—government—university program directed at improving manufacturing technology. We need a national strategy for productivity improvement that brings together government, business, labor, and academia in a cooperative, rather than adversary, relationship. We will have to remove many of the disincentives to innovation and find new ways to capitalize on our diversity and our proven creative and inventive abilities. Just as MITI capitalizes on Japan's homogeneity, we must find new ways to foster, encourage, and channel our innovative diversity.

At present, Westinghouse is working with the National Science Foundation and the universities of Rhode Island, Florida, and Wisconsin on technology development programs. Along with the Robotics Institute of Carnegie-Mellon University, we are developing "seeing," "feeling," and "thinking" robotic systems for several of our factories. We are also very interested in the Air Force's ICAM program to coordinate sophisticated design and manufacturing techniques now used by industry on a piecemeal basis. This program attempts to integrate design, analysis, fabrication, materials handling, and inspection and to develop hardware and software demonstration manufacturing cells in selected aerospace plants. . . .

The application of automated systems in manufacturing will have several major effects on the people involved in production. It will make our jobs more interesting and challenging; it will enhance job security; and it will multiply the productivity increases.

Workers today are looking for greater job satisfaction through greater involvement and increased sophisticated. New technologies provide this added dimension to the workplace. For instance, draftsmen use CAD today to perform work that was normally performed by engineers just five or ten years ago. Engineers, in turn, are freed to delve into even more technically sophisticated areas. As a peripheral advantage, the critical need for technical manpower is partially satisfied.

To manage technological change, we must manage our human resources better. For example, we must commit ourselves to ensuring that none of our workers is laid off because of technological changes, as long as they are willing to be retrained and accept new job assignments. Our experience at Westinghouse has been that employees displaced by robots normally move up to better, more challenging work. . . .

In Westinghouse, by putting the programs for people first, we expect to multiply the productivity improvements that are gained through technology and capital investments. With participative management, for instance, employees welcome advanced technology because they feel in charge of it.

"The Race to Build a Supercomputer"

WILLIAM D. MARBACH

One day in 1981, Michael L. Dertouzos, the director of the renowned Computer Laboratory at the Massachusetts Institute of Technology, received from a colleague just back from Japan a draft of a research paper. It outlined Japanese proposals for long-range research projects in advanced computer science—plans to build revolutionary artificial intelligence computers and supercomputers a thousand times faster than today's machines. To Dertouzos's ears, the document had a familiar ring. "I looked at it and I started panicking, panicking, panicking," he recalls. "I said, 'My God, this is the research charter for my laboratory. These guys have stolen it.'"

The Japanese had in fact taken nothing but the initiative, yet Dertouzos immediately saw the threat: Japan's JIPDEC plan, as it was then called, was a carefully conceived blueprint of the research and engineering needed to leapfrog the U.S. computer industry and destroy its world supremacy. Worse, even though American universities had produced the basic research the Japanese would rely on, American companies were as serenely unaware of danger as the battleships that swung at anchor in Pearl Harbor more than 40 years ago. "My good friends in the U.S. corporations were deeply asleep," Dertouzos says.

Today the battle lines are drawn. Armed with fresh commitments of money and manpower, the U.S. is taking on Japan for control of the advances technologies that will dominate computing in the late 1980s and the 1990s. Nor is this simply a struggle for an industry: entire economies will be reshaped by the coming radical changes in information processing. Supercomputer speed is already being used commercially for aircraft design, oil, and mineral exploration, weather forecasting and computer circuit design—all of which require vast amounts of calculation. Supercomputers may soon be put to work in the automobile and shipbuilding industries, and pressed into the service of genetic engineers and economic forecasters.

The supersecret National Security Agency, the cryptographers' "Puzzle Palace," is already a heavy user of today's supercomputers. And the Pentagon's futuristic laser weapons systems based in space will depend on supercomputers. "This assault is far more serious to our future than the automobiles sold from Japan, because the computer is at the root of every major future change," Dertouzos warns. "The Japanese recognize that whoever controls the information revolution has, in effect, some form of increased geopolitical control."

Until now the U.S. has dominated advanced computer technologies: the world's supercomputers have all been American-made. There are 74 in operation, and they are very powerful machines, capable of performing several hundred million operations per second. They are so fast and their electronic circuitry is so dense that giant refrigeration units must pump a freon-gas coolant through the machines just to keep them from melting down.

Yet the current supercomputers are only at the threshold of what computer designers think can be achieved; the next generation of advanced supercomputers will make today's machines look like handheld calculators. "We have problems that would take 500 to 1,000 hours to solve [on today's supercomputers]," says David Nowak, division leader for computational physics at Lawrence Livermore National Laboratory, where a cluster of seven supercomputers—known as "Octopus"—is used for nuclear weapons research. Before the end of the century, computer scientists hope to develop machines that not only crunch numbers at high speed but also exhibit artificial intelligence—computers that can think and reason somewhat like human beings and that can understand information conveyed by sight, speech, and motion.

The question is, which nation's scientists will get there first? . . .

The Pentagon's Defense Advanced Research Projects Agency (DARPA) is more than any other single agency in the world, responsible for the shape of advanced computer science today—and for many technologies now in widespread commercial use. Over the past 20 years, DARPA has poured half a billion dollars into computer research, in the process virtually creating the science of artificial intelligence. The first supercomputer, built in 1964, was a DARPA project. Computer time sharing, a fundamental advance, came out of work sponsored by DARPA; so did packet-switched networks, the workhorses of today's telecommunications data networks. And computer graphics—now used on desktop computers and video-arcade screens as well as in F-10 cockpits—is a DARPA-sponsored invention.

DARPA's next priority is a push for advanced supercomputing and artificial intelligence technologies that may cost as much as $1 billion. DARPA plans to do everything the Japanese have set out to accomplish—and more.

"Dual-Use" Technology, 1991

JEFF BINGAMAN AND BOBBY R. INMAN

The collapse of the Soviet Union overturned the assumptions upon which United States military security rested for 40 years. When President Bush was asked to describe the threat to which defense planning should now be directed, he responded,

From Jeff Bingaman and Bobby R. Inman, "Broadening Horizons for Defense R & D," *Issues in Science and Technology* (Fall 1992): 80–85.

"unpredictability, uncertainty, and instability." Such a future will mean that technology, always a bulwark of America's national security, will become even more important.

For technology to be an effective "strategic reserve," however, U.S. defense technology policy must be fundamentally revised. These revisions must take account of the relative decline of U.S. technological leadership, both military and civilian, since the 1960s. . . .

. . . [I]n important dual-use technologies—those with both military and civilian applications—the Department of Defense (DOD) has lost its technological leadership. Although defense technology investments still powerfully affect the commercial sector, the defense technology base is increasingly dependent upon developments in the larger and more dynamic commercial area.

. . . [D]espite this growing dependence, the commercial technology base has become less and less accessible to the Department of Defense. . . .

This inefficiency is particularly striking at a time of growing convergence between the underlying technologies that support military and commercial activities. Electronics, computers, software, and advanced materials are among the technologies critical to economic competitiveness as well as to advanced weapon systems. Thus, even though defense and commercial *products* continue to diverge, the supporting *technologies* are converging.

. . . [W]e must move toward a single, cutting-edge technology base that will serve military and commercial needs—a national technology base. Such a change would allow DOD to draw more easily from the commercial sector to meet national security needs. . . .

Of the many steps needed to build a strong national technology base, an essential one involves broadening the mission of the Defense Advanced Research Projects Agency (DARPA) to include more dual-use technology development. . . .

DARPA was established as the Advanced Research Projects Agency (ARPA) in 1958, in the wake of *Sputnik*, to oversee the military space program. ARPA soon lost most of its space-related work to another new agency, the National Aeronautics and Space Administration (NASA), but following President Kennedy's election in 1960, ARPA (and later DARPA) was given a charter to pursue basic and applied research in a wide range of fields of military interest.

In its 34-year history, DARPA has pioneered a remarkable number of important technologies. Some of them are uniquely military in character—phased-array radar, infrared detection systems, precision-guided munitions and stealth technology. Many others have had broad civilian, as well as military, applications. DARPA almost single-handedly created the discipline of materials science, paving the way for high-strength, lightweight composites that are finding their way into everything from tennis rackets to jet aircraft. But the agency is probably best known for its pioneering work in electronics, which produced packet-switched computer communications, computer networking, time-sharing, computer graphics, and major developments in artificial intelligence and robotics. As John Deutch, the former provost of MIT, has observed, "The computer strength of the United States came out of DARPA."

What made DARPA—an agency with only 165 employees, nearly half of them support staff, and a $1.5 billion budget—so successful? At least in the computer field, a major factor—perhaps the major factor—was the agency's ability to finance visionary research with only indirect military applications. Indeed, DARPA's official history documents the agency's unabashed emphasis on advanced computer technology with broad commercial applications. . . .

In the agency's prime, DARPA managers consciously promoted industrial spinoffs. But in the past two decades, DARPA has fallen victim to three sets of debilitating pressures.

The first set of pressures resulted in the addition of the word "Defense" to ARPA's name in 1972. The late 1960s and early 1970s were a time of cynicism—especially on university campuses—about the Pentagon's impact on society. That cynicism culminated in the Mansfield amendment to the 1970 Defense Authorization Act, which directed DOD to concentrate on research with direct defense applications. . . .

Budgetary pressures have also had an impact, forcing a more constricted emphasis on immediate applications. . . .

The third, and most recent, set of pressures on DARPA has been political in nature. The view that government should not pick winners and losers has been interpreted by key people in the executive branch to mean that DARPA should not support any technology with significant commercial application. Support for dual use technology has gone from being an ideal to a pejorative. . . .

Former DARPA director Richard Cooper told a Senate hearing that . . . "Every ARPA director, to my knowledge—and I have known them all and have had close relationships with them all—[has] done the thing that the White House dislikes the most. That is, they have [promoted a particular] company and got its first product to the point where the government could buy it. In many cases—in most cases—those products were dual-use products. We did it quietly. We didn't talk about it. . . ."

Political pressures have led to administration budgets that have systematically shortchanged critical dual-use technologies with broad commercial applications. . . .

Since 1988, Congress has countered the administration by adding several hundred million dollars a year to DARPA's budget for dual-use technologies. . . . [T]ypically, Congress specifies a dollar amount and a technology—say, $75 million for high-definition display systems—and leaves it to DARPA to spend the money largely as it sees fit. Moreover, Congress' identification of which technologies to supplement reflects a broad industry consensus rather than any narrow political interest.

. . . [A] growing share of congressional additions to DARPA's budget is for "critical technology partnerships," which are even more open-ended. The only requirement is that DARPA fund dual-use projects, preferably in high-risk areas, in which industry, often in conjunction with universities and federal labs, contributes roughly half the funds. . . .

The response from industry . . . has been dramatic. . . .

In sum, the answer to the question "Why ARPA?" is apparent. DARPA's traditional operating style is well-suited to a post-Cold War era, in which DOD must increasingly have access to commercial technology and work with private firms. The agency is fast on its feet when a technological opportunity arises and just as quick to eliminate unpromising projects. The list of firms that owe their existence to DARPA—MIPS, Sun Microsystems, Thinking Machines, and Orbital Sciences, among others—is testament to the agency's historic ability to support important dual-use technologies.

. . . Now it is time to . . . make statutorily explicit that the dual-use trend is not only legitimate but also essential. . . .

... ARPA would be charged with moving the nation toward a strong, unified, national technology base. The DOD would benefit by getting faster and cheaper access to commercial technology. ...

We are entering an era in which it is imperative that we link our economic policy and our military policy. That marks a departure from past practice, which treated national security and industrial competitiveness as separate, and often contradictory, goals.

ESSAYS

In the first selection, economists Nathan Rosenberg and Richard Nelson discuss the centrality of university research to technological change since World War II. They make a generally positive assessment of the university-military relationship while recognizing the challenges imposed by the end of the Cold War. The authors are skeptical about calls for increased private sector support for university research and strongly recommend against dismantling the federal support system for science and technology. Their essay also shows how historical analysis can inform contemporary public policy debates.

The second essay, from Paul Edwards's *The Closed World,* narrows the discussion to a specific case of engineering research: computers and information processing. Edwards chronicles how military support of World War II computer research extended into the cold war, and how academic entrepreneurship and bureaucratic politics helped to shape postwar computer science. Political strategies associated with containing communism pushed research toward total command and control systems. Yet few if any of those involved in the development of these systems, Edwards argues, fully understood the political logic that drove their work, let alone its larger implications. What, then, were their motives and goals, and how did these attitudes influence their technological designs?

The third essay, by David Noble, examines another military-sponsored technology—numerically controlled machine tools—and critically assesses their social costs and implications. He suggests, among other things, that such "command technologies" have been biased against the interests of small producers and working people.

Universities and Industrial Research

NATHAN ROSENBERG AND RICHARD R. NELSON

While large-scale public support of university research was unthinkable prior to World War II, the war-time successes completely changed that picture. Vannevar Bush . . . was the director of the war-time Office of Scientific Research and Development, which was responsible for mobilizing much of this effort. Bush wrote an influential document, *Science, The Endless Frontier,* which put forth the case for large-scale post-war support by the federal government of the American scientific enterprise. There were three major parts to the Bush proposal.

From Nathan Rosenberg and Richard R. Nelson, "American Universities and Technical Advance in Industry," *Research Policy* 23 (1994): 323–348, © 1994 Elsevier Science B. V. All rights reserved.

First, the U.S. government should not let the capability for military R & D, assembled during the war, atrophy, but rather should continue to sustain a level and mix of funding adequate to preserve those capabilities. With the rise of the Cold War in the late 1940s and early 1950s this policy became manifest in large-scale funding of military R & D. While the bulk of that funding went to support work on military systems and components carried out in industry, a sizeable amount of money flowed to universities to support work on computers, electronics more generally, materials, and the applied sciences and engineering disciplines that were relevant to military technologies.

The second part of the proposal was for significant public support of medical R & D. Here the universities from the beginning have been the largest recipient of government funding, with the National Institutes of Health the principal funder.

The third part of the post-war strategy articulated in *Science, The Endless Frontier,* was for the federal government to assume responsibility for supporting basic research at the universities, in a broader sense. After several false starts, this responsibility became manifest in the establishment, in 1950, of the National Science Foundation.

Federal funding of academic research, which probably amounted to about a quarter of total academic research support in the mid-1930s, increased enormously, and by 1960 was accounting for over 60% of the total. The total academic research enterprise increased more than tenfold in nominal terms between 1935 and 1960, and more than doubled again by 1965. . . . Rapid growth continued from 1965 until 1980 or so. It is estimated that real academic research funding grew at a rate of about 3% a year over this period.

With the vast expansion of resources employed in the university enterprise, and the very great expansion in the funding role of the federal government, there came about an equally dramatic transformation in the character of university research.

We shall argue shortly that solutions to practical problems continue to dominate the articulated rationale for most university research. However, there was a major shift in the nature of university research towards the basic end of the spectrum. In contrast with the pre-World War II era when proponents of basic research had to fight hard against a dominant applications orientation, in the environment after World War II "basic research" became not only respectable, but widely perceived as what the universities ought to be doing. By the mid-1960s the American system was clearly providing world leadership in most fields of science. Statistics of Nobel Prizes tell part of the story, but the best indicator is the flow of students from Europe to the United States for their graduate training, a reversal of the situation prior to the war.

But while American universities became the pre-eminent centers of basic research and graduate education, the dominant rationale for most of the research funding continued to be the expectation that the research would yield practical benefits. The National Science Foundation is indeed committed to the support of basic research for its own sake, with the broad rationale that the research sooner or later will yield social benefits, but the NSF has accounted for less than one-fifth of federal support for university research over the post-war period. The Department of Defense and two other government agencies that are allied with Defense in many ways, NASA and the Department of Energy (earlier the Atomic Energy Commission), have accounted for much more, roughly one-third in total. This share has remained virtually constant since 1960, but is likely to fall significantly in the coming years. In the years through 1960 the National Institutes of Health provided roughly comparable funds, about a third of the federal total. After 1960 NIH funding of university research increased greatly, and the NIH presently is by far the largest federal supporter of academic research, now accounting for almost half of total federal support.

The mission orientation of the biggest funders of academic research, and their particular fields of interest, is reflected in the distribution of research funding by field. Funded research in the engineering disciplines exceeds funded research in the physical sciences. The interests and money of the DOD and kindred organizations thus show through very clearly. . . .

. . . [E]xcept for the period between the mid-1960s and the mid-1970s, over 30% of university research has been on projects that are explicitly labelled as "applied research" or even "development." Here the Department of Defense and related agencies would appear to be the principal clients.

The changing composition of funding sources is additionally reflected in the changing output of university research. In view of the fact that more than half of the university research funding since the 1960s has come from DOD, DOE, NASA and the NIH, one would expect that this would be reflected in an increase in the role played by university research in defense and space technology and in health and medicine. Indeed, the role of universities in these areas has been very substantial since 1945.

In fact, a large part of university defense-related research funding in the postwar years built directly upon an earlier military research program . . . the development of the electronic digital computer. MIT, which had done important earlier work on techniques of electronic computation in the late 1930s (work with which Vannevar Bush had been closely associated), played an even more prominent role in the postwar years. MIT's research in this field had been supported by the Rockefeller Foundation and then, on a substantially larger scale, as part of Project Whirlwind. Project Whirlwind, supported by the Office of Naval Research for the development of general-purpose computer programming capabilities, had achieved some important successes. These included Jay Forrester's invention of a magnetic storage system in 1949. After the Soviets detonated an atomic bomb in August 1949, the Air Force proposed that Whirlwind be incorporated in a highly ambitious national air defense system, called SAGE (Semi-Automatic Ground Environment). The first portion of the SAGE system went into operation in June 1958. . . .

The link between federal research priorities and university research's contribution to technical advance is further strengthened by an examination of the biotechnology revolution. Since World War II, the federal government has devoted substantial resources toward medical research and the life sciences. The genetic engineering revolution that began in the mid-1970s represents a clear payoff from this investment. However, over 20 years passed before university researchers were able to synthesize the first human genes, a synthesis based upon the identification of the double helix structure of the DNA molecule in the early 1950s. Research at Stanford, UCSF, and Harvard was critical in the development of the methods for this pathbreaking innovation. . . .

. . . [N]umerous "start-up" firms with close connections to universities have operated on the assumption that the performance of good science was a sufficient condition for the achievement of financial success. Biogen, whose CEO in the early 1980s was a Harvard Nobel Prize-winning biologist, is symptomatic of biotech firms that concentrated on good science with little financial discipline or attention to "downstream" product development. It survived after its stock fell from $23 in 1983, when it first went public, to around $5 by the end of 1984, only as a result of drastic managerial reorganization. . . . [B]iotechnology represents an important industrial sector with a strong contemporary reliance on university research. Not surprisingly, the links between university research and industry are closer in this industry than in many others.

As a result of the changes we have been describing, research aimed at helping local civilian industry and agriculture, which was the hallmark of the American university research enterprise prior to World War II, became a much smaller part of the total picture in the postwar era. American university research that was aimed at solving practical problems for local economic needs dwindled (at least relatively) because defense and health-related problems became the dominant foci and the rationale for university research funding. Large parts of the earlier traditional enterprise were . . . very much hands-on, dirt-under-the-nails work, and the post World War II notion that the proper role for academic research was to make scientific and technical breakthroughs militated against this kind of work. . . .

. . . [W]hile the relative share of university research directly aimed to help civilian industry has declined greatly from what it was before World War II, many universities did remain in the role of helping local industry. Engineering schools like RPI and Georgia Tech continued to serve local industry, even if MIT and, even more so, Cal Tech drew away from that function. Federal and state funding for agricultural research actually increased over the postwar period, even if it became a relatively very small part of total university research funding.

The rise of concerns about the competitiveness of American industry that marked the 1980s rekindled notions that a major explicit objective of American universities ought to be to service civilian industry. The end of the Cold War and the erosion of the credibility of national security as a rationale for public support of universities has also led to a rethinking of old missions. . . .

We began this essay by remarking on the significant increase in the fraction of academic research funded by industry over the past two decades, and the rapid growth in the number and size of university-industry research centers. Many in universities clearly see all this as just the beginning, and anticipate a significant further increase of industry funding of academic research. Many of those concerned with government policies towards universities also foresee this development, anticipating that in the coming years industry funding will reduce the need of government funds to support the academic research enterprise. But while at first this sounds like a harmony of consistent anticipations and expectations, there are strong reasons for skepticism.

In the first place, many of the academics hoping for a significant further increase in industrial funding also hope for this to occur without much change in what academics actually do or in how their research is oriented. Many academics clearly have a firm belief in what has been called the "linear model" of technological advance, seeing unfettered research by academics as providing the basis for technological innovations in industry, with the process not calling for strong industry influence over what the academics actually do. . . .

The industry views . . . suggest, on the other hand, considerable industry skepticism over the ability of academics to contribute directly to industrial innovation, which probably reflects a drawing back from more hopeful and less realistic beliefs held earlier in the 1980s. To a considerable extent the industry views expressed . . . were that the academics should stick with the basic research they are doing, and heed their training functions, and stop thinking of themselves as the source of technology. These views also suggest that it is highly unlikely that industry funding of academic research is going to increase much in the coming years.

We believe that expectations held by some about what university research, if suitably reoriented, can contribute directly to industrial innovation, are quite unrealistic, and so also beliefs about how much funding of academic research private industry is likely to shoulder. At the same time we disagree with those academics and others who argue for a simple continuation of the status quo. We do think that the times call for a major rethinking about what Americans ought to expect of their university research system and in particular about how university research ought to relate to industry. We believe the issue of competitiveness is a serious one. We also believe that American universities can help restore competitiveness in those technologies that their research illuminates. However, it is important to sort out when universities are capable of helping and where, while there may be problems, university research does not seem to be an appropriate answer.

While much of the attention recently has been on the weakness of American industry in product and progress development, we think it a mistake to see universities as a likely source of solution here. Less attention has been given to the erosion of industrial research, as contrasted with design and development, in a number of industries where industrial research traditionally has been very strong, particularly in electronics. Here university research can be of more help.

Actually, as we have noted, the present danger is that the university contribution may decline. The end of the Cold War has eroded the rationale that has served over the past 40 years to provide the justification for government support of university research in a number of fields of vital importance to American industry. The first order of business, in our view, is to assure that government support of university research in the engineering disciplines and applied sciences, such as materials and computer science, not be orphaned by sharp cutbacks in military R & D that are almost certain to occur over the coming years. One element that is essential is to articulate clearly that a major purpose of government funding of university research in these fields is to assist American industry. . . .

. . . [I]f such research is to be fruitful there must be close communication and interaction between those who do research, and those who are responsible for product and process design and development. If university research is to pick up more of the role that industrial research has been serving, this would seem to mean that there needs to be close links between university researchers doing the research, and their scientific and technical colleagues in industry. These exist in important areas of defense technology, and in technologies relating to agriculture and health. The new university–industry research centers extend the range of such connections. If university research is to play a more helpful role in industrial innovation, the connections need to be further extended and strengthened.

Does this mean, as some people seem to argue, that universities should get much more into the business of helping industry develop particular new products and process? As a general rule, we don't think so. . . .

. . . [W]e think it ill-advised to try to get university researchers to work on specific practical problems of industry, or on particular product or process development efforts. In general, university researchers are poorly equipped for judging what is likely to be an acceptable solution to a problem and what is not. University researchers are almost always insufficiently versed in the particulars of specific product markets to make good decisions about appropriate tradeoffs. Equally important, such work provides few results that are respected or rewarded in academic circles, unlike research that pushes forward conceptual knowledge in an applied science or engineering discipline.

What of the practical problem-solving that marked earlier days of American university research, the research on boilers or the processing of ores, that used to be quite common on university campuses? That kind of work is still there, often associated with education programs for engineers who will go out into local industry, or in business "incubator" programs at places such as Georgia Tech. It is there in larger scale and more systematic form in institutions affiliated with universities, but not an integral part of them, where research is undertaken to serve the needs of particular national industries (e.g., Carnegie-Mellon's Center for Iron and Steelmaking Research, or the Forest Products Laboratory at the University of Wisconsin).

By and large, there programs have grown up in fields where industrial research is not strong. They are a substitute for industrial R & D, or represent a locus for it outside of industry itself. The industries in question tend to be, although not always, made up of small firms without R & D facilities, and often the technologies in question lack a sound underlying scientific base. . . .

These kinds of programs can be very valuable to industries whose firms do little R & D of their own. They are an important part of the activities of many universities. However, after a certain size is surpassed, their locus at universities becomes more a matter of historical happenstance of convenience than a particular source of strength. They could exist just as well as separate organizations.

In any case, we do not think that the emphasis of university research ought to be here, or that a revamped policy of federal-support of university research which places the emphasis on contributions to industrial technical advance ought to be oriented to this kind of work. It is in research, not commercial design and development, that universities excel. . . .

A shift in emphasis of university research toward more extensive connections with the needs of civilian industry can benefit industry and the universities if it is done in the right way. That way, in our view, is to respect the division of labor between universities and industry that has grown up with the development of the engineering disciplines and applied sciences, rather than one that attempts to draw universities deeply into a world in which decisions need to be made with respect to commercial criteria.

Why Build Computers?

PAUL N. EDWARDS

For two decades, from the early 1940s until the early 1960s, the armed forces of the United States were the single most important driver of digital computer development. Though most of the research work took place at universities and in commercial firms, military research organizations such as the Office of Naval Research, the Communications Security Group (known by its code name OP-20-G), and the Air Comptroller's Office paid for it. Military users became the proving ground for initial concepts and prototype machines. As the commercial computer industry began to take shape, the armed forces and the defense industry served as the major marketplace. Most historical accounts recognize the *financial* importance of this backing in early work on computers. But few, to date, have grasped the deeper significance of this military involvement.

At the end of World War II, the electronic digital computer technology we take for granted today was still in its earliest infancy. It was expensive, failure-prone, and ill-understood. Digital computers were seen as calculators, useful primarily for accounting and advanced scientific research. An alternative technology, analog computing, was relatively cheap, reliable (if not terribly accurate) better developed, and far better supported by both industrial and academic institutions. . . . [A]nalog computing was more easily adapted to the control applications that constituted the major uses of computers in battle. Only in retrospect does it appear obvious that command, control, and communications should be united within a single technological frame (to use Wiebe Bijker's term) centered around electronic digital computers.

Why, then, did military agencies provide such lavish funding for digital computer research and development? What were their near-term goals and long-term visions, and how were these coupled to the grand strategy and political culture of the Cold War? How were those goals and visions shaped over time, as computers moved out of laboratories and into rapidly changing military systems?

I will argue that military support for computer research was rarely benign or disinterested—as many historians, taking at face value the public postures of funding agencies and the reports of project leaders, have assumed. Instead, practical military objectives guided technological development down particular channels, increased its speed, and helped shape the structure of the emerging computer industry. I will also argue, however, that the social relations between military agencies and civilian researchers were by no means one-sided. More often than not it was civilians, not military planners, who pushed the application of computers to military problems. Together, in the context of the Cold War, they enrolled computers as supports for a far-reaching discourse of centralized command and control—as an enabling, infrastructural technology for the closed-world political vision. . . .

During World War II, virtually all computer research (like most scientific research and development) was funded directly by the War Department as part of the war effort. But there are particularly intimate links between early digital computer

From Paul N. Edwards, *The Closed World: Computers and the Politics of Discourse in Cold War America* (Cambridge, MA: MIT Press, 1996), pp. 43–49, 52–53, 58–64, 65–66, 70–73.

research, key military needs, and the political fortunes of science and engineering after the war. These connections had their beginnings in problems of ballistics. . . .

[Vannevar] Bush was perhaps the single most important figure in American science during World War II, not because of his considerable scientific contributions but because of his administrative leadership. As war approached, Bush and some of his distinguished colleagues had used their influence to start organizing the scientific community for the coming effort. After convincing President [Franklin] Roosevelt that close ties between the government and scientists would be critical to this war, they established the National Defense Research Committee (NDRC) in 1940, with Bush serving as chair. When the agency's mandate to conduct research but not development on weapons systems proved too restrictive, Bush created and took direction of an even larger organization, the development-oriented Office of Scientific Research and Development (OSRD), which subsumed the NDRC. The OSRD coordinated and supervised many of the huge science and engineering efforts mobilized for World War II. By 1945 its annual spending exceeded $100 million; the prewar *total* for military R & D had been about $23 million.

Academic and industrial collaboration with the military under the OSRD was critically important in World War II. Research on radio, radar, the atomic bomb, submarines, aircraft, and computers all moved swiftly under its leadership. Bush's original plans called for a decentralized research system in which academic and industrial scientists would remain in their home laboratories and collaborate at a distance. As the research effort expanded, however, this approach became increasingly unwieldy, and the OSRD moved toward a system of large central laboratories.

Contracts with universities varied, but under most of them the university provided laboratory space, management, and some of the scientific personnel for large, multidisciplinary efforts. The Radio Research Laboratory at Harvard employed six hundred people, more of them from California institutions than from Harvard itself. MIT's Radiation Laboratory, the largest of the university research programs, ultimately employed about four thousand people from sixty-nine different academic institutions. Academic scientists went to work for industrial and military research groups, industrial scientists assisted universities, and the military's weapons and logistics experts and liaison officers were frequent visitors to every laboratory. The war effort thus brought about the most radical disciplinary mixing, administrative centralization, and social reorganization of science and engineering ever attempted in the United States.

It would be almost impossible to overstate the long-term effects of this enormous undertaking on American science and engineering. The vast interdisciplinary effort profoundly restructured scientific research communities. It solidified the trend to science-based industry—already entrenched in the interwar years—but it added the new ingredient of massive government funding and military direction. MIT, for example, "emerged from the war with a staff twice as large as it had had before the war, a budget (in current dollars) four times as large, and a *research* budget ten times as large—85 percent from the military services and their nuclear weaponeer, the AEC." Eisenhower famously named this new form the "military-industrial complex," but the nexus of institutions is better captured by the concept of the "iron triangle" of self-perpetuating academic, industrial, and military collaboration.

Almost as important as the institutional restructuring was the creation of an unprecedented *experience* of community among scientists and engineers. Boundaries between scientific and engineering disciplines were routinely transgressed in the wartime labs, and scientists found the chance to apply their abilities to create useful devices profoundly exciting. For example, their work on the Manhattan Project bound the atomic physicists together in an intellectual and social brotherhood whose influence continued to be felt into the 1980s. Radiation Laboratory veterans protested vigorously when the lab was to be abruptly shut down in December 1945 as part of postwar demobilization; they could not believe the government would discontinue support for such a patently valuable source of scientific ideas and technical innovations. Their outcry soon provoked MIT, supported by the Office of Naval Research (ONR), to locate a successor to the Rad Lab in its existing Research Laboratory of Electronics. Connections formed during the war became the basis . . . for enduring relationships between individuals, institutions, and intellectual areas. . . .

This trend, and the politics it reflected, resulted from three concurrent developments in postwar American politics. First, in the rapid transition from World War II to the Cold War, the war's key events served as anchoring icons for postwar policies. Wartime institutions became blueprints for their postwar counterparts. Second, the emerging politico-military paradox of a peacetime Cold War generated a perceived need for new technology, justifying vast military investments in research. Finally, fierce public debates about postwar federal support for science and technology had ended in stalemate. Plans for a National Science Foundation suffered long delays, and military agencies were left to fill the resulting vacuum. . . .

In his famous 1945 tract *Science: The Endless Frontier*, composed at President Roosevelt's request as a blueprint for postwar science and technology policy, Vannevar Bush called for a civilian-controlled National Research Foundation to preserve the government-industry-university relationship created during the war. In his plea for continuing government support, Bush cited the Secretaries of War and Navy to the effect that scientific progress had become not merely helpful but utterly essential to military security for the United States in the modern world. . . .

Bush's MIT colleague Edward L. Bowles, Radiation Laboratory "ambassador" to government and the military, advocated an even tighter connection. Bowles wrote of the need to "systematically and deliberately couple" scientific and engineering schools and industrial organizations with the military forces "so as to form a continuing, working partnership." . . .

Bush's efforts were rebuffed, at first, by [President Harry] Truman's veto of the bill establishing the National Science Foundation (NSF). The populist president blasted the bill, which in his view "would . . . vest the determination of vital national policies, the expenditure of large public funds, and the administration of important government functions in a group of individuals who would be essentially private citizens. The proposed National Science Foundation would be divorced from . . . control by the people."

With major research programs created during the war in jeopardy, the War Department moved into the breach, creating the Office of Naval Research in 1946. In a pattern repeated again and again during the Cold War, national security provided the consensual justification for federally funded research. The ONR, conceived as a temporary stopgap until the government created the NSF, became the major federal force in science in the immediate postwar years and remained important throughout the 1950s. Its mandate was extremely broad: to fund basic research ("*free* rather than directed research"), primarily of an unclassified nature.

Yet the ONR's funding was rarely, if ever, a purely altruistic activity. The bill creating the office mentioned the "paramount importance [of scientific research] as related to the maintenance of future naval power, and the preservation of national security"; the ONR's Planning Division sought to maintain "listening posts" and contacts with cutting-edge scientific laboratories for the Navy's possible use. Lawmakers were well aware that the ONR represented a giant step down the road to a permanent federal presence in science and engineering research and a precedent for military influence. House Committee on Naval Affairs Chairman Carl Vinson opposed the continuing executive "use of war powers in peacetime," forcing the Navy to go directly to Congress for authorization.

By 1948 the ONR was funding 40 percent of *all* basic research in the United States, by 1950 the agency had let more than 1,200 separate research contracts involving some 200 universities. About half of all doctoral students in the physical sciences received ONR support. ONR money proved especially significant for the burgeoning field of computer design. It funded a number of major digital computer projects, such as MIT's Whirlwind, Raytheon's Hurricane, and Harvard's Mark III. The NSF, finally chartered in 1950 after protracted negotiations, did not become a significant funding source for computer science until the 1960s (in part because computer science did not become an organized academic discipline until then). Even after 1967, the only period for which reliable statistics are available, the NSF's share of total federal funding for computer science hovered consistently around the 20 percent mark, while Department of Defense obligations ranged between 50 and 70 percent, or 60 to 80 percent if military-related agencies such as the Department of Energy (responsible for atomic weapons research) and NASA (whose rockets lifted military surveillance satellites and whose research contributed to ballistic missile development) are included. . . .

What sort of influence did this military support have on the development of computers? . . .

First, military funding and purchases in the 1940s and 1950s enabled American computer research to proceed at a pace so ferocious as to sweep away competition from Great Britain, the only nation then in a position to become a serious rival. At the end of World War II the British possessed the world's only functioning, fully electronic digital computer (Turing's Colossus), and until the early 1950s its sophistication in computing at least equaled that of the United States. . . .

With its financial resources limited by the severe demands of postwar reconstruction, the British government failed to pursue the field with the intensity of the United States. British researchers and producers were in general left to more ordinary commercial and technical resources. By the time large-scale commercial markets for computers developed in the early 1960s, British designs lagged behind American models. Unable to keep up, the fledgling British computer industry declined dramatically: though British firms totally dominated the British market in the 1950s, by 1965 more than half of computers operating in Britain were U.S. made.

Second, the military secrecy surrounding some of both British and American research impeded the spread of the new technology. Most academic researchers felt advances would come faster in an atmosphere of free exchange of ideas and results. They pressed to reestablish such a climate, and in many cases—such as that of the IAS computer, whose technical reports and plans were widely disseminated—they succeeded. But the wartime habits of secrecy died hard, and in the course of the Cold War tensions between military and commercial interests rose. In August 1947 Henry Knutson of the ONR's Special Devices Center informed Jay Forrester, director of the MIT Whirlwind computer project, that "the tendency is to upgrade the classification [of military-funded research projects] and that all computer contracts are now being reconsidered with the possible view of making them confidential." Much of the Whirlwind work was, in fact, classified. (Indeed, in the 1950s MIT spun off the Lincoln Laboratories from its university operations because of the huge volume of classified research on air defense, including computers.) In the late 1940s, Forrester sometimes had trouble recruiting researchers because so many people refused to work on military projects. John Mauchly, to cite another kind of postwar security issue, was accused of being a communist sympathizer (he was not) and was denied a clearance.

Though many of the military-sponsored computer projects were not classified in the direct sense, informal self-censorship remained a part of postwar academic research culture. As Paul Forman has argued, "strictly speaking there was in this [post-World War II] period no such thing as unclassified research under military sponsorship. 'Unclassified' was simply that research in which some considerable part of the responsibility for deciding whether the results should be held secret fell upon the researcher himself and his laboratory." Forman cites the ONR's Alan Waterman and Capt. R. D. Conrad, writing in 1947, to the effect that "the contractor is entirely free to publish the results of his work, but . . . we expect that scientists who are engaged on projects under Naval sponsorship are as alert and as conscientious as we are to recognize the implications of their achievement, and that they are fully competent to guard the national interest."

Third, even after mature commercial computer markets emerged in the early 1960s, U.S. military agencies continued to invest heavily in advanced computer research, equipment, and software. In the 1960s the private sector gradually assumed that bulk of R & D funding. IBM, in particular, adopted a strategy of heavy investment in research, reinvesting over 50 percent of its profits in internal R & D after 1959. The mammoth research organization IBM built gave it the technical edge partly responsible for the company's dominance of the world computer market for the next two decades. To compete, other companies eventually duplicated IBM's pattern of internal research investment.

Despite the extraordinary vitality of commercial R & D after the early 1960s, the Pentagon continued to dominate research funding in certain areas. For example, almost half of the cost of semiconductor R & D between the late 1950s and the early 1970s was paid by military sources. Defense users were first to put into service integrated circuits (ICs, the next major hardware advance after transistors); in 1961, only two years after their invention, Texas Instruments completed the first IC-based computer under Air Force contract. The Air Force also wanted the small, lightweight ICs for Minuteman missile guidance control. In 1965, about one-fifth of all American IC sales went to the Air Force for this purpose. Only in that year did the first commercial computer to incorporate ICs appear. ICs and other miniaturized electronic components allowed the construction of sophisticated digital guidance computers that were small, light, and durable enough to fit into missile warheads. This, in turn, made possible missiles with multiple, independently targetable reentry vehicles (MIRVs), which were responsible for the rapid growth of nuclear destructive potential in the late 1960s and early 1970s. ICs were the ancestors of today's micro-processors and very-large-scale integrated circuitry, crucial components of modern cruise missiles and other "smart" weaponry.

Another instance was the nurturance of artificial intelligence (AI) by the Advanced Research Projects Agency (ARPA, later called DARPA, the Defense Advanced Research Projects Agency), which extended from the early 1960s until the final end of the Cold War. AI, for over two decades almost exclusively a pure research area of no immediate commercial interest, received as much as 80 percent of its total annual funding from ARPA. . . .

Artificial intelligence per se was only one of many kinds of computer research [that ARPA's Information Processing Technologies Office (IPTO)] backed; ARPA budgets did not even include AI as a separate line item until 1968. Numerous other IPTO-funded projects reaped major advances. Perhaps most significant of these was the ARPANET computer network, which eventually spawned the MILNET military network and the modern worldwide network of networks known as the Internet. Other ARPA-supported work has included supercomputing (as in the ILLIAC IV) and advanced microprocessor research (including work on gallium arsenide semi-conductors and very-large-scale integrated circuits). IPTO supported advanced computing and AI not only at MIT and Stanford but at Rand, Carnegie-Mellon, SRI, SDC, BBN . . . and seven other "centers of excellence."

As the project with the least immediate utility and the farthest-reaching ambitions, AI came to rely unusually heavily on ARPA funding. As a result, ARPA became the primary patron for the first twenty years of AI research. Former director Robert Sproull proudly concluded that "a whole generation of computer experts got their start from DARPA funding" and that "all the ideas that are going into the fifth-generation [advanced computing] project [of the mid-1980s]—artificial intelligence, parallel computing, speech understanding, natural-languages programming—ultimately started from DARPA-funded research." In the late 1980s, DARPA remained the largest single funding source within the military for computer and behavioral sciences. Since its founding, IPTO has typically provided between 50 and 80 percent of the federal government's share, which is usually by far the largest share, of AI research budgets in the academic centers it funds. . . .

. . . ARPA also supported such other important innovations as timesharing and computer networking. In 1983, with its Strategic Computing Initiative (SCI), DARPA led a concerted Pentagon effort to guide certain critical fields of leading-edge computer research, such as artificial intelligence, semiconductor manufacture, and parallel processing architectures, in particular directions favorable to military goals.

Thus the pattern of military support has been widespread, long-lasting, and deep. In part because of connections dating to the ENIAC [Electronic Numerical Integrator and Calculator, the first American electronic digital computer] and before, this pattern because deeply ingrained in postwar institutions. But military agencies led cutting-edge research in a number of key areas even after a commercial industry became well established in the 1960s. As Frank Rose has written, "the computerization of society . . . has essentially been a side effect of the computerization of war." . . .

We have explored the origin of military support, its extent, and some of its particular purposes. Now we must return once again to the question posed by this chapter's title, this time at the level of more general institutional and technical problems.

Why did the American armed forces establish and maintain such an intimate involvement with computer research?

The most obvious answer comes from the utilitarian side of the vision captured in General [William] Westmoreland's "electronic battlefield" speech [in 1969]: computers can automate and accelerate important military tasks. The speed and complexity of high-technology warfare have generated control, communications, and information analysis demands that seem to defy the capacities of unassisted human beings. Jay Forrester, an MIT engineer who played a major role in developing the military uses of computing, wrote that between the mid-1940s and the mid-1950s

> the speed of military operations increased until it became clear that, regardless of the assumed advantages of human judgment decisions, the internal communication speed of the human organization simply was not able to cope with the pace of modern air warfare. . . . In the early 1950s experimental demonstrations showed that enough of [the] decision making [process] was understood so that machines could process raw data into final weapon-guidance instruction and achieve results superior to those then being accomplished by the manual systems.

Computers thus improved military systems by "getting man out of the loop" of critical tasks. Built directly into weapons systems, computers assisted or replaced human skills in aiming and operating advanced weapons, such as antiaircraft guns and missiles. They automated the calculation of tables. They solved difficult mathematical problems in weapons engineering and in the scientific research behind military technologies, augmenting or replacing human calculation. Computers began to form the keystone of what the armed forces now call "C^3I"—command, control communications, and intelligence (or information) networks, replacing and assisting humans in the encoding and decoding of messages, the interpretation of radar data, and tracking and targeting functions, among many others.

I will argue that this automation theory is largely a retrospective reconstruction. In the 1940s it was not at all obvious that *electronic digital* computers were going to be good for much besides exotic scientific calculations. Herman Goldstine recalled that well into the 1950s "most industrialists viewed [digital] computers mainly as tools for the small numbers of university or government scientists, and the chief applications were thought to be highly scientific in nature. It was only later that the commercial implications of the computer began to be appreciated." Furthermore, the field of analog computation was well developed, with a strong industrial base and a well-established theoretical grounding. Finally, analog control mechanisms (servomechanisms) had seen major improvements during the war. They were readily available, well-understood and reliable.

Howard Aiken, the Harvard designer of several early digital computers, told Edward Cannon that "there will never be enough problems, enough work, for more than one or two of these [digital] computers," and many others agreed. . . .

The utilitarian account of military involvement in computer development . . . fails to explain one of the major paradoxes of military automation. Computers were used first to automate calculation, then to control weapons and guide aircraft, and later to analyze problems of command through simulation. The final step in this logic would be the eventual automation of command itself; intermediate steps would centralize it and remove responsibilities from lower levels. Military visionaries and defense intellectuals continually held out such centralization as some kind of ulti-mate goal, as in General Westmoreland's dream of the electronic battlefield. By the mid-1980s, DARPA projects envisioned expert systems programs to analyze battles, plot strategies, and execute responses for carrier battle group commanders. The Strategic Computing Initiative program announcement claimed that in "the projected defense against strategic nuclear missiles . . . systems must react so rapidly that it is likely that almost complete reliance will have to be placed on automated systems" and proposed to develop their building blocks. DARPA's then-director Robert Cooper asserted, in an exchange with Senator Joseph Biden, that with sufficiently powerful computers, presidential errors in judgment during a nuclear confrontation might be rendered impossible: "we might have the technology so he couldn't make a mistake."

The automation of command clearly runs counter to ancient military traditions of personal leadership, decentralized battlefield command, and experience-based authority. By the early 1960s, the beginning of the [Secretary of Defense Robert] McNamara era and the early period of the "electronic battlefield," many military leaders had become extremely suspicious of the very computers whose development their organizations had led. Those strategists who felt the necessity and promise of automation described by Jay Forrester were opposed by others who saw that the domination of strategy by preprogrammed plans left no room for the extraordinarily contingent nature of battlefield situations. In 1964, Air Force Colonel Francis X. Kane reported in the pages of *Fortune* magazine that "much of the current planning for the present and future security of the U.S. rests on computerized solutions." It was, he wrote, impossible to tell whether the actual results of such simulated solu-tions would occur as desired, because

> we have no experience in comparing the currently accepted theory of predicting wars by computer with the actual practice of executing plans. But I believe that today's planning is inadequate because of its almost complete dependence on scientific methodology, which cannot reckon with those acts of will that have always determined the conduct of wars. . . . In today's planning the use of a tool—the computer—dictates that we depend on masses of data of repeated events as one of our fundamental techniques. We are ignor-ing individual experience and depending on mass experience instead.

Also in the early 1960s occasional articles in the armed forces journal *Military Review* began warning of "electronic despotism" and "demilitarized soldiers" whose tasks would be automated to the point that the men would be deskilled and become soft. Based on interviews with obviously disaffected commanders, *U.S. News & World Report* reported in 1962–under the banner headline "Will 'Computers' Run Wars of the Future?"—that "military men no longer call the tunes, make strategy decisions and choose weapons. In the Pentagon, military men say they are being forced to the side-lines by top civilians, their advice either ignored or not given proper hearing. . . . In actual defense operations, military commanders regard themselves as increasingly dependent on computer systems." While these reports certainly exaggerated the actual role of computers in military planning and especially in military operations at the time, their existence shows that the view of computers as a solution to military problems faced internal opposition from the start. They also demonstrate how deeply an ideol-ogy of computerized command and control had penetrated into U.S. military culture.

The automation theory alone, then, explains neither the urgency, the magnitude, nor the specific direction of the U.S. military effort in computing. Rather than explain how contests over the nature and potential of computers were resolved, the utilitarian view writes history backwards, using the results of those contests to account for their origins.

Nor does the utilitarian view explain the pervasive military *fascination* with computers epitomized by General Westmoreland's speech in the aftermath of Vietnam. "I see," he proclaimed, "an Army built into and around an integrated area control system that exploits the advanced technology of communications, sensors, fire direction, and the required automatic data processing—a system that is sensitive to the dynamics of the ever-changing battlefield—a system that materially assists the tactical commander in making sound and timely decisions." This is the language of vision and technological utopia, not practical necessity. It represents a dream of victory that is bloodless for the victor, of battle by remote control, of speed approaching the instantaneous, and of certainty in decision-making and command. It is a vision of a closed world, a chaotic and dangerous space rendered orderly and controllable by the powers of rationality and technology.

Why build computers? In this chapter I have tried to show that not only the answers, but also the very question, are complex. Their importance to the future of U.S. military power was by no means obvious at the outset. To understand how it became so, we must look closely at the intricate chains of technological advances, historical events, government policies, and emergent metaphors comprising closed-world discourse. For though policy choices at the largest levels determined research directions, in some cases quite specifically, defining digital computation as relevant to national priorities was not itself a policy issue. Instead it involved a complicated nexus of technological choices, technological traditions, and cultural values. In fact, digital computer research itself ended up changing national priorities.

Command Performance

DAVID NOBLE

Everyone has heard at least some of the war stories about radar, nuclear energy, electronics, computers, high-performance aircraft, and control and communication systems. All of these technologies, and the list is endless, were created to serve purposes peculiar to the military: proximity fuses for bombs, submarine and aircraft detection, combat communications, rocketry and missile warfare, gunfire control, ballistics calculations, command and control defense networks, high-speed, versatile-flight aircraft, and nuclear weapons. Yet, despite these original objectives, it is a common perception that such military-born technologies as these "spill over," as the story goes, into civilian use, where they are then adapted for a host of other more benign and even beneficial purposes. This is the conventional account of the role of the military in technological development. Essentially, this military role is characterized

From David F. Noble, "Command Performance: A Perspective on the Social and Economic Consequences of Military Enterprise," in M. R. Smith, ed., *Military Enterprise and Technological Change: Perspectives on the American Experience* (Cambridge, MA: MIT Press, 1985), pp. 329–335, 340–346.

in two ways. First, it is what economists would call an "externality" as far as the civilian economy is concerned; military-born technologies enter the economy from "outside," so to speak, in a random, unsystematic way. (Of course, this is the way economists view all technological development; for them, military technologies merely combine two externalities, the military, or government, and technology.) Second, the military influence on the development of the technologies is only temporary and is restricted to the actual military uses of the technologies, for weaponry and the like. That is, the military influence does not permanently mark the technologies nor does that military influence in any way spill over along with the technologies when they undergo transfer from the military to the civilian arenas.

I would like to suggest that this conventional view of the role of the military in technological development is problematic on both counts. First, the military role has not been the "externality" that it appears to be when viewed through the lens of the neoclassical economist. Rather, it has been central to industrial development in the United States since the dawn of the industrial revolution. Lewis Mumford among others has been arguing this for some time, but it has been terribly difficult for us to shake the economistic habits as well as the peculiarly American blindness to the presence of the military. Seymour Melman, in his writings about Pentagon capitalism and the permanent war economy, has perhaps contributed more than anyone else to our understanding of the centrality of the military since World War II. But this is not just a postwar phenomenon, as we will see. Second, the influence of the military on the technologies is not temporary, something removed when the technologies enter the civilian economy. The influence spills over in the specific shape of the technologies themselves and in the ways they are put together and used, with far-reaching economic and social consequences that have barely been examined. Professor Melman has described some of the consequences of the military's role in our economy: the vast military monopoly of material, technical, and human resources that might be used to meet human needs were they not diverted toward nonproductive, wasteful, and extremely dangerous military objectives; the corrupting influence of cost-maximizing military procurement and contracting practices, which has given rise to generations of managers who are incapable of truly independent, innovative, efficient, or economical production and to legions of technical personnel who are incompetent to produce for a competitive market or otherwise meet such nonmilitary specifications as cheapness, simplicity, accessibility, and the like. But there are still other ways, more subtle perhaps, in which the military shapes technological and industrial development, with consequences that are no less profound.

In 1965 the Air Force produced a half-hour film, *Modern Manufacturing: A Command Performance,* to promote the use of numerical control manufacturing methods in the military-oriented aerospace industry. The new technology had been developed over the previous decade and a half under Air Force aegis. The film offers a good reflection of the scope of the military's penetration into private industry, ranging from aircraft manufacture to machine tools, electronic controls and communications, and computers (Republic Aviation, Lockheed, Hughes, Giddings and Lewis, Pratt and Whitney, Sundstrand, Kearney and Trecker, Raytheon, and IBM are all in the film). It also illustrates what I will refer to as the dominant characteristics of the military approach to industrial development, characteristics which, together, constitute a system of thinking that informs, embraces, and transcends the particular technological developments themselves. For simplicity, I have reduced these to three basic preoccupations: performance, command, and "modern" methods.

By performance I mean the emphasis placed upon meeting military objectives and what follows necessarily from it. These objectives include, for example, combat readiness, tactical superiority, and strategic responsiveness and control; and these objectives demand such things as—in the case of the Air Force—fast, versatile, and powerful aircraft, keeping up with the arms race for ever more sophisticated weaponry, and worldwide communications and control. And these secondary objectives require another set of manufacturing specifications: the capability to manufacture highly complex yet reliable parts for high-speed aircraft and missiles (airfoils, variable thickness skins, integrally stiffened wing sections, etc.); short lead time and turnaround time to accommodate rapid design changes; and, perhaps most important, the interchangeability, reproducibility, and compatibility vital to an integrated system, what Merritt Roe Smith has aptly called "the uniformity principle." "Tapes can be sent anywhere in the world," the narrator of the film boasts, "to produce interchangeable parts." These military performance objectives are justified in the name of national survival and so too are the product specifications and manufacturing criteria that follow from them. Note that cost has not yet been mentioned. Certainly, it is an important consideration, but only a secondary one, insofar as it is "consistent with reliability and reproducibility," to quote the film again. There is no direct concern whatsoever for meeting market demands or social or human needs.

In a talk at MIT in 1979, British design engineer Michael Cooley referred to management as "a bad habit inherited from the church and the military." I do not know about the church's influence upon management, but the military's is certainly clear. The military term for management is command, a rather straightforward notion that means the superior gives the orders and the subordinate executes them, with no ifs, ands, or buts. It is the ideal of managers everywhere. In the private sector it follows, with more or less legitimacy, from the pursuit of profit, control, and the will to power. In the military it follows from the need to meet performance objectives. Uniformity in manufacture, for example, presupposes command, direct and uncompromised. The film noted above well illustrates this point. First, it was made for top management, not the workforce who would actually be doing the work. The film's theme, the proposed and promised aim of modern manufacturing was "to shorten the chain of command" and "greatly reduce the opportunities for a breakdown in communication." This means less human intervention between order and execution and those who remain will perform "reliably," according to "fixed instructions" that are "not subject to human error or emotion." Thus there will be no reliance upon the autonomy, skill, initiative, or creativity of people who stand between the commander and the machinery. The dream, the supreme management fantasy, is well depicted at the beginning of the film when the top manager voices his commands into the microphone: "orders to the plant." "Humans do what they do best," create, so long as by "humans" we mean top management; on the other hand, "machines do what they do best," the automatic following of orders, down to the last detail.

This brings us to the last characteristic military preoccupation: modern methods. Modern manufacturing means a fetish for machinery which won't talk back, a preoccupation with capital-intensive production. Modern means numerically controlled production machinery, computers, assembly robots, plotters and drafting machines, inspection, testing equipment, transfer machines, machines for automatic welding, forming, and pipe bending. These are the "elements of our plan of the future." People, except for top management and designers, disappear from view almost entirely. Indeed, "modern" specifically means machines, to be contrasted with "conventional," meaning people. But conventional also means "backward" or "primitive," and this gives force to the modernizing drive. This is illustrated, in a racist and pictorially (though unintentionally) humorous way, by scenes of half-clad natives making iron by hand and even operating a lathe in a thatched hut. The message is clear: conventional means reliance upon people and people mean error, emotion, primitiveness. The ideal of the military, and of the managers who have inherited the military habit, is the automatic factory (factory on, factory off). In the meantime the military system of manufacture means a highly regimented system of people, temporary place holders for the robots of the future, who are placed and disciplined by the machinery which has come under direct management control.

Performance, command, modern methods—these then are the dominant characteristics of the military approach to industry, justified in the name of national security and enforced throughout industry by the system of military procurement contracts. The Department of Defense "expects defense contractors to maintain a modern base in their facilities," the film concludes. Within the military framework, all of this makes perfect sense; it is logical, supremely rational. But it becomes irrational in other contexts, as the military approach spills over, permeates, and diffuses throughout the economy, carried in the form of performance requirements, habits of command, and machine designs—irrational because in other contexts the objectives are different. The focus is on meeting social and human needs through the production of cheap goods and services; meeting the demands of a competitive market; fostering the kinds of things all Americans profess to value: self-reliance, democracy, life, liberty, and the pursuit of happiness. The rationality of the military is not always compatible with these objectives; indeed, it is often destructive of them. It increases costs while using up valuable resources; it devalues human judgment, skill, autonomy, self-reliance, initiative, and creativity; it leads to the actual depletion and atrophy of the store of inherited human skills; in its fetish for capital-intensive production, it contributes to the dislocation and displacement of untold numbers of workers and possibly to massive structural unemployment; it fosters, in its emphasis on command, what Mumford has called an "authoritarian" rather than a "democratic" technics, and thus, in the name of order, creates social instability and mounting industrial tensions; in its insistence on uniformity and system integration, it fosters ever increasing complexity and, its correlates, greater inflexibility and unreliability; and, finally, it places human beings, the subject of society, of history, or production, in a subordinate role to military objectives, to the commands that flow from those objectives, and to the machinery that automatically executes those commands. Nothing could be more irrational or more frightening.

It might appear to some, by this time, that I am simply against progress, against technology, against mechanization and automation per se. This is not true. Indeed, quite the contrary. I applaud new ways of doing things as much as the next person. I find many of the particular machines illustrated in the film marvelous. But I try to discipline myself, temper my fascination and enthusiasm, by looking hard at the proposed uses of the technologies and the likely consequences, the human and social costs, the potential for greater or less happiness. This is what I understand to be rationality. Progress for what? What kind of progress? Progress for whom? . . .

Numerical control [a computerized method of manufacturing known as "NC"] was largely underwritten by the U.S. Air Force, including research and development, software development, actual purchase of machinery for contractors, and training of programmers and operators. Total government subsidy of NC development and implementation was over $60 million. As already indicated, the *performance* objectives were high-speed aircraft and missiles, requiring complex machining capability and uniformity. The NC revolution, as it came to be called, was fueled by the Korean War and the Cold War of the 1950s and 1960s. The *command* imperative entailed direct control of production operations not just with a single machine or within a single plant, but worldwide, via data links. The vision of the architects of the NC revolution involved much more than the automatic machining of complex parts; it meant the elimination of human intervention–a shortening of the chain of command—and the reduction of remaining people to unskilled, routine, and closely regulated tasks. It is no surprise, then, that Air Force development of NC involved no worker or union participation.

The way to achieve all this was through *modern methods,* that is, numerical control, which is the translation of part specifications into mathematical information that can be fed directly by management into a machine without reliance upon the skills or initiative of the machinist. The whole fantasy was the fully automatic, computer-controlled factory, still being pursued by the Air Force Integrated Computer-Aided Manufacturing (ICAM) Program. A December 1980 Air Force request for proposals on computer manufacturing systems reads: "Sources are sought which have the experience, expertise and production base for establishing a Flexible Manufacturing System for parts. This FMS should be capable of providing a technically advanced production facility for the manufacture of aerospace batch-manufactured products. The system shall be capable of automatically handling and transporting parts, fixtures, and tools, automatically inspecting part dimensional quality and incoming tool quality; integrated system control with machinability data analysis; computer aided process planning and scheduling and other capabilities that would provide a totally computer-integrated machining facility." The Air Force advertisement announcing this request for proposals also points out that "extensive subcontracting to aerospace and other manufacturers, machine tool vendors, universities and other technology companies is expected." All will get caught up in the military quest for the automatic factory.

Essentially, numerical control is the technical realization of management control envisioned by the directors of the [U.S. Army] Ordnance Department back in the nineteenth century. Gauges, patterns, jigs and fixtures, process planning, time studies—over the years all were designed to get the workforce to perform, manually or with machinery, in a specified way, machine-like. NC is a giant step in the same direction; here management has the capacity to bypass the worker and communicate directly to the machine via tapes or direct computer link. The machine itself can thereafter pace and discipline the worker. Essentially, this transforms skilled batch work into continuous process, assembly-line work. From the military point of view, it is the command performance, supremely rational, the dream come true. But economically and socially, it raises as many problems as it solves.

During the 1940s machine tool manufacturers and control engineers were experimenting with many forms of new equipment for metalworking, trying to put to use wartime developments in electronics and servo-control systems. They came up with improved tracer-controlled machines, plugboard-type controls, and record-playback controls—an ingenious development whereby a machinist made a first part manually while the motions of the machine were recorded on magnetic tape; thereafter the tape was simply played back to recreate the machine motions and duplicate the part. These technologies were ideally suited for small batch automatic production, where a change in set-up was required for each short run of parts. For set-up (programming) and operation, all of these systems relied upon the traditional store of machinist skills and were therefore readily accessible to most metalworking enterprises. But because of the development of NC, they never got very far in either full development or actual use. NC development was dictated by the performance and command objectives of the Air Force; these other technologies, which could not be used effectively to make highly complex parts and, most important, which relied upon the skills and resources of workers, were thus perceived from the start as anachronistic and primitive. In fact, they represented a significant advance on current methods.

NC was the brainchild of John Parsons, a Michigan manufacturer who was trying to meet the demanding military specifications for helicopter rotor blade templates. He elaborated his ideas when he saw a proposed design for an integrally stiffened wing section of a Lockheed fighter, and subsequently sold them to the Air Force. The Air Force eventually contracted with MIT to build the first NC milling machine and then went on to underwrite the software development, the promotion, and the procurement of the new technology—a bulk order purchase that finally elicited the sustained interest of machine tool and electronic control manufacturers.

It is important to note that, as with the uniformity system, industry generally did not share the Air Force's enthusiasm for the new technology, and for good reason. Although NC was theoretically ideal for complex machining, it was not necessarily ideal for the vast majority of metalworking orders that were not so demanding. NC was also very costly, not only for the hardware but also for the software and computers required to calculate endless amounts of information for the machine controls. NC was also notoriously unreliable, and the programming involved was excessive and time-consuming. With technologies such as record-playback, an analog system that was programmed by manual direction or by following the contour of a pattern, there was no need for computers, programmers, or excessive training of personnel. In addition, the programming was right the first time. In terms of manufacturing needs of the metalworking industry, therefore; it would have been rational to proceed with both technologies, the one for the bulk of metalworking operations, the other (NC) for subsidized military work. But the needs of the Air Force proved hegemonic: when it gave the signal for the development of NC and guaranteed lucrative returns for machine tool and control manufacturers, everyone jumped aboard. All industrial and technical efforts were geared to meet Air Force specifications. Other developments, which might have proved more accessible, more practical, and more economical for the metalworking industry as a whole were abandoned. The Air Force wanted highly sophisticated five-axis machines and a complex, expensive software systems to go with them (the APT system) and enforced their use through the contract system. Machine manufacturers meanwhile concentrated on the most expensive designs, confident that for their subsidized customers in the aerospace industry, cost was not a factor.

Performance, command, modern methods: it all made perfect sense for the Air Force. But the economic and social costs were great. Some very promising technical possibilities were foreclosed in the wake of the rush to numerical control. The great expense of the machinery that was manufactured and the overhead requirements of the programming system made the diffusion of NC into the metalworking industry very slow. The contract system fostered concentration in the metalworking industry because it favored the larger shops able to underwrite the expense of NC and APT. In the vast majority of metalworking establishments, there was no gain from the technical advances in automation until the 1970s.

The commercial competitiveness of U.S. machine manufacturers was also undermined by the concentration on NC. In April 1979, at the hearings of the House of Representatives Committee on Science and Technology, Congressman Ritter of Pennsylvania observed that Japan and Germany invested in machinery for commercial rather than military use. Predictably, Presidential Science Advisor Frank Press assured the congressman that defense expenditures "spill over" into commercial use. But Congressman Ritter was onto something quite significant. While American manufacturers were concentrating on highly sophisticated machinery and the APT software system, Japanese and German manufacturers emphasized cheapness, accessibility, and simplicity in their machine designs and software systems. The result is obvious: in 1978 the United States became a net importer of machine tools for the first time since the nineteenth century, and we still can't compete.

Finally, for workers—and this includes the technical personnel as well as production people—modernization orchestrated according to the Air Force objectives has been disastrous, marked by deskilling, downgrading, routinization, and powerlessness. Autonomy and initiative are giving way to precisely prescribed tasks and computer monitoring and supervision. This is happening even though the latest generations of NC machines, equipped with microprocessors at the machine, now make it possible as never before for the operator to program and edit at the machine and to regain control over more sophisticated technology. The technology is rarely used that way, however, especially in military-oriented plants. There the trend is to integrate these CNC (computer numerical control) machines into a larger DNC (direct numerical control) network under central command. (At a factory in Kongsberg, Norway, for example, workers have successfully struggled to regain control over the editing of machines—except for those who work on the military F-16.) Again, a technical possibility that might mean low costs, higher quality, and better working conditions is foreclosed by military imperatives. Unions are being seriously weakened by the new systems and military strategies. The military requirements of "strategic decentralization" of plants, for example, confronts the unions as runaway shops subsidized by the state. The military demand for interchangeability and communication networks appears to the union as satellite-linked duplicate plants that undermine the power of the strike.

The exaggerated emphasis on capital-intensive methods and automation increases system unreliability (an effect perhaps most obvious in the military itself) while at the same time eliminating irreplaceable human skills—a trend even John

Parsons, the inventor of NC, finds insane and shortsighted. (Parsons was trained in manufacturing by an all-around Swedish machinist, precisely the type of person being lost.) In addition, the military imperatives contribute to dislocation and displacement and ultimately to structural unemployment. This ultimate social cost is now being endured by workers everywhere, invisible and silently. But that low profile will not last long, for it will soon become obvious to all of us that there is simply no place for these people to go—no farms, no factories, no offices. Faith in the inevitable new industry which will absorb them rings hollow. Even the computer and control industries are themselves undergoing automation. Meanwhile the Air Force ICAM Project proceeds apace. Recently, it must be noted, they offered a contract for a study of the social implications of Integrated Computer-Aided Manufacture. But this is no cause for rejoicing. The contract went to Boeing, one of the major users of the latest automated technology. . . .

It should now be obvious that the military has played a central role in industrial development and that this role has left an indelible imprint on that development: the imprint of performance, command, and modern methods. . . . [W]hile the military influence has not been all bad, neither has it been an unmixed blessing. [It suggests] rather that we must take a closer look at what is happening under the military aegis. . . . On whose behalf ought the government to foster technological development? Progress for whom? . . . What exactly are the presumed economic benefits and what have been the social costs? Again, progress for whom and for what? Finally, the computer revolution in manufacturing: what role has the military played in undermining the competitive viability of U.S. industry? How has it promoted industrial concentration? How has it contributed to the deskilling of workers and the degrading of working conditions, the unreliability of our productive plants, the intensification of management power and control at the expense of workers and unions? And, perhaps most crucial, to what extent has it created a yet-to-be-reckoned-with structural unemployment, our own twentieth century "world turned upside down," to borrow Christopher Hill's phrase. Again, what kind of progress are we talking about here, and progress for whom?

Performance, command, modern methods: these words do not appear in the U.S. Constitution nor are the subtle yet profound and pervasive transformation they imply ever voted upon. The role of the military in shaping our technologies, our productive activities, our social organizations, the power relations between us—in shaping our lives, in short—has gone relatively unnoticed and unrecorded. It is time we gave the matter some serious attention, subjected it to critical scrutiny, brought it under democratic control. It is time we began to answer the fundamental questions: what kind of progress do we want? What kind of progress can we, as a society, afford?

↟↟ F U R T H E R   R E A D I N G

Flamm, Kenneth. *Creating the Computer: Government, Industry, and High Technology* (Washington, DC: The Brookings Institution, 1988).

Koistinen, Paul. *The Military-Industrial Complex: A Historical Perspective* (New York: Praeger, 1980).

Leslie, Stuart W. *The Cold War and American Science: The Military-Industrial-Academic Complex at MIT and Stanford* (New York: Columbia University Press, 1993).

Mackenzie, Donald. *Inventing Accuracy: A Historical Sociology of Nuclear Missile Guidance* (Cambridge, MA: The MIT Press, 1990).

Mendelsohn, Everett, Merrit Roe Smith, and Peter Weingart, eds. *Science, Technology and the Military.* 2 vols. (Dordrecht, The Netherlands: Kluwer Academic Publishers, 1988).

Noble, David F. *Forces of Production: A Social History of Automation* (New York: Alfred A. Knopf, 1984).

Norberg, Arthur L., and Judy E. O'Neill. *Transforming Computer Technology: Information Processing for the Pentagon, 1962–1986* (Cambridge: MA: The MIT Press, 1996).

Pursell, Carroll W., Jr., ed. *The Military-Industrial Complex* (New York: Harper & Row, 1972).

Sapolsky, Harvey. *Science and the Navy: The History of the Office of Naval Research* (Princeton, NJ: Princeton University Press, 1990).

Smith, Merritt Roe, ed. *Military Enterprise and Technological Change: Perspectives on the American Experience* (Cambridge, MA: The MIT Press, 1985).

Zachary, G. Pascal. *Endless Frontier: Vannevar Bush, Engineer of the American Century* (New York: The Free Press, 1997).

CHAPTER
13

Countdown to Cyberspace:
1974–1990

✝✝

In the youth politics of the Vietnam War era, the identity of computers and advanced electronics was clear: they were the brain and nerves of "the system" in its most active (dangerous) guises. Twenty years later, the political meaning of numberless personal computers wired to the Internet was, for some, just as evident: "The net sure feels like freedom to me," posted one visitor to the Unabomber home page in 1996, noting that Ted Kaszynski had missed that particular shift in meaning, if he was even aware of the new technology. How was it that ideas about personal and collective freedom (even empowerment) came to be embodied in the enabling technologies of the "military-industrial complex"? Were new ideas and meanings simply responsive to technological developments, to a "microelectronics revolution"? Who was set free, and how?

Most of the following readings address identity, empowerment, and powerlessness among technologies that can only be described as "advanced." They span the period in which personal computers went from being hobbyist kits, to mass-market machines, to nodes on a fledgling Internet. Some of that story is told in the essays and documents included here, but other machines with restructuring potential were also being deployed, resisted, and re-signified in the same period. This chapter will look at relationships Americans had (or imagined having) with several types of microelectronic technologies.

The idea of confiscating or "liberating" advanced technology from existing power collectives was a peripheral and controversial position in leftist politics through the 1970s and early 1980s. The alternative technology movement imagined wind and solar power as successor technologies to nuclear energy. Emphasis was on invention; no one spoke of "liberating" nuclear plants. Under the slogan "Small Is Beautiful" (the title of a book by E. F. Schumacher), some activists rejected even advanced alternative systems in favor of the local and easily made. Many feminists developed powerful discourses against technology in general as inherently masculinist. The left, then as now, was not a united front.

Neither did technological signification on the right remain static. Christian broadcasters, pioneering the use of satellite dishes, built strong coalitions against the mainstream media. Abortion politics proved a particularly confused (or rich) nexus of technologies, metaphors, and ideas about power over instruments and bodies.

471

But other "appropriations" of advanced technology took place at the periphery *of activist movements. The male hobbyists who nurtured the personal computer are an intriguing case—what were the politics of their artifacts? And what of the women who, in unprecedented numbers, joined the U.S. military in the recruitment crisis following the Vietnam War? Their heightened contact with weapons of war created multiple crises in feminist and masculinist politics, and undermined basic gender inscriptions within the armed forces. Some attributed both these changes to a "microelectronic revolution," in which machinery became lighter and smaller as a matter of course. Miniaturization was clearly a trend within electrical engineering by the 1970s, but, as we saw in previous chapters, so were "supercomputers." And how can technical change account for women firing guns and repairing jet engines?*

"We are cyborgs," wrote Donna Haraway in an influential 1985 essay, "theorized and fabricated hybrids of machine and organism." To activists of the 1970s this would have sounded like a Taylorist military experiment. But Haraway was a feminist, and her "cyborg manifesto" was meant as a challenge, a wake-up call to the left. With a different set of intentions, science fiction author William Gibson coined the term cyberspace *in 1984.* Cyborg *and* cyberspace *became political words with radical meaning to the generation coming of age in the mid-to-late 1980s. To others they represented the submergence of an activist liberal politics.*

In 1979, speaking in a different context, the black lesbian author Audre Lorde said that "the master's tools will never dismantle the master's house." How had "the master's tools"—in the form of high technology—been seized by the early 1990s, and by whom? Were they dismantling, merely remodeling, or instituting a new mastery? Were (are) any other tools available?

⋈ D O C U M E N T S / E S S A Y S

The line between "document" and "essay" in this chapter collapses. Two of the following selections are by professional historians. Others are by sociologists, science fiction authors, and activists, some of whom write as historians. At least one of the historians also writes as an activist.

In the first selection, from *Computer Lib* (1974), activist Ted Nelson argues that computers might be stolen away from a professional "priesthood" by those he calls "fans." From what position is Nelson speaking, and what does he mean by "liberation"?

The second piece, by historians Martin Campbell-Kelly and William Aspray, chronicles the development of the personal computer between the mid-1970s and the early 1980s. The authors place Nelson and computer liberationists in the context of other cultures—hobbyists, business people, and IBM. How did the development of personal computing fulfill, or not fulfill, Nelson's expectations?

The third selection is from sociologist Sherry Turkle's *The Second Self.* Turkle studied early personal computer hobbyists in the Route 128 electronics region of Massachusetts in the late 1970s. How does Turkle's portrait fit with Campbell-Kelly and Aspray's model of hobbyist and computer liberation subcultures?

Fourth is a brief passage from William Gibson's science fiction novel *Neuromancer.* Gibson's novel of a future dystopia was published in 1984, the time (and title) of George Orwell's famous dystopian novel of 1948. The characters in Gibson's novel have a technology that Orwell's lacked—"cyberspace." Very few people in 1984 were aware of computer networking. Is Gibson's cyberspace similar to our own, or was it a vision particular to the 1980s?

Fifth is an excerpt from historian Donna Haraway's influential "Cyborg Manifesto," published in 1985. Haraway's move to expropriate high technology for feminist politics was revolutionary and, to some dangerous. What does Haraway mean when she says, "We are cyborgs," and why does she see this as crucial to feminism and socialism? How does her image of the cyborg differ from Gibson's?

The sixth selection is from Mike Davis' *City of Quartz* published in 1990, two years before the Rodney King beating and the Los Angeles riots. The technologies at work in Davis' Los Angeles range from sophisticated micro-electronics to simple bus benches. Is Davis' landscape the antithesis of the dreams of liberation presented in other selections, or are the two somehow related?

The seventh selection, by DeeDee Halleck, is alternately history, political commentary, and biographical narrative by a media activist whose career began in the 1970s. (The account was published in 1991.) How does Halleck's description of video technology compare to our current language about the Internet? Why doesn't she mention computer networking? How does the Halleck essay relate to the Davis piece?

Last, science fiction author Bruce Sterling presents his short "History of the Internet" (1993). Nelson had spoken of "liberation"; Turkle dwelt on "control" and worried that computers might be an "opiate." How, at the beginning of the 1990s, might the Internet have embodied the strategies and hopes for empowerment and/or control that we've traced through this chapter?

Computer Lib, 1974

TED NELSON

Knowledge is power and so it tends to be hoarded. Experts in any field rarely want people to understand what they do and generally enjoy putting people down.

Thus if we say that the use of computers is dominated by a priesthood, people who spatter you with unintelligible answers and seem unwilling to give you straight ones, it is not that they are different in this respect from any other profession. Doctors, lawyers and construction engineers are the same way.

But computers are very special, and we have to deal with them everywhere, and this effectively gives the computer priesthood a stranglehold on the operation of all large organizations, of government bureaus, and anything else that they run. Members of Congress are now complaining about control of information by the computer people, that they cannot get the information even though it's on computers. Next to this it seems a small matter that in ordinary companies "untrained" personnel can't get straight questions answered by computer people; but it's the same phenomenon.

. . . Guardianship of the computer can no longer be left to a priesthood. I see this as just one example of the creeping evil of Professionalism . . . There may be some chance, though, that Professionalism can be turned around. Doctors, for example, are being told that they no longer own people's bodies. . . .

This is not to say that computer people are trying to louse everybody up on purpose. Like anyone trying to do a complex job as he sees fit, they don't want to be bothered with idle questions and complaints. Indeed, probably any group of insiders would have hoarded computers just as much. If the computer had evolved from the telegraph (which it just might have), perhaps the librarians would have hoarded it conceptually as much as the math and engineering people have. But things have gone too far.

From Ted Nelson, *Computer Lib* (Redmond, WA: Tempus Books of Microsoft Press, 1987), pp. 4–5, 31–32, 37, 107. First Published in 1974.

People have legitimate complaints about the way computers are used, and legitimate ideas for ways they should be used, which should no longer be shunted aside. . . .

With this book I am no longer calling myself a computer professional. I'm a computer *fan,* and I'm out to make you one. (All computer professionals were fans once, but people get crabbier as they get older, and more professional.) A generation of computer fans and hobbyists is well on its way, but for the most part these are people who have had some sort of an In. This is meant to be an In for those who didn't get one earlier.

The computer fan is someone who appreciates the options, fun, excitement, and fiendish fascination of computers. Not only is the computer fun in itself, like electric trains; but it also extends to you a wide variety of possible personal uses. (In case you don't know it, the price of computers and using them is going down as fast as every other price is going up. So in the next few decades we may be reduced to eating soybeans and carrots, but we'll certainly have computers.)

Somehow the idea is abroad that computer activities are *uncreative,* as compared, say, with rotating clay against your fingers until it becomes a pot. This is categorically false. Computers involve imagination and creation at the highest level. Computers are an involvement you can really get into, regardless of your trip or your karma. They are toys, they are tools, they are glorious abstractions. So if you like mental creation, toy trains, or abstractions, computers are for you. If you are interested in democracy and its future, you'd better understand computers. And if you are concerned about power and the way it is being used, and aren't we all right now, the same thing goes. . . .

Public thinking about computers is heavily tinged by a peculiar image which we may call the Myth of the Machine. It goes as follows: there is something called the Machine, which is Taking Over The World. . . . Symbolic of this is of course Charlie Chaplin, dodging the relentless, repetitive, monotonous, implacable, dehumanizing gears of a machine he must deal with in the film *Modern Times. . . .*

. . . What people mainly refuse to see is that *machines in general aren't like that,* relentless, repetitive, monotonous, implacable, dehumanizing. Oh, there are some machines like that, particularly the automobile assembly line. But the assembly line was designed the way it is because it gets the most work out of people. It gets the work it does out of people by the way it exerts pressure.

So here we see the same old trick: people building a system and saying it has to work that way because it's a machine, rather than because that's how I designed it.

To make the point clearer, let's consider some other machines.

The *automobile* is a machine, but it is hardly the repetitive, "dehumanized" thing we usually hear about. It goes uphill, downhill, left and right, fast and slow. It may be decorated. It is the scene of many warm human activities. And most importantly, *automobiles are very much the extension of their owners,* exemplifying life-style, personality, and ideology. Consider the Baja Buggy Volkswagen and the ostentatious cushy Cadillac. Consider the dashboard ornament and the bumper sticker. The Machine, indeed.

The *camera* is a machine, but one that allows its user to freeze and preserve the views and images of the world he wants.

The *bicycle* is a machine, but one that brings you into personal and non-polluting contact with nature, or at least that stylized kind of nature accessible to bicycle paths.

To sum up, then, The Machine is a myth. The bad things in our society are the products of bad systems, bad decisions and conceivably bad people, in various combinations. Machines per se are essentially neutral, though some machines can be built which are bad indeed, such as bombs, guns and death-camps. . . .

. . . In over a decade in the field I have not ceased to marvel at the way people's personalities entwine with the computer, each making it his own—or rejecting it— in his own, often unique and peculiar way, deeply reflecting his concerns and what is in his heart. Yes, odd people are attracted to the computer, and the bonds that hold them are not those of casual interest.

In fact, people tend to *identify* with it.

In this light we may consider the often-heard remarks about computers being rigid, narrow, and inflexible. This is of course true in a sense, but the fact that some people stress it over and over is an important clue to something about them. My own impression is that the people who stress this aspect are the comparatively rigid, narrow and inflexible people.

Other computer experts, no less worthy, tell us the computer is a supertoy, the grandest play machine ever to be discovered. These people tend to be the more outgoing, generous and playful types.

In a classic study, psychiatrist Bruno Bettelheim examined a child who *thought he was a machine,* who talked in staccato monosyllables, walked jerkily and decorated the side of his bed with gears. We will not discuss here the probable origins and cure of this complex; but we must consider that identifying with machines is a crucial cultural theme in American society, an available theme for all of us. And it well may be that computer people are partaking of this same self-image: in a more benign form, perhaps, a shift of gears (as it were) from Bettelheim's mechanical child, but still on the same track.

Some of the computer high-school kids I've known, because of their youth, have been even more up-front about this than adults.

I know one boy, for instance, whose dream was to put a 33ASR Teletype on wheels under radio control, and alarm people at the computer conference by having it roll up to them and clatter out questions impersonally. (If you knew the kid—aloof and haughty-seeming—you might think that's how he approaches people in real life).

I know a high school boy (not a computer expert) who programmed a computer to type out a love story, using the BASIC "print" command, the only one he knew. He could not bring himself to write the love story on paper.

The best example I can think of, though, took place at the kid's booth . . . at a computer conference. One of the more withdrawn girls was sitting at an off-line video terminal, idly typing things onto the screen. When she had gone, a sentence remained. It said:

I love you all, but at a distance.

. . . Computers are COMPLETELY GENERAL, with no fixed purpose or style of operation. In spite of this the strange myth has evolved that computers are somehow "mathematical."

Actually von Neumann, who got the general idea about as soon as anybody (1940s), called the computer

THE ALL-PURPOSE MACHINE.

(Indeed, the first backer of computers after World War II was a maker of multi-lightbulb signs. It is an interesting possibility that if he had not been killed in an airplane crash, computers would have been seen first as text-handling and picture-making machines, and only later developed for mathematics and business.)

We would call it the All-Purpose Machine here, except that for historical reasons it has been slapped with the other name.

But that doesn't mean it has a fixed way of operating. On the contrary.

COMPUTERS HAVE NO NATURE AND NO CHARACTER,

save that which has been put into them by whoever is creating the program for a particular purpose. Computers are, unlike any other piece of equipment, perfectly BLANK. And that is how we have projected on it so many different faces. . . .

Computer people may best be thought of as a new ethnic group, very much unto themselves. Now, it is very hard to characterize ethnic groups in words, and certain to give offense, but if I had to choose one word for them it would be *elfin*. . . .

One common trait of our times—the technique of obscuring oneself—may be more common among computer people than others. . . . Perhaps a certain disgruntlement with the world of people fuses with fascination for (and envy of?) machines. Anyway, many of us who have gotten along badly with people find here a realm of abstractions to invent and choreograph, privately and with continuing control. A strange house for the emotions, this. Like Hegel, who became most eloquent and ardent when he was lecturing at his most theoretical, it is interesting to be among computer freaks boisterously explaining the cross-tangled ramifications of some system they have seen or would like to build.

(A syndrome to ponder. I have seen it more than once: the technical person who, with someone he cares about, cannot stop talking about his ideas for a project. A poignant type of Freudian displacement.)

A sad aspect of this, incidentally, is by no means obvious. This is that the same computer folks who chatter eloquently about systems that fascinate them tend to fall dark and silent while someone *else* is expounding his own fascinations. You would expect that the person with effulgent technical enthusiasms would really click with kindred spirits. In my experience this only happens briefly: hostilities and disagreements boil out of nowhere to cut the good mood. My only conclusion is that the same spirit that originally drives us muttering into the clockwork feels threatened when others start monkeying with what has been controlled and private fantasy.

This can be summed up as follows: NOBODY WANTS TO HEAR ABOUT ANOTHER GUY'S SYSTEM.

The Shaping of the Personal Computer

MARTIN CAMPBELL-KELLY AND WILLIAM ASPRAY

The enabling technology for the personal computer, the microprocessor, was developed during 1969 to 1971 in the semiconductor firm Intel. . . .

When Intel first began operations in 1968, it specialized in the manufacture of semiconductor memory and custom-designed chips. Intel's custom-chip sets were

From Martin Campbell-Kelly and William Aspray, *Computer: A History of the Information Machine* (New York: Harper Collins Basic Books, 1996), pp. 236–257.

typically used in calculators, video games, electronic test gear, and control equipment. In 1969 Intel was approached by the Japanese calculator manufacturer Busicom to develop a chip set for a new scientific calculator—a fairly up-market model that would include trigonometrical and other advanced mathematical functions. The job of designing the chip set was assigned to Ted Hoff.

Hoff decided that instead of specifically designed logic chips for the calculator, a better approach would be to design a general-purpose chip that could be programmed with the specific calculator functions. Such a chip would of course be a rudimentary computer in its own right, although it was some time before the significance of this dawned inside Intel.

The new calculator chip, known as the 4004, was delivered to Busicom in early 1971. . . .

It would have been technically possible to produce an affordable personal computer (costing less than $2,000, say) anytime after the launch of the 4004, in November 1971. But it was not until nearly six years later that a real consumer product emerged, in the shape of the Apple II. The long gestation of the personal computer contradicts the received wisdom of its having arrived almost overnight. It was rather like the transition from wireless telegraphy to radio broadcasting, which the newspapers in 1921 saw as a "fad" that "seemed to come from nowhere"; in fact, it took several years, and the role of the hobbyist was crucial. . . .

The computer hobbyist was typically a young male technophile. Most hobbyists had some professional competence. If not working with computers directly, they were often employed as technicians or engineers in the electronics industry. This typical hobbyist had cut his teeth in his early teens on electronic construction kits, bought through mail-order advertisements in one of the popular electronics magazines. Many of the hobbyists were active radio amateurs. But even those who were not radio amateurs owed much to the "ham" culture, which descended in an unbroken line from the early days of radio. After World War II, radio amateurs and electronic hobbyists moved on to building television sets and hi-fi kits advertised in magazines such as *Popular Electronics* and *Radio Electronics.* In the 1970s, the hobbyists lighted on the computer as the next electronic bandwagon.

Their enthusiasm for computing had often been produced by the hands-on experience of using a minicomputer at work or in college. The dedicated hobbyist hungered for a computer at home for recreational use, so that he could explore its inner complexity, experiment with computer games, and hook it up to other electronic gadgets. However, the cost of a minicomputer—typically $20,000 for a complete installation—was way beyond the pocket of the average hobbyist. To the nonhobbyist, why anyone would have wanted his own computer was a mystery: It was sheer techno-enthusiasm, and one can no more explain it than one can explain why people wanted to build radio sets sixty years earlier when there were no broadcasting stations.

It is important to understand that the hobbyist could conceive of hobby computing only in terms of the technology with which he was familiar. This was not the personal computer as we know it today; rather, the computing that the hobbyist had in mind in the early 1970s was a minicomputer hooked up to a teletype equipped with a paper-tape reader and punch for getting programs and data in and out of the machine. While teletypes were readily available in government surplus shops, the most expensive part of the minicomputer—the central processing unit—remained much too costly for the amateur. The allure of the microprocessor was that it would reduce the price of the central processor by vastly reducing the chip count in the conventional computer.

The amateur computer culture was widespread. While it was particularly strong in Silicon Valley and around Route 128 [in Massachusetts], computer hobbyists were to be found all over the country. The computer hobbyist was primarily interested in tinkering with computer hardware; software and applications were very much secondary issues.

Fortunately, the somewhat technologically fixated vision of the computer hobbyists was leavened by a second group of actors: the advocates of "computer liberation." It would, perhaps, be overstating the case to describe computer liberation as a movement, but there was unquestionably a widely held desire to bring computing to ordinary people. Computer liberation was particularly strong in California, and this perhaps explains why the personal computer was developed in California rather than (say) around Route 128.

Computer liberation sprang from a general malaise in the under-thirty crowd in the post-Beatles, post–Vietnam War period of the early 1970s. There was still a strong anti-establishment culture that expressed itself through the phenomena of college dropouts and campus riots, communal living, hippie culture, and alternative lifestyles sometimes associated with drugs. Such a movement for liberation would typically want to wrest communications technologies from vested corporate interests. In an earlier generation the liberators might have wanted to appropriate the press, but in fact the technology of printing and distribution channels were freely available, so that the young, liberal-minded community was readily able to communicate through magazines such as *Rolling Stone* as well as a vast underground press. On the other hand, computer technology was unquestionably not freely available; it was mostly rigidly controlled in government bureaucracies or private corporations. The much vaunted computer utility was, at $10 to $20 per hour, beyond the reach of ordinary users.

The most articulate spokesperson for the computer liberation idea was Ted Nelson, the financially independent son of the Hollywood actress Celeste Holm. Among Nelson's radical visions of computing was an idea called hypertext, which he first described in the mid-1960s. *Hypertext* was a system by which an untrained person could navigate through a universe of information held on computers. Before such an idea could become a reality, however, it was necessary to "liberate" computing: to make it accessible to ordinary people at a trivial cost. In the 1970s Nelson promoted computer liberation as a regular speaker at computer hobbyist gatherings. He took the idea further in his self-published books *Computer Liberation* and *Dream Machines,* which appeared in 1974. While Nelson's uncompromising views and his unwillingness to publish his books through conventional channels perhaps added to his anti-establishment appeal, this created a barrier between himself and the academic and commercial establishments.

. . . Nelson influenced mainly the young, predominantly male, local Californian technical community.

It is important to understand that personal computing in 1974, whether it was the vision of computer liberation or that of the computer hobbyist, bore little resemblance to the personal computer that emerged three years later—that is, the configuration of a self-contained machine, somewhat like a typewriter, with a keyboard and screen, an internal microprocessor-based computing engine, and a floppy disk for long-term data storage. In 1974 the computer-liberation vision of personal computing was a terminal attached to a large, information-rich computer utility at very low cost, while the computer hobbyist's vision was that of a traditional minicomputer. What brought together these two groups, with such different perspectives, was the arrival of the first hobby computer, the Altair 8800. . . .

In January 1975 the first microprocessor-based computer, the Altair 8800, was announced on the front cover of *Popular Electronics.* The Altair 8800 is often described as the first personal computer. This was true only in the sense that its price was so low that it could be realistically bought by an individual. In every other sense the Altair 8800 was a traditional minicomputer. Indeed, the blurb on the front cover of *Popular Electronics* described it as exactly that: "Exclusive! Altair 8800. The most powerful minicomputer project ever presented—can be built for under $400."

The Altair 8800 closely followed the marketing model of the electronic hobbyist kit: It was inexpensive ($397) and was sold by mail order as a kit that the enthusiast had to assemble himself. In the tradition of the electronics hobbyist kit, the Altair 8800 often did not work when the enthusiast had constructed it; and even if it did work, it did not do anything very useful. The computer consisted of a single box containing the central processor, with a panel of switches and neon bulbs on the front; it had no display, no keyboard, and not enough memory to do anything useful. Moreover, there was no way to attach a device such as a teletype to the machine to turn it into a useful computer system.

The only way the Altair 8800 could be programmed was by entering programs in pure binary code by flicking the hand switches on the front. When loaded, the program would run; but the only evidence of its execution was the change in the shifting pattern of the neon bulbs on the front. This limited the Altair 8800 to programs that only a dedicated computer hobbyist would ever be able to appreciate. Entering the program was extraordinarily tedious, taking several minutes—but as there were only 256 bytes of memory, there was a limit to the complexity of programs that could be attempted.

The Altair 8800 was produced by a tiny Albuquerque, New Mexico, electronics kit supplier, Micro Instrumentation Telemetry Systems (MITS). The firm had originally been set up by an electronics hobbyist, Ed Roberts, to produce radio kits for model airplanes. . . . The Altair 8800 was unprecedented and in no sense a "rational" product—it would appeal only to an electronics hobbyist of the most dedicated kind, and even that was not guaranteed.

Despite its many shortcomings, the Altair 8800 was the grit around which the pearl of the personal-computer industry grew during the next two years. The limitations of the Altair 8800 created the opportunity for small-time entrepreneurs to develop "add-on" boards so that extra memory, conventional teletypes, and audio-cassette recorders (for permanent data storage) could be added to the basic machine. Almost all of these start-up companies consisted of two or three people—mostly computer hobbyists hoping to turn their pastime to profit. A few other entrepreneurs developed software for the Altair 8800.

In retrospect, the most important of the early software entrepreneurs was Bill Gates, the co-founder of Microsoft. Although his ultimate financial success has been almost without parallel, his background was quite typical of a 1970s software nerd—a term that conjures up an image of a pale, male adolescent, lacking in social skills, programming by night and sleeping by day, oblivious to the wider world and the need to gain qualifications and build a career. This stereotype, though exaggerated, contains an essential truth; nor was it a new phenomenon—the programmer-by-night has existed since the 1950s. Indeed, programming the first personal computers had many similarities to programming a 1950s mainframe: There were no advanced software tools, and programs had to be hand-crafted in the machine's own binary codes so that every byte of the tiny memory could be used to its best advantage.

Gates, born in 1955 in Seattle to upper-middle-class parents, was first exposed to computers in 1969, when he learned to program in BASIC using a commercial time-sharing system on which his high-school rented time. He and his close friend, Paul Allen, two years his senior, discovered a mutual passion for programming. . . .

The launch of the Altair 8800 in 1975 transformed Gate's and Allen's lives. Almost as soon as they heard of the machine, they recognized the software opportunity it represented and proposed to MITS' Ed Roberts that they should develop a BASIC programming system for the new machine. . . .

Gates and Allen formed a partnership they named Micro-Soft (the hyphen was later dropped), and after six weeks of intense programming effort they delivered a BASIC programming system to MITS in February 1975. . . . Gates abandoned his formal education. During the next two years, literally hundreds of small firms entered the microcomputer software business, and Microsoft was by no means the most prominent.

The Altair 8800, and the add-on boards and software that were soon available for it, transformed hobby electronics in a way not seen since the heyday of radio. In the spring of 1975, for example, the "Homebrew Computer Club" was established in Menlo Park, on the edge of Silicon Valley. Besides acting as a swap shop for computer components and programming tips, it also provided a forum for the computer-hobbyist and computer-liberation cultures to meld. . . .

While it had taken the mainframe a decade to be transformed from laboratory instrument to business machine, the personal computer was transformed in just two years. The reason for this rapid development was that most of the subsystems required to create a personal computer already existed: keyboards, screens, disk drives, and printers. It was just a matter of putting the pieces together. Hundreds of firms—not just on the West Coast, but all over the country—sprang up over this two-year period. They were mostly tiny start-ups, consisting of a few computer hobbyists or young computer professionals; they supplied complete computers, add-on boards, peripherals, or software. Within months of its initial launch at the beginning of 1975, the Altair 8800 had itself been eclipsed by dozens of new models produced by firms such as Applied Computer Technology, IMSAI, North Star, Cromemco, and Vector. . . .

Most of the new computer firms fell almost as quickly as they rose, and only a few survived beyond the mid-1980s. Apple computer was the rare exception in that it made it into the Fortune 500 and achieved long-term global success. Its initial trajectory, however, was quite typical of the early hobbyist start-ups.

Apple was founded by two young computer hobbyists, Stephen Wozniak and Steve Jobs. Wozniak grew up in Cupertino, California, in the heart of the booming West Coast electronics industry. Like many of the children in the area, electronics was in the air they breathed. Wozniak took to electronics almost as soon as he could think abstractly; he was a talented hands-on engineer, lacking any desire for a deeper, academic understanding. He obtained a radio amateur operating license while in sixth grade. . . .

While Wozniak was a typical, if unusually gifted, hobbyist, Steve Jobs bridged the cultural divide between computer hobbyism and computer liberation. That Apple Computer ultimately became a global player in the computer industry is largely due to Jobs's evangelizing of the personal computer, his ability to harness Wozniak's engineering talent, and his willingness to seek out the organizational capabilities needed to build a business.

Born in 1955, Jobs was brought up by adoptive blue-collar parents. Although not a child of the professional electronics-engineering classes, Jobs took to the electronic hobbyism that he saw all around him. While a capable enough engineer, he was not in the same league as Wozniak. . . .

Something of a loner, and not academically motivated, Jobs drifted in and out of college in the early 1970s before finding a well-paid niche as a games designer for Atari. An admirer of the Beatles, like them Jobs spent a year pursuing transcendental meditation in India and turned vegetarian. Jobs and Wozniak made a startling contrast: Wozniak was the archetypal electronic hobbyist with social skills to match, while Jobs affected an aura of inner wisdom, wore open-toed sandals, had long, lank hair, and sported a Ho Chi Minh beard.

The turning point for both Jobs and Wozniak was attending the Homebrew Computer Club in early 1975. Although Wozniak knew about microprocessors from his familiarity with the calculator industry, he had not up to that point realized that they could be used to build general-purpose computers and had not heard of the Altair 8800. But he had actually built a computer, which was more than could be said of most Homebrew members at that date, and he found himself among an appreciative audience. He quickly took up the new microprocessor technology, and within a few weeks had thrown together a computer based on the Mostek 6502 chip. He and Jobs called it the "Apple," for reasons that are now lost in time, but possibly for the Beatles' record label.

While Jobs never cared for the "nit-picking technical debates" of the Homebrew computer enthusiasts, he did recognize the latent market they represented. He therefore cajoled Wozniak into developing the Apple computer and marketing it, initially through the Byte Shop. The Apple was a very crude machine, consisting basically of a naked circuit board, lacking a case, a keyboard, or screen, or even a power supply. Eventually about two hundred were sold, each hand-assembled by Jobs and Wozniak in the garage of Job's parents.

In 1976 Apple was just one of dozens of computer firms competing for the dollars of the computer hobbyist. Jobs recognized before most, however, that the microcomputer had the potential to be a consumer product for a much broader market if it were appropriately packaged. To be a success as a product, the microcomputer would have to be presented as a self-contained unit in a plastic case, able to be plugged into a standard household outlet just like any other appliance; it would need a keyboard to enter data, a screen to view the results of a computation, and some form of long-term storage to hold data and programs. Most important, the machine would need software to appeal to anyone other than an enthusiast. First this would be BASIC, but eventually a much wider range of software would be required. This, in a nutshell, was the specification for the Apple II that Jobs passed down to Wozniak to create.

For all his naïveté as an entrepreneur Jobs understood, where few of his contemporaries did, that if Apple was to become a successful company, it would need access to capital, professional management, public relations, and distribution channels. None of these was easy to find at a time when the personal computer was unknown outside hobbyist circles. Jobs's evangelizing was called on in full measure to acquire these capabilities. During 1976, while Wozniak designed the Apple II, Jobs secured venture capital from Mike Markkula, to whom he had been introduced by his former employer at Atari, Nolan Bushnell. Markkula was a thirty-four-year-old former Intel executive who had become independently wealthy from stock options. Through Markkula's contacts, Jobs located an experienced young professional manager from the semiconductor industry, Mike Scott, who agreed to serve as president of the company. Scott would take care of operational management, leaving Jobs free to evangelize and determine the strategic direction of Apple. The last piece of Jobs's plan fell into place when he persuaded the prominent public relations company Regis McKenna to take on Apple as a client.

Throughout 1976 and early 1977, while the Apple II was perfected, Apple Computer remained a tiny company with fewer than a dozen employees occupying 2,000 square feet of space in Cupertino, California. . . .

During 1977 three distinct paradigms for the personal computer emerged, represented by three leading manufacturers: Apple, Commodore Business Machines, and Tandy, each of which defined the personal computer in terms of its own existing culture and corporate outlooks.

If there can be said to be a single moment when the personal computer arrived in the public consciousness, then it was at the West Coast Computer Faire in April 1977, when the first two machines for the mass consumer, the Apple II and the Commodore PET, were launched. Both machines were instant hits, and for a while they vied for market leadership. At first glance the Commodore PET looked very much like the Apple II in that it was a self-contained appliance with a keyboard, a screen, and a cassette tape for program storage, and with BASIC ready-loaded so that users could write programs.

The Commodore PET, however, coming from Commodore Business Machines—a firm that had originally made electronic calculators—was not so much a computer as a calculator writ large. For example, the keyboard had the tiny buttons of a calculator keypad rather then the keyboard of a standard computer terminal. Moreover, like a calculator, the PET was a closed system, with no potential for add-ons such as printers or floppy disks. Nevertheless, this narrow specification and the machine's low price appealed to the educational market, where it found a niche supporting elementary computer studies and BASIC programming; eventually several hundred thousand machines were sold.

. . . The Apple II was . . . far more appealing to the computer hobbyist because it offered the opportunity to engage with the machine by customizing it and using it for novel applications that the inventors could not envisage.

In August 1977 the third major computer vendor, Tandy, entered the market, when it announced its TRS-80 computer for $399. Produced by Tandy's subsidiary, Radio Shack, the TRS-80 was aimed at the retailer's existing customers, who consisted mainly of electronic hobbyists and buyers of video games. The low price was achieved by the user having to use a television set for a screen and an audiocassette recorder for program storage. The resulting hook-up was no hardship to the typical Tandy customer, although it would have been out of place in an office.

Thus, by the fall of 1977, although the personal computer had been defined physically as an artifact, a single constituency had not yet been established. For Commodore the personal computer was seen as a natural evolution of its existing calculator line. For Tandy it was an extension of its existing electronic-hobbyist and video games business. For Apple the machine was initially aimed at the computer hobbyist.

Jobs's ambition and vision went beyond the hobby market, and he envisioned the machine also being used as an appliance in the home—perhaps the result of his experience as a designer of domestic video games. This ambiguity was revealed by the official description of the Apple II as a "home/personal computer." The advertisement that Regis McKenna produced to launch the Apple II showed a housewife doing kitchen chores, while in the background her husband sat at the kitchen table hunched over an Apple II, seemingly managing the household's information. The copy read:

> The home computer that's ready to work, play and grow with you. . . . You'll be able to organize, index and store data on household finances, income taxes, recipes, your biorhythms, balance your checking account, even control your home environment.

These domestic projections for the personal computer were reminiscent of those for the computer utility in the 1960s, and were equally misguided. Moreover, the advertisement did not point out that these domestic applications were pure fantasy—there was no software available for "biorhythms," accounts, or anything else.

The constituency for the personal computer would be defined by the software that was eventually created for it. . . .

The biggest market, initially, was for games software, which reflected the existing hobbyist customer base:

> When customers' walked into computer stores in 1979, they saw racks of software, wall displays of software, and glass display cases of software. Most of it was games. Many of these were outer space games—*Space, Space II, Star Trek.* Many games appeared for the Apple, including Programma's simulation of a video game called *Apple Invaders.* Companies such as Muse, Sirius, Broderbund, and On-Line systems reaped great profits from games.

Computer games are often overlooked in discussions of the personal-computer software industry, but they played an important role in its early development. Programming computer games created a corps of young programmers who were very sensitive to what we now call human/computer interaction. The most successful games were ones that needed no manuals and gave instant feedback. . . .

The market of packaged software for business applications developed between 1978 and 1980, when three generic applications enabled the personal computer to become an effective business machine: the spreadsheet, the word processor, and the database. All these types of software already existed in the ordinary mainframe computer context, typically using a time-sharing terminal, so it was not obvious at the outset that the personal computer offered any advantage as a business machine.

The first application to receive wide acceptance was the VisiCalc spreadsheet. The originator of VisiCalc was a twenty-six-year-old Harvard MBA student, Daniel Bricklin. . . .

Bricklin's program used about 25,000 bytes of memory, which was about as big as a personal computer of the period could hold, but was decidedly modest by mainframe standards. The personal computer, however, offered some significant advantages that were not obvious at the outset. Because the personal computer was a stand-alone, self-contained system, changes to a financial model were displayed almost instantaneously compared with the minute or so it would have taken on a conventional computer. This fast response enabled a manager to explore a financial model with great flexibility, asking what were later known as "what if?" questions. It was almost like a computer game for executives.

When it was launched in December 1979, VisiCalc was an overnight success. Not only was the program a breakthrough as a financial tool but its users experienced for the first time the psychological freedom of having a machine of one's own, on one's desk, instead of having to accept the often mediocre take-it-or-leave-it services of a computer center. Moreover, at $3,000, including software, it was possible to buy an Apple II and VisiCalc out of a departmental, or even a personal, budget. . . .

Word processing on personal computers did not develop until about 1980. . . .

The first successful firm to produce word-processing software was MicroPro, founded by the entrepreneur Seymour Rubinstein in 1978. Rubinstein, then in his early forties, was formerly a mainframe software developer. He had a hobbyist interest in amateur radio and electronics, however, and when the first microcomputer kits became available, he bought one. He recognized very early on the personal computer's potential as a word processor. . . .

During 1980, with dozens of spreadsheet and word-processing packages on the market and the launch of the first database products, the potential of the personal computer as an office machine became clearly recognizable. At this point the traditional business machine manufacturers, such as IBM, began to take an interest. . . .

IBM was not, in fact, the giant that slept soundly during the personal-computer revolution. IBM had a sophisticated market research organization that attempted to predict market trends. The company was well aware of microprocessors and personal computers. Indeed, in 1975 it had developed a desktop computer for the scientific market (the model 5100), but it did not sell well. . . .

Once the personal computer became clearly defined as a business machine in 1980, IBM reacted with surprising speed. The proposal that IBM should enter the personal-computer business came from William C. Lowe, a senior manager who headed the company's "entry-level systems" in Boca Raton, Florida. . . .

For nearly a century IBM had operated a bureaucratic development process by which it typically took three years for a new product to reach the market. Part of the delay was due to IBM's century-old vertical integration practice, by which it maximized profits by manufacturing in-house all the components used in its products: semiconductors, switches, plastic cases, and so on. Lowe argued that IBM should instead adopt the practice of the rest of the industry by outsourcing all the components it did not already have in production, including software. Lowe proposed yet another break with tradition—that IBM should not use its direct sales force to sell the personal computer but should instead use regular retail channels.

Surprisingly, in light of its stuffy image, IBM's top management agreed to all that Lowe recommended, and within two weeks of his presentation he was authorized to go ahead and build a prototype, which had to be ready for the market within twelve months. The development of the personal computer would be known internally as Project Chess.

IBM's relatively late entry into the personal computer market gave it some significant advantages. First, it could make use of the second generation of microprocessors (which processed sixteen bits of data at a time instead of eight); this would make the IBM personal computer significantly faster than any other machine on the market. IBM chose to use the Intel 8088 chip, thereby guaranteeing Intel's future prosperity.

Although IBM was the world's largest software developer, paradoxically it did not have the skills to develop software for personal computers. Its bureaucratic software development procedures were slow and methodical, and geared to large software artifacts: the company lacked the critical skills needed to develop the "quick-and-dirty" software needed for personal computers.

IBM initially approached Gary Kildall of Data Research—the developer of the CP/M operating system—for operating software for the new computer, and herein lies one of the more poignant stories in the history of the personal computer. For reasons now muddied, Kildall blew the opportunity. One version of the story has it that he refused to sign IBM's nondisclosure agreement, while another version has him doing some recreational flying while the dark-suited IBMers cooled their heels below. In any event, the opportunity passed Digital Research by and moved on to Microsoft. Over the next decade, buoyed by the revenues from its operating system for the IBM personal computer, Microsoft became the quintessential business success story of the late twentieth century, and Gates became a billionaire at the age of thirty-one. Hence, for all of Gates's self-confidence and remarkable business acumen, he owes almost everything to being in the right place at the right time.

The IBM entourage arrived at Bill Gates and Paul Allen's Microsoft headquarters in July 1980. It was then a tiny (thirty-two-person) company located in rented offices in downtown Seattle. It is said that Gates and Allen were so keen to win the IBM contract that they actually wore business suits and ties. Although Gates may have appeared a somewhat nerdish twenty-nine-year-old who looked fifteen, he came from an impeccable background, was palpably serious, and showed a positive eagerness to accommodate the IBM culture. For IBM, he represented as low a risk as any of the personal-computer software firms, almost all of which were noted for their studied contempt for Big Blue. It is said that when John Opel, IBM's president, heard about the Microsoft deal, he said, "Is he Mary Gates's son?" He was. Opel and Gates's mother both served on the board of the United Way.

At the time that Microsoft made its agreement with IBM for an operating system, it did not have an actual product, nor did it have the resources to develop one in IBM's time scale. However, Gates obtained a suitable piece of software from a local software firm, Seattle Computer Products, for $30,000 cash. Eventually, the operating system, known as MS-DOS, would be bundled with almost every IBM personal computer and compatible machine, earning Microsoft a royalty of between $10 and $50 on every copy sold. . . .

Early in 1981, only six months after the inception of Project Chess, IBM appointed the West Coast—based Chiat Day advertising agency to develop an advertising campaign. Market research suggested that the personal computer still lay in the gray area between regular business equipment and a home machine. The advertising campaign was therefore ambiguously aimed at both the business and home user. The machine was astutely named the IBM Personal Computer, suggesting that the IBM machine and the personal computer were synonymous. For the business user, the fact that the machine bore the IBM logo was sufficient to legitimate it inside the corporation. For the home user, however, market research revealed that although the personal computer was perceived as a good thing, it was also seen as intimidating—and IBM itself was seen as "cold and aloof." The Chiat Day campaign attempted to allay these fears by featuring in its advertisements a Charlie Chaplin lookalike and alluding to Chaplin's famous movie *Modern Times.* Set in a futuristic automated factory, *Modern Times* showed the "little man" caught up in a world of hostile technology, confronting it, and eventually overcoming it. The Charlie Chaplin figure reduced the intimidation factor and gave IBM "a human face." . . .

The IBM Personal Computer was given its press launch in New York on 12 August. There was intense media interest, which generated many headlines in the computer and business press. In the next few weeks the IBM Personal Computer became a runaway success that exceeded almost everyone's expectations, inside and outside the company. While many business users had hesitated over whether to buy an Apple or a Commodore or a Tandy machine, the presence of the IBM logo convinced them that the technology was for real: IBM had legitimated the personal computer. There was such a demand for the machine that production could not keep pace, and retailers could do no more than placate their customers by placing their names on a waiting list. Within days of the launch, IBM decided to quadruple production.

During 1982–83 the IBM Personal Computer became an industry standard. Most of the popular software packages were converted to run on the machine, and the existence of this software reinforced its popularity. This encouraged other manufacturers to produce "clone" machines, which ran the same software.

The Second Self, 1982

SHERRY TURKLE

The subjects of my study are men and women who bought personal computer systems in the four years that followed the 1975 announcement of the "Altair"—the first computer small enough to sit on a desktop, powerful enough to support high-level language programming, and that you could build for only $420. My study began in 1978 with a questionnaire survey answered by 95 New England computer hobbyists (their names had been drawn from the roster of a home computer club and from the subscription list of a personal computer magazine), and continued during 1978 and 1979 with nearly 300 hours of conversation with 50 individuals who owned home computers. What I found can be read historically: a study of the pioneer users of an increasingly ubiquitous technology. But most central to the intent of this essay is to use the story of the early hobbyists as a window into the highly personal ways in

From Sherry Turkle, *The Second Self: Computers and the Human Spirit* (New York: Simon & Schuster, 1984), pp. 182–199. First published in *Social Studies of Science* 12 (1982).

which individuals appropriate technologies. It is a case study of the "subjective computer," the computer as a material for thinking, for feeling, for "working through."

My emphasis on the subjective is at odds with a widespread ideology that quickly grew up around the emergent computer hobbyist culture. The Altair, aimed at a strictly hobby market, was followed by other small systems—the Pet, the Sol, and, most successfully, the Radio Shack TRS-80 and the Apple, marketed to less specialized audiences of small businessmen and curious householders. With this explosion of hardware came a lot of rhetoric about a personal computer revolution. Most of the talk, both from the companies that marketed the machines and from those who claimed to be the most visionary spokesmen for the people who bought them, was about all of the things that a home computer could do for you. The utilitarian, "genie in the bottle," ideology is expressed in the content of hobbyist conventions and magazines, filled with articles on how to make your home computer dim your lights, control your thermostat, run an inventory system for your kitchen or toolroom. And it is also found in writing on the personal computer from outside the hobbyist world. . . .

This instrumental view is an important ingredient of the hobbyist ideology but it is not the whole story. In the course of my work I found a very different answer from within. Most hobbyists do make their computers "strut their stuff," but their sense of engagement and energy are found primarily in the non-instrumental uses of the technology. When asked in a questionnaire "What first attracted you to computers?" more than half the respondents gave reasons that were highly subjective. In response to an open-ended question, 26 percent said that they were first attracted to computers by an appeal that was intellectual, aesthetic, involved with the fun of what I would call "cognitive play." They wrote of "puzzle solving," of "the elegance of using computer techniques to handle problems," of the "beauty of understanding a system of many levels of complexity." They described what they did with their home computers with metaphors like "mind stretching" and "using the computer's software to understand my wetware." Another 26 percent wrote of reasons for getting involved that seemed more emotional than intellectual. They wrote of the "ego boost" or "sense of power" that comes from knowing how to run a computer, of the "prestige of being a pioneer in a developing field," of the "feeling of control when I work in a safe environment of my own creation."

The hobbyists who responded to my survey seemed familiar with . . . people who ask them what they do with their computers and who won't take "cognitive play" for an answer. David, a 19-year-old undergraduate at a small engineering school, put it this way: "People come over and see my computer and they look at it, then they look at me, then they ask me what useful thing I do with it, like does it wash floors, clean laundry or do my income tax—when I respond no, they lose interest." David said that when he started out, he was attracted to the computer because "I like the idea of making a pile of hardware do something useful, like doing real time data processing . . . like picking up morse code with an amateur radio and transcribing it automatically into text," but in his list of things that he currently does with his computer, an instrumental discourse is most notable for its absence:

> Conway's GAME OF LIFE in assembly code was a challenge, forced me to "think logically," and gave the pleasure of making something work the way I wanted it to . . . Having control from the bottom level of program for that game made me feel comfortable, safe, sort of at home.

Thirteen percent of those who responded to my questionnaire told a similar story. Like David, they began their relationship with personal computation for instrumental reasons (they had an image of a job to do, a specific task), but they became absorbed by the "holding power" of something else. A full two-thirds of my survey sample either began with or ended up with a primary interest in what I have called the "subjective computer," the computer seen in its relationship to *personal meaning*. Clearly, to understand what people are doing with their home computers we must go beyond the "performance criteria" shared by the hobbyist magazines and the *Wall Street Journal*. . . .

The elusiveness of computational processes and of simple descriptions of the computer's essential nature, the tension between local simplicity and global complexity, all contribute to making the computer an object of projective processes, an exemplary "constructed object." Different people apprehend it with very different descriptions and invest it with very different attributes. In views of the computer's internal process, individuals project their models of mind. In descriptions of the computer's powers, people express feelings about their own intellectual, social, and political power—or their lack of it.

. . . In my own studies of people's emotional relationships with technologies, airplanes emerge as startlingly like computers in respect to the issues they raise for their hobbyists. Specifically, both are powerful media for working through the issue of control. . . .

. . . Bob is a computer professional, a microprocessor engineer who works all day on the development of hardware for a large industrial data system. He has recently built a small computer system for his home and devotes much of his leisure time to programming it. . . . Although Bob works all day with computers, his building and programming them at home is not more of the same. At work he sees himself as part of a process that he cannot see and over which he feels no mastery or ownership: "Like they say, I'm just a cog." At home Bob works on well defined projects of his own choosing, projects whose beginning, middle, and end are all under his control. He describes the home projects as a compensation for the alienation of his job. He works most intensively on his home system when he feels furthest away from any understanding of "how the whole thing fits together at work." . . .

. . . Most hobbyists have relationships with computation at work which involve sharing the machine with countless and nameless others. In personal computation they see a chance to be independent and alone. The machine comes to them virgin. They have full possession. . . . Bob, like many of the other hobbyists I spoke with, is a middle-level worker in the computer industry. He does not feel very good about the importance of his job. Proving that he is "better than any dumb compiler" gives a sense of importance.

Using the computer to assert control was a central theme in my interviews with hobbyists. It was expressed directly, and also wove itself into four other issues that characterize the hobbyists' "subjective computer." These are using the computer to strengthen a sense of identity; to construct a completely intelligible piece of reality that is experienced as "transparent" and safe; to articulate a political ideology; and to experience a sense of wholeness that is absent in one's work life. It is these four issues to which I now turn. . . .

In achieving a sense of mastery over the computer, in learning about the computer's "innards," people are learning to see themselves differently. Among other things, they are learning to see themselves as "the kind of people who can do science and math." This was most striking among hobbyists who had no technical background. But it also came up among hobbyists who did see themselves as "technical people" but who for one reason or another had gotten "scared out of real science."

Barry is 28 years old, an electronics technician at a large research laboratory. He went to college for two years, hoping to be an engineer, then dropped out and went to technical school. He has always loved to tinker with machines and to build things. His current job is to calibrate and repair complex instruments, and he is very happy with it because he gets a chance "to work on a lot of different equipment." But he came to his job with a feeling of having failed, of not being "analytic," "theoretical," of not being capable of "what is really important in science."

> Ever since I was a child I always had an interest in science, but I never had the opportunity or the passion to go back and finish college and get a real degree in science. I don't think I have a theoretical mind. I got all D's in mathematics. I have a more practical mind . . . I always had a great deal of difficulty with mathematics in college which is why I never became an engineer. I just could not seem to discipline my mind enough to break mathematics down to its component parts, and then put it all together and really do it.

Five years ago, Barry bought a programmable calculator and started "fooling around with it and with numbers the way I have never been able to fool around before," and says that "it seemed natural to start working with computers as soon as I could." To hear him tell it, numbers stopped being theoretical, they became concrete, practical and playful, something he could tinker with.

> I'll pick up the calculator, and if I don't know how to do a problem I'll play with the calculator a few minutes, or a few hours and figure it out. It's not so much that the calculator does a particular calculation, but you do so many, have so much contact with the numbers and the results and how it all comes out that you start to see things differently . . . The numbers are in your fingers.

When the calculator and the computer made numbers seem concrete, the numbers became "like him," and Barry felt an access to a kind of thinking that he had always felt "constitutionally" shut out of: "While I write in assembler I feel that mathematics is in my hands . . . and I'm good with my hands."

Barry claims to have "grown out of" his aspiration to be an engineer. He says he doesn't keep engineering as a pipedream or think of his computer skills as something that could make it real. In terms of his career he says that "nothing has changed." But a lot has changed. Barry has always thought of himself as a bundle of aptitudes and ineptitudes that define him as the kind of person who can do certain things and cannot do others. Working with the computer has made him reconsider his categories.

> I really couldn't tell you what sort of thing I'm going to be doing with my computer in six months. It used to be that I could tell you exactly what I would be thinking about in six months. But the thing with this, with the computer, is that the deeper you get into it, there's no way an individual can say what he'll be thinking in six months, what I'm going to be doing. But I honestly feel that it's going to be great. And that's one hell of a thing.

For Barry, the world has always been divided between the people who think they know what they'll be thinking in six months and those who don't. And in his mind, his home computer has gotten him across that line and "That's one hell of a thing." For Barry, part of what it means to have crossed the line is to start to call the line into question. When he was in school, his inability to do the kind of mathematics he had "respect" for made him lose respect for himself as a learner. The computer put mathematics in a form that he could participate in. Barry has three children, has bought them their own calculators, and encourages them to "mess around with the computer." He feels that they are going through the same problems with math and science that he had and he wants them to have "a better start." For Barry, the computer holds the promise of a better start, not because it might teach his children a particular subject, but because it "might change their image of themselves. They might think of themselves as learners."

Personal computers are certainly not the only hobby that people use to enhance their sense of identity. For my informants, "hobbies" have always been a way of life. Almost 90 percent of them had been involved in a hobby other than computation, most usually in another "technical" hobby, such as photography, ham radio, or model railroading. Fifteen percent of the hobbyists surveyed were using their computers to "augment" their participation in another hobby—for example, using the computer to keep an inventory of motorcycle parts, figure out ideal compression ratios for racing cars, interface with amateur radio equipment. For nearly a third of them, their home computer had completely replaced another hobby. People spoke of these abandoned hobbies as "fun" and as "good experiences," but their remarks about past hobbies underscored several ways in which in our day and time a computer hobby can be special. In particular, people spoke about their "switch to the computer" as making them part of something that was growing and that the society at large "really cared about."

Gregory is in his mid-forties, and has been in the electronics industry for all of his working life, as a technician, a programmer, and currently as a products designer. For two years, his computer shared space in his study with an elaborate model railroad system. A year and half before I met him he had bought a new hard copy printer and a graphics plotter. In the overcrowding that followed, the trains had finally found their way to storage in the basement.

> Nobody ever really paid attention to my model railroad stuff, although a lot of the circuitry that I did for those trains was just as complex as what I'm now doing with my computer. But people would look at the train and they would say "that's cute." The computer is my own thing, but it's part of the real world too. When my kid got involved with my trains, he was just into my hobby. But if my kid becomes good at the computers, it will mean something.

I heard many echoes of Gregory's phrase, "it's part of the real world too." Hobbyists spoke about the computer offering them a connection with something beyond the hobby. For some, having a computer and "getting good at it" means crossing a frontier that separates "tinkering" from "real technology." They feel that the world sees their computer hobby as serious (several commented that friends and neighbours hardly even look at it as a hobby, as though the word were reserved for frivolities), and they start to see themselves that way too. Most first-generation hobbyists have technical educations, but many of them, like Barry, feel they have never been part of what is most exciting and important in the scientific and technical cultures. They see themselves as the low men on the totem pole. Working with computers, even small computers, feels technologically "avant garde." A smaller group of hobbyists (but a group whose numbers are growing as new generations of personal computers become more accessible to the nonspecialist) have always felt completely left out of the scientific and technical worlds. For them, owning a computer can mean crossing a "two cultures" divide.

Alan, a 29-year-old high school French teacher who describes himself as "having a love affair with a TRS-80," has always felt he wasn't "smart enough to do science."

> After *Sputnik,* when I was in grade school and then in Junior High, there was all that fuss, all the kids who were good in math got to be in special classes. Rockets were going up . . . men trying to go to the moon. Decisions about things. Scientists seemed to be in charge of all that.

Alan majored in French ("It was easy for me . . . my mother is from Montreal") and took up carpentry as a hobby. And although he was good at it, it only reinforced his sense of not being able to do intellectual things, which in his mind meant not being able to "do anything technical." When Barry began to do mathematics with his calculator, he felt that he started to cross a line to become the kind of person who could expect change and excitement in his intellectual life. For Alan, his TRS-80 led him across a line to become a member of a different culture, a scientific culture, a culture of "powerful people." . . .

Hobbyist's descriptions of what it is like to work with their own computers frequently referred to the idea that the computer provides a safe corner of reality. Other hobbies can give a similar sense of security but often exact a price. For example, people can feel safe but limited. Alan, the French major, now "in love with his TRS-80," felt secure in his carpentry hobby, but he experienced it as a safety that came from refusing challenge. "It was an 'artsy' hobby. I couldn't see myself any other way." The computer is more likely than most other media to allow the experience of playing worlds (let us call them "microworlds") that are secure and also adventurous enough to allow for mind-stretching explorations. Almost all of the hobbyists I interviewed described some version of a limited, safe, and transparent microworld that was embodied in their personal computer. For Alan just the fact of working with a computer created such a world. For others, it was more specific: a morse code microworld; a text editor microworld; and, most generally, the assembly language microworld.

This use of the computer as a place to build a microworld is particularly salient for children when they are put in computational environments in which they have access to programming. . . .

Deborah at 11 years old was the baby of her family, the youngest of three children. Her childhood had been spotted with illness which further exaggerated her "baby" position. The members of her family were always doing things for her, insisting that she was not old enough to do the things that she wanted to do most: take out the laundry, baby-sit, stay over at a friend's house, choose her own hair style and her own clothes. Dependent on others at home, very overweight, and with an image of herself as sick and weak, Deborah had little sense of her own boundaries, her ability to say no, to assert control. Even at 11, she had become involved with a crowd of older kids who were smoking, drinking, using drugs.

Towards the end of her eleventh year a LOGO computer came into Deborah's classroom as part of an educational experiment. At first, she found the computer frightening and threatening: until one day she hit upon the idea of confining the designs she made with the computer to ones in which the lines always came together in multiples of 30 degrees. She called it her "30 degrees world."

This restriction defined for her a space in which she felt safe but in which she was able to produce designs of great ingenuity and complexity. When I interviewed her two years later I found that she had used her experience with the "30 degrees world" as a kind of model, an experience-to-think-with. In her mind it represented how you could take control and make things happen by the judicious use of constraint. In Deborah's words, it was the first time that she ever "laid down her own laws." It was a turning point in her ability to take control of other situations. She lost 20 pounds, has given up smoking and drugs, and says that she "only sometimes" has a drink.

For Deborah and for many adult hobbyists the sense of safety with the computer derived from the feeling of working in a sphere of intelligibility and transparency, a sphere that is protected, much as the space of a psychotherapeutic or psychoanalytic relationship is set off, bracketed. People talked about feelings safe and secure in the world they had built with their home computers, a world where there were few surprises and "things didn't change unless you wanted them to." Of course, there was much talk of problems, of false starts, of frustrations. There are "bugs" in hardware and in programs. Things don't work; things go wrong. But bugs, with time, are either fixed or become "known" bugs. Joe is an insurance salesman in a small North California suburb who owns a second-hand Commodore Pet "with a lot of hardware problems." To Joe the bugs in his system "have become almost like friends": "I turn on the machine and I systematically check for my 'old friends,' and I swear, finding them there has a certain reassuring element." . . .

The use of the computer as a medium for building a transparent and intelligible world brings us to how it can be used to think through questions of political ideology. Fred sells components for a large electronics supply house. He narrowly escaped starvation in a prisoner of war camp during World War II, and from that experience he says that he took "a sense of optimism," "I mean, if there is something out there and you want to do it—do it, understand it, act." Fred has tried to live that way. He is active in local politics; he keeps up with the news; he writes letters to the editor of his town newspaper. He bought his TRS80 on an impulse because "it seemed that you wouldn't be able to understand American society any more if you didn't know about computers." When it comes to working with his computer, Fred wants to know "exactly how things work": "There is a big gap in my own mind between the fact that an electrical circuit can be on or off and the binary number system . . . and again from there to the BASIC language. I've got to understand all of that. . . .

. . . Hobbyists associate images of computational transparency and of "knowing how the machine works" with a kind of politics where relations of power will be transparent, where people will control their destinies, where work will facilitate a rich and balanced cognitive life, and where decentralized power will follow from decentralized information resources.

For many hobbyists a relationship with their home computer carries longings for a better and simpler life in a more transparent society. *Co-Evolution Quarterly,*

Mother Earth News, Runner's World, and *Byte Magazine* lie together on hobbyists' coffee tables. Small computers become the focus of hopes of building cottage industries that will allow people to work out of their homes, have more personal autonomy, not have to punch time cards, and be able to spend more time with their family and out of doors.

Some see personal computers as a next step in the ecology movement: decentralized technology will mean less waste. Some see personal computers as a way for individuals to assert greater control over their children's education, believing that computerized curricula will soon offer children better education at home than can be offered in today's schools. Some see personal computers as a path to a new populism: personal computer networks will allow citizens to band together to send mail, run decentralized schools, information resources, and local governments.

. . . [M]any of the computer hobbyists I have interviewed talk about the computers in their livingrooms as windows onto a future where relationships with technology will be more direct, where people will understand how things work, and where dependence on big government, big corporations, and big machines will end. They imagine the politics of this computer-rich future by generalizing from their special relationship to the technology, a relationship characterized by simplicity and a sense of control. . . .

Over 40 percent of those who responded to my survey worked, or had once worked, as computer programmers. The programmer is typically in a situation where he or she is in touch with only a very small part of the problem that is being worked on. Increasingly, programmers work in large teams where each individual has very little sense of the whole, of how it all fits together. Programmers have watched their opportunities to exercise their skill as a whole activity being taken away (for those who are too young, the story of the process remains alive in the collective mythology of the shop). They have watched their work being routinized, being parcelled out into the well defined modules that make up the tasks of the structured programming team. They mythologize a golden age. This lived experience at work made programmers particularly sensitive to the parcellization of knowledge and to the alienation from a sense of wholeness in work. And they bring this sensitivity to their home computer hobbies.

Hannah worked as a programming consultant for a large business system for ten years before starting her own consulting company through which she offers her services to other computer hobbyists. To her, nothing is more depressing than working on a tiny piece of a problem. In her old job, "most of the time I didn't even know what the whole problem was." She likes working with computers at home because she has more control of her time and can spend more time with her family. But she says that what is most important about working with a personal computer is that "I can finally think about a whole problem." Hannah's feelings were widely shared among the hobbyists I interviewed, most notably among programmers, ex-programmers, and "team engineers." Images of lack of intellectual balance, of fragmentation, of not being connected, came up often, with the computer at home usually placed in the role of righting what had been wrong at work. As Hannah put it: "With my computer at home I do everything. I see my whole self, all my kinds of thinking." . . .

In studying the hobbyist experience I have found people, largely people with technical backgrounds, in intense involvement with machines. They describe their work (or rather their leisure) with the computer as different from what they have done before with other hobbies. They describe it as an involvement with greater personal consequence. Some of the sense of consequence comes from an historical moment: the computer hobby is seen as signifying a place in the "avant garde." Although in some circles "computer person" is a term of derision, the hobbyist experiences it with pride. Some of the sense of consequence comes from experiencing an individualistic and independent relationship with computation that can be mythologized as belonging to a now-past "golden age" of the programmer. But most of the sense of consequence comes from the holding power and intensity of the time spent with the computer. What is there about these people and these machines that makes possible relationships of such power and such intensity?

For me, the relationships that hobbyists form with their home computers can be partially captured with a metaphor of the "mind" and the "body" of the machine. The "mind" of the computer is that side of computation that involves thinking in terms of high-level programs. In this metaphor, relating to the "body" of the computer means not only working on hardware, but also, and indeed especially, working with programs in a way that is as close as possible to the machine code—that is to say, as close as possible to the core of the computer, its central processing unit (CPU). In terms of this metaphor I have found that the prototypical hobbyist is trying to get into a relationship with the body (rather than the mind) of the machine, to assert power and control in the relationship with the computer, and to create safe worlds of transparent understanding. In trying to find concepts for thinking more clearly about what draws the hobbyist to this kind of relationship with the CPU and about what its meaning might be, I find three issues particularly salient. I think, moreover, that, although I formulate them here in terms of computers, they are relevant to understanding relationships with other technologies as well.

The first issue goes back to control. The hobbyist complains of a work situation where everyone suffers from the constant presence of intermediaries. Bureaucracies stand between the programmer and the computer, a bureaucracy that schedules the computer, that decides its up and down time, that apportions the work for its software design and decides on priorities and procedures for access to it. At work, when something goes wrong with the system it is usually the fault of an intermediary person, one of the many "somebody elses" who deal with the machine. Or it may be the fault of a technical intermediary, one of the many elements in the computer system that mediate between the user and the bare machine: a compiler, an interpreter, an operating system, someone else's program. At home, the hobbyists feel themselves as working directly with the CPU, in complete and direct control of the machine's power. And when something does blow up, the situation has a special immediacy. It is between them and the bare machine. . . .

The issue of control was often explicitly recognized by the hobbyists I interviewed. But they lacked a language for naming a second issue which has to do with a notion referred to as "syntonicity" within the psychoanalytic tradition. Syntonicity implies that we should look for "body-to-body" identification in every powerful relationship with a technology—the body of the person and the body of the machine.

It implies that we should understand the appeal of machine language in terms of people's ability to identify with what is happening inside the machine. The CPU of the hobbyist computer lends itself to personal identification with its primary action: moving something that is conceptually almost a physical object (a byte of information) in and out of some thing (a register) that is almost a physical place. The metaphor is concrete and spatial. One can imagine finding the bytes, feeling them, doing something very simple to them, and passing them on. For many of the people that I met in the hobbyist culture, getting into this kind of identification feels safe. It makes the machine feel real.

There is a third issue raised by the hobbyists relationship to the CPU. It is an aesthetic one. The generation of hobby computers that was born in the 1970s are very primitive machines. The hobbyist thinks of much about them as "klugey," a computerist's way of saying that one is dealing with a comprise, a collection of patches whose structure has been dictated by arbitrary corporate decisions, by economic necessities. The corner of the hobbyist machines that seems to them to have the greatest "intellectual integrity," that distills what they feel to be tradition of some of the best ideas in computer science, that comes closest to being "clean," is the CPU. And so it is natural for the hobbyist to seek the closest possible contact with it. For a culture in which there is a widely shared aesthetic of simplicity, intelligibility, control, and transparency, getting into the "un-klugey" part of the machine and working in machine code seems the most aesthetically satisfying way to use the personal computer as an artistic medium. . . .

I would like to conclude with some personal reflections on personal computation and political metaphor. As an ethnographer, I use interviews and observations to enter sufficiently into people's lives to develop a sympathetic understanding of how they look at the world. And then I take this experience and try to distill from it those elements that will make the lives of the people I have been studying intelligible and meaningful to others. The hobbyists I interviewed are excited, enthusiastic, satisfied with what they are doing with their machines. It seems appropriate to report this enthusiasm and to try to capture a sense of the pleasures and satisfaction that these individuals are getting from developing "non-alienated" relationships with their computers, from "understanding" machine systems from the "bottom up," and from feeling satisfied that they have finally found models of transparency for thinking about the kind of political order they would like to live in.

But this picture also has a darker side. The "pleasing populism" of the hobbyists I interviewed is not in itself unproblematic. Will the individual satisfactions of personal computation (which seem to derive some of their power from the fact that they are at least in part responsive to political dissatisfactions) take the individual away from collective politics? People will not change unresponsive political systems or intellectually deadening work environments by building machines that are responsive, fun, and intellectually challenging. They will not change the world of human relations by retreating into a world of things. It would certainly be inappropriate to rejoice at the holistic and humanistic relationships that personal computers offer if it turns out that, when widespread, they replace religion as an opiate of the masses.

Cyberspace, 1984

WILLIAM GIBSON

"The matrix has its roots in primitive arcade games," said the voice-over, "in early graphics programs and military experimentation with cranial jacks." On the Sony, a two-dimensional space war faded behind a forest of mathematically generated ferns, demonstrating the spacial possibilities of logarithmic spirals; cold blue military footage burned through, lab animals wired into test systems, helmets feeding into fire control circuits of tanks and war planes. "Cyberspace. A consensual hallucination experienced daily by billions of legitimate operators, in every nation, by children being taught mathematical concepts . . . A graphic representation of data abstracted from the banks of every computer in the human system. Unthinkable complexity. Lines of light ranged in the nonspace of the mind, clusters and constellations of data. Like city lights, receding. . . ."

. . . He settled the black terry sweatband across his forehead, careful not to disturb the flat Sendai dermatrodes. He stared at the deck on his lap, not really seeing it. . . .

He closed his eyes.

Found the ridged face of the power stud.

And in the bloodlit dark behind his eyes, silver phosphenes boiling in from the edge of space, hypnagogic images jerking past like film compiled from random frames. Symbols, figures, faces, a blurred, fragmented mandala of visual information.

Please, he prayed, *now—*

A gray disk, the color of Chiba sky.

Now—

Disk beginning to rotate, faster, becoming a sphere of paler gray. Expanding—

And flowed, flowered for him, fluid neon origami trick, the unfolding of his distanceless home, his country, transparent 3D chessboard extending to infinity. Inner eye opening to the stepped scarlet pyramid of the Eastern Seaboard Fission Authority burning beyond the green cubes of Mitsubishi Bank of America, and high and very far away he saw the spiral arms of military systems, forever beyond his reach.

And somewhere he was laughing, in a white-painted loft, distant fingers caressing the deck, tears of release streaking his face.

A Cyborg Manifesto

DONNA HARAWAY

This chapter is an effort to build an ironic political myth faithful to feminism, socialism, and materialism. Perhaps more faithful as blasphemy is faithful, than as reverent worship and identification. Blasphemy has always seemed to require taking things very seriously. I know no better stance to adopt from within the secular-religious, evangelical traditions of United States politics, including the politics of socialist feminism.

From William Gibson, *Neuromancer* (New York: Ace Books, 1984), pp. 51–52.

From Donna Haraway, *Simians, Cyborgs, and Women* (London: Free Association Books, 1991), pp. 149–155, 176–179, 180–181.

Blasphemy protects one from the moral majority within, while still insisting on the need for community. Blasphemy is not apostasy. Irony is about contradictions that do not resolve into larger wholes, even dialectically, about the tension of holding incompatible things together because both or all are necessary and true. Irony is about humour and serious play. It is also, a rhetorical strategy and a political method, one I would like to see more honoured within socialist-feminism. At the centre of my ironic faith, my blasphemy, is the image of the cyborg.

A cyborg is a cybernetic organism, a hybrid of machine and organism, a creature of social reality as well as a creature of fiction. Social reality is lived social relations, our most important political construction, a world-changing fiction. The international women's movements have constructed "women's experience," as well as uncovered or discovered this crucial collective object. This experience is a fiction and fact of the most crucial, political kind. Liberation rests on the construction of the consciousness, the imaginative apprehension, of oppression, and so of possibility. The cyborg is a matter of fiction and lived experience that changes what counts as women's experience in the late twentieth century. This is a struggle over life and death, but the boundary between science and social reality is an optical illusion.

Contemporary science fiction is full of cyborgs—creatures simultaneously animal and machine, who populate worlds ambiguously natural and crafted. Modern medicine is also full of cyborgs, of couplings between organism and machine, each conceived as coded devices, in an intimacy and with a power that was not generated in the history of sexuality. . . . Modern production seems like a dream of cyborg colonization work, a dream that makes the nightmare of Taylorism seem idyllic. And modern war is a cyborg orgy, coded by C^3I, command-control-communication-intelligence, an \$84 billion item in 1984's US defense budget. . . .

By the late twentieth century, our time, a mythic time, we are all chimeras, theorized and fabricated hybrids of machine and organism; in short, we are cyborgs. The cyborg is our ontology; it gives us our politics. The cyborg is a condensed image of both imagination and material reality, the two joined centres structuring any possibility of historical transformation. In the traditions of "Western" science and politics—the tradition of racist male-dominant capitalism; the tradition of progress; the tradition of the appropriation of nature as resource for the productions of culture; the tradition of reproduction of the self from the reflections of the other—the relation between organism and machine has been a border war. The stakes in the border war have been the territories of production, reproduction, and imagination. This chapter is an argument for *pleasure* in the confusion of boundaries and for *responsibility* in their construction. It is also an effort to contribute to socialist-feminist culture and theory in a postmodernist, non-naturalist mode and in the utopian tradition of imagining a world without gender, which is perhaps a world without genesis, but maybe also a world without end. The cyborg incarnation is outside salvation history. . . .'

The cyborg is a creature in a post-gender world.

. . . In a sense, the cyborg has no origin story in the Western sense—a "final" irony since the cyborg is also the awful apocalyptic *telos* of the "West's" escalating dominations of abstract individuation, an ultimate self united at last from all dependency, a man in space. An origin story in the "Western," humanist sense depends on the myth of original unity, fullness, bliss and terror, represented by the phallic mother from whom all humans must separate, the task of individual development and of history, the twin potent myths inscribed most powerfully for us in psycho-analysis and Marxism. . . .

The cyborg is resolutely committed to partiality, irony, intimacy, and perversity. It is oppositional, utopian, and completely without innocence. . . .The cyborg does not dream of community on the model of the organic family, this time without the oedipal project. The cyborg would not recognize the Garden of Eden. . . . Cyborgs are not reverent; they do not re-member the cosmos. They are wary of holism, but needy for connection. . . . The main trouble with cyborgs, of course, is that they are the illegitimate offspring of militarism and patriarchal capitalism, not to mention state socialism. But illegitimate offspring are often exceedingly unfaithful to their origins. Their fathers, after all, are inessential.

. . . I want to signal three crucial boundary breakdowns that make the following political-fictional (political-scientific) analysis possible. By the late twentieth century in United States scientific culture, the boundary between human and animal is thoroughly breached. The last beachheads of uniqueness have been polluted if not turned into amusement parks—language, tool use, social behaviour, mental events, nothing really convincingly settles the separation of human and animal. And many people no longer feel the need for such a separation; indeed, many branches of feminist culture affirm the pleasure of connection of human and other living creatures. Movements for animal rights are not irrational denials of human uniqueness; they are a clear-sighted recognition of connection across the discredited breach of nature and culture. . . .

. . . There is much room for radical political people to contest the meanings of the breached boundary. The cyborg appears in myths precisely where the boundary between human and animals is transgressed. Far from signalling a walling off of people from other living beings, cyborgs signal disturbingly and pleasurably tight coupling. Bestiality has a new status in this cycle of marriage exchange.

The second leaky distinction is between animal-human (organism) and machine. Pre-cybernetic machines could be haunted; there was always the spectre of the ghost in the machine. This dualism structured the dialogue between materialism and idealism that was settled by a dialectical progeny called spirit or history, according to taste. But basically machines were not self-moving, self-designing, autonomous. They could not achieve man's dream, only mock it. They were not man, an author to himself, but only a caricature of that masculinist reproductive dream. To think they were otherwise was paranoid. Now we are not so sure. Late twentieth-century machines have made thoroughly ambiguous the difference between natural and artificial, mind and body, self-developing and externally designed, and many other distinctions that used to apply to organisms and machines. Our machines are disturbingly lively, and we ourselves frighteningly inert. . . .

Who cyborgs will be is a radical question; the answers are a matter of survival. Both chimpanzees and artefacts have politics, so why shouldn't we?

The third distinction is a subset of the second: the boundary between physical and non-physical is very imprecise for us. Pop physics books on the consequences of quantum theory and the indeterminacy principle are a kind of popular scientific equivalent to Harlequin romances as a marker of radical change in American white heterosexuality: they get it wrong, but they are on the right subject. Modern machines are quintessentially microelectronic devices: they are everywhere and they are invisible. Modern machinery is an irreverent upstart god, mocking the Father's ubiquity and spirituality. The silicon chip is a surface for writing. . . . Writing, power, and technology are old partners in Western stories of the origin of civilization, but miniaturization has changed our experience of mechanism. Miniaturization has turned out to be about power; small is not so much beautiful as pre-eminently dangerous, as in cruise missiles. Contrast the TV sets of the 1950s or the news cameras of the 1970s with the TV wrist bands or hand-sized video cameras now advertised. Our best machines are made of sunshine; they are all light and clean because they are nothing but signals, electromagnetic waves, a section of a spectrum, and these machines are eminently portable, mobile—a matter of immense human pain in Detroit and Singapore. People are nowhere near so fluid, being both material and opaque. Cyborgs are ether, quintessence.

The ubiquity and invisibility of cyborgs is precisely why these sunshine-belt machines are so deadly. They are as hard to see politically as materially. They are about consciousness—or its simulation. They are floating signifiers moving in pickup trucks across Europe, blocked more effectively by the witch-weavings of the displaced and so unnatural Greenham women, who read the cyborg webs of power so very well, than by the militant labour of older masculinist politics, whose natural constituency needs defense jobs. Ultimately the "hardest" science is about the realm of greatest boundary confusion, the realm of pure number, pure spirit, C^3I, cryptography, and the preservation of potent secrets. The new machines are so clean and light. Their engineers are sun-worshippers mediating a new scientific revolution associated with the night dream of post-industry society. The diseases evoked by these clean machines are "no more" than the minuscule coding changes of an antigen in the immune system, "no more" than the experience of stress. The nimble fingers of "Oriental" women, the old fascination of little Anglo-Saxon Victorian girls with doll's houses, women's enforced attention to the small take on quite new dimensions in this world. There might be a cyborg Alice taking account of these new dimensions. Ironically, it might be the unnatural cyborg women making chips in Asia and spiral dancing in Santa Rita jail whose constructed unities will guide effective oppositional strategies.

So my cyborg myth is about transgressed boundaries, potent fusions, and dangerous possibilities which progressive people might explore as one part of needed political work. One of my premises is that most American socialists and feminists see deepened dualisms of mind and body, animal and machine, idealism and materialism in the social practices, symbolic formulations, and physical artefacts associated with "high technology" and scientific culture. From *One-Dimensional Man* (Marcuse, 1964) to *The Death of Nature* (Merchant, 1980), the analytic resources developed by progressives have insisted on the necessary domination of technics and recalled us to an imagined organic body to integrate our resistance. Another of my premises is that the need for unity of people trying to resist world-wide intensification of domination has never been more acute. But a slightly perverse shift of perspective might better enable us to contest for meetings, as well as for other forms of power and pleasure in technologically mediated societies.

From one perspective, a cyborg world is about the final imposition of a grid of control on the planet, about the final abstraction embodied in a Star Wars apocalypse waged in the name of defence, about the final appropriation of women's bodies in a masculinist orgy of war. From another perspective, a cyborg world might be about lived social and bodily realities in which people are not afraid of their joint kinship with animals and machines, not afraid of permanently partial identities and contra-dictory standpoints. The political struggle is to see from both perspectives at once because each reveals both dominations and possibilities unimaginable from the other vantage point. Single vision produces worse illusions than double vision or many-headed monsters. Cyborg unities are monstrous and illegitimate: in our present political circumstances, we could hardly hope for more potent myths for resistance and recoupling. . . .

Writing is pre-eminently the technology of cyborgs, etched surfaces of the late twentieth century. Cyborg politics is the struggle for language and the struggle against perfect communication, against the one code that translates all meaning perfectly, the central dogma of phallogocentrism. That is why cyborg politics insist on noise and advocate pollution, rejoicing in the illegitimate fusions of animal and machine. These are the couplings which make Man and Woman so problematic, subverting the struc-ture of desire, the force imagined to generate language and gender, and so subverting the structure and modes of reproduction of "Western" identity, of nature and culture, or mirror and eye, slave and master, body and mind. . . .

To recapitulate, certain dualisms have been persistent in Western traditions; they have all been systemic to the logics and practices of domination of women, people of colour, nature, workers, animals—in short, domination of all constituted as others, whose task is to mirror the self. Chief among these troubling dualisms are self/other, mind/body, culture/nature, male/female, civilized/primitive, reality/appearance, whole/part, agent/resource, maker/made, active/passive, right/wrong, truth/illusion, total/partial, God/man. The self is the One who is not dominated, who knows that by the service of the other, the other is the one who holds the future, who knows that by the experience of domination, which gives the lie to the autonomy of the self. To be One is to be autonomous, to be powerful, to be God; but to be One is to be an illu-sion, and so to be involved in a dialectic of apocalypse with the other. Yet to be other is to be multiple, without clear boundary, frayed, insubstantial. One is too few, but two are too many.

High-tech culture challenges these dualisms in intriguing ways. It is not clear who makes and who is made in the relation between human and machine. It is not clear what is mind and what body in machines that resolve into coding practices. In so far as we know ourselves in both formal discourse (for example, biology) and in daily practice (for example, the homework economy in the integrated circuit), we find ourselves to be cyborgs, hybrids, mosaics, chimeras. Biological organisms have become biotic systems, communications devices like others. There is no fundamen-tal, ontological separation in our formal knowledge of machine and organism, of technical and organic. The replicant Rachel in the Ridley Scott film *Blade Runner* stands as the image of a cyborg culture's fear, love, and confusion.

One consequence is that our sense of connection to our tools is heightened. The trance state experienced by many computer users has become a staple of science-fiction film and cultural jokes. Perhaps paraplegics and other severely handicapped people can (and sometimes do) have the most intense experiences of complex hy-bridization with other communication devices. Anne McCaffrey's pre-feminist *The Ship Who Sang* (1969) explored the consciousness of a cyborg, hybrid of girl's brain and complex machinery, formed after the birth of a severely handicapped child. Gender, sexuality, embodiment, skill: all were reconstituted in the story. Why should our bodies end at the skin, or include at best other beings encapsulated by skin? From the seventeenth century till now, machines could be animated given ghostly souls to make them speak or move or to account for their orderly development and mental capacities. Or organisms could be mechanized—reduced to body understood as resource of mind. These machine organism relationships are obsolete, unnecessary. For us, in imagination and in other practice, machines can be prosthetic devices, intimate components, friendly selves. . . .

There are several consequences to taking seriously the imagery of cyborgs as other than our enemies. Our bodies, ourselves; bodies are maps of power and identity. Cyborgs are no exception. A cyborg body is not innocent; it was not born in a garden; it does not seek unitary identity—and so generate antagonistic dualisms without end (or until the world ends); it takes irony for granted. One is too few, and two is only one possibility. Intense pleasure in skill, machine skill, ceases to be a sin, but an aspect of embodiment. The machine is not an *it* to be animated, worshipped, and dominated. The machine is us, our processes, an aspect of our embodiment. We can be responsible for machines; *they* do not dominate or threaten us. We are responsible for boundaries; we are they. Up till now (once upon a time), female embodiment seemed to be given, organic, necessary; and female embodiment seemed to mean skill in mothering and its metaphoric extensions. Only by being out of place could we take intense pleasure in machines and then with excuses that this was organic activity after all, appropriate to females. Cyborgs might consider more seriously the partial, fluid, sometimes, aspect of sex and sexual embodiments. Gender might not be global identity after all, even if it has profound historical breadth and depth.

The ideologically charged question of what counts as daily activity, as experience, can be approached by exploiting the cyborg image. Feminists have recently claimed that women are given to dailiness, that women more than men somehow sustain daily life, and so have a privileged epistemological position potentially. There is a compelling aspect to this claim, one that makes visible unvalued female activity and names it as the ground of life. But *the* ground of life? What about all the ignorance of women, all the exclusions and failures of knowledge and skill? What about men's access to daily competence, to knowing how to build things, to take them apart, to play? What about other embodiments? Cyborg gender is a local possibility taking a global vengeance. Race, gender, and capital require a cyborg theory of wholes and parts. There is no drive in cyborgs to produce total theory, but there is an intimate experience of boundaries, their construction and deconstruction. There is a myth system waiting to become a political language to ground one way of looking at science and technology and challenging the informatics of domination—in order to act potently.

One last image: organisms and organismic, holistic politics depend on metaphors of rebirth and invariably call on the resources of reproductive sex. I would suggest that cyborgs have more to do with regeneration and are suspicious of the reproductive matrix and of most birthing. For salamanders, regeneration after injury, such as the loss of a limb, involves regrowth of structure and restoration of function with the constant possibility of twinning or other odd topographical productions at the site of former injury. The regrown limb can be monstrous, duplicated, potent. We have all been injured, profoundly. We require regeneration, not rebirth, and the possibilities for our reconstitution include the utopian dream of the hope for a monstrous world without gender.

Cyborg imagery can help express two crucial arguments in this essay: first, the production of universal, totalizing theory is a major mistake that misses most of reality, probably always, but certainly now; and second, taking responsibility for the social relations of science and technology means refusing an anti-science metaphysics, a demonology of technology, and so means embracing the skilful task of reconstructing the boundaries of daily life, in partial connection with others, in communication with all of our parts. It is not just that science and technology are possible means of great human satisfaction, as well as a matrix of complex dominations. Cyborg imagery can suggest a way out of the maze of dualisms in which we have explained our bodies and our tools to ourselves. . . . It means both building and destroying machines, identities, categories, relationships, space stories. Though both are bound in the spiral dance, I would rather be a cyborg than a goddess.

Los Angeles Before the Riots, 1990

MIKE DAVIS

The carefully manicured lawns of Los Angeles's Westside sprout forests of ominous little signs warning: "Armed Response!" Even richer neighborhoods in the canyons and hillsides isolated themselves behind walls guarded by gun-toting private police and state-of-the-art electronic surveillance. Downtown, a publicly-subsidized "urban renaissance" has raised the nation's largest corporate citadel, segregated from the poor neighborhoods around it by a monumental architectural glacis. . . . In the Westlake district and the San Fernando Valley the Los Angeles Police barricade streets and seal off poor neighborhoods as part of their "war on drugs." In Watts, developer Alexander Haagen demonstrates his strategy for recolonizing inner-city retail markets: a panoptican shopping mall surrounded by staked metal fences and a substation of the LAPD in a central surveillance tower. . . .

Welcome to post-liberal Los Angeles, where the defense of luxury lifestyles is translated into a proliferation of new repressions in space and movement undergirded by the ubiquitous "armed response." This obsession with physical security systems, and, collaterally, with the architectural policing of social boundaries, has become a zeitgeist of urban restructuring, a master narrative in the emerging built environment of the 1990s. Yet contemporary urban theory, whether debating the role of electronic technologies in precipitating "postmodern space," or discussing the dispersion of urban functions across poly-centered metropolitan "galaxies," has been strangely silent about the militarization of city life so grimly visible at the street level. Hollywood's pop apocalypses and pulp science fiction have been more realistic, and politically perceptive, in representing the programmed hardening of the urban surface in the wake of the social polarizations of the Reagan era. Images of carceral inner cities (*Escape from New York, Running Man*), high-tech police death squads (*Blade Runner*),

From Mike Davis, *City of Quartz* (New York: Vintage Books, 1992), pp. 223–229, 232—237, 250–253, 302–307, 316. First published in 1990.

sentient buildings (*Die Hard*), urban bantustans (*They Live!*), Vietnam-like street wars (*Colors*), and so on, only extrapolate from actually existing trends.

Such dystopian visions grasp the extent to which today's pharaonic scales of residential and commercial security supplant residual hopes for urban reform and social integration. The dire predictions of Richard Nixon's 1969 National Commission on the Causes and Prevention of Violence have been tragically fulfilled: we live in "fortress cities" brutally divided between "fortified cells" of affluent society and "places of terror" where the police battle the criminalized poor. The "Second Civil War" that began in the long hot summers of the 1960s has been institutionalized into the very structure of urban space. The old liberal paradigm of social control, attempting to balance repression with reform, has long been superseded by a rhetoric of social warfare that calculates the interests of the urban poor and the middle class as a zero-sum game. In cities like Los Angeles, on the bad edge of postmodernity, one observes an unprecedented tendency to merge urban design, architecture and the police apparatus into a single, comprehensive security effort.

This epochal coalescence has far-reaching consequences for the social relations of the built environment. . . . the market provisions of "security" generates its own paranoid demand. "Security" becomes a positional good defined by income across to private "protective services" and membership in some hardened residential enclave or restricted suburb. As a prestige symbol—and sometimes as the decisive borderline between the merely well-off and the "truly rich"—"security" has less to do with personal safety than with the degree of personal insulation, in residential, work, consumption and travel environments, from "unsavory" groups and individuals, even crowds in general. . . .

. . . [T]he neo-military syntax of contemporary architecture insinuates violence and conjures imaginary dangers. In many instances the semiotics of so-called "defensible space" are just about as subtle as a swaggering white cop. Today's upscale, pseudo-public spaces—sumptuary malls, office centers, culture acropolises, and so on—are full of invisible signs warning off the underclass "Other." Although architectural critics are usually oblivious to how the built environment contributes to segregation, pariah groups–whether poor Latino families, young Black men, or elderly homeless white females—read the meaning immediately.

The universal and ineluctable consequence of this crusade to secure the city is the destruction of accessible public space. The contemporary opprobrium attached to the term "street person" is in itself a harrowing index of the devaluation of public spaces. To reduce contact with untouchables, urban redevelopment has converted once vital pedestrian streets into traffic sewers and transformed public parks into temporary receptacles for the homeless and wretched. The American city, as many critics have recognized, is being systematically turned inside out—or, rather, outside in. The valorized spaces of the new megastructures and super-malls are concentrated in the center, street frontage is denuded, public activity is sorted into strictly functional compartments, and circulation is internalized in corridors under the gaze of private police.

The privatization of the architectural public realm, moreover, is shadowed by parallel restructurings of electronic space, as heavily policed, pay-access "information orders," elite data-bases and subscription cable services appropriate parts of the invisible agora. Both processes, of course, mirror the deregulation of the economy and the recession of non-market entitlements. The decline of urban liberalism has been accompanied by the death of what might be called the "Olmstedian vision" of public space. Frederick Law Olmsted, it will be recalled, was North America's Haussmann, as well as the Father of Central Park. In the wake of Manhattan's "Commune" of 1863, the great Draft Riot, he conceived public landscapes and parks as social safety-values, *mixing* classes and ethnicities in common (bourgeois) recreations and enjoyments. As Manfredo Tafuri has shown in his well-known study of Rockefeller Center, the same principle animated the construction of the canonical spaces of the La Guardia—Roosevelt era.

This reformist vision of public space—as the emollient of class struggle, if not the bedrock of the American *polis*—is now as obsolete as Keynesian nostrums of full employment. In regard to the "mixing" of classes, contemporary urban America is more like Victorian England than Walt Whitman's or La Guardia's New York. In Los Angeles, once-upon-a-time a demi-paradise of free beaches, luxurious parks, and "cruising strips," genuinely democratic space is all but extinct. The Oz-like archipelago of Westside pleasure domes—a continuum of tony malls, arts centers and gourmet strips—is reciprocally dependent upon the social imprisonment of the third-world service proletariat who live in increasingly repressive ghettoes and barrios. In a city of several million yearning immigrants, public amenities are radically shrinking, parks are becoming derelict and beaches more segregated, libraries and playgrounds are closing, youth congregations of ordinary kinds are banned, and the streets are becoming more desolate and dangerous.

. . . Even as the walls have come down in Eastern Europe, they are being erected all over Los Angeles. . . .

This conscious "hardening" of the city surface against the poor is especially brazen in the Manichaean treatment of Downtown microcosms. In his famous study of the "social life of small urban spaces," William Whyte makes the point that the quality of any urban environment can be measured, first of all, by whether there are convenient, comfortable places for pedestrians to sit. This maxim has been warmly taken to heart by designers of the high-corporate precincts of Bunker Hill and the emerging "urban village" of South Park. As part of the city's policy of subsidizing white-collar residential colonization in Downtown, it has spent, or plans to spend, tens of millions of dollars of diverted tax revenue on enticing, "soft" environments in these areas. Planners envision an opulent complex of squares, fountains, world-class public art, exotic shrubbery, and avant-garde street furniture along a Hope Street pedestrian corridor. In the propaganda of official boosters, nothing is taken as a better index of Downtown's "liveability" than the idyll of office workers and up-scale tourists lounging or napping in the terraced gardens of California Plaza, the "Spanish Steps" or Grand Hope Park.

In stark contrast, a few blocks away, the city is engaged in a merciless struggle to make public facilities and spaces as "unliveable" as possible for the homeless and the poor. . . .

. . .[T]he city, self-consciously adopting the idiom of urban cold war, promotes the "containment" (official term) of the homeless in Skid Row along Fifth Street east of the Broadway, systematically transforming the neighborhood into an outdoor poorhouse. But this containment strategy breeds its own vicious circle of contradiction. By condensing the mass of the desperate and helpless together in such a small space, and denying adequate housing, official policy has transformed Skid Row into probably the most dangerous ten square blocks in the world—ruled by a grisly succession of "Slashers," "Night Stalkers" and more ordinary predators. Every night on Skid Row is Friday the 13th, and, unsurprisingly, many of the homeless seek to escape the "Nickle" during the night at all costs, searching safer niches in other parts of Downtown. The city in turn tightens the noose with increased police harassment and ingenious design deterrents.

One of the most common, but mind-numbing, of these deterrents is the Rapid Transit District's new barrelshaped bus bench that offers a minimal surface for uncomfortable sitting, while making sleeping utterly impossible. Such "bumproof" benches are being widely introduced on the periphery of Skid Row. Another invention, worthy of the Grand Guignol, is the aggressive deployment of outdoor sprinklers. Several years ago the city opened a "Skid Row Park" along lower Fifth Street, on a corner of Hell. To ensure that the park was not used for sleeping—that is to say, to guarantee that it was mainly utilized for drug dealing and prostitution—the city installed an elaborate overhead sprinkler system programmed to drench unsuspecting sleepers at random times during the night. The system was immediately copied by some local businessmen in order to drive the homeless away from adjacent public sidewalks. Meanwhile restaurants and markets have responded to the homeless by building ornate enclosures to protect their refuse. Although no one in Los Angeles has yet proposed adding cyanide to the garbage, as happened in Phoenix a few years back, one popular seafood restaurant has spent $12,000 to build the ultimate bag-lady-proof trash cage: made of three-quarter inch steel rod with alloy locks and vicious outturned spikes to safeguard priceless moldering fishheads and stale french fries.

Public toilets, however, are the real Eastern Front of the Downtown war on the poor. Los Angeles, as a matter of deliberate policy, has fewer available public lavatories than any major North American city. On the advice of the LAPD (who actually sit on the design board of at least one major Downtown redevelopment project), the Community Redevelopment Agency bulldozed the remaining public toilet in Skid Row. Agency planners then agonized for months over whether to include a "freestanding public toilet" in their design for South Park. As CRA Chairman Jim Wood later admitted, the decision not to include the toilet was a "policy decision and not a design decision." The CRA Downtown prefers the solution of "quasi-public restrooms"—meaning toilets in restaurants, art galleries and office buildings—which can be made available to tourists and office workers while being denied to vagrants and other unsuitables. The toiletless no-man's-land east of Hill Street in Downtown is also barren of outside water sources for drinking or washing. A common and troubling sight these days are the homeless men—many of them young Salvadorean refugees—washing in and even drinking from the sewer effluent which flows down the concrete channel of the Los Angeles River on the eastern edge of Downtown.

Where the itineraries of Downtown powerbrokers unavoidably intersect with the habitats of the homeless or the working poor, as in the . .. zone of gentrification along the norther Broadway corridor, extraordinary design precautions are being taken to ensure the physical separation of the different humanities. For instance, the CRA brought in the Los Angeles Police to design "24-hour, state-of-the-art security" for the two new parking structures that serve the Los Angeles *Times* and Ronald Reagan State Office buildings. In contrast to the mean streets outside, the parking structures contain beautifully landscaped lawns or "microparks," and in one case, a food court and a historical exhibit. Moreover, both structures are designed as "confidence-building" circulation systems—miniature paradigms of privatization—which allow white-collar workers to walk from car to office, or from car to boutique, with minimum exposure to the public street. The Broadway Spring Center, in particular, which links the Ronald Reagan Building to the proposed "Grand Central Square" at Third and Broadway, has been warmly praised by architectural critics for adding greenery and art (a banal bas relief) to parking. It also adds a huge dose of menace—armed guards, locked gates, and security cameras—to scare away the homeless and poor.

The cold war on the streets of Downtown is ever escalating. The police, lobbied by Downtown merchants and developers, have broken up every attempt by the homeless and their allies to create safe havens of self-organized encampments. "Justiceville," founded by homeless activist Ted Hayes, was roughly dispersed; when its inhabitants attempted to find refuge at Venice Beach, they were arrested at the behest of the local council person (a renowned environmentalist) and sent back to the inferno of Skid Row. The city's own brief experiment with legalized camping—a grudging response to a series of exposure deaths in the cold winter of 1987—was ended abruptly after only four months to make way for construction of a transit repair yard. Current policy seems to involve a perverse play upon Zola's famous irony about the "equal rights" of the rich and the poor to sleep out rough. As the head of the city planning commission explained the official line to incredulous reporters, it is not against the law to sleep on the street per se, "only to erect any sort of protective shelter." To enforce this prescription against "cardboard condos," the LAPD periodically sweep the Nickle, confiscating shelters and other possessions, and arresting resisters. Such cynical repression has turned the majority of the homeless into urban bedouins. They are visible all over Downtown, pushing a few pathetic possessions in purloined shopping carts, always fugitive and in motion, pressed between the official policy of containment and the increasing sadism of Downtown streets. . . .

This comprehensive urban security mobilization depends not only upon the imbrication of the police function into the built environment, but also upon an evolving social division of labor between public- and private-sector police services, in which the former act as the necessary supports of the latter. As *Police Chief* magazine notes, "harsh economic realities of the 1980s"—for instance, the tax revolt, rising rates of crime against property, and burgeoning middle-class demands for security—have catalyzed "a realignment of relationships between private security and law enforcement." The private sector, exploiting an army of non-union, low-wage employees, has increasingly captured the labor-intensive roles . . . while public law enforcement has retrenched behind the supervision of security macrosystems (maintenance of major crime date bases, aerial surveillance, jail systems, paramilitary responses to terrorism and street insurgency, and so on). The confusing interface between the two sectors is most evident in the overlapping of patrol functions in many neighborhoods and in the growing trend to subcontract jailing (with the privatized supervision of electronic home surveillance as another potentially lucrative market).

In many respects this division of labor is more elaborated in Los Angeles than elsewhere, if only because of the LAPD's pathbreaking substitutions of technological capital for patrol manpower. In part this was a necessary adaption to the city's dispersed form; but it has also expressed the department's particular definition of its relationship to the community. Especially in its own self-perpetuated myth, the LAPD is seen as the progressive antithesis to the traditional big-city police department with its patronage armies of patrolmen grafting off the beat. As reformed in the early 1950s by the legendary Chief Parker (who admired above all the elitism of the Marines), the LAPD was intended to be incorruptible because unapproachable, a "few good men" doing battle with a fundamentally evil city. *Dragnet's* Sergeant Friday precisely captured the Parkerized LAPD's quality of prudish alienation from a citizenry composed of fools, degenerates and psychopaths.

Technology helped insulate this paranoid *esprit de corps.* In doing so, it virtually established a new epistemology of policing, where technologized surveillance and response supplanted the traditional partolman's intimate "folk" knowledge of specific communities. Thus back in the 1920s the LAPD had pioneered the replacement of the flatfoot or mounted officer with the radio patrol car—the beginning of dispersed, mechanized policing. Under Parker, ever alert to spinoffs from military technology, the LAPD introduced the first police helicopters for systematic aerial surveillance. After the Watts Rebellion of 1965 this airborne effort became the cornerstone of a policing strategy for the entire inner city. As part of its "Astro" program LAPD helicopters maintain an average nineteen-hour-per-day vigil over "high crime areas," tactically coordinated to patrol car forces, and exceeding even the British Army's aerial surveillance of Belfast. To facilitate ground-air synchronization, thousands of residential rooftops have been painted with identifying street numbers, transforming the aerial view of the city into a huge police-grid.

The fifty-pilot LAPD airforce was recently updated with French Aerospatiale helicopters equipped with futuristic surveillance technology. Their forward-looking infra-red cameras are extraordinary night eyes that can easily form heat images from a single burning cigarette, while their thirty-million-candlepower spotlights, appropriately called "Nightsun," can literally turn the night into day. Meanwhile the LAPD retains another fleet of Bell Jet Rangers capable of delivering complete elements of SWAT personnel anywhere in the region. Their training, which sometimes includes practice assaults on Downtown highrises, anticipates some of the spookier Hollywood images (for example, *Blue Thunder* or *Running Man*) of airborne police terror. A few years ago a veteran LAPD SWAT commander (apparently one of the principals in the infamous SLA holocaust in Southcentral Los Angeles) accidentally shot his own helicopter out of the sky while practicing a strafing run with a machine-gun.

But the most decisive element in the LAPD's metamorphosis into a technopolice has been its long and successful liaison with the military aerospace industry. Just in time for the opening of the 1984 Los Angeles Olympics, the department brought on line ECCCS (Emergency Command Control Communications Systems), the most powerful, state-of-the-art police communications systems in the world. First conceptualized by Hughes Aerospace between 1969 and 1971, ECCCS's design was refined and updated by NASA's Jet Propulsion Laboratory, incorporating elements of space technology and mission control communications. After the passage of a $42 million tax override in May 1977, the City Council approved Systems Development Corporation of Santa Monica as prime contractor for the system, which took more than seven years to build.

The central hardware of ECCCS is encased in security comparable to a SAC missile silo in Montana. Bunkered in the earthquake-proofed and security-hardened

fourth and fifth sublevels of City Hall East (and interconnecting with the Police pentagon in Parker Center), Central Dispatch Center coordinates all the complex itineraries
and responses of the LAPD using digitalized communication to eliminate voice congestion and guarantee the secrecy of transmission. ECCCS, together with the LAPD's
prodigious information-processing assets, including the ever-growing databases on
suspect citizenry, have become the central neutral system for the vast and disparate,
public and private, security operations taking place in Los Angeles.

. . . Having brought policing up to the levels of the Vietnam War and early
NASA, it is almost inevitable that the LAPD, and other advanced police forces, will
try to acquire the technology of the Electronic Battlefield and even Star Wars. . . .
Ex-Los Angeles police chief, now state senator, Ed Davis (Republican—Valencia)
has proposed the use of a geosynclinical space satellite to counter pandemic car theft
in the region. Electronic alarm systems, already tested in New England, would alert
police if a properly tagged car was stolen; satellite monitoring would extend coverage over Los Angeles's vast metropolitan area. . . .

The image here is ultimately more important than the practicality of the proposal,
since it condenses the historical world view and quixotic quest of the postwar LAPD:
good citizens, off the streets, enclaved in their high-security private consumption
spheres; bad citizens, on the streets (and therefore not engaged in legitimate business), caught in the terrible, Jehovan scrutiny of the LAPD's space program. . . .

. . . It is necessary to recall that the revolutionary rhetoric of the 1960s was
sustained by the real promise of reformism. . . . Moreover in the superheated
summit of the Vietnam boom, young Black men at last began to find their way, in
some substantial number, into factory and transportation jobs, while Black women
thronged into the lower levels of the pink-collar workforce. And, for teenagers and
the younger unemployed, the federal government supplied a seasonal quota of temporary "weed-pulling" jobs and bogus training schemes to cool out the streets during the long summers.

But the illusion of economic progress was shortlived. By 1975—the tenth anniversary of the Watts Rebellion . . . a special report by the *Times* found that the "the
Black ghetto is not a viable community . . . it is slowly dying." In the face of double-
digit unemployment (1975 was a depression year for Southland Blacks), overcrowded schools, high prices, and deteriorating housing, "the fighting mood of
the 1960s has been replaced by a sick apathy or angry frustration." With rebellion
deterred by the paramilitarization of the police and the destruction of the community's radical fringe, *Times* writer John Kendall described despair recycled as gang
violence and Black-on-Black crime.

Seen from a perspective fifteen years further on, it is clear that the *Times,* and
other contemporary observers, did not fully appreciate the complexity of what was
happening in Southcentral Los Angeles. Although the image of overall community
demoralization was accurate enough, a sizeable minority was actually experiencing
moderate upward mobility, while the condition of the majority was steadily worsen-
ing. In simplified terms, Los Angeles's Black community became more internally
polarized as public-sector craftworkers, clericals, and professionals successfully entrenched themselves within city, county, and federal bureaucracies, while the semi-
skilled working class in the private sector was decimated by the dual impact of job
suburbanization and economic internationalization. . . .

... Working-class Blacks in the flatlands—where nearly 40 per cent of families live below the poverty line—have faced relentless economic decline. While city resources (to the tune of $2 billion) have been absorbed in financing the corporate renaissance of Downtown, Southcentral L.A. has been markedly disadvantaged even in receipt of anti-poverty assistance, "coming far behind West Los Angeles and the Valley in access to vital human services and job-training funds." Black small businesses have withered for lack of credit or attention from the city, leaving behind only liquor stores and churches.

Most tragically, the unionized branch-plant economy toward which working-class Blacks (and Chicanos) had always looked for decent jobs collapsed. As the Los Angeles economy in the 1970s was "unplugged" from the American industrial heartland and rewired to East Asia, non-Anglo workers have borne the brunt of adaptation and sacrifice. The 1978–82 wave of factory closings in the wake of Japanese import penetration and recession, which shuttered ten of the twelve largest non-aerospace plants in Southern California and displaced 75,000 blue-collar workers, erased the ephemeral gains won by blue-collar Blacks between 1965 and 1975. Where local warehouses and factories did not succumb to Asian competition, they fled instead to new industrial parks in the South Bay, northern Orange County or the Inland Empire—321 firms since 1971. An investigation committee of the California Legislature in 1982 confirmed the resulting economic destruction in Southcentral neighborhoods: unemployment rising by nearly 50 per cent since the early 1970s while community purchasing power fell by a third.

If Eastside manufacturing employment made a spectacular recovery in the 1980s, it offered little opportunity for Blacks, as the new industry overwhelmingly consisted of minimum-wage sweatshops, super-exploiting immigrant Latino labor in the production of furniture or non-durables like clothes and toys. (Borrowing the terminology of Alain Lipietz, we might say that a "Bloody Taylorism now operates within the ruined shell of Fordism." This extinction of industrial job opportunities has had profound gender as well as socioeconomic ramifications for the Black labor force. Young Black women have been partially able to compensate for community deindustrialization by shifting into lower-level information-processing jobs. Young Black working-class men, on the other hand, have seen their labor-market options (apart from military service) virtually collapse as the factory and truckdriving jobs that gave their fathers and older brothers a modicum of dignity have either been replaced by imports, or relocated to white areas far out on the galactic spiral-arms of the L.A. megalopolis—fifty to eighty miles away in San Bernardino or Riverside counties.

Equally, young Blacks have been largely excluded from the boom in suburban service employment. . . . it is a stunning fact—emblematic of institutional racism on a far more rampant scale than usually admitted these days—that most of California's 1980s job and residential growth poles—southern Orange County, eastern Ventura County, northern San Diego County, Contra Costa County, and so on—have Black populations of 1 per cent or less. At the same time, young Blacks willing to compete for more centrally located, menial service jobs find themselves in a losing competition with new immigrants, not least because of clear employer opinions about labor "docility." As a result, unemployment amongst Black youth in Los Angeles County— despite unbroken regional growth and a new explosion of conspicuous consumption—remained at a staggering 45 per cent through the late 1980s. . . . The scale of pent-up demand for decent manual employment was also vividly demonstrated a few years ago when *fifty thousand* predominantly Black and Chicano youth lined up for miles to apply for a few openings on the unionized longshore in San Pedro.

. . . As the political muscle of affluent homeowners continues to ensure residential segregation and the redistribution of tax resources upwards, inner-city youth have been the victims of a conscious policy of social disinvestment. The tacit expendability of Black and brown youth in the "city of the angels" can be directly measured by the steady drainage of resources—with minimum outcry from elected officials—from the programs that serve the most urgent needs. . . .

Job alternatives for gang members have been almost nonexistent, despite widespread recognition that jobs are more potent deterrents to youth crime than STEP laws or long penitentiary sentences. As Charles Norman, the veteran director of Youth Gang Services, observed in 1981: "You could pull 80 per cent of gang members, seventeen years old or younger, out of gangs if you had jobs, job training and social alternatives." . . . As the LAPD's budget crept above $400 million in 1988, the City Council begrudgingly approved a $500,000 pilot program to create one hundred jobs for "high-risk" youth. In the vast escalation of hostilities since the mid 1980s, this pathetic program is the only "carrot" that the City has actually differed to its estimated 50,000 gang youth. . . .

. . . In Los Angeles there are too many signs of approaching helter-skelter: everywhere in the inner city, even in the forgotten poor-white boondocks with their zombie populations of speed-freaks, gangs are multiplying at a terrifying rate, cops are becoming more arrogant and trigger-happy, and a whole generation is being shunted toward some impossible Armageddon.

Watch Out, Dick Tracy, 1991

DEEDEE HALLECK

Dick Tracy used advanced technology. He was the comic hero with the two-way radio wristwatch. He was also a cop, and cops can usually get the technology they need. But in 1948 I, a knobby-kneed eight-year-old girl, had a Dick Tracy watch, which made me the most technologically advanced of my family, not to mention on my block. No one in our neighborhood even had a TV set at that time. I got my two-way radio watch by sending in Kix (or was it Shredded Wheat?) box tops with a quarter and a self-addressed, stamped envelope. It was a classic case of military research benefiting the consumer. The cops got their equipment and we Kix eaters shared in the advancement of science. I was ecstatic. It didn't matter that it didn't work. Neither did the infinitely most frustrating battery-operated walkie-talkie my younger sister got in the late fifties. The Dick Tracy watch had no pretensions. It *was* pretend, I didn't expect it to work. It was adapted for the home market. It was the idea that counted.

DeeDee Halleck, "Watch Out, Dick Tracy: Popular Video in the Wake of the Exxon Valdez," from *Techno-culture* ed. Constance Penley and Andrew Ross (Minneapolis: University of Minnesota Press, 1991) excerpts from pp. 211–228. Copyright © 1991 by the Regents of the University of Minnesota. Reprinted by permission.

From the cereal box to the TV set, the military is a part of everyday life in the United States. The merger between GE and RCA has only made more obvious the kinds of symbiosis that the military has had from the beginning with the major media corporations. General Electric and RCA have been two of the biggest military contractors since World War II. NBC was a subsidiary of RCA and is now a part of the megamilitary corporation the merger created. Collusion of military and communication technology isn't new. The first large U.S. corporation was Western Union, which had its western expansion subsidized by Congress as a wartime expense for the Union during the Civil War. Native Americans fought this expansion by cutting the wires and on occasion felling the telegraph poles with axes. Resistance to the relentless advance of corporate communications seems just as futile today, if not more so. What recourse exists in a world ringed with satellites and stitched with microwave links? . . .

The profound alienation and impotence that most people feel about technology has overshadowed any embryonic thoughts we might have had about the liberatory potential of most machines. But people are more willing to struggle against nuclear power proliferation than against the toxic effects of our communication system. The widespread sense of technological impotence is increased by maintaining the myth that the development of communication technology is inherently based in a military arena. It is clear that everyone but the radical right and the corporations have been effectively intimidated. How can we challenge the media if RCA/GE is in charge? . . .

With the introduction of home video and public access television, there has been a media *evolution,* if not a video *revolution.* Video technology is being used by a vast number of people in ways that have begun to challenge the passive consumption model that has dominated electronic communication ever since department stores first began to sponsor radio concerts to sell sofas and radios over the air (for listening to those same concerts in one's own home).

Bertolt Brecht's famous treatise on the emancipatory possibilities of radio drew its inspiration from the inherent "democratic" potential of transmission itself. There is no reason electronic transmission—broadcasting as opposed to receiving—cannot be a popular-based activity. There is no law of the apparatus that decrees that it is only *reception* of radio signals that is widespread. *Broad*casting (including radio and television and cable distribution and satellite transmission) always contains the potential of multiple transmitters: multiple sites of transmissions and multiple messages to be transmitted. . . .

. . . [T]here are many . . . features of the consumer video phenomenon that are worthy of our attention. In fact, it is evident that pockets of resistance have arisen that have the potential to evolve into more highly organized and autonomous centers of democratic communications.

Equipment manufacturers have every interest in selling ever-increasing numbers of machines, and, to guarantee a mass market, the machines have to be priced low enough for everyone either to have one or to feel that one is not entirely out of reach. The level of competition has ensured that television picture quality has developed at increasingly higher levels and at ever-lowering prices. However, the corporate program suppliers (i.e., commercial television and the movie companies) have an obvious interest in maintaining control over the programs that are consumed and distributed, and, more important, over whether and how they are duplicated. . . .

The masters of video technology have been successful at marketing elements of active control even for hitherto passive viewing. Early Sony ads stressed the "time-shifting" possibilities: one could change the flow of television transmission to watch specific programs selectively, at one's convenience. One of the most attractive features of a VCR is the control it gives to viewing: still frame, fast forward, rewind, repeat—these are controls that allow a selective and critical viewing in an active mode. VCR users are unwilling to rest as passive viewers. The consuming public demands that the machines they buy produce *and reproduce* and have the capacity to time-shift images.

From the beginning of photography, equipment manufacturers have attempted to encourage a certain type of image production. In the early days of consumer photography, equipment was sold to the home market by promoting portraits of family members, family milestones, get-togethers, and remembrance of travel. This "domestication" of imagery was continuous with the domestic fate of women: safe in the home, the kitchen, and occasionally on vacation. For almost an entire century a certain (usually gender-specific) passivity has been promoted in the imagery of Kodak ads and especially in their instruction books, where almost 100% of the *subjects* for the novice camera users are women.

In their advertising and hobby books, Eastman Kodak never suggested that Brownie owners take pictures of their workplaces, or that they record their rank-and-file strikes. Nor did Kodak promote the use of still photography to document water pollution or industrial waste (especially since they are on the top of the list of industrial polluters).

With the development of the "home movie" camera, the subjects were the same as those in still photography, only now they waved to the camera. Eight-millimeter movie cameras and super-8 rigs were marketed as live-action snapshots. With the introduction of consumer video, home camcorders, like still photography and home-movie cameras before them, are pushed as adjuncts of the bourgeois heterosexual family. . . .

However, there are several areas of difference between video camcorders and snapshot or even home move cameras: the first difference is the *size of investment.* Video cameras are more expensive than Brownie cameras, and consumers are apt to want to get more use from them than a yearly glimpse of the kid's birthday.

A second difference is in the *site of display.* Photos fit neatly into special albums piled on coffee tables and in gilt frames on bureau tops. . . . The viewing is an extended family ceremony. Homemade video, however, has its place not in a separate and ceremonial realm. It is shown on the family TV set, which, although it is located as the "hearth" of the modern home, is the central receiver of external "reality," the window on the world outside; in this respect, it can be defined as a public space.

A third difference between home video and snapshot photograph and home movies is the *use of sound.* . . . One needs something to say. Consequently, home videos tend to have more content.

There is also a *narrowing of the gap* between "amateur" images and "professional" ones. With home movies, we always knew they weren't MGM. The size of the image, the clarity of registration, the skillful use of lighting all made "the movies" look very different from home movies. With video that differential is less evident. The new video cameras obviate the use of lights, and the resolution of detail is approaching that of some network programming. . . .

Finally, an important difference has been the *expansion of the video market beyond individuals to organizations and groups.* Video is purchased by businesses and groups in a way that never happened with still photography and home movies. Golf clubhouses, day-care centers, ballet classes, and biology labs are potential camcorder users. . . . As a result, video handbooks break with the wife-and-kids-posing images that adorn photo textbooks. Video sales pitches include shots of everyone from nuns to Cuna Indians shooting video. The stereotype of domestic use is broken. Consumer cameras show up at town council meetings, school board tax hearings, rent strikes, block parties, and Rotary Club meetings. Camcorders are becoming a fact of civic life not easily dismissed. To be widely sold video has had to be serious (and fun), public (and private), and accessible across gender and racial boundaries. It has been marketed, in other words, as nothing less than a popular tool.

The most far-reaching aspect of popular video use in the United States has been the growth of the public access movement. Access to channels and studio space and equipment is part of the cable franchising process in cities and towns across the country. This movement has been underreported and misunderstood by both mainstream press and media critics. It is a grass-roots movement of tremendous potential, although it varies a great deal in details from city to city. In certain cities (Dallas, Somerville, Portland, Austin, Burlington, Pocatello, and Atlanta are a few examples) a good mix of artists, media activists, community organizers, labor unions, and politicians has made public access an important, viable outlet for community information, organization, and creativity.

In those cities where public access TV is thriving, there is also a good audience for the access channels, or rather many audiences, for when access works best, it is "narrowcasting"—providing programming for communities of interest, answering specific informational needs. In Milwaukee, a group of deaf persons was able to produce a weekly "signed" show so successfully that they inspired a group of partially blind persons to get training and do a series themselves. They received an oversized monitor through a grant to disabled persons and devised a system for using headphones for guests to signal their camera cues, since the normal hand signals weren't readily perceived. Among the thousands of groups using public access are welfare rights groups, Latin America solidarity organizations, the United Farm Workers Union, and local affiliates of Amnesty International.

I have been involved with cable access since 1976, when I was part of a group called Image Union, formed to cover the Democratic National Convention. At that time we cablecast for five hours a night for five nights on Manhattan cable access. In the early days of video, when there were few portapaks, experimental work was done for the most part in collectives. These groups, such as Video Freex, TV TV, and Raindance, shared equipment and space and were the first groups to garner grants from the public arts councils as collectives. Although they made tapes for several years, few of the early video artists were actively involved in producing for television. Video art tended to be shown in closed-circuit situations, in galleries, museums, and media centers. . . .

However, by the late 1970s there were several alternative series running regularly on public access in New York. . . . The audiences were small, but loyal. The most radical effect of these often wildly outrageous programs was to add a bit of leavening to the often weighty seriousness of public access talk shows. . . .

In 1981, I was one of the founders of the access series *Paper Tiger Television.* These programs have been developed not only as programming on Manhattan Cable (and several other systems around the country) but as a model series for creative low-budget use of studio, small-format cameras, and local resources. The Paper Tiger Collective has now produced almost two hundred programs of media criticism, from "Herb Schiller Reads the *New York Times*" to "Donna Haraway on the *National Geographic.*" The ultimate value of this series lies less in the impact of any of the individual programs than in the overall effort to create television formats that are site specific to public access. . . .

Because of this, Paper Tiger drew a number of enthusiasts from around the country, and we were able to make contact with other progressive access users, many of whom expressed the desire to exchange programming. It was out of these discussions that we were able to form the Deep Dish Satellite Network, a collaborative organization of access activists and producers, to share our programming via the commercial satellites. . . .

Most of the programs have been magazine-type shows, each tackling a specific social issue. For example, one program is called *Home Sweet Homefront.* Produced by Louis Messaih, it combines footage on the struggles for housing from many different communities, from Philadelphia, New York's Lower East Side, and Minneapolis, among others. The community video footage is ironically framed with Mumford-esque clips from housing films from the New Deal. The program neatly juxtaposes homeless activists with the liberal rhetoric of a bygone era. The show paints a vivid picture of a major crisis in locally specific terms. In direct contrast to the decontextualized and atomized way these issues are portrayed in the nightly network news, the local struggles are recontextualized in this program and given an additional historical frame of reference. Other Deep Dish shows have focused on the farm foreclosure crisis, pesticides, women's issues, and racism. Each combines local clips to form a larger national picture of the issue.

. . . Deep Dish uses the technology to create communities of interest that prove to the video producers and the organizing groups that their work is part of a larger movement. Letters of support to Deep Dish have one phrase that is most often repeated: "Now we know we are not alone."

Deep Dish has also received letters from home satellite owners, a potential audience that now numbers more than four million. The majority of dish owners are in isolated rural areas without any other source of television signals. This individual satellite audience has been fully appreciated by Christian broadcasters, who use them for fund-raising and for proselytizing to other viewers. The right wing in this country has proved effective in the creation, through media technology, of an audience and a community that transcend geographic boundaries with technology. The right's early use of direct mail and computer lists was only tardily replicated by environmentalist and antimilitarist groups. However, in recent years we have seen the successful development of Peacenet, a progressive computer network. Peacenet provides electronic mail and computer data bases in such fields as environmental research, media analysis, Latin American refugee assistance, and antinuclear organizing. Many individuals and groups have come to rely on the circuits of data and exchange thereby provided. This network will be an important resource for any future networking possibilities in the video community.

In spring of 1989, I received a notice through Peacenet that a solidarity group in California was organizing a presentation in connection with the tenth anniversary of the Nicaraguan revolution: an hour interview with Daniel Ortega. The San Francisco group had set up down-links across the country (similar to the reception locations set up for boxing championships) in auditoriums in ten large cities. The message would come "live" to solidarity groups gathered for the celebration. After receiving the Peacenet memorandum via my computer, I contacted the San Francisco group and sent them the Deep Dish address list; more than four hundred stations that had picked up and played our last series. The group mailed out notices to this select list. This mailing, combined with the organization's own mailing list of solidarity groups and individuals, created a formidable network for the program. It was transmitted from Managua on July 22, 1989, and received by several hundred access stations across the country. The combination of computer networking, solidarity work, and video transmission formed a wide network that combined narrow-casting and broad information dissemination. This sort of consortium of organizations and expertise can be tapped in the future.

Why hasn't the left done this sort of thing before? Satellite networking has been commonplace among right-wing Christians for years. Although they have been able to con thousands of dollars by playing on the desperation of the faithful, most of the pledge dollars go into buying cars and spilt-level homes for the preachers. The actual dollars spent on the satellites and the technology are minimal. This sort of network is cheap when weighed against the price of mailing and duplication costs of more ob- solete methods of program distribution. But the left has not made use of this oppor- tunity. To this day, it is still uncommon for progressive groups to use technology in this way. . . .

. . . It seems more humane, more real, more pure to organize a rally or to create a refugee camp than to create a TV network. It is easier to get funds for a film about a coal strike than it is to fund a film about the lies the media are telling about the coal company. It is easier to organize a speaking tour than it is to organize the cir- culation of a television series. Unfortunately, the right in this country doesn't have these inhibitions.

Meanwhile, on main street, popular video has arrived and it is growing lustily. Video camcorders combined with community organizations have begun to cause ripples in the sands of the TV wasteland. The creative use of technology that Mum- ford dreamed of is alive in hundreds of small studios, in trailer parks, in community- controlled mobile TV vans, and in high school rec rooms. It's called public access. The rank and file are seizing the time and channels.

> One of the most interesting uses of video is a self defense against the police. For years African-Americans and Latinos have been victimized by excessive police force. Every year several hundred young men die in police custody or in street struggles with under- cover cops. Camcorder video has enabled communities to document these incidents. For years, police have videotaped demonstrations and community organizations. But as mass sales of video recorders have increased, harassed communities have taken to watching the police. "It's the democratization of surveillance," said Larry Sapadin, Director of AIVF (The Association of Independent Video and Filmmakers).

Watch out, Dick Tracy! We've got you covered.

From ARPANET to Internet

BRUCE STERLING

Some thirty years ago, the RAND Corporation, America's foremost Cold War think-tank, faced a strange strategic problem. How could the U.S. authorities successfully communicate after a nuclear war?

Postnuclear America would need a command-and-control network, linked from city to city, state to state, base to base. But no matter how thoroughly that network was armored or protected, its switches and wiring would always be vulnerable to the impact of atomic bombs. A nuclear attack would reduce any conceivable network to tatters.

And how would the network itself be commanded and controlled? Any central authority, any network central citadel would be an obvious and immediate target for an enemy missile. The center of the network would be the very first place to go. RAND mulled over this grim puzzle in deep military secrecy, and arrived at a daring solution. The RAND proposal (the brainchild of RAND staffer Paul Baran) was made public in 1964. In the first place, the network would have no central authority. Furthermore, it would be designed from the beginning to operate while in tatters.

The principles were simple. The network itself would be assumed to be unreliable at all times. It would be designed from the get-go to transcend its own unreliability. All the nodes in the network would be equal in status to all other nodes, each node with its own authority to originate, pass, and receive messages. The messages themselves would be divided into packets, each packet separately addressed. Each packet would begin at some specified source node, and end at some other specified destination node. Each packet would wind its way through the network on an individual basis.

The particular route that the packet took would be unimportant. Only final results would count. Basically, the packet would be tossed like a hot potato from node to node, more or less in the direction of its destination, until it ended up in the proper place. If big pieces of the network had been blown away, that simply wouldn't matter; the packets would still stay airborne, lateralled wildly across the field by whatever nodes happened to survive. This rather haphazard delivery system might be "inefficient" in the usual sense (especially compared to, say, the telephone system)—but it would be extremely rugged.

During the '60s, this intriguing concept of a decentralized, blastproof, packet-switching network was kicked around by RAND, MIT and UCLA. The National Physical Laboratory in Great Britain set up the first test network on these principles in 1968. Shortly afterward, the Pentagon's Advanced Research Projects Agency decided to fund a larger, more ambitious project in the USA. The nodes of the network were to be high-speed supercomputers (or what passed for supercomputers at the time). These were rare and valuable machines which were in real need of good solid networking, for the sake of national research-and-development projects.

In fall 1969, the first such node was installed in UCLA. By December 1969, there were four nodes on the infant network, which was named ARPANET, after its

From Bruce Sterling, "Short History of the Internet," *The Magazine of Fantasy and Science Fiction* (February 1993).

Pentagon sponsor. The four computers could transfer data on dedicated high-speed transmission lines. They could even be programmed remotely from the other nodes. Thanks to ARPANET, scientists and researchers could share one another's computer facilities by long-distance. This was a very handy service, for computer-time was precious in the early '70s. In 1971 there were fifteen nodes in ARPANET; by 1972, thirty-seven nodes. And it was good.

By the second year of operation, however, an odd fact became clear. ARPANET's users had wrapped the computer-sharing network into a dedicated, high-speed, federally subsidized electronic post-office. The main traffic on ARPANET was not long-distance computing. Instead, it was news and personal messages. Researchers were using ARPANET to collaborate on projects, to trade notes on work, and eventually, to downright gossip and schmooze. People had their own personal user accounts on the ARPANET computers, and their own personal addresses for electronic mail. Not only were they using ARPANET for person-to-person communication, but they were very enthusiastic about this particular service—far more enthusiastic than they were about long-distance computation.

It wasn't long before the invention of the mailing-list, an ARPANET broadcasting technique in which an identical message could be sent automatically to large numbers of network subscribers. Interestingly, one of the first really big mailing-lists was "SF-LOVERS," for science fiction fans. Discussing science fiction on the network was not work-related and was frowned upon by many ARPANET computer administrators, but this didn't stop it from happening.

Throughout the '70s, ARPA's network grew. Its decentralized structure made expansion easy. Unlike standard corporate computer networks, the ARPA network could accommodate many different kinds of machine. As long as individual machines could speak the packet-switching lingua franca of the new, anarchic network, their brand-names, and their content, and even their ownership, were irrelevant.

The ARPA's original standard for communication was known as NCP, "Network Control Protocol," but as time passed and the technique advanced, NCP was superceded by a higher-level, more sophisticated standard known as TCP/IP. TCP, or "Transmission Control Protocol," converts messages into streams of packets at the source, then reassembles them back into messages at the destination. IP, or "Internet Protocol," handles the addressing, seeing to it that packets are routed across multiple nodes and even across multiple networks with multiple standards—not only ARPA's pioneering NCP standard but others like Ethernet, FDDI, and X.25.

As early as 1977, TCP/IP was being used by other networks to link to ARPANET. ARPANET itself remained fairly tightly controlled, at least until 1983, when its military segment broke off and became MILNET. But TCP/IP linked them all. And ARPANET itself, though it was growing, became a smaller and smaller neighborhood amid the vastly growing galaxy of other linked machines.

As the '70s and '80s advanced, many very different social groups found themselves in possession of powerful computers. It was fairly easy to link these computers to the growing network-of-networks. As the use of TCP/IP became more common, entire other networks fell into the digital embrace of the Internet, and messily adhered. Since the software called TCP/IP was public-domain, and the basic technology was decentralized and rather anarchic by its very nature, it was difficult to stop people from barging in and linking up somewhere-or-other. In point of fact, nobody wanted to stop them from joining this branching complex of networks, which came to be known as the "Internet."

Connecting to the Internet cost the taxpayer little or nothing since each node was independent, and had to handle its own financing and its own technical requirements. The more, the merrier. Like the phone network, the computer network became steadily more valuable as it embraced larger and larger territories of people and resources.

A fax machine is only valuable if everybody else has a fax machine. Until they do, a fax machine is just a curiosity. ARPANET too, was a curiosity for a while. Then computer-networking became an utter necessity.

In 1984 the National Science Foundation got into the act through its Office of Advanced Scientific Computing. The new NSFNET set a blistering pace for technical advancement, linking newer faster, shinier supercomputers, through thicker, faster links, upgraded and expanded, again and again, in 1986, 1988, 1990. And other government agencies leapt in: NASA, the National Institutes of Health, the Department of Energy, each of them maintaining a digital satrapy in the Internet confederation. . . .

ARPANET itself formally expired in 1989, a happy victim of its own overwhelming success. Its users scarcely noticed, for ARPANET's functions not only continued but steadily improved. The use of TCP/IP standards for computer networking is now global. In 1971, a mere twenty-one years ago, there were only four nodes in the ARPANET network. Today [1993] there are tens of thousands of nodes in the Internet, scattered over forty-two countries, with more coming on-line every day. Three million, possibly four million people use this gigantic mother-of-all-computer-networks. . . .

Why do people want to be "on the Internet"? One of the main reasons is simple freedom. The Internet is a rare example of a true, modern, functional anarchy. There is no "Internet Inc." There are no official censors, no bosses, no board of directors, no stockholders. In principle, any node can speak as a peer to any other node, as long as it obeys the rules of the TCP/IP protocols, which are strictly technical, not social or political. . . .

. . . ARPA's network, designed to assure control of a ravaged society after a nuclear holocaust, has been superceded by its mutant child the Internet, which is thoroughly out of control, and spreading exponentially through the post-Cold War electronic global village. The spread of the Internet in the '90s resembles the spread of personal computing in the 1970s, through it is even faster and perhaps more important.

λλ *F U R T H E R   R E A D I N G*

Benedikt, Michael. *Cyberspace: First Steps* (Cambridge, MA: MIT Press, 1992).

Flamm, Kenneth. *Creating the Computer* (Washington, DC: Brookings Institution, 1988).

Forester, Tom, ed. *Computers in the Human Context: Information Technology, Productivity, and People* (Cambridge: MA: MIT Press, 1989).

Garson, Barbara. *The Electronic Sweatshop* (New York: Simon & Schuster, 1988).

Kidder, Tracy. *The Soul of a New Machine* (Boston: Little, Brown, 1981).

Long, Franklin, and Alexandra Oleson, eds. *Appropriate Technology and Social Values—A Critical Appraisal* (Cambridge, MA: American Academy of Arts & Sciences, 1980).

Penley, Constance, and Andrew Ross, eds. *Technoculture* (Minneapolis: University of Minneapolis Press, 1991).

Shaiken, Harley. *Work Transformed: Automation and Labor in the Computer Age* (New York: Holt, Rinehart, and Winston, 1985).

Star, Susan Leigh, ed. *The Cultures of Computing* (Oxford, England: Blackwell Publishing, 1995).

Sterling, Bruce. *The Hacker Crackdown: Law and Order on the Electronic Frontier* (New York: Bantam Books, 1992).

Turkle, Sherry. *Life on the Screen* (New York: Simon and Schuster, 1995).

Zuboff, Shoshanna. *In the Age of the Smart Machine: The Future of Work and Power* (New York: Basic Books, 1988).

Credits